TEACHING ELEMENTARY LANGUAGE ARTS

THIRD EDITION

TEACHING ELEMENTARY LANGUAGE ARTS

Dorothy Rubin
Trenton State College

The Library
Saint Francis College
Fort Wayne, Indiana 46808

HOLT, RINEHART AND WINSTON

New York   Chicago   San Francisco   Philadelphia   Montreal   Toronto   London
Sydney   Tokyo   Mexico City   Rio de Janeiro   Madrid

Library of Congress Cataloging in Publication Data
Rubin, Dorothy.
    Teaching elementary language arts.

    Includes bibliographies and index.
    1. Language arts (Elementary) I. Title.
LB1575.R82 1985   372.6'044   84-25200

ISBN 0-03-071042-1

CBS COLLEGE PUBLISHING
Holt, Rinehart and Winston
The Dryden Press
Saunders College Publishing

With love to my understanding and supportive husband, Artie,
my precious daughters, Carol and Sharon,
my delightful grandchildren, Jennifer and Andrew, my charming sons-in-law, John and Seth,
and my dear brothers and sister.

PREFACE

A book for the latter part of the 1980s must be one that reflects the times. It must help teachers be more current, more effective, more creative, more understanding of the variety of children in the classroom, more knowledgeable, more accountable, and better teachers. *Teaching Elementary Language Arts* is intended to be such a book. The third edition retains all of the features of the first and second editions that have made them such popular books among professors, students, and inservice teachers, while broadening their scope and coverage. New chapters have been added for two reasons: to help teachers implement the language arts ideas, materials, and methods presented, and to help them plan for and accommodate the children with special needs, whom they will probably encounter in their regular classrooms.

Although the breadth and scope of *Teaching Elementary Language Arts* have increased, its substantiveness and readability have not been compromised. The text still emphasizes both the blend of theory and practice and, especially, the interrelatedness of the language arts, including reading. It focuses on the language arts as thinking processes and on students as active consumers of information.

In order to understand the "whys" of teaching methods and practices in the area of language arts, you should comprehend those psychological foundations and researches on which this book is based. However, this is not a "theory" text, since a practical approach is emphasized throughout to help teachers effectively implement the language arts program. The material is presented so that it will be enjoyable as well as informative.

The text presents psychological principles and/or historical perspectives in the language arts, followed by exercises that illustrate practical applications in classroom teaching situations.

Part One deals with the foundation on which a good language arts program should be built. Unless teachers are aware of individual differences, the ways in which language is acquired by the child, and the importance of creativity in the life of a child, they will not be able to implement the proposed language arts program well. Part One also presents material that allows teachers to gain insight into themselves as teachers, to be perceptive of the physical environment in their classrooms, and to be aware of the complex of variables operating in the world of their students. These factors, combined with principles of good classroom management, will make better teachers.

Part Three continues to deal with those factors that enhance the teaching–learning situation. I also discuss various organizational patterns stressing both techniques for individualizing instruction and the impact of microcomputers in the language arts classroom. I present information on diagnosis and evaluation and emphasize that these are important ongoing processes. I also present information on the characteristics of children with special needs, with particular emphasis on borderline children, gifted children, and children who speak nonstandard English. In addition, I stress that the language arts should be integrated into all content areas, and present a special chapter to help teachers do this.

Part Two contains the subject matter of the language arts and discusses both the development and implementation of skills that a good language arts teacher needs. All the chapters in Part Two have Diagnostic Checklists for each language arts area. Model Lesson Plans are given as further illustrations. The two chapters on children's acquisition of composing skills reflect current research in a logical, sensible way. I cover the essentials of the "process approach" in a practical manner and give suggestions on how to make the approach work.

In this text the child is the focal point around which the teacher orchestrates language arts activities, providing a learning environment that allows a child the freedom to participate, interact, and experience.

Sensitivity is a key word in education—and that is all to the good. Unless teachers, however, know how children develop certain skills, know the subject matter of language arts, and are aware of methods to help children attain needed skills, there will be no real teaching.

I wish to emphasize that this book does not dictate one approach to the language arts. Controversies are explained from several viewpoints in order both to help teachers see through an "either/or" dichotomy and to utilize elements from each that best suit the needs of students. By explaining and analyzing the various outlooks and methods prevalent in the language arts field, a practical approach to teaching is developed throughout the text.

Acknowledgments

I would like to thank my editor, Earl McPeek, for his valuable suggestions and support; my project editor, Jeanette Ninas Johnson, for her patience, kindness, consideration, and help; and my copy editor, Kathy Nevils, for her careful scrutiny of the manuscript. I'd like also to express my gratitude to the following professors for their scholarly suggestions and very helpful reviews of my manuscript: Esther Alvino, Glassboro State College; Joanne E. Bernstein, Brooklyn College; Joan Glazer, Rhode Island College; Mary Anne Hall, Georgia State University; Marciene Mattleman, Temple University; Nancy Quisenberry, Southern Illinois University; Terry S. Sallinger, University of Texas at El Paso; and Margaret S. Wheeler, Ball State University. In addition, I would like to express my appreciation to the administration of Trenton State College and particularly to Dr. Phillip Ollio, Dean of the School of Education, and Dr. Leon Durkin for their continued support. Finally, I'd like to give special thanks to Sharon Johnson for her creative suggestions and to Carol Smith for taking such excellent photographs in a timely manner in the Monticello, Arkansas, school system.

D. R.

CONTENTS

PART TWO

THE SUBJECT MATTER OF THE LANGUAGE ARTS 59

PART THREE

ENHANCING LANGUAGE ARTS INSTRUCTION   351

TEACHING
ELEMENTARY
LANGUAGE ARTS

Introduction:
A Scenario

The child is the starting-point, the center, and the end. His development, his growth, is the ideal. It alone furnishes the standard.

John Dewey

Ms. Hart arrived especially early the first day of school to make sure everything in her classroom was in order. When she arrived, she was relieved to see that everything was as she had left it the day before, and that the custodian had not changed her desk arrangements.

Ms. Hart had worked for a long time to prepare her classroom for her students. She looked at the Communication bulletin board and smiled. "It does look pretty good," she said to herself. She was especially pleased with her Jigsaw bulletin board because it made the room look so bright and cheerful. (She had known there was a reason for saving all that gift-wrapping paper.) "The cutouts of various sizes and designs with the words PUZZLED? ASK QUESTIONS! should certainly attract attention," she thought to herself.

Ms. Hart had arranged the desks and chairs in clusters of four in a semicircle. She wanted to allow for easy access to all the learning centers, which were placed around the periphery of the room. (See the diagram on page 2.) At the far left, she had placed her grandmother's hooked rug and rocking chair. Surrounding the

rug at right angles were the bookcases filled with books at various readability levels. Ms. Hart had read practically all of the books for her college course in children's literature. The colorful book jackets that she had collected through the years were on display on top of the bookcases. Ms. Hart beamed when she looked at the warm, homey setting. "Children should enjoy reading there, and it will be perfect for storytelling or for reading stories to the class," she thought.

Ms. Hart's anthill, goldfish aquarium, and plants had been placed near the science center. Because of Ms. Hart's special interest in words and vocabulary expansion, she had prepared a special learning sequence in this area. She would help the children see how the learning of a few word parts could help them in learning many of the terms used in the metric system. Ms. Hart felt especially proud of her media corner, which housed the media equipment, and in which the listening and music learning centers were located. Ms. Hart had prepared some of the tapes for the listening center, and she had brought in some of her favorite tapes for the music appreciation learning sequences. She hoped that her puppet stage would stimulate children to make their own puppets, write scripts, and present puppet shows. The math

MS. HART'S CLASSROOM

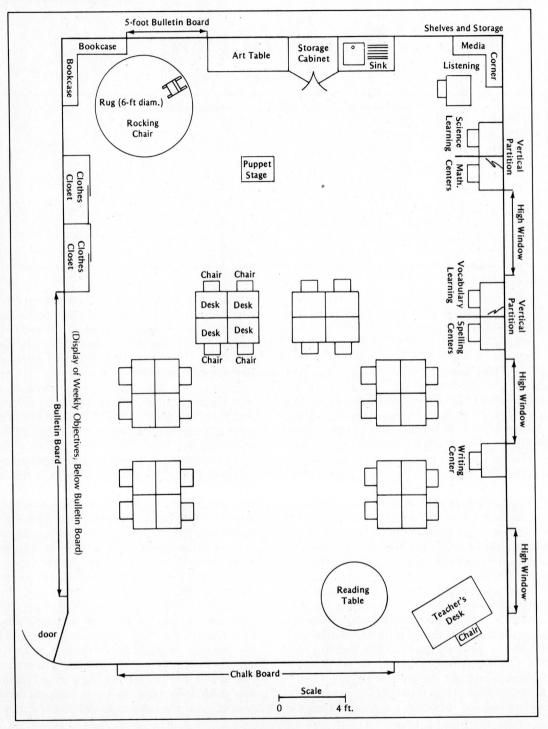

center, writing center, art tables, and round reading table for group work were all as she had placed them. Even the line she had strung for the hanging of the groups' weekly behavioral objectives was still there.

Ms. Hart sighed and thought, "What a lot of work!" And she was right. It had taken a great amount of time, effort, planning, decision making, and work to organize this classroom for optimum teaching and learning.

Ms. Hart is a new teacher. She is excited about her fourth-grade teaching assignment, and she wants to be a perfect teacher—well, almost perfect. After looking over everything in the classroom, Ms. Hart feels that she is starting in the right direction. She has tried to make the room into an attractive and inviting learning environment that reflects her philosophy of education.

Ms. Hart realizes, however, that this is only the first step. She still has not decided on how to organize for instruction within her self-contained classroom. She respects the fact that each student is a unique individual; the importance of individual differences was stressed in many of her college courses. She agrees with the principle of adapting instruction to the needs, interests, and ability levels of each of her students, and she wants to organize an educational program within her classroom based on individual differences. Ms. Hart's problem is in deciding on the kind of program. There are so many individualized programs. The one thing that Ms. Hart is certain about is that she wants a program that provides for both group and individual instruction.

Ms. Hart is making a good start. She has established a physical environment that is conducive to both individual and group activities. The kind of organizational pattern Ms. Hart chooses will depend on the students she has. Some organizational patterns work better with some groups of students than with others. Also, some patterns work better in one curriculum area than in another.

Ms. Hart will have to wait a little while to see what works best with her group of students. She will probably try a few plans. First, she must learn about each of her students. Through observation, informal tests, and standardized tests she can gain information to help her determine what will work best for her unique group of students. There is no one correct way to organize for instruction. There are a number of ways, and, as already stated, some work better for certain groups of students and teachers than others. Ms. Hart will find this out.

Ms. Hart will certainly find out a lot of things after working with her students. Experience is, after all, the best teacher. However, usually the most fruitful experiences are those that are based on intelligent insight and a fund of information. Ms. Hart is probably on her way to having a very good year because she has received a great amount of help from her college courses; she is a creative individual; she has good reasoning ability; she loves children; and she loves to teach.

Teaching Elementary Language Arts has been written to help preservice and inservice teachers gain the competence they need to help children to be better listeners, speakers, readers, writers, and thinkers. Nothing is taken for granted. The emphasis in this book is on helping teachers gain the necessary skills, as well as the methods for teaching these skills. Also, it is hoped that it will help teachers to recognize that the language arts are thinking processes that are all interrelated and that permeate the whole school curriculum.

THE FOUNDATION OF THE LANGUAGE ARTS

PART ONE

ONE

Introducing the Language Arts

WHAT ARE THE LANGUAGE ARTS AND HOW ARE THEY INTERRELATED?

The language arts are listening, speaking, reading, and writing.

Did you know that elementary-school children spend a large percentage of their time supposedly listening? That is, for a large period of time in elementary school someone is speaking and the students may or may not be engaged in the act of listening.

After you have finished reading Chapter 6 of this book, you will be able to make the children's listening time in class more effective and you will also comprehend how listening affects the other language arts areas. Perhaps, you will become a better listener yourself.

How shy children can be encouraged to engage in oral expression more freely is an important part of the language arts also. The solution to this problem as well as other speech-related questions will be found in Chapter 7.

Do you think you would be able to encourage your students to read on their own? You will know how to do so after finishing Chapter 10.

And how many activities can you think of to make written expression more enjoyable for your students? Examples of such stimulating activities will be found in Chapters 11 and 12.

Now you know that the major components of language arts are listening, speaking, reading, and writing, but you still are not aware of the wide range of topics included in each area. To help you to visualize the composition and organization of the subject matter of the language arts as presented in this textbook, see Table 1.1.

Although the language arts areas in this book are divided into separate chapters in order to make them more comprehensible, it is important to recognize and stress the interrelatedness of the language arts. This fundamental relatedness can be deduced from observations of children's development of oral and written expression, which usually follows the sequence listening, speaking, reading, and writing. To reinforce the importance of this sequence in the reader's mind, this book follows the same sequential order. Because of this developmental sequence a problem encountered in one segment of the language arts will usually carry over to another, while proficiency in one segment usually facilitates the acquisition of another area. For example, in order for children to be able to speak correctly, they must be able

---

TABLE 1.1   SUBJECT MATTER OF LANGUAGE ARTS

Section One—Aural–Oral Communication
   Chapter 6—Listening
   Chapter 7—Speaking

Section Two—Reading
   Chapter 8—Reading: An Integral Part of the
      Language Arts
   Chapter 9—Vocabulary Development in the
      Language Arts Program
   Chapter 10—Children's Literature

Section Three—Writing
   Chapter 11—Creative Writing
   Chapter 12—Practical Writing
   Chapter 13—Spelling
   Chapter 14—Handwriting
   Chapter 15—Grammar

---

to hear sounds correctly, and the sounds must convey meaning for them.

A young child kept asking his mother for carrots every Sunday after he came home from Sunday School. Finally, his mother decided to ask the child's Sunday School teacher about this phenomenon. The teacher had no explanation to give the mother. When they asked the child he said that the teacher had said, "Eat carrots for me." The teacher realized the child was misinterpreting "He careth for me," as "Eat carrots for me."

Another young child became almost hysterical when her parents tried to open the window in her room to let in some fresh air. "No, no," she screamed, "the giraffe will get me! The giraffe will get me!" At first the parents were perplexed until they realized that their daughter probably meant, "The draft will get me."

Many teachers know of similar examples. One of the most common substitution errors made is "My country 'tis a bee, sweet land of liver tree," for "My country 'tis of thee, Sweet land of liberty."

The Pledge of Allegiance to the Flag is also often misheard and therefore misrecited. For example, children have been heard to say, "I pledge allegiance to the . . . for Richard Stanz" and "one nation invisible. . . ."

DECODING AND ENCODING IN THE LANGUAGE ARTS

The language arts, which employ common word symbols, involve the intake (listening and reading) and the outgo (speaking and writing) of language. *Encoding* and *decoding* are technical terms that explain what takes place in the acts of listening, speaking, reading, and writing. For example, when you speak, you encode the sounds so that they are meaningful; when you listen, you decode and interpret the meanings. Writing involves the encoding of sounds in graphic (written) symbols, whereas reading involves the decoding and interpreting of the graphic form.

Figure 1.1 portrays the encoding and decoding process as it is used in communicating messages. In this model Speaker A first conveys a message to Listener B, who, after decoding and interpreting the message, becomes Speaker B. Speaker B then conveys a message to Listener A, who decodes and interprets the message and becomes Speaker A again. The communication cycle is now complete.

The same sequence would be followed for writing and reading, substituting writer for speaker and reader for listener, as is shown in the model.

COMMUNICATION AND LANGUAGE

When Confucius was asked what he would do if he had the responsibility for administering a country, he said that he would improve language. If language is not correct, he stated, then what is said is not what is meant; if what is said is not what is meant, then what ought to be done remains undone; if this remains undone, morals and arts would deteriorate; if morals and arts deteriorate, justice will go astray; if justice goes astray, the people will stand about in helpless confusion.

Confucius (c. 551–479 B.C.)

You can well imagine what would happen if there were no language. Would there be any communication? In answering this question one would have to say it depends on the definition of "language," which is used by different

FIGURE 1.1   MODEL OF ENCODING AND DECODING IN COMMUNICATION

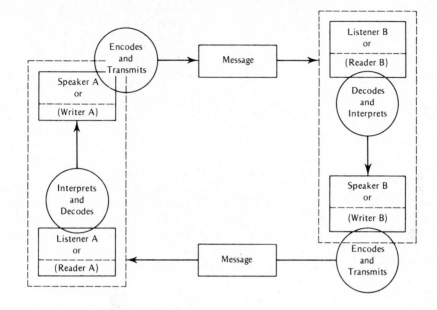

people to mean many different things. *Webster's Third International Dictionary* gives the following as its first definition of "language": "The words, their pronunciation, and the methods of combining them used and understood by a considerable community and established by long usage." Further on it also gives the following broader definition: "A systematic means of communicating ideas or feelings by the use of conventionalized signs, sounds, gestures, or marks having understood meanings." According to the latter definition, one can talk of kinesics, which involves gestures that may or may not accompany speech as language; or one can speak of the language of flowers, bees, computers, and so on. However, in *linguistics*, which concerns itself with the science of language, the term *language* refers to human speech. Since kinesics and the others mentioned are nonvocal and nonlingual, they would not be considered language by most linguists. (See the following section and Chapter 7 for more on kinesics.)

In linguistics, *language* would be defined in the following way: *Language is a learned, shared, and patterned, arbitrary system of vocal sound symbols with which people in a given culture can communicate with one another*. From this definition it can be stated that language is vocal, requiring commonality of agreement on the vocal sounds chosen to stand for ideas or objects. The term "patterned" in the definition of language refers to the recognition that word meanings depend on the position or placement of the words in a sentence. For example, in the following sentences the words "train" and "left" have different meanings based on their position in the sentences.

1. *Train* your dog to lift his *left* paw.
2. Since I *left* so late, I may miss my *train*.

Let us look at another example involving commonality of meaning. If two persons are conversing with one another and Individual A says to Individual B, "They put my dog on the litter," B might have difficulty in understanding A because "litter" has many different meanings. Does "litter" refer to a "stretcher" or does it mean "disorder"? It is difficult to discern the meaning of "litter" from the context (the words surrounding a word that can shed light on its meaning) of this sentence. However, if Individual A says, "They carried my dog on the litter to place him in the ambulance," there would be less chance for confusion because both people would be able, from the context of this sentence, to recognize a commonality of meaning for the noise "litter."

Communication could not take place unless a consensus of word meanings existed between Individuals A and B. Using Humpty Dumpty's rules, could communication take place?

"And only *one* for birthday presents, you know. There's glory for you!"

"I don't know what you mean by 'glory,' " Alice said.

Humpty Dumpty smiled contemptuously. "Of course you don't—till I tell you. I meant 'there's a nice knockdown argument for you.' "

"But 'glory' doesn't mean 'a nice knockdown argument,' " Alice objected.

"When *I* use a word," Humpty Dumpty said in rather a scornful tone, "it means just what I choose it to mean—neither more nor less."

"The question is," said Alice, "Whether you *can* make words mean so many different things."

"The question is," said Humpty Dumpty, "which is to be master—that's all."[1]

Would communication always take place if individuals have a consensus of word meanings? The answer would have to be, "It depends," for the term "communication" also seems to evoke a number of different meanings. To some persons, watching television, reading a book, or listening to a lecture all involve communication. This may be due to the fact that some dictionaries define communication as "the act of imparting, conferring or delivering from one to another; as, the communication of knowledge, opinions, or facts."[2] This definition is not very precise because it implies that communication can be a one-way process;

that is, merely giving. However, in order for communication to take place, there must be an *exchange* of ideas; there must be a sharing of common understanding between or among individuals.

The following should help give you a better understanding of language:

1. Language is man-made.
2. Language changes.
3. Language is primarily a system of sounds.
4. Sounds are arranged into words.
5. The method of sound production helps to convey meaning.
6. Words are made up of vocal sounds plus meaning.
7. Words are organized into patterns that convey unique meanings.
8. There are no right or wrong words for things, but common usage is employed in word meanings.
9. New words are derived as a society advances.
10. Language needs and uses are determined by a specific society.
11. Language helps transmit culture to the child.
12. Language is used for various functions or purposes.
13. Language helps satisfy various needs.
14. Language is important for establishing understanding in a human environment; it is important for communication.

(See "Language Development Theories" in Chapter 3 for a discussion of the functional aspects of the language of a child.)

As stated earlier, linguists are primarily concerned with the oral aspects of language. In the language arts, however, we are just as concerned with the written. Therefore, for us in language arts, language is both an oral and written expression of ideas. Lack of common word meanings between a speaker and a listener or between a writer and a reader will result in faulty communication.

This textbook is concerned with helping readers to be more perceptive to the world around them via the language arts. The more proficient students are in listening, speaking, reading, and writing, the more able they will be to contribute to the culture in which they live and the more they can benefit from that culture.

[1] Lewis Carroll, *Through the Looking Glass* (New York: Grosset & Dunlap), pp. 216–217.

[2] *Webster's New Twentieth-Century Dictionary, Unabridged,* 2d ed. (Cleveland, Ohio: World, 1970), p. 367.

FIGURE 1.2 COMMUNICATION HAS NOT TAKEN PLACE BETWEEN SMIDGENS AND THE ACE FINANCE CO.

Humans advance through language; it influences our acquisition of concepts. Helen Keller, who became blind and deaf in early infancy, exemplified the importance of language, its interrelationships, and what a phenomenal feat is involved in the child's acquisition of language. In her own words she describes her awakening to language:

As the cool stream gushed over one hand she [Helen Keller's teacher] spelled into the other the word water, first slowly, then rapidly. I stood still, my whole attention fixed upon the motions of her fingers. Suddenly I felt a misty consciousness as of something forgotten—a thrill of returning thought; and somehow the mystery of language was revealed to me. I knew then that "w-a-t-e-r" meant the wonderful cool something that was flowing over my hand. That living word awakened my soul, gave it light, hope, joy, set it free! . . .

I left the well-house eager to learn. Everything had a name, and each name gave birth to a new thought. As we returned to the house every object which I touched seemed to quiver with life. That was because I saw everything with the strange, new sight that had come to me.[3]

COMMUNICATION AND NONVERBAL BEHAVIOR

Human communication is actually a combination of words and gestures. Walburga von Raffler-Engel, a world-renowned linguist who has done extensive research in the area of nonverbal behavior, feels that the nonverbal component is as vital to communication as words. Engel differentiates between and among *body language*, *kinesics*, and *social movements*. She states that "the term *kinesics* should be reserved for message-related motions, and the more general term of *body language* for all other movements."[4] *Body language* is used to express the mood of an individual. For example, people walking back and forth or fidgeting with their hands are expressing signs of nervousness or anxiety. This may indeed relay a message to onlookers; however, the action movements are not *purposely communicative*. *Kinesics*, on the other hand, is associated with message-related body movements; it is *purposely communicative*. Kinesics either accompanies speech or is used in place of speech. For example, American speakers may communicate that they feel someone is crazy by *saying* that, while at the same time making circular movements around their temples, or just by making circular movements around their temples without speaking. *Social movements* are those body movements that children may be taught,

[3]Helen Keller, *The Story of My Life* (New York: Doubleday, 1954), p. 36.

[4]Walburga von Raffler-Engel, "The Unconscious Element in Intercultural Communication," in *The Social and Psychological Contexts of Language*, Robert N. St. Clair and Howard Giles, eds. (Hillsdale, N.J.; Lawrence Erlbaum Assoc., 1980), p. 113.

whereas kinesic motions usually are those acquired with verbal language. Greetings are in the category of social movements, and so methods of greeting one another would vary with cultural groups. Black Americans may use the highly stylized "soul handshake," other Americans may merely shake hands, the Japanese may greet each other with a bow, and so on.[5]

Unless teachers who are working with children from various cultures recognize that differences exist in the nonverbal behavior between and among cultures, communication may not take place. While Americans use the kinesic motion or gesture of circular movements around the temple to indicate someone is "nutty," Germans will touch their foreheads with their index fingers. Another example in the social movements area shows how misunderstanding can take place because of lack of communication due to nonverbal behavior: Many Chicano and black children in the past had been taught that it is a sign of respect to look down while speaking to an elder; it is considered a sign of respect *not* to look the person in the face. Other Americans are generally taught that well-bred persons look directly at the person to whom they are speaking. American teachers who see a child looking down while they are speaking to him or her usually infer that the child is either discourteous or not paying attention. Misreading of a child's nonverbal behavior will cause confusion for a child and put up needless barriers between a child and a teacher.

THE LANGUAGE ARTS, THINKING, AND INSTRUCTION

The language arts (listening, speaking, reading, and writing) are thinking processes. Therefore, the better an individual is in thinking, the better listener, speaker, reader, and writer he or she should be. It is possible, however, for an individual to be a good thinker but not to be proficient in the language arts. In other words, it is possible for someone to lack knowledge of specific language arts skills, even though he or she has the ability to organize, analyze, synthesize, and evaluate information. For example, a person may understand something when it is read aloud to him, but he may not be able to read the material himself because he has difficulty decoding words from the printed page. Similarly, another person may have good ideas, but she may have difficulty communicating in writing because she lacks skill in capitalization, punctuation, sentence structure, and so on.

It is also possible that some students may have difficulty in thinking, because they have not had experiences in working at higher levels of cognition; that is, it is possible that teachers have neither required nor challenged students to answer questions that demand a high level of thinking, nor engaged them in activities that demand such levels of thinking. (See the sections on concept development in Chapter 3.) If we say that the language arts are thinking processes, it would be a contradiction not to engage students in thinking activities when teaching the language arts.

Recent research about the human brain and cognition has shown that the human brain is actively involved in selecting, transforming, organizing, and remembering information.[6] In many ways, it is analogous to a computer's information-processing system. However, the human brain, unlike the computer, is constantly reprogramming itself, generating new strategies, and learning new information. This research on the brain and cognitive processes has implications for learning and teaching. If we look at the brain as an active consumer of information, able to interpret information and to draw inferences from it, as well as ignore some information and selectively attend to other information, we give the learner "a new, more important active role and responsibility in learning from instruction. . . ."[7] Good listeners, speakers, readers, and writers are active consumers of information and good thinkers.

Teachers who look upon their students as active consumers of information will present a

[5]Walburga von Raffler-Engel, "We Do Not Talk Only with Our Mouths," *Language Quarterly* 4 (December 1977): 1–3.

[6]Merlin C. Wittrock, "Education and the Cognitive Processes and the Brain," *The National Society for the Study of Education, Seventy-seventh Yearbook,* Part II (Chicago 1978) : 64.

[7]Ibid., p. 101.

language arts program that encourages students to work at various levels of cognition. These teachers will teach the language arts so that language arts and thinking skills are integrated. For example, writing as a thinking process requires students to attain basic skills, as well as such skills as analyzing, categorizing,

synthesizing, evaluating, and so on. Throughout this book the emphasis is on helping teachers to help their students to become more proficient listeners, speakers, readers, writers, and thinkers—and, consequently, better students in all their content classes.

SUMMARY

The various areas of language arts—listening, speaking, reading, and writing—are interrelated, and children develop command over language in the sequential order listed. The languages arts involve intake (or decoding) and outgo (or encoding) of language, and a communication model for these processes was presented earlier in the chapter.

After defining language as the learned, shared, and patterned, arbitrary system of vocal sound symbols used in communication, the

components for effective interchange were listed with emphasis on common word meanings. The importance of nonverbal behavior to human communication was emphasized, and the terms *body language, kinesics,* and *social movements* were explained. Language arts were also stressed as thinking processes. Therefore, good listeners, speakers, readers, and writers are active consumers of information and good thinkers.

SUGGESTIONS FOR THOUGHT
QUESTIONS AND ACTIVITIES

1. What would the world be like if all written matter were completely destroyed? What kind of communication would we have? What would happen to the educational establishment?

2. Try to communicate with another person without speaking. Get a number of people to team up with a partner and attempt to establish some form of communication without speaking. Then set up a communications system. Analyze what procedures you had to follow to set up the system.

3. At the first class meeting, have students who do not know one another form groups of four to six. Have the students talk among themselves to learn about each other's likes, interests, backgrounds, names, and so forth. After a while have the students put each of their names on a slip of paper. The group as a whole, using a part of each person's name, creates a new word with a meaning that somewhat reflects each person in the group. Each newly created word must conform to a part of speech so that when it is combined with the other newly cre-

ated words to form a sentence it will be structurally correct and make sense. After the sentence with the newly created words is put on the board for the class, each member is introduced using the newly created word and what it stands for. Example:

Persons in Group	Word Created	Part of Speech	Meaning of Word
John	Jonic	Adjective	Cheerful
Michael	Pechael	Verb	Likes
Deidre	Eido	Noun	Individual
Cynthia	Thial	Adjective	Social
Jennifer	Enniferings	Noun	Events

A jonic eido pechaels thial enniferings.
A cheerful individual likes social events.[8]

Ask students to explain what they have learned about language from this activity.

[8]Adapted from Kenneth Cadenhead, "Using Language in a Special Way to Get Acquainted," *Language Arts* 53 (October 1976): 772–773.

SELECTED BIBLIOGRAPHY

Bickerton, Derek. *Roots of Language.* Ann Arbor: Karoma Publishers, 1981.

Knapp, Mark. *Essentials of Nonverbal Communication.* New York: Holt, Rinehart and Winston, 1980.

Pei, Mario. *All About Language.* Philadelphia: J.B. Lippincott, 1954.

Pellegrini, Anthony D., Johanna S. DeStefano, and Deborah L. Thompson. "Saying What You Mean: Using Play to Teach 'Literate Language.' " *Language Arts* 60 (March 1983): 380–384.

von Raffler-Engel, Walburga. "Developmental Kinesics: Cultural Differences in the Acquisition of Nonverbal Behavior," in *Child Language.* New York: International Linguistic Association, 1975, 195–204.

———. "We Do Not Talk Only with Our Mouths." *Language Quarterly* 4 (December 1977): 1–3.

———. "The Unconscious Element in Intercultural Communication," in *The Social and Psychological Contexts of Language.* Robert N. St. Clair and Howard Giles, eds. Hillsdale, N. J.: Lawrence Erlbaum Associates, 1980.

TWO

Understanding the Individual Differences of Children

The classic fable of "The Animal School" by G. H. Reavis illustrates the importance of recognizing that individual differences exist among students.

THE ANIMAL SCHOOL

Once upon a time the animals decided they must do something heroic to meet the problems of a "New World." So they organized a school. They adopted an activity curriculum consisting of running, swimming, and flying. To make it easier to administer the curriculum it was decided that all of the animals should take all of the subjects.

The duck was excellent in swimming. In fact, he was far better than his instructor, but he could not do more than make passing grades in flying and was very poor in running. Since he was so slow in running, he had to remain after school and drop swimming in order to practice running. This was kept up until his web feet were badly worn and he was only average in swimming. But average was acceptable in the school—so nobody worried about that except the duck.

The rabbit started at the top of the class in running, but had a nervous breakdown because of so much make-up work in swimming. The squirrel was excellent in climbing until he developed frustration in the flying class where his teacher insisted that he start from the ground up instead of from the treetop down. He also developed "Charlie Horses" from over-exertion and then got a "C" in climbing and a "D" in running.

The eagle was indeed a problem child and was disciplined severely. In the climbing class, he beat all others to the top of the tree, but insisted on using his own way to get there. At the end of the year an abnormal eel that could swim exceedingly well, run, climb, and fly a little, had the highest average and was made valedictorian.

> The prairie dogs stayed out of school and fought the tax levy because the administration refused to add digging and burrowing to the curriculum. They apprenticed their child to a badger and joined with the groundhogs and gophers to start a very successful private school.
>
> Does this little Fable have a moral?

A good language arts program cannot exist unless teachers take the individual differences of their students into account. Perceptive teachers sensitive to the uniqueness of each of their students will be better able to plan a program based on their students' needs. Because the principle of providing for the individual differences of students is the backbone of the language arts program, this chapter is being presented in Part One. Throughout this book the necessity for providing for the individual differences of students is emphasized.

Some important individual differences that influence language development and, consequently, school achievement are shown in Figure 2.1. (No weighting of the relative importance of the factors is given.) This chapter will explain how these factors may affect individual school performance.

FIGURE 2.1   INDIVIDUAL DIFFERENCES

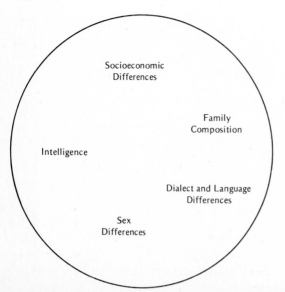

Socioeconomic
Differences

Family
Composition

Intelligence

Dialect and Language
Differences

Sex
Differences

Why humans behave as they do is a fascinating question. For example, why is it that two children with similar Intelligence Quotient (IQ) scores have different achievement behaviors? We cannot discuss the cause of children's behavior in any substantive way in this text, but many excellent books are devoted specifically to this topic. Yet it is important for the language arts teacher to have some understanding of the various factors that make up individual difference and we will consider some of these now.

INTELLIGENCE

It is difficult to pick up a newspaper, journal, or magazine without finding some reference to achievement or intelligence. Usually when intelligence—specifically an intelligence test—is brought up, the atmosphere becomes highly charged. Hardly anyone seems to regard IQ objectively.

Intelligence refers to the ability to reason abstractly or to solve problems. Since intelligence is a construct—that is, it is something that cannot be directly observed or directly measured—testing and research have necessitated an operational definition. Such a definition coined in the early part of the century is still much quoted: "Intelligence is what the intelligence test measures."[1] There are a variety of tests designed to measure intelligence, yet no test exists that actually measures intelligence. In other words, intelligence tests cannot adequately determine an individual's absolute limits or the potential of the intelligence. Yet many persons, both lay and professional, actually behave as if the intelligence test will tell all.

This state of affairs may be due to the nature–nurture controversy. Advocates of the nature side believe that heredity is the sole de-

---

[1]E. G. Boring, "Intelligence as the Tests Test It," *New Republic* 35 (1925): 35–37.

terminant of intelligence, and that no amount of education or quality of environment can alter intelligence. Those who believe in the nurture side claim that intelligence is determined in great part by the environment. For them, intelligence can be affected if the child is exposed to different environments and education. Most professionals take an in-between position, saying that intelligence may be determined by an interaction between heredity and environment. "Heredity deals the cards and environment plays them."[2] Yet the heredity theory dies hard.

The majority position which believes that intelligence is determined by some combination of heredity and environment brings up the question as to *which* factor is more important. Conflicting studies reported in this area attribute different percentages to each factor. The controversy continues to rage, as does the confusion surrounding what intelligence tests actually do measure.

Most intelligence tests are highly verbal, and studies have shown that persons who do well on vocabulary tests also seem to do well on intelligence tests.[3] If a child has language problems—or if a dialect of English or a language other than English is spoken at home—the child could easily have difficulty in performing well in school. IQ tests are valid mainly for a middle-class standard English curriculum, and they predict the ability of an individual to do well in such environments. The positive correlation or agreement between individuals' IQs and their ability to do work in school is neither very high nor low. There are factors other than IQ that determine an individual's success in school. One very important factor for school success is *motivation*—the desire, drive, and sustained interest to do the work.

The IQ test is an imperfect tool that helps teachers and parents to better understand the abilities of children. If students are doing very well in school, and if, according to their IQ scores, they are only supposed to be doing average work, one would be misusing the IQ test by thinking, "Stop, you're not supposed to be doing that well."

[2]Lee J. Cronbach, *Educational Psychology* (New York: Harcourt Brace, 1954), p. 204.
[3]Leona Tyler, *The Psychology of Human Differences* (New York: Appleton-Century-Crofts, 1965), p. 80.

The IQ test also helps show teachers the wide range of levels of ability in their classes. If teachers are aware of the wide span of mental age of their students, they can design a program based especially on individual needs. (See Chapter 17.)

However, teachers are cautioned not to see the IQ test as a perfect predictor of a child's ability to do work in school, for there are other factors, discussed in the remainder of this chapter, which influence school achievement.

Intelligence and the Language Arts

Because the language arts are thinking processes, it seems reasonable to assume that highly able persons, who have the abilities to learn and to think at high levels of abstraction, should be good listeners, speakers, readers, and writers. To a degree this is so, and many gifted children learn to speak at an early age, have extensive vocabularies, and learn to read before they come to school (see Chapter 17). However, not all gifted children become good listeners, speakers, readers, or writers, which confirms the statement made in the previous section that there are factors besides intelligence that contribute to success in the language arts and, consequently, to school achievement.

In Chapter 1 it was stated that students who have difficulty thinking at high levels of cognition may have the ability to do so but may not have been challenged or expected to do such kinds of thinking. In the 1980s the emphasis is on helping students to become better thinkers. This is evidenced in some of the latest language arts series. For example, Harper & Row English has a special component in its elementary series (K–8) devoted to language and reasoning. Skills such as categorizing, recognizing relationships, differentiating between fact and opinion, and so on are presented as part of the language arts lesson so that students can see how important these skills are to being good listeners, speakers, readers, writers, and thinkers.

SEX DIFFERENCES

Are females really the weaker sex? Why are there more male underachievers in elementary-school grades? Why are there more remedial readers among boys than girls? Why do males usually receive poorer grades in school than females? Since there are more adult males in important positions in society, does this mean that males are smarter than females?

There are vast differences between males and females besides the obvious physical ones. Females seem to have a biological precocity evident from birth onward.[4] "Girls develop faster than boys, and this rate of development begins during the fetal period."[5] Males, however, give off more carbon dioxide than females,[6] which means that boys need to take in more food and consequently produce more energy. Even though the male matures later than the female, his oxygen intake is greater and continues so throughout life.[7] It has been hypothesized that sex differences in behavior may be due to these differences in metabolism.

These factors may affect the readiness levels of children in listening, speaking, reading, and writing—the language arts. Teachers must realize that some primary-grade boys may not be as mature as some girls of the same chronological age. They should not be expected to do equally well on tasks that necessitate the use of specific hand muscles—such as handwriting. Similarly, teachers should not expect these more immature male students to be able to "sit still" as long as some more mature female students, or to have a comparable attention span. Teachers should know that, although studies reveal no significant differences between males and females in general intelligence.[8,9] there are differences in specific aptitudes. For example, males in general, according to the studies, are superior in mathematical

ability and in the area of science, but in the area of rote memory females are usually superior.[10] It also has been consistently shown that girls usually surpass boys in verbal ability. From infancy to adulthood, females usually express themselves in words more readily and skillfully than males. Researches show that in general girls seem to learn to talk a little earlier; are usually somewhat superior during the preschool years in articulation, intelligibility, and correctness of speech sounds; and learn grammar and spelling more readily and are less likely to be stutterers.[11]

It is important to note that the studies in this area are not definitive. More recent studies show that for "large unselected populations the situation seems to be one of very little sex difference in verbal skills from about 3 to 11, with a new phase of differentiation occurring at adolescence."[12] Comparisons of males and females on a variety of tests have made it clear that girls and women do not have larger vocabularies than boys and men.

It has been hypothesized, and the evidence is mounting, that both language differences between the sexes in the early years and male superiority in quantitative reasoning and science may be due to cultural factors. Beginning in the late 1960s, many changes in our society occurred to bring about more equality for women in the job market. Today women find it much easier to enter such fields as law, business, engineering, and so on. Even in the 1980s, however, females are not choosing to go into the fields of mathematics or of the hard sciences in large numbers. One reason may be that "males have been expected to be more competent than females at a variety of tasks."[13] Another reason closely related to competence expectations may be that "few counselors encourage girls to pur-

[4]Amram Scheinfeld, *Women and Men* (New York: Harcourt Brace, 1944), pp. 58–71.

[5]Paul H. Mussen, John J. Conger, and Jerome Kagan, *Child Development and Personality*, 5th ed. (New York: Harper & Row, 1979), p. 112.

[6]Stanley M. Garn and Leland C. Clark, Jr., "The Sex Difference in the Basal Metabolic Rate," *Child Development* 24 (September–December 1953): 215–224.

[7]Ibid., p. 222.

[8]Scottish Council for Research in Education, *The Intelligence of a Representative Group of Scottish Children* (London: University of London Press, 1939).

[9]Scottish Council for Research in Education, *The Trend of Scottish Intelligence* (London: University of London Press, 1949).

[10]Tyler, *Psychology*, pp. 244–245.

[11]Ibid., pp. 243–244; see also Mussen, Conger, and Kagan, *Child Development*, p. 340; and Robert R. Reilly and Ernest L. Lewis, *Educational Psychology* (New York: Macmillan, 1983), pp. 314–315.

[12]Eleanor E. Maccoby and Carol N. Jacklin, *The Psychology of Sex Differences* (Stanford, Ca.: Stanford University Press, 1974), p. 85.

[13]Marlene E. Lockheed, "Competence Expectations and Sex Differences in Task Influence: A Meta Analysis," paper presented at the Annual Meeting of the American Psychological Association, Washington, D.C., August 23–27, 1982, p. 3.

sue studies and careers in mathematics and physical science."[14]

Whatever the reasons for women's failure to enter certain disciplines, stereotypes die hard. Some parents still reward behavior in females that does not correlate with achievement. The result is females who learn to be more docile, to have less initiative, to be less independent, and to be less aggressive than their male counterparts. Males are also not exempt from sex stereotyping in the 1980s. Some parents still pressure their sons into being "rougher" or "tougher" than they may like to be out of a stereotype of what a male should be.

A long time is required for changes to be noted in test results. It will be interesting to note whether or not sex differences shown in test results will remain in spite of the impact of the movement to counter sexism in texts and in certain aspects of society. Perhaps these and other influences will change the results of earlier research on sex differences, not only in the interest and learning spheres, but also in the biological realm. Now that many women are working and competing with males, insurance companies may have to revise their actuarial tables for females in which women had longer life expectancy than males after the childbearing years. This trend has, however, not manifested itself in the first half of the 1980s.

It is to be hoped that by recognizing that sex differences exist, teachers will be more aware of the halo effect[15] and can be on the alert for it. For example, girls typically receive higher grades in school than boys in the area of overall "work" achievement because teachers tend to rate girls higher on such specific traits as deportment and handwriting.

Furthermore, girls are known to be more perceptive of the external environment than boys,[16] so that they can "size up" teachers more readily and therefore are more able to give teachers what they think is wanted.

By recognizing the existence of sex differences, teachers will be able to plan more effectively for students. They will be more able to dispel sex-stereotyping myths, which not only hinder effective planning but also interfere with the learning process. Teachers' own thinking concerning sex differences may perhaps be changed to avoid a number of sex-stereotyping pitfalls. They will recognize that all girls are not alike and that all boys are not similar. Children are not plastic prototypes of one another but unique entities. Not all boys are aggressive and competitive; nor are all girls docile, dependent, and verbal.

DIALECT AND LANGUAGE DIFFERENCES

According to *Webster's New Collegiate Dictionary,* the term *standard English* is defined as "the English that with respect to spelling, grammar, pronunciation, and vocabulary is substantially uniform, though not devoid of regional differences, that is well established by usage in the formal and informal speech and writing of the educated, and that is widely recognized as acceptable wherever English is spoken and understood."

The term *dialect* is more difficult to define, however. To some persons, a dialect of English is any variation of standard English; to others, it is merely a means of expressing oneself; and to still others, it is a variety of language related to social class, educational level, geography, gender, and ethnicity. From these definitions, we can see that standard English could then be considered a dialect and that the definition of dialect is obviously intertwined with that of language. If we were to define dialect in a broad sense, we would be concerned with the language of a geographic area; if we were to define it in a specific sense, we would be looking at the language of a neighborhood, a family, or even an individual (idiolect). Generally, however, when we refer to dialect, we are talking about a structured subsystem of a language, with definite phonological and syntactic structures, that is spoken by a group of people united not only by their speech but also by fac-

[14]Patricia Lund Casserly, "Helping Able Young Women Take Math and Science Seriously in School," reprint from *New Voices in Counseling the Gifted* (Dubuque, Iowa: Kendall/Hunt, 1979), p. 1.

[15]The halo effect is a response bias that contaminates an individual's perception in the area of rating; that is, a person may rate another individual high on general characteristics because of one or two good impressions or rate the person low overall because of one or two bad impressions.

[16]Herman A. Witkin, et al., *Personality Through Perception* (New York: Harper & Row, 1954).

tors such as geographic location and/or social status.[17]

For some persons the term *dialect* seems to have negative connotations associated with it. This is unfortunate because we all speak a dialect. "Dialects inevitably arise within all languages because all languages inevitably change."[18] If the geographical separation between groups of people is very great, and the separation lasts long enough, "the dialects may diverge from each other so much that they become two distinct languages."[19] (Persons who speak different languages do not understand one another, whereas persons who speak different dialects do.)

In the United States, standard English is considered the "prestige" dialect and where regional dialects differ very little from each other, perhaps almost exclusively in pronunciation, we would be more likely to speak of an "accent" than a "dialect."[20] In this book, whenever the term *nonstandard English* is used, it refers to a variation of standard English owing to socioeconomic and cultural differences in the United States. Other terms such as *black English, variant English,* and nonstandard Negro English have been used in a similar vein.

Controversy exists among linguists (persons who study language) over the origin of black English. Some linguists feel that black English is merely a variety of southern American English, which has become a social dialect because of the southern blacks' migration to other parts of the United States after World War II. William Labov and others, however, feel differently. Reacting to a 1979 case concerning the Ann Arbor school system, Labov claims the case helped clarify linguists' views toward black English. Here is the substance of the testimony according to Labov that was given by the linguists at the trial concerning black English and teachers:

1. The black English vernacular is a subsystem of English with a distinct set of phonological and syntactic rules that are now aligned in many ways with the rules of other dialects.

2. It incorporates many features of southern phonology, morphology, and syntax. Blacks, in turn, have exerted influence on the dialects of the South where they have lived.

3. It shows evidence of derivation from an earlier Creole, which was closer to the present-day Creoles of the Caribbean.

4. It has a highly developed aspect (the nature of the action of the verb), quite different from other dialects of English, which shows a continuing development of its semantic structure.[21] [See the following section on "Nonstandard English."]

Children who speak a variation or dialect of English or another language are not inferior to children speaking standard English, nor is their language inferior. Research by linguists has shown that many variations of English are highly structured systems and not accumulations of errors in standard English. For example, William Labov states that "it is most important for the teacher to understand the relation between standard and nonstandard and to recognize that nonstandard English is a system of rules, different from the standard but not necessarily inferior as a means of communication."[22]

Children speaking in a dialect of English have no difficulty communicating with one another. However, any dialect that differs from standard English structure and usage will usually cause communication problems for children in school and in society at large. Many expressions used by children who speak a variation of English may be foreign to teachers, and many expressions used by teachers may have different connotations for the students. The similarities between the dialects of English and standard English can also cause misunderstandings between students and teachers because both groups may feel they "understand"

[17]Jean Malmstrom and Constance Weaver, *Transgrammar: English Structure, Style, and Dialects* (Glenview, Ill.: Scott, Foresman, 1973), p. 338.

[18]Peter Desberg, Dale E. Elliott, and George Marsh, "American Black English and Spelling," in *Cognitive Processes in Spelling,* Uta Frith ed. (New York: Academic Press, 1980), p. 70.

[19]Ibid., p. 71.

[20]John P. Hughes, *The Science of Language* (New York: Random House, 1962), p. 26.

[21]William Labov, "Objectivity and Commitment in Linguistic Science: The Case of the Black English Trial in Ann Arbor," *Language Society* 11 (August 1982): 192.

[22]William Labov, *The Study of Nonstandard English* (Urbana, Ill.: National Council of Teachers of English, 1970), p. 14.

what the others are saying when, in actuality, they may not.

Children who come from homes where a language other than English is the dominant one may also have language difficulties when they enter school unless they are truly bilingual. The dictionary definition of *bilingual* states that one must be "capable of using two languages."[23] However, many schoolchildren who speak a language other than standard English at home are not bilingual. These children may hear only "noises" when they first enter school, because the English sounds have little or no meaning for them. They will often confuse the language spoken at home with their newly acquired English and vice versa. It is not a question of one language being better than or preferred over another, but rather one of helping children to get along in the dominant social, economic, and political culture and to become a part of it. Unless students learn to communicate in standard English as well as in a dialect or another language, they will have difficulty in finding their "places in the sun" in the economy.

Nonstandard English

Children who speak nonstandard English may have more problems than children who come from homes in which a foreign language is spoken because more status is generally attributed to a foreign language. It is reported in a large-scale Educational Testing Service study of Title I reading programs that teachers do hold negative attitudes toward nonstandard language.[24] Other studies with similar findings have also reported that the negative attitudes have influenced teacher practices. For example, "teachers tend to rate black English speaking students as lower class, less intelligent, and less able to do well academically than standard English speaking students."[25] In the Ann Arbor school-system case, Judge Charles W. Joiner, a United States district court judge, wrote that "a language barrier develops when teachers, in helping the child switch from the home [black English] language to standard English, refuse to admit the existence of a language that is the acceptable way of talking in his local community."[26]

The rejection of the child's language "may more deeply upset him than rejection of the color of his skin. The latter is only an insult, the former strikes at his ability to communicate and express his needs, feelings—his self."[27] The language of children who do not speak standard English has been an effective means of communication for them until they come to school. If such children are made to feel inferior because of their language by a teacher who constantly attacks their speech as incorrect, they may not attempt to learn standard English. (See Chapter 17 for a more extensive coverage of children who speak nonstandard English.)

HOME ENVIRONMENT

Socioeconomic class, parents' education, and the neighborhood in which children live are some of the factors that shape children's home environments. Studies have shown that the higher the socioeconomic status, the better the verbal ability of the child.[28] Children who have good adult language models and are spoken to and encouraged to speak will have an advantage in the development of language and intelligence. Parents who behave in a warm, democratic manner and provide their children with stimulating, educationally oriented activities, challenge their children to think, encourage independence, and reinforce their children, are preparing them very well for school.

Children who come from homes where parents have only an elementary-school education, where many people live in a few rooms, and where unemployment among the adults in the home is common will usually be at a disadvantage in language learning (see Chapter 3).

[26]Reginald Stuart, *The New York Times*, July 13, 1979, p. 8.

[27]E. Brooks Smith, Kenneth S. Goodman, and Robert Meredith, *Language and Thinking in the Elementary School* (New York: Holt, Rinehart and Winston, 1976), pp. 46–47.

[28]Walter D. Loban, *Language Development: Kindergarten through Grade Twelve*, Research Report No. 18 (Urbana, Ill.: National Council of Teachers of English, 1976).

[23]*Webster's New Twentieth-century Dictionary*, Unabridged, 2d ed. (Cleveland, Ohio: World, 1970), p. 182.

[24]Mary K. Monteith, "Black English, Teacher Attitudes, and Reading," *Language Arts* 57 (November–December 1980): 910.

[25]Ibid.

Teachers should also be aware of the adult composition of the child's home environment. Whether a child is reared by both parents, a single parent, a servant, by grandparents, or by foster parents will affect the child's attitudes and behavior. A child who is reared by a female single parent may behave differently from one reared by a male single parent, for instance. The death of one parent or of another family member will usually cause emotional stress in the child. A divorce can also be a traumatic experience for children. Teachers who are aware of the home environment and are sensitive to sudden changes in this important area are in a better position to understand and help such students.

The number of children born into a family and the order in which they are born affect the achievement levels of individuals, at least to some degree. Research is still being done on these factors, but it has been hypothesized that firstborn children do better both in school and in life than other children in the family. Children without siblings have been shown to be more articulate for the most part than a child who is a product of a multiple birth (e.g., twins or triplets) or a singleton (one child born at a time) who has other brothers and sisters.[29] Also, it appears that in both higher- and lower-class homes children who come from families where there are one to three children do better in verbal reasoning than children who come from homes where there are four or more children.[30]

Studies have shown that the only child, who is more often in the company of adults, has more chances of being spoken to by the surrounding grown-ups than is the case when there are many children in the family. Then, too, twins seem to have less need to communicate with others because they have a close relationship.

Singletons with siblings also have "interpreters" near at hand; that is, older siblings who can often understand a younger child's messages so well that the younger child need not attempt more effective communication.

All of these factors form part of the learning climate in the home and influence the degree and amount of learning in the school.

[29]Mildred A. Dawson and Miriam Zollinger, *Guiding Language Learning* (New York: Harcourt, Brace & World, 1957), pp. 36–37; Didi Moore, "The Only-Child Phenomenon," *The New York Times Magazine*, Section 6, January 18, 1981, 26–27, 45–48; see also Mussen, Conger, and Kagan, *Child Development*, pp. 370–372.

[30]Mollie S. Smart and Russell C. Smart, *Children: Development and Relationships*, 4th ed. (New York: Macmillan, 1982), p. 361.

SUMMARY

Intelligence can be defined as the ability to reason abstractly and to solve problems, but there seems to be no hard and fast way of measuring either intelligence or of predicting how well a child will do in school. There are, however, a number of factors that a teacher must recognize when concerned about the individual differences in children. One such factor is sex differences, particularly the differences between young boys and girls in growth and learning abilities. Another difference is in the home life of the child. In some homes more than one language is spoken, in others a dialect prevails. Also, the differences in the education of a student's parents, the socioeconomic class of the family, the neighborhood in which a student lives, and the composition of the family must be recognized as creating differences. Such factors should be taken into account if the teacher is to give each pupil the best possible education.

Since research generalizations are often based on averages, we tend many times to talk of "average" children, but they don't really exist. It must be emphasized—and often—that each child is an individual who reacts differently because of many variables that make the student separate and unique, with his or her special assets, liabilities, and needs.

SUGGESTIONS FOR THOUGHT QUESTIONS AND ACTIVITIES

1. Given two hypothetical students, X and Y, construct a comparison chart showing how one child's chances for success in school are better than the other child's chances because of certain factors. State five factors, and describe and explain how each affects the child's chances for success in school.

2. Explain why children who speak nonstandard English may have more problems in school than persons who speak a foreign language such as French.

3. You have been asked to give a talk to parents about intelligence. What will you say?

4. Prepare a position paper on the schools' responsibility to children who speak nonstandard English.

SELECTED BIBLIOGRAPHY

Bassett, G. W., and Betty Watt. *Individual Differences: Guidelines for Educational Practices.* London: Allen & Unwin, 1978.

Clarke-Stewart, Alison, and Joanne Koch. *Children: Development through Adolescence.* New York: Wiley, 1983.

Hamilton, Stephen F. "Socialization for Learning: Insights from Ecological Research in Classrooms," *Reading Teacher* 37 (November 1983): 150–156.

Labov, William. *The Study of Nonstandard English.* Urbana, Ill.: National Council of Teachers of English, 1970.

———. "Objectivity and Commitment in Linguistic Science: The Case of the Black English Trial in Ann Arbor." *Language in Society* 11 (August 1982): 165–201.

Maccoby, Eleanor E. *Social Development: Psychological Growth and the Parent–Child Relationship.* New York: Harcourt Brace Jovanovitch, 1980.

Mussen, Paul H., and Mavis Hetherington. *Handbook of Child Psychology: Socialization, Personality and Social Development,* vol 4. New York: Wiley, 1983.

Reilly, Robert R., and Ernest L. Lewis. Chapter 11 "Sex Differences and Gender Role Development," in *Educational Psychology.* New York: Macmillan, 1983.

THREE

Understanding Language and Concept Development in the Child

RELATIONSHIP OF LANGUAGE TO SCHOOL ACHIEVEMENT AND OTHER FACTORS

When young children first come to school, we can wonder what their chances are for success. Will they achieve or will they become roll-call statistics in the nonachievement ledger?

The answers to these questions depend on the children's past experiences, as well as the difference factors discussed in Chapter 2. Figure 3.1 illustrates how the quality of language development depends on the interrelationships of the basic ingredients—the factors of intelligence, home environment, sex differences, cultural differences, and family make-up.

Children who are advanced in language development tend to achieve better in school than those who are not.[1] Studies show that high-achieving readers come from homes with enriched verbal environments, whereas low-achieving readers come from homes in which little conversation takes place with the parents.[2]

This report on the language ability of "disadvantaged children" comes from an English writer:

Twenty-four children of one-and-a-half to two years old, living in an orphanage, were divided into two groups, matched for "measured intelligence"—as far as it could be measured at that age: what is clear is that both groups showed *low* ability. Each of the twelve in one group was sent to be looked after by an adolescent girl living in a mental home: the other group was left at the orphanage. After two years the group that had been living with the girls showed extraordinary increases in measured intelligence (well over twenty points), while those in the orphanage showed a *decrease* of similar proportions. What is more astounding still is that after *twenty-one years*, the experimenter was able to trace the children and discovered that the average of the final school achievement of the group looked after in infancy by the girls was twelfth grade (work normal for seventeen-to-eighteen-year-olds) whereas the average for the other group was fourth grade (work normal for nine-to-ten-year-olds).[3]

The importance of having someone to talk to, especially in the crucial years from two to

---

[1]Walter D. Loban, *Language Development: Kindergarten through Grade Twelve*, Research Report No. 18 (Urbana, Ill.: National Council of Teachers of English, 1976).

[2]Esther Milner, "A Study of the Relationship between Reading Readiness in Grade One School Children and Patterns of Parent–Child Interaction," *Child Development* (June 22, 1951): 95–112.

[3]James Britton, *Language and Learning* (Middlesex, England: Penguin, 1970), pp. 94–95.

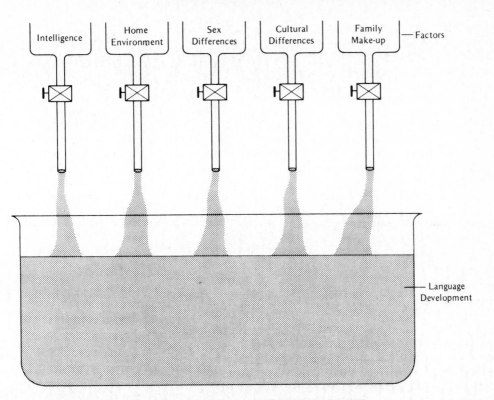

FIGURE 3.1   FACTORS AFFECTING THE LANGUAGE DEVELOPMENT OF THE CHILD

five, has been substantiated by many studies. From these, as well as from the discussion in Chapter 2, it can be seen how closely interrelated are the areas of language, intelligence, early home environment, and school achievement. Furthermore, one can begin to realize how language plays a vital role in the development of intelligence and the reality of success in school.

Let us now turn to the development of language.

LANGUAGE DEVELOPMENT THEORIES

There is no general agreement among linguists, who are individuals engaged in the systematic study of language, on how a child acquires language. One group claims that language is not innate or inborn. According to this group, the child possesses general abilities for learning, but no specific ability for the learning of language. Another group claims that the human brain is biologically suited for language development. Based on this view, the human brain is unique in its ability to acquire language, which is, thus, an innate human characteristic. In other words, in addition to the general abilities for learning, there is a special ability for language learning.

In the 1970s, researchers started concentrating on studying the functional aspects of language, which is concerned with how a child constructs a "meaning potential." This group of researchers focuses on interaction between the child and other human beings in a specific cultural and social setting. Michael A. K. Halliday, a leader in this area, has suggested a set of functions that the very young child must master to attain a "meaning potential." The "set of functions" appears in an approximate order, with the "informative function" coming significantly last. According to Halliday, "It is conceivable that these functions determine the initial development of language in all cultures; if so this would have major implications for our understanding of the evolution of language."[4]

The suggested set of language functions that Halliday postulates is as follows:[5]

1. *Instrumental:* "I want" function of language; it serves to satisfy the child's material needs; it enables him or her to obtain the goods and services wanted.
2. *Regulatory:* "Do as I tell you" function of language; directed toward a specific individual and concerned with influencing the individual; different from the instrumental function where the focus is on the goods or services rather than the person supplying it.
3. *Interactional:* "Me and you" function of language; used by child to interact with persons, especially persons important to him or her such as a parent; includes greetings and responses to calls.
4. *Personal:* "Here I come" function of language; used to express the child's own uniqueness; it is used to express the child's attitudes, interests, dislikes, and so on.
5. *Heuristic:* "Tell me why" function of language; concerns exploration of environment; this turns into a variety of questioning forms; it begins with the demand for a name for some specific object, which is a means of categorizing; then becomes concerned with more specific meanings.
6. *Imaginative:* "Let's pretend" function of language; the child creates an environment of his or her own; a world that turns from sound into story and make believe and ultimately into poetry and imaginative writing.
7. *Informative:* "I've got something to tell you" function of language; this does not emerge in the child's life until considerably after the others; it is used to communicate information to persons who do not already possess it.

Regardless of which theory one advocates, most would agree that the acquisition of language is a most important aspect of the child's intellectual development during the preschool years. Young children must determine, solely from the speech around them, the rules that govern language usage, so that they are able to understand and to produce well-constructed sentences. Amazingly, this difficult and complex task is accomplished by almost all children!

STAGES IN LANGUAGE DEVELOPMENT

A theoretical model describing the process of language learning consistent with recent research, but not dependent on the innateness assumption, follows.[6] In this model children's language development is divided into a number of stages that overlap; that is, children enter into higher stages well before they have completed earlier (lower) stages. The age at which children enter the various stages is dependent on individual differences. The ages given are approximations and are supplied by the author of this text. (See Figure 3.2 for age approximations for the various language-acquisition stages.)

Stage One: Random

In the random stage, children are involved in vocalizing, cooing, gurgling, babbling, and make most of the sounds that they will need in articulation later on. Children vary the way they use their lips, mouths, and tongues. The sounds children produce are a chance assortment, but adults hear them as the *phonemes* (smallest units of speech sounds) of language. Often children's babbling is composed of consonant–vowel links, such as Ma-ma-ma or Da-da-da. These first sounds are usually greeted with joy and delight by children's parents. No matter

[4]Michael Alexander Kirkwood Halliday, *Learning How to Mean: Explorations in the Development of Language* (New York: Elsevier North-Holland, 1975), p. 37.

[5]Ibid., pp. 18–37.

[6]E. Brooks Smith, Kenneth S. Goodman, Robert Meredith, *Language and Thinking in School,* 2d ed. (New York: Holt, Rinehart and Winston, 1976), pp. 17–26.

how unintelligible the sounds, the parents will perceive them to be words meaning "Mama" and "Daddy." Parents are excited because they feel that their children have spoken. They will many times repeat the sounds of "Ma ma" and "Da da," and reward the children with extra attention and smiles every time they produce these sounds. Such reinforcement usually causes children to repeat the response. Such imitative utterances are often referred to as *echoic speech*.

Stage Two: Unitary

In the unitary stage children develop deliberate units of language that are often limited to one syllable. The length of each utterance is a function of the child's level of physical development and control over his or her sound-producing mechanism, since the processes of language development and physical maturation are simultaneous. For example, one-year-old children usually have only a one-digit word span (the children can only retain and repeat one digit). The word that the children use is an abbreviation for their association with the total situation. Single words are used to convey whole sentences. Sometimes a single utterance is used to signify a variety of adult sentences. For example, "See" may mean "I see you" or "Let me see it." The child's use of such single-word utterances to express complex ideas is often referred to as *holophrastic speech*.

Children's speech has been described as "telegraphic."[7] Their early forms of speech include those words that convey a major meaning from the speech heard. Children are able to get and convey the message even though it is beyond their digit span. In *telegraphic speech*, when the children use more than one word, the word order of adult speech is preserved.

How are children able to extract the most meaningful words from fairly complex utterances? One explanation is that content words are those that parents may have practiced with the children one at a time. For example, the parents may use association; that is, they pair a real apple with the word sound "apple." When

the children repeat the word the parents may reinforce them by smiling and saying "Good." Content words also receive the most stress in a sentence, and may therefore be the easiest to discern.

Stage Three: Expansion and Delimiting

In expanding speech children go from one- or two-syllable utterances to adult language structure. At approximately eighteen or twenty months children's first two-word utterances usually appear. These consist of words from two classes. The first, called the pivot class, is small, contains words of high frequency, and may be in either the first or second position. Each pivot word is usually fixed in one or the other, however. First or second position merely refers to the place of the word in a given sentence. The second, called the open class, contains all other words. In speaking, the children combine a single pivot word with other words. For example, "See Mommy," "See Daddy," "See kitty," "See baby." (*See* is the pivot word.) In the examples, "Gimme that," "Gimme bunny," "Gimme cookie," *gimmie* is the pivot word. In the examples, "Baby off," "Mommy off," "Blanket off," *off* is a pivot word that appears in the second position. Some two-word utterances may serve a number of speech purposes. For example, "Mommy play," might mean "Mommy is playing" or "I want Mommy to play with me."

Researchers in language development, considering the problem of how children's telegraphic speech becomes elaborated, supposed that a constant exposure to adult speech may be a sufficient basis for children to enlarge their own speech. However, from observing parent–child interactions, it was found that parents often "model," that is, reiterate their child's message in an expanded pattern. For example, if a child says "Kitty drink," the parent is apt to say, "Yes, the kitty is drinking his milk." The parents help children to see that their utterances are correct for the situation and add other appropriate language elements that are grammatical.

If parents "overload" the information that is presented to children at this stage by using too many words, the children will probably not get the message. For example, Gertrude L. Wyatt,

[7]Roger Brown and Ursula Bellugi, "Three Processes in the Child's Acquisition of Syntax." *Harvard Educational Review* 34 (1964): 133–151.

an authority on language problems, writes of four-and-one-half-year-old twins who were having difficulty in speaking because their mother flooded them with too much information. The boys were looking at a picture book with their mother when this dialogue took place:

STEVE: How do aya-pa go?

MOTHER (who has understood Steve's question): It takes an elephant fifteen years to reach mature size. Elephants are mammals with an enormous appetite.

The language pattern that the mother presented did not fit the boys' stage of development. As a result, communication between mother and sons broke down. The mother's rapid speech and sophisticated vocabulary had overloaded the boys' receiving systems to the point where they were unable to distinguish and remember single sounds and sequences of sounds.[8]

By thirty-six months of age some children are using varieties of complete English sentences. Through the gradual expansion of speech, the child, by about four years of age, has mastered the features of adult speech.

Stage Four: Structural-Awareness

So that children can express their increasingly abstract ideas and feelings, they must come to the stage of structural awareness, where they are able to generalize and find pattern and order in speech. As children begin to use plurals and to vary their verb forms, the most common type of mistake they make indicates that the rules they follow are overgeneralized and do not include exceptions. For example, irregular verbs are regularized, making the past tense of "I go," "I goed."

Stage Five: Automatic

In the automatic stage children have internalized grammar, so that they can generate a large number of sentences that are grammatical although they cannot explain why by conscious reasoning. Children are usually at this stage when they are ready to enter kindergarten.

[8]Gertrude L. Wyatt, "In the Beginning Is the Word," *New York Times*, October 19, 1969.

Stage Six: Creative

At the creative stage children are involved in inventing their own language. Although many of the phrases they use may be trite, expressing the attitudes of their peer group or community, they fulfill the children's needs.

Figure 3.2 illustrates the language development stages just discussed.

Summary of Stages

It appears that children learn language by *association* (pairing the real object with the sound of the word), *reinforcement* (any positive stimulus, such as praise, which usually causes the individual to repeat a given response), *imitation* (children's attempting to voice the sounds initially voiced by the parent figures), and *elaboration* (expanding a word into a complete sentence).

Children may have difficulty in acquiring language if they are not exposed to elaborated speech patterns and if they are not listened to. (See Chapter 7 for a discussion of the child's development of articulation.)

MOTOR DEVELOPMENT AND THE ACQUISITION OF LANGUAGE

As children are gaining language and cognitive skills, they are also in the process of developing motor skills. In the first year of life, children achieve phenomenal feats in motor development. They go from a prone position to a vertical one; they go from supporting their head in a prone position to walking. From approximately 12 to 18 months, children are usually concentrating on perfecting their newly acquired motor skills. As a result, they usually do not seem to concentrate as much on their speaking vocabulary.

One of the most comprehensive studies done on vocabulary growth shows that from birth to 18 months the child acquires about 22 words; however, from 18 to 24 months, the child's vocabulary growth increases significantly, and the child develops a vocabulary of about 272 words. From 24 months onward, the child's vocabulary continues to increase at a rapid pace. At six years of age the child's speak-

FIGURE 3.2 MODEL OF LANGUAGE DEVELOPMENT STAGES SHOWING THE CLOSE OVERLAP OF ANY ONE STAGE WITH THE IMMEDIATE NEIGHBORING STAGES (ages are approximated and supplied by the author). *Source:* Adapted from E. Brooks Smith, Kenneth S. Goodman and Robert Meredith. *Language and Thinking in School* 2d ed. (New York: Holt, Rinehart and Winston, 1976).

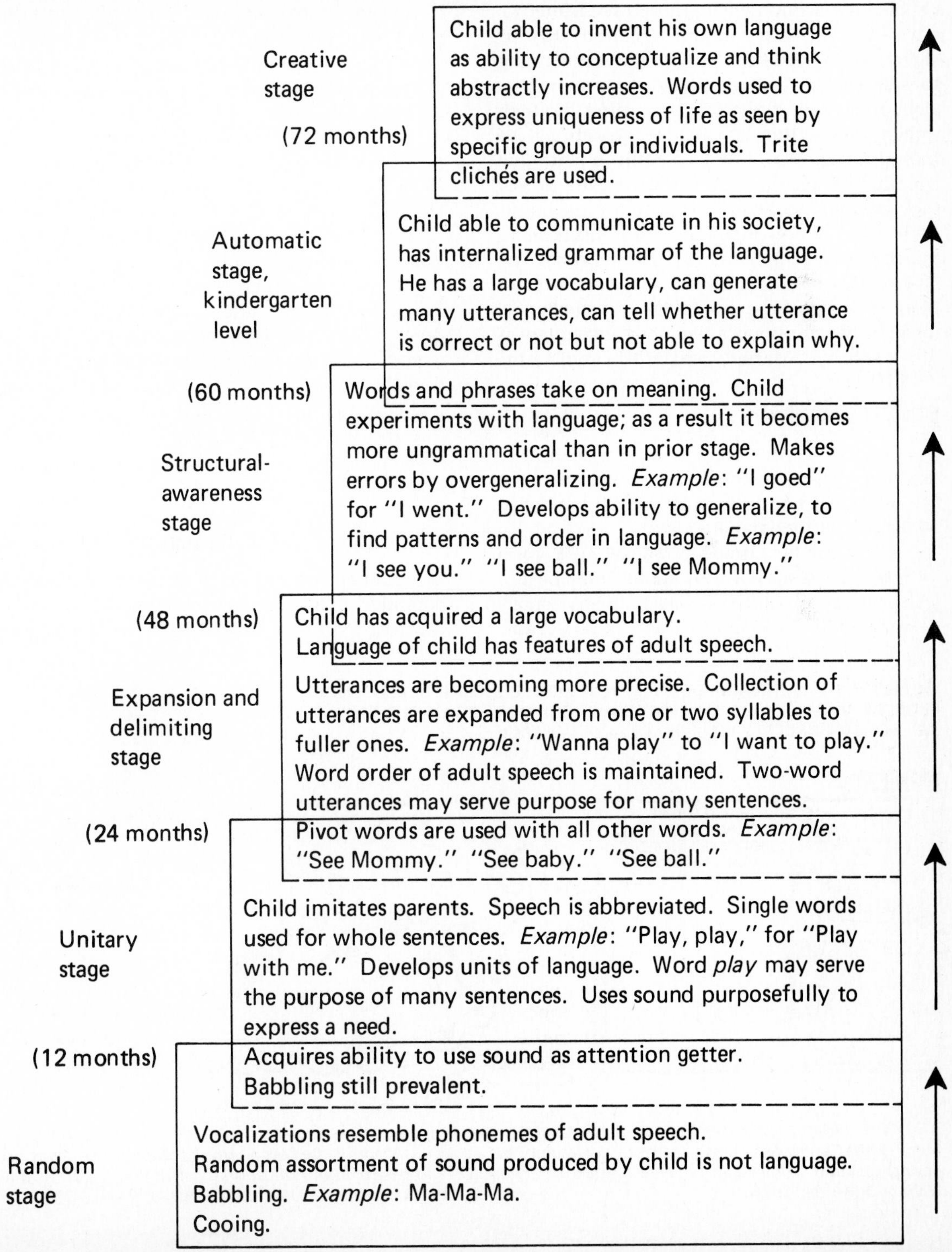

Creative stage

(72 months)

Child able to invent his own language as ability to conceptualize and think abstractly increases. Words used to express uniqueness of life as seen by specific group or individuals. Trite clichés are used.

Automatic stage, kindergarten level

Child able to communicate in his society, has internalized grammar of the language. He has a large vocabulary, can generate many utterances, can tell whether utterance is correct or not but not able to explain why.

(60 months)

Structural-awareness stage

Words and phrases take on meaning. Child experiments with language; as a result it becomes more ungrammatical than in prior stage. Makes errors by overgeneralizing. *Example:* "I goed" for "I went." Develops ability to generalize, to find patterns and order in language. *Example:* "I see you." "I see ball." "I see Mommy."

(48 months)

Child has acquired a large vocabulary. Language of child has features of adult speech.

Expansion and delimiting stage

Utterances are becoming more precise. Collection of utterances are expanded from one or two syllables to fuller ones. *Example:* "Wanna play" to "I want to play." Word order of adult speech is maintained. Two-word utterances may serve purpose for many sentences.

(24 months)

Pivot words are used with all other words. *Example:* "See Mommy." "See baby." "See ball."

Unitary stage

Child imitates parents. Speech is abbreviated. Single words used for whole sentences. *Example:* "Play, play," for "Play with me." Develops units of language. Word *play* may serve the purpose of many sentences. Uses sound purposefully to express a need.

(12 months)

Acquires ability to use sound as attention getter. Babbling still prevalent.

Random stage

Vocalizations resemble phonemes of adult speech. Random assortment of sound produced by child is not language. Babbling. *Example:* Ma-Ma-Ma. Cooing.

ing vocabulary is a little over 2500.[9] Since the study was done in the 1920s, it is probable that children's development is more precocious today. However, even though children may be saying more words earlier, and may be learning to walk sooner, it is reasonable to assume that while they are in the process of perfecting their walking skills, their vocabulary growth will be more limited. Also, it is important to state that even though children are not saying the words, they continue to acquire vocabulary meanings during the period that they are concentrating on motor development. In other words, the children's listening vocabulary is much greater than their speaking vocabulary. (Actually, all through life, a person's listening vocabulary is greater than his or her speaking vocabulary.)

CONCEPT DEVELOPMENT

Concept development is closely related to language development. Unless children attain the necessary concepts, they will be limited in all aspects of the language arts.

A *concept* is a group of stimuli with common characteristics. These stimuli may be objects, events, or persons. Concepts are usually designated by their names, such as book, war,

man, woman, animal, teacher, and so forth. All these concepts refer to classes (or categories) of stimuli. Some stimuli do not refer to concepts; Miss Dawn, the hairdresser, Hemingway's "The Killers," World War II, and the Super Bowl are examples. These are particular (not classes of) stimuli, persons, or events.[10]

Concepts are needed to reduce the complexity of the world. When children learn that their shaggy pets are called dogs, they tend to label all other similar four-footed animals as "dogs." This is because young children overgeneralize, tending to group all animals together, and have not yet perceived the differences between and among various animals. Unless children learn to discern differences, the class of words that they deal with will become exceptionally unwieldy and unmanageable. However, if children group each object in a class by itself, this too will bring about difficulties in coping with environmental stimuli, because it will also be such an unwieldy method.

Piaget and Concept Development

Concept development is closely related to cognitive (thinking) development. Jean Piaget, a renowned Swiss psychologist, has written on

FIGURE 3.3 LANGUAGE DEVELOPMENT AND CONCEPT DEVELOPMENT ARE CLOSELY RELATED. NOT UNDERSTANDING ONE MEANING OF THE WORD *TOAST*, THE BOY INCORRECTLY INTERPRETS ADULT SPEECH.

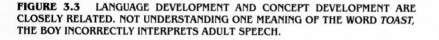

FIGMENTS   By Dale Hale

[9]M. E. Smith, "An Investigation of the Development of the Sentence and the Extent of Vocabulary in Young Children," *University of Iowa Studies in Child Welfare* 3 (No. 5), 1926.

[10]John P. DeCecco, *The Psychology of Learning and Instruction: Educational Psychology,* 2d ed. (Englewood Cliffs, N.J.: Prentice-Hall, 1974), p. 288.

children's cognitive development in terms of their ability to organize (which requires conceptualization), classify, and adapt to their environments.

According to Piaget,[11] the mind is capable of intellectual exercise because of its ability to categorize incoming stimuli adequately. Schemata (structured designs) are the cognitive arrangements by which this takes place. As children develop and take in more and more information, it is necessary to have some way to categorize all the new information. This is done by means of schemata, and, as children develop, their ability to categorize also grows. That is, children should be able to differentiate, to become less dependent on sensory stimuli, and to gain more and more complex schemata. Children should be able to categorize a cat as distinct from a mouse or a rabbit. They should be able to group cat, dog, and cow together as animals. Piaget calls the processes that bring about these changes in children's thinking *assimilation* and *accommodation*.

Assimilation does not change an individual's concept but allows it to grow. It is a continuous process that helps the individual to integrate new, incoming stimuli into existing schemata or concepts. For example, when children tend to label all similar four-footed animals as dogs, the children are assimilating. They have assimilated all four-footed animals into their existing schemata.

If the child meets stimuli that cannot fit into the existing schema, then the alternative is either to construct a new category or to change the existing category. When a new schema or concept is developed, or when an existing schema is changed, this is called accommodation.

Although both assimilation and accommodation are important processes that the child must attain in order to develop adequate cognition, a balance between the two processes is necessary. If children overassimilate, they will have categories that are too large to handle and, similarly, if they overaccommodate, they will have too many categories, as we have already seen. Piaget calls the balance between

the two *equilibrium*. A person having equilibrium would be able to see similarities between stimuli and thus properly assimilate them, and would also be able to determine when new schemata are needed for adequate accommodation of a surplus of categories.

As children develop cognitively they proceed from more global (generalized) schemata to more particular ones. For the child there are usually no right or wrong placements, but only better or more effective ones. That is what good education is all about.

Concepts are necessary to help students acquire increasing amounts of knowledge. For example, in school, as one proceeds through the grades, learning becomes more abstract and is expressed in words, using verbal stimuli as labels for concepts. Many teachers take for granted that those spoken concept labels are understood by their students, but this is not always so. Many times these concepts are learned either incompletely or incorrectly. This example illustrates incomplete concepts for the tourist and immigrant.

All tourists may be obviously American whereas all the immigrants may be obviously Mexican. The tourists may be well dressed, the immigrants poorly dressed, and so on. If the natural environment is like a grand concept-formation experiment, it may take the child a long time to attain the concepts *tourist* and *immigrant;* indeed, the environment may not be as informative as the usual experimenter since the child may not always be informed, or reliably informed, as to the correctness of his guesses. No wonder a child might form the concept that a tourist is a well-dressed person who drives a station wagon with out-of-state license plates![12]

When children come to school the teacher must assess their concept-development level, then help them to add the attributes necessary and relevant for the development of particular concepts, while aiding them to delete all those concepts that are faulty or irrelevant.

[11]Jean Piaget, *The Origins of Intelligence in Children* (New York: International Universities Press, 1952).

[12]John Carroll, "Words, Meanings, and Concepts," in *Thought & Language: Language and Reading,* Maryanne Wolf, Mark K. McQuillan, and Eugene Radwin, eds. (Cambridge, Mass.: *Harvard Educational Review,* 1980), p. 42.

Organizing Information and Concept Development

The better strategies we have for processing information, the better able we are to retain the information. For example, read the following words; then cover the words, and see how many you remember.

thimble, suit, butter, table tennis, button, football, thread, cloth, hat, hockey, bread, baseball, salt, handball, cereal, shoes, needle, sugar, shirt, tennis, socks

Now read the following words; then cover the words, and see how many you remember.

Groceries	Sports	Clothing	Sewing
bread	baseball	hat	needle
butter	football	shoes	thread
sugar	tennis	suit	thimble
salt	table tennis	shirt	button
cereal	hockey	socks	cloth
	handball		

Wasn't it easier to remember the second group of words than the first? The reason for this is because the second group of words is in categories; the words are organized for you. You are familiar with all the categories, so it is easy for you to remember what words would belong to the various categories. In learning information, we are able to remember better information that is related to material we already have met. We are active consumers of information, and as active consumers, we must attend to the information and determine how it is to be processed. If we have a category that would hold this information, we assimilate this information into our existing schemata. If not, we have to build a new category for the information.

Concept Development and Semantic Mapping (Graphic Organizing)

Semantic mapping is "a graphic representation used to illustrate concepts and relationships among concepts such as classes, properties, and examples."[13] Semantic mapping is a technique for organizing information; it helps to give structure or order. It helps persons to see the relationships among concepts, and it shows the various ways that information can be organized or categorized in more general or more specific categories. Using semantic maps to help us to see the relationships between and among ideas is not new; it is an offshoot of diagraming, and it is closely related to outlining. Figure 3.4 is an example of a simplified semantic map of the concept *living organisms* going from the most general to more specific. Although a specialized vocabulary exists for semantic mapping, teachers do not really need it in order to help students see how concepts are related and that the more general a category is the more abstract it is, and the more specific a category is the more concrete it is.

Rather than using semantic maps to help students see the relationships among categories, teachers can use sets such as in Figure 3.5 (see "Sets and Outlining" in Chapter 12).

Teachers can also use outlines (see "Outlining" in Chapter 12) to help students see relationships. For example:

I. Living Organisms
  A. Plants
    1. Trees
      a. Evergreens
        (1) Spruce
  B. Animals
    1. Humans
      a. Men
        (1) Arthur Hale

Concept Development and the Educationally Disadvantaged Child

In our schools there are many educationally disadvantaged[14] children who need special help. These children come to school with attitudes and values that are different from average children. Their "fatalistic attitude, orientation toward the present, and 'keep out of

---

[13]David P. Pearson and Dale D. Johnson, *Teaching Reading Comprehension* (New York: Holt, Rinehart and Winston, 1980), p. 232.

[14]The term "disadvantaged" is applied to those students who come from low socioeconomic-status homes. These children are disadvantaged in school because they may lack the concept-development experiences and the vocabulary that are needed in order to achieve well in school.

FIGURE 3.4   SIMPLIFIED SEMANTIC MAP FOR LIVING ORGANISMS

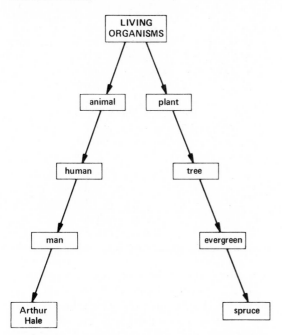

trouble' outlook hardly encourages the risk, exploration, and effort required to succeed academically."[15] Similarly, their vocabularies are "different." Although children who live in low socioeconomic environments may have rich,

FIGURE 3.5   THE USE OF SETS TO ILLUSTRATE RELATIONSHIPS FOR THE UNIVERSE OF LIVING ORGANISMS

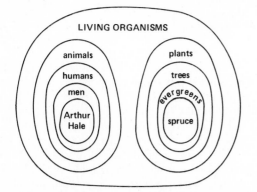

expressive vocabularies of their own, they will not be the same vocabulary that is predominantly used in middle-class schools and curriculums.

In helping educationally disadvantaged children to develop concepts, the teacher must help them to attain concepts that are of greatest concern, interest, and use to them. Teachers should give special attention to vocabulary development and categorizing skills because these are crucial for acquiring concepts. More will be said about this in upcoming sections in this chapter, as well as in other chapters in this book (see Chapter 9).

Concept Development in Primary Grades K–3

Preschool children learn concepts, for the most part, from direct experience. Unless young children have had direct sensory experiences, they will have difficulty in concept development.

When children enter kindergarten they may know the following concepts: above and below, on top of, underneath, next to, the middle one, start, stop, go, come, sit, stand, and so on. They may not know this type of concept, however: the one before, the next one, double, like, and unlike. Nor are they likely to recognize grapheme–phoneme (letter–sound) correspondences or number names for quantities.[16] It is important to state, however, that individual differences exist among children entering kindergarten, and some young children entering kindergarten can read and have some number names for quantities.

Kindergarten children are learning to group many objects. For example, under the class Games, they learn to group different kinds of games such as Candyland, Frustration, Lotto, and so on. Pears, apples, bananas, plums, and so forth would go under the class Fruit.

In the primary grades children are learning simple concepts such as over and under, big and little. Proceeding from a concrete to a more abstract level the pupils learn to classify things such as dogs and animals, days and weeks,

[15]Robert R. Reilly and Ernest L. Lewis, *Educational Psychology* (New York: Macmillan, 1983), p. 367.

[16]Robert M. Gagné, *Conditions of Learning and Theory of Instruction,* 4th ed. (New York: Holt, Rinehart and Winston, 1985).

© 1974 by NEA, Inc.

"YOU GOTTA SPEAK PLAIN ENGLISH TO MY MOM! YOU ASK FOR BREAD AND YOU GET BREAD ... ASK FOR MONEY!"

pennies and money, and so on. For example, a child can name his or her dog "Champ," who is a pet, and as a pet it is also in the class of animals.

As children grow in their use of listening, speaking, and reading skills, their concept development continues. They learn that some words designate different levels of things and feelings: They put on their *coats* but they use *coats* of paint on the toy. These two uses illustrate a *homograph*.

The children learn about different kinds of elevators, forms, cities. They develop the relational concepts of afraid, brave, proud, faraway, and so on. They learn about associations and how some words are associated with certain ideas and objects. For example, they would associate *farmer, barn, cows, pigs, chickens,* and so on with farm. They learn the meaning of figures of speech, such as: "The trees trembled in the night" or "The wind roared its disapproval."

The students should also be learning the concepts of *synonyms* (words that mean the same or nearly the same) and *antonyms* (words that mean the opposite) in isolation and in context. As children gain skill in working with such concepts as classification, synonyms, antonyms, and word associations, they are gaining the ability to recognize and work with word relationships (analogies).

SUMMARY

Success in school depends in great part on children's language development. Whether language is an innate ability, as some authorities believe, or is a result of a human brain uniquely able to acquire language, young children learn to speak the language of those around them and, furthermore, learn the grammar involved in producing well-constructed sentences. This is generally accomplished in six interlocking stages, for which a model is given in the text. In order to grow in their use of language, children must also begin to develop concepts by which they group words and organize them. Piaget calls the processes that bring about changes in thinking *assimilation* and *accommodation*. As their ability to develop new concepts grows, children are learning and gaining knowledge.

It is important for teachers to identify the level of concept development among the children in their classes. Particularly with children from low socioeconomic areas, teachers must not make assumptions about concept development, but must try to determine actual levels.

SUGGESTIONS FOR THOUGHT
QUESTIONS AND ACTIVITIES

1. Choose a preschool child from among your acquaintances. Observe and record the verbal behavior of the child during a half-hour play period. Discuss your observations with the class. (Take into account limited data.)

2. Choose a preschool child from among your acquaintances. Engage the child in a conversation. Try to determine at what language development stage the child is. Use Figure 3.2 on page 29 to help you. Also, give specific examples as evidence to share with the class.

3. Discuss the interrelatedness of language development and school success.

SELECTED BIBLIOGRAPHY

Brown, Roger, and Ursula Bellugi. "Three Processes in the Child's Acquisition of Syntax." *Harvard Educational Review* 34 (1964): 133–151.

Carroll, John B. "Words, Meanings and Concepts," in *Thought and Language, Language and Reading.* Maryanne Wolf, Mark K. McQuillan and Eugene Radwin, eds. Cambridge, Mass.: *Harvard Educational Review,* 1980, pp. 26–50.

Dale, Philip S. *Language Development: Structure and Function,* 2d ed. New York: Holt, Rinehart and Winston, 1976.

Dyson, Anne Haas, and Celia Genishi. "Research Currents: Children's Language for Learning." *Language Arts* 60 (September 1983): 751–757.

Edwards, A. D. "Language Difference and Educational Failure." *Language Arts* 59 (May 1982): 513–519.

Halliday, M. A. K. *Learning How to Mean: Explorations in the Development of Language.* New York: Elsevier, 1975.

Lindfors, Judith W. *Children's Language and Learning.* Englewood Cliffs, N.J.: Prentice-Hall, 1980.

Loban, Walter D. *Language Development: Kindergarten through Grade Twelve.* Research Report No. 18. Urbana, Ill.: National Council of Teachers of English, 1976.

McNeill, D. *The Acquisition of Language: The Study of Developmental Psycholinguistics.* New York: Harper & Row, 1970.

Piaget, Jean. *The Language and Thought of the Child.* New York: Harcourt Brace, 1926.

Pinnel, Gay Su, ed. *Discovering Language with Children.* Urbana, Ill.: National Council of Teachers of English, 1980.

Wells, Gordon. *Learning through Interaction: The Study of Language Development.* London: Cambridge University Press, 1981.

Wood, Barbara S. "Children and Communication: Verbal and Nonverbal Language," in *Language Development,* 2d ed. Englewood Cliffs, N.J.: Prentice-Hall, 1981.

FOUR

Developing Creativity in the Language Arts Program

I see the mind of a five year old . . . as a volcano with two vents, destructiveness and creativeness. And I see that to the extent that we widen the creative channel we atrophy the destructive one. . . .[1]

Sylvia Ashton-Warner

THE YOUNG CHILD AND CREATIVITY

It is said that children come to school curious, uninhibited, filled with enthusiasm and the desire to know, but as they proceed through school, these talents are squelched. Carl Rogers, a well-known clinical psychologist, claims, "In education we tend to turn out conformists, stereotypes, individuals whose education is 'completed,' rather than freely creative and original thinkers."[2] Another psychologist, H. A. Anderson, says, "Creativity was in each of us as a small child. In children creativity is a universal. Among adults it is almost nonexistent."[3] Others decry the stifling of the child's natural gifts by surrounding adults and blame them for destroying the child's ability to create.[4]

These statements imply that our schools are not assuming the responsibility that John Dewey, an eminent philosopher and educator, felt was an especially crucial one—that of giving free rein to the child's imagination and allowing it to flourish.[5]

Language arts teachers must be well acquainted with creativity. A good physical environment is a necessary first step in helping to establish an atmosphere where creativity can reign. (See "Classroom Physical Environment" in Chapter 5.) More is needed to encourage and stimulate creativity, however. Teachers must have some understanding and insight into the creative process itself. They must also have a knowledge of techniques to spark the creativity in students.

HOW IS CREATIVITY DEFINED AND MEASURED?

Confusion exists about the meaning of the term *creativity* because it can mean so many

[1]Sylvia Ashton-Warner, *Spinster* (New York: Simon & Schuster, 1959), p. 221.

[2]Carl Rogers, "Toward a Theory of Creativity," in *Creativity and Its Cultivation,* Harold H. Anderson, ed. (New York: Harper & Row, 1959), p. 69.

[3]Ibid., p. xii.

[4]Hughes Mearns, *Creative Youth* (New York: Doubleday, 1926), p. viii.

[5]John Dewey, *The Child and the Curriculum and the School and Society* (Chicago: University of Chicago Press, 1902), p. 61.

different things to so many different people. Some define creativity as "something new." Yet what may be new to one may not be new to another. If we use a definition such as this, anyone, regardless of intellectual capacity, can be considered creative. Other definitions of creativity are based on that of divergent thinking—for example, the many different ways of doing things, which has been derived from J. P. Guilford's three-dimensional model of intelligence that represents intellect in terms of operations, content, and products.

However, since the dimension of creativity is not measured on IQ tests, E. P. Torrance, an educational psychologist at the University of Georgia, developed tests of creative thinking which he based on his investigations of classroom situations where he felt creativity was fostered. Torrance defines creativity "as the process of becoming sensitive to problems, deficiencies, gaps in knowledge, missing elements, disharmonies, and so on; identifying the difficulty; searching for solutions, making guesses, or formulating hypotheses about the deficiencies; testing and retesting these hypotheses and possibly modifying and retesting them; and finally communicating the results."[6] The tests are supposed to measure fluency or the number of relevant ideas; flexibility or the number of shifts in thought or changes in categories of response; originality or the number of statistically infrequent responses; and elaboration or the number of different ideas employed in working out the specifics of an overall idea.

S. J. Parnes, President of Creative Education Foundation at Buffalo University, gave his definition at a symposium on creativity in the early sixties: a combination of imagination plus knowledge plus evaluation.[7] Although there is no universally agreed-on definition of creativity, Parnes' seems to incorporate all the necessary elements. It also delimits and qualifies a broad definition, whereby anything new to the individual connotes creativity. It seems reasonable that the more knowledge individuals have, no matter in what area, the more able they will be to generate many different ideas—if they have the requisite imagination. Similarly, the more intelligent the individuals, the more able they will be to evaluate their product. Therefore, an individual who is more intelligent is bound to be more capable of greater creativity than someone who is less intelligent—all other things being equal. In actuality, since "other" variables are rarely equal, it does not necessarily follow that people of great intelligence will be more creative than people of less intelligence.

J. W. Getzels and P. W. Jackson's study of two groups of students, one of which was composed of supposedly high creatives who were not gifted and the other of which was composed of gifted students who were not highly creative, was of great significance because it brought the concept and importance of creativity to the attention of educators. The researchers found that the high-IQ group was not necessarily the high creative group and, although both groups of students achieved equally well, different characteristics distinguished the two groups. After studying the data more closely, it was found that all the students had relatively high IQs and were able; for example, the mean IQ of the high-creative group was 127; whereas the mean IQ of the high-intelligence group was 150.[8]

Some persons have used this study in their claim that one does not need to be intelligent in order to be creative. This is not so when we define creativity in an absolute sense. For example, the discovery of a new vaccine or a new technique in surgery would necessitate special knowledge and intelligence, but other factors are needed to make one truly creative. The characteristics that distinguish one group of able students from another include those salient features that may determine creative behavior. High-creatives are more concerned with their "self-ideal" and are not as influenced by impositions from the teacher or society. A sense of humor was another factor, according to the Getzels and Jackson study, which set high-creatives apart from high-gifted students.

[6]E. P. Torrance, "Scientific Views of Creativity and Factors Affecting Its Growth," in *Creativity and Learning*, Jerome Kagan, ed. (Boston: Houghton Mifflin, 1967), pp. 73–74.

[7]S. J. Parnes, Symposium on Creativity, University of Maryland, Summer 1963.

[8]J. W. Getzels and P. W. Jackson, *Creativity and Intelligence: Explorations with Gifted Students* (New York: Wiley, 1962), p. 24.

HIGH-CREATIVE SUBJECT

This man is flying back from Reno where he has just won a divorce from his wife. He couldn't stand to live with her anymore, he told the judge, because she wore so much cold cream on her face at night that her head would skid across the pillow and hit him in the head. He is now contemplating a new skidproof face cream.

HIGH-IQ SUBJECT

Mr. Smith is on his way home from a successful business trip. He is very happy and he is thinking about his wonderful family and how glad he will be to see them again. He can picture it, about an hour from now, his plane landing at the airport and Mrs. Smith and their three children all there welcoming him home again.

For example, one test used a projective technique, a method in which the individual tends to put himself or herself into the situation depicted. Students were presented with a picture stimulus perceived as a man sitting in an airplane reclining seat on a return trip. Above are samples of the comments given by a high-IQ subject and a high-creative subject.[9]

A possible explanation for the difference in response between the two groups may be that very able students, who are achievement oriented and grade conscious, will attempt to "size up" the teacher at the beginning of the term, try to "figure out" what is wanted and then attempt to give the teacher exactly that. It's not that these students are not able to be creative but that they have learned while going to school that "creativity" is not rewarded; and they act accordingly. They have been conditioned not to be divergent. Creative students, on the other hand, tend to be unique; they seem to abhor routine and organized tasks. They often appear disorganized, even though they may not be.

The creative individual is less predictable than other persons. "The more creative a person is, the harder he or she is to predict with any precision. And if what is created were pre-

dictable, it could no longer be described as creative."[10] The unpredictability factor is what makes research on creativity difficult.

When students are asked to write their autobiographies, most students probably just state their vital statistics. This may show that high-IQ children answer in what they feel is the expected direction. The question is: Would they answer in this way if they were encouraged to be creative?

THE CREATIVE PROCESS

Creativity cannot be commanded. It needs time. If teachers want to help students to be creative, they must have an understanding of this process.

According to psychologists there seem to be four stages to the creative act for most people: (1) preparation, (2) incubation, (3) illumination, and (4) verification.[11]

Preparation involves all the necessary background experience and skills an individual must have in order to be creative in a given area. As was previously mentioned in Parnes' definition of creativity, "knowledge" is an important ingre-

[9]Ibid., p. 39.

[10]Leona E. Tyler, *Thinking Creatively* (San Francisco, Ca.: Jossey-Bass, 1983), p. 200.

[11]G. Wallas, *The Art of Thought* (New York: Harcourt Brace, 1926).

FIGURE 4.1 THE MORE KNOWLEDGE AND IMAGINATION INDIVIDUALS HAVE, THE MORE CREATIVE THEY CAN BE.

© 1960 United Feature Syndicate, Inc.

dient. The more knowledge people have, the more able they are to be creative. Creativity and knowledge of basic skills are not mutually exclusive. They work hand in hand. The teacher can help students by making sure all are receiving the necessary tools. Those who say, "Let them just create; knowledge gets in the way," and so forth, are not helping to set the proper stage to prepare for creativity. An engineer-lawyer discussing engineering education says:

Engineering education should encourage students to strive for the mastery of fundamentals, the discovery of the relatedness of things, and the cultivation of excellence. But it should also be a creative experience, stimulating the imagination of students and helping them to prepare themselves for the contests and the challenges of an imperfect world. It should encourage them to believe they can do the "impossible" from time to time, even if it means doing violence to precedent.[12]

The importance of recognizing the tools necessary for creativity has been sidetracked because of the overuse and misuse of the term *creativity*. Persons who have achieved in the creative area usually devote a great portion of their lives to the field in which they work. Competency and creativity demand good preparation.

Incubation is the second stage in the creative process. This stage is not visible. It is the time when individuals appear to be thinking about anything but the problem, yet they may actually be mulling it over in their minds.

Illumination is that moment of insight when a spark is lit and a solution seems at

[12]Daniel V. DeSimone, "Education for Innovation," *Spectrum* IEEE 5 (January 1968): 83.

hand. A Nobel Prize-winning scientist describes illumination this way:[13]

I just wander about, without especially clear ideas or preconceived notions so far as I know, and now and then something pops up—boom!—something that is entirely new, that leads to new lines of research.

Verification is the final stage, where the "hunch" (the hypothesis) is subjected to testing and refinement. The same Nobel Prize-winner describes his manner of work:[14]

But while I am working I usually do not know where I am going. I just follow hunches. I dream up all sorts of theories at night and then disprove them in the laboratory the next day. Checking a hunch, sometimes I see some discrepancy, something unexpected—then I follow it up. Success depends on whether the hunch was good or bad.

NURTURING CREATIVITY

Creativity is not something that "just happens." If we want divergent thinkers (persons who can see many different ways to solve problems) and individuals who are and continue to be intelligent risk-takers, we must create an environment that values these traits and we must involve students in creative experiences. If teachers are not creative—if they are frightened and bothered by divergency—they will be unable to create the proper physical, emotional, and intellectual climate essential for the development of creativity.

A creative atmosphere is one that pervades everything that is done in the classroom. On the first school day the manner in which the students are greeted will determine, to a certain extent, how free students will feel to be different.

Teachers must provide stimulating activities for students when they first begin school. Torrance has developed a tentative hierarchy of creative skills that he feels might be taught to children. His six levels range from the young child's learning to produce new combinations

through the manipulation of sounds, colors, and shapes to the child's being able to carry through the sequence of creative problem-solving.[15]

In the following section are some exercises that have been used on the first few days of class with intermediate-grade students, as well as with college language arts students. They help to establish rapport, to awaken many students as to how "set" they are, and also to show how the verbal behavior of the teacher influences students.

To illustrate how rigid many students are, and how a teacher's verbal behavior influences students, it can be shown that beginning with the question of how clever someone is can cause anxiety, especially on the first day of class when a student wants to make a good impression. This challenge may bring about less effective functioning. The second question about how well the students know Roman numerals, and a repetition of the words, can cause students to think about an answer in the area only of Roman numerals, where their minds have been "set" (see activity 2 of the "Creativity Exercises").

Another exercise in creative thinking designed to avoid rigidity is to put this dot matrix on the board:

$$\begin{matrix} \bullet & \bullet & \bullet \\ \bullet & \bullet & \bullet \\ \bullet & \bullet & \bullet \end{matrix}$$

Tell the students to connect the dots with four straight lines going through each dot only once and without lifting the pencil from the paper. To solve this new problem students must use a very important clue, that of *going beyond*. Most people confine themselves to the set of the original square, but the problem can only be solved if one goes beyond.

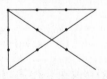

[13]Albert Szent-Gyorgyi, "The Strategy of Life," *Science and Technology* (New York: International Communications, June 1966), p. 49.

[14]Ibid.

[15]E. Paul Torrance, *Encouraging Creativity in the Classroom* (Dubuque, Iowa: W. C. Brown, 1970), pp. 40–53.

Creativity Exercises

1. In the following line drawing, how many squares do you see?

Most people say 16. Ask them to look again. They are usually puzzled. *Hint:* What is the definition of a square? Now look again. How many do you see now? At this point some call out 17, 18, or 19. They are getting the idea. They are looking beyond the obvious.

Solution: There are 30 different squares: 16 each of 1×1; 9 each of 2×2; 4 each of 3×3; and one of 4×4.

2. How clever are you? How many know their Roman numerals well? Think of Roman numeral nine, then subtract three. By adding one symbol to Roman numeral nine, you should be able to come up with the answer.

After some time the teacher often has to provide the answer. IX is put on the board, and an "S" is added before the number to produce six.

3. Ask students to say aloud the words that are being spelled orally:

Mac Arthur Mac Duffy Mac Guiness Mac Kinney Mac Namara Machinery

4. The teacher says, "We're going to be involved with some rhyming words and spelling. Spell *could, would, should.* Spell *cake, bake, make, lake.* Spell *Polk* as in President Polk. Now, who can spell the name for the white of an egg? How many of you spelled *yolk* rather than *albumen*?

5. Three murderers killed their victim in a sauna. They left the sauna without the weapon. The police came and found no trace of the weapon. How was the victim killed and what was the weapon used?

Solution: The victim was stabbed with an icicle. The teacher can make this activity into one that encourages students to ask questions in the form of hypotheses by telling the students that he or she will help them solve the mystery if they ask questions that require only a "Yes" or "No" response.

6. Following are some words. See if you can determine which words would fit between A and horrible?
A   be   _____ _____ _____ _____ _____ horrible.

Solution: The words that would fit would be in an alphabetical sequence, with each succeeding word having one extra letter, for example: A be car down every father garages horrible.

Brainstorming

Brainstorming, generating many different ideas without inhibition, is a technique that has been popularized in business and industry. It can be used very effectively in the classroom situation to help stretch students' imaginations. The process is an excellent way to break the ice among students on any level. It helps them to work together while creating an atmosphere conducive to creativity.

Certain principles must be followed so that brainstorming will be truly effective:

1. Anything goes.
2. No criticisms.
3. Build on another's ideas.

It has been found that those who generate the most ideas in a brainstorming session most often also have the ideas of highest quality.[16]

Before getting students involved in group-brainstorming, they should try self-brainstorming. Students can be given a stimulus to which they must react, "stretching their imaginations" while observing the three principles listed here. They can write down all of their ideas; after a few minutes, time is called. The student with the greatest quantity of ideas reads his or her list to the whole class. If someone in the class has an idea not on this original list, that idea is added. (This also makes for a very good listening activity for students.) Only after all the ideas have been stated does evaluation take place.

In group-brainstorming students choose one person who is a very fast writer to record oral ideas called out as soon as they are thought up. The same principles prevail for group-brainstorming as for self-brainstorming. But in the group the temptation to criticize

[16]Alex F. Osborn, *Applied Imagination,* 3d ed. (New York: Scribner's, 1963), p. 156.

must be overcome. These topics could be used for both group- and self-brainstorming sessions:

1. Many different uses of a brick
2. Many different uses of a pin
3. Many different uses of a paper clip
4. Many different uses of a coat hanger
5. Many different uses of a paper bag
6. Many different uses of a button
7. Many different uses of a rubber band
8. Many different uses of a pencil
9. Many different uses of a block
10. Many different uses of a paper carton
11. State all elements that an "ideal school" would have.
12. State what you would build on the moon, if you were going there on a trip.
13. State all the kinds of automation devices you can think of.

Students should be helped to understand that "different uses" does not include, for example: "A brick can be used to build a house. A brick can be used to build a wall. A brick can be used to build a chimney." It would include such things as: "A brick can be used as a bed warmer, to write with, to carve out and use as an ashtray, to use as a missile," and so on.

Brainstorming activities can lead to a number of very exciting language arts projects. In one fifth-grade class, students were group-brainstorming the many different uses of a half-pint milk carton. After they had evaluated some of their ideas, many of the children wanted to carry them out. As a result, a number of new groups were formed. One group made puppets and a stage out of the cartons. Then they started to write scripts for their puppets. The Fifth Grade Thespian Group was born. They not only gave original shows to their own class but also presented shows for many of the other classes. The kindergarten children enjoyed them, and upper-grade children looked forward to these informal productions as well. Announcements to advertise coming attractions were written by the Thespian Group, which was usually joined by other children who helped with artwork and new productions.

Some students made robots and other imaginary creatures out of the milk containers and wrote stories about them.

Another brainstorming activity that children would enjoy would be to have them choose a room in the house and then to ask them to brainstorm as many things as possible that they could find in that room that begin with a certain letter. For example, "Name as many things as possible that you could find in the kitchen that start with c. Most children will probably state such things as cake, cupboard, cookie, candy, and so on. The creative child, however, would be prone to state some of the following: crumbs, calories, cholesterol, critters, and so on.[17]

Brainstorming, while helping to establish a nonthreatening environment, can also be a springboard to creative writing! (See Chapter 11.)

A good language arts program cannot exist without the necessary ingredient of creativity. When creativity is a living process that permeates the teaching-learning activities, the classroom atmosphere is charged with electricity and becomes a very special place. When this atmosphere does not exist, however, results may be unfortunate.

This poem describes how creativity in a child can be almost thwarted. If you were this child's teacher, how would you have reacted?

GREEN SKY, BLUE GRASS

Oh happy day,
Oh day so bright,
Let me catch you,
Just for a moment,
And let me feel you!

Yes, I'll draw you,
My happy day, with
Bright, happy colors.
Pretty day, I'll draw you
With a green sky and blue grass—
All in a smiling sea of yellow.
Happy and oh so free,
Let me draw you!

Then I heard a laugh,
A snicker, a sneer.
"Green sky, blue grass?

[17]This brainstorming activity was suggested by Dr. Joanne E. Bernstein.

Everyone knows that
Grass is green and
Skies are blue and
Seas aren't yellow and . . ."

But I didn't hear any more,
Because I had lost my happy day—
It disappeared so fast
I didn't see it go.
And I was sad and tired
And didn't know what to do.

Then I heard another voice,
A bright, happy voice,

Like my day.
And it said, "What a pretty picture!
What beautiful colors!"

And then I found
My happy, carefree day again.
My pretty day with
Green skies and
Blue grass in a
Sea of yellow.
And I had caught my day.
And for a moment I was free
Like my day.

Sharon Anne Rubin

SUMMARY

Whatever the ingredients of creativity are, they are difficult to measure. Most studies have shown that creativity and intelligence seem to go together, but a high IQ does not guarantee imagination, humor, or creative ability. Time and understanding seem to be involved in the four-stage model of the creative act given in this text. These stages include preparation, incubation, illumination, and verification. When creativity is recognized, it can be nurtured by the teacher. Getting students to go beyond rigid mind-sets, to brainstorm either by themselves or in groups, and to develop activities and new ways of looking at things are some suggestions for making the classroom a special place.

SUGGESTIONS FOR THOUGHT QUESTIONS AND ACTIVITIES

1. Choose an object and then brainstorm the many different ways that the object can be used.
2. Use brainstorming techniques to make a list of the many different topics that could be used for brainstorming activities in the language arts.
3. You have been asked to give a talk on the place of creativity in the school. You will be addressing other teachers. What will you say, and what suggestions will you make?
4. Have students brainstorm the many different uses of a metal coat hanger.
5. Observe a classroom for a day. Determine whether the students are involved in any activities that would encourage or stimulate creative thought.

SELECTED BIBLIOGRAPHY

Getzels, J. W., and P. W. Jackson. *Creativity and Intelligence: Explorations with Gifted Students.* New York: Wiley, 1962.

Guilford, J. P. "Traits of Creativity," in *Creativity and Its Cultivation: Interdisciplinary Symposia on Creativity,* H. H. Anderson, ed. New

York: Harper and Brothers, 1959, pp. 142–161.

Lowenfeld, Viktor, and W. Lambert Brittan. *Creative and Mental Growth,* 7th ed. New York: Macmillan, 1982.

Osborn, Alex F. *Applied Imagination: Principles and Procedures of Creative Problem-solving,* 3d ed. New York: Scribner's, 1979.

Stanley, Julian C., ed. *Gifted and the Creative: A Fifty-Year Perspective.* Baltimore, Md.: Johns Hopkins University Press, 1978.

Torrance, E. P., and J. Pansy Torrance. *Is Creativity Teachable?* Bloomington, Ind.: Phi Delta Kappa, 1973.

FIVE

The Teacher as Manager of the Language Arts Program

It is the supreme art of the teacher to awaken joy in creative expression and knowledge.

Albert Einstein

There are a number of factors that profoundly influence children's learning in school. These factors range from teachers' insight into their own personalities to the physical surroundings, including school plant, classroom, walls of the rooms, corridors, play area, and so on. All of these variables will determine how teachers organize for learning and how they manage the learning environment. Although teachers are not managers in the business sense, they are responsible for a group of pupils and are interested in the "largest return" for an investment of time, energy, and money. Many persons would frown on looking at human behavior as an "output" and would claim that such an attitude is dehumanizing. But is it?

Are not teachers interested in making a positive, beneficial difference to the learning of their students? "A teacher is a person engaged in interactive behavior with one or more students for the purpose of effecting a change in those students."[1] In order to accomplish this goal teachers must have teaching strategies and also ways to evaluate whether the desired learnings have been achieved. And, they must not make unfounded assumptions about the abilities of their students.

It is not possible to give an exhaustive, in-depth discussion of all the components with which teachers must deal in this chapter. However, unless teachers understand their roles, the firm foundation on which a strong language arts program can be mounted cannot be established. In the *Second Handbook of Research on Teaching* Robert Dreeben states:

[The] teacher's primary task is to design and engage pupils in learning activities sufficiently engrossing that pupils find those activities substantially more attractive than proscribed alternatives (which often have attractions of their own). Under these circumstances, maintaining "the students' absorption in the task at hand" and getting their attention are tasks of great immediacy and importance both for instructional and managerial reasons.[2]

How teachers gain students' attention and keep them engaged in these tasks is a most im-

[1] John D. McNeil and W. James Popham, "The Assessment of Teacher Competence," in *Second Handbook of Research on Teaching.* Robert M. W. Travers, ed. (Chicago: Rand McNally, 1973), p. 219.

[2] Robert Dreeben, "The School as a Workplace," in *Second Handbook of Research on Teaching,* Robert M. W. Travers, ed. (Chicago: Rand McNally, 1973), p. 466.

portant concern of educators. The successful accomplishment of this concern depends on the teaching technique and incentives that are used, the teacher's personality and motivating techniques, challenging seat work, the ability to make smooth transitions from one topic to another, and a knowledge of individual differences.

TEACHER PLANNING FOR LEARNING

Teacher planning is an essential part of the language arts program, as well as any other program. Planning helps guide teachers in making choices about what to include in the language arts program, how to organize the program, and how to develop it. Effective planning also helps teachers to clarify their thinking about objectives, students' needs, interests, and readiness levels, as well as choice of motivating techniques. Good planning guarantees the wisest use of time, assuring that balance and sequence will prevail in teaching–learning activities.

DECISION MAKING, PLANNING, AND MATERIALS FOR A LANGUAGE ARTS PROGRAM

Planning for the language arts program includes decision making. When the teacher decides to arrange the desks in the classroom in a semicircle rather than in straight rows, a decision has been made based on the teacher's values. The teacher who recognizes the importance of students' visual contact for more effective aural (listening) and oral (speaking) communication will develop a program different from the one for children who are always sitting behind one another.

Similarly, teachers who choose a variety of materials from many sourses are making decisions that will affect the kind of language arts program they will present. Their programs will be different from those of teachers who use only one source for materials. If teachers decide they want to use a multimedia approach to teaching, further decisions concerning the kinds of materials employed in their lessons must also be made. For example, will the lesson be more effective if only printed materials—such as books, bulletins, or pamphlets—are used, or should cartoons and charts be brought into the classroom? Cartoons give some comic relief if they are at the comprehension level of the students, and charts graphically illustrate some of the points made in the written material. Such questions as to whether the print is too small, or whether the words used in printed materials are at the children's reading level, must also be considered if evaluation of children's accomplishments with the material is to be valid.

Should visual aids such as pictures (photographs of individuals, places, animals, objects), picture slides, television, filmstrips, videotapes, or motion pictures be used? This decision would depend on the amount of time allotted to the lesson, the availability of the visual aids, facilities provided, and whether there were other more effective ways to obtain the desired objectives.

Should audio aids—such as tape recorders, record players, the radio, or plays—be brought into class? Again the answer would depend on the objectives and what is being stressed in a particular lesson. For example, if the lesson focuses on some aspect of speech improvement, a video- or audiotape recorder would be an invaluable tool, if it is properly used.

Teachers must decide on the kinds of concrete materials they will need for the language arts program. Often such decisions must be made months before the materials are to be used because of the long lead time necessary for delivery. In this case planning must take place before the beginning of the school year. This would be particularly true if the teacher wants students to learn to express themselves, for instance, as in puppet making. If the teacher wants to coordinate a writing lesson with an art period, various kinds of construction paper and other art supplies must be made available to give children the choice of a range of materials.

It can be seen that planning and decision making are ongoing processes that complement one another. The better the planning and the more timely the decision making, the more effective the language arts program will be.

STUDENT–TEACHER PLANNING

Student–teacher planning is rapidly becoming accepted by teachers and is effective if properly used. The role of the teacher in planning with students must consist of a judicious balance between accepting students' contributions and managing and controlling the teaching–learning situation. For pupil–teacher planning to be productive, teachers must recognize that students' involvement in some decisions will help these students to become more self-reliant and more interested in the planned activity.

Teachers must also realize that student–teacher planning will only work if students are helped to plan. Such planning should begin in the primary grades, where the teacher and children discuss and plan the topics and activities that they will engage in during morning and afternoon sessions. The teacher can assure wise decision making by helping students to understand why they should not plan certain activities consecutively. They should also state scheduling constraints, such as group plans, seat work, special art periods, special music periods, and so on.

In the language arts areas students should be given opportunities to express the kinds of activities in which they would like to engage. For example, if students are interested in puppetry, creative dramatics, or writing skits, time for these activities should be planned.

SCENARIO: TEACHER–PUPIL PLANNING

Lower-intermediate grade: ten boys, nine girls, one female teacher. A suburban school with children from a middle socioeconomic background. The classroom contains desks clustered together in groups of four. Learning centers are visible in easily accessible areas.

Time: beginning of the school day
Date: middle of the week (middle of the school year)

ACTION

Children arrive in classroom. They are smiling and chatting with one another. Mrs. Hill greets each of her students and seems to have something special to say to each. After the children have settled down, Mrs. Hill asks if anyone has anything special that they would like to share with the class. Four children raise their hands. Mrs. Hill asks each to share his or her special item. After the children share their special items, Karen comes to the front of the room and reads her favorite poem. Mrs. Hill thanks her and then she reminds Seth that tomorrow he will be reading his special poem to the class. "Remember," Mrs. Hill says, "you do not have to know the poem by heart. The poem you choose to read to the class should be one that you enjoy and that you think your classmates will enjoy hearing. I'm very pleased with the poems everyone has chosen to share with us. Some of them have also been really funny."

A child comes to the chalkboard, on which a large sheet of paper is attached with masking tape. Mrs. Hill says, "Cynthia is ready to write our plans for the day. Let's help her. Don't forget to carry over any of our unfinished plans from yesterday."

A child raises his hand. Mrs. Hill calls on him. The child says, "Yesterday, we said that we would finish making our hand puppets and that we would begin working on our scripts for the puppet shows." "Good," says Mrs. Hill, "let's put that down." Many of the children in the class show agreement by saying "yes," by vigorously shaking their heads, or by making some affirming comment to a neighbor. Another child raises her hand. Mrs. Hill calls on her. "We challenged Mr. Smith's class in dodgeball yesterday." "That's right, we did, didn't we? Well, I've talked to Mr. Smith and we've decided if it's all right with you that we would begin the tournament this afternoon."

A child raises her hand. "We have to continue working on our science experiments." Another child raises his hand and says that Mrs. Hill had asked that someone remind her and the class to set aside some time to work on their word-puzzle booklets. Another child raises her hand and says that they were supposed to leave time to work in their groups on role-playing their special stories on life in colonial times. Mrs. Hill says, "I'd like to add something, too. Let's put down continuing to work with the metric system in our learning center, writing a story about a child's life in the colonial period, reading groups, math groups, and working on individual projects in our learning centers."

This is what the plans looked like:

Finish making hand puppets.
Work on scripts for puppet shows.
Dodgeball tournament with Mr. Smith's class after lunch.
Continue work on science experiments.
Work on word-puzzle booklets.
Role-play stories on life in colonial times.
Work with the metric system.
Write a story on a child's life in the colonial period.
Reading groups.
Math groups.
Work on individual projects in learning centers.

Mrs. Hill thanks Cynthia for writing everything so clearly on the large newsprint paper. She then asks if anyone has any questions. Seth raises his hand. Mrs. Hill calls on him. Seth says, "Mrs. Hill, you said that as long as we finished our special assignments we could work in any of our interest areas that we wanted. Well, John, Mary, and I will need extra time to work on our science experiment, and we need to do it today. Is that all right?" "Why don't I meet with the three of you in a moment to discuss this and see what we can work out."

Children without any cue from Mrs. Hill begin work at their seats, in learning centers, and in groups. Mrs. Hill walks around the room, nods approval to some, says "good" to others, and stops to ask a question or two. She then goes to meet with John, Mary, and Seth.

TEACHING AND THE LESSON PLAN

Lesson plans are tools or aids for teachers. They serve as guides and are necessary for good teaching. Although experienced teachers use more succinct lesson plans than a novice would, the plans are always useful. It is not necessary for experienced teachers to put down every question that they will ask or write in every detail, because they are better able to anticipate children's questions and utilize students' cues to provide meaningful and interesting lessons.

The beginning teacher, on the other hand, is more insecure and so tends to prepare more detailed lesson plans. This is good until experience takes over. Although the detail of the planning will vary according to the individual instructor, the parts included in the lesson plan are similar.

The success of any lesson depends on the preplanning and preparation for the lesson, as well as its execution. If students' past experiences, interests, and previous learnings are not considered in the plan, there is less likelihood for a successful lesson. Similarly, the teacher must estimate the proper amount of time necessary for the lesson, know the availability of materials and books needed for the lesson, and have prepared any special charts, displays, work papers, and so forth that are to be used in the lesson.

Many times a lesson may act as a springboard for a number of other lessons. Subsequent lessons may extend, reinforce, review, or provide application.

PARTS OF THE DAILY LESSON PLAN

The lesson plan presented here has five parts.

OBJECTIVES

Objectives should be stated in behavioral terms (that which can be directly observed and measured). This part is primarily for the instructor. The more precise teachers are in stating objectives, the better they will be able to plan and execute a successful lesson.

INTRODUCTION

The introduction includes the following three areas:

a. Relating the lesson to the students' past experiences
b. Using motivating techniques to gain the attention and interest of students
c. Informing pupils about the purpose for the lesson

Students' knowledge of the objectives of the lesson is important because it helps them to know what they are expected to accomplish.

DEVELOPMENT

This is the "heart" of the lesson. Each step in the sequence is enumerated. (The more experienced the teacher is, the less detail is given.) The questions, examples, materials, and activities used to help the students to attain the objectives are stated.

SUMMARY AND EVALUATION

a. The summary ties the loose ends together and makes sure that learning is complete.
b. The behavioral objective should be restated, and the evaluation should consist of evidence that the desired outcomes have been achieved.
c. The progress and interest of the children may be noted and standards of work evaluated.
d. Next steps and assignments may be defined.

PRELIMINARY PREPARATIONS

This involves any special arrangments that are necessary for the execution of the lesson plan, such as the arrangement of furniture in the classroom and special equipment or materials.

CLASSROOM PHYSICAL ENVIRONMENT

The discussion so far in this chapter has focused on the teacher and planning. However, as already stated, the physical environment in which teachers and pupils are housed can and does affect the teaching–learning situation, as well as the teachers' and students' behavior.

Environmental psychology, which is still in its infancy, is a field of extreme importance. It focuses on behavior in relation to physical settings. "Physical settings—simple or complex— evoke complex human responses in the form of feelings, attitudes, values, expectancies, and desires and it is in this sense as well as in their known physical properties that their relationships to human experience and behavior must be understood."[3]

It is important for teachers to recognize that the constraints of the classroom physical setting will influence behavior as well as the ongoing activities. Windowless rooms and fixed desks will evoke one kind of student behavior; classrooms with windows and mobile desks and walls will evoke a different kind. For example, if a teacher arranges students' desks in five straight rows, five desks to a row, and emphasizes that the desks must remain in these exact positions, students' physical, emotional, and social behavior will be restricted. A certain atmosphere exists in the class, and the teacher is looked on as authoritarian and dominant. In such an environment communication can only take place with students adjacent to, behind, or in front of the individual. Since desks may not be moved, communication is not very satisfactory, and there are a number of other difficulties:

It almost encourages shy children to be inarticulate and to rely on the teacher to be their interpreter. The girl who answers a question or offers a comment from the front of the room may be quite inaudible to those sitting behind her, and she will certainly be unable to see their reaction to what she says. The boy who speaks from a seat near the back will probably

be heard by the rest of the class, since he will have to use more volume in order to be heard by the teacher; but he will be little better informed than the girl at the front about the reactions of his fellow pupils, since he will be looking, for the most part, at the backs of their heads. Some children enter cheerfully into the competition to secure the teacher's attention and approval. Others find the whole situation threatening and become intellectually crippled by it. Others, of course, prefer to form their own systems of communication in their own part of the classroom.[4]

Such a classroom obviously does not lend itself to a good language arts environment where students feel free to communicate, probably because of the teacher's lack of knowledge in the area of proxemics.

Proxemics concerns the relationship of humans and space. It is a form of nonverbal communication, which can have an effect on pupil–teacher, as well as pupil–pupil, communication. The placement of the teacher in the room and seating of students at the front, center,

---

[3]Harold M. Proshansky, William H. Ittleson and Leanne G. Rivlin, "The Influence of the Physical Environment on Behavior: Some Basic Assumptions," in *Environmental Psychology*, Harold M. Proshansky, William H. Ittleson and Leanne G. Rivlin, eds. (New York: Holt, Rinehart and Winston, 1970), p. 28.

[4]Elizabeth Richardson, "The Physical Setting and Its Influence on Learning," in *Environmental Psychology*, Harold M. Proshansky, William H. Ittleson and Leanne G. Rivlin, eds. (New York: Holt, Rinehart and Winston, 1970), p. 387.

side, or back of the classroom will determine to a degree the kind of verbal communication that can take place.[5]

Other factors that teachers must take into account in the physical environment of the classroom concern heating, lighting, and acoustics. A room that is too hot or too cold, or one in which there are many competing stimuli, or one filled with glare, will detrimentally affect the learning behavior of children.

Teachers must recognize that the physical setting of the classroom is an important and dynamic part of the learning environment because of the direct force it exerts on students' physical and mental well-being. The physical, emotional, and social environment all interact and help to establish the teaching–learning climate.

Throughout this textbook, where appropriate, the various environments of the classroom have been analyzed in relation to the specific area under discussion. The emphasis has been on maintaining a comfortable, nonthreatening environment where mutual respect and trust can reign and where there is a balance of competition and cooperation.

A good language arts program cannot prevail where children feel intimidated, are isolated, and are reluctant to express themselves.

TEACHER ASSUMPTIONS

Teachers should recognize the dynamic interplay of variables described so far throughout this chapter. The more teachers know about their students, the better they are able to plan well for them. However, teachers must be cautioned against the *self-fulfilling prophecy*—where teachers' assumptions about children come true, at least in part, because of the attitude of the teachers, which in turn becomes part of the children's reactions in the classroom. For example, if a child comes from a home environment not conducive to learning, the teacher may assume this child cannot learn beyond a certain level and thus may treat the child accordingly. If this happens, then the teacher's

[5]*See* Peter Delefes and Barry Jackson, "Teacher–Pupil Interaction as a Function of Location in the Classroom," *Psychology in the Schools* 9 (April 1972): 119–125.

assumptions could become part of the child's own self-concept, further reinforcing the teacher's original expectations.

THE TEACHER AS THE KEY TO A GOOD LANGUAGE ARTS PROGRAM

Although a school may have the best equipment, the most advanced school plant, a superior curriculum, and children who want to learn, it must have "good teachers" so that the desired kind of learning can take place. With today's emphasis on accountability, the spotlight is even more sharply focused on "the Teacher." When conversation turns to "teacher evaluation," *everyone* seems to be an expert. Despite the surge in educational research, however, no definitive agreement exists as to how to evaluate teachers. If we were to go back through the ages we would find such familiar comments as:

The teachers today just go on repeating in rigamarole fashion, annoy the students with constant questions and repeat the same things over and over again. They do not try to find out what the students' natural inclinations are, so that the students are forced to pretend to like their studies; nor do they try to bring out the best in their talents. As a result, the students hide their favorite readings and hate their teachers, are exasperated at the difficulty of their studies, and do not know what good it does them. Although they go through the regular course of instruction, they are quick to leave when they are through. This is the failure of education today.

Confucius (c. 551–479 B.C.)

When he [Abelard's teacher] lit the fire, he filled the house with smoke not with light.

Peter Abelard (A.D. 1079–1142)

However difficult it is to generate universally agreed-upon statements and evaluative criteria, teachers must realize that they are always under scrutiny, formalized or not. For example, the first day that teachers enter their classrooms, the way they walk, their facial expressions, the way they speak, what they say, how they say it, their voices, their mannerisms, what they are wearing, their ages, their modus operandi, even their genders—all these and more affect their students, regardless of grade level. Will teachers measure up?

There are no precise measurements for determining what makes a good language arts teacher, nor are there commonly accepted instruments for determining "good-teacher" traits in general. One might ask, "Shouldn't a language arts teacher be superior in the area of communication skills?" All teachers *should* be able to express themselves well, for we usually gain our first impression of individuals from their ability to communicate. How many of us have been impressed with a beautiful or handsome face only to have the image shattered when the person began to speak?

Good teachers are insightful about themselves and sensitive to the individual differences in their students. This is especially true of language arts teachers. They also recognize that there are certain skills and knowledge that they need in order to be called teachers.

A teacher who is enthusiastic, warm, and friendly; who knows the interests, needs, and readiness levels of individual students in the class; who uses the experiences and interests of the students to plan cooperatively for them; who employs a variety of teaching procedures such as discussion, review, questioning, and discovery; who uses a wide variety of materials and resources; and who knows adequate techniques for student evaluation is *a good teacher*.

Self-Evaluation

Good teachers evaluate themselves continuously in terms of how well their students do and how well they perform in relation to established criteria.

A self-evaluation method using videotape can be effective in giving teachers insight into their teaching performance. Teachers can list certain criteria as a guide for evaluation of performance; videotape themselves in action at different times of the day during different activities over one week; and then view the tapes to rate their abilities with these measures in mind. To ensure objective rating, other teachers whom the teacher respects and trusts could be invited to comment on the teacher's performance. Student evaluation should also be encouraged.

Here are a number of questions that teachers can ask themselves in order to determine the effectiveness of their classroom performance:

1. Did I capitalize on students' interests?
2. Did I help to stimulate the students?
3. Was I usually enthusiastic about the lesson?
4. Was I clear in the presentation of objectives for the lesson?
5. Were my questions clear and easily understood?
6. Were my questions thought-provoking?
7. Did I use positive reinforcement?
8. Did I provide for individual differences?
9. Did I allow for adequate student–teacher interaction?
10. Did I allow adequate time for group discussions?
11. Was I always prepared?
12. Did I use various materials?
13. Did I speak clearly and distinctly, varying the pitch, tone, and volume of my voice?
14. Was I always able to make myself heard?
15. Did I make good use of the language arts periods?
16. Did I adequately prepare for the students in the various language arts lessons?
17. Did I use the games and gamelike activities as an integral part of the language arts lesson, rather than as ends in themselves?
18. Did I use games and gamelike activities and simulation activities to help children to overlearn certain skills?
19. Did I help students to understand the purposes of teacher-made and standardized tests?
20. Did I use teacher-made tests for diagnostic purposes?
21. Did I use teacher-made tests for review purposes?

The only way that many of these questions can be adequately answered is by observation of students' behavior. By videotaping lessons, teachers can better observe classroom behavior, including their own. This method will help teachers to evaluate progress in teaching areas in which they are weak by comparing videotapings over a period of time.

Evaluating the Teacher in Action

What criteria are used in judging teacher performance? The accompanying boxed material shows two hypothetical teachers in action. Which teacher is more effective?[6]

[6]Although these are two hypothetical classroom scenes, similar events can readily be observed in many schools.

SCENARIO ONE

Upper-elementary grade: 11 girls, 4 boys, 1 male teacher. An inner-city school with children from a low socioeconomic background. The classroom contains five straight rows of desks, five to a row. In the upper right front of the classroom a TV set is prominently in view. The front chalkboards contain these instructions:

Bd. #1—Do pp. 81–84 in your English books.
Bd. #2—Two sentences about Halloween are on the board.
Bd. #3—Class spelling words. Spelling book p. 40. Write each word five times neatly.

The children are told to:

1. Finish the story.
2. Make interesting sentences.
3. Proofread.

ACTION

Children arrive in classroom after recess. They are still energized from their outdoor activities and some generalize this feeling to the classroom environment. They are highly agitated about some event that has occurred in the playground. The teacher sits on the sidelines and says nothing. The children exchange accusations with one another. After about five minutes the teacher walks to the front of the room and points to board #1, board #2, and to board #3. He says: "Do this work!" The teacher then walks to the back of the room with one boy. He and the boy sit down at a desk at the far end of the room and play chess for one hour and ten minutes.

Let's see what took place during this hour: One quite physically mature girl—we'll call her Jane—is still apparently rather agitated about events that had transpired during recess. She points a finger of accusation at a very heavy-set girl—whom we'll call Laurie—who is seated at a nearby desk. "It's all your fault," Jane says. "No, it isn't," says Laurie. At this point another girl, sitting next to Jane, also turns and points to Laurie and says vehemently, "Oh yes it is. I was standing in front of you and I heard you." Now two more girls and Jane stop what they are doing (they were supposed to be working on word-usage problems in their language books) and also attack Laurie verbally. The accused Laurie, who has apparently learned how to survive such bombardments, completely ignores them. She does not raise her head from her book. She appears to be working on spelling words. Jane, who has never attempted to do any work, stands up, goes to the TV set, and turns it on. She sits down in the chair in front of the TV set and glues her attention to it. At this point everyone in the classroom also looks at the TV set—everyone, that is, except the chess players, the teacher, and one boy.

After about one hour and ten minutes (at 2:20) the teacher, Mr. D. Ense, terminates the chess game and goes to the front of the room, pointing in rapid succession at boards #1, #2, and #3. Then he says, "You know this has to be all finished before you can go home. [The class will be dismissed at 2:45.] Those who haven't been doing their work had better get to it."

COMMENT

Since a learning experience constitutes an interaction between a learner and the environment, we could say that the students were having learning experiences of a kind. However, what kind of learning was taking place is another matter. For effective learning, the teacher must try to structure and organize the classroom situation in such a way as to stimulate experiences and maximize total learning. The preplanning, the organization of learning experiences, and other preliminaries necessary for effective learning are not readily visible when an operating classroom is being observed. They must be inferred from the ongoing activities seen in the classroom. However, whatever the organizational pattern, if proper attention has been paid to the "learning prerequisites" and if they have been well planned, the results would be readily discernible in the learning behavior of the children.

It is difficult to infer that desired learning was taking place from the behavior of these students. The only child who was totally engrossed in the task was the boy playing chess with the teacher. Although chess is a challenging game, for a teacher to spend one hour and ten minutes with only one child, while the rest are left to fend for themselves, represents a misapportionment of time and a poverty of judgment. Mr. D. Ense could have taught more of the children to play chess, and could then have overseen several games with the objective of helping students to develop strategies necessary for playing and winning the game.

We should also wonder about Jane, the girl who did not appear to be doing anything. Jane is only at a first-grade reading level. The work she was asked to do was not within her readiness. How could she read a fifth-grade English book, which was the one assigned by the teacher? And why should she learn to spell words that she can't even read?

Using the questions given in the section "Self-Evaluation," how would you rate Mr. D. Ense's teaching performance?

SCENARIO TWO

Upper-elementary grade: 14 girls, 12 boys, 1 female teacher. Same inner-city school.

The classroom contains desks clustered together in groups of four. In the front of the room there are six desks in a semicircle facing a chalkboard. A large map is visible. A bulletin board has an exhibit called "Creative Stories from Other Continents" on display, including a list of the continents and various countries being studied. Next to the list are spelling words related to the countries and continents being considered.

Another board contains class plans for the day. The teacher is working with a group of six at the chalkboard. Children who are at their desks seem to be engrossed and busy.

ACTION

The teacher, Ms. K. Now, says, "We've been working with different continents and countries and we have combined this with our language arts lesson and working with the newspaper. Yesterday we allowed our imaginations to roam, and we wrote some very creative stories. We've talked about some of the countries and their leaders who have been in the news lately. Who remembers some of the countries and leaders we have been talking about?"

A child raises his hand and suggests Japan and Hirohito.

Ms. K. Now says, "Yes. Why were we talking about Hirohito?"

A student raises her hand and tells about the President's visit with the Japanese emperor and where and why this visit took place.

Ms. K. Now responds with "Good!" She then asks that someone go to the board to point out Japan on the map.

Many children enthusiastically raise their hands. Someone is chosen who quickly and correctly points out the country.

"Good," Ms. K. Now says. She then asks, "Who are two women leaders who have been in the news that we have also talked about? I'll give you a hint. The first name of one of the women is spelled almost exactly like the country she headed."

Many children raise their hands again. The teacher calls on a boy who proudly says, "Indira Gandhi." He also offers to point out India on the map. The teacher thanks him and nods, and the student quickly points out India.

A discussion ensues about why India has been in the news so much. The teacher then asks the name of the other famous woman leader who has been in the news. A girl is called on and answers correctly. She says, "Mrs. Thatcher, the Prime Minister of England."

The teacher says, "Good. You really seem to know your world affairs and your countries. Let's see how good you are in categorizing countries according to their continents. I have an outline map for each one of you, and I'd like you to see if you can put the continents in the right areas and then insert the countries that I have listed on the board. Does anyone have any questions? Let's do one together to make sure everyone understands."

She points to an area on one of the outline maps, and asks, "Can everyone see where I am pointing? Okay, what is this continent?"

Almost everyone calls out, "North America!"

"Correct," says Ms. K. Now. "Looking at the list on the board, which country would you place in this continent and approximately where would you put it?"

Again, many of the children call out the correct answer.

"Good. Let's see how many of you can finish this on your own."

The children start working and Ms. K. Now goes around the room checking other papers and stopping to help those who need it. After some time has elapsed, the teacher goes over the correct answers with the group to give them feedback on the results. She helps students summarize what they have done and asks them to check the news for exciting things that are happening in other areas of the world so that they can add those to their list.

"Tomorrow," Ms. K. Now says, "we're going to be combining outlining with our study of continents and countries. Then we're going to use the outline as a guide to learn more about the country we choose to study. I would like you to think about which country you want to get to know better. At your seats, review some of the things we talked about concerning outlines. This sheet should help you."

During the lesson with this group, other children moved about the room freely. Two children came to the front of the room to ask the teacher questions. After getting an answer the children returned to their seats. Rather than calling another group to the front of the room, the teacher asked the class what game they would like to play when she had finished with the group at the bulletin board. When the game was over, the teacher continued reading a Sherlock Holmes story to the children, but first she challenged the children to try to solve the mystery in the story.

The next scheduled activity concerned description. This was a "whole class" activity. Each student had a number of mystery items in a box or bag. A student would have to describe a hidden item using only one sense. The words used to describe the items were written on the board. These words would then be used in the pupils' writing. Lastly, Ms. K. Now and her students discussed their plans for the next day.

COMMENT

From observation of the students, desirable learning seems to be taking place in this classroom. The teacher is sensitive to individual differences in students. Pupil–teacher planning is in evidence. She used a variety of teaching materials and methods, and she employed stimulating techniques and encouraged creativity. She correlated the language arts to other subject-matter areas. Pre-planning and organizing for learning were evident from these ongoing activities. Ms. K. Now appears to be an effective teacher.

SUMMARY

Teachers are managers of the teaching–learning environment because they are responsible for a group of students and because their purpose is to make a positive and beneficial difference to their students' learning. Good planning, the use of lesson plans as aids, the inclusion of students in planning, and a good physical environment greatly influence the teaching–learning program. Teachers themselves are key factors in the teaching-learning environment. Knowledge of self-fulfilling prophecy and self-evaluation helps teachers gain greater insights into themselves.

SUGGESTIONS FOR THOUGHT QUESTIONS AND ACTIVITIES

1. After reading Part Two, design a language arts minilesson that uses videotape. Rate yourself as a teacher according to some of the criteria presented in this chapter.

2. As a teacher how would you evaluate whether you had presented a good language arts lesson?

3. Think of two teachers you have had in school. One should be someone you feel was your best teacher; the other should be one you feel was the worst. State the characteristics of each. Compare your list of characteristics with others generated by the class.

4. Read the following short selection. Then determine whether any language arts principles are being violated. If a principle is being violated, explain how the principle is being violated by the teacher and state the language arts principle(s).

Ms. X asks all the second-graders in her class to open to page 26 in the language book. She says, "Since so many persons had trouble with the inductive phonics lesson the other day, everyone will review it again. No questions. Let's begin. I have everything planned for you and I want to make sure we finish it all. Sit up straight. Don't turn around. Pay attention. I know we've been working one hour straight, but we have to finish."

5. You have been asked to give a talk to your colleagues on the factors that make teachers good classroom managers. What will you say?

6. Observe a classroom for a period of time. Try to determine whether you think the teacher is a good classroom manager. State how you made your decision.

7. Evaluate a few classrooms to determine whether they have a good physical environment.

SELECTED BIBLIOGRAPHY

Ashton-Warner, Sylvia. *Teacher.* New York: Simon and Schuster, 1963.

Barker, Roger. *Ecological Concepts:* Stanford, Ca.: Stanford University, 1968.

Charles, C. M. *Elementary Classroom Management.* New York: Longman, 1983.

Cooper, Harris, and Thomas Good. *Pygmalion Grows Up.* New York: Longman, 1982.

Holt, John. *How Children Fail.* rev. ed. New York: Delacorte, 1982.

Kounin, Jacob S. *Discipline and Group Management in Classrooms.* New York: Holt, Rinehart and Winston, 1970.

THE
SUBJECT MATTER
OF THE
LANGUAGE ARTS

PART TWO

SIX

Aural Responsiveness: Listening

Gilbert and Sullivan, in their comic opera *Pirates of Penzance*, illustrate the dire consequences that can occur from faulty listening. In the opera we learn how Frederic, the well-born hero, has been wrongly doomed to a life of piracy by Ruth, his nursemaid:

> I was a stupid nursery-maid,
> on breakers always steering,
> And I did not catch the word aright,
> through being hard of hearing.
> Mistaking my instructions, which
> within my brain did gyrate,
> I took and bound this promising
> boy apprentice to a pirate.
> A sad mistake it was to make,
> and doom him to a vile lot:
> I bound him to a pirate—you—
> instead of to a pilot!

The importance of listening is evident in many ways in our everyday lives: for example, the telephone; the sound motion picture (which replaced silents); the prominent place in home entertainment of radio and television; and the dubbing of foreign films with oral text replacing written subtitles to make them more acceptable to worldwide audiences. Can one imagine the world without oral communication?

An individual's adequate development of listening skills is important for advanced learning and thinking. Listening to the ideas of others allows us to compare them with our own and helps us to become more critical thinkers. By learning to listen to others, students are better able to discern the purpose of the speakers, the way they organize their ideas, and their use of developmental materials. Such students are better prepared to resist double-talk and meaningless generalizations and to acquire new information.

A study relating personality to the way of listening concludes that:

The ideal listener primarily keeps an open, curious mind. He listens for new ideas everywhere, integrating what he hears with what he already knows. He is also self-perceptive and thus listens to others with his total being or self. Thus he becomes personally involved with what he hears. Being this aware he is not willing to blindly follow the listening crowd. He maintains conscious perspectives on what is going on instead. He looks for ideas, organization and arguments but always listens to the essence of things. Knowing that no two people listen the same, he stays mentally alert by outlining, objecting, approving, adding illustrations of his own. He is introspective but he has the capacity and desire to critically examine, un-

FIGURE 6.1   LISTENING IS AN IMPORTANT SKILL THAT NEEDS TO BE DEVELOPED IN YOUNG CHILDREN.

© 1958 United Feature Syndicate. Inc.

derstand and attempt to transform some of his values, attitudes, and relationships within himself and with others. He focuses his mind on the listening and listens to the speaker's ideas, but he also listens with feeling and intuition.[1]

Listening is to language arts as the sense of seeing is to the art of painting. Before artists are able to express themselves in some esthetic form, they must first have perceived the world around them visually. Only then can they begin to build and integrate these images into a more meaningful perception of their experiences. In a similar manner, listening is basic to the language arts. Embryonic language artists must first accumulate listening experiences so that they can build, integrate, and assimilate these experiences and be able to express themselves more meaningfully.

After you have finished reading this chapter you should be able to answer the following questions:

1. How important is listening? Why?
2. How are listening skills developed?
3. Can listening skills be taught? How?
4. What are some teaching tactics?
5. What should a teacher know about the various levels of listening? Why?
6. What are some listening activities that would enhance listening at the various levels?
7. What is an effective listener?
8. What should a teacher know about the relationship of listening to other language arts areas?

[1]Elizabeth Mae Pflaumer, "A Definition of Listening," in *Listening: Readings*, Sam Duker, ed. (Metuchen N.J.: Scarecrow Press, 1971), pp. 46–47.

LEVELS OF LISTENING

In order to have a better understanding of the hierarchical and cumulative nature of listening, a discussion of the various levels of listening is necessary.[2] From highest to lowest in the hierarchy of listening, the three levels are auding, listening, and hearing. The lowest level,[3] *hearing,* refers to sound waves being received and modified by the ear. Someone in the process of hearing physically perceives the presence of sounds, but would not be able to make out what the sounds are; they would merely be noise. Hearing, being a purely physical phenomenon, cannot be taught.

Listening is in the middle of the hierarchy of listening, in which individuals become aware of sound sequences. They are able to identify and recognize the sound sequences as known words, if the words are in their listening capacity; that is, they have heard the words before, and they know what the words mean.

Auding is at the highest level of the hierarchy and involves not only giving meaning to the sounds but assimilating and integrating the oral message. An individual at the auding level would be able to gather the main idea of a spoken passage, discern analogies and inferences, and perform all the other high-level comprehension skills that are usually associated with reading. (See "Helping Children Acquire Comprehension Skills" in Chapter 8.) Creative problem solving as well as critical listening are also skills included in this level. Although we are looking at each level as a separate entity, the act of listening is not divided into parts, but functions as a whole.

Special note: Unless otherwise qualified, such as in the discussion on the hierarchy of listening, whenever the term "listening" is used in this text it will refer to auding, the highest level of listening.

Factors Affecting Hearing, the Lowest Level

Auditory Acuity *Auditory acuity* has to do with the physical response of the ear to sound

vibrations. If individuals have organic ear damage, they will not be able to hear properly, if at all, depending on the extent of the damage. Auditory acuity is the ability to respond to various frequencies (tones) at various intensities (level of loudness).

Human speech comprises frequencies ranging from 125 to 8,000 Hertz (Hz).[4] The intensity or loudness level found in everyday speech will range typically from the 55 decibels (db) of faint speech to the 85 decibels of loud conversation. When hearing is tested, a person's ability to hear is checked across the entire speech-frequency range. If persons require more than the normal decibel level to hear sounds at certain frequencies, they are most probably exhibiting a hearing loss.

The most critical frequencies for listening to speech lie in the frequency range between 1,000 and 2,500 Hz, because the majority of word cues are within this range. Frequencies above 2,500 Hz contribute to the fineness with which we hear such sounds as: /b, d, f, g, s, t, v, sh, th, and zh /(Webster's symbols).

An audiometer is used for precise measurement of hearing loss by audiologists. Teachers, however, can make a lot of informal measurements on their own. They can observe their students to notice if any of the following behavior is present:

Does the child appear to be straining to push himself or herself closer to the speaker?

Does the child speak either very softly or very loudly?

Does the child have difficulty in following simple directions?

Does the child turn up the sound of the record player or tape recorder?

Does the child have difficulty pronouncing words?

Does the child seem confused?

Although these questions could be posed for a number of other problems, a teacher should have the student checked for possible hearing loss if one or more of these symptoms is manifested.

---

[2]Stanford E. Taylor, *Listening: What Research Says to the Teacher* (Washington, D.C.: National Education Association, 1969).

[3]Ibid.

[4]*Hertz* is the accepted international scientific word for "cycles per second," named after the great nineteenth-century German physicist who proved the existence of electromagnetic waves.

Auditory Fatigue *Auditory fatigue* is a temporary hearing loss due to continuous or repeated exposure to sounds of certain frequencies such as a monotonous tone or droning voice. It has been shown that exposure to continuous loud noises over an extended period of time could be permanently harmful to an individual's hearing ability. Listening to music at a very high volume or being constantly exposed to cars and trucks rumbling through highway tunnels can have deleterious effects on hearing.

Binaural Considerations When individuals are in the presence of two or more conversations, they must be able to direct their attention to only one of the speakers in order to be able to get the essence of what is being said. The more readily listeners are able to separate the sound sources, the more they will be able to get messages correctly. *Binaurality* thus refers to the ability of listeners to increase their reception sensitivity by directing both ears to the same sound.

Masking *Masking* will occur when other sounds interfere with the message being spoken. Background noises drowning out a speaker or noisy classrooms or simultaneous group discussions will retard hearing ability.

Factors Affecting Listening, the Middle Level

Listening involves the way in which one identifies and recognizes sounds. Unless people are attentive to sounds, they will not understand their meaning, and meaning of sounds is an important part of listening. Sustained attention is concentration. If individuals are physically or mentally unwell, their chances for attending, and thus listening, are slim. Speakers play an important role in maintaining sustained attention. If they are boring, disliked, or unenthusiastic, they will not be as readily listened to as speakers who are interesting, liked, enthusiastic, and who use motivating techniques. Similarly, the physical environment of the classroom plays an important role in maintaining sustained attention. If the room is too hot or cold, if the chairs are uncomfortable, if there

are provisions for writing, if the lighting is adequate and free of glare, if the acoustics are good, and if there are visual distractions—all these play a part in whether listening occurs.

Factors Affecting Auding, the Highest Level

Auding is the highest level of listening, as we have seen. Auding is not only the ability to discriminate between one word and another, or one syllable and another, it also involves the individual's ability to assimilate the spoken message using an individual's total experience. The thinking skills used during auding are quite similar to those employed during speaking, reading, and writing. Since the average speaking rate is 150 words per minute, the individual has time to formulate thoughts about what is being said, if what is being said is in the experience of the auditor. If the words are not in the listener's listening capacity, or if the topic is beyond the scope of his or her experience, the listener will not understand what is being said. An individual who knows nothing about linguistics will have difficulty in comprehending an advanced lecture on this topic. A person with a background in linguistics may also have difficulty with the lecture if the words being used by the speaker are not familiar.

Figure 6.2[5] on page 65 depicts the three stages of hearing, listening, and auding.

RELATIONSHIP OF LISTENING TO OTHER LANGUAGE ARTS AREAS

The child's initial learning of language comes through listening; it is the foundation for the sequential development of language arts. If children do not listen effectively, they almost assuredly will have difficulty in all other areas of the language arts. If children hear "dat" for "that" or "dis" for "this," they will say "dat" and "dis." Later, when they have to read "that" or "this," they may have difficulty because these words are not in their listening experience. The written symbol would not remind them of a sound with which they are familiar. Similarly, if children cannot read the word "that" and it is not in their listening capacity, they will not be

[5]Taylor, *Listening,* p. 5.

FIGURE 6.2.   THE TOTAL ACT OF RECEIVING AUDITORY COMMUNICATION

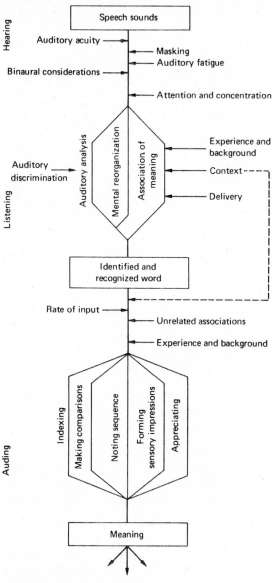

retarded. Many children with hearing problems have often been improperly diagnosed as being mentally retarded because of their language difficulty. It would not be far off the mark to say, "We speak what we hear."

From descriptive studies of acquisition of language, it has been found that children learn language from the speech around them. They learn the rules that govern usage of words so that they can comprehend and produce properly constructed speech. Since skill in listening is so very closely related to speech development and, subsequently, effective oral development, knowledge of the various aspects of listening becomes essential for the proper understanding of the development of speech.

Auditory Discrimination and Memory Span Auditory discrimination, which is the ability to distinguish between sounds, is essential for the acquisition of language and for learning to read. The essence of what speech clinicians have learned concerning auditory discrimination can be summarized:

1. There is evidence that the more nearly alike two phonemes are in phonetic [relating to speech sounds] structure, the more likely they are to be misinterpreted.

2. Individuals differ in their ability to discriminate among sounds.

3. The ability to discriminate frequently matures as late as the end of the child's eighth year. A few individuals never develop this capacity to any great degree.

4. There is a strong positive relation between slow development of auditory discrimination and inaccurate pronunciation.

5. There is a positive relationship between poor discrimination and poor reading.

6. While poor discrimination may be at the root of both speech and reading difficulties, it often affects only reading or speaking.

7. There is little if any relationship between the development of auditory discrimination and intelligence, as measured by most intelligence tests.[6]

able to write it. If children are going to communicate effectively, they must learn to hear even subtle differences and similarities among sounds.

Listening and Speaking

Studies with deaf and hard-of-hearing children reveal that their speech has been severely

[6]Joseph W. Wepman, "Auditory Discrimination, Speech and Reading," *Elementary School Journal* 60 (1960): 326.

For children who speak a nonstandard dialect of English or for whom English is a second language, it is well to bear in mind that the acquisition of speech sounds for any given dialect is learned very early in life and is usually established by the time the child starts school. These children especially need help in auditory discrimination if they are to learn standard English.

Auditory memory span is essential for individuals who must judge whether two or more sounds are similar or different. In order to make such comparisons, the sounds must be kept in memory and retrieved for comparison. Auditory memory span is defined as "the number of discrete elements grasped in a given moment of attention and organized into a unity for purposes of immediate reproduction or immediate use."[7] A deficiency in memory span will hinder effective listening.

Listening and Reading Comprehension

In the elementary grades, when children are learning to read, students of low and average achievement usually prefer to listen rather than to read independently. These children gain more comprehension and retention from listening because of the important added cues they receive from the speaker, such as stress given to words or phrases, facial expressions, and so on.[8] Children who are very able and who have had success in reading achievement usually prefer to read because these children can set their own rate of reading for maximum comprehension and retention. They don't wish to be constrained by the fixed oral rate of the teacher.

The case where students can understand a passage when it is read to them, but cannot understand it when they read it themselves indicates that the words are in the students' listening capacity, but that they have not gained the skills necessary for decoding words from their written forms.

It may be that some words are in the children's listening capacity (for example, they know the meaning of the individual words when they are said aloud), but they still might not be able to assimilate the words into a meaningful concept. The instructor will have to help these children in concept development and in gaining the necessary reading comprehension and listening skills. A person who does not do well in listening comprehension skills will usually not do well in reading comprehension skills. Help in one area usually improves the other, because both listening and reading contain some important similar skills. As a matter of fact, listening capacity or comprehension tests are often given to students to determine their reading capacity. (See "Informal Teacher Assessment of Listening Comprehension Skills" later in this chapter, as well as "Listening and Reading" in Chapter 8.)

THE ACTIVE LISTENER

Listening is the active aural intake of language. The listener is involved in decoding and interpreting a message from the speaker. Hearing sound symbols that are called *phonemes*, analogous to the Morse code, the listener must be able to decode the various sounds that stand for symbols. In order to decode, listeners must be able to hear differences between and among the various sounds of their language. If you were to ask a salesperson about the price of an item and were told fifty cents a pound, how can you be sure that the salesperson didn't say ninety cents a pound or five dollars a pound? You might say, "Because with my ears I heard that person say fifty cents rather than ninety cents. Fifty cents sounds *different* from ninety cents."

The buyer-listener might think he or she heard fifteen rather than fifty cents because of the similarly of the sounds. The emotional bias toward wanting to hear the lower price could also influence the listener.

Phonemes have no meaning in themselves except as they are combined into a specific pattern to form a *morpheme*, which is the smallest word unit that carries meaning. Morphemes are

[7]Virgil A. Anderson, "Auditory Memory Span as Tested by Speech Sounds," *American Journal of Psychology* 52 (1939): 95.

[8]Robert Ruddell, "Oral Language and the Development of Other Language Skills," *Elementary English* 43 (May 1966): 489–498.

[9]Thomas Jolly, "Listen My Children and You Shall Read," *Language Arts* 57 (February 1980): 214–217.

combined into an arrangement that gives the sentence its unique meaning.

The listener must be able to assimilate the flow of sound symbols into meaningful concepts or no communication can occur. If a listener heard the sentence, "I blibed the blob," the sounds cannot be assimilated into meaningful concepts because "blibed" and "blob" are nonsense words. Similarly, if listeners heard the delightful poem "Jabberwocky" recited by Alice in *Through the Looking Glass,* they would be as perplexed as Alice concerning its meaning. Read one stanza and see if you agree.

> 'Twas brillig, and the slithy toves
> Did gyre and gimble in the wabe:
> All mimsy were the borogoves,
> And the mome raths outgrabe.

Active listeners when they decode a message have strategies for processing information—they know what information to attend to and what to ignore. They are able to make predictions about what the speaker will say and to be as objective as possible about the speaker. The active listener tries to determine the stance of the speaker and concentrate on the speaker's message rather than other distractions. While listening, the active listener tries to determine how his or her ideas relate to what is being voiced, as well as what the central theme of the speaker is. The active listener is constantly trying to determine whether he or she understands the message and what inferences can be made about it.

Active listening is hard work that requires various levels of thinking ability. Active listeners are active consumers of information; they interact with the speaker; they interpret, analyze, synthesize, and evaluate information, as well as go beyond the information to come up with alternate solutions, techniques, and so forth. The active listener is the *ideal* listener.

DEVELOPMENT OF LISTENING

"Listen! Listen to me!" Children want to be heard. Whether their parents spend time listening to them, whether they encourage them to express themselves will affect the kind of listening the children are able to do, as well as influence their oral expression.

By the time children come to school they have emerged from an egocentric view of the world, where everything they do and say concerns *me, my,* or *I.* In this egocentric world, children speak in parallel, in a collective monologue. They are not in the role of listeners; that is, young children usually have difficulty grasping another person's view because they are so concerned with their own. Therefore, there is less communication. According to Jean Piaget, the eminent Swiss psychologist, not until the children need to be social do they need to become logical in their speaking.

Read the following noncommunicative, egocentric speech of a preschooler:

> Mlle. L. tells a group of children that owls cannot see by day.
>
> Lev: "Well, I know quite well that it can't."
>
> Lev (at a table where a group is at work): "I've already done 'moon' so I'll have to change it."
>
> Lev picks up some barley-sugar crumbs: "I say, I've got a lovely pile of eyeglasses."
>
> Lev: "I say, I've got a gun to kill him with. I say, I am the captain on horseback. I say, I've got a horse and a gun as well.[10]

If children are to learn effectively in school, they must first learn to listen. Since they have spent their early childhood years in egocentric thought, they have not developed this skill adequately. When children come to school they participate in dialogue, which is a giving and receiving of ideas between two persons. Though they must listen, children still need someone to listen to them.

When Lev emerged from egocentric speech, he was able to engage in a communicative conversation with other children of his age:

> Pie: (6.5 years old) "Now you shan't have it [the pencil] because you asked for it."
>
> Hei: (6.0 years old) "Yes I will, because it's mine . . ."
>
> Pie: "Course it isn't yours. It belongs to everybody, to all the children."

[10]Barry J. Wadsworth, *Piaget's Theory of Cognitive Development* (New York: David McKay Co., 1971), p. 66.

LEV (6.0 years old): "Yes, it belongs to Mlle. L. and all the children, to Ai and to My too."

PIE: "It belongs to Mlle. L., because she bought it and it belongs to all the children as well."[11]

Dialogue between children and their classmates and between teachers and children is very important in children's development of listening skills and in making their thinking more objective. Teachers should listen to children; observe them at play and work; introduce new materials and ideas to them; add information; raise questions; allow opportunities for children to raise questions as well; and *talk* with children about what they see, think, and feel. From listening to children, teachers can learn about children's interpretation of the world around them. It is essential that teachers show they respect their pupils' ideas and act as models of "good listeners" for them. Children must have sufficient practice or "play" in the intake and outgo of language. Unless children are given ample opportunities to engage in listening and "being listened to," they may not develop their listening ability adequately. (See "Developing Vocabulary from Literature" in Chapter 9 for a discussion on how children can be more active consumers of information.)

PURPOSES FOR LISTENING

People read for different purposes; they listen for different purposes, too. "It might be extremely unprofitable to listen creatively or casually to an emotionally charged appeal requiring action of some sort by the listener. It would be extremely unpleasant to always listen to social conversations critically. Therefore, the individual must not only learn to listen carefully, but learn to listen appropriately in order to get the most [or the least] from what is heard."[12]

In a conversation with a friend we are attentive listeners. In listening to a story being read, we may listen for the main idea, a sequence of events, specific details, supporting evidence, and so on. However, in listening to a dramatic presentation we may merely listen with appreciation. When listening to a politician or a commercial, we should listen critically.

[11]Ibid., p. 66.
[12]John Gilbert Way, "Teaching Listening Skills," *Reading Teacher* (February 1973): 474.

Critical Listening—An Important Auding Skill

We are living at a time when individuals, from early childhood onward, are daily exposed to a plethora of news, advertisements, and information from the mass media. From past experiences we have learned that what is presented as fact may actually be suspect. One way that teachers can help to lessen the impact of propaganda or half-truths is to emphasize critical listening skills in the classroom. *Critical listening* refers to that high level of listening skill whereby the individual is able to detect bias, propaganda, and so on in oral presentations. Critical listening is "the process of examining spoken materials in the light of related, objective evidence, comparing the ideas with some standard or consensus, and then concluding or acting upon the judgment made."[13]

Critical listening incurs special difficulties that arise from face-to-face relationships. The speaker's voice, gestures, and the general reaction of the audience can influence the listeners' thinking and interpretation. The listeners must also adjust their intake of information based on a pace set by the speaker.

These statements may seem contradictory to what was previously discussed concerning differences between reading and listening. It was earlier stated that the speaker's voice, expressions, mannerisms, and so on enhance comprehension for the listeners by helping them with certain cues that are not present while reading. However, for *critical* listening, the speaker's voice, gestures, expressions, and so on may actually impede the exercise of the critical faculty of listening because of the particular persuasiveness of the speaker. Such a speaker may be able to sway even antagonistic audiences to a one-sided view. An example would be the almost hypnotic effect that Adolf Hitler had on his German audiences at mass meetings during the 1930s.

Critical listening requires that students be able to engage in many levels of thinking, while

[13]Sara Lundsteen, "Teaching and Testing Critical Listening," in *Elementary School Language Arts: Selected Readings*, Paul C. Burns and Leo M. Schell, eds. (Chicago: Rand McNally, 1969), p. 158.

still being effective listeners. The thinking skills include those in the cognitive domain, such as knowledge, comprehension, application, analysis, synthesis, and evaluation.

In the primary grades the teachers should be establishing the foundation for effective critical listening. Children must have many experiences all through school in working at various cognitive levels, as well as training in listening concentration skills and in listening comprehension skills.

Students should be helped to know what to note about a speaker, so that they can detect the presence of propaganda or bias. They also should be taught methods of logical reasoning so that they can detect fallacies in the speaker's arguments.

The Institute for Propaganda Analysis has identified several devices or basic techniques of propaganda (see Table 6.1 on page 70). The teacher could tape-record speeches using each of these propaganda strategies and have students decide what tactic is being used and give examples.[14]

The questions that listeners should ask themselves about a speaker involve the "newness" of the material being presented, its relevance, the competence of the speaker, the sources of information, and the attitude of the speaker.

Listening for Appreciation

Teachers should set aside some time every day for appreciative listening. During this time the emphasis should be completely on enjoyment. Appreciative listening is listening for deriving pleasure and enjoyment from poems, stories, music, or any other art form that fits some mood, feeling, or interest. The skill of appreciative listening should be developed in early childhood. Children who are accustomed to listening for appreciation will be better able to enhance their learning–listening ability by sharpening their concentration and memory skills.

Young children enjoy listening to stories, poems, music, and to the delightful sounds of

language itself. (See "Vocabulary of the Senses" in Chapter 9 and "Poetry of the Senses" in Chapter 11.) Teachers can help children appreciate the works of others by creating a good affective environment and by helping children to identify with the mood of the poem or music. For example, the teacher can play a polka record. After the record is played, the teacher should elicit from the children how the music made them feel. Did it make them feel good? Happy? Like dancing? Poetry is another excellent vehicle for developing appreciative listening. Young children learn early that many Mother Goose poems are as good as music because they help you run, skip, jump, trot, gallop, swing, and hop.

Children delight in poems that stress alliteration. *Alliteration* is the repetition of (usually) the initial consonant sound or sounds in two or more neighboring words or syllables. Young children are fascinated by alliteration because it seems to tickle their sound sense. Because of this, tongue twisters are especially relished by children. Who hasn't enjoyed listening to and saying, "She sells seashells at the seashore"?

Onomatopoeia is another poetic technique that appeals to children's ears. Onomatopoeia is the use of words whose sound suggests the sense of the word. For example, in Langston Hughes's poem "African Dance," you can hear and feel the beating of the drums from the following:

> And the tom-toms beat,
> And the tom-toms beat.

Of course, rhythm and rhyme are also loved by children. What child hasn't delighted in Dr. Seuss's *Cat in the Hat?* What child or adult hasn't enjoyed listening to Edward Lear's amusing limericks?

> There was an Old Man with a beard,
> Who said, "It is just as I feared!—
> Two Owls and a Hen,
> Four Larks and a Wren,
> Have all built their nests in my beard!"

Listening to stories that are well read or well told is also an excellent means to help de-

---

[14]Adapted from Thomas R. Lewis and Ralph G. Nichols, *Speaking and Listening* (Dubuque, Iowa: W. C. Brown, 1965), pp. 56–58.

TABLE 6.1   BASIC PROPAGANDA TECHNIQUES

Type of Propaganda	Examples
1. *Name-calling:* Denouncing a person by tagging him or her with a widely condemned label.	Fascist, chisler, Red, and so on.
2. *Glittering generalities:* Seeking acceptance of ideas by associating them with words widely accepted and approved.	Freedom, businesslike, American, Christian, democratic, and so on.
3. *Transfer:* Citing respected sources of authority, prestige, or reverence in such a way as to make it appear they approve the proposal.	The home, the Constitution, will of the people, public education, the Church, the flag, and so on.
4. *Testimonial:* Using testimonials from famous people to build confidence in a product.	For TV commercials or certain causes—actors, athletes, personalities, and so on.
5. *Card-stacking:* Building on half-truths.	Through careful selection of favorable evidence and an equally careful omission of unfavorable or contrary evidence.
6. *Plain folks:* Seeking favor through establishing someone as "just one of the group."	Presidential candidates photographed in Indian war bonnets or politicians shown milking cows, and so on.
7. *Bandwagon:* Going along; since everybody is doing some certain thing, we ought to do it too.	A commercial saying, "The majority of people eat Crunchies. Are you one of them?"

velop appreciative listening skills. Being transported to another land, century, or world can challenge our imaginations and uplift our souls. (See "Nonstandard English and Its Implications for Instruction" in Chapter 17 for further discussion on the importance of reading stories aloud to children.)

CLASSROOM MANAGEMENT FOR LISTENING TRAINING

Time Spent in Oral Communication

There must be a balance between oral (speaking) and aural (listening) activities in school. The teacher must understand that first-grade children are not used to sitting still for long periods of time. They need a rhythm of rest and activity. Although there are individual differences in the attention spans of children, expecting children to spend forty-five minutes to one hour at their desks while listening is most unrealistic. Young children become restless after ten to fifteen minutes of listening.

Most teachers do not seem to realize how much time children spend "listening" in school. When teachers are asked to list those areas in which schoolchildren spend the most time, they usually state reading and give a low listing to listening. A much-quoted research has shown

that children in elementary school listen at least 57.5 percent of class time.[15] This percentage may rise to about 90 percent in high school. As early as 1926, before the advent of television, a researcher stated, "Listening ability is the most frequently used of the forms of communication. Of the total time spent in communication with verbal symbols, it occupies almost three times as much time as reading, and four times as much as writing."[16] In a 1952 study, it was found that of the time adults spend in communication through verbal symbols, 42.1 percent is listening, 31.9 percent talking, 15.0 percent reading, and 11.0 percent writing. Of the total waking time spent in such communication, 29.5 percent is spent in listening, 21.5 percent talking, 10.0 percent reading, 6.9 percent writing, 2.7 percent miscellaneous activities, and 29.4 percent in no form of communication.[17] Today persons are probably writing even less and spending more time in oral communication.

[15]Miriam E. Wilt, "A Study of Teacher Awareness of Listening as a Factor in Elementary Education," *Journal of Educational Research* 43 (April 1950): 626–636.

[16]Paul T. Rankin, "The Measurement of the Ability to Understand Spoken Language" (Ph.D. diss., University of Michigan, 1926); *Dissertation Abstracts* 12 (1952): 848.

[17]Ibid., pp. 847–848.

Although research has substantiated the importance of listening and has shown that students spend the most time in this area, many schools may still lack programs for the sequential development of this important skill. It is often either taken for granted that students can "listen" without any aid, or it is assumed that students are somehow gaining the necessary skills. With the emphasis on reading, due to the increasing number of reading failures in school, some feel that more time should be given to reading than to listening. Ironically, the lack of training in listening skills may well be impeding the development not only of reading but also of speaking and writing.

Providing the Listening Environment

The relationship and importance of listening to language arts and other subject-matter courses have been established. Good listening takes training, and teachers should incorporate direct listening training sessions into each school day to ensure that listening skills will be systematically developed. Such lessons are an essential part of the child's curriculum and should not be neglected or taken for granted. However, no listening skills can be developed unless the child's hearing organs are functioning properly. Even if there are no organic hearing difficulties, there may be other factors that will affect adequate listening.

An environment must be provided where students feel free to share their ideas with one another and are able to listen to others without distraction. Some of the factors that affect both the quality of living in the classroom and the listening climate include the physical, emotional, social, and intellectual environments.

The physical environment refers to any observable factors in the setting that could affect the behavior of an individual. A desirable physical environment would include an arrangement of classroom furniture that is best suited for ongoing listening activities. The furniture should be functional, comfortable, and easily movable. The sound and noise level from the outside or neighboring classrooms should be minimal. The room should be properly ventilated, with a comfortable temperature and humidity range. There should be glareless lighting. Materials,

such as tape recorders, earphones, and record players, should be easily accessible. A specific area should be set aside for individuals or a group of children who can use these materials without disturbing other children. A good physical environment contributes to the good overall quality of classroom living and helps set the stage for a satisfactory emotional, social, and intellectual environment.

The emotional environment should be one in which children do not feel threatened, and where they are not fearful or overly anxious. A warm, friendly, nonthreatening atmosphere is set by the teacher's acceptance, respect, and understanding of each child. A teacher who is consistent and fair, as well as stable and emotionally mature, will help provide an effective place to study. A discipline technique, one used to control a misbehavior, must be fair, firm, clear, and administered without anger. The teacher must avoid outbursts of anger, threats, or arbitrary and willful punishments.

The social environment is somewhat dependent on the presence of a positive emotional environment, so that students will reflect it by being more accepting of others. Children who gain recognition and approval in the classroom are more ready to give recognition and approval to others. Teachers can learn about the social relations of the children in their classes by means of a *sociogram*, a map or chart showing the interrelationships of the children in the classroom and identifying those who are "stars" or "isolates." By means of the sociogram, the teacher can group children more effectively. Teachers who encourage students to express themselves, to explore many ways of solving problems, to make intelligent guesses, who are open-minded, and who allow for mistakes are helping to establish a good intellectual environment.

Students who feel comfortable with one another, who are not threatened, who are secure and physically comfortable will be more ready to learn and better able to listen.

Setting Purposes for Listening in the Classroom

The teacher should help children to set purposes for the various kinds of listening that they will be doing. "Show and tell" listening is different from critical listening. In the former, where a child shares some event or idea with the class, the listeners are involved in appreciative listening; in the latter the listeners are involved in making comparisons, judging whether the speaker is qualified, evaluating what is being said, and looking for biases.

Organizing and Planning for Listening

Teachers should plan to spend at least fifteen minutes of each school day in direct listening-training activities. The listening lesson should be based on the needs, interests, and readiness levels of the pupils. Some of the activities would involve the whole class, whereas others might involve a group of children or only one child. The students can participate not only in the planning of some of the lessons but also in providing ideas for them. Listening learning centers can be developed by both the teacher and children.

TEACHING TACTICS IN LISTENING

Some effective "teaching tactics" that teachers can use to develop good listening habits in their students are given below:

1. *In the first place, children need to recognize that the teacher places a high value on good listening habits.* Teachers should make it clear that attentive listening is sincerely appreciated. A comment to the class such as, "It certainly is helpful to have a class that listens so thoughtfully to the opinions of the other children," is a positive approach which gives status to good listening.

2. *Capitalize on that last "five-minute period" of the day.* This is the time to briefly review the highlights of the day so that the children will have something constructive to tell their parents when asked, "What did you do in school today?" These last five minutes not only promote thoughtful listening, they also provide an excellent opportunity to develop good relations with the parents.

3. *Develop a good speaking voice and help the children to do likewise.* The voices of both teacher and children reflect honest inter-

est in what is being said. A pleasant voice coupled with evident enthusiasm invites others to listen. Thus it is evident that the speaker, too, plays an important part in developing the art of listening. For this reason, oral reports especially should always be most carefully prepared.

4. *Sometimes give tests orally.* Instead of having children always given tests which involve reading, have them write answers to test items which you dictate.

5. *Avoid being a "parrot."* Oftentimes some of the children will pay little attention to what is being said by their classmates or the teacher. In such instances some teachers will repeat these statements or questions "so that everyone can hear." This practice may encourage some of the children not to listen in the first place. However, there may be times when pupils' comments or questions may truly not be understood and in these instances the pupils themselves should be called upon for clarification.

6. *If a pupil has been absent, have another pupil summarize for him or her what was done while the pupil was gone.* This practice will encourage pupils to listen thoughtfully in order to recall the main points of a report or a discussion. In turn, the absent pupil will be inclined to listen carefully to the summary, and thus the practice is a good experience for both pupils.

7. *Afford children opportunities to listen to a variety of sources.* Children should not only listen thoughtfully to the teacher and to the other children's "talk" but to other sources such as playbacks on the tape recorder, television, sociodramas, assembly programs, radio, dramatizations, dialogues, and oral reports. Listening to oral reading by the pupils might especially be stressed, as it seems to have been largely overlooked in recent language arts programs.

8. *Guide the children in making a chart listing the characteristics of a good listener.* Such standards as (1) asks intelligent questions and (2) respects speakers' rights to their opinions might illustrate points in *The Good Listener's Code.*

9. *Have the children discuss why they should be good listeners.* This experience in calling forth their own reasons may help the

children convince themselves as to the importance of listening well. It would be especially helpful if they list and debate the *whys of good listening.*

10. *Encourage pairs of children to interview each other about their hobbies.* Following these interviews, the children could report the findings of their interviews to the entire class.

11. *Ask children to give oral summaries of what has been discussed or reported.* This activity fosters interest and gives purpose to the listening situation.

12. *Provide the children with ample practice in writing from dictation.* Start with short sentences and gradually increase the length and difficulty. Normally, say the sentences only once. If the children wish, they may utilize their personal form of shorthand. After a paragraph has been dictated, ask the children to point out the main idea and perhaps a key word.

13. *By using the sociodrama, have a group of children dramatize both good and poor listening situations.* In terms of the negative, one sociodrama could show an inattentive, restless audience, listeners being disturbed by an inattentive pupil; speakers who do not understand their subjects or who use distracting mannerisms or poor voice projection. *Of course, dramatizations or sociodramas in which the "positive" approach is used are very important and should follow the negative presentation.* Following these presentations, class discussion should bring out a number of important points connected with effective listening.

14. *Use the tape recorder.* Many occasions lend themselves to the use of this instrument. For example, a tape recording could be made of a class discussion followed by the pupils noting and evaluating the main points made during the discussion. Then, when the tape is played back, they could compare the main points which they had listed with what they now hear for a second time.

15. *Help children recognize the importance of listening carefully for names when they are being introduced to others.* Good listening habits pay dividends in this listening situation—and encourage the practice of listening carefully in order to remember.

16. *Be a good listener yourself.* By the process of osmosis children often do as they see others do. When the teacher listens with sincere interest to what the children themselves say, the latter will catch the habit of both attentiveness and courtesy in listening. Perhaps this is the most important method of all in helping children to become courteous, thoughtful listeners.[18]

Another teaching tactic would be to invite students to ask relevant questions of a speaker during and after his or her talk. Also, after the talk, some students can be asked to summarize orally the talk, as well as the questions asked. In addition a discussion about the talk can take place. Active involvement of listeners during and after the talk will help students become better listeners.

INFORMAL TEACHER ASSESSMENT OF LISTENING COMPREHENSION SKILLS

The informal assessment is not concerned with determining organic ear malfunctions. If a teacher feels that a student is having difficulty that might be physiological, he or she should go through the proper referral procedures and inform the principal, school nurse, and parents so that the child can be properly diagnosed by professionally trained personnel. Many times a child is diagnosed as having a "hearing impairment" problem and labeled as having perceptual learning problems when the difficulty is not due to physiological factors but to experiential ones.

In order to determine the student's level of listening at the auding level, the teacher could easily develop a diagnostic instrument by choosing selections based on the student's concentration and vocabulary ability according to grade levels. These selections can vary in length for grades one to six. A grade-one selection would be approximately 50 words, whereas a grade-six selection would be approximately 150 words. The number of comprehension questions asked would depend on the specific grade level or ability levels of students. For the

[18]Guy Wagner, "What Schools Are Doing: Teaching Listening," *Education* (November, 1967): 184–186. Copyright 1967 by Bobbs-Merrill, Indianapolis, Ind.

PRIMARY-GRADE–LEVEL LISTENING SKILLS

During or by the end of the *kindergarten–primary* years the child . . .

Responds to simple verbal questions, directions, and statements.
Listens with comprehension to short discussions.
Listens critically, recognizing gross discrepancies and distinguishing fact from fancy.
Recognizes words that rhyme.
Listens and matches tones.
Listens and responds to rhythm in music.
Locates the source of a sound.
Identifies voices of peers and others.
Listens in order to reproduce sounds, such as animal noises.
Becomes sensitive in rhyme and rhythm in poetry.
Appreciates beauty in the language or in poetry.
Begins to see word pictures in poetry and prose.
Can hear most likenesses and differences in beginning, final, and medial sounds.
Follows sequential development of a story.
Remembers order of events in correct sequence up to five steps.
Derives meaning from intonation.
Identifies with the characters in literature.
Shows increased attention span.
Grows in awareness of the value and the use of words.
Shows enrichment of ideas.
Listens for a specific purpose: details—funny part—exciting part—word pictures—sequence—main ideas—comparisons.
Learns to be a good member of an audience.
Increases ability to make inferences.
Listens in order to relate, to compare, and to apply information.
Senses effective speech on the part of others.
Recognizes oral clues.
Begins to determine the purpose of the speaker.
Recognizes onomatopoeic terms.
Raises pertinent questions in discussion.
Perceives cause and effect relationships.
Responds emotionally, sensing the feeling of the speaker or story character.*

*Source: Curriculum Bulletin of the Malcolm Price Laboratory School, University of Northern Iowa, Iowa City, Iowa.

first grade the teacher could ask three or four questions, whereas in sixth grade, six or seven questions could be asked. The questions should require students to do thinking at various levels of difficulty. For example, teachers should construct questions that require students to do inferential reasoning, that is, to answer questions whereby the answers are not directly stated in the selection, for example, the drawing of conclusions. Critical-thinking questions would require students to pass personal judgment on the truthfulness, accuracy, or value of something, for example, differentiating between fact and opinion. Teachers need to also ask students questions that require them to recall information that is directly stated in the selection. The ability to recall details is necessary for answering higher-level thinking questions. In addition, if students have difficulty recalling details, this may indicate a concentration problem.

LISTENING ACTIVITIES FOR ALL CHILDREN

Although many opportunities may present themselves each day for excellent listening activities, the teacher should also plan these activities.[19] The boxed material on page 74 and 77 lists listening skills that students should attain. Teachers can use this as a checklist to determine whether enough opportunities have been provided to students for developing listening skills. Examples of activities are also presented so that teachers can develop exercises on their own. Many can be adapted for group or individual administration, or audiotaped by teachers and incorporated into the listening learning center.

Some examples of activities for developing or improving primary-grade-level listening skills follow.

Auditory Discrimination Activities

Present three words to children with similar initial consonant sounds and one word with a different initial consonant sound. Have children state the words with similar consonant sounds. Present three words to children with similar final consonant sounds and one word with a different consonant sound. Have children state the word with different final consonant sound. State four words to children of which three are rhyming words and one is not. Have children state the three rhyming words.

Have children listen to a tape of city sounds.
Have children pick out all the sounds they hear.
Have children listen to a tape of country sounds.
Have children pick out all the sounds they hear.
Have children listen to a tape of school sounds.
Have children pick out all the sounds they hear.

[19]Although activities are being presented at specific levels they can be adapted for any grade level.

Concentration and Following-Directions Exercises:

These concentration and following-directions exercises can be adapted for any grade level. In kindergarten and grade one the teacher can use these activities:

Following Directions Orally "Listen carefully. I am going to tell you a few things to do. Let's see who can do them all correctly. Is everyone listening? Fine. When I point to you, that pupil should do all the things that I have told him or her to do. Ready, here we go.

"Stand up, raise your right hand, and put number six on the front chalkboard."
"Stand up, go to the back of the room, and hop on your right foot."

The teacher can either increase or decrease the number of directions according to the ability levels of the students.

Some other concentration activities that could be used at the primary-grade levels include following-directions and specific subject-matter skills. Since the purpose of the activity is to determine concentration skill, the instructor should make sure that the children know the meanings of all the words in the activities and that they understand and can apply the concepts.

The following exercise involves squares, circles, triangles, and numbers. The children have received this sheet:

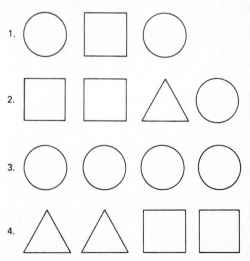

Instructions "Listen carefully. We are going to see how well we can listen and follow directions. Before beginning, we will do one together. On the board I have put a square, a circle, and a triangle. I will state some directions to you. I will then call on someone to follow them. Is everyone listening? Good! Put a three in the circle, a one in the square, and a four in the triangle."

After the teacher has called on someone to do the example, these instructions are given:

1. Put a cross in the first circle, a dot in the last circle, and a one in the square.
2. Put a check in the second square, a one in the first square, and a three in the triangle.
3. Put a two in the second circle, a three in the first circle, and a one in the last circle.
4. Put a four in the first triangle, a six in the second square, and a two in the second triangle.

Listening, Handwriting, and Following-Directions Activities[20]

The teacher can easily combine the handwriting lesson with a listening activity. Children can be asked to listen carefully and see how well they can follow directions and how well they can construct the letter *b*. When the teacher has everyone's attention she or he should say, "Listen carefully. I'm going to give you some directions that involve the construction of the letter *b*. You are not to do anything until I have given you the complete directions for each line."

1. On the first line make two capital letter *B*s, three small letter *b*s, and write the word *boat*.
2. On the second line make three capital letter *B*s, write the word *baby*, and make one small letter *b*.
3. On the third line make two small letter *b*s, write the word *book*, and write the sentence *Betty buys books*.

After the children have finished each line, the teacher can call on individual children who

[20]This section, "The Flannel Box and Following-Directions Activities," and "Listening for Information (Careful Listening)" are drawn from Dorothy Rubin, *The Primary-Grade Teacher's Language Arts Handbook* (New York: Holt, Rinehart and Winston, 1980).

have the correct answers to construct the letters and words on the chalkboard.

The Flannel Box and Following-Directions Activities

The flannel box is a four-sided flannel board. It is made out of plywood, and each side is covered with flannel.

Four children are able to use the box at one time. The teacher initiates the activity. Each child is equipped with similar flannel pieces. The teacher gives directions to the children to make a certain design. The children must place the flannel pieces in the correct order to make the design. Different children are called on to go to the flannel board and to be direction-givers.

This activity helps children to be better direction-givers as well as to listen more carefully.

Listening for Information (Careful Listening)

Tell your children that they are going to listen to a story and that, after the story, they are going to discuss why it's important to listen *carefully*.

The phone rings in the Stewart house. Jane picks up the phone. "Hello," she says. "Hello," says Mrs. Brown, "is your mother home?" "No," answers Jane. "Would you give her a message for me, please?" "Yes," says Jane. "Please tell your mother that we are meeting at Mrs. Drake's house, not Mrs. Crane's. Also tell her to bring the paper plates, not the cups. Do you have that, Jane? Should I repeat it for you?" "Oh, no," says Jane, "I'll remember."

When Jane's mother came home, Jane said, "Mom, Mrs. Brown phoned. She told me to tell you that they are meeting at Mrs. Crane's house and that you should bring paper cups."

"Oh dear," says Mrs. Stewart. "I don't have any paper cups. I'll have to go out to buy some. Also, Mrs. Crane's house is so far away. Oh well . . ."

Ask the children what Jane should have done to help her remember the message.

1. Write down the message.
2. Ask that it be repeated.
3. Repeat the message herself.

Have children construct their own "listening for information stories" and share them with the group.

Sample Listening Comprehension Activities

1. Children listen to a short story and suggest titles for it.

2. In random order teacher reads a sequence of words that can be categorized. Children then select the categories.

3. Students are presented with the following kinds of questions or statements (inference activities), and they must determine who is talking.

a. Number, please?
b. Calling all cars.
c. It is time to go to bed.
d. Always read silently first.
e. All aboard!

4. The teacher makes up a silly story in which the events are out of sequence. The children must listen carefully and put the events in proper sequence. The children can be challenged to make up their own mixed-up stories. They then challenge their classmates to put their stories in proper order.

Examples of some activities to develop listening concentration and comprehension skills at the intermediate-grade level follow.

Concentration and Following-Directions Exercises:

Digit Span Forward In order to develop concentration, which is sustained attention, digit-span exercises are given based on a graduated level of difficulty. The instructor should caution students that concentration demands an individual's complete attention. It would be

---

INTERMEDIATE-GRADE–LEVEL LISTENING SKILLS

During or by the end of the *intermediate* years the child . . .

Shows increasing desire to learn through listening, as an individual and as a member of a group.
Shows increasing responsibility for listening efficiently and effectively.
Responds to more complicated verbal questions, directions, and statements.
Listens to peers, as well as to instructors and other speakers, to get information and knowledge and to develop understanding.
Recognizes and respects the needs of others for group listening.
Accepts responsibility of raising questions when the ideas of the speaker have not been understood.
Shows increased skill in offering constructive criticism when reacting to reports, comments, and other activities of classmates and teachers.
Follows an argument, a discussion, a problem-solving situation, and so on in order to contribute effectively to the development of group understandings.
Responds emotionally to good poetry and prose.
Is gaining sympathetic understanding of people of other times and other places through listening to good literature.
Is gaining understanding of life through vicarious experiences in listening.
Begins to recognize the use of words in influencing the listener.
Shows increased awareness of shades of meaning of words.
Identifies, enjoys, and uses figures of speech.*

*Source: Curriculum Bulletin of the Malcolm Price Laboratory School, University of Northern Iowa, Iowa City, Iowa.

a paradox for someone to be relaxed and concentrating at the same time. Students must focus all their efforts on the stimuli being presented. The teacher should instruct students in the following way: "Listen carefully. I am going to say some numbers, and when I am through I want you to write them exactly the way I have said them. I will state the numbers only once and at a rate of one per second. All right, let's begin. Remember, listen carefully and do not write them until I am finished giving you the whole sequence."

Following is a sample list of numerals at a span from 2 to 9. This exercise can be used with younger children after they have learned to write the digits 0 to 9. A teacher can also use these exercises in the early grades in another way. The teacher would instruct young children to: "Listen carefully. I am going to say a group of numbers and right after I stop, I will point at someone and that child will repeat them. Let's all listen and see whether the numbers are *exactly* the way I said them."

Numbers for Digits Forward

Span
(2)   85
(3)   374
(4)   7295
(5)   52874
(6)   362915
(7)   8514739
(8)   16952738
(9)   739584162

Digit Span Backward   Exercises involving the repetition of digits backward are more difficult and demand more concentration than repeating digits forward. Since many students have difficulty with this exercise a few examples should be given by the teacher before starting. The level at the beginning of the exercise should assure success for all students. The teacher says: "Listen carefully. I am going to say some numbers, and I want you to be able to repeat them backward. For example, if I should say 7-3-1, you should say 1-3-7. Since we are going to work with the whole class (or a

group of students), rather than saying the numbers backward, you will write them backward. Do not first write them forward and then turn them backward. You must write them backward immediately. Ready now; listen carefully." The rate is one per second.

Numbers for Digits Backward

Span
(2)   61
(3)   195
(4)   9583
(5)   94158
(6)   483692
(7)   5836192
(8)   18362749

The instructor can use the norms in Table 6.2 to determine the level of students. The norms should also serve as a guide for preparing concentration exercises for various age levels.

Verbal Memory Exercise   "Listen carefully. I will state pairs of words one after the other. I will then state only one word from each pair and you will have to tell me the mate of the

TABLE 6.2   TERMAN 1937 REVISION NORMS FOR DIGITS FORWARD AND DIGITS BACKWARD

Year Level	Digits Forward	Digits Backward
2½	2	—
3	3	—
4½	4	—
7	5	3
9	5	4
10	6	4
12	6	5
14	7	5
*SA I	7	6
SA II	8	7
SA III	9	7

*Superior Adult
Source: Table compiled from data contained in Lewis M. Terman and Maud A. Merrill, *Measuring Intelligence* (Boston: Houghton Mifflin, 1937), and prior work by Terman.

word. For example, I will say: 'man/woman' 'apple/cake.'

When I say 'man' alone, you will have to say 'woman.'

When I say 'apple' alone, you will have to say 'cake.' "

The teacher can increase the pairs of words from two to three to four and so on. This activity can be made into a game, or the whole class or a group of children, depending on the grade level, can write the words.

Following Directions   A sample activity to improve direction-following and concentration skills is given below. The instructor can adapt the exercise according to the readiness levels of students. Before proceeding with the activity, the teacher must be sure that all the vocabulary words are in the listening capacity of the children so that the children can state the meanings of all the words in the directions. This exercise can also serve as a review to determine whether children are able to use the words when they are presented orally in a sentence. Students receive the two boxed diagrams on a sheet of paper.

The teacher instructs the students, "Listen carefully while I give you some directions. Do not start to follow the directions until after I have finished reading the whole sentence to you."

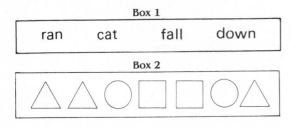

Box 1

| ran | cat | fall | down |

Box 2

Directions

1. **In Box 1 circle the second letter of the second word, and in Box 2 put a dot in the center figure.**
2. **In Box 2 put a check in the second triangle, and a cross on the first letter of the third word in Box 1.**
3. **Put a dot in the first circle in Box 2, a cross in the last figure in Box 2, and a circle around the second letter of the last word in Box 1.**

Sample Listening Comprehension Activities

1. Read a story to the students. Have them give the main idea of the story.
2. Read a short story in which events are in an illogical order; have children order them logically.
3. Listen to a political speech. Have children point out any use of appeals to emotion.
4. Read short paragraphs and have children write what would happen next.

Listening Comprehension and the Newspaper

The teacher reads a human interest article from the newspaper. The students are told to listen carefully because they will be challenged to state the events of the story in proper sequence.

The students are told to listen carefully to a newspaper article for anything that does not make sense. The teacher reads a short article in which he or she has inserted words that do not make sense. The children are challenged to state the inserted words that did not make sense.

The teacher reads an editorial on something of interest to the community. The teacher and the children discuss what techniques the writer used to try to influence readers to his or her views.

The teacher reads an interesting article from a local newspaper. He or she asks students questions that relate to the article.

The teacher reads a few sentences from different parts of the newspaper. The students are challenged to state from what parts of the paper the sentences were taken. The excerpts should be from such sections as the sports section, movie section, theater section, editorial section, news section, advertisement section, fashion section, and so on.

The teacher reads the weather reports from different parts of the country. The children are told to concentrate very carefully to see if they can answer questions about the weather in different parts of the country.[21]

[21]These newspaper activities are drawn from Dorothy Rubin, *The Intermediate-Grade Teacher's Language Arts Handbook* (New York: Holt, Rinehart and Winston, 1980).

STUDENT'S NAME:
          GRADE:
       TEACHER:

DIAGNOSTIC CHECKLIST FOR AURAL RESPONSIVENESS (LISTENING)

PART 1

LISTENING (ORGANIC)	OBSERVATION DATES

Symptoms

1. The child is absent due to ear infection.
2. The child speaks very softly.
3. The child speaks very loudly.
4. The child speaks in a monotone.
5. The child complains of noises in head.
6. The child turns head to one side to hear.
7. The child reads lips while listening.
8. The child asks to have things repeated.
9. The child cups hand behind ear to listen.

PART 2

AUDITORY DISCRIMINATION (SAMPLES)	YES	NO

1. The child can state whether the following sets
of words are similar or different:

Tim	Tom
bit	bet
none	none
fan	van
saw	saw
down	pawn

2. The child can state another word that begins
like

four
Tom
pan
some
down

3. The child can state another word that ends like

look
jump
can
pot

4. The child can state another word that rhymes
with

PART 2 (Continued)

AUDITORY DISCRIMINATION (SAMPLES)	YES	NO
look		
fat		
tan		
bake		

5. The child can give the letter that stands for the first sound heard in

	YES	NO
bury		
mother		
zone		
curb		
label		
jewel		
yell		

6. The child can give the two letters that stand for the first two sounds heard in

	YES	NO
plan		
twin		
stone		
swan		
float		
snag		
cry		
glove		

7. The child can give the two letters that stand for the first sound heard in

	YES	NO
chair		
shame		
thumb		
phone		

8. The child can give the letter that stands for the last sound heard in

	YES	NO
plan		
mom		
rug		
hare		
buzz		
lake		

PART 3

LISTENING CONCENTRATION (SAMPLES)	YES	NO

1. The child is able to repeat sets of digits in proper order:

	YES	NO
a. forward		
b. backward		

PART 3 (Continued)

LISTENING CONCENTRATION (SAMPLES)	YES	NO
2. The child is able to follow orally presented sets of directions.		

PART 4

LISTENING COMPREHENSION (SAMPLES)*	YES	NO
1. Literal listening: The child, after listening to a passage, can answer questions that relate to information explicitly stated in the passage.		
2. Interpretive listening: The child, after listening to a passage, can answer questions dealing with		
a. finding the main idea		
b. generalization		
c. "reading between the lines"		
d. reasoning cause and effect		
e. conclusions		
f. semantic variation of meaning		
3. Critical listening: The child, after listening to a passage, can answer questions dealing with		
a. propaganda		
b. fact or opinion		
c. fantasy or reality		
d. objectivity or subjectivity		
4. Creative listening: The child, after listening to a passage, can answer questions dealing with divergent thinking.		

PART 5

LISTENING FOR APPRECIATION	YES	NO
The child voluntarily chooses to listen to records, tapes, and so on.		

*The length and difficulty of the selection used is determined by the grade level. Also, this is not an inclusive list of listening comprehension skills.

SUMMARY

It has been established that listening is the foundation of the language arts program, and its relationship to the other language arts areas has been discussed. The development of listening skills in the child, as well as the hierarchical nature of listening—which includes hearing, listening, and auding—were presented. The development of critical listening, which is necessary to detect bias and propaganda, was explored and shown to be an important listening skill. Emphasis on this skill in the schools was advocated because of the constant exposure of the public to special pleading in the mass media. It was also suggested that teachers set aside some time every day for appreciative listening, which is listening for enjoyment.

In addition, the role of the active listener was described.

The second half of the chapter was concerned with the instruction and development of students as effective listeners. Classroom management and environments conducive to the teaching of listening skills were discussed. Numerous teaching tactics and listening training exercises were presented, variations of which can be used with children at all grade levels. A "Diagnostic Checklist for Aural Responsiveness (Listening)" was also presented.

As a further aid, two examples of listening lesson plans follow.* Using these as a guide, see if you can construct a plan of your own.

LESSON PLAN I: UPPER-PRIMARY-GRADE LEVEL*

OBJECTIVES

1. The children will be able to identify differences in the sounds and tones of various musical instruments.
2. The children will be able to describe the sounds of various instruments and use their imaginations to state what the musical sounds make them think of.
3. The children will be able to write a title and a short story for one of the musical selections.

PRELIMINARY PREPARATION

1. Make up bulletin board entitled "Musical Sounds." On the bulletin board, have pictures of famous musicians playing their instruments.
2. Have available a record player and the records "Instruments of the Orchestra" and "Bear Dance" from *Hungarian Sketches* by Bela Bartok.
3. Have the following words and phrases on the board: brass instruments, trumpet, French horn, trombone, tuba
4. If possible, have available real instruments. (These could be borrowed from the music department on the day of the music lesson, or the music teacher could bring in these instruments on the day of the lesson to demonstrate the unique sounds of each.)

INTRODUCTION

"We've been working with various musical instruments because many of you said that you would like to learn more about them. What are the instruments that we de-

---

*Formats for lesson plans will vary somewhat to show flexibility in style.

cided to work with first?" "Yes, they are called brass instruments. Can someone find those words on the board for me?" "Good. Can someone tell me the names of the brass instruments that we have already worked with?" "Good. Can someone find these words on the board and point out the instrument on the bulletin board?" "Very good. Today, I brought in a record for you to listen to. The record has some new brass instruments in it. We will be working with these today. See if you can hear them. Close your eyes and allow your imaginations to roam. Try to imagine what is happening. Try to think of a good title for the musical piece. Listen carefully to see whether you can tell which instrument is being used." (Play "Bear Dance" from *Hungarian Sketches* by Bela Bartok.)

DEVELOPMENT

1. After the children have listened to the record, ask them what they thought of as they listened to the record. What kinds of sounds did they hear? Did the sounds remind them of anything or anyone?

Examples: Write suggestions on board. Reinforce each suggestion made, e.g., "You seem to have a very good imagination." Examples include

large clumsy animals
giants or monsters
big machines

What in the music made you think of these things?

Examples: Reinforce each comment: "That's a good description of the music," and so on. Examples include

very loud sounds
fast speed
tones repeated over and over
very high then very low tone
a lot of excitement

What might this animal or monster be doing?

chasing
running
dancing
rushing

2. The children are asked if they recognize any of the brass instruments they had learned about the other day. The children are asked whether they heard any new sounds. The children are then asked to state words that describe the new sounds. For example:

deep	sad
low	funny
harsh	loud
gloomy	etc.

3. The children are then told that these sounds were made by two instruments that they will be learning about today. They are the trombone and the tuba. (Point to words on board.)

"This record has the sounds of the trombone and the tuba. First we will listen to the trombone." (Point to the picture.) "It goes up and down the scale to show you how high it can go and how low. Then there will be a few short pieces to show you what it sounds like when it is playing music."

(Play "Instruments of the Orchestra," Side 3.)

"Next is the tuba." (Point to picture.) Play selection; then turn off record player.

4. "What two new instruments did we listen to today?" "Good, show us the words on the board." "The pictures." "That's right." "What do they sound like?"

deep	sad
low	loud
harsh	funny
gloomy	

Why do you think these instruments were used to represent a dancing bear? Examples of replies:

A bear is clumsy.

He makes low, loud noises.

It sounds like a growl, etc.

5. "Let's play 'Bear Dance' once more. Listen closely and see if you hear the trombone and the tuba. Hold up your left hand if you hear the trombone, and hold up your right hand if you hear the tuba."

6. If time permits, have the children divide into groups of four. Each group is challenged to come up with a title for the selection just reheard and a short story telling what they think is taking place.

7. Each group shares its title and story with the class.

8. The teacher tells the children the name of the musical selection. The children discuss whether they think the title fits the selection.

SUMMARY

The main points of the lesson are pulled together. The children are told that tomorrow they will listen to a musical piece that has all four of the brass instruments that they have learned about. They will be asked to identify the instruments when they are played, to make up a title for the musical selection, and to write a short story about it. (The musical selection is "Circus Music.")

LESSON PLAN II: INTERMEDIATE-GRADE LEVEL

OBJECTIVES

1. The students will be able to identify the various sounds presented on the tape recorder.

2. The students will be able to state the mood that certain recorded sounds suggest.

3. The students will be able to state how certain sounds give us information.

PRELIMINARY PREPARATION

Have blinds or curtains closed. Have tape recorder ready and children seated in a circle around the recorder.

INTRODUCTION

"We have been involved with many different kinds of listening exercises. We have talked about how important it is to listen and how some people are better listeners than others because they have had to depend more on this sense than on the sense of sight. Today we're going to be involved with a special listening activity. Will everyone please close his or her eyes." [While their eyes are closed, turn off the lights.] Play eerie music on the tape recorder playback. After a minute turn off the tape and ask the children to open their eyes. [Keep lights out.] Ask whether anyone can tell you what they thought of when they heard the music played. If they were seeing a movie what would they expect to happen if they heard such music? Tell the students that this special listening activity involves their ability to identify many different familiar sounds when presented on the tape recorder. They will also hear many different kinds of sounds and music presented in films, and they will have to determine what they think will happen or is happening when these sounds are played.

DEVELOPMENT

Tell the children to listen carefully and see if they can pick out and remember all the sounds that are played. When the tape recorder is stopped, one student will identify and remember one of the sounds and then that person will call on someone else to identify another sound. The children will continue to call on one another until they have identified all of the sounds. Say, "Is everyone ready? Good! Now, listen carefully!"

The sounds presented are: car honking, children talking, dishes being washed, leaves rustling in the wind, people walking, people running, running water, keys moving on a key chain, the jingling of coins in a pocket, and a bowling ball hitting pins. After all the sounds have been identified, the students are asked if they can think of any sounds they would like to record. They can then record some familiar school sounds and have other children guess what the sounds are.

Now tell the students that the sounds they are going to hear are usually heard in movies and on the radio to help to set the mood of a story. "Listen carefully and tell me what else the music says to us." Play the tape with sad music, happy music, eerie music, gay music. The following recordings can be used:

Sad music—Chopin's "Dirge"

Happy music—Music from the movie *Snow White and the Seven Dwarfs:* "Whistle While You Work"

Eerie music—"Night on Bald Mountain"—Moussorgsky, arranged by Rimski-Korsakov

Gay music—Any waltz by Strauss or "The Beer Barrel Polka"

After each mood piece is played, children are encouraged to tell how it makes them feel and also to state what they would expect to happen if they heard this music in a film, on the radio, on television.

SUMMARY

Pull main points of lesson together by restating the objectives and having the students determine whether these have been achieved.

SUGGESTIONS FOR THOUGHT QUESTIONS AND ACTIVITIES

1. Develop a listening activity for fun, perhaps one involving directions to be followed by primary-grade students. By intermediate-grade students.

2. There are children in your classroom who never seem to pay attention and who hardly ever follow directions. How would you go about determining what their problems are? How would you try to help them overcome these problems?

3. Develop a *creative* lesson plan on some aspect of listening.

4. List some creative listening activities.

5. Prepare some critical listening questions for intermediate-grade students that could be used with a particular short oral selection of your own choosing.

6. Prepare some creative listening questions for the same selection as in Question 5.

7. Discuss those factors that should be taken into account in determining whether a good listening environment exists for learning.

8. State some skills you would like your students to achieve that were not presented in this chapter.

9. Prepare a lesson plan in listening to use with children who have auditory discrimination problems.

10. Explain how you would develop an appreciative listening program in the primary grades. In the intermediate grades.

11. Create a learning center for the development of critical listening skills.

SELECTED BIBLIOGRAPHY

Burley-Allen, Madelyn. *Listening: The Forgotten Skill.* New York: Wiley, 1982.

Devine, Thomas G. *Listening Skills Schoolwide: Activities and Programs.* Urbana, Ill.: National Council of Teachers of English, 1982.

Duker, Sam, ed. *Teaching Listening in the Elementary School: Readings.* Metuchen, N.J.: Scarecrow Press, 1971.

Froese, Victor. "Hearing/Listening/Auding: Auditory Processing," in *Research in the Language Arts: Language and Schooling,* Victor Froese and Stanley B. Straw, eds. Baltimore: University Park Press, 1981.

Lundsteen, Sara. *Listening: Its Impact on Reading and the Other Language Arts.* Champaign, Ill.: National Council of Teachers of English, 1979.

Pearson, David P., and Linda Fielding. "Research Update: Listening Comprehension." *Language Arts* (September 1982): 617–629.

Rubin, Dorothy. "Developing Listening Skills," in *The Primary-Grade Teacher's Language Arts Handbook.* New York: Holt, Rinehart and Winston, 1980.

———. "Developing Listening Skills," in *The Intermediate-Grade Teacher's Language Arts Handbook.* New York: Holt, Rinehart and Winston, 1980.

Wright, Jone Perryman, and Lester Laminack. "First Graders Can Be Critical Listeners and Readers. *Language Arts* (February 1982): 133–136.

SEVEN

Oral Communication and Speech Improvement

There is all the difference in the world between having something to say and having to say something.

John Dewey

Talking wasn't allowed in the school I went to. You only spoke if you were called on to recite or answer a question. Anyone caught talking at other times was looked on with disdain by the teacher. A chronic violator of the silence rule was usually severely disciplined.

Fortunately, times have changed. We recognize the importance of oral expression, and we recognize that school is a place for talking—for giving free play to children's communicative instincts. A classroom in which children can spontaneously interact with one another and teachers is necessary for oral communication. A good classroom should not be silent. It should be one in which children's ideas are heard, respected, encouraged, and shared.

Children need many opportunities to express themselves, to try out ideas, and to get feedback. When children interact with adults, they are testing their own language. Children's language grows when it receives reinforcement from adults, and children's self-concepts are enhanced when they feel that what they have to say is valuable. Listening to children and re-specting what they have to say encourages them to engage in more conversations. The more conversations that children engage in, the better listeners they become because to engage in a meaningful conversation, they must listen to the speaker. (See Chapter 6.)

This chapter is concerned with the classroom teachers' ability to provide an effective oral communication and speech improvement program that is also *fun* for the students. This chapter is divided into two parts. The first part presents the oral expression (speech stimulation) activities such as finger play, choral speaking, puppetry, and so on, that are vital to all oral communication and speech improvement programs. The second part is concerned with speech improvement. The topics and materials of this part are designed to help teachers who may feel inadequate in the speech improvement area to gain confidence in their ability to present a good speech improvement program in the classroom. Teachers are shown how to determine standards of speech normality in their students. In order to make the teacher aware of the kinds of speech defects that separate the average child from the speech-handicapped child, a listing and description of these defects are presented.

After you have finished reading this chapter you should be able to answer these questions:

1. How can a teacher organize the classroom for the development of effective oral communication?
2. What types of activities are included in an oral communication program?
3. What oral expression activities can primary-grade level children participate in?
4. What oral expression activities can intermediate-grade level children participate in?
5. What kinds of activities should the teacher include in a speech improvement program for primary or intermediate students?
6. How can television be made part of the educative process?
7. What are the differences between speech improvement and speech correction?
8. What is the classroom teacher's role in the area of speech disorders?
9. Do all children develop speech sounds at the same age? Elaborate on the answer.
10. What are the most common speech defects in children?
11. How can teachers help children correct some speech defects?

CLASSROOM ENVIRONMENT CONDUCIVE TO EFFECTIVE ORAL EXPRESSION

The necessity for providing a good physical, emotional, social, and intellectual environment was discussed in Chapter 6 and is applicable here. An environment in which listening occurs without distractions will also be more conducive to oral expression. If students know that others are listening to them, they will be motivated to speak effectively in order to convey their messages.

Physical Environment

Classroom desks and chairs should be arranged so that all students can see and hear the speaker. Obstacles obstructing students' view should be removed, for they act as deterrents to both speakers and listeners trying to communicate. If the speakers' expressions and manner—their total nonverbal behavior—are ef-

fective in relaying the message, then the whole class should be able to see as well as hear them. Speakers faced with an audience that is constantly twisting and turning in their seats will be distracted. Speakers who feel they have lost their audience may lose confidence, and this will affect their delivery.

A classroom that is too warm, too cold, drafty, or peppered with posters and displays may distract the audience and prevent speakers from performing at their highest level of competence.

Emotional Environment

So that children will volunteer to give oral reports or talks or become involved in discussions, creative dramatics, puppetry, and so on, they must be in a nonthreatening environment. They must feel that what they have to say is important and that others want to listen to them. They must be secure about not being ridiculed or criticized. The classroom situation must be friendly, sympathetic, and understanding.

Social Environment

Children who feel accepted by their peers and teacher will more often volunteer to engage in oral expression activities. The teacher who is aware of the individual personalities of students and who uses a sociogram to discover more about the students' social relationships can more intelligently assemble groups for discussions, group reports, and so on.

Teachers should also recognize that their own behavior toward students influences the children's behavior toward those same students.

In the primary grades boys and girls usually work and play together indiscriminately, but by the intermediate grades this pattern alters to a more deliberately homogeneous sex pattern. During the past few decades, this primary-grade pattern seems to be changing, however. In many first-, second-, and third-grade classes boys will only choose boys for play and social interaction, while girls will only choose girls. Teachers should be aware of this phenomenon in their classrooms and act accordingly when they group children for oral expression activities; that is, they should try to mix boys and girls.

Intellectual Environment

Students who are in an intellectually stimulating environment and are engaged in a variety of activities will have many things to talk about, discuss, and report on.

ORAL EXPRESSION ACTIVITIES (SPEECH STIMULATION ACTIVITIES)

When children come to school they have usually acquired basic adult language patterns and are engaging in meaningful oral expression. The teacher needs to encourage children's language development with activities that stimulate speech.

Speech stimulation activities involve the speech arts. They not only help to develop better speech, voice, and body movements necessary for effective speech, but are also enjoyable activities in which children usually love to participate. A variety of activities should be incorporated in the oral communication program in order to provide for all students' needs and interests.

The oral expression (speech stimulation) activities included here are:

Conversation
Telephoning
Discussion
Giving talks
Finger play
Creative dramatics
Puppetry
Storytelling
Choral speaking

Some special activities on role playing, pantomime, nonverbal behavior, haptics (nonverbal communication through touch), and voice usage are also included.

Conversation

Socialization is a process that prepares an individual to live in society. Human beings are social animals. The better we know one another, the better we are able to get along with one another. It is through social discourse such as conversation that we learn more about our friends and neighbors and, many times, about ourselves as well. The need to converse with one another is seen daily in any classroom, whether it is a university graduate class or a kindergarten. When an instructor is interrupted during a class period and must stop to talk to a visitor or leave the class for a short while, what happens? Practically anyone can predict the students' behavior in this situation. They start talking to one another. No prompting is necessary, sometimes to the dismay of the teacher.

Children naturally like to talk, to exchange pleasantries, ideas, comments, and so on. The teacher must understand this need in students and provide not only an environment where students will feel free to engage in spontaneous, informal, and nonstructured talks with one another but also provide time for this to take place.

Since children as well as adults spend most of their time in conversational oral discourse, teachers should help students to be more adept at this skill. Being a good conversationalist helps individuals to be freer to communicate with others and thus enhances self-concept.

Telephoning

Can you imagine life without the telephone? Would you agree that hardly a day goes by when you do not use the phone? Many children speak on the phone for a variety of purposes at very early ages. This does not mean that they use the phone well or effectively, however. Teachers ought to help children communicate better through use of the telephone.

Primary-grade children should learn how to answer the telephone in a courteous and pleasant manner. They should learn how to dial the operator's number and, in case of an emergency, how to dial the police department's number, the fire department's number, or the hospital's number. The children should learn how to state their message in a direct and calm manner. Simulated conversations using the *teletrainer*,[1] available through many local telephone business offices, can help children be

---

[1] The teletrainer is an amplifier and control unit that produces a dial tone, ringing, and a busy signal, and completes the circuit between the two phone units by means of a long cord.

PRIMARY-GRADE TELEPHONING

SCENARIOS

Child calls the fire department to report a fire.

Child calls the police to report that his or her dog is missing.

Child calls information for help in finding an out-of-town telephone number.

Child calls the operator to report reaching a wrong number.

Child calls a friend to find out about a homework assignment.

Child calls a friend to invite the friend for dinner.

Child calls a sick friend to find out how the friend is feeling.

Child phones his or her parents to tell them that he or she will be late.

Child calls the doctor because someone has just become very ill, and no one else is home.

---

better telephone users. Examples of scenarios for simulated telephone conversations are above. Each scenario requires two children—the caller and the receiver of the call—and the teacher, who will operate the teletrainer switchboard. (If teletrainer equipment is not available, the teacher can have the children engage in simulated telephone conversations using toy phones.) In each scenario, the child must dial the number correctly, speak clearly, use good telephone manners, and role-play the part for the suggested scenario.

Intermediate-grade-level children should continue to acquire telephoning skill. Following are examples of scenarios for simulated conversations and role-playing. If teletrainer equipment is used, the teletrainer switchboard can be operated by one of the students.

INTERMEDIATE-GRADE TELEPHONING

SCENARIOS

Child dials long-distance information to get a telephone number.

Child dials the operator to report reaching a wrong number on an in-state long-distance call.

Child calls the police to report a serious accident.

Child calls a business firm to leave a message for one of his or her parents.

Child calls the operator to report receiving a wrong number on an out-of-state call.

Child uses the yellow pages of the telephone directory to find a business firm that sells a special item that he or she needs. The child phones a few business firms to find out whether they have the special item, the cost of the item, and other pertinent information about the item.

Child calls the newspaper editor to report something exciting that happened at school.

USING THE TELETRAINER.

Discussion

Although the terms "conversation" and "discussion" are used interchangeably, and children engage in informal discussions during work and play, differences exist between the two. As already stated, conversation is informal, spontaneous, and nonstructured, whereas classroom discussions are usually formal, more structured, directed, involved with specific purposes, and demand the cooperation of many persons.

Group Discussions in the Primary Grades Group discussions can be initiated by a number of stimuli. Every day innumerable opportunities present themselves for group discussions. The children may have had a story read to them that has caused some excitement or controversy. They may have seen a television show or movie that has stimulated them, or some event in the news may have sparked a need for clarification or discussion. In order to make discussions meaningful and beneficial, certain standards should be set by the students and the teacher.

1. Everyone must respect the rights of each person to state his or her opinion.
2. When someone is speaking, all persons should be courteous and attentive.

3. Speakers have the responsibility to make themselves heard, to stick to the point, and to speak clearly so that they can be understood.
4. All persons should try to contribute to the discussion.
5. Individual children should try not to dominate the discussion.

Group Discussions in the Intermediate Grades In the intermediate grades all of these standards would also apply. However, there are some more advanced skills that such children should develop.

1. Everyone should develop the ability to participate in meetings conducted according to a basic parliamentary procedure.
2. Each child should learn to act as a leader in discussion by:
   a. keeping all speakers on the topic
   b. helping all to contribute, sometimes by asking questions
   c. not allowing a few people to dominate
   d. not letting arguments begin
   e. not allowing emotions to rule
   f. pulling main points of discussion together
3. Children should learn to disagree politely.
4. All persons should be able to listen for supporting evidence related to the main topic of discussion.

A listing of the various forms of discussion is given below for teachers:

1. *Informal Discussion:* This can evolve at any time in the classroom with or without apparent leadership. It usually includes a grouping of some children who have a common interest or problem.

2. *Round Table:* This takes place without an audience. A number of members informally discuss something under the direction of a leader.

3. *Panel Discussion:* Approximately four to eight equally informed participants, under the direction of a leader, engage in a discussion before an audience. The topic or problem is informally presented from many views. A question-and-answer period from the audience usually follows.

4. *Dialogue:* An expert is questioned by another individual who is also well informed in the area. Television programs use this format when

interviewing public figures. Teachers can employ this technique when an authority on a specific topic is invited to visit the classroom. Some students can take a special assignment to become more informed in this area, and then act as the expert in questioning the guest.

5. *Debate:* Two different sides of an issue are presented in a formal manner. Provisions for full class participation can be achieved by allowing questions from the floor. For an effective debate the students involved must be well informed.

Giving Talks

Time should be set aside each week for special talks given by individuals on topics of interest. Talks not only help students to present ideas in a logical and sequential fashion but also give them practice in using appropriate voice quality, rhythm, rate, and volume, and in speaking in front of an audience. They can also practice good body posture, facial expressions, gestures, and body movements during talks.

Informal Oral Reporting In the primary grades informal oral reporting is the most frequent talk activity. "Show and tell" is a first-grade activity in which pupils share some event with their classmates or tell about some new acquisition. Although some teachers use sharing time at the beginning of the school day to "calm children down," it can be an excellent technique to draw out the shy child and to give more aggressive children an opportunity to stand in the limelight. In order to gain the attention of the group, children soon learn that they must have something interesting to say; they also must be able to say it so that others will continue to listen.

From "show and tell" sharing,[2] primary-grade children can be encouraged to share some information about a television show that they especially like, a movie that they have just

²In some school districts, such terms as "meeting time" and "sharing time" have replaced "show and tell" in order to emphasize more the *telling* rather than the *showing*.

"SHOW AND TELL" OR "SHARING TIME"

seen, or a story that they have either read or had read to them.

Teachers should not only encourage this type of oral reporting, but should also assist children presenting the talks to make them enjoyable for listeners. Teachers, by asking specific questions, will help the reporter not only to recall some pertinent facts but will also keep rambling to a minimum.

Reinforcement should be given, praising the student for an interesting point or some descriptive phrases that help listeners to get a better picture of what is being said.

Formal Oral Reporting In the intermediate and upper grades students present formal reports. These differ from informal oral reports in that they require study and preparation of background material.

When primary-grade children give formal oral reports, the length of time for the talk should be just a few minutes and preparation should also be limited in scope. It should be stressed that those second- and third-grade pupils who are reading at a fifth- or sixth-grade level are able to do research with help from the teacher, and give oral reports that will provide an opportunity for enrichment for them.

Certain standards should be set for talks in order to make them worthwhile and meaningful. These guidelines might be beneficial for both the teacher and students in the primary grades:

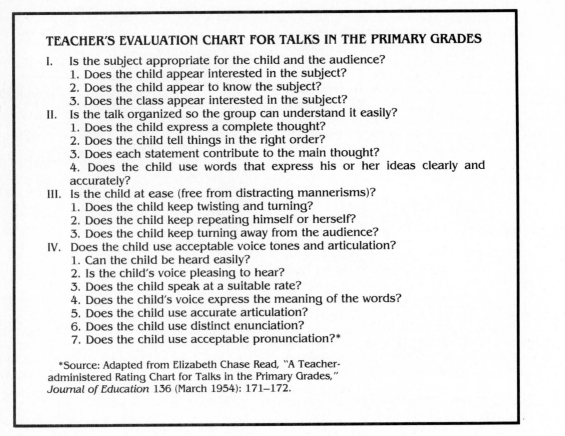

TEACHER'S EVALUATION CHART FOR TALKS IN THE PRIMARY GRADES

I.   Is the subject appropriate for the child and the audience?
1. Does the child appear interested in the subject?
2. Does the child appear to know the subject?
3. Does the class appear interested in the subject?
II. Is the talk organized so the group can understand it easily?
1. Does the child express a complete thought?
2. Does the child tell things in the right order?
3. Does each statement contribute to the main thought?
4. Does the child use words that express his or her ideas clearly and accurately?
III. Is the child at ease (free from distracting mannerisms)?
1. Does the child keep twisting and turning?
2. Does the child keep repeating himself or herself?
3. Does the child keep turning away from the audience?
IV. Does the child use acceptable voice tones and articulation?
1. Can the child be heard easily?
2. Is the child's voice pleasing to hear?
3. Does the child speak at a suitable rate?
4. Does the child's voice express the meaning of the words?
5. Does the child use accurate articulation?
6. Does the child use distinct enunciation?
7. Does the child use acceptable pronunciation?*

*Source: Adapted from Elizabeth Chase Read, "A Teacher-administered Rating Chart for Talks in the Primary Grades," *Journal of Education* 136 (March 1954): 171–172.

Finger Play

Finger play is a speech-stimulation activity especially suitable for kindergarten and first-grade children. If properly presented, it can be most effective in helping children to learn sequential order in speaking and to develop good body movements and gestures. Finger play is an excellent medium for the shy or withdrawn child who is reticent to speak. Since finger-play activities can be presented with the participation of the whole group, children who have speech difficulties usually participate.

Finger plays involve simple rhyming stories that are readily dramatized. Here are some suggestions for presenting finger-play activities.

Steps in Learning Finger Play

1. Teacher presents finger-play activity to be learned by children.

2. Children thoroughly learn the rhyme that accompanies the finger-play activity.
3. Next, children learn the finger actions.
4. The rhyme and the finger actions are joined. The teacher softly and slowly accompanies the students' recitation.
5. The children, without the teacher, are asked to perform the first line of the finger play, then the second line, and so on until all the lines have been individually completed.
6. The children perform the whole finger-play activity by themselves.

Teachers should act as encouragers, reinforcers, and helpers. For finger play to be both fun and educationally worthwhile, children must feel free to participate. Children should be invited to participate, but they should not be pressured if they are reluctant. If teachers are

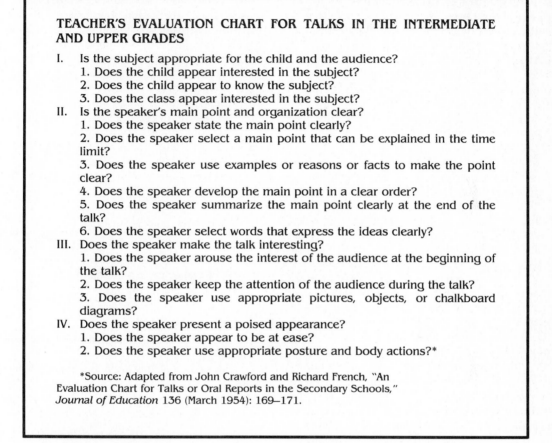

TEACHER'S EVALUATION CHART FOR TALKS IN THE INTERMEDIATE AND UPPER GRADES

I.   Is the subject appropriate for the child and the audience?
     1. Does the child appear interested in the subject?
     2. Does the child appear to know the subject?
     3. Does the class appear interested in the subject?
II. Is the speaker's main point and organization clear?
     1. Does the speaker state the main point clearly?
     2. Does the speaker select a main point that can be explained in the time limit?
     3. Does the speaker use examples or reasons or facts to make the point clear?
     4. Does the speaker develop the main point in a clear order?
     5. Does the speaker summarize the main point clearly at the end of the talk?
     6. Does the speaker select words that express the ideas clearly?
III. Does the speaker make the talk interesting?
     1. Does the speaker arouse the interest of the audience at the beginning of the talk?
     2. Does the speaker keep the attention of the audience during the talk?
     3. Does the speaker use appropriate pictures, objects, or chalkboard diagrams?
IV. Does the speaker present a poised appearance?
     1. Does the speaker appear to be at ease?
     2. Does the speaker use appropriate posture and body actions?*

*Source: Adapted from John Crawford and Richard French, "An Evaluation Chart for Talks or Oral Reports in the Secondary Schools," *Journal of Education* 136 (March 1954): 169–171.

enthusiastic and generous in their praise, they will soon have everyone in the class involved.[3]

Creative Dramatics and Speaking

Creative dramatics offers many opportunities for the development of the "creative spirit," and lends itself as well to the improvement of voice, vocabulary, diction, and thinking. This is a natural for children, because their play is so full of pretending, imagination, and imitation.

Brian Way, who has made significant contributions to the field of creative dramatics, states in an interview that "drama, linked with other forms of creative expression, allows youngsters to see the whole of themselves— senses, imagination, language, emotion, intellect—to deal with those things which are necessary and mandatory in school."[4] Unfortunately, he feels that many teachers have tried drama in the classroom[5] with poor results and, as a result, are reluctant to try it again. This is regrettable because creative drama in the classroom can be used to stimulate all the language

[3] The length of the finger-play activity will depend on the individual differences of the students.

[4] David Dillon, "Perspectives: Drama As a Sense of Wonder—Brian Way," *Language Arts* (March 1981): 359.

[5] Creative dramatics is sometimes referred to as drama in the classroom, improvisational drama, educational drama, and informal classroom drama.

arts, as well as help persons learn about themselves and others. "Active participation in creating classroom drama broadens students' experiences, clarifies information, generates new ideas, and improves attitudes toward learning."[6] Creative dramatics, if used properly, therefore, can be an effective teaching and learning tool.

Before we proceed further, we should distinguish between creative dramatics and play productions. Creative dramatics is for the children, themselves, not for an audience; it is informal. In this form, it is usual for the children to make up their own story and dialogue, as well as act them out. Creative dramatics is spontaneous and unrehearsed. The teacher can stimulate the activity by setting a certain scene and having students act out the parts, or by encouraging students to generate ideas of their own by asking penetrating questions.

If teachers have not worked with creative dramatics before or if they have had bad experiences with it in the classroom, they should proceed slowly. That is, they should engage their students in creative dramatics for no more than two minutes, and it should be related to the students' ongoing activities. For example, teachers can transform course material into a three-dimensional activity by having students get into groups of three to make still photographs to illustrate what they are studying. The teacher tells students that they are going to pose for a quiet photograph to put into a book. The photograph could be the President of the United States shaking hands with a famous person, or a scientist working in a lab, or any picture the teacher wishes the students to capture. If students have been successful in this endeavor, they could advance to bringing to life their photographs, that is, acting them out. Each time, the period of concentration could be extended, but only by a few seconds.[7]

Teachers should begin with simple activities that give children experience in using their bodies and voices to express a message. They could begin, first, by using only their bodies (pantomime), then only their voices, and, finally, putting the two together. The activities could also go from teacher-guided ones to those developed by groups of children. In addition, creative dramatics could be performed by the whole class in unison, by one group of children at a time, or by an individual child alone. Creative dramatics can be an effective teaching tool if teachers integrate it with various subject-matter areas and plan properly for its use.

Here are suggestions for children five through seven years of age.

Procedure The teacher might ask, "How many have heard Mother or Father call the dentist? What did they say? Who can pretend to be Mother or Father calling the dentist?"

The conversation would probably go something like this:

"Is this Dr. Jones?

"I would like to make an appointment to have my teeth checked.

"May I have one this week? One tooth is bothering me.

"Thank you."

A dramatization of a boy or girl feeding a dog can be motivated by the teacher in the same way: "How many children have a dog or cat? How many have fed them? Show us how you did it."

One example of such a dramatization might be the following:

Here, Shawn; here, Shawn; here, Shawn. Look what I have for you. It's a nice bone. We had rib roast today and Mother gave me this bone. No, don't jump all over me. I'll give it to you. Here you are. Look at him run with it. He's afraid somebody will take it away from him.

Other possibilities would include:

Someone cutting the grass
Someone watering the lawn
Someone cleaning the house
Child putting sick doll to bed

[6]National Council of Teachers of English and Children's Theatre Association of America NCTE and CTAA Committee, "Forum: Informal Classroom Drama," *Language Arts* (March 1983): 371.
[7]Dillon, "Perspectives," p. 359.

Child running a lemonade stand
Child calling friends to come to play
Child going to bed
Child getting up and dressing
Children visiting the zoo
Someone shopping at the supermarket
Child eating supper
Child building an airplane

Self-consciousness at the beginning can be reduced by allowing several children to dramatize the same thing at the same time, encouraging each child to act as he or she thinks best and not imitating what the others are doing. As they develop in dramatic ability and gain confidence, one child may perform alone. Gradually, more difficult situations can be acted such as:

Two children talking about a game
Several children playing going to the library
One child being a storekeeper while others come to buy
Several children giving a simple circus performance
Children dramatizing animals, while other children visit the zoo and talk about the habits and actions of the animals

The teacher can tell a story and then have the children act it out, supplying their own dialogue. Poems can be acted out by the children as well. Many Mother Goose rhymes are excellent acting sources for kindergarten and first-grade children. Such characters as Humpty Dumpty, Jack and Jill, Little Miss Muffet, Mary and her lamb, and Georgie Porgie are fun to portray. The opportunities for creative dramatics are bound only by the creative limitations of the teacher.

By second grade many children can be more independent in creative dramatics. They can take the initiative in choosing a story that they would like to "act out" for the class. A group of second-graders might decide to present "The Three Billy Goats Gruff," a favorite with most children. The performers should be encouraged to make all decisions concerning casting, props, and number of rehearsals. The teacher's role is that of questioner, suggester, encourager, and reinforcer. The teacher can ask questions to stimulate children's thinking about a problem or can make some positive suggestions for solving the problem. The children should be encouraged to try their ideas, but they should know that the teacher is available for assistance if needed. The children's efforts should be praised, and their endeavors should be shown as worthwhile.

Role Playing: An Extension of Creative Play

Role playing is a form of creative dramatics that is natural to children. They either choose or are appointed to specific roles, the scenario is set, but the dialogue is spontaneously developed. In a fifth- or sixth-grade class the scenario might be a discipline problem serious enough to warrant calling both parents to school. A meeting is set up in the principal's office. The child, the mother, the father, the teacher, and the principal are present. The players have been told the scenario. It is up to them to act out the drama.

Role playing often helps teachers gain insights into the feelings of students, and to discover what is important to them. This technique can also help students develop keener perception of how it feels to be in certain situations.

The teacher is cautioned, when choosing children to play particular roles, against obvious assignments; for example, having an "isolate" play a popular student or the "star" in the classroom play an "isolate." Discretion must be used in role playing so that students are not embarrassed or ridiculed. Children should not be forced to play a role in which they might feel uncomfortable.

Pantomime

Pantomime is creative dramatics without speech. Students use only their faces and bodies to convey a thought or action. Pantomime usually helps students become more sensitive to what they see, and to learn about the importance of facial expressions and body movements in conveying and receiving messages.

Primary-grade pupils seem to use pantomime naturally in their everyday activities. They especially enjoy playing "make-believe" or "pretend" type of games in which they imitate some

person, animal, or object. These children can pantomime many everyday situations such as:

Waking up in the morning
Getting dressed
Eating lunch
Reading a book
Sweeping the floor

Intermediate-grade students might try more difficult themes such as :

Playing baseball
Showing enthusiasm
Exhibiting fear
Being too hot
Being too cold
Crying
Acting bored
Feeling tired
Moving through a crowded bus
Having a difficult time conversing on the telephone

When pantomiming, students must carefully think about and analyze the moods, situa-tions, or ideas they wish to act out in order to determine how best to convey them. Imitation of facial expressions and body movements re-quires keen observation.

"Reflections" is a good game to use with pantomime for both primary- and intermediate-grade students. This game uses sets of two players in which one student is the "mirror" and the other is the "image." The "image" students make different faces or body movements for the "mirror" students to reflect.

Nonverbal Behavior: Its Role in Oral Communication and Creative Dramatics

The human being communicates both ver-bally and nonverbally, and the total message lies in the combination of the two modalities.[8] (See Chapter 1.) *Kinesics*, the gestures that may or may not accompany speech, help to convey and clarify meaning. For example, an arched eyebrow tells us that a person is skepti-cal about what is being said, and is a gesture that if put into words would say "Do you really want me to believe that?" Upturned palms com-bined with a shrug of the shoulders tell us that a person is confused. That person might be saying, "I don't know." Body movements por-tray a person's moods and feelings as readily as words. For example, a person's posture can tell us whether he or she is anxious or relaxed. Following are some suggestions for activities that can help students be more perceptive to the messages conveyed by nonverbal behavior:

1. Students can videotape some persons while role playing. Students then can view the tape to identify the kinesic motions that individ-ual role players use while speaking, the *vocal* nonverbal behaviors (ohs, ahs, screams, and so forth, that are vocal but express no words by themselves), and body movements.

2. Students can view a foreign film and re-cord some of the representative nonverbal be-havior of the actors and actresses.

[8]Walburga von Raffler-Engel, "Total Communica-tive Redundancy: The Neglected Factor in Foreign Language Research," paper presented at the Los An-geles Second Language Research Forum, 1978.

3. Children from different cultural backgrounds can try to communicate some message using some form of nonverbal behavior.

4. Students, with eyes closed, listen to a videotape of two persons talking. The students then open their eyes to view the videotape. The students are asked to compare the listening and viewing of the tapes to determine whether they were able to get the complete message from only listening. If videotapes are not available, two students can role-play the two sequences for the class.

5. Students can view television shows to observe the various kinds of facial gestures and body movements that individuals use when they speak.

Haptics: Nonverbal Communication Through Touch   The study of *haptics*, nonverbal communication through touch, is relatively new; most of the research in this area has been done mainly with visually impaired or handicapped children. Haptics offers many possibilities for helping all kinds of students to become more sensitive to the effect that "touch" has on communication. When one is speaking, "a touch" at the right time helps convey meaning, for different ways of touching may convey different feelings or meanings. A pat on the back by a parent to a child and a pat on the behind by a football player to another player after a good scrimmage both mean "well done." A handshake or the touching of hands are forms of greeting.

Videotaping spontaneous class conversations during recess can allow students to observe how touch aids communication. Students can then role-play different kinds of touch techniques and have their classmates interpret what they are trying to convey.

Puppetry

Some children who are reluctant to participate in storytelling, creative dramatics, or role playing find *puppetry* a fine outlet for creative expression. Through the manipulation of puppets, these children overcome much of their shyness and fear of speaking in front of an au-

dience. By projecting their feelings and thoughts into the puppets, they make them come alive.

Puppetry is a means of acting by using one's hands. The hands become the characters. The suggestions listed here will aid puppeteers in giving a successful performance.

Suggestions to Students on How to Be a Good Puppeteer

1. Know your script or story by heart if you are performing in front of an audience without a stage. Even when performing behind a stage, know the script or story very well. (Puppets may, of course, be used in a more informal manner; that is, children can use puppets in different situations in which the dialogue is completely spontaneous.)

2. Keep your eyes on the puppet.

3. Move the puppet that is talking, and have other puppets looking at the one that is speaking.

4. Help puppets make expressions by moving their heads and bodies. For example, a sad puppet would be turned slowly away from the audience, whereas a happy puppet might be bouncing up and down looking at the audience. Your voice will also help to convey the desired effect.

5. Avoid jerky movements with your puppets. Let them make graceful entrances and exits. Do not just snatch them out or pop them in.

In the primary grades many Mother Goose poems and fairy tales lend themselves well to dramatizations with puppets. Intermediate-grade pupils might also use fairy tales, as well as their favorite stories from children's literature. They might want to write their own plays or stories and make puppets needed for the characters in the play.

Once puppet shows have been created, they can be taken to a wider audience—other classes, parents, a home for the aged—where the show's impact can be evaluated by the audience and where the students involved can achieve a sense of pride in what they have accomplished.

Making Puppets   Primary-grade children can make stick puppets and hand puppets, which are both easy to construct and manipu-

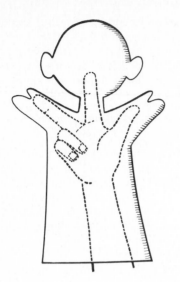

material (such as nylon stockings) and tie it loosely where you want the neck, leaving room to insert your index finger. Sew on features and a piece of cloth around the "chin" to cover your hand (see illustration).

Line the palm of a mitten with red cloth and sew on two button eyes where your knuckles are. If you like, add yarn whiskers or yarn hair sewn to the wristband. This puppet makes an interesting "creature" of any kind. Floppy ears can make it a dog; a cardboard horn on the tip of the nose will make it a unicorn. Should you want to make this puppet on a larger scale, use a piece of material that fits over your arm like a loose sleeve and terminates at your fingers in two sections, the bottom for your thumb and the top for your fingers. Add the red mouth lining, eyes, hair, ears, etc., and you will have a more elaborate, long-necked creature, such as a giraffe or dragon (see illustration).

late. Only biodegradable and recyclable material should be considered for building puppet-show sets or creating the puppets themselves. This helps children to develop an ecological conscience and to become more sensitive to their environment.

Stick puppets can be constructed from cardboard by stapling the front and back of the figures together over a long thin stick. Hand puppets may also be made from vegetables such as potatoes, carrots, yams, and turnips, or from bags, socks, Styrofoam, and Spongex.

One type of hand puppet consists of a head and loose garments and usually has no legs. The index finger fits into the neck (see illustration),[9] and the thumb and middle finger fit into the sleeves; the garment conceals the hand.

A hand puppet can also be made of a sock, handkerchief, or paper bag, which covers the hand. Here are some suggestions for making hand puppets.[10]

A sock can be fashioned into a puppet in two ways: Simply put your hand into it, as you would into the mitten, and work your fingers for a mouth; or, stuff the toe of the sock with soft

[9]Eleanor Boylan, *How to Be a Puppeteer* (New York: McCall, 1970), p. 13.
[10]Ibid., pp. 20–21.

For a paper-bag puppet, draw a face at the bottom of the bag where it folds flat, making sure that the mouth is in the center of the crease. Then put your hand into the bag and open and shut the crease so that the mouth "speaks" (see illustration).

A Styrofoam ball and a popsicle stick make a delightful puppet. Take a piece of cloth about eight or nine inches square and, holding the stick erect, drape the cloth over it; thrust the covered end of the stick into the ball (see illustration).

Choral Speaking

Choral speaking helps children to improve their speech while having fun. It is a way of saying aloud, in unison, a poem or a prose selection by a group trying to catch the spirit and rhythm of the piece. The selection must be one that lends itself to unison speaking.

Participation in this activity helps students not only to appreciate good literature but to gain a better understanding of poetry. In order to give a good rendition of a poem, students must be able to interpret the mood and thought of the selection.

Choral speaking also helps shy youngsters to "forget themselves" and become less self-conscious. Once children have gained confidence in their ability to speak, they will be less reticent to speak before an audience.

The teacher can employ choral speaking effectively in kindergarten with appropriate material to help children enjoy the sounds and rhythm of poetry.

Types of Choral Speaking There are various types of choral speaking in which children can take part. In *Line-a-Child,* individual children speak different lines. For example, in the following Mother Goose nursery rhyme, "Solomon Grundy," the entire class could speak the first and eighth lines, while six individual children speak the second, third, fourth, fifth, sixth, and seventh lines. For further interest a contrast of voices can be used so that children with light, bright voices speak the first three lines, and children with rich, heavy voices speak the last three lines.

Solomon Grundy

ALL	Solomon Grundy born on Monday,
1ST CHILD	Christened on Tuesday,
2D CHILD	Married on Wednesday,
3D CHILD	Very ill on Thursday,
4TH CHILD	Worse on Friday,
5TH CHILD	Died on Saturday,
6TH CHILD	Buried on Sunday,
ALL	This is the end of Solomon Grundy.

Mother Goose

Other selections from Mother Goose that can be used with *Line-a-Child* choral speaking include "Here Sits the Lord Mayor"; "One, Two, Buckle My Shoe"; "This Little Cow"; and "For Want of a Nail." Other good choices are "One and One" by Mary Dodge and "The Owl" by Alfred, Lord Tennyson.

In antiphonal poems the heavy and light voices speak to each other. The Mother Goose rhymes "Willy Boy, Willy Boy"; "Baa Baa Black Sheep"; "Little Girl, Little Girl"; "Pussy Cat, Pussy Cat"; "Jennie Come Tie"; and "Little Dog, Little Dog" are examples of this type of verse. Another example follows:

Lady Moon

1ST-HALF CLASS	Lady Moon, Lady Moon, where are you roving?
2D-HALF CLASS	"Over the sea."
1ST-HALF CLASS	Lady Moon, Lady Moon, whom are you loving?
2D-HALF CLASS	"All that love me."
1ST-HALF CLASS	Are you not tired with rolling, and never
	Resting to sleep?
	Why look so pale and so sad, as forever
	Wishing to weep?
2D-HALF CLASS	"Ask me not this, little child, if you love me;
	You are too bold:
	I must obey my dear Father above me,
	And do as I'm told."
1ST-HALF CLASS	Lady Moon, Lady Moon, where are you roving?
2D-HALF CLASS	"Over the sea."
1ST-HALF CLASS	Lady Moon, Lady Moon, whom are you loving?
2D-HALF CLASS	"All that love me."

Lord Houghton

In *cumulative choral reading* a small group reads one section and is joined by a second group that reads the second section; they are joined by a third group that reads the third section. Usually no more than five groups should be used to build the cumulative effect. The emphasis in this kind of reading becomes more forceful and poem usually sounds louder and faster with each group and line. Here is an example of a poem that can be used with cumulative choral reading.

African Dance

GROUP 1	The low beating of the tom-toms,
GROUPS 1 AND 2	The slow beating of tom-toms,
GROUPS 1–3	Low . . . slow.
GROUPS 1–4	Slow . . . low—
GROUPS 1–5	Stirs your blood.
GROUPS 1–5, LOUDLY	Dance!
GROUP 1, SOFTLY	A night-veiled girl
GROUPS 1 AND 2, SOFTLY	Whirls softly into a
GROUPS 1–3, SOFTLY	Circle of light
GROUPS 1–4, SOFTLY	Whirls softly . . . slowly,
GROUPS 1–5, SOFTLY	Like a wisp of smoke around the fire—
GROUPS 1–5	And the tom-toms beat,
GROUPS 1 AND 2	And the tom-toms beat,
GROUPS 1–4	And the low beating of the tom-toms
GROUPS 1–5, LOUDLY	Stirs your blood.

Langston Hughes

The reading emphasis of "African Dance" should grow more forceful, and the poem should become louder and faster with each line, indicating the increasing intensity of the drum beat. In the second verse, there should also be an increasing intensity of feeling, but the reading should be more melodious and softer than in the first verse. In the last stanza the voices should reach an explosive crescendo.

When class members speak the refrain while one or several students tell the story they are *refrain speaking*. A verse that lends itself to this type of choral speaking follows:

A Farmer Went Trotting

GROUP 1	A farmer went trotting upon his grey mare,
ALL	Bumpety, bumpety, bump!
GROUP 1	With his daughter behind him so rosy and fair,

ALL	Lumpety, lumpety, lump!
GROUP 2	A raven cried "croak!" and they all tumbled down,
ALL	Bumpety, bumpety, bump!
GROUP 2	The mare broke her knees, and the farmer his crown,
ALL	Lumpety, lumpety, lump!
GROUP 3	The mischievous raven flew laughing away,
ALL	Bumpety, bumpety, bump!
GROUP 3	All vowed he would serve them the same next day,
ALL	Lumpety, lumpety, lump!

Mother Goose

Part speaking presents a selection by groups of students in such a way that the sequence and continuity of ideas expressed in the poem are maintained. Each group speaks a part of the selection, the groups being divided according to the kinds of voices indicated by the poem; for example, low voices would read a part appropriate for heavy voices, whereas higher voices would read a part that calls for light voices.

The following poem lends itself to part speaking:

WHERE GO THE BOATS?

Dark brown is the river,
  Golden is the sand,
It flows along forever,
  With trees on either hand.

Green leaves a-floating,
  Castles of the foam,
Boats of mine a-boating—
  Where will all come home?

On goes the river
  And out past the mill,
Away down the valley,
  Away down the hill.

Away down the river,
  A hundred miles or more,
Other little children
  Shall bring my boats ashore.

Robert Louis Stevenson

In *unison speaking* the group reads the entire poem where it maintains one mood or one theme throughout. The students then decide what divisions they wish to make, which help portray the meaning of the poem more clearly to the audience. Unison or group choral reading is not a separate technique or form but merely uses any or all types of choral reading for the most effective casting of a poem.

A Choral-Speaking Technique To proceed with a choral-speaking program teachers should first attempt to release the class from tension, for *relaxation* is necessary for effective choral speaking. Breathing exercises can be used to relax students, and to help them to learn proper breathing. In breathing activities such as puffing, blowing, sighing, and yawning, emphasize swelling at the waist or belt line on the intake of air. This should help to discourage shoulder and upper-chest breathing. Another relaxing activity has children responding to the teacher's oral reading of a poem with rhythmical body movements. The teacher's reading should bring out the rhythms and music of the poem.

After these "warm up" activities students are ready for choral reading. During this phase the teacher presents meaningful segments of a selection to students, who silently follow the reading by making the proper lip and mouth movements. The segments are presented again, and this time the pupils whisper the lines. Finally, pupils recite the lines as the teacher silently mouths or whispers them.

Storytelling

The traditional definition of storytelling is "the oral interpretation of literature and folklore." In the traditional definition, no props or theatrical tricks are used. The storyteller, the story, a place to tell the story, and a receptive audience are all that is needed. Today, a number of persons combine storytelling with creative dramatics or use puppets or other props to help them to convey their story. Whatever technique of storytelling the storyteller uses, the key is in finding a story that is just right for that person—a story that the storyteller enjoys. Storytellers must also use the language of the story well, and their voice, gestures, and body movements must all work together to convey that certain magic that good storytellers have.

Storytelling is an art that can be learned. Teachers should not only encourage their children to be storytellers, but they too should set an example for their students.

Every week the teacher and students can plan for sharing and storytelling. Children may either relate their experiences or tell a story to the class. In the primary grades students should be encouraged to relate their experiences without much emphasis on form. However, by the intermediate grades the teacher and students can set some guidelines for storytelling. Here are some suggestions:

1. Only tell stories with which you are very familiar.
2. Prepare a list of characters.
3. Outline the action and plot.
4. Keep the story moving.
5. Use your voice and body to help to tell the story.
6. Look at your audience.

Voice Usage Activities

To help pupils improve their voice quality and to learn about the varieties of pitch, a tape recorder should be used so that students can listen to themselves. The teacher should plan systematic periods for voice–speech improvement to help students establish a relaxed and easy attitude. They should also be helped to listen with awareness and attention.

"The Three Bears" is a good story to use in the primary grades for teaching volume, pitch, or voice quality. Children act out the story, interchanging the roles of father, mother, and baby bear.

Activity for Developing a Pleasing Voice Quality An example of an activity for developing a pleasing voice quality in early-primary-grade students follows:

Teacher reads story. "Lenny the Tiger liked to eat a lot. The problem was that every time he ate a lot, he became very very sleepy. He would become so sleepy after he ate that he would fall asleep wherever he was. If anyone tried to awaken Tiger, he would be very angry, because then he would yawn all day long."

TEACHER: "Can you describe Tiger?"
CHILD: "He liked to eat a lot and he always fell asleep."
TEACHER: "Can you tell us what he did all day after he was awakened?"
CHILD: "He would yawn."
TEACHER: "Let's all yawn like Tiger."
(All the children yawn.)
TEACHER: "How do you think Tiger sounded when he was angry? Who would like to sound like Tiger and say, 'Leave me alone!' "
CHILD: "Leave me alone."
TEACHER: "Good, let's all say, 'Leave me alone.' "
CHILDREN: "Leave me alone."
TEACHER: "How did your throats feel when you said that? Did they hurt? Did you feel your muscles tighten? Let's yawn again."
(The children yawn.)
TEACHER: "How did that feel? Did your throats feel easy and relaxed?"
CHILDREN: "It felt easy."
TEACHER: "When we talk, should we allow our throats to become tight?"
CHILDREN: "No."
TEACHER: "Good, when we talk, our voices should not be hurting but should feel easy. Our throats should not be tight; they should be relaxed."

TELEVISION: MAKING IT PART OF THE EDUCATIVE PROCESS

It is a fact that children spend a great amount of time watching television. In the early 1970s researchers reported that preschool children may average about four hours a day, and 9- and 10-year-olds may average about four to six hours a day.[11] More than a decade later the Nielsen Report, which gives information on individuals' viewing habits, reports that on a

[11]Aletha H. Stein, "Mass Media and Young Children's Development," *71st Yearbook for the National Society for the Study of Education,* Part II, Ira J. Gorden, ed. (Chicago: University of Chicago Press, 1972), pp. 181–202.

weekly basis 2- to 5-year-olds watch television for about 27 hours 9 minutes and 6- to 11-year-olds watch for about 24 hours 50 minutes.[12] Rather than bemoaning this state of affairs, let us channel children's enjoyment of television into constructive instructional paths (see "Television Reporting" in Chapter 12).

Television requires listening and viewing; communication requires interaction—an exchange of ideas. The challenge is to make television part of the communicative process rather than a one-way process. How to do this is, of course, the key. Some suggestions follow that may be helpful. These suggested activities can be used with both primary- and intermediate-grade level children unless otherwise specified. Obviously the materials used would vary according to the ability levels of the children involved.

1. Use television in the classroom.
    a. Have children discuss the shows that they watch and why they watch the shows that they do.
    b. If videotapes and videocassettes are available, you might tape a favorite situation comedy and watch it together. A discussion should follow of the characters, plot, dialogue, and message that the writer is trying to convey.
    c. Watch some special educational program together. Prepare students for the program. Set purposes for the viewing. Follow up with a discussion.
    d. Listen to a tape recording of two different commercials that promote two different products. Then view a videotape of the same two commercials. Discuss which medium is more effective in getting its message across.
2. Correlate out-of-school television viewing with your language arts program.
    a. Discuss the various commercials that appear on television and what makes them so memorable.
    b. Analyze the most popular commercials to try to determine why they became so popular.
    c. Discuss the propaganda tactics used in different commercials seen on television (for intermediate-grade level).
    d. Have students watch a number of television news shows at home, and have them read a number of newspapers. Then have them make a comparison/contrast between the two media concerning the coverage of news, sports, entertainment, weather, and so on (for intermediate-grade level).
    e. Encourage students to write a script for their favorite television character.
    f. Encourage children to role-play their favorite television characters in a given scenario.
    g. Encourage students to present a puppet show based on their favorite television program or their favorite characters.
    h. Have students watch a play or special television movie based on a book. Then have students read the book on which the television show is based. The students can compare the television production with the book.
    i. Students can present character sketches to the class portraying the main character of a television show, and the rest of the class is challenged to figure out who the character is.
    j. Some students could present a scene from a television show and then challenge the rest of the class to name the show.

SPEECH IMPROVEMENT

Most of us are aware of George Bernard Shaw's play *Pygmalion (My Fair Lady),* and of how a great transformation takes place in the heroine due mainly to improvement in her speech. Professor Higgins' technique as the story's speech therapist was so effective in bringing about the desired verbal changes in Eliza, the ragged cockney flower girl, that she was able to enter the English upper class at least for a time. This beguiling story demonstrates that good speech can be learned, provided that one is motivated enough to want to learn. The play dramatically underlines the maxim that we are judged by what we say *and how we say it.*

Shaw's play has a happy ending, but in reality it would be difficult to improve and correct someone's speech at Eliza's age, unless,

[12]*Nielsen Annual Report on Television,* (Northbrook, Ill., A.C. Nielsen Co., 1984), pp. 8–9.

like Eliza, one spent night and day doing nothing else.

Fortunately, speech improvement programs are part of, and integrated with, many ongoing elementary-school programs. Increased knowlede of the development of language in the child and of the important interrelatedness of speech to all other forms of language arts learning has stimulated teachers to use speech improvement programs. These not only include speech sound education (articulation) but also help students to express themselves more clearly and audibly and to use their voices and bodies as assets in conveying a message.

While all children need and can benefit from speech improvement programs, only a small percentage may need speech correction or speech therapy. Special speech correction is needed for those who exhibit speech defects that distract listeners and distort or entirely lose the speaker's message. Although speech correction is in the domain of the school speech clinician, the classroom teacher can also provide some correction when it is developmental in nature. The separation of "speech improvement" from "speech correction" can be misleading, because some speech improvement does involve correction. The confusion can be overcome if one thinks in terms of degree. While classroom teachers can help some children who show inadequately developed speech, they cannot help those with more severe developmental problems, as well as those with other kinds of disorders.

To summarize, the term "speech improvement" is used when the ongoing classroom program is discussed; "speech correction" is applied to children who are helped by a clinician.

Classroom teachers are not expected to be, nor should they be, speech diagnosticians. They should be able to distinguish children's speech problems that can be helped in the regular classroom from those requiring referral to the school clinician.

Although the school clinician serves as a consultant to the speech improvement program, the clinician's primary responsibility is in clinical speech services: to identify the children who require special services; provide those services through identification and selection of children for therapy and a clinical program of diagnosis, direct and indirect remedial methods, and consultative services.[13]

The Teacher's Role in Speech Improvement

In Chapter 5 the teacher is discussed as the key person in the classroom. Effective or not, the teacher will make a difference in the kind of education the children get. In the speech area the teacher has a double-barreled effect: first, by guiding the speech improvement program through the school year; and second, by serving as a model of (one would hope) desirable speech for many children. One of the skills that marks an excellent teacher is good speech, together with the ability to communicate orally. In all activities in which teachers engage—including directions given in class—whether intentionally or not, they set examples for students on how to speak. Teachers must, therefore, be conscious of their speech patterns, their mannerisms, their speech delivery, their diction, and the overall effect their speech has on students.

Teachers should attempt to evaluate their speech behavior critically. Videotape is an excellent tool to use for self-assessment purposes (see Chapter 5). Teachers can tape themselves while engaged in different activities at various times of the day to determine how they measure up as speech models. Here are some questions to ask yourself in self-evaluation.

When I speak, do my actions, facial expressions, and gestures enhance or distract from my delivery?

Do I appear bored or am I "alive" and enthusiastic?

Do I speak loudly enough for everyone to hear, or is my voice too loud?

Would I enjoy listening to myself? For example, does my voice have variety?

Do I pronounce my words clearly and carefully?

Am I confusing my audience because I am not sure enough about my topic?

[13]Clayton L. Bennett, "Communications Disorders in the Public Schools," in *Handbook of Speech Pathology and Audiology*, Lee Edward Travis, ed. (New York: Appleton-Century-Crofts, 1971), p. 978.

Is the information that I am giving reliable and accurate?

How new is it?

Have I chosen the words at the level of my audience?

Am I logical?

Do I keep repeating myself?

Is my vocabulary varied?

Do I talk too much?

Do I try to understand other people's points of view?

Do I listen to others?

Do I try to bring humor into my talks?

Do I present information in interesting ways?

A good teacher does not have to be a speech expert to be aware of the relationship of speech to other language arts areas. A child who has difficulty in speaking may have difficulty with reading, writing, spelling, phonics, and so on.

A teacher does not have to be a speech pathologist, either, to recognize the most common speech problems children bring to school. As has been said, the teacher should know which problems can be handled in class and which should be referred to professionals. The good teacher designs a school speech program to correct faulty speech habits and to help children communicate more effectively through oral expression. Children must learn to recognize that people with overt speech problems sometimes cannot assume leadership roles because of their inability to express themselves adequately or to address an audience.

DEVELOPMENT OF SPEECH SOUNDS IN CHILDREN

Before teachers can wisely plan the speech improvement program best suited to the needs of their students, they should know something about the chronological development of speech sounds. Studies have shown that children at successive ages should be able to "produce correctly" each of the English sounds. The words "produce correctly" mean that the child can make the specific articulatory or phonetic movements so that they are acceptable to a linguistic community. (While children are acquiring speech sounds, they are also involved in the more complex activity of learning a language with all its rules or subsystems of rules [see Chapter 3].)

Studies have shown that infants at various ages utter a certain number of phonemes (smallest units of speech sounds). The average child utters approximately seven phonemes at about months 1 and 2, and twenty-seven phonemes at about 29 and 30 months. Researchers have also reported that vowel sounds are more frequent than consonant sounds in infants before their first year. After one year of age the infant makes more consonant than vowel types of utterances, and by age two and one-half the child's vowel repertoire equals that of an adult.

The consonant sound development of the child includes only four in the first 2 months of life; by approximately 5 or 6 months about six more consonant sounds appear. By 29 or 30 months the child's consonant profile approximates that of an adult.[14]

In order to learn a system of phonemes one must be able to produce phonetic features such as voicing, nasality, and so on. According to linguists, the phonetic features are already in children's repertoires when they start to learn the phoneme system of English.

Variables Affecting Articulatory Development

It should be noted that individual differences may exist in children's ability to articulate specific sounds. Certain variables may influence when a child produces a sound. For example, a number of studies have shown a low positive correlation between intelligence and articulatory errors. This correlation is an inverse one and is more pronounced for those with IQs below 70, that is, the lower the IQ, especially below 70, the greater the chance for articulatory errors.

Studies of the relationship between socioeconomic status and articulatory development have revealed more articulatory errors among

[14]Harris Winitz, *Articulatory Acquisition and Behavior* (New York: Appleton-Century-Crofts, 1969), pp. 9–14.

children from lower socioeconomic classes. However, this relationship is similar to that between intelligence and articulation; it, too, is a low positive one.

Ordinal position studies (order of birth) have found that first born children articulate better. Studies of intersibling age difference found that articulation improved with increased age difference. The greater the difference between the ages of siblings, the better the articulation. An only child's articulation is better than that of a child from a home with many siblings. The explanation for these findings might be that first born children, only children, and siblings with larger intersibling age difference have a greater opportunity to spend time with their parents while learning phoneme production.[15]

Teachers should be aware that IQs below 70, birth order, and socioeconomic status may impede the articulatory development of the children in their classrooms, and they should make allowance for such differences.

CHILDREN'S SPEECH PROBLEMS

Children who have difficulty in speaking or who have a speech problem will avoid speaking. To some they may appear shy or introverted, but they may really be frustrated. Rather than causing themselves embarrassment or embarrassing those around them, they may prefer to remain silent. This will affect their work in school, their relations with their peers and others, and their feelings about themselves. They will be limited in their activities because social intercourse is the most common form of human communication. They will also be at a disadvantage in making themselves understood. They will refuse to speak on the telephone, and discussions and talks will be avoided.

A speech problem may on occasion actually be detrimental to health. The mother of a 10-year-old girl who is a stutterer said that one day, while the girl was with her grandfather, he had severe pains in his chest, indicating a possible heart attack. The girl was terrified. Although he asked her to phone his doctor, whose number was on the table, the child could not speak into the receiver. While most 10-year-olds would be terrified under these circumstances, they would be able to use the phone to call the doctor, parent, or ambulance. This is an example of a child who needs special help in speech correction and who should be referred to a speech clinician.

Children who use "dat" for "that" and "dis" for "this" in their daily speech do not need speech therapy, unless they cannot make the "th" sound. They have learned to speak this way from adult figures around them. Similarly, children who come from another part of the country where a different dialect is spoken may sound "different" to their classmates, but they should not be categorized as having a speech defect. (See Chapter 17 for a discussion of nonstandard English.) Other children—whose voices are noticeably thin or weak, or who speak without inflection—may be doing so, however, as the result of a poor self-concept and not necessarily as a result of a speech defect.

Many children come to school with infantile speech habits. Since they have been speaking that way for a long while they will need motivation and help in overcoming such habits. These children must recognize that they have a problem and then learn how to correct the habit. They will need the teacher's patience, understanding, and protection from ridicule.

The classroom teacher can also help with some simple lisping problems. If a child is still lisping at the end of the first grade, he or she should be referred for special help. Stuttering is a more difficult problem, however, and usually requires special work, since it is most often caused by a complex of variables involving both emotional and physiological factors.

The teacher should be careful not to confuse some barriers to effective communication with speech defects or speech/language disorders. "A speech/language disorder is a serious interference or obstruction of the communicative act that reduces or prevents its intended impact on the listener."[16] Many times teachers,

---

[15]Ibid., pp. 141–147.

[16]Jon Eisenson and Mardel Ogilvie, *Communicative Disorders in Children* (New York: Macmillan, 1983), p. 14.

parents, or other persons may "perceive some less serious interferences in communication as speech/language disorders. In these instances, however, the interferences are often applicable only to a particular class of listeners or to a particular setting.[17] There are five types of such interferences:

1. *Nonstandard pronunciations and language usage.* In this instance many or most of the child's classmates understand him or her with little or no difficulty.
2. *Regional dialects.* Again, children from the child's home region undoubtedly understand the communicative effort.
3. *Poor oral reading.* This difficulty occurs only in one setting.
4. *Articulation and fluency patterns.* When normal for the developmental stage of the child, but not at an adult level, the other children usually can interpret the message, often better than the teacher.
5. *Psychological disturbance.* Psychological disorders may manifest themselves as a speech/language symptom. Cooperating specialists can help teachers plan programs of speech/language improvement in such instances.[18]

Usually, such speech difficulties can be handled by the classroom teacher with the aid of a speech therapist or specialist.

Types of Speech Defects

Speech defects usually cannot be handled in an ordinary classroom. Eight types of speech defects include:

1. Articulatory defects
2. Stuttering
3. Voice defects
4. Cleft palate speech
5. Cerebral palsy speech
6. Retarded speech development
7. Language impairment associated with brain damage
8. Speech defects due to impaired hearing.[19]

[17]Ibid., pp. 14–15.
[18]Ibid.
[19]Jon Eisenson and Mardel Ogilvie, *Speech Correction in the Schools* (New York: Macmillan, 1963), p. 4.

The questionnaire on pages 110–111, "Analysis of Speech Defects," is provided for teachers as an aid in determining whether students have any speech defects. A preponderance of "yes" answers would indicate that the teacher should consult with a speech therapist.

The teacher must accept a child whatever the problem or handicap, and must help other children to encourage the child to become an effective, contributing member of the class. The child with a speech problem must be made to feel respected and wanted. Although such a child is usually aware of the speech defect, the child should not feel that he or she is being singled out negatively because of it.

Articulatory Problems

Articulatory problems are the most frequently found speech defects in children. Teachers can provide sound production education training in their regular classrooms. Articulatory problems are most often caused by faulty learning rather than an oral or dental malformation. Speech therapists have discovered that the most frequently occurring articulatory errors are likely to center around eight consonant sounds: /r/, /s/, /l/, /sh/, /h/, /th/, /ch/, /f/. Of these, the /r/, /s/, /l/, and /th/ usually are most difficult for primary-grade children. (It is interesting to note that the consonant sounds are most difficult for children. It appears that vowels are, on the whole, mastered early.)

Some articulatory difficulties arise due to the substitution, distortion, omission, or slighting of phonemes in children's speech-sound production. When teachers become aware of some of these errors they should refer the children to speech clinicians. However, some errors can be treated with a program in speech-sound education in the regular classroom.

VOICE USAGE IN ORAL EXPRESSION

A good speaking voice should be easily heard, pleasing, and expressive of meaning and mood. To be pleasing and expressive, a child's voice must possess five qualities:

1. A pleasing quality
2. Adequate volume

ANALYSIS OF SPEECH DEFECTS

ARTICULATORY DEFECTS

Does the child substitute one sound for another?
Does the child omit sounds?
Does the child distort sounds?
Is the child very hard to understand?

STUTTERING

Is the child disturbed by his or her dysfluency?
Does the child repeat sounds or syllables or words more than the child's classmates?
Is the child's speech decidedly arhythmical?
Does the child block frequently?
Does the child have difficulty in getting his or her words out?

VOCAL DIFFICULTIES

Is the child's voice noticeably unpleasant in quality?
Is the child's pitch higher or lower than most of the child's classmates?
Is the child's voice monotonous?
Is the child's voice husky?
Is the child's voice too loud?
Is the child's voice too weak?
Is the child difficult to hear in class?

CLEFT PALATE SPEECH

Is there an obvious cleft of the teeth ridge or palate?
Is the child's voice excessively nasal?
Are the child's /p/, /b/, /t/, /d/, /k/, and /g/ inaccurate?
Are some of the child's other consonants distorted?

CEREBRAL PALSY SPEECH

Does the child have obvious tremors of the musculature in phonation and breathing?
Is the child's speech slow, jerky, and labored?
Is the child's rhythm of speech abnormal?

DELAYED SPEECH

Is the child's speech markedly retarded in relation to that of the child's classmates?
Does the child omit and substitute sounds substantially more than the child's classmates?
Does the child use shorter and simpler sentences than those of classmates?
Does the child use fewer phrases and prepositions than those of classmates?

LANGUAGE IMPAIRMENT

Is the child's comprehension of language markedly retarded?

Does the child seem to be inconsistent in the ability to understand as well as to use language?

Is the profile of the child's linguistic abilities uneven? (For example, can the child read much better than spell? Is the child surprisingly good in arithmetic and yet quite poor in either reading or writing?)

SPEECH DEFECT DUE TO IMPAIRED HEARING

Does the child have frequent earaches and colds?

Does the child have running ears?

Does the child omit sounds or substitute one sound for another?

Does the child distort sounds?

Does the child speak too softly?

Does the child frequently ask you to repeat what you have said?

Does the child turn his or her head to one side as you speak?

Does the child watch you closely as you speak?

Does the child make unusual mistakes in the spelling words you dictate?

Does the child misinterpret your questions or instructions frequently?

Does the child do better when given written instructions than when given oral instructions?

Does the child seem more intelligent than his or her work indicates?*

*Source: Jon Eisenson and Mardel Ogilvie, *Speech Correction in the Schools* (New York: Macmillan, 1963), pp. 10–12.

Child's Name:
Grade:
Date:

INVENTORY OF SPEECH PROBLEMS

1. Is voice:
   a. loud?   _____
   b. too low?   _____
   c. nasal?   _____
   c. hoarse?   _____
   e. monotonous?   _____
   f. pitched abnormally high?   _____
   g. pitched abnormally low?   _____

2. Is rate of speech:
   a. too slow?   _____
   b. too rapid?   _____

3. Is phrasing poor?
4. Is speech hesitant?
5. Is there evidence of articulatory difficulties such as:
   a. distorting sounds?
   b. substituting one sound for another?
   c. omitting sounds?
6. Is there evidence of vocabulary problems such as:
   a. repetition of phrases?
   b. limited vocabulary?
7. Is there evidence of the child's negative attitudes toward oral communication such as:
   a. not engaging in discussions or conversations?
   b. not volunteering to give a talk or oral report?

3. Variety in duration of words
4. Appropriate phrasing and smoothness
5. Variety of pitch[20]

Not only does a child imitate the language of the people in the surrounding environment, but his or her voice is also an imitation of someone's voice at home. When the child comes to school he or she may decide to choose the teacher as a model. Therefore, it must be stressed again that the teacher has the responsibility to serve as a good example.

Many factors affect a child's voice usage. A child who is aggressive may speak loudly and harshly, whereas a shy, timid child may speak quietly. Physical illness or emotional tension will also be reflected in the child's voice.

DEVELOPING THE SPEECH IMPROVEMENT PROGRAM

Planning

In order to be able to plan a program appropriate to the needs of particular students, the teacher must first evaluate their speech performance. The chart on page 111 and above

[20]Wilbert Pronovast and Louise Kingman, *The Teaching of Speaking and Listening in the Elementary School* (New York: Longman, Green, 1959), p. 111.

serves as a guide for cataloging a pupil's speech faults in both the primary and intermediate grades.

To use this instrument the teacher can either (1) listen to the speech sounds and patterns of students during ordinary classroom activities, and mark the chart appropriately, or (2) tape some special oral activity in which students' production of speech sounds and patterns is noted.

Pupil–Teacher Planning After the teacher has determined that there will be time devoted each day for speech improvement activities and has chosen a number of possible activities based on children's needs, the teacher should invite the students to participate in the planning and final selection of activities and topics. If the students participate in determining when the special talks, creative dramatics, or work with puppets will occur, and if they have a say in the kinds of activities they will be doing, the chances for a successful speech program will be enhanced.

Including the children in the planning process does not mean that teachers abdicate their role in the classroom, however. Both teachers and students should have a voice in the allocation of time as well as the choice of topics. If differences arise and choices need to be made, the teachers and students should give reasons for their choices.

Time Spent in Activities

Since almost all children need help in speech improvement, the program should be related to many ongoing classroom activities. Speech activities can be integrated with the language arts, as well as with many other subject areas. Almost all school activities afford time for oral expression, when pupils should be encouraged to talk about matters that interest them. Time should be set aside each day for talks to involve individual children, or a group, or the whole class. The amount of time spent in this area will depend on the specific grade level and activity. In the first grade the teacher might

---

STUDENT'S NAME:
   GRADE:
   TEACHER:

DIAGNOSTIC CHECKLIST FOR ORAL COMMUNICATION AND SPEECH IMPROVEMENT (see specific inventory checklists given within chapter)

	Yes	No
Speech (general): The child's speech is		
1. distinct		
2. inaudible		
3. monotonous		
4. expressive		
Nonverbal Communication: The child		
1. uses facial expressions effectively		
2. uses hands effectively		
3. uses body movements effectively		
Vocabulary (general): The child's vocabulary is		
1. meager		
2. rich		
3. accurate		
4. incorrect		
Sentences		
1. The child uses incomplete sentences.		
2. The child uses simplistic sentences.		
3. The child uses involved sentences.		
4. The child uses standard English.		
5. The child uses a variation of English.		
6. English is not the dominant language of the child.		
The child engages in conversation freely.		
The child respects other persons when he or she is speaking.		

	Yes	No
The child enters into class discussions.		
The child can describe in his or her own words an event that has occurred.		

The child freely engages in these activities:
1. creative dramatics
2. role playing
3. choral speaking
4. finger play (primary grades)
5. puppetry
6. pantomime
7. "show and tell" (primary grades)
8. informal reports
9. formal reports (intermediate grades)
10. debates (intermediate grades)
11. storytelling

set aside 15 minutes a day for special talks, while in the second grade 20 minutes might be set aside. In third and fourth grades 25 to 30 minutes might be allotted for talks, and in fifth and sixth grades the allotment could be 30 to 35 minutes.

There is no set rule for time allotment. Teachers must take the needs, interests, and readiness levels of their students into account when planning such activities. In some first-grade classes, where the children are very immature and their attention span is quite short, 15 minutes could be too long. In another first-grade class of more mature children with a longer attention span, however, 15 minutes might not be long enough.

The time spent in any area should be just enough so that the pupils do not become restless. Spending a shorter amount of time in an activity and stopping while students are still interested help to insure that they will look forward to the next speech improvement activity.

Avoiding Sex Stereotyping in Choice of Speech Topics and Activities

The specific interests of boys and girls are in large part determined by what society cate-gorizes as "masculine" or "feminine." On the whole, today girls do not compromise their femininity nor boys their masculinity if they choose interests that diverge from what used to be the expected for each sex.

Teachers must avoid classifying oral expression activities or topics for discussion as either "masculine" or "feminine." When planning lists of topics for class discussions with students, they should avoid making such remarks as, "Oh, this is a topic that will be fun for boys," or "Girls would really enjoy working in this area." Teachers should display equal enthusiasm for all topics and show that they will allow pupils to choose any one that interests them. Students will perform much better if they have chosen a topic because of genuine interest rather than because it is expected.

Tongue Twisters Help Untwist Tongues

A number of children have learned poor speech habits, and one of these involves not moving the tongue and lips when speaking. Tongue twisters are excellent for training students to move their lips and tongues; they are also a good ice-breaker. Tongue-twisters are sentences that are hard to say because almost every word begins with the same sound. To say a tongue twister correctly, students must concentrate very hard to move their lips and tongue.

At first, teachers should have their students practice the tongue twister very slowly, and the students should exaggerate the movements of their lips and tongue. After they have learned the tongue twister and can say it well they should try to say it faster and faster. For children who cannot read, teachers can recite the tongue twister to them until they have learned it.

Teachers can encourage students to make up their own tongue twisters and use these to challenge their classmates to say them faster and faster.

SUMMARY

This chapter has provided the teacher with the necessary background information and activities for carrying out an oral communication and speech improvement program in the regular classroom. The teacher's role and the importance of the teacher as a good speech model were emphasized, and the ingredients necessary to provide a nonthreatening environment conducive to oral expression were given. Articulatory development, as well as the factors that may affect it—such as socioeconomic status, intelligence, number of siblings, order of birth—were also discussed. The more practical aspects of an oral communication and speech improvement program were presented, including setting aside time each day for speech training, organizing for oral expression, and choosing types of oral expression activities for the speech program. Oral expression activities (speech stimulation activities), including talks, discussions, conversation, choral speaking, finger play, creative dramatics, role playing, and puppetry—were discussed to enable teachers to employ them in class. A "Diagnostic Checklist for Oral Communication and Speech Improvement" was also presented.

As a further aid, two examples of speech lesson plans follow. Using these as a guide, see if you can construct a plan of your own.

LESSON PLAN I: EARLY PRIMARY-GRADE LEVEL

OBJECTIVES

1. The students will be able to correctly recite the words and sounds in proper sequence of Edward Lear's alphabet rhymes.

2. The students will be able to differentiate among different sounds orally presented.

INTRODUCTION

"Yesterday we were talking about a book that I read to you. Who remembers the name of it? Yes! Good! It was called *May I Bring a Friend?** Now, who remembers what it was about? Yes, it was about animals visiting the king and queen. Do you remember how carefully we had to listen so we could remember the exact order in which they visited, and then made our picture story? Who still remembers the order? Very good! Listen carefully to the music that is played on the tape recorder while Jane shows the picture story to us. The music should make all the sounds that the animals make.

"Today we are going to learn some rhymes which are 'ear ticklers.' Listen carefully and tell me why I said that they would tickle your ears."

DEVELOPMENT

Lear's rhymes are presented to the class. After the children have heard the verses, the children are asked why the teacher called them ear ticklers. (Because of the sounds.) They may also be called tongue twisters.

A familiar example of a tongue twister can be given—"She sells seashells by the seashore." The teacher explains that to be able to recite this verse, the class must make their mouths and tongues do exactly what they want. They will have to speak clearly and not too fast, or their tongues will run away from them. The Lear poem is recited again, and the class is asked to listen. The children are then asked to give another reason why they had to listen carefully. (Because it's like the first verse. In order to know in what order the words appear it is necessary to listen carefully.) The first line of the poem is said aloud by the teacher: "A was once an apple-pie." The whole class repeats the line. The teacher then says:

> Pidy
> Widy
> Tidy
> Pidy
> Nice insidy,
> Pidy
> Nice insidy,
> Apple pie!

The whole class repeats the verse. Both parts are then put together and the class repeats both parts. The same procedure is followed for verses B, C, and D.

The children are next divided into four groups. Each group recites its part in proper sequence. The teacher practices verse A with the first group, verse B with the second group, verse C with the third group, and verse D with the fourth group. Now the groups say the verses one after another, each group reciting only its part. The children's recitation can be taped and played back so that they can hear themselves. They then discuss the taping of their production.

SUMMARY

The teacher asks the children what they did. A new poem was learned and recited on tape. Careful listening let them learn their parts and know what came next.

*Beatrice Schenk De Regniers, *May I Bring a Friend?* (New York: Atheneum, 1964).

LESSON PLAN II: INTERMEDIATE-GRADE LEVEL

OBJECTIVE

The students, after listening to a tape recording of various sounds, will be able to create characters and dialogue to match the sounds.

INTRODUCTION

"Who remembers some of the things we've been doing in creative dramatics? Yes, good. We have listened to stories and then acted them out. We've also created our own characters and had our classmates try to guess who we were. Listen to this tape recording for a moment."
Play some eerie music.
"What does this remind you of? Yes, I agree, it sounds scary. Today, we're going to listen to various sounds on the tape and from these create characters and dialogue that would seem to match the sounds."

DEVELOPMENT

"Let me play this eerie sound again. If we were to create a character to match this sound, what kind of character could we make up? How do you think he or she would sound or speak? What do you think he or she would say? Let's think about this for a moment and develop a character together. Any suggestions? Good! We could have a 'mad scientist,' who has just created a 'nonbeing.' How would the scientist sound? What would the scientist say? How would the scientist act? Who would like to play this role for us? Look at all these hands. I see we have lots of potential 'mad scientists.'

"Judy, would you like to try? Good.

"Harry, would you like to try? Good.

"Now that we seem to have the idea, I'm going to have you go into groups of four. I will play various sounds on the tape and then each group will decide on the character that they think best matches the tape, the way he or she would sound, and what he or she would say. We'll present our characters after each sound taping. Are there any questions? Fine. Let's go into the same groups we were in for the puppet activity."

(Students in groups listen to sounds, create characters, and present them to the class.)

SUMMARY

"What have we done today? Who can briefly summarize it for us? Good. We've listened to tape-recorded sounds and we've created characters and dialogue to match the sounds. Were we successful? Yes, we were able to do this. Who has some ideas on how to follow up on this activity?

"Very good! Do all of you want to take Leslie's suggestion?

"Fine, then each group, using its own tape recorders, will try to tape a sound and have the rest of us create characters for the sound."

SUGGESTIONS FOR THOUGHT QUESTIONS AND ACTIVITIES

1. You have children in class who are very quiet, follow directions, and are able to do the required work. Would you call on them often? Explain your answer. What would you do to engage these children in more interaction sessions? Because children are quiet, does this necessarily mean they have problems? Explain your answer.

2. Develop a creative lesson plan in the area of speech improvement. What elements would go into the plan? How would it develop? What goals do you have in mind?

3. Generate some tongue twisters to help children "untwist their tongues."

4. Develop some stimulating situations to encourage creative dramatics in the primary and intermediate grades.

5. Develop some activities that will initiate oral-interaction sessions among primary-grade and intermediate-grade students.

6. Discuss techniques that will help to develop "good speakers."

SELECTED BIBLIOGRAPHY

Brooks, William D. *Speech Communication.* Dubuque, Iowa: Wm. C. Brown, 1981.

Diedrich, William M., and Jeff Bangert. *Articulation Learning.* San Diego, Ca.: College-Hill, 1980.

Eisenson, Jon, and Mardel Ogilvie. *Communication Disorders in Children.* New York: Macmillan, 1983.

Rubin, Dorothy. "Developing Speaking Skills," in *The Primary-Grade Teacher's Language Arts Handbook.* New York: Holt, Rinehart and Winston, 1980.

———. "Developing Speaking Skills," in *The Intermediate-Grade Teacher's Language Arts Handbook.* New York: Holt, Rinehart and Winston, 1980.

Willbrand, Mary L., and Richard D. Rieke. *Teaching Oral Communication in Elementary Schools.* New York: Macmillan, 1983.

Creative Dramatics

Heinig, Ruth, and Lyda Stillwell. *Creative Dramatics for the Classroom Teacher,* 2d ed. Englewood Cliffs, N.J.: Prentice-Hall, 1981.

McCaslin, Nellie. *Creative Drama in the Classroom,* 3d ed. New York: Longman, 1980.

Siks, Geraldine B. *Drama With Children,* 2d ed. New York: Harper & Row, 1983.

Way, Brian. *Development through Drama.* London: Longman, 1967.

Youngers, Judith S. "The Process and Potential of Creative Dramatics for Enhancing Linguistic and Cognitive Development," in *Research in the Language Arts: Language and Schooling,* Victor Froese and Stanley B. Straw, eds. Baltimore: University Park, 1981.

Nonverbal Behavior

Thompson, James. *Beyond Words: A Nonverbal Communication in the Classroom.* New York: Scholastic Book Services, 1973.

von Raffler-Engel, W. *Children's Acquisition of Kinesics.* Scarsdale, N.Y.: Campus Film Distributors, 1974. (Color film)

Wood, Barbara. *Children and Communication: Verbal & Non-Verbal Language Development.* Englewood Cliffs, N.J.: Prentice-Hall, 1976.

Pantomime and Mime

Howard, Vernon. *Pantomimes, Charades and Skits,* rev. ed. New York: Sterling, 1974.

Walker, Katherine. *Eyes on Mime: Language without Speech.* New York: John Day, 1969.

Finger Plays

Brown, Marc. *Finger Rhymes.* New York: E. P. Dutton, 1980.

Colville, M. Josephine. *The Zoo Comes to School: Finger Plays and Action Rhymes.* New York: Macmillan, 1973.

Shely, Patricia. *All-Occasion Finger Plays for Young Children.* Cincinnati, Ohio: Standard, 1978.

Puppets

Boylan, Eleanor. *How to Be a Puppeteer.* New York: McCall, 1970.

Gates, Frieda. *Easy to Make Puppets* (Gr. K–3). Chippewa Falls, Wisc.: Harvey House, 1976.

Hunt, Tamara, and Nancy Renfro. *Puppetry and Early Childhood Education.* Austin, Tex.: Renfro Studios, 1981.

Luckin, Joyce. *Easy to Make Puppets* (Gr. 3–10). Boston: Plays, 1975.

Storytelling

Bauer, Caroline Feller. *Handbook for Storytellers.* Chicago: American Library Association, 1977.

Chambers, Dewey. *Literature for Children: The Oral Tradition; Storytelling and Creative Drama,* 2d ed. Dubuque, Iowa: Wm. C. Brown, 1977.

Champlin, Connie. *Puppetry and Creative Dramatics in Storytelling.* Austin, Tex.: Renfro Studios, 1981.

Groff, Patrick. "Let's Update Storytelling." *Language Arts* 54 (March 1977): 272–277, 286.

Ross, Ramon Royal. *Storyteller,* 2d ed. Columbus, Ohio: Merrill, 1980.

EIGHT

Reading: An Integral Part of the Language Arts

David is a quiet boy with an endearing smile. He is small in stature and not well-dressed; he is determined to learn to read. Although he is in the fourth grade, David cannot read. "I want to read," he told his teacher. "My father bring one big book when he came home at night. He say it for me to read. I read. You see." David has hope, so he comes to school each day. But how much longer will he do so? Will he succeed in entering and mastering the land of books filled with those magic symbols called words? Will he unlock these symbols and discover the wonders of far-off places? David is waiting. Will we, as teachers, be able to help him?

It would be both foolhardy and presumptuous to assume that one or two chapters in a language arts text could perform the Herculean task of preparing teachers to help the Davids of this country learn to read. Special reading courses are needed for that. Most schools of education have at least one required course in reading for education majors that gives special emphasis and importance to reading. This does not mean, however, that reading must or should be separated from the rest of the language arts

areas. As a matter of fact, reading is so closely related to the other language arts that a problem in one area will usually overflow into others.

This chapter presents a few selected topics in reading that are of particular interest to the language arts teacher. The emphasis throughout this chapter is on how reading is related to the other language arts areas. This chapter will present also a special section on the integration of reading and writing. After you read this chapter, you should be able to answer these questions:

1. How is reading related to the other language arts areas?
2. Why is it important to learn how to read?
3. How is reading defined?
4. What are the relationships between reading and listening?
5. How are reading and listening comprehension related?
6. How are reading and writing related?
7. How can teachers use reading as a springboard for writing?

8. How can writing help students to be better readers?
9. What is the language-experience approach to teaching reading?
10. How does the language-experience approach incorporate all of the language arts?
11. What is an experience story?

IMPORTANCE OF LEARNING TO READ

The significance of the child's early years in reading achievement has been amply documented; however, this should not be used as an excuse for not helping the child when he or she comes to school. Rather than putting blame on social, political, and economic factors, over which teachers and children have little control, more *should* be done in the schools.

The importance of learning to read in the early grades cannot be overstated. The longer a child remains a nonreader, the less likely are his or her chances to get up to grade level or ability level, even with the best remedial help. Underachievers in reading tend to have many emotional and social problems, and these are compounded as the child progresses through school.

Teachers want to help children to learn—that is their intent. Those teachers who cannot help students soon lose confidence in themselves, and their own self-concept is impaired. This feeling eventually gets picked up by their students. As was stated earlier, it would be an impossible task to prepare teachers to help all children to learn to read in a single chapter. By making teachers more aware of the interrelationship of reading to other language arts, they will be better able to integrate reading with the rest of the teaching program and to recognize that aid in one area reinforces another. Aware teachers will provide more reading opportunities for their students, as well as strengthening their foundation for reading. Reading in the elementary grades should not be relegated to that one period during the day specifically devoted to the reading group. Before we discuss how reading is related to the other language arts areas, we should first define reading and discuss the reading process.

DEFINING READING[1]

John is able to decode correctly all the words in a passage; however, he cannot answer any questions on the passage. Is John reading? Susie makes a number of errors in decoding words, but the errors she makes do not seem to prevent her from answering any of the questions on the passage. Is Susie reading? Maria reads a passage on something about which she has very strong feelings; she has difficulty answering the questions based on the passage because of her attitude. Is she reading? José can decode the words in the passage, and he thinks that he knows the meaning of all the words. However, José cannot answer the questions on the passage. Is José reading?

To answer the questions just posed, we would have to state: They depend on our definition of reading. A definition of reading is necessary because it will influence what goals will be set in the development of the reading program. A teacher who sees reading as a one-way process, consisting simply of the decoding of symbols or the relating of sounds to symbols, will develop a different type of program from one who looks upon reading as getting meaning from the printed page.

There is *no single, set definition of reading*. As a result, it is difficult to define it simply. A broad definition that has been greatly used is that reading is the bringing to and the getting of meaning from the printed page. This implies that readers bring their backgrounds, their experiences, as well as their emotions, into play. Students who are upset or physically ill will bring these feelings into the act of reading, and this will influence their interpretive processes. A person well versed in reading matter will gain more from the material than someone less knowledgeable. A student who is a good critical thinker will gain more from a critical passage than one who is not. A student who has strong dislikes will come away with different feelings

---

[1]This section, "Reading Comprehension," and "Reading Comprehension Taxonomies" are largely drawn from Dorothy Rubin, *Teaching Reading and Study Skills in Content Areas* (New York: Holt, Rinehart and Winston, 1983).

and understandings from a pupil with strong likings.

If reading is defined as the bringing to and the getting of meaning from the printed page, Susie is actually the only child who is reading because she is the only one who understands what she is reading. Although John can verbalize the words, he has no comprehension of them. Maria can also decode the words, but her strong feelings about the topic presented in the selection have prevented her from getting the message that the writer is conveying. José can decode the words and knows the meanings of the individual words, but either he is not able to get the sense of the whole passage or he does not know the meaning of the words in another context. Word recognition is necessary for reading comprehension, but it does not guarantee that reading comprehension will take place. Without reading comprehension, there is no reading.

Reading as a Total Integrative Process

By using a broad or global definition of reading, we are looking upon reading as a total integrative process that includes the following domains: (1) the *affective,* (2) the *perceptual,* and (3) the *cognitive.*

The Affective Domain The affective domain includes our feelings and emotions. The way we feel influences greatly the way we look upon stimuli on a field. It may distort our perception. For example, if we are hungry and we see the word *fool,* we would very likely read it as *food.* If we have adverse feelings about certain things, these feelings will probably influence how we interpret what we read. Our feelings will also influence what we decide to read. Obviously, attitudes exert a directive and dynamic influence on our readiness to respond.

The Perceptual Domain In the perceptual domain, perception can be defined as giving meaning to sensations or the ability to organize stimuli on a field. How we organize stimuli depends largely on our background of experiences and on our sensory receptors. If, for example, our eyes are organically defective, those perceptions involving sight would be distorted.

In the act of reading, visual perception is a most important factor. Children need to control their eyes so they move from left to right across the page. Eye movements influence what the reader perceives.

Although what we observe is never in exact accord with the physical situation,[2] readers must be able to accurately decode the graphemic (written) representation. If, however, readers have learned incorrect associations, this will affect their ability to read. For example, if a child reads the word *was* for *saw* and is not corrected, this may become part of his or her perceptions. If children perceive the word as a whole, in parts, or as individual letters, this will also determine whether they will be good or poor readers. More mature readers are able to perceive more complex and extensive graphemic patterns as units. They are also able to give meaning to mutilated words such as

Perception is a cumulative process that is based on an individual's background of experiences. The perceptual process is influenced by physiological factors as well as affective ones. As already stated, a person who is hungry may read the word *fool* as *food.* Similarly, a person with a biased view toward a topic being read may delete, add, or distort what is being read.

The Cognitive Domain The cognitive domain includes the areas involving thinking. Under this umbrella we would place the area of comprehension. Persons who have difficulty in thinking (the manipulation of symbolic representations) would obviously have difficulty in reading. Although the cognitive domain goes beyond the perceptual domain, it builds and depends on a firm perceptual base. That is, if readers have faulty perceptions, they will also have faulty concepts.

[2]Julian E. Hochberg, *Perception* (Englewood Cliffs, N.J.: Prentice-Hall, 1964), p. 3.

Teachers, however, can aid students in developing thinking skills by helping them acquire necessary strategies and by giving them practice in using these strategies (see Chapter 3).

READING COMPREHENSION

Comprehension is a construct; that is, it cannot be directly observed or directly measured. We can only infer that someone "understands" from the overt behavior of the person. *Webster's Third International Dictionary* defines *comprehension* as "the act or action of grasping (as an act or process) with the intellect," and *intellect* is defined as "the capacity for rational or intelligent thought especially when highly developed." Obviously, the more intelligent an individual is, the more able he or she is to comprehend. What may not be so obvious is that persons who have difficulty understanding may have this difficulty because they have not had certain experiences that require higher levels of thinking; they may not have learned how to do high-level thinking. Such people will have problems in all language arts areas. (See "The language Arts, Thinking, and Instruction" in Chapter 1.)

Reading comprehension is a complex intellectual process involving a number of abilities. The two major abilities involve word meanings and verbal reasoning. Without word meanings and verbal reasoning, there would be no reading comprehension; and, as stated earlier, without reading comprehension, there would be no reading. Most persons would agree with these statements; disagreement, however, exists when we ask, "How does an individual achieve comprehension while reading?" In 1917, Edward Thorndike put forth his statement that "reading is a very elaborate procedure, involving a weighing of each of many elements in a sentence, their organization in the proper relations one to another, and the cooperation of many forces to determine final response."[3] He stated further that even the act of answering simple questions includes all the features characteristic of typical reasoning. Today investigators are still exploring reading comprehension in attempts to understand it better, and through the years many have expounded and expanded upon Thorndike's theories.

For the past two decades, research into the process of understanding has been influenced by the fields of psycholinguistics and cognitive psychology. As a result, terms such as surface structure, deep structure, microstructure, macrostructure, semantic networks, schemata, story grammar, story structure, and so on have invaded the literature. The studies that have been done are not conclusive; that is, from the studies it is not possible to say that if a reader were to follow certain prescribed rules, he or she would most assuredly have better comprehension.

Although it is difficult to definitively state how persons achieve comprehension while reading, studies seem to suggest that good comprehenders appear to have certain characteristics.[4] Good comprehenders are able to do inferential reasoning; they can state the main or central ideas of information; they can assimilate, categorize, compare, make relationships, analyze, synthesize, and evaluate information. Good comprehenders engage in meaningful learning by assimilating new material to concepts already existing in their cognitive structures;[5] that is, good comprehenders relate their new learning to what they already know. Also, good comprehenders are able to think beyond the information given; they are able to come up with new or alternate solutions. In addition, they seem to know what information to ignore and what to attend to.

---

[3]Edward L. Thorndike, "Reading as Reasoning: A Study of Mistakes in Paragraph Reading," *Journal of Educational Psychology* 8:6 (June 1917): 323.

[4]Barbara M. Taylor, "Children's Memory for Expository Text After Reading," *Reading Research Quarterly* 15:3 (1980): 399–411; B. J. Bartlett, "Top-level Structure as an Organizational Strategy for Recall of Classroom Text," unpublished doctoral dissertation, Arizona State University, 1978; and John P. Richards and Catherine W. Hatcher, "Interspersed Meaningful Learning Questions as Semantic Cues for Poor Comprehenders," *Reading Research Quarterly* 13:4 (1977–1978): 551–552.

[5]Richards and Hatcher, ibid., p. 552.

READING COMPREHENSION TAXONOMIES

A number of reading comprehension taxonomies exist and many appear similar to one another. This is not surprising. Usually the persons who develop a new taxonomy do so because they are unhappy with an existing one for some reason and want to improve upon it. As a result they may change category headings, but keep similar descriptions of the categories, or they may change the order of the hierarchy, and so on. Most of the existing taxonomies are adaptations in one way or another of Bloom's taxonomy of educational objectives in the cognitive domain, which is concerned with the thinking that students should achieve in any discipline. Bloom's taxonomy is based on an ordered set of objectives ranging from the more simplistic skills to the more complex ones. Bloom's objectives are cumulative in that each one includes the one preceding it. And most taxonomies that have been evolved are also cumulative.

Of the many persons who have tried to categorize reading comprehension, one attempt that is often referred to is Barrett's *Taxonomy of Reading Comprehension*. Barrett's taxonomy consists of four levels: literal comprehension, inferential comprehension, evaluation, and appreciation. In this text, an adaptation of Nila Banton Smith's model is used, and, at first glance, it may appear to be similar to Barrett's. The differences become obvious when we look at the skills subsumed under each of the first three levels. In the model used in this book, literal-type questions are those that require a low-level type of thinking; skills such as the finding of the main idea of a paragraph would not be included under the literal level. However, in Barrett's taxonomy, "recognition or recall of main ideas" is included in his literal level. Finding the main idea of a paragraph is not easy even if it is directly stated in the paragraph; students must do more than a low-level type of thinking to determine that something stated in the paragraph is the main idea. In other words, any time that a student must interpret what he or she is reading, the student is required to do reasoning that is beyond merely recalling what is in the text.

Also, in this text, appreciation is not in the hierarchy because appreciation has a hierarchy of its own. While it is possible for us to appreciate something we have read or that is read to us at any level of the hierarchy, we would probably have the highest appreciation, however, at the level at which we had the greatest understanding. (See "What Is Reading for Appreciation?" in Chapter 10.)

Categorizing Reading Comprehension

Comprehension involves thinking. As there are various levels in the hierarchy of thinking, so are there various levels of comprehension. Higher levels of comprehension would obviously include higher levels of thinking. The following model adapted from Nila Banton Smith divides the comprehension skills into four categories.[6] Each category is cumulative in building on the others. The four comprehension categories are (1) literal comprehension, (2) interpretation, (3) critical reading, and (4) creative reading.

Literal Comprehension Literal comprehension represents the ability to obtain a low-level type of understanding by using only information explicitly stated. This category requires a lower level of thinking skills than the other three levels. Answers to literal questions simply demand that the pupil recall from memory what the book says.

Although literal-type questions are considered a low-level type of thinking, it should *not* be construed that reading for details to gain facts that are explicitly stated is unimportant in content-area courses. A fund of knowledge is important and necessary; it is the foundation for high-level thinking. If, however, teachers ask only literal-type questions, students will not graduate to higher levels of thinking.

Interpretation Interpretation is the next step in the hierarchy. This category demands a

[6]Nila Banton Smith, "The Many Faces of Reading Comprehension," *Reading Teacher* 23 (December 1969): 249–259, 291.

higher level of thinking ability because the questions in the category of interpretation are concerned with answers that are not directly stated in the text but are suggested or implied. To answer questions at the interpretive level, readers must have problem-solving ability and be able to work at various levels of abstraction. Obviously, children who are slow learners will have difficulty working at this level as well as in the next two categories. (See Chapter 17.)

The interpretive level is the one at which the most confusion exists when it comes to categorizing skills. The confusion concerns the term *inference*. The definition of inference is: Something derived by reasoning; something that is not directly stated but suggested in the statement; a logical conclusion that is drawn from statements; a deduction; an induction. From the definition we can see that inference is a broad reasoning skill involving analysis and synthesis and that there are many different kinds of inferences. All of the reading skills in interpretation rely on the reader's ability to "infer" the answer in one way or another. However, by grouping all the interpretive reading skills under inference, "some of the most distinctive and desirable skills would become smothered and obscured."[7]

Some of the reading skills that are usually found in interpretation are as follows:

Determining word meanings from context
Finding main ideas
"Reading between the lines" or drawing inferences[8]
Drawing conclusions
Making generalizations
Recognizing cause-and-effect reasoning
Recognizing analogies

Critical Reading Critical reading is at a higher level than the other two categories because it involves evaluation, the making of a personal judgment on the accuracy, value, and truthfulness of what is read. To be able to make judgments, a reader must be able to collect, interpret, apply, analyze, and synthesize the information. Critical reading includes such skills as the ability to differentiate between fact and opinion, the ability to differentiate between fantasy and reality, and the ability to discern propaganda techniques. Critical reading is related to critical listening because they both require critical thinking.

Creative Reading Creative reading uses divergent thinking skills to go beyond the literal comprehension, interpretation, and critical-reading levels. In creative reading, the reader tries to come up with new or alternate solutions to those presented by the writer (see Chapter 4).

HELPING CHILDREN ACQUIRE COMPREHENSION SKILLS

All children need help in developing higher-level reading comprehension skills. If teachers persist in asking only literal-type comprehension questions that demand a simple convergent answer, high-level skills will not be developed.

Unfortunately, much of what goes on in school is at the literal comprehension level. Teachers usually ask questions that require a literal response and children that answer this type of question are generally looked upon as being excellent students. It is to be hoped that this will change now that many reading task forces across the country are emphasizing the teaching of higher-level comprehension skills.

Rather than asking a question that would call for a literal response, the teacher must learn to construct questions that call for higher levels of thinking. This should begin as early as kindergarten and first grade. For example, the children are looking at a picture in which a few children are dressed in hats, snow pants, jackets, scarves, and so on. After asking the children what kind of clothes the children in the picture are wearing, the teacher should try to elicit from his or her students the answers to the following questions: "What kind of day do you think it is?" "What do you think the children are going to do?"

---

[7]Ibid., pp. 255–256.
[8]Although, as already stated, all the interpretive skills depend on the ability of the reader to infer meanings, the specific skill of "reading between the lines" is the one that teachers usually refer to when they are teaching *inference*.

This type of inference question is at a very simple level because it is geared to the readiness and cognitive development level of the children. As the children progress to higher levels of thinking they should be confronted with more complex interpretation or inference problems. It is important that the teacher work with the children according to their individual readiness levels. The teacher should expect all of the children to be able to perform, but should avoid putting them in situations that frustrate rather than stimulate them.

Critical reading skills are essential for good readers. Teachers can use primary graders' love of fairy tales to begin to develop some critical reading skills. For example, after the children have read "Little Red Riding Hood," the teacher can ask several questions:

1. Should Little Red Riding Hood have listened to her mother and not spoken to a stranger? Explain.
2. Would you help a stranger if your mother told you not to speak to a stranger? Explain.
3. Do you think a wolf can talk? Explain.
4. Do you think that this story is true? Explain.
5. Do you think Little Red Riding Hood is a good girl? Explain.

Creative reading questions are probably the most ignored by teachers. To help children in this area, teachers need to learn how to ask questions that require divergent rather than convergent answers. A teacher who focuses only on the author's meaning or intent and does not go beyond the text will not be encouraging creative reading. Some questions to stimulate divergent thinking on the part of the reader would be the following:

1. After reading "Little Red Riding Hood," can you come up with another ending for the story?
2. After reading about John, can you come up with a plan for the kind of vacation he would like?
3. After reading the story about the cat that escaped from the well, can you come up with some ideas as to how he was able to escape?
4. Based on your reading about John and his family, what kind of trip would you plan to make them happy?

Divergent answers, of course, require more time than convergent answers. Also, there is no one correct answer.

Following is a short reading selection and examples of the four different types of comprehension questions. These are presented so that the teacher can gain practice in recognizing the different types of questions at the four levels.

One day in the summer, some of my friends and I decided to go on an overnight hiking trip. We all started out fresh and full of energy. About halfway to our destination, when the sun was directly overhead, one-third of my friends decided to return home. The remaining four of us, however, continued on our hike. Our plan was to reach our destination by sunset. About six hours later as the four of us, exhausted and famished, were slowly edging ourselves in the direction of the setting sun, we saw a sight that astonished us. There, at the camping site, were our friends who had claimed that they were returning home. It seems that they did indeed go home, but only to pick up a car and drive out to the campsite.

The following are the four different types of comprehension questions:

Literal comprehension: What season of the year was it in the story? What kind of trip were the persons going on?

Interpretation: What time of day was it when some of the people decided to return home? How many persons were there when they first started out on the trip? In what direction were the hikers heading when they saw a sight that astonished them? At what time did the sun set?

Critical reading: How do you think the hikers felt when they reached their destination? Do you feel that the persons who went home did the right thing by driving back to the site rather than hiking? Explain.

Creative reading: What do you think the exhausted hikers did and said when they saw those who had supposedly gone home?

RELATIONSHIP OF READING TO OTHER LANGUAGE ARTS AREAS

The interrelatedness of the various language arts areas to reading cannot be emphasized enough. Students meeting difficulties in one facet will generally carry the problem over to another aspect of the language arts. If we ask why David, in the fourth grade, is not reading, his teacher claims that he was tested the year before and was found to have impaired hearing. Digging into the problem further, we find that David had been "tested" by another teacher in the school, who knew little about the study of hearing. When David's teacher is asked if referrals had been made for more professional opinions and testing, we are told that it doesn't really pay to bother, because all special personnel from the psychologist to the remedial reading teachers are overloaded and the teacher would only be wasting his or her time.

By pinning the label "hearing impairment problem" on David the teacher is psychologically relieved of responsibility. David, however, has not yet lost his determination to learn to read. He does not have a hearing problem. He has a language problem, which might be mistaken for a hearing impairment difficulty in the third or fourth grade. David comes from a bilingual home where Spanish is the dominant language. He has difficulty discriminating between sounds in English; therefore, he needs help in auditory discrimination. If David does not hear English words correctly, how can he be expected to say them correctly, or, for that matter, read or write them? To David, many of the words in English are mere noises, because the words are not in his listening vocabulary. David needs help in learning the English language.

To help David and others like him to become more competent in English, a teacher must know the methods of teaching English as a second language using aural–oral approaches before involving a child in the act of reading. Such children must learn to "listen," so they will be able to make auditory discriminations in standard English. The teacher must also determine whether children have adequate visual perception. The concept of left and right, which is so important for learning to read, should also be established; in other words, children need to understand that they start to read and write at the left and proceed to the right for each line. Children such as David must be helped to build concepts not previously developed. They should be given concrete objects

and their labels, and helped to develop the concepts of opposites, rhyming, size, relativity, similarity, and so on. Nothing can be taken for granted. (See Chapters 3 and 17.)

Now let us take up the particulars of how listening, speaking, and writing are closely related to reading.

Listening and Reading

In Chapter 6 we learned that students spend a great amount of time in school listening, and throughout this book, we stress the importance of listening to all the other language arts areas. In this section, we will see how listening is of particular importance to reading. Reading comprehension depends on comprehension of the spoken language, and students who are sensitive to the arrangement of words in oral language are usually more sensitive to the same thing in written language. Listening helps students to enlarge their vocabulary and to learn many expressions they will eventually see in print. During the day, teachers explain word meanings and what the text says, as well as read stories aloud to children and encourage them to guess at word meanings. Students listen to other students read orally, talk about books, and explain their contents.

Listening and reading are closely related; this makes sense since they both share some similar skills, and, as already mentioned in Chapter 6, a person inadequate in listening comprehension will probably not do well in reading comprehension. Also, both listening and reading comprehension require students to have the ability to think at various levels of difficulty; persons who lack necessary thinking skills will not be able to be either good listeners or readers. It was also stated in Chapter 6 that it is possible for some students to understand a passage when it is orally read to them, but they cannot understand it when they read it themselves. This indicates that the students have the thinking ability necessary to understand the written passage, but they have probably not gained the skills for decoding words from their written forms.

From the previous paragraph, it would appear that help in listening comprehension should enhance reading comprehension and vice versa. Researchers going as far back as the 1930s seem to support this view. For example, an investigation made in 1936 found that children who did poorly in comprehension through listening were also poor in reading comprehension.[9] Research in 1955 on the relationship between reading and listening found that practice in listening for detail will produce a significant gain in reading for the same purpose.[10] More recent studies have also found that training in listening comprehension skills will produce significant gains in reading comprehension[11] and that reading and listening have similar thinking skills.[12]

Although there are many common factors involved in the decoding of reading and listening—which would account for the relationship between the two areas—listening and reading are, nonetheless, separated by unique factors. The most obvious is that listening calls for *hearing*, whereas reading calls for *seeing*. As has already been stated, in the area of listening, the speakers are doing much of the interpretation for the listeners by their expressions, inflections, stresses, and pauses. Similarly, the listeners do not have to make the proper grapheme (letter)-phoneme (sound) correspondences because these have already been done for them by the speakers. It is possible for students to achieve excellent listening comprehension but not to achieve as well in reading.

Readers must make the proper grapheme–phoneme correspondences themselves and organize these into the proper units to gain meaning from the words. Readers must also be able to determine the shades of meaning implied by the words, to recognize any special figures of speech, and finally to synthesize the unique ideas expressed by the passage.

The relationship between listening and reading ability is succinctly summarized by these four rules:

1. **When auding[13] ability is low, reading ability tends more often to be low.**
2. **When auding ability is high, reading ability is not predictable.**
3. **When reading ability is low, auding ability is not predictable.**
4. **When reading ability is high, auding ability is, to a very small extent, predictable—and likely to be high.[14]**

Speaking and Reading

Students usually read more easily those things that they have talked about. Also, talking about a selection often helps persons to clarify their thinking; it gels experiences; it makes them real; it reinforces them, and so on. Oral statements in a class discussion can be recorded and become reading material for the students. The students could analyze the statements to determine whether they are sound and logical. Then suggestions could be given to enhance class discussions.

Through oral language, teachers can learn about the interests of students and build on these in choosing books. Students share favorite stories and passages with others by reading aloud. Many times, pupils will dramatize a story they have found in their reading. Also, discussion topics may emanate from stories. In addition, teachers can learn about students' think-

[9]William E. Young, "The Relation of Reading Comprehension and Retention to Hearing Comprehension and Retention," *Journal of Experimental Education* 5 (September 1936): 30–39.

[10]Annette P. Kelty, "An Experimental Study to Determine the Effect of Listening for Certain Purposes Upon Achievement in Reading for Those Purposes," *Abstracts of Field Studies for the Degree of Doctor of Education* 15 (Greeley: Colorado State College of Education, 1955): 82–95.

[11]Sybil M. Hoffman, "The Effect of a Listening Skills Program on the Reading Comprehension of Fourth Grade Students," Ph.D. Dissertation, Walden University, 1978.

[12]Thomas Sticht et al., *Auding and Reading: A Developmental Model* (Alexandria, Va.: Human Resources Research Organization, 1974); Walter Kintsch and Ely Kozminsky, "Summarizing Stories After Reading and Listening," *Journal of Educational Psychology* 69 (1977): 491–99.

[13]*Auding* refers to the highest level of listening. It is defined as listening plus comprehension. The term "listening" is many times used to mean auding (see Chapter 6).

[14]John Caffrey, "The Establishment of Auding-age Norms," *School and Society* 70 (November 12, 1949): 310.

ing ability from listening to them. For example, if some students can answer questions well when they have listened to a story read aloud to them, but they have difficulty answering questions after having read a story silently, the teacher will recognize that these students probably have some kind of decoding problem rather than a comprehension problem. Teachers can also learn about their students' ability to comprehend what they are reading from listening to their oral statements in class or group discussions.

Writing and Reading[15]

Without writing, there would be no reading. Writing reinforces word recognition and discourse structure, and increases familiarity with words. Through writing, students are able to gain a better understanding of the author's task in getting his or her ideas across. Writing can make students keener analyzers of reading; writing is a thinking process. As writers, we are also readers looking over our own shoulder and trying to determine whether what we have written makes sense and whether it accurately expresses what we wanted to convey. Writing forces us to pay attention to the logical arrangement of our words into sentences and to the arrangement of our sentences into a paragraph. As readers, we use the sequence and organization of ideas to help us comprehend the writer's message as well as to help us remember. If we read widely, we will have a broad range of topics from which to draw for our own writing. Also, through reading we will come to recognize what skills are necessary to be a good writer. Reading helps us acquire knowledge and often furnishes the stimulus for creative writing. Reading helps us to develop vocabulary and a language sense and helps us to become familiar with a variety of sentence structures used in both speaking and writing. Reading good literature exposes us to the beauty of language written in such a way that it seems to capture a sentiment or thought perfectly.

An integrated reading–writing approach

stresses the teaching of the two together in such a way that each acts as a stimulus and aid for the other. By combining the instruction of reading and writing, students can become more sensitive to the kinds of strategies writers use to convey their ideas and readers use to receive the ideas. Writing, as well as reading, will be seen as a problem-solving process that requires specific skills and reasoning ability (see "The Writing Process" in Chapter 11).

It is important to state that writing and reading should only be taught together when feasible. In other words, teachers must be aware of their purposes and recognize that an integrated reading–writing approach does not do away with direct instruction in reading nor with direct instruction in writing.

It probably comes as no surprise that correlational studies show "that better writers tend to be better readers (of their own writing as well as of other reading material), that better writers tend to read more than poorer writers, and that better readers tend to produce more syntactically mature writing than poorer readers."[16] Similarly, persons are not surprised to learn that studies suggest that poor readers are usually also poor writers. What may be surprising is that persons are using writing as a means to helping poor readers gain skill in reading.[17] Actually, this makes sense since writing requires reading and rereading in order to attain a polished paper. Let's follow a writer as she attempts to create a short story to see how closely related the processes of writing and reading are. (See Scenario, page 130.)

When students write, teachers can help them to understand the relationship between writing and reading by having them analyze what they do when writing. Also, after they have a finished product, or what they feel is a finished product, they could submit their product for review. Reviewers, randomly chosen from a group of students, would read the writer's work

---

[15]This section is largely drawn from Rubin, *Teaching Reading and Study Skills in Content Areas.*

[16]Sandra Stotsky, "Research on Reading/Writing Relationships: A Synthesis and Suggested Directions," *Language Arts* (May 1983) : 636.

[17]Irene W. Gaskins, "A Writing Program for Poor Readers and Writers and the Rest of the Class, Too," *Language Arts* 59 (November–December 1982) : 854.

SCENARIO

Lynn is a well-known and celebrated writer, who is envied by many because she is so prolific and appears to write with great ease. Lynn knows differently, however. She needs one more story for her book of short stories, which she has been working on all year. Thinking about this one for a month now, she has the central theme in her mind's eye. To write this story, she'll have to do a bit of research because the main character is a Southerner who used to live on a large plantation. Even though Lynn writes fiction, and this story will be a mystery, most of her work has been acclaimed because she uses authentic settings and relies heavily on historical facts. In other words, Lynn does her homework before beginning stories or books. She reads all about the time period she is writing about, the place, and the types of characters who inhabited the various place or places. After researching their way of life, customs, habits, and so on, Lynn sits down to write.

Lynn, however, does not just sit and write, write, write. Contrary to what many persons believe, Lynn writes, reads what she has written, revises, rereads, revises again, rereads, and then goes on. The pattern of writing, revising, rereading, and so on continues throughout the writing.

and then write a review of it. Each reviewer would write his or her own review. The author would then have to read the review and incorporate the suggestions in his or her work if the author agrees with them. If the author does not agree with them, however, he or she would have to write a rebuttal explaining why. From the preceding procedures, students should recognize that writing requires reading and that reading can be a stimulus for writing. The following section presents a few other suggestions that teachers can use to combine reading and writing instruction.

Instructional Techniques The suggestions that follow should help students to become better writers as well as better readers because the emphasis is on making students keener analyzers and, therefore, better thinkers.

1. Have students write a paragraph on a particular topic. After they have written the paragraph, have them reread it to determine its main idea and to verify whether the main idea

is the one desired. Then have them check to see if all of their sentences develop the main idea.

2. Have students read a number of different paragraphs, and then have them determine the main idea of each. After this, have them see how the writer develops his or her main idea; that is, through what technique (comparison/contrast, examples, sequence of events, and so on).

3. Have students read a number of topic sentences and have them state what they expect to follow from these.

4. Present students with a topic sentence and have them write a paragraph using it. Have them state how they developed the paragraph, that is, what technique they used to develop the paragraph.

5. Have students read a selection and, after they have read the selection, have them write a summary of it. Then give them a test on the selection. Give the students another selection to read, which they do not summarize. Give them a test on the selection. Have them compare

their results. (See Chapters 11 and 12 for more on the integration of reading and writing.)

THE LANGUAGE-EXPERIENCE APPROACH

Although there are a number of approaches that teachers can use in teaching reading, only the language-experience approach (LEA) will be presented because it is one that utilizes all the language arts. It is important to state, however, that most teachers use a combination of approaches in the teaching of reading and that the language-experience approach is usually used in conjunction with other approaches.

Utilizing the experiences of children, the language-experience approach is a nonstructured emerging reading program based on the inventiveness of both teacher and students. In sharp contrast to approaches predetermined by exact guidelines and materials, the language-experience approach to reading brings together all the language arts skills. Persons advocating this approach do not attempt to distinguish between the reading program and other language activities.

In the language-experience approach children's speech determines the language patterns of what they will read, and the children's experiences determine the content. The emphasis is not on decoding from the printed page but rather on speaking to express a thought, followed by the encoding of that thought into written form. Since the written material is composed of the children's experiences, they will have more of an incentive to learn to read it. A word of caution is in order. The teacher must be careful to determine whether the children can actually decode the written symbols or whether they have just memorized what they have said. The children may act as though they are reading, but they may not be making any grapheme-phoneme associations.

The teacher using the language-experience approach must also help students gain facility in word-recognition skills. One difficulty is that word-attack skills are often neglected, because the needs of the children are not as clearly recognized as when other approaches are used. Nor does the experience approach have a se-

quential, predetermined guide. As a result, the teacher must know the sequence of skills and teach them as part of the program. The word-attack skills needed for independence in the language-experience approach are similar to those necessary for any other approach—phonics, structural analysis, context clues, and so on. All the skills that make an effective reader should be emphasized.

Teachers do not have to use an exclusive language-experience approach for their whole reading program. Even for the very experienced teacher, it is not recommended that this be the only approach. A varied reading program is the most likely to be successful for the greatest number of students.

The Experience Story

One tool used as a basic teaching technique is the experience story, which provides for the development and expression of concepts on a very personal and meaningful level. It has the added virtue of permitting growth in most of the language skills.

The experience story is written cooperatively after the class has had a real or a vicarious learning experience. The technique is useful with all students at various ability levels. When used with able students, it provides a model against which individuals can evaluate their own writing efforts. The time spent on the experience story may vary from one class period to several days, depending on the complexity of the concept and the ability of the class.

Types of Experiences Used for Experience Stories The opportunities are unlimited, but the best are those that provide for the development of meaning in a stimulating discussion. Examples include picture description and interpretation; map explanation and interpretation; report on a field trip; summaries of answers to problems; summaries of stories, television shows, and movies; original stories; explanation of the facilities in a new school; descriptions of holidays or special events.

Steps in the Development of an Experience Story *Readiness.* The teacher structures the actual experience for the group or individual. Following the experience, the teacher guides a discussion during which the class or the child:

Reviews the experience

Uses the vocabulary to be utilized in writing the story

Lists the important points to be included in the story

Sets up standards for the construction of the story

Writing the Story. The pupils suggest sentences that are discussed and probably improved before being written on the board by the teacher. Then the organization follows. A listing is made of the important points described, based on the natural sequence of the experience. The entire story is read, evaluated, and improved by the class working together.

Example of an Experience Story Mrs. Smith and her class had visited a local bakery in the morning. For a snack, they had eaten some of the cookies and cupcakes that they had gotten from the bakery. The children were taken on a tour of the bakery. They saw how clean everything was, and they also watched the baker decorate a large birthday cake.

After the children returned to their classroom, Mrs. Smith had the children discuss their experiences. Mrs. Smith asked them about what they had seen and encouraged them to discuss their own baking experiences. She also asked them about the special clothes the baker and his assistant wore. The children, in addition, discussed the varieties of breads and cakes that they saw in the local bakery.

After the children discussed their experiences, Mrs. Smith went over some of the special terms that they would need to write their experience story. Here are some of the words that were listed:

bakery	bus
baker	dessert
cookies	enjoy
cake	local (word explained)
bread	taste
dough	tour (word explained)

Here are some of the points that were listed that would help in writing the story:

Going to the bakery
What we saw at the bakery
What we tasted at the bakery
Coming back to school

Mrs. Smith and the children then discussed the standards for the story. They decided that each child should have a chance to give a sentence for the story, that the sentence should fit into the story, and that the sentence should make sense.

The children suggested the following sentences for the story:

Today we went to visit a local bakery.
We went on the bus to the bakery.
A woman met us at the bakery.
She took us on a tour of the bakery.
We saw lots of cakes, breads, and cookies.
We watched the baker decorate a cake.
The bakery was very clean.
The baker wore a white apron and a large white hat.
The baker gave us some cookies to eat.
They tasted good.
We went back on the bus.
We came back to school.
We enjoyed our visit to the bakery.

After each sentence was given, it was read aloud again by Mrs. Smith. Mrs. Smith then had the child who dictated the sentence read it aloud. After the whole story had been written, Mrs. Smith called on the children to read each

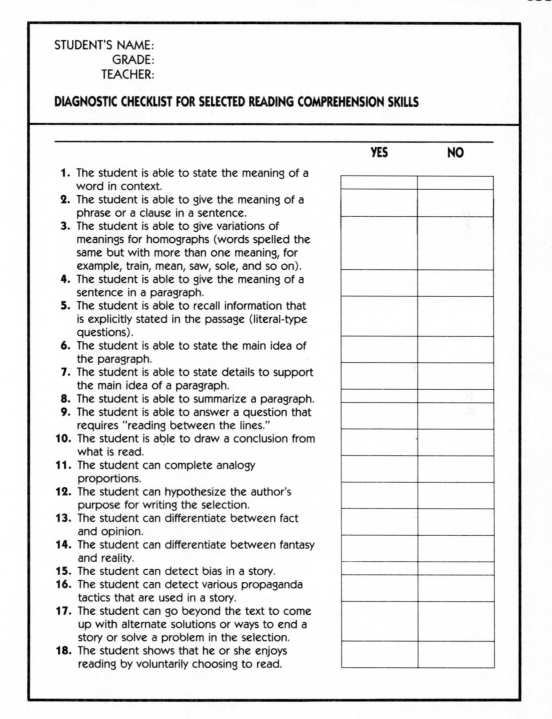

STUDENT'S NAME:
    GRADE:
    TEACHER:

DIAGNOSTIC CHECKLIST FOR SELECTED READING COMPREHENSION SKILLS

	YES	NO
1. The student is able to state the meaning of a word in context.		
2. The student is able to give the meaning of a phrase or a clause in a sentence.		
3. The student is able to give variations of meanings for homographs (words spelled the same but with more than one meaning, for example, train, mean, saw, sole, and so on).		
4. The student is able to give the meaning of a sentence in a paragraph.		
5. The student is able to recall information that is explicitly stated in the passage (literal-type questions).		
6. The student is able to state the main idea of the paragraph.		
7. The student is able to state details to support the main idea of a paragraph.		
8. The student is able to summarize a paragraph.		
9. The student is able to answer a question that requires "reading between the lines."		
10. The student is able to draw a conclusion from what is read.		
11. The student can complete analogy proportions.		
12. The student can hypothesize the author's purpose for writing the selection.		
13. The student can differentiate between fact and opinion.		
14. The student can differentiate between fantasy and reality.		
15. The student can detect bias in a story.		
16. The student can detect various propaganda tactics that are used in a story.		
17. The student can go beyond the text to come up with alternate solutions or ways to end a story or solve a problem in the selection.		
18. The student shows that he or she enjoys reading by voluntarily choosing to read.		

sentence. She then asked if anyone thought that he or she could read the whole story. Mrs. Smith encouraged the children by telling them that she felt that they could read the story and that if they needed any help, she would supply it.

SUMMARY

This chapter explores the relationship of reading to the other language arts areas. It begins with a discussion of the importance of reading and demonstrates that reading should be integrated with the rest of the teaching program. Because the definition of reading will influence the reading program, this chapter presents reading as a total integrative process, including the affective, perceptual, and cognitive domains. Under the cognitive domain is reading comprehension.

Throughout the chapter, it is stressed that reading is a thinking act and that good readers are good thinkers. Although researchers still do not agree on how persons achieve reading comprehension, studies seem to suggest that good comprehenders have such characteristics as the ability to do inferential reasoning, to assimilate, compare, categorize, analyze, synthesize, and evaluate information, among a host of other skills. Reading taxonomies are also discussed, and reading comprehension is categorized into a hierarchy of four levels: literal comprehension, interpretation, critical reading, and creative reading. After a discussion of each category, suggestions are given to help teachers to construct questions that would require students to go beyond the literal-type comprehension level.

Special emphasis is given to the relationship of reading to the other language arts and, in particular, to the interrelationship of reading to listening and writing. It is shown how reading and listening comprehension require similar thinking skills, how reading is a stimulus for writing, and how writing helps persons to be better analysts of reading. Since the language-experience approach emphasizes the interrelatedness concept, this approach is discussed, and suggestions are given for the development of an experience story. A "Diagnostic Checklist" for Selected Reading Comprehension Skills" is also given.

As a further aid, two examples of lesson plans follow. Using these as a guide, see if you can construct a third one.

LESSON PLAN I: UPPER-PRIMARY-GRADE LEVEL

OBJECTIVES

1. The children will listen to a short, silly story and then cooperatively write one.
2. The children will be able to state words that contain the phonogram *oon*.
3. The children will read their story and make up comprehension questions for it.

PRELIMINARY PREPARATION

Pictures of various familiar fairy tales are on display. Large paper attached to board.

INTRODUCTION

"We've been reading a number of silly stories. Who can tell me some? Good. Yesterday, I promised to reread you one of your favorite stories. Who remembers what it is? Yes, good. I have it here. It's one of the stories I read to you at the beginning of the year. It's a silly story and one that made you laugh." The teacher reads the short story aloud to the children. After she reads it aloud, she tells them that they will write a silly story together, and after they write it, they will read it and make up some questions for it.

DEVELOPMENT

"Before we begin our story, I would like you to make up some questions for the story I just read." The teacher calls on a few children who have raised their hands. After each child gives his or her question, the teacher writes it on the board. The teacher tells the students that she has some questions also, and she gives hers. The teacher tells her students that she is very proud of them because they are becoming such good question askers. "Now," she says, "let's write a silly story together." The teacher suggests that they continue to write about their imaginary friend Kippa Kappa. Here is the story they wrote:

Once, a long time ago, there lived a cheerful and friendly animal called Kippa Kappa. He lived in outer space in a village called Kippa Kump, near the earth's moon. Although Kippa Kappa was cheerful and friendly, he was very lonely because he had no friends. One day Kippa Kappa told his mother and father that he was leaving Kippa Kump in order to travel to other villages in search of friends.

Kippa Kappa started on his journey. He walked and walked. Soon he became tired and hungry. He stopped and, lo and behold, he saw his favorite moon food growing. What do you think Kippa Kappa's favorite moon food is? In case you don't know, moon food is very different from earth food. On the moon, words are eaten as food. Kippa Kappa's favorite moon food is a word with "oon" in it. The children helped Kippa Kappa pick some of his favorite food. He picked a coon, a spoon, a noon, a soon. Kippa Kappa liked his delicious food. However, he was still hungry. The children helped Kippa Kappa find some other moon food.

After the story was written, the teacher read it aloud. She then called on children to read it. After that she had the children make up some questions about the story.

SUMMARY

The teacher helps the students pull the main points of the lesson together. She tells them that tomorrow they will see how well they can answer the questions they made up about their story.

LESSON PLAN II INTERMEDIATE-GRADE LEVEL

OBJECTIVES

1. The students will be able to allow their imaginations to roam and state how various school items would feel if they could think and talk.
2. The students will be able to act out how they think a specific school item would feel if it could think and speak.

3. The students will be able to write a paragraph about their object.

4. The students will be able to state the main idea of their paragraph.

INTRODUCTION

"We have been doing a great amount of creative dramatics over the past few months. Who can tell me some of the things that we have done? Good! Now close your eyes and see if you can tell me who or what might be talking."

The teacher in a falsetto voice says, "I'm so glad that I'm purple and not green, red, or blue. It feels so good to come out of my box. It's so dark in there. I wonder if any of my friends will be chosen to come out, too. It's so cramped in my box. I wonder what the children will want me to do for them today. I hope they don't use too much of me because I'll soon disappear. Also, I hate to be sharpened. Who wouldn't?"

The children are challenged to guess who or what was talking. After the children respond, "A crayon," the teacher says, "Good, it was a crayon. Today we are going to discuss how you think different things in the class would feel if they were able to think and speak. After we do this, we will go into groups and act out 'a day in the life of the thing we choose.' Then we will write a paragraph about our object and see if we can state the main idea of our paragraph."

DEVELOPMENT

"First, what are some items in the classroom that we could talk about and act out? Yes. Good. We can talk about a pencil, a sheet of paper, and chalkboard. What else? Good, the window, the chalk, the ball, our books, and so on. I see that you are getting the idea. Now, let's go back to our crayon. What do you think a crayon would talk about in its box? Very good. How do you think a crayon feels if it is not chosen? Very good. What do you think a crayon thinks of when it is being used? Children, all of your comments have been very good. You are really using your imaginations. We are now going to break up into groups. Each group will choose an item in the class-room. The group will then prepare a little skit in which the item tells us how it feels. Only the group knows what item it has chosen."

The children divide into groups. After a while the teacher calls on the group to perform its skit. The children in the class try to guess what the item is.

The teacher then asks each student to write a paragraph about the item he or she has chosen. In addition, the teacher asks each student to state the main idea of his or her paragraph after it is written. Before the students begin to write, the teacher reviews with them the technique they had learned for finding the main idea of paragraphs. Then the teacher gives the students time to do the work. After about one-half hour, the teacher asks some of the students to read aloud their paragraphs. The teacher tells the students to listen carefully to see if they can state the main idea of each paragraph. The teacher asks the person who has written the paragraph whether his or her main idea statement was the same as that given by the student or students.

SUMMARY

The main points of the lesson are pulled together. The teacher tells the children that tomorrow they will write a story about the objects they had chosen, and they will then state the central idea of the story.

SUGGESTIONS FOR THOUGHT QUESTIONS AND ACTIVITIES

1. State and explain each of the four levels of comprehension presented in this chapter.

2. You have just been appointed to a special school committee that is interested in interrelating reading with the other language arts areas. What will you say?

3. How are listening and reading related?

4. State some ideas for experience stories.

5. You have just been appointed to a special primary-grade reading committee. Your task is to acquaint the teachers with the language-experience approach to reading. How would you do this so that teachers would want to incorporate this type of approach into their reading programs?

6. There is talk in your school of separating reading from the rest of the language arts program and perhaps having a special teacher for reading instruction. How do you feel about this? Present your arguments.

7. Explain how reading can be a stimulus for writing.

8. Explain how writing can help make persons better readers.

9. Brainstorm some activities that would combine reading and writing.

SELECTED BIBLIOGRAPHY

Cowen, John E., ed. *Teaching Reading through the Arts.* Newark, Del.: IRA, 1983.

Downing, John. *Reading and Reasoning.* New York: Springer-Verlag, 1979.

Hall, MaryAnne. *Teaching Reading As a Language Experience,* 3d ed. Columbus, Ohio: Merrill, 1981.

Holt, Suzanne L., and JoAnne L. Vacca. "Reading with a Sense of Writer: Writing with a Sense of Reader." *Language Arts* 58 (November–December 1981): 937–941.

Jensen, Julie M., ed. "Theme: Reading and Writing." *Language Arts* 60 (May 1983).

Lehr, Fran. "Developing Critical and Creative Reading and Thinking Skills." *Language Arts* 60 (November–December 1983): 1031–1035.

Rubin, Dorothy. *The Teacher's Handbook of Reading/Thinking Exercises.* New York: Holt, Rinehart and Winston, 1980.

————. *The Teacher's Handbook of Primary-Grade Reading/Thinking Exercises.* New York: Holt, Rinehart and Winston, 1982.

————. *A Practical Approach to Teaching Reading.* New York: Holt, Rinehart and Winston, 1983.

————. *Writing and Reading—The Vital Arts.* New York: Macmillan, 1983.

Stauffer, Russell. *The Language–Experience Approach to the Teaching of Reading.* New York: Harper & Row, 1980.

Stotsky, Sandra. "Research on Reading/Writing Relationships: A Synthesis and Suggested Directions." *Language Arts* 60 (May 1983): 627–642.

Wixson, Karen K. "Questions about a Text: What You Ask about Is What Children Learn." *Reading Teacher* 37 (December 1983): 287–293.

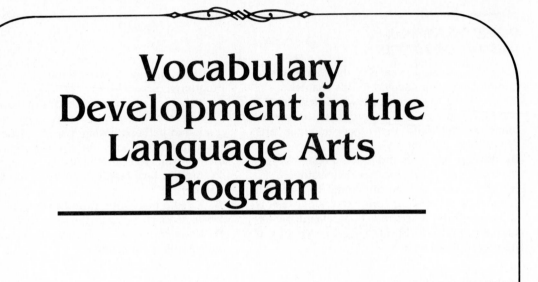

NINE

Vocabulary Development in the Language Arts Program

A number of years ago, a young man whom I had been trying to help said to me that he had great animosity toward me. When he said this, I was stunned, but I kept my composure and asked him why he felt this way. The young man replied, "Because you are trying to help me." His reply confused me even more, so I probed further. "What do you mean by *animosity*"? I asked. "Oh," the young man said, "I like you a lot." "Oh," I said, feeling both relief and concern at the same time. "Frank," I asked, "Have you used the word *animosity* before?" "Oh, sure," beamed Frank, "it's one of my favorites, so I use it a lot."

The preceding anecdote is a true one. Frank had heard the word *animosity*. He liked the way it sounded, so he used it often. Fortunately, for him, persons with whom he used the word didn't take offense (I can see why—he was 6'4" tall) or they didn't know what the word meant either.

I did tell Frank the meaning of *animosity* and discussed with him the importance of only using words whose meanings are known (see Chapter 1).

A good vocabulary and good reading go hand in hand. Unless students know the meanings of words, they will have difficulty in understanding what they are reading. A good vocab-

ulary is necessary not only for reading but for all the other language arts areas also; the more words students have in their listening capacity (ability to know the meaning of words when they are said aloud), the better their ability to be good speakers, readers, and writers. Obviously, in order to listen, speak, read, and write, we need to know word meanings. Acquiring word meanings is an important language arts skill, and one that should continue not only all through school but all through life. Because of its importance, it is being presented in a chapter by itself, and the emphasis in this chapter is on vocabulary expansion.

After you have finished reading this chapter, you should be able to answer the following questions:

1. What is the relationship of vocabulary to concept development?
2. What word-recognition strategies do students use?
3. What is a vocabulary consciousness?
4. What are some vocabulary expansion strategies?
5. How can knowledge of combining forms help students gain word meanings?
6. What is the role of context in gaining word meanings?

7. What should students know about the connotative meaning of words?
8. What is the role of the dictionary in vocabulary expansion?
9. What is the role of vocabulary in gaining content concepts?
10. What are examples of some fun-with-words activities?
11. What are some primary-grade-level vocabulary skills?
12. What are some intermediate-grade-level vocabulary skills?

CONCEPT DEVELOPMENT AND WORD MEANINGS

In Chapter 3, we stressed that students more advanced in language development are also usually more advanced in concept development and consequently are better readers and achievers in school. This fact makes sense because of the interrelatedness of vocabulary development and concept development. The first step in acquiring concepts concerns vocabulary because concepts are based on word meanings; without vocabulary, there would be no concepts because there would be no base for the development of concepts.

The second step in acquiring concepts is gathering data, that is, specific information about the concept to be learned. In doing this, students use their strategies for processing information—they select data that are relevant, ignore irrelevant data, and categorize those items that belong together. Concepts are formed when the data are organized into categories. Let's see how a young child may acquire the concept *pet:*

Andrew is fortunate because he lives in a home that is large enough for pets. Andrew, who is four years old, has a cat, a dog, and fish as pets. He has always had pets. His mother and father use the word *pets* when they refer to the kitty, dog, and fish; they use also the labels *kitty, doggie,* and *fish,* as well as the pets' special names. In Andrew's natural environment he has gained a great amount of data concerning pets. He has learned that pets are animals that live in your home, pets such as dogs and cats are gentle, and you can play with them. He has also learned that you cannot play with some pets such as

fish; these you can only watch. In addition he has learned that all pets need to be taken care of and that they do not eat the same things.

Andrew, at four, is quite verbal and can tell you a lot about his pets because he has grown up with them. His mother and father also have talked to him about pets and have read aloud to him many books about animals. Andrew knows that a lion, tiger, elephant, giraffe, and so on would not be pets. He has seen these animals in books and on TV, and he has visited them at the zoo. Thus, Andrew is learning the difference between wild animals and tame animals. When you talk to him about pets, he can tell you those that would make good pets and those that would not. He laughs when you suggest that he have a lion as a pet. He gets hysterical with laughter when you suggest that the cat live in the fish bowl or that the fish live out of water. He becomes very serious when you recommend that the fish play with the cat. "No, no!" he says, "The cat will eat my fish."

At four, Andrew has gained the concept *pet.* He knows what data to ignore and what data he should include in his concept formation of *pet.* He gained this concept easily because of his background of experiences. Think for a moment about another four-year-old, however.

Alice lives in a two-room apartment in the inner city. This four-year-old has five other brothers and sisters, and is next to the youngest. Her parents both work, and her older sister takes care of her and her other brothers and sisters. (Although this child may appear stereotyped, unfortunately many such children exist.) What kind of information will she gain concerning pets? Where she lives there are dogs that roam the streets in packs, and you can hear their howls at night. There are also large numbers of cats who must daily forage in the streets for food. When Alice was two, she was attacked by a wild dog, and as a result, she is still afraid of any dog. When she sees a rat in the apartment, she runs in fright and tells her sister that she has just seen a kitty.

Alice's experiences are certainly different from Andrew's, and this will obviously affect her concept formation of *pet,* a term not even used in her home. The word is not in her listening capacity, so Alice does not have a base or a foundation upon which she can adequately build the concept *pet.*

If students are to advance in concept development, their vocabulary development must also advance. Students deficient in vocabulary development will usually be deficient in concept development and vice versa. Studies have shown that "vocabulary is a key variable in reading comprehension and is a major feature of most tests of academic aptitude. . . ."[1]

VOCABULARY DEVELOPMENT AND INDIVIDUAL DIFFERENCES

For a vocabulary program to be successful, teachers must recognize that individual differences exist among the amount and kind of words that their students possess. For example, when kindergarten and first-grade children come to school, the words in their listening capacity will vary based on their home environment. Some children come to school with a rich and varied vocabulary, whereas others have a more limited and narrow vocabulary. Some children may come to school with a rich and varied vocabulary that can be used with their peers and at home, but it may not be one that is useful to them in school. For example, some children may possess a large lexicon of street vocabulary and expressions, while others may speak a dialect of English that may contain its own special expressions and vocabulary.

When children first come to school, teachers should recognize that these young children's listening vocabulary is larger than their speaking vocabulary and obviously larger than their reading and writing vocabulary. However, as children go through the grades, it is possible for a student's reading vocabulary to include words that may not be in his or her listening capacity; that is, the student may have gained the meaning of the word from context clues rather than from having heard it. As a result, the student may be able to "read" the word, but he or she may not be able to pronounce it. It seems apparent, then, that those students who are

good readers and who read frequently will have a larger vocabulary than those who do not spend time reading.

Teachers can learn a great deal about students' reading habits by observing the vocabulary they use in writing. Some students can pronounce a word correctly, but use it incorrectly. Others are unable to correctly pronounce a word, but can use it correctly in writing. The latter, as already stated, have acquired their vocabulary through reading, and they may greatly surprise their teachers with their written productions.

Although most persons' speaking vocabulary tends to be more limited than their reading or writing vocabularies, there are some students who can express themselves better orally. Teachers should recognize that not all students who are verbal are good writers, and, conversely, not all good writers are good orators.

In helping children to expand their vocabularies, teachers will need to assess their students' stock of words so that they can build a program based on their needs. Students who have a good vocabulary, who are curious about words, and who are interested in increasing their stock of words will need a program different from those students who are weak in vocabulary and who rely primarily on overworked words or clichés. The former group of students has developed a vocabulary consciousness; whereas the latter has not.

Vocabulary Consciousness

When students recognize the power of words and their ability to have different meanings based on surrounding words, they are building a vocabulary consciousness. This vocabulary consciousness grows and matures when students independently search out word meanings. Teachers can help awaken and advance this awareness in students by helping them to acquire tools in addition to the dictionary to expand their vocabulary.

Vocabulary consciousness grows when students do the following:

1. **Become aware of words they do not know**
2. **Have a desire to unlock the meanings of unfamiliar words**

[1]Walter M. MacGinitie, "Language Development," *Encyclopedia of Educational Research,* 4th ed. (London: Collier-Macmillan Ltd., 1969), p. 693.

3. Are interested in gaining insight into the strategies for recognizing words and for expanding vocabulary
4. Try to determine the meaning of words from the context and from their knowledge of word parts
5. Learn the most-used combining forms
6. Jot down words they do not know and look them up later in the dictionary
7. Keep a notebook handy to write down words that they have missed in their vocabulary exercises
8. Learn to break down words into word parts to learn their meanings
9. Maintain interest in wanting to expand vocabulary

ROLE OF THE LANGUAGE ARTS TEACHER IN VOCABULARY DEVELOPMENT

Language arts teachers need to help students recognize how knowledge of word meanings is essential for precision and clarity in language. Also, they need to help their students gain strategies for vocabulary expansion. Several methods exist. One way for a teacher to show students that he or she feels vocabulary study is important is to devote time to it. Another is to be a good role model, that is, to use a good vocabulary oneself. For example, when a teacher is presenting information, discussing something, or merely conversing with students, he or she could use an unfamiliar word and pair this word with a synonym. If students hear the word often enough, many will get its meaning. Another tactic teachers can use is to challenge students to use more descriptive words in their writing and in their oral reports. One of the most important roles of the teacher in vocabulary development is, of course, to expose the children to lots of books. A good literature program is an excellent way to help children expand their vocabulary. (More will be said about this later in the chapter, as well as in other chapters.)

In addition, it is important that language arts teachers, rather than relying only on incidental methods, *directly* teach students strategies for developing their vocabulary. Language arts teachers and students should plan to set aside time during the week for vocabulary study. (More will be said about this in upcoming sections in this chapter.)

Language Arts Teachers and Vocabulary Aids in Textbooks

Language arts teachers should help acquaint their students with the many aids that textbook writers provide for their readers. At the beginning of the term teachers should spend time with students to discuss the various techniques used in their textbooks to help students acquire vocabulary. Nothing should be taken for granted. Most textbook writers use a combination of aids such as the following: context clues, marginal notes, footnotes, parenthetical explanations, illustrations, glossaries, pronunciation keys, word lists, italicized words, bold print, and so on. Teachers should familiarize students with each of the aids to ascertain that students can use them effectively.

Choosing Vocabulary Words for Study

Teacher judgment plays an essential role in determining which words will be selected for special emphasis, as well as the number of words, the kind, and the method of presentation. Language arts teachers should choose for study those words that students will need to gain key concepts in the areas that they are studying. Also, they should present students with the most common combining forms; that is, the combining forms from which a great number of words are derived. It is just not possible to specifically state all those words that students at each grade level will need because of the individual differences of the students. Using a number of techniques, teachers will have to assess the vocabulary ability of students to determine the type of vocabulary program they should present as well as the type of words their students need.

One technique a teacher can use is word lists, which give the words that persons at various levels both will meet most frequently in reading and will require in writing. Disadvantages exist, however. Word lists are usually given to assess students' word-recognition vocabularies, and these require individual administration, a process that is quite time consuming. Also, it is possible for a student to be able to pronounce a word correctly because he or she has excellent word-analysis skills but not know its meaning. Conversely, a student may not be able to pronounce the word but may know its meaning when it is said aloud. Another problem with word lists is determining which ones to use.[2]

Written vocabulary tests are probably more effective than word lists because they are not as time consuming, and they give teachers a good gauge of a student's meaning vocabulary. Teachers need to recognize, however, that a student who has decoding problems will obviously have difficulty taking the vocabulary test. Again, it is possible that the student may know the meaning of the word when it is said aloud but not be able to figure out the pronunciation of the written word. Such students will need help in building their decoding skills rather than in building a meaning vocabulary. This point is being stressed so that language arts teachers will recognize that differences exist between a student's listening and reading vocabularies, and that a good vocabulary expansion program takes these factors into account.

A good technique that teachers could use in choosing words for vocabulary study is to peruse their students' reading assignments to select all those words that they feel are necessary for students to understand what they are reading. Even if these words are defined in their books, it would be a good idea for the teacher to present these words before their students read them in print. If students have met a number of key words beforehand, they will be reinforced when they meet the words in their reading, and this recognition will help to improve their reading comprehension. Teachers should especially be on the lookout for words with multiple meanings that are used frequently in everyday language because such words can cause difficulty for students. (The rest of this chapter helps readers gain insight into word-recognition strategies and gives numerous examples of how teachers can present vocabulary to their primary-grade and intermediate-grade students, as well as help these students expand their vocabulary.)

WORD-RECOGNITION STRATEGIES

Language arts teachers are generally involved in teaching reading and, particularly, in helping students learn to read. Word-recognition skills are associated with learning to read, and phonics, in particular, is associated with learning to read. This section will provide background on how students recognize words. However, the word-recognition strategies stressed in this chapter will be those primarily associated with word meaning, namely, context clues, structural analysis, and the dictionary.

Pronunciation[3]

Word recognition is necessary to be able to read. No one would disagree with that statement; however, persons do disagree on what word recognition encompasses. In this book, *word recognition* is looked upon as a twofold process that includes both the recognition of printed symbols by some method so that the word can be pronounced and the attachment or association of meaning to the word after it has been properly pronounced.

When we read, we are intent on getting the message and appear to do so automatically and in one step. We don't notice the individual letters, groups of letters, or even every word. If we are good readers, this is what should be taking place. It isn't until we stumble on an unfamiliar word that we become aware of the individual letters that are grouped together to form a word. The reason we stopped reading is because the word we stumbled on has interfered with our getting the message. The question is: Do you remember what you did when a word interfered with your understanding of what you were reading? To understand better the concept that word recognition is a twofold process, that there are a number of strategies that can be used to figure out how to pronounce a word as well as strategies that can be used to determine the meaning of a word, and that these strategies are not necessarily the

[2]See Mary Monteith, "A Whole Word List Catalog," *Reading Teacher* 29 (May 1976): 844–846.

[3]This section is adapted from Dorothy Rubin, *A Practical Approach to Teaching Reading* (New York: Holt, Rinehart and Winston, 1982).

same, we will be involved in a number of exercises involving nonsense and actual words.

As already stated, the strategies for determining how to pronounce a word are different from those that are used to unlock the meaning of the word. Read the following sentence:

I don't like *cland* food.

You should have stumbled on the nonsense word *cland*. Imagine that you do not know that *cland* is a nonsense word. Let's look at the kinds of strategies we could and could *not* use to help us to gain the pronunciation of a word *independently*.

STRATEGY 1: Phonic analysis and synthesis

DEFINITION: Phonics is a decoding technique that depends on students' being able to make the proper grapheme (letter)–phoneme (sound) correspondences. *Analysis* has to do with the breaking down of something into its component parts. *Synthesis* has to do with the building up of the parts of something into a whole.

ANALYSIS: Break down *cland* into the blend *cl* and the phonogram (graphemic base) *and*.

We have met the blend *cl* before in such words as *climb* and *club*.

We have met the phonogram *and* before in such words as *sand* and *band*.

We therefore, know the pronunciations of *cl* and *and*.

SYNTHESIS: Blend together the *cl* and *and*.

Using this technique, we should be able to pronounce *cland*.

STRATEGY 2: Whole word or "look and say" method

DEFINITION: The whole word or "look and say" method, which is also referred to as the sight method, has to do with the teacher's or any other individual's directing a student's attention to a word and then saying the word. The student must make an association between the oral word and the written word, and he or she shows this by actually saying the word.

This technique is a useful word-recognition strategy that helps us to learn to pronounce words, but it will not help us to figure out the pronunciation of unfamiliar words independently.

STRATEGY 3: Ask someone to pronounce the word for you.

This could be done, but it would be similar to the "look and say" method, and it would not help us to figure out the word independently.

STRATEGY 4: Context clues

DEFINITION: By *context* we mean the words surrounding a word that can shed light on its meaning. When we refer to context clues, we mean clues that are given in the form of definitions, examples, comparisons or contrasts, explanations, and so on, which help us figure out word meanings.

This is a word-recognition technique, but it is not one that helps us to figure out the pronunciation of words. It is one that is used for helping us to gain the meaning of a word.

STRATEGY 5: Structural analysis and synthesis (word parts)

DEFINITION: Structural analysis and synthesis have to do with the breaking down (analysis) and building up (synthesis) of word parts such as prefixes, suffixes, roots (bases), and combining forms.

Structural analysis is most often used in conjunction with phonic analysis. Knowledge of word parts such as prefixes, suffixes, and roots helps us to isolate the root of a word. After the root of a word is isolated, phonic analysis is applied. If the word parts are familiar ones, then we can blend together the word parts to come up with the pronunciation of the word.

Structural analysis is a helpful word-recognition technique that can aid with the pronunciation of words, but it will not help us to figure out the pronunciation of *cland* unless we apply phonic analysis because *cland* as a nonsense word is an unfamiliar root (base) word.

Structural analysis is especially helpful in figuring out the pronunciation of an unfamiliar word if the word is composed of familiar word parts such as prefixes, suffixes, and roots. The technique to use is similar to that used with phonic analysis and synthesis. For example, let's see how we would go about figuring out how to pronounce the italicized word in the following sentence using structural analysis and synthesis.

The salesperson said that the goods were not *returnable*.

STRUCTURAL ANALYSIS: Break down the word into its parts to isolate the root.

re   turn   able

If we had met *re* before and if we had met *able* before, we should know how to pronounce them. After we have isolated *turn,* we may recognize it as a familiar word and know how to pronounce it.

STRUCTURAL SYNTHESIS: Blend together *re, turn,* and *able.*

If *turn* is not a familiar root word for us, then we could apply phonic analysis to it and after that blend it together with the prefix *re* and the suffix *able.*

STRATEGY 6: Look up the pronunciation in the dictionary.

This is a viable method, but you may not have a dictionary handy, and by the time you look up the pronunciation of the word, you may have lost the trend of what you were reading.

Let's list those techniques that can help us to figure out the pronunciation of words:

1. Phonic analysis and synthesis
2. Whole word or "look and say"
3. Asking someone
4. Structural analysis and synthesis
5. Looking up the pronunciation in the dictionary

Word Meanings

Being able to pronounce a word is important, but it does not guarantee that we will thereby know the meaning of the word. As pre-

viously stated, word recognition is a twofold process: The first involves the correct pronunciation, and the second involves meaning. After we have pronounced a word, we have to associate the word with one in our listening capacity in order to determine the meaning of the word; that is, we need to have heard the word before and know what the word means. Obviously, the larger our stock of listening vocabulary, the better able we will be to decipher the word. However, even though we can pronounce a word such as *misanthropic,* it doesn't mean that we can associate any meaning to it. If we have never heard the word before, it would not be in our listening vocabulary; therefore, the pronunciation would not act as a stimulus and trigger an association with a word that we have stored in our memory bank. Let's see the techniques that we can use to help us unlock words that we have never encountered before.

STRATEGY 1: Context

By *context* we mean the words surrounding a particular word that can help shed light on its meaning. (Context clues are especially important in determining the meanings of words, and because of their importance, special emphasis is given to this area in this chapter.) Read the following sentence:

Even though my *trank* was rather long, I wouldn't take out one word.

From the context of the sentence you know that the nonsense word *trank* must somehow refer to a sentence, paragraph, paper, or report of some kind. Even though you had never met *trank* before, the context of the sentence did throw light on it. You know from the word order or position of the word (syntax) that *trank* must be a noun, and words such as *word* and *long* give you meaning (semantic) clues to the word itself. There are times, however, when context is not too helpful so that other strategies must be used.

STRATEGY 2: Structural analysis and synthesis for word meaning

Read the following sentence:

We asked the *misanthrope* to leave.

From the position of the word *misanthrope* in the sentence, we know that it is a noun; however, there is not enough information to help us figure out the meaning of *misanthrope*. Structural analysis could be very useful in situations where there are insufficient context clues, and the word consists of a number of word parts.

ANALYSIS: Break down *misanthrope* into its word parts.

Mis means either "wrong" or "hate," and *anthropo* means "humankind."

SYNTHESIS: Put together the word parts. It doesn't make sense to say, "Wrong humankind," so it must be *hate* and *humankind*. Since *misanthrope* is a noun, the meaning of *misanthrope* would have to be "hater of humankind."

Structural analysis is a powerful tool, but it is dependent on your having at your fingertips knowledge of word parts and their meanings. If you do not have these at hand, you obviously need another strategy. (More will be said about structural analysis later on in this chapter.)

STRATEGY 3: Ask someone the meaning of the word.

This at times may be the most convenient if someone is available who knows the meaning of the word.

STRATEGY 4: Look up the meaning in the dictionary.

If you cannot figure out the word independently rather quickly so that your trend of thought is not completely broken, the dictionary is a valuable tool for word meanings.

Let's list those techniques that can help us figure out the meaning of words:

1. Context of a sentence
2. Structural analysis and synthesis
3. Asking someone
4. Looking up the meaning in the dictionary

There are times when it is possible for context clues to help with the correction of mispronounced words that are in the listening capacity of the reader but not yet in his or her reading vocabulary. Here is such an example. A student is asked to read the following sentence:

The horse went into the barn.

The student reads the sentence as follows:

The *harse* went into the barn.

The reader then self-corrects and rereads the sentence correctly. What has taken place? The first pronunciation of *harse* was obtained from graphic clues. As the student continued to read, the context of the sentence indicated to the student that the mispronounced word should be *horse* rather than *harse*. Since *horse* was in the person's listening capacity, the student was able to self-correct the mispronunciation. In this case, the context clues helped the reader to correct the mispronunciation of *horse*.

It is important to state that the reader would not have been able to self-correct if the word *horse* had not been in his or her listening capacity and if he or she had not heard it correctly pronounced.

It is also important to state that readers usually use a *combination* of word-recognition strategies.

Many of the sections that follow will expand on this area of gaining word meanings.

GAINING WORD MEANINGS THROUGH CONTEXT

In 1918, Chief Justice Oliver Wendell Holmes said the following concerning a word:

A word is not a crystal, transparent and unchanged; it is the skin of a living thought and may vary greatly in color and content according to the circumstances and the time in which it is used.

Because many words have more than one meaning, the meaning of a particular word is determined by the position (syntax) of the word in a sentence and from meaning (semantic) clues of the surrounding words. By *context* we mean the words surrounding a word that can shed light on its meaning.

Studies done on the teaching of word meanings seem to show that students learn unfamiliar words best when the new word is presented in a meaningful, familiar context so that the learner can see how the word is used, as well as when the word is used. The student can then assimilate the new information into his or her existing schemata or categories. The ability to relate the word to what is already known aids the learner in retaining the word's meaning.[4]

Teachers should make a concerted effort to help students learn the various types of context clues that writers and speakers use. One way to do this is for teachers to present their students with many written and oral sentences and then to challenge them to determine the meanings of some of the key words in the sentences. Teachers should try to elicit from their students how they figured out the word meanings. After a discussion of the various tactics that the students used, teachers could share with their students information about context clues. The sections that follow should help language arts teachers to become more adept in directly teaching context clues to their students.

Context Clues

1. If a writer or speaker wants to ascertain that the reader or listener will get the meaning of a key word, he or she will define, explain, or describe the word in the same sentence or in a following one. For example, in the preceding section, the word *context* has been defined because it is a key word in the section. In the following example the writer or speaker actually gives us the definition of a word. You should help students to recognize that sentences such as this are generally found in textbooks.

[4]Joan Gipe, "Investigating Techniques for Teaching Word Meanings," *Reading Research Quarterly* 14:4 (1978–1979): 624–644.

Example

The pictures in your mind formed by the words in the poem are called *imagery*.

2. Notice how the writer in the next example gives the reader the meaning of two words by using synonyms (words similar in meaning to others). Notice also how this makes the writing more expressive and clear and avoids repetition.

Example

Ms. Brown had told her *constituents* to *trust* her; however, from the returns of the election, we can see that the *voters* obviously did not have *faith* in her.

3. In the next example, notice how the writer *describes* the word that he wants the reader to know.

Example

Jonathan Smith is a *diligent* young man who works from morning to night, but he never complains.

Special Notes

a. The word *or* may be used by the writer when he or she uses another word or words with a similar meaning. *Example:* Andrew felt ill after he had eaten rancid, or spoiled, butter.

b. The words *that is* and their abbreviation *i.e.* usually signal that an explanation will follow. *Example:* The human being is a biped, that is, an animal having only two feet. *Or,* The human being is a biped, i.e., an animal having only two feet.

4. Many times authors or speakers help us get the meaning of a word by giving us examples illustrating the use of the word. In the following sentence notice how the examples that the writer gives in her sentence help us determine the meaning of the word *illuminated*.

Example

The lantern *illuminated* the cave so well that we were able to see the crystal formations and even spiders crawling on the rocks.

(From the sentence you can determine that *illuminated* means "lit up.")

5. Another technique writers employ that can help us gain the meaning of a word is *comparison.* Comparison usually shows the similarities between persons, ideas, things, and so on. For example, in the following sentence notice how we can determine the meaning of *passive* through the writer's comparison of Paul to a bear in winter.

Example
Paul is as *passive* as a bear sleeping away the winter. (From the sentence you can determine that *passive* means "inactive.")

6. *Contrast* is another method writers use that can help the reader to figure out word meanings. Contrast is usually used to show the differences between persons, ideas, things, and so on. In the following sentence we can determine the meaning of *optimist* because we know that *optimist* is somehow the opposite of one "who is gloomy and expects the worst."

Example
My sister Marie is an *optimist,* but her boyfriend is one who is always gloomy and expects the worst to happen. (From the sentence you can determine that *optimist* means "one who expects the best" or "one who is cheerful.")

Special Notes
a. The writer may use the words *for example* or the abbreviation *e.g.* to signal that examples are to follow. *Example: Condiments,* e.g., pepper, salt, and mustard, make food taste better. (From the examples of condiments we can determine that condiments are seasonings.)
b. Many times such words as *but, yet, although, however,* and *rather than* signal that a contrast is being used. *Example:* My father thought he owned an *authentic* antique chest, but he was told recently that it was a fake. (From the sentence the reader can tell that *authentic* is the opposite of fake; therefore, *authentic* means "not false but genuine or real.")

Context Clues to Homographs

Many words that are spelled the same have different meanings. These words are called *homographs.* The meaning of a homograph is determined by the way the word is used in the sentence. For example, the term *run* has many different meanings. (One dictionary gives 134 meanings for *run.*) In the listed sentences, notice how *run's* placement in the sentence and context clues help readers figure out the meaning of each use.

1. Walk, don't *run.*
2. I have a *run* in my stocking.
3. Senator Jones said that he would not *run* for another term.
4. The trucker finished his *run* to Detroit.
5. She is going to *run* in a ten-mile race.
6. The play had a *run* of two years.

In Sentence 1 *run* means "go quickly by moving the legs more rapidly than at a walk."
In Sentence 2 *run* means "a tear or to cause stitches to unravel."
In Sentence 3 *run* means "be or campaign as a candidate for election."
In Sentence 4 *run* means "route."
In Sentence 5 *run* means "take part in a race."
In Sentence 6 *run* means "continuous course of performances."

From these examples, we can see that the way the word is used in the sentence will determine its meaning. As already stated, words that are spelled the same but have different meanings are called *homographs.* Some homographs are spelled the same but do not sound the same. For example, *refuse* means "trash," but it also means "to decline to accept." In the first sentence, *refuse* (ref' use) meaning "trash" is pronounced differently from *refuse* (re fuse') meaning "to decline to accept" in the second sentence. In reading, we can determine the meaning of *refuse* from context clues. For example:

1. During the garbage strike there were tons of uncollected *refuse* on the streets of the city.
2. I *refuse* to go along with you.

As already shown, readers should be able to grasp the meaning of homographs from the

THE BORN LOSER

© 1975 by NEA, Inc.

sentence context (the words surrounding a word that can shed light on its meaning). Here are some examples. Note the many uses of *capital* in the following sentences.

1. That is a *capital* idea.
2. Remember to begin each sentence with a *capital* letter.
3. The killing of a police officer is a *capital* offense in some states.
4. Albany is the *capital* of New York State.
5. In order to start a business, you need *capital*.

Each of the preceding sentences illustrates one meaning for *capital*.

In Sentence 1 *capital* means "excellent."
In Sentence 2 *capital* means "referring to a letter in writing that is an uppercase letter."
In Sentence 3 *capital* means "punishable by death."
In Sentence 4 *capital* means "the seat of government."
In Sentence 5 *capital* means "money or wealth."

Teachers must help students to be careful to use correctly those words with many meanings.

Special Note
Confusion may exist among the terms *homonym, homophone,* and *homograph* because some authors are using the more scientific or linguistic definition for the terms and others are using the more traditional definition. *Homonyms* have traditionally been defined as words that sound alike, are spelled differently, and have different meanings; for example, *red, read.* However, many linguists use the term *homophone* rather than homonym for this meaning. Linguists generally use the term *homonym* for words that are spelled the same, pronounced the same, but have different meanings; for example, *bat* (the mouselike-winged mammal) and *bat* (the name for a club used to hit a ball). *Bat* (baseball bat) and *bat* (animal) would traditionally be considered a homograph (words that are spelled the same but have different meanings), but linguists usually define *homographs* as words that are spelled the same but have *different pronunciations* and *different meanings;* for example, *lead* (dense metal) and *lead* (verb).

The teacher should be aware that different English textbooks may be defining the three terms somewhat differently and should be familiar with the various systems and definitions in use.

In this book the generic definition of *homograph* is used; that is, homographs are words that are spelled the same but have different meanings, and the words may or may not be pronounced the same.

CONNOTATIVE MEANINGS

Intermediate-grade-level children should begin to realize that when we speak or write we often rely more on the *connotative* meanings of words than on their *denotative* meaning to express our real position on the topic discussed. The connotative meaning of a word includes the denotative meaning, the direct, specific meaning of the word. The connotative meaning, however, also includes all *emotional senses* associated with the word. The connotative use of a word, therefore, involves an understanding of more than a simple definition. When you respect a word's connotative meanings, you will use the word precisely and effectively.

"Credulous" and "trusting" are two words that have a similar denotative meaning, "ready to believe or to have faith in." However, if you refer to someone as a "trusting person," you are saying he or she has the admirable trait of believing the best of someone or something. If you refer to the same person as "credulous," you are saying that he or she lacks judgment, that he or she foolishly believes anything. Although both words have the same denotative meaning, in their very different connotative senses one is complimentary and the other belittling or insulting. Connotative meanings are obviously vital to the art of saying the right thing the right way. Writers rely on connotative meanings all the time, especially when they want to influence their readers. Whether a word influences, positively ("trusting") or negatively ("credulous") makes a great difference to what is actually conveyed.

Many words also have different overtones or associations for different persons. For example, the term "mother" can elicit images of apple pie, warmth, love, and kindness for one, whereas for another it can mean beatings, hurt, shame, fear, and disillusionment.

Some words lend themselves more readily to emotional overtones or associations than others. For example, the term "home" can bring forth both good or bad associations based on the past experiences of the individual. However, the term "dwelling," which has the same specific definition as "home," does not bring forth the emotional overtones of "home."

Teachers can help their students recognize that a number of words have substitutes that more aptly express the meaning that an author wishes to communicate. Students can be challenged to come up with words that carry negative, positive, or neutral meanings. For example, a building that people live in could be a barn, a castle, or a dwelling.

COMPLETING ANALOGIES

Working with analogies, or word relationships, requires high-level thinking skills. Stu-

dents must have a good stock of vocabulary and the ability to see relationships. Students who have difficulty in classification will usually have difficulty working with analogies.

Some primary-grade-level children can begin to be exposed to simple analogies based on relationships with which they are familiar.[5] Analogies are relationships between words or ideas. In order to be able to make the best use of analogies or to complete an analogy statement or proportion, the children must know the meanings of the words and the relationship of the pair of words. For example: *Sad is to happy as good is to* _____ . Many primary-grade-level children know the meanings of *sad* and *happy* and that *sad* is the opposite of *happy*; they would, therefore, be able to complete the analogy statement or proportion with the correct word—*bad*.

Some of the relationships that words may have to one another are similar meanings, opposite meanings, classification, going from particular to general, going from general to particular, degree of intensity, specialized labels, characteristics, cause–effect, effect–cause, function, whole–part, ratio, and many more. The preceding relationships do not have to be memorized. Tell your students that they will gain clues to these from the pairs making up the analogies; that is, the words express the relationship. For example: "*pretty* is to *beautiful*"—the relationship is degree of intensity (the state of being stronger, greater, or more than); "*hot* is to *cold*"—the relationship is one of opposites; and "*car* is to *vehicle*"—the relationship is classification.

Special Notes

a. In the primary grades the term *word relationships* should be used with the students rather than *analogies*. You might want to introduce the term *analogy* to some of your highly able upper-primary-grade-level children and intermediate-grade-level children. Highly able children especially enjoy working with analogies.

[5]See Sister Josephine, C.S.J., "An Analogy Test for Preschool Children," *Education* (December 1965): 235–237.

b. In introducing some of the relationships that pairs of words can have to one another, you should, of course, use words that are in your student's listening capacity.

DEFINING WORD-PART TERMS

To help students use word parts as an aid to increasing vocabulary, we should define some terms. There are a great number of words in our language that combine with other words to form new words, for example, "grandfather" and "chairperson" (compound words). You may also combine a root (base) word with a letter or a group of letters, either at the beginning (prefix) or end (suffix) of the root word, to form a new, related word, for example, "replay" and "played." *Affix* is a term used to refer to either a prefix or a suffix.

In the words *replay* and *played, play* is a root or base, *re* is a prefix, and *ed* is a suffix. A *root* is the smallest unit of a word that can exist and retain its basic meaning. It cannot be subdivided any further. *Replay* is not a root word because it can be subdivided to *play*. *Play* is a root word because it cannot be divided further and still retain a meaning related to the root word.

Derivatives are combinations of root words with either prefixes or suffixes or both. *Combining forms* are usually defined as roots borrowed from another language that join together or that join with a prefix, a suffix, or both a prefix and a suffix to form a word. Many times the English combining form elements are derived from Greek and Latin roots. In some vocabulary books, in which the major emphasis is on vocabulary expansion rather than on the naming of word parts, *combining forms* are defined in a more general sense to include any word part that can join with another word or word part to form a word or a new word.[6] More will be said about word parts in upcoming sections. Special emphasis is given to the use of word parts for vocabulary expansion in the upcoming section dealing with intermediate-grade-level vocabulary skills.

---

[6]Dorothy Rubin, *Gaining Word Power* (New York: Macmillan, 1978); Dorothy Rubin, *Vocabulary Expansion I* (New York: Macmillan, 1982).

THE DICTIONARY AND VOCABULARY EXPANSION

Even though the dictionary is a necessary tool and one with which all students should be familiar, it should not be used as a crutch; that is, every time students meet a word whose meaning is unknown to them, they should first try to use their knowledge of combining forms and context clues to unlock the meaning. If these techniques do not help and the word is essential for understanding the passage, then they should look up the meaning.

Teachers should help their students to recognize that different dictionaries may use different pronunciation keys and to be on the lookout for this. The pronunciation key is composed of words with diacritical marks. To know how to pronounce a word in a particular dictionary, students must familiarize themselves with the pronunciation key in that dictionary. For example, look at the way that five different dictionaries present a few similar words in Table 9.1.

If your students had no knowledge of the pronunciation key of the specific dictionary, they would have had difficulty in pronouncing the word. Pronunciation guides are generally found at the beginning of dictionaries. Many dictionaries also have a simplified pronunciation key at the bottom of every page.

The Dictionary as a Tool in Vocabulary Expansion

Although children use picture dictionaries in the primary grades more as an aid to writing than in vocabulary expansion, if young readers discover the wonders of the dictionary they can enrich their vocabulary. Primary-grade picture dictionaries consist of words that are generally in the children's listening, speaking, and reading vocabularies. They consist of alphabetized lists of words with pictures and can serve as the children's first reference tool, helping them to unlock words on their own and making them more independent and self-reliant. The children can also learn multiple meanings from a picture dictionary, for example, when they see the word "saw" presented with two pictures representing a tool and the act of seeing.

In the intermediate grades dictionaries serve more varied purposes, and there is emphasis

TABLE 9.1 COMPARISON OF THE PRONUNCIATION OF THREE WORDS IN FIVE DIFFERENT DICTIONARIES.

Word	Webster's New Twentieth Century Dictionary	Webster's Third New International Dictionary	Random House Dictionary of the English Language	The American Heritage Dictionary of the English Language	Funk & Wagnalls Standard College Dictionary
1. coupon	cōu'pon	′k(y)ü, pän	ko͞o' pon	ko͞o' pŏn	ko͞o' pon
2. courage	cōur' āge	′kər· ij	kûr'ij	kûr'ij	kûr'ij
3. covet	cŏv' et	′kəvət	kuv'it	kŭv'it	kuv'it

on vocabulary expansion. Children delight in learning new words. If properly encouraged by the teacher, vocabulary expansion can become an exciting hunting expedition, where the unexplored terrain is the vast territory of words.

At any grade level teachers can show by their actions that they value the dictionary as an important tool. If a word seems to need clarification and if the student cannot figure out its meaning from context clues or combining forms, students should be asked to look it up in the dictionary. Although at times it may seem more expedient to simply supply the meaning, students should be encouraged to look it up for themselves. If pupils discover the meaning of the word on their own, they will be more apt to remember it.

In order to build a larger meaning vocabulary the teacher could use a number of motivating techniques to stimulate vocabulary expansion. Pupils can be encouraged to keep a paper bag attached to their desks in which they put index cards with words on one side and word meanings they have looked up on the other. Sometime during the day students can be encouraged to challenge one another, with one student calling out the meanings of a word and another student supplying the word. This technique should make the dictionary one of the students' most treasured possessions.

PRIMARY-GRADE-LEVEL VOCABULARY SKILLS

During or by the end of the kindergarten-primary years, children should have attained

concepts such as *over, under, big, little, the one before, the one after,* and so on (see "Concept Development in Primary Grades K–3" in Chapter 3). These children should recognize that many words have more than one meaning, that antonyms are word opposites, and that synonyms are words similar in meaning. They should be beginning to learn the meaning of some figures of speech and acquiring a vocabulary consciousness. Primary-grade children should also be increasing their vocabulary from literature and incorporating many of their new words in oral and written expression. Furthermore, they should be able to solve word riddles, figure out word meanings from context clues, look up a word in the dictionary, and begin to build words using word parts.

Vocabulary of the Senses

All children usually enjoy words that appeal to the senses. Young children especially enjoy the words that they can almost taste and feel when they say them because of their sounds. As preschoolers, they savored many words by repeating them very slowly over and over again; the sounds of the words were fun to say. Now, with primary-grade students, teachers can take advantage of children's delight in words that appeal to the senses by helping them develop a vocabulary of the senses.

A technique a teacher can use is to ask children to give a word for various animal sounds. For example, a cow "moos," a cat "meows," a dog "barks" or "bays," a sheep "baas," a chick "peeps," and a bull "bellows." Then a word can be given for the sounds of nature. For example, the wind "howls," the brook "babbles," the trees "rustle," and so on. This technique can be continued for the sense of sight, of touch, and so on.

Vocabulary of Sounds Activities

Activity 1   The students look at a number of pictures such as a teakettle, a bell, a cow, a rooster, a trumpet, an airplane getting ready for take off, and so on; and then they give the characteristic sound of each.

Activity 2   The children are given a number of phrases with a blank for each phrase. A list of words is written on the board. The teacher states each word. The children must choose a word from the word list that *best* describes the sound of the object in the phrase. Here is a sample of the activity:

Word List: whir, clink, slush, creak, hiss

Phrases

1. The _____ of the coin
2. The _____ of the propellers
3. The _____ of the door
4. The _____ of the teakettle
5. The _____ of the snow

Vocabulary of Feelings Activities

Activity 1   Discuss with children the meaning of *mood*. Have them look at pictures that show persons in various moods. Ask the children to describe the persons' expressions in the pictures, and then have them generate a number of words that they feel best portrays the person's mood. Here are examples of some words to describe persons' expressions or moods.

happy	stern	frightened
silly	mean	tired
glad	cheerful	relieved
angry	disappointed	sorry
confused	surprised	worried

Activity 2   Have students role-play certain moods, and then have the other students guess what the mood is.

Activity 3   Have students look through various magazines and cut out pictures that illustrate different moods. Have them also label each picture. Then have them write a sentence telling why they feel the person in the picture is in the mood he or she is in.

Developing Vocabulary from Literature

Teachers can use literature to help their students expand their vocabulary and concepts if they prepare their students for the reading experience and choose carefully the book. For example, before reading aloud a book or selection to children, the teacher should try to relate the book to the students' past experiences, present some key words to the students, and set purposes for the reading of the story. This type of readiness will prepare the children for the story and help them to get the most from it. During the story the teacher should encourage the children to interject comments and to make predictions about what they think will take place or happen next in the story. After the story is finished, the teacher should ask the students to give their feelings about the story and to tell what they liked or did not like about the story. The teacher could select some key phrases or sentences from the story and ask the children about these. Also, the teacher could use a number of speech-stimulating activities to encourage the children to discuss the story using many of the terms from the story.

Such activities help make students more active consumers of information and give them an opportunity to use words from the story. (See "A Rich Oral Program" in Chapter 17.) An especially good activity that encourages children to use story words involves the choosing of familiar books that have repetitive language. During the reading aloud of the story, the teacher pauses at some key points in the story, and the children chorus the repetitive section.

There are times, however, when the teacher does want to encourage children to listen carefully. For example, the teacher can encourage students to listen to him or her read aloud a story such as *Mike Mulligan and His Steam Shovel* so that they can state all the things that Mary Anne is able to do. By listening carefully, the children gain a better understanding of what a steam shovel can do. The type of book and teacher purposes will determine the amount of student interaction and careful listening.[7]

Building Vocabulary Using Word Parts

It is not too soon to begin in the primary grades to help children to learn about word parts such as prefixes, suffixes, and roots in order to expand their vocabulary. (See the section presented earlier in this chapter for an explanation of word-part terms.) Here are some activities that can be used with primary-grade-level children that use word parts.

Vocabulary Expansion Activities

Activity 1   Building Compound Words and Making Silly Sentences. The children are told that compounds are words that combine with other words to make new words. Two lists of words are given to the children. The children are told to combine words from both lists to make a new word. After they have combined the words to make a new word, they should make up a silly sentence. Here is a sample of this activity:

Words to Form Compound Words   *Compound Words*

grand	fish	_____
cow	room	_____
ear	mother	_____
crab	boy	_____
bed	drum	_____

Sample answers:
  1. ear + drum = eardrum. Have you ever seen an ear drum?
  2. crab + fish = crabfish. Have you ever seen a crab fish?

[7]See Dorothy Cohen's article "Word Meaning and the Literary Experience in Early Childhood" in *Elementary English* 46 (November 1969): 914–925, for a bibliography of excellent books that help children gain understandings of terms.

Activity 2   Fishy Compounds. Present the children with riddles such as the following, and tell them to see how many fish they can catch. Tell them also that each fish they catch must be a compound word.

1. What fish goes well with peanut butter?
2. What fish can you use as a weapon?
3. What fish is a color?
4. What fish brings light?

Answers:
  1. jellyfish 2. swordfish 3. bluefish
4. sunfish

If children work individually on the compound word activities, it would be a good idea to go over the answers together in a group so that interaction and discussion can further enhance vocabulary development, as well as clear up any confusion or questions.

Building Words Using Prefixes, Suffixes, and Roots

Prefixes	*Roots*	*Suffixes*
re—again, back	kind	er—one who
un—not	cook	y—having, full of

Activity 1   Challenge the children to make as many words as they can using various word parts. Have them add a number of their own word parts, and then have them put some of their words into sentences.

Activity 2   Have a child put a root word on the board. Then have another child add a prefix or suffix to the root word to make a new word.

Activity 3   Have children write a number of root words on slips of paper. Put these slips of paper in a large bag. Then have the children write a prefix or a suffix on a slip of paper. Each root word, prefix, and suffix should be on a separate slip of paper. Have the children pull out one slip of paper and make a word using the word part.

INTERMEDIATE-GRADE-LEVEL VOCABULARY SKILLS

During or by the end of the intermediate years, children should be using correctly many words that have more than one meaning, and they should be able to use synonyms and antonyms effectively in speaking and writing. They should be able to use context clues and word parts to figure out word meanings, as well as be gaining skill in acquiring the connotative meaning of words. Not only are these children able to work with analogies, solve word riddles, and build words using word parts, but they are continuing to acquire a vocabulary consciousness and increasing their vocabulary. Intermediate-grade-level students are more adept in categorizing things into more general or more specific categories, and they show that they enjoy using new words by incorporating them in their oral and written expression.

In the intermediate grades, students should be guided to a mastery of vocabulary. If they are fascinated by words, they generally want to know the longest word in the dictionary, and many enjoy pronouncing funny or nonsensical sounding words such as *supercalifragilisticexpialidocious*.

Vocabulary Expansion Instruction Using Word Parts

Vocabulary expansion instruction depends on the ability levels of students, their past experiences, and their interests. If they are curious about sea life and have an aquarium in the classroom, this could stimulate interest in such combining forms as *aqua* meaning "water," and *mare* meaning "sea." The combining form *aqua* could generate such terms as *aquaplane, aqueduct,* and *aquanaut.* Since *mare* means "sea," students could be given the term *aquamarine* to define. Knowing the combining forms *aqua* and *mare,* many will probably respond with "sea water." The English term actually means "bluish-green." The students can be challenged as to why the English definition of aquamarine is bluish-green.

A *terrarium* can stimulate discussion of words made up of the combining form *terra.*

When discussing the prefix *bi,* students should be encouraged to generate other words that also contain *bi,* such as *bicycle, binary, bilateral,* and so on. Other suggestions follow.

Write the words *biped* and *quadruped* in a column on the board, along with their meanings. These words should elicit guesses for groups of animals. The teacher could ask such questions as: "What do you think an animal that has eight arms or legs would be called?" "What about an animal with six feet?" And so on. When the animals are listed on the board, the students can be asked to look them up in the dictionary so that they can classify them.

The students can also try to discover the combining forms of the Roman calendar.[8]

Martius	Sextilis
Aprilis	September
Maius	October
Junius	November
Quintilis	December

(Students should discover that the last six months were named for the positions they occupy.)

Another set of words made from combining forms describing many-sided geometric figures (polygons) are:

3 sides	trigon
4 sides	tetragon
5 sides	pentagon
6 sides	hexagon
7 sides	septagon
8 sides	octagon

When presenting the combining forms *cardio, tele, graph,* and *gram,* place the following vocabulary words on the board:

cardiograph	telegraph
cardiogram	telegram

After students know that *cardio* means "heart" and *tele* means "from a distance," ask them to try to determine the meaning of *graph,* as used in *cardiograph* and *telegraph.* Have them try to figure out the meaning of *gram,* as used in *telegram* and *cardiogram.* Once students are able to define *graph* as an instrument or machine and *gram* as message, they will hardly ever confuse a *cardiograph* with a *cardiogram.*

---

[8]See Loraine Dun, "Increase Vocabulary with the Word Elements, Mono through Deca," *Elementary English* 47 (January 1970): 49–55.

When students are exposed to such activities, they become more sensitive to their language. They come to realize that words are made, that language is living and changing, and that as people develop new concepts they need new words to identify them. The words *astronaut* and *aquanaut* are good examples of words that came into being because of space and undersea exploration.

Students come to see the power of combining forms when they realize that, by knowing a few combining forms, they can unlock the meanings of many words. For example, by knowing a few combining forms, students can define correctly many terms used in the metric system, as well as other words. Here is a scenario to illustrate this.

SCENARIO:

The teacher, Ms. Johnson, tells her students that they will be studying the metric system. To help them learn many of the terms in the metric system, she will present a lesson on combining forms. Ms. Johnson explains to her students what combining forms are. She then asks them which is longer, a centimeter or a millimeter. She tells them that by knowing a few terms they could very easily answer a number of such questions. She presents the following list of combining forms to her students and asks them to memorize the combining forms and their meanings.

deca	ten
deci	tenth
cent, centi	hundred, hundredth
mill, milli	thousand, thousandth
kilo	thousand

Ms. Johnson also tells her students that *centi, milli,* and *deci* are usually used to designate "part of." Ms. Johnson asks the students if they think they have memorized the few combining forms. She gives them a little quiz in which she covers up the meanings and asks the students to write the meaning or meanings for each of the combining forms. She then covers up the combining forms and asks the students to write the combining forms.

Ms. Johnson then presents the combining form *meter*, explaining that the combining form *meter* means "to measure." The term *meter*, however, means a unit of length equal to approximately 39.37 inches in the metric system. Ms. Johnson then presents the following words to her students and asks them to try to write the meaning of each by using their knowledge of combining forms.

decameter	(10 meters)
decimeter	($\frac{1}{10}$ meter)
centimeter	($\frac{1}{100}$ meter)
millimeter	($\frac{1}{1000}$ meter)
kilometer	(1,000 meters)

After going over the meanings with her students, she puts a number of other words on the board and asks her students to try to figure out the meanings of the words by using their knowledge of combining forms.

decade	(10 years)
century	(100 years)

centennial(100th anniversary; pertaining to a period of 100 years)
million   (1,000,000)
decimate (to destroy one tenth of)

Ms. Johnson tells her students that all through the term she will be presenting combining forms to them to help them expand their vocabulary and to help them to read their mathematics and other content-area books better.

Ms. Johnson was true to her word. Here are examples of some other combining forms and words derived from them that she presented to her students:

poly = many	polygon = many-sided figure
gon = figure having (so many) sides	trigon = three-sided figure
tri = three	tetragon = four-sided figure
tetra = four	pentagon = five-sided figure
penta = five	hexagon = six-sided figure
hexa = six	septagon = seven-sided figure
septa = seven	octagon = eight-sided figure
octa = eight	symmetrical = same
sym = same	equivalent = equal
equi = equal	

Also, throughout the term, Ms. Johnson would continuously remind her students that the combining forms she was presenting to them were only a base; that is, they were a springboard for them to build on. She would often challenge her students to find other words that use the same combining forms and to add to their list of combining forms. Each week she would request students to bring in two new combining forms and challenge classmates to give their meanings.

Ms. Johnson was also very careful to caution her students that many times the literal definitions of the prefixes, suffixes, or combining forms may not be exactly the same as the dictionary meaning. For example, *automobile*. An *automobile* refers to a four-wheeled vehicle, whereas the literal translation of its combining forms is "self-moving."

Vocabulary Expansion Instruction for Students Weak in Vocabulary

Working with students who are especially weak in vocabulary requires a relatively structured approach, one that emphasizes the systematic presentation of material at graduated levels of difficulty in ways somewhat similar to those used in the teaching of English as a second language. Each day roots, combining forms, prefixes, and suffixes should be presented with a list of words composed from these word parts. Emphasis is placed on the meanings of the word parts and their combinations into words rather than on the naming of the word parts. For example, *bi* and *ped* are pronounced and put on the chalkboard. Their meanings are given. When *biped* is put on the board, the students are asked by the teacher if they can state its meaning.

The terms presented for study should be those that students will hear in school, on television, or on radio, as well as those they will meet in their reading. The word parts should be presented in an interesting manner, and those that combine to form a number of words should be given. When students see that they are meeting these words in their reading, they will be greatly reinforced in their learning.

To provide continuous reinforcement, daily "nonthreatening" quizzes on the previous day's words may be given. Students should receive the results of such quizzes immediately, so that any faulty concepts may be quickly corrected. The number of words that are presented would depend on individual students.

The possibilities for vocabulary experiences in the classroom are unlimited. Teachers must have the prefixes, suffixes, and combining forms at their fingertips in order to take advantage of the opportunities that present themselves daily. Table 9.2 provides a list of some often used word parts and vocabulary words derived from these word parts.

Vocabulary Expansion Activities

Activity 1   Silly Compounds. The students are given a number of sentences with clues, and they are told that the answer to the clue is a compound word. Here are some samples.

1. The first nut is combined with a girl's name. (hazelnut)
2. The second nut is combined with a tree. (beechnut)
3. The first foot is combined with something you write. (footnote)
4. The second foot is combined with the antonym of *dark*. (footlight.)
5. The first head is combined with something that makes things bright. (headlight)
6. The second head is combined with a throughfare. (headway)

Activity 2   Building Vocabulary. The teacher presents the students with a number of combining forms with their meanings, as well as a number of words derived from these combining forms and sentences that have blanks. The students have to figure out which words fit the blanks.

TABLE 9.2.   SOME OFTEN-USED WORD PARTS AND VOCABULARY DERIVED FROM THEM

Prefixes	Combining Forms	Vocabulary Words
a—without	anthropo—humanity or human	anthropology, apodal
ante—before	astro—star	astronomy, astrology
arch—main, chief	audio—hearing	audiology, auditory, audition, audible
bi—two	auto—self	automatic, autocracy, binary, biped
cata—down	bene—good	benefit, catalog
circum—around	bio—life	biology, biography, autobiography
hyper—excessive	chrono—time	chronological, hypertension
hypo—under	cosmo—world	microcosm, cosmology
in—not	gamy—marriage	monogamy, bigamy, polygamy
inter—between, among	geo—earth	interdepartmental, geology
mis—wrong, bad	gram—written or drawn	telegram, mistake
mono—one, alone	graph—written or drawn, instrument	telegraph, monarchy
post—after	logo—speak	theology, logical, catalog
pre—before	macro—large	macrocosm, macron, preface
re—backward, again	micro—small	microscope, transatlantic
trans—across	mis—hate	misanthrope, misogynist
	poly—many	polyglot
	retro—backward	retrorocket
Suffixes		
able—able to	scope—instrument for seeing	microscope
ible—able to	phobia—fear	monophobia
ology—the study of	theo—god	theocracy
tion—the act of	pseudo—false	pseudoscience

Activity 3 Homographs (Words with Many Meanings). The teacher presents the students with a number of sentences that have blanks. The students have to insert a word that is spelled the same but has different meanings that would fit all the blanks of the sentence and make sense. Here are some samples.

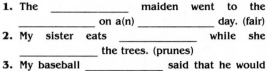

1. The _____ maiden went to the _____ on a(n) _____ day. (fair)
2. My sister eats _____ while she _____ the trees. (prunes)
3. My baseball _____ said that he would _____ me in math while we were riding in the _____ . (coach)

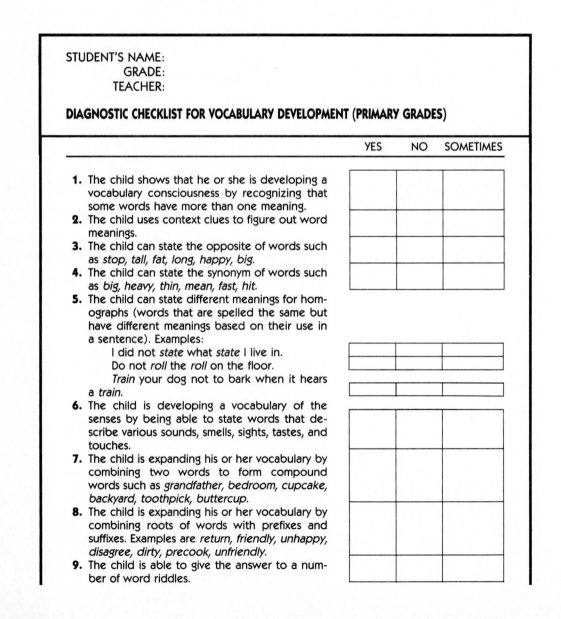

STUDENT'S NAME:
       GRADE:
     TEACHER:

DIAGNOSTIC CHECKLIST FOR VOCABULARY DEVELOPMENT (PRIMARY GRADES)

	YES	NO	SOMETIMES
1. The child shows that he or she is developing a vocabulary consciousness by recognizing that some words have more than one meaning.			
2. The child uses context clues to figure out word meanings.			
3. The child can state the opposite of words such as *stop, tall, fat, long, happy, big.*			
4. The child can state the synonym of words such as *big, heavy, thin, mean, fast, hit.*			

5. The child can state different meanings for homographs (words that are spelled the same but have different meanings based on their use in a sentence). Examples:
    I did not *state* what *state* I live in.
    Do not *roll* the *roll* on the floor.
    Train your dog not to bark when it hears a *train.*			

6. The child is developing a vocabulary of the senses by being able to state words that describe various sounds, smells, sights, tastes, and touches.			
7. The child is expanding his or her vocabulary by combining two words to form compound words such as *grandfather, bedroom, cupcake, backyard, toothpick, buttercup.*			
8. The child is expanding his or her vocabulary by combining roots of words with prefixes and suffixes. Examples are *return, friendly, unhappy, disagree, dirty, precook, unfriendly.*			
9. The child is able to give the answer to a number of word riddles.			

10. The child is able to make up a number of word riddles.
11. The child is able to classify various objects such as fruits, animals, colors, pets, and so on.
12. The child is able to give words that are associated with certain objects and ideas. Example: hospital—*nurse, doctor, beds, sick persons, medicine,* and so on.
13. The child is able to complete some analogy proportions such as *Happy* is to *sad* as *fat* is to _____.

14. The child shows that he or she is developing a vocabulary consciousness by using the dictionary to look up unknown words.

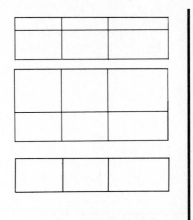

STUDENT'S NAME:
GRADE:
TEACHER:

DIAGNOSTIC CHECKLIST FOR VOCABULARY DEVELOPMENT (INTERMEDIATE GRADES)

	YES	NO	SOMETIMES
1. The student recognizes that many words have more than one meaning.			
2. The student uses context clues to figure out the meanings.			
3. The student can give synonyms for words such as *similar, secluded, passive, brief, old, cryptic, anxious.*			
4. The student can give antonyms for words such as *prior, most, less, best, optimist, rash, humble, content.*			
5. The student can state different meanings for homographs (words that are spelled the same but have different meanings based on their use in a sentence). Examples: It is against the law to *litter* the streets. The man was placed on the *litter* in the ambulance. My dog gave birth to a *litter* of puppies.			
6. The student is able to use word parts to figure out the word meanings.			
7. The student is able to use word parts to build words.			
8. The student is able to complete analogy statements or proportions.			

9. The student is able to give the connotative meaning of a number of words.
10. The student is able to work with word categories.
11. The student is able to answer a number of word riddles.
12. The student is able to make up a number of word riddles.
13. The student uses the dictionary to find word meanings.
14. The child shows that he or she is developing a vocabulary consciousness by using the dictionary to look up unknown words.

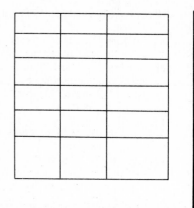

SUMMARY

Vocabulary development is an essential part of the language arts program because the more words students have in their listening capacity, the better speakers, listeners, readers, and writers they have the ability to be. Concept development and language development are interrelated, so students who are more advanced in language are also usually more advanced in concept development. This chapter is concerned with helping teachers acquire information about the importance of vocabulary development and how they can help students to expand their vocabularies. The role of the language arts teacher in vocabulary development is explored; emphasis is given to individual differences, and it is stressed that teachers can help students acquire a vocabulary consciousness by helping students' acquire the tools they need. As a result, the various ways that students use to determine word meanings and expand vocabulary are explored. Context clues are explained, and examples of different types are given. Combining forms are also explained and given as a viable approach to help students figure out word meanings and expand their vocabulary. Although a number of word-recognition strategies are presented, the emphasis in this chapter is on those related to word meaning and vocabulary expansion. Special sections are presented on primary-grade-level and intermediate-grade-level vocabulary skills and activities, including a diagnostic checklist for each level.

As a further aid, two examples of vocabulary lesson plans follow. Using these as a guide, see if you can construct a third one.

LESSON PLAN 1:   LOWER-PRIMARY-GRADE LEVEL

OBJECTIVES

1. The children will be able to give words that best describe the sense of touch portrayed in a number of presented pictures.
2. The children will be able to give the opposites of words relating to touch.
3. The children will be able to state words to fit the blanks of sentences read aloud by the teacher.

PRELIMINARY PREPARATION

1. Pictures depicting the sense of touch
2. Two pictures—one portraying a small clown carrot and the other showing a large clown carrot
3. A rose in a vase
4. Sentences to be read aloud by the teacher:
   a. The sandpaper feels very _____ .
   b. The cactus plant feels very _____ .
   c. The chalkboard feels very _____ .

INTRODUCTION

"Let's review some of the things we've been working with. We've been working with words that sound just like the sound they make. Who can give me some of them? Good, I like *plunk, clang, plop, clink,* and *gobble.* We've been working with our five senses. What are they? Very good. Sight, touch, smell, hearing, and taste. We've also been working with words that are opposites. Look at this picture. What do you see? Yes, a very big carrot dressed like a clown. Look at this picture. What do you see? Good, a very little carrot dressed like a clown. What is different about these two pictures? Good, in one the clown carrot is little, and in the other the clown carrot is big. What do we call these words? Yes, opposites. Today we will put together some of the things we've been working with. We will combine opposites with the sense of touch."

DEVELOPMENT

"Let's look at this picture. What do you see? Yes, a little girl falling off her tricycle. Do you think the little girl hurt herself? Yes, she probably did. How do you know this? Good, because she is riding on the sidewalk. How do you think the sidewalk feels? Yes, *rough, scratchy,* and *hard.* I'll put these words on the board. Now, let's look at this picture. What do you see? Yes, a little boy who fell on the grass. Do you think the little boy hurt himself? I agree, he probably didn't. Why not? Very good, because the grass is *soft.* I'll put the word *soft* on the chalkboard. Let's look at these two pictures. What do you see? Yes, one picture shows a girl riding her bicycle on a bumpy road, and another picture shows a boy riding his bicycle on a smooth road. Which is easier to ride on? I agree. Let's put the words *smooth* and *bumpy* on the board."

The teacher then picks up the vase on her desk, which contains a rose with thorns. She asks some children to touch the petals very, very gently and then to tell how they feel. She writes what they say on the board. She asks some other children to touch the stem with thorns gently and to say how that feels. She writes what they say on the board.

The teacher repeats all the words on the board. She asks the children to give her words that are opposites. After this, she reads aloud the three sentences with a missing word. She asks the children to supply a word that would make sense in the sentence. A number of words could fit. The word does not have to be one from the board.

SUMMARY

The teacher elicits from the students what they did today. She helps them to pull the main points of the lesson together. She then tells them that tomorrow they will be working with sense words that have to do with smell.

LESSON PLAN II: INTERMEDIATE-GRADE LEVEL

OBJECTIVES

1. Students will be able to use pantomime to act out the meanings of words.

2. Students will be able to use the pantomime clues to figure out the words and give at least one synonym for the word.

PRELIMINARY PREPARATION

Slips of paper with words written on them, such as *haughty, modest, exhausted, famished, content, aggressive,* and *dictator* are in a small box on a table.

INTRODUCTION

"Today we're going to work with pantomime in a special way. First, let's review some of the things we said about pantomime. Yes, we try to communicate without talking. We let our bodies speak for us. Let's try a few pantomimes just to warm up. I'd like you to think that you are different machines. Don't tell us which ones. We'll try to guess from your movements." The teacher calls on individual children to pantomime a machine. Other students try to guess what the machine is. After a few of these pantomimes, the teacher says, "We've worked with pantomime, and we've worked with expanding our vocabulary. Today we're going to combine vocabulary and pantomime."

DEVELOPMENT

The teacher tells the students that he or she has chosen some of the words that they have worked with and that each has been written on a slip of paper. The teacher then says that the class will be divided into groups, and a person from each group will choose a slip of paper and try to get his or her teammates to guess the word written on the paper. After the word has been guessed, the team must come up with at least one synonym or antonym for the word. The teacher also tells the students that he or she will keep time.

The students divide into groups of five. The teacher tells the groups to take a few moments to decide on the order in which they want to go. The teacher also tells everyone to watch very carefully because if the group doesn't guess the word, any of the other groups can have a chance to guess the word.

The teacher asks the students if they have decided on the order. They say that they have. The teacher then asks which group would like to start. He or she chooses a group and tells the first student to choose a slip from the box. The game proceeds until all the groups have had at least one or two chances.

After the game the teacher asks the students to write each of the words that they pantomimed in a sentence.

SUMMARY

The teacher helps the students to pull together the main points of the lesson. He or she tells them that tomorrow they will be working with words and their connotative meanings.

SUGGESTIONS FOR THOUGHT QUESTIONS AND ACTIVITIES

1. You have been asked to give a talk to your colleagues concerning the importance of vocabulary development in the elementary grades. What will you say?

2. You have been asked about developing a special vocabulary course for upper-elementary-level students using a combining forms approach. How do you feel about this? What will you say?

3. Develop some creative vocabulary activities for primary-grade-level children.

4. Develop some creative vocabulary activities for intermediate-grade-level children.

5. What combining forms would you choose to present to children in fifth grade? How would you go about making your decision concerning which to present? What kinds of activities would you provide? How would you present the combining forms?

6. How would you help children to acquire a vocabulary consciousness?

SELECTED BIBLIOGRAPHY

Beck, Isabel L., and Margaret G. McKeown. "Learning Words Well—A Program to Enhance Vocabulary and Comprehension." *Reading Teacher* 36 (March 1983) : 622–625.

Burke, Eileen M. "Using Trade Books to Intrigue Children with Words." *Reading Teacher* 32 (November 1978): 144–48.

Mattleman, Marciene S., and Herman Mattleman. *Expanding Language Skills.* Portland, Me: J. Weston Walch, 1981.

Mayher, John S., and Rita S. Brause. "Learning Through Teaching: Teaching and Learning Vocabulary." *Language Arts* 60 (November–December 1983) : 1008–1016.

Rubin, Dorothy. *Gaining Word Power.* New York: Macmillan, 1978.

———. *The Teacher's Handbook of Reading/Thinking Exercises.* New York: Holt, Rinehart and Winston, 1980.

———. "Developing Vocabulary Skills." In *The Primary-Grade Teacher's Language Arts Handbook.* New York: Holt, Rinehart and Winston, 1980.

———. "Developing Vocabulary Skills." In *The Intermediate-Grade Teacher's Language Arts Handbook.* New York: Holt, Rinehart and Winston, 1980.

———. *The Teacher's Handbook of Primary-Grade Reading/Thinking Exercises.* New York: Holt, Rinehart and Winston, 1982.

———. *Vocabulary Expansion I.* New York: Macmillan, 1982.

———. *Vocabulary Expansion II.* New York: Macmillan, 1982.

TEN

Creative Communication through Children's Literature

There is no frigate like a book
  To take us lands away,
Nor any coursers like a page
  Of prancing poetry.
This traverse may the poorest take
  Without oppress of toll;
How frugal is the chariot
  That bears a human soul!

Emily Dickinson

STUDENT: Today I am a princess, tomorrow a scientist, and the next day an astronaut. I don't know what I will be next week. It depends on which book I choose to read.

A good literature program should provide for the varying interests of students at all grade and ability levels. It should help to bring joy, delight, and hope to children. A book is "good" only if children enjoy it; if it helps children to broaden their views, to better understand themselves and their emotions. A good book satisfies intellectual hunger and helps children to awaken to the intelligent love of the beautiful, which is esthetic appreciation. Literature provides students with a limitless fertile terrain of vicarious experiences; it is so rich a source of both information and meaningful insights, that its role in the language arts must be examined in considerable depth.

The relationship of literature to the language arts areas is a very close and important one. An adequate foundation in the areas of listening, speaking, and learning to read should manifest itself in the children's literature program in that children will voluntarily choose to read books, and teachers will be more successful in generating enthusiasm, excitement, and love for books. The more vicarious experiences children have through books, the more they will converse and write, producing reinforcement in various language arts areas. Figure 10.1 is an

FIGURE 10.1 INTERACTIVE FEEDBACK LOOP MODEL

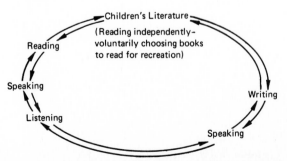

interactive feedback loop model that shows the reinforcement among some of the language arts areas through children's literature. The figure illustrates how literature acts as a stimulus for writing and reading, and how these, in turn, stimulate oral expression.

The children's literature chapter will include a number of topics that the elementary-school teacher will use in order to establish and maintain a good ongoing literature program for all students.

After you have finished reading this chapter you should be able to answer the following questions:

1. Are there many differences between children's and adults' books? Explain.
2. Should children be allowed to read the Hardy Boys and the Nancy Drew books? Explain.
3. How would you provide an atmosphere conducive to recreational reading in your classroom?
4. What are some techniques that will interest children in books?
5. How would you help children to select books?
6. What should you know about stereotyping in books?
7. What is bibliotherapy? Explain.
8. What kinds of books would you provide for the children in your classroom?
9. How can you provide for book sharing in the classroom?
10. What is the role of humor in children's books?
11. What are some of the current themes that interest children?
12. What should you know about the portrayal of the aged in books?
13. What is the place of book reporting in the children's literature program?
14. What is the place of poetry in the school program?
15. Are all children able to understand figures of speech? Explain.
16. What should you know about readability formulas?
17. What are some reference books that you could use as an aid in helping your students to choose books?
18. What library skills would you teach to primary- and intermediate-grade-level students?
19. What is the relationship between role modeling and reading?

BACKGROUND AND DEVELOPMENT OF CHILDREN'S LITERATURE

In the *Republic* Plato, the fifth-century B.C. Greek philosopher, asks: "What kind of education shall we give them all? We shall find it difficult to improve on the time-honored distinction between the training we give to the body and the training we give to the mind and character." Plato is discussing the kind of education that young children should receive in their first stage. He recommends using stories of two kinds, true stories and fiction. He also says:

We start to train the mind before the body. And the first step, as you know, is always what matters most, particularly when we are dealing with those who are young and tender. That is the time when they are taking shape and when any impression we choose to make leaves a permanent mark. Shall we, therefore, allow our children to listen to any stories written by anyone, and to form opinions the opposite of those we think they should have when they grow up? Then it seems that our first business is to supervise the production of stories, and choose only those we think suitable, and reject the rest. We shall persuade mothers and nurses to tell our chosen stories to their children and so mold their minds and characters rather than their bodies. The greater part of the stories current today we shall have to reject.[1]

Plato lists explicit kinds of stories that should be rejected, such as those that misrepresent gods and heroes. He would also forbid those in which a father is mistreated by his son, nor would he permit stories of wars and plots and battles among gods. Thus, concern about children's reading matter dates back to antiquity.

Plato realized that the early years of childhood are very important in that what children are exposed to will greatly influence their later life. Plato's ideas were only a utopian dream, however.

Not much was actually done concerning children's literature until the second half of the eighteenth century. During this period, children recited "poetry" such as:

> Yes, I was ever born in sin.
> And all my heart is bad within.

[1]Plato, *Republic*, trans. H. D. P. Lee (Baltimore: Penguin, 1961).

Children at this time were treated as miniature adults, and this included the selection of their reading material. Even Shakespeare, whose range of views was so wide, seldom makes use of love of children as a motive. When he does introduce children into one of his plays, he makes them precocious and priggish—children playing at being grown-ups.

In the eighteenth century a number of educational philosophers became interested in the child. As a result, some literature was written specifically for children to both interest and instruct them. It wasn't until the end of the eighteenth and the beginning of the nineteenth centuries, however, that literary standards for children's literature began to emerge.

Today the pendulum has swung far in the other direction:

Many of my readers seem amazed by the fact that I began to write for children in my late years. The desire to create for them usually manifests itself when the writer is still young himself, not far removed from his own childhood. I was driven to it by deep disenchantment in the literary atmosphere of our epoch. I have convinced myself that while adult literature, especially fiction, is deteriorating, the literature for children is gaining in quality and stature. The child, which until the middle of the 19th century was nothing but a passive and uncritical listener of stories that tired mothers and nannies improvised at his bedside, in our time has become a consumer of great growing literature—a reader who cannot be deluded by literary fads and barren experiments. No writer can bribe his way to the child's attention with false originality, literary puns and puzzles, arbitrary distortions of the order of things, or muddy streams of consciousness which often reveal nothing but a writer's boring and selfish personality. I came to the child because I see in him a last refuge from a literature gone berserk and ready for suicide.[2]

DIFFERENCES BETWEEN CHILDREN'S AND ADULTS' BOOKS

What differentiates children's literature from adult literature? Some persons claim that there

is no difference. P. L. Travers has said, "There is no such thing as a children's book. There are simply books of many kinds, and some of them children read."[3] According to Natalie Babbitt, an author of children's books, although everyone can tell a child's book from one for adults, the difficulty lies in discerning the essential nature of the difference. Babbitt does not believe that books for adults are serious while books for children tend to amuse, and she cites *Winnie-the-Pooh, Wind in the Willows,* and *How the Grinch Stole Christmas* as books read by people of all ages who find them both serious in intent and entertaining. Children's books deal with emotions, just as adult books do—love, hate, pride, fear of death, violence, and grief. Among them *Sleeping Beauty, Wind in the Willows,* and *Heidi* all deal with love. *Toad of Toad Hall* is concerned with pride; and *The Yearling* expresses grief. *Charlotte's Web* is unforgettable in its approach to dying and death. *Ali Baba* and *Jack and the Giant Killer* deal with violence.

Babbitt claims that the one emotional theme found in children's literature that is not found in adult literature is that of joy, and children's books generally have a "happy ending." She claims that this applies especially to those we remember the longest.[4] The "happy or satisfying ending" is closely related to "hope"—no matter how unpromising the circumstances, it is not too late. We must all hope, and for children, hope is a part of life.

A distinctive children's literature has a uniqueness which relates to the nature of children. The individual works are literary, however, and it must remain the responsibility of the critics . . . to preserve both those qualities which are literary and those which are childlike. It is also their responsibility to insist that there is no place in children's literature for the condescending, the childish, or the unliterary.[5]

[2]Isaac Bashevis Singer, "Children's Books," *New York Times Book Review* (November 9, 1969).

[3]Natalie Babbitt, "Children's Books," *New York Times Book Review* (November 8, 1970).
[4]Ibid.
[5]Betty M. Brett and Charlotte S. Huck, "Research Update: Children's Literature—The Search for Excellence," *Language Arts* 59 (November–December 1982): 882.

WHAT IS READING FOR APPRECIATION?

Webster's New Collegiate Dictionary defines appreciation as "1 a: sensitive awareness; especially the recognition of aesthetic values; b: judgment, evaluation: especially a favorable critical estimate; c: an expression of admiration, approval, or gratitude; 2: increase in value." When we talk about reading appreciation, we usually are talking about sensitive awareness, especially the recognition of aesthetic values. The emphasis in appreciative reading is usually completely on enjoyment. *Appreciative reading* in this book is defined as reading to derive pleasure and enjoyment from books that fit some mood, feeling, or interest.

Some persons feel that an individual cannot attain "appreciation" unless he or she has a complete understanding at the highest level of what is being read. For these persons, reading for appreciation would be at the highest level in a hierarchy of reading. In this book, however, appreciative reading is regarded as a separate domain with a hierarchy of its own. It is, therefore, possible for an individual to gain appreciation for a piece of literature even though he or she does not have a complete understanding of it. According to this, a poem can be enjoyed because of its delightful sounds, rhythm, or language, even though it is not understood. Of course, the greater the understanding, the higher the appreciation, but appreciation is still possible without complete understanding at various lower levels.

IMPORTANCE OF PROVIDING TIME FOR A READING-FOR-APPRECIATION PROGRAM

Every good reading program must have a component dedicated to appreciative reading. Learning to read and reading to learn are important parts of any reading program, but appreciative reading is what determines whether persons will read and continue to read throughout their lives. If children develop an appreciation of books at an early age, it will be more difficult for other activities and media to compete. One important factor is the decision to have a reading-for-appreciation program. Many educators give lip service to the appreciation component of the reading program, but they do not

implement it. The only way educators can show they value this program is to set aside time for it. In doing this, there is a chance for success.

Young people have to contend with many enjoyable activities that compete for their time and attention; reading for pleasure is often given a low priority in the competitive battle. By setting time aside during the school day for reading for enjoyment, educators would be giving students a chance to whet their appetites for books. What is especially encouraging is that the Drop Everything and Read Program (DEAR) seems to be sweeping the country. Many school systems have initiated DEAR in their schools, and the response to it has been excellent. DEAR is a very simple program to institute, but it needs the backing and commitment of *all* school personnel for it to work. Certain times during the week are set aside when *all persons* in the school system drop everything and read. (*Sustained Silent Reading* [SSR] rather than *DEAR* is the more familiar phrase used for practice in independent silent reading. The original phrase was Uninterrupted Sustained Silent Reading [USSR].)

DEAR or SSR requires that teachers follow certain rules:

1. Each student must read.
2. The teacher must read at the same time that the students read.
3. Students read for a specified time period.
4. Students are not responsible for any reports on what they have read, and no records are kept of what students have read.
5. Students choose any reading material that they like.[6]

SSR is obviously easier to initiate in the elementary grades than in the upper grades; however, it can be practiced in the upper grades if teachers are committed to the importance of having students engage in independent silent reading and if proper provisions are made so that it fits smoothly into the content program. The idea of having a bell ring and everyone from the superintendent to the custo-

[6]Adapted from Robert A. McCracken, "Initiating Sustained Silent Reading," *Journal of Reading* (May 1971): 521–524, 582.

FIGURE 10.2   FITTING THE BOOK TO THE CHILD AND GETTING THE CHILD TO OPEN THE BOOK HELPS "HOOK" THE CHILD ON BOOKS.

dian Drop Everything and Read (DEAR) is intriguing and may work in some school systems; however, common sense dictates that this can cause some difficulties. For example, what if a student in a science class is in the middle of dissecting a frog or involved in a very intricate experiment? What if a student in an art class is in the middle of a project that demands immediate attention? What if a student is in the midst of solving a very complicated problem that requires extensive concentration? What should these students do? The bell to drop everything and read may prove very frustrating for these individuals. Also, what if these students are in a special classroom or laboratory? They may be able and willing to drop everything and read, but the facilities may not be conducive to reading.[7]

DEAR or SSR is an excellent idea, but the program can work only if, as stated earlier, *all* teachers are committed to making it work. Content-area teachers should be involved in plan-

ning when the period for SSR should take place in their classes, and they should provide many types of reading matter for their students. Of course, even if a school system or individual school is not committed to having an SSR program, any individual teacher can initiate and implement one in his or her own class.

ROLE MODELING AND READING

When the character Fonze of the television series "Happy Days" took out a library card in a particular episode, librarians across the country were swamped with requests for library cards by persons who had never had one before. An analysis of the results of young children's watching "Sesame Street" found that a significant number of children who watched "Sesame Street" entered school with prolearning and proreading attitudes even though the attainment of these attitudes was not the objective of the program.[8] It has been hypothesized that be-

---

[7]Marilyn Joy Minton, "The Effect of Sustained Silent Reading upon Comprehension and Attitudes among Ninth Graders," *Journal of Reading* (March 1980): 502.

[8]Pamela M. Almeida, "Children's Television and the Modeling of Proreading Behaviors," in *Television and Education*, Chester M. Pierce, ed., (Beverly Hills: Sage Press, 1978), pp. 56–61.

cause children like to watch other children on television, "peer role-modeling of reading behaviors could motivate and reinforce positive attitudes toward reading."[9]

Teachers at all grade levels who are enthusiastic about books and portray this enthusiasm to their students will infect their students with this enthusiasm. Some researchers reported in the literature how one junior-high-school teacher's habit of silently reading a newspaper for the first five minutes or so of his class stimulated other students in his class to model his behavior.[10] A teacher who is seen to be deeply immersed in a book during the lunch hour will also have a marked influence on students.

SETTING THE ENVIRONMENT FOR THE ENJOYMENT OF READING IN THE CLASSROOM

Teachers who are enthusiastic about books will infect their students with that enthusiasm. As already stated, a teacher obviously absorbed in reading will also have a marked influence on students. The teacher's responsibility does not end there, however. The teacher must set the stage, provide the materials, and plan with students for recreational reading.

First, the classroom must be an inviting place to read. It should be airy, light, and physically comfortable. The emphasis on books should be clearly visible. For example, bulletin boards should have recommended booklists at all interest and readability levels. Award-winning books, book jackets from a number of popular children's books, students' recommendations and evaluations of various books, as well as artwork depicting a scene or characters in books, should be on display.

Lots of books should be provided for the children at all interest and readability levels. (See "Criteria for Selecting Books" later in this chapter.) Newspapers, magazines, and other printed matter of interest to children should be available. Filmstrips, records, and films of favorite stories should also be kept handy for the children's use.

Next, a special place to read is necessary! A section or corner of the room should be readily accessible to all the students, where a few comfortable chairs, some large comfortable pillows, and a scatter rug are placed. This is the reading corner.

Now, time must be provided so that children can read. This book period is separate from the weekly visit to the library and is not dependent on whether children have free time only because they have finished all their "other work." Every day the teacher and children should plan for a book time, when the class just enjoys literature. After the teacher has helped students to choose their books and settle down, the teacher, too, should read.

WHETTING CHILDREN'S INTEREST IN BOOKS

"Daddy, read me a story, please."
"Mommy, tell me a story."
"Mommy, daddy, I want to tell you a story. Listen."

The secret of it all lies in the parents' reading aloud to and with the child.

E. B. Huey (1908)

The time spent by parents and children sharing books and stories is precious and never forgotten. Such reading activity brings parents and children together; it is an experience of love and warmth.

Those parents who spend time listening to their children and reading aloud to them are not only helping their children to be more proficient language users, but also starting their children on the road to becoming lifelong readers.

When children come to school, teachers should continue to whet children's interest in books by reading aloud. Studies have shown that such reading aloud helps prepare children for reading.[11] (See "A Rich Oral Program" in Chapter 17 and "Developing Vocabulary from Literature" in Chapter 9.)

During the week there are many opportunities for the teacher to read to students. Books

[9]Ibid., p. 59.

[10]Robert A. McCracken and Marlene J. McCracken, "Modeling Is the Key to Sustained Silent Reading," *Reading Teacher* (January 1978): 407.

[11]William H. Teale, "Parents Reading to Their Children: What We Know and Need to Know," *Language Arts* 58 (November–December 1981): 902–912.

that are chosen to be read in full to the children should be those that will interest all children. For example, one fifth-grade class loved Sherlock Holmes stories; however, the vocabulary was too difficult for a number of the students, even though the stories were at their interest level. Therefore, the teacher either used synonyms for difficult words or defined them. There are many such books in which the teacher can use word imagery to clarify the meanings of unfamiliar words. These techniques do not take away from the quality of the story as a story but, rather, enhance it.[12]

The teachers must read with expression. They should imagine themselves to be actors or actresses and literally "give it their all." If they are reading effectively, the teachers should have gained the complete attention of the students.

Children love to be told stories. For that matter so do adults. Storytelling is an art, and must be practiced to be effective. It is different from reading, and many teachers find this difficult and very time-consuming. Some schools have special librarians who are adept at storytelling. (See Chapter 7.)

Another technique that teachers can use to interest children in books is to have several students orally report on books that they have read and that they feel others would also enjoy. In presenting such reports students must explain why they enjoyed the books, tell about some of the exciting parts, but not give away the endings.

A technique children enjoy using to interest others in books is creative dramatics. A group of students who have read the same book can present skits highlighting exciting parts in the book. (See Chapter 7.)

One fifth-grade teacher sets time aside each day to read to her students. She chooses a book based on her students' maturation and general interest levels and reads a chapter or a certain number of pages each day. At the end of her reading, she usually asks her students what they think will happen next. After she has

finished reading the entire book, she asks her students whether they agree with the author's ending. After a discussion of the ending and the book, she usually asks her students to write either another ending or another adventure or episode for the main character in the book.

Another technique that this teacher uses is to have students share with the class a book that they especially liked. In doing this, she encourages the students to read aloud some special sections from the book.

CRITERIA FOR SELECTING BOOKS

There are a number of factors that should be considered in selecting books for children. Criteria concerned with knowledge of children and what they enjoy in a book include:

1. *Theme:* What the story is all about.
2. *Plot:* These grow out of good themes. Children like heroes and heroines who have obstacles to overcome, conflicts to settle, and difficult goals to win. (It is possible for the characters of a story to determine what direction a story will take and as a result influence the plot, but this is generally within the confines of the theme.)
3. *Characterization:* As children mature in their reading tastes, they go from enjoyment of tales of action with stereotyped characters to characters who are individual, unique, and memorable.
4. *Style:* A difficult quality to define, but its ab-

[12]*See* Dorothy H. Cohen, "Word Meaning and the Literary Experience in Early Childhood," *Elementary English* 46 (November 1969): 914–925, for a listing of books and examples.

sence is noticeable in books that are repetitious, boring, labored, and so on.

5. *Setting:* Concerns time and place of the story. It should enhance the plot, characters, and the theme of the story.

6. *Format:* Deals with the presentation of material, illustrations, quality of paper used, and binding. The illustrations should be attractive and pleasing to the eye as well as consistent with the story. The quality of the paper should not detract from the reading, and the print of the book should be appropriate for the reader.[13]

A book that hinders a child from finding his or her identity, which portrays the child in a stereotyped role, is a book that would be considered poor reading for all children.

When selecting books for a class library, teachers should try to put themselves in the position of their children and ask: How would I feel if I read this book? Would this book make me come back for another one? Will this book interest me? Are these books on many readability levels? Does the book portray the minority child as an individual? Are the minority adults protrayed in a nonchildlike manner? Are the characters supplied with traits and personalities that are positive? Are the minority individuals in various social positions?

If the answers are "yes," the teacher should choose the book. But even one "no" answer should make the teacher reexamine the book.

If we were to think of all the different racial, religious, and ethnic groups that live in the United States—such as Indian, Mexican, Spanish, French, black, and so on—many children would be considered to be culturally different. In the *good* literature books, minorities are not portrayed in a stereotyped fashion. They are presented sympathetically and with sensitivity.

Regardless of the group to which children belong, the books they read must help them to feel good about themselves. They must help children view themselves in a positive light, achieve a better self-concept, and give them a feeling of worth.

The importance of learning about other groups of people through literature is aptly expressed in the following:

I never felt the world-wide importance of the children's heritage in literature more than on a day when I stood with Mrs. Ben Zvi, wife of the [then] President of Israel, in the midst of the book boxes she had filled for the centers in Jerusalem where refugee boys and girls were gathered for storytelling and reading of the world's great classics for children. "We want our boys and girls to be at home with the other children of the world," she said, "and I know of no better way than through mutual enjoyment of the world's great stories."[14]

Good books can open doors through which can pass better understanding, mutual respect, trust, and the hope of people living together in harmony and peace.

Avoiding Sex Stereotyping

Change in sex stereotyping of females in books started to become more evident in the early 1970s. For example, the 1973 Caldecott award went to *The Funny Little Woman* by Arlene Mosel, which concerns an inventive Japanese woman who outwits the gods. The Newbery award-winner, *Julie of the Wolves,* by Jean George, concerns a 13-year-old Eskimo girl who, married to a simpleton, escapes and with resourcefulness is able to survive by making friends with a pack of wolves. In both books initiative and independence are shown as virtues in females even though they are traits traditionally rewarded in males and so portrayed.

Since the 1960s, science-fiction books, which were usually considered in the male domain, have tended to be oriented toward both sexes, where both males and females play central roles. Some books in this category are Madeleine L'Engle's *A Wrinkle in Time,* Robert O'Brien's *The Silver Crown,* Patricia Wrightson's *Down to Earth,* and H. M. Hoover's *Rains of Eridan* and *The Delikon.*

In helping children choose books, the teacher should not differentiate between "male"

---

[13]Adapted from Charlotte Huck, Children's Literature in the *Elementary School,* 3d ed. updated (New York: Holt, Rinehart and Winston, 1979), pp. 6–14.

[14]Dora V. Smith, "Children's Literature Today," *Elementary English* 47 (October 1970): 778.

and "female" books. In fact, the teacher should not "push" any book on any child. Books at all interest levels should be made available randomly to all children. Teachers should, however, be aware that sex-preference research[15] suggests that boys and girls in grades 7, 9, and 11 prefer protagonists to be their own sex and that "boys' preferences for male protagonists became significantly stronger as grade level increased, whereas girls' preferences for female protagonists decreased significantly as grade level increased."[16]

Children's Interests

Every summer Jennifer visits her grandparents for a few weeks, and every summer for five consecutive summers she has gone to the library with her grandparents and has taken out a number of Madeline and Babar books. Jennifer loves them and she can read every one on her own, but she still loves to have her granny read them to her. Jennifer, who is seven years old, has been reading on her own since she was four years old. She loves to read. Watching her read is a delight because she giggles and laughs out loud at the funny parts, and she insists on reading some of the silly parts to the persons around her. Jennifer has found the joy of reading.

When you ask Jennifer why she likes the Madeline and Babar books, she tells you that they are fun to read, and there are more of them. It appears that many series books appeal to children because it is comforting for them to know that there are more of them after they have finished one book. When children fall in love with a character, they like to meet the character again and again in different situations. Also, if a book makes a child feel good, that child, like Jennifer, likes to read it over and over again to recapture the feeling.

In school, teachers have a responsibility to keep children's love of books alive, as well as to help spark others to want to read for pleasure. As already stated, one way to do this is for teachers to show that they value reading for pleasure by providing time for students to do independent reading. Another way is for teachers to care enough about their students to take the time to find out about their interests and concerns. The teacher must then use this information to provide a wide selection of books for his or her students so that they can choose their own books. (While studies have shown that students usually prefer to choose their own books for recreational reading,[17] teachers can still help children to explore the world of books available to them. See "Developing Children's Taste in Book Selection" later in this chapter.)

There are a number of ways that teachers can find out about students' interests. The simplest way is to ask them; that is, the teacher has the students fill out a form in which they state their interests or books they would like to have in their class library. A less direct way would be to have students complete incomplete sentences such as the following:

If I were stranded on an island, I would like to have the following book: ————————————.

I prefer to ——————— more than anything else.

Most reading-interest studies have been based on asking children what they would like to read rather than on what they actually read. A rare study was done on books actually borrowed from the library by children. In grades four through six these books were taken out in order of popularity: *Henry Huggins, Charlotte's Web, Mrs. Piggle Wiggle, Encyclopedia Brown, Homer Price, All-of-a-Kind-Family, The Black Stallion, The Tenggren Tell-It-Again Book, John Henry* (Keats), *The Red Balloon, Stuart Little, The Mouse on the Motorcycle, Dot for Short, Pinocchio,* and *Peter Pan* (abridged by Josette Frank.)[18]

It was also reported that jokes and riddles were in first place for nonfiction popularity. A reflection of the times was shown in the chil-

---

[15]Karen C. Beyard-Tyler and Howard J. Sullivan, "Adolescent Reading Preferences for Type of Theme and Sex of Character," *Reading Research Quarterly* XVI:1 (1980):104–120.

[16]Ibid., p. 104.

[17]Dixie Lee Spiegel, *Reading for Pleasure: Guidelines* (Newark, Del.: International Reading Association, 1981), p. 37.

[18]Donald J. Bisset, "Literature in the Classroom," *Elementary English* 50 (February 1973):235.

dren's choices of sport books—Judo and jujitsu were the favorites.[19]

Even though children continue to enjoy such classics as *Charlotte's Web*, the Madeline and Babar books, the Little Pear books, and so on, each decade there seems to be a certain genre of books that gains popularity. In the 1980s, it appears to be books about romance, divorce, puzzle books (such as the ones in which children create their own endings), self-help books, and science-fiction books.

Teachers should recognize that children generally have many interests and that often we tend to underestimate what they can do, as well as what they will respond to. For example, Northrop Frye, the eminent literary critic, states that "children can respond to tragedy and irony as well as to comedy and romance, and that children want difficulty; if they are practicing jumping over hurdles, they want the highest hurdle they can possibly get over, not a low one that they know they can manage."[20]

One area that teachers have not sufficiently exploited is children's sense of humor. Have you ever seen a child read something, start laughing hysterically, leave his or her seat, and bring over a friend to read what made him or her laugh? Didn't it make you feel like also going over to see what was so funny? Laughter is infectious, and it often helps us in troubled times. The point is that teachers should use children's delight in "funny" words and the way they sound, as well as knowledge of children's development of a sense of humor to interest students in books that would appeal to their funnybone. Teachers should also choose such books to read aloud. In this way, children will realize that the classroom is a place for laughter, not just "work."[21]

Children Like Nonfiction, Too

Teachers should capitalize on children's curiosity about the world around them to intro-

duce them to nonfiction. Interestingly, one way to do this is via fiction. When students are studying a particular subject area, the teacher should make available a number of books related to the topic under study. Fiction should "tease" the child's imagination so that he or she will want to find out more about what the author has written. Nonfiction should be at the students' reading ability levels and able to answer a number of the students' questions.

A unit on the life-cycle of a frog can be an excellent stimulus for encouraging reading and for introducing children to informational books. The unit activities help children gain the background they will need for reading informational books; the children learn the technical vocabulary they will meet in print, as well as a conceptional framework about the frog's life-cycle, and probably most important, they want to read more about the frog.[22] (See "Literature in Content-Area Classes" in Chapter 19.)

Readability and Interest Levels

There are usually one or two books that are very popular and make the rounds of almost all the children in the class. Although this book may be at the interest level of most of the children, it may not be at all of their reading ability levels. There are always a few children who feel left out because they can't read these books. They may take out the books and either walk around with them or make-believe that they are reading them. By having the book in their possession they may feel they can gain the esteem they need.

The teacher should not embarrass such students, but should carefully choose substitutes at their reading ability levels, to gain their interest. The teacher should speak individually to such a child and say, "I know how much you like books about heroes. Well, I was looking through this book the other day and I immediately thought of you. I just felt that you would enjoy this book." The teacher should then try to have the student read the first page. Once the child starts by reading the first page, the battle

---

[19]Ibid.

[20]Northrop Frye, "Foreword," in *The Child As Critic* by Glenna Davis Sloan, (New York: Teachers College Press, in press), p. xiv.

[21]See "The Sound of Literature: Laughter" in *Early Childhood Literature* by Eileen Burke (Boston: Allyn & Bacon, in press) for a discussion of humor in children's literature.

[22]Amy A. McClure, "Integrating Children's Fiction and Informational Literature in a Primary Reading Curriculum," *Reading Teacher* 35 (April 1982): 784–789.

is almost won. The student will usually continue because the book is at both his or her reading ability and interest levels.

The teacher should have an ample supply of books at various readability and interest levels. To aid teachers in obtaining a proper selection, they can consult the *Elementary School Library Collection*. This reference work gives estimates of children's interest levels and reading difficulties for all the books listed. Having such books available is the essential first part. The other part is helping students choose books based on both their interest and reading ability levels. Unfortunately, as has been shown, a book may be at a child's interest level, but the child may be unable to read it independently.

Readability formulas are used to determine the reading difficulty of written material. While most readability formulas are based on both sentence length and syllabication, some may also use word lists. Limitations exist, however. Readability formulas do not take other variables—such as children's experiential background, maturation, purpose of reading, and so on—into account. They also do not measure the abstractness of ideas nor the literary style nor quality of the written material. Readability formulas are also unreliable, since different formulas on similar material may not produce the same scores. When a readability formula produces a score of grade four, it does not mean that all fourth graders will be able to read the book because "one cannot assume that the formula will correctly predict how a particular reader will interact with a particular book."[23] Although readability formulas are imperfect tools, they do have value, for they give some idea of the difficulty of a book for specific groups of readers.

For example, *The Lion* by René DuBois would be of interest to preschool, kindergarten, and first-grade children. According to the Spache Readability formula for grades one to three, however, the book would be near the 3.5-grade level. This means it would have to be read to younger children. At the other end of the scale,

there may be students in upper grades with difficulty in reading, who may be at a reading level as low as preprimer. These students desperately need books at their interest levels. Fortunately, during the past decade, more books have been published with the high interest but low readability levels required by such students.

Regardless of which readability formula teachers use, they should be familiar with the methods for estimating readability. Teachers do not have to work out the exact estimates for each book, but by observing the sentence length and syllables, or sentence length and kinds of words, that is, the difficulty of the words used in a paragraph, they can estimate whether a book is at the proper level for their students to read independently. (See Appendix C for an example of a readability formula.)

Although it is difficult to completely ascertain what makes a book easy or hard, the following are "readability pluses" that parents, teachers, and librarians might look for in a book.

Readability is excitement. A punchy beginning. Forceful and colorful language. Variety in style, including both long and short sentences. A subject that appeals to the reader. Interesting pictures and other illustrations.

Readability is familiarity. Plain talk and an informal style, especially for readers with difficulty in standard English. The words and expressions of ordinary speech. The familiar sentence patterns of spoken language. Material that deals with something the reader knows about and has experience with. Unfamiliar ideas explained in terms of familiar ideas.

Readability is clarity. A low percentage of abstract words. Difficult ideas explained and not clumped together. Paragraphs not too long or complicated. Ideas developed in logical order. Introductions and summaries where suitable.

Readability is visibility. Type large enough to read comfortably. Lines not so long that the eye has trouble finding the beginning of the next line. Paper and ink that lets type stand out sharply—black ink on whitish nonglare paper is best. Plenty of light, without glare. Distance between eyes and print close enough for comfortable reading, but not too close.

Readability is a good book. It's the symmetry and warmth a poem transmits to you. It's a quality that

---

[23]Bob Lange, "Readability Formulas: Second Looks, Second Thoughts," *Reading Teacher* 35 (April 1982): 859.

computers find indigestible because it defies precise statistical analysis.[24]

Child Development Characteristics

Teachers who are knowledgeable about the social, emotional, physical, and intellectual de-

velopment of their students will be better able to help them choose books. "Both authors and critics must take into account the nature of child growth and development, for to do otherwise is to deny both the nature of children and the existence of a distinctive children's literature."[25]

Table 10.1 suggests a listing of books based on children's developmental stages.

[24]Allen M. Blair, "Everything You Always Wanted to Know About Readability but Were Afraid to Ask," *Elementary English* 48 (May 1971): p. 443.

[25]Brett and Huck, "Research Update," p. 880.

TABLE 10.1   BOOKS FOR AGES AND STAGES

Preschool and Kindergarten—Ages 3, 4, and 5

Characteristics	Implications	Examples
Rapid development of language	Interest in words, enjoyment of rhymes, nonsense, repetition, and cumulative tales. Enjoy retelling folktales and stories from books without words.	*Mother Goose* *The Gingerbread Boy* Burningham, *Mr. Gumpy's Outing* Gág, *Millions of Cats* Hutchins, *Rosie's Walk* Rockwell, *The Three Bears* Spier, *Crash! Bang! Boom!* Watson, *Father Fox's Pennyrhymes* Wezel, *The Good Bird*
Very active, short attention span	Require books that can be completed in one sitting. Enjoy participation through naming, touching, and pointing. Should have the opportunity to hear stories several times each day.	Burningham, *ABC* Burningham, *The Cupboard* Carle, *Do You Want to Be My Friend?* Carle, *The Very Hungry Caterpillar* Kunhardt, *Pat the Bunny* Wildsmith, *Puzzles*
Children themselves are the center of their world; interest, behavior, and thinking are egocentric.	Like characters with whom they can clearly identify; can only see one point of view.	Buckley, *Grandfather and I* Keats, *The Snowy Day* Preston, *Where Did My Mother Go?* Wells, *Noisy Nora*
Curious about their world	Stories about everyday experiences, pets, playthings, home, people in their immediate environment are enjoyed.	Cohen, *Will I Have a Friend?* Hoban, *Best Friends for Frances* Keats, *Peter's Chair* Rockwell, *My Doctor*
Building concepts through many firsthand experiences	Books extend and reinforce children's developing concepts.	Anno, *Anno's Counting Book* Hoban, *Big Ones, Little Ones* Hoban, *Count and See* Jensen, *Sara and the Door* Showers, *The Listening Walk*
Having little sense of time; time is "before now," "now," and "not yet."	Books can help children begin to understand the sequence of time.	Burningham, *Seasons* Carle, *The Grouchy Ladybug* Tresselt, *It's Time Now* Zolotow, *Over and Over*

TABLE 10.1   (continued)

Preschool and Kindergarten—Ages 3, 4, and 5

Characteristics	Implications	Examples
Learning through imaginative play	Enjoy stories that involve imaginative play; like personification of toys and animals.	Burton, *Mike Mulligan and His Steam Shovel* DeRegniers, *May I Bring a Friend?* Ets, *Just Me* Freeman, *Corduroy* McPhail, *The Train*
Seeking warmth and security in relationships with adults.	Like to be close to the teacher or parent during storytime; the ritual of the bedtime story begins literature experiences at home.	Brown, *Goodnight Moon* Clifton, *Amifika* Flack, *Ask Mr. Bear* Hutchins, *Good-Night, Owl!* Minarik, *Little Bear* Sharmat, *I Don't Care*
Beginning to assert their independence; taking delight in their accomplishments	Books can reflect emotions.	Barrett, *I Hate to Go to Bed* Brown, *The Runaway Bunny* Krauss, *The Carrot Seed* Lexau, *Benjie* Preston, *The Temper Tantrum Book* Watson, *Moving*
Beginning to make value judgments about what is fair and what should be punished	Require poetic justice and happy endings in the stories.	Bulla, *Keep Running, Allen* Hutchins, *Titch* Piper, *The Little Engine That Could* Potter, *The Tale of Benjamin Bunny* Potter, *The Tale of Peter Rabbit*

Primary—Ages 6 and 7

Characteristics	Implications	Examples
Continuing development and expansion of language	Daily story hour provides opportunity to hear qualitative and creative language of literature.	Poetry of Aileen Fisher, Karla Kuskin, David McCord, Robert Louis Stevenson, and others Preston, *Squawk to the Moon, Little Goose* Steig, *Amos and Boris* Tresselt, *A Thousand Lights and Fireflies*
Increasing attention span	Prefer short stories, or may enjoy a continued story provided each chapter is a complete incident.	Flack, *Walter the Lazy Mouse* Lobel, *Frog and Toad Together* Parish, *Amelia Bedelia*
Striving to accomplish skills demanded by adults	Children are expected to learn the skills of reading and writing. Need to accomplish this at their own rate and feel successful. First reading experiences should be enjoyable.	Cohen, *When Will I Read?* Conford, *Impossible, Possum* Duvoisin, *Petunia* Guilfoile, *Nobody Listens to Andrew* Kraus, *Leo the Late Bloomer*
Learning still based upon immediate perception and direct experiences	Use informational books to verify experience; watch guinea pigs, or record changes in a tadpole *prior* to using a book.	Brady, *Wild Mouse* Hoban, *Look Again!* Selsam, *The Amazing Dandelion* Silverstein, *Guinea Pigs, All about Them*

TABLE 10.1   (continued)

Primary—Ages 6 and 7		
Characteristics	**Implications**	**Examples**
Continuing interest in the world around them—eager and curious; still see world from their egocentric point of view.	Need wide variety of books; TV has expanded their interests beyond their home and neighborhood.	Aliki, *Green Grass and White Milk* Fuchs, *Journey to the Moon* Koren, *Behind the Wheel* Lionni, *Fish Is Fish* Swinton, *Digging for Dinosaurs*
Vague concepts of time	Simple biographies and historical fiction may give a feeling for the past, but accurate understanding of chronology is beyond this age group.	Aliki, *A Weed Is a Flower* Dalgliesh, *The Bears on Hemlock Mountain* Hutchins, *Clocks and More Clocks* Turkle, *Obadiah the Bold*
More able to separate fantasy from reality; developing greater imagination	Enjoy fantasy; like to dramatize simple stories.	Ness, *Sam, Bangs, and Moonshine* Sendak, *Where the Wild Things Are* Slobodkina, *Caps for Sale* Tolstoy, *The Great Big Enormous Turnip*
Beginning to develop empathy and understanding for others	Adults can ask such questions as, "What would you have done?" "How do you think Stevie felt about Robert?"	Hill, *Evan's Corner* Steptoe, *Stevie* Wolf, *Ann's Silent World* Yashima, *Crow Boy*
Have a growing sense of justice; demand applications of rules, regardless of circumstances	Expect poetic justice in books	Freeman, *Dandelion* Hutchins, *The Surprise Party* Udry, *Let's Be Enemies* Zemach, *The Judge*
Developing humor; enjoy incongruous situations, misfortune of others, and slapstick	Encourage appreciation of humor in literature. Reading aloud for pure fun has its place in the classroom. Enjoy books that have surprise endings, play on words, and broad comedy.	Allard, *The Stupids Have a Ball* Barrett, *Animals Should Definitely Not Wear Clothing* DuBois, *Lazy Tommy Pumpkinhead* Kuskin, *Just Like Everyone Else* Segal, *Tell Me a Mitzi*
Beginning sexual curiosity	Teachers need to accept and be ready to answer children's questions about sex.	Gruenberg, *The Wonderful Story of How You Were Born* Mayle, *"Where Did I Come From?"* Sheffield, *Where Do Babies Come From?*
Physical contour of the body is changing; permanent teeth appear; learn to whistle and develop other fine motor skills	Books can help children accept physical changes in themselves and differences in others.	Keats, *Whistle for Willie* McCloskey, *One Morning in Maine* Rockwell, *I did It*
Continuing search for independence from adults	Need opportunities to select books of their own choice. Should be encouraged to go to the library on their own.	Ardizzone, *Tim to the Rescue* Steptoe, *Train Ride* Taylor, *Henry the Explorer* Waber, *Ira Sleeps Over*
Continuing need for warmth and security in adult relationships	Books may emphasize universal human characteristics in a variety of lifestyles.	Clark, *In My Mother's House* Gill, *Hush, Jon* Reyher, *My Mother Is the Most Beautiful Woman in the World* Scott, *Sam* Zolotow, *Mr. Rabbit and the Lovely Present*

TABLE 10.1   (continued)

Middle Elementary—Ages 8 and 9

Characteristics	Implications	Examples
Attaining independence in reading skill, and may read with complete absorption. Others may still be having difficulty in learning to read. Wide variation in ability and interest. Research indicates boys and girls developing different reading interests during this time.	Discover reading as an enjoyable activity; prefer an uninterrupted block of time for independent reading. During this period, many children become avid readers.	Blume, *Tales of a Fourth-Grade Nothing* Clymer, *My Brother Stevie* Clover, *Bread-and-Butter Indian* Dahl, Danny: *The Champion of the World* Fox, *Maurice's Room* Greene, *Philip Hall Likes Me, I Reckon Maybe* Konigsburg, *From the Mixed-Up Files of Mrs. Basil E. Frankweiler* Robinson, *The Best Christmas Pageant Ever* Schulz, *Hooray for You, Charlie Brown* Selden, *The Cricket in Times Square* Steele, *Winter Danger*
Interest in hobbies and collections is high.	Enjoy how-to-do-it books and series books; like to collect and trade paperback books; begin to look for books of one author.	Bond, *A Bear Called Paddington* Cleary, *Ramona and Her Father* Simon, *The Paper Airplane Book* Stein, *The Kids' Kitchen Takeover* Wilder, *"Little House"* series
Seek specific information to answer their questions; may go to books that are beyond their reading ability to search out answers.	Require guidance in locating information; need help in use of library, card catalog, and reference books.	Gallob, *City Leaves, City Trees* Macaulay, *Castle* McWhirter, *The Guinness Book of World Records* Sarnoff, *A Great Bicycle Book*

Later Elementary—Ages 10, 11, and 12

Characteristics	Implications	Examples
Rate of physical development varies widely. Rapid growth precedes beginning of puberty; girls about two years ahead of boys in development and reaching puberty. Boys and girls increasingly curious about all aspects of sex.	Continued sex differentiation in reading preferences; guide understanding of growth process and help children meet personal problems.	Blume, *Are You There God? It's Me, Margaret* Blume, *Then Again, Maybe I Won't* Donovan, *I'll Get There, It Better Be Worth the Trip* Ravielli, *Wonders of the Human Body* Winthrop, *A Little Demonstration of Affection*
Understanding and accepting the gender role is a developmental task of this period. Boys and girls develop a sense of each other's identity.	Books may provide impetus for discussion and identification with others meeting this task.	Cleaver, *Trial Valley* George, *Julie of the Wolves* Greene, *A Girl Called Al* Jones, *Edge of Two Worlds* L'Engle, *The Moon by Night*

TABLE 10.1 (continued)

Later Elementary—Ages 10, 11, and 12

Characteristics	Implications	Examples
Increased emphasis on peer group and sense of belonging; deliberate exclusion of others; expressions of prejudice.	Emphasize unique contribution of all. In a healthy classroom atmosphere discussion of books can be used for values clarification.	Armstrong, *Sounder* Levoy, *Alan and Naomi* Neville, *Berries Goodman* Westall, *The Machine Gunners*
Changing family patterns. Highly critical of siblings. By end of period may challenge parents' authority.	Books may provide some insight into these changing relationships.	Byars, *The Pinballs* Hopkins, *Mama* Mann, *My Dad Lives in a Downtown Hotel* Rodgers, *Freaky Friday* Wersba, *The Dream Watcher*
Begin to have models other than parents; may draw them from TV, movies, sports figures, and books. Beginning interest in future vocation.	Biographies may provide appropriate models. Career books may open up new vocations and provide useful information.	Carruth, *She Wanted to Read: The Story of Mary McLeod Bethune* Goldreich, *What Can She Be? A Lawyer* Lee, *Boy's Life of John F. Kennedy* Naylor, *How I Came To Be a Writer* Robinson, *Breakthrough to the Big League*
Sustained, intense interest in specific activities.	Children spend more time in reading at this age than any other. Tend to select books related to one topic; for example, horses, sports, or a special hobby.	Glubok, *The Mummy of Ramose* Graham, *Great No-Hit Games of the Major Leagues* Moeri, *A Horse for X, Y, Z* Ravielli, *What Is Tennis?* Ross, *Racing Cars and Great Races*
Reflecting current adult interest in the mysterious, occult, and supernatural.	Enjoy mysteries, science fiction, and books about witchcraft.	Christopher, *Wild Jack* Duncan, *A Gift of Magic* Hunter, *The 13th Member* L'Engle, *A Swiftly Tilting Planet* Sleator, *Blackbriar*
Highly developed sense of justice and concern for others. Innate sympathy for weak and downtrodden.	Like "sad stories" about handicapped persons, sickness, or death.	Byars, *Summer of the Swans* Greene, *Beat the Turtle Drum* Platt, *Hey, Dummy* Robinson, *David in Silence*
Increased understanding of the chronology of past events. Beginning sense of their place in time. Able to see many dimensions of a problem.	Literature provides the opportunity to examine issues from different viewpoints. Need guidance in being critical of biased presentations.	Frank, *Anne Frank: The Diary of a Young Girl* Hickman, *The Valley of the Shadow* Hunt, *Across Five Aprils* Lester, *To Be a Slave* Tunis, *His Enemy, His Friend* Uchida, *Journey to Topaz*
Search for values. Interested in problems of the world. Can deal	Valuable discussions may grow out of teacher's reading aloud	Babbitt, *Tuck Everlasting* Collier, *My Brother Sam Is Dead*

TABLE 10.1   (continued)

Later Elementary—Ages 10, 11, and 12		
Characteristics	Implications	Examples
with abstract relationships; becoming more analytical.	prose and poetry to this age group. Questions may help students gain insight into both the content and literary structure of a book.	Cunningham, *Dorp Dead* Dunning, *Reflections on a Gift of Watermelon Pickle and Other Modern Verse* Engdahl, *Enchantress from the Stars* Kohl, *The View from the Oak* Slote, *Hang Tough, Paul Mather* Wojciechowska, *Shadow of a Bull*

Based on Charlotte S. Huck, *Children's Literature in the Elementary School*, 3d ed. updated (New York: Holt, Rinehart and Winston, 1979), pp. 31–36.

CHILDREN AS CRITICS

Who is to judge whether a book has value for children? Are children given a chance to judge the books that they read?

As was stated earlier in this chapter, the criteria to use in determining selection of books for children should include knowledge of children and what they enjoy in a book. Merely saying that a book is an award-winner, as judged by adults, does not mean that the book will be enjoyed by children. It may be that the award-winners chosen by adults have adult values and are reflections of what they think a good book for children should be.

Some awards, however, are given to books based on children's nominations: The Georgia Children's Book Award, the Dorothy Canfield Fisher Memorial Children's Book Award, the Junior Book Award, the Young Readers' Choice Award, the William Allen White Children's Book and the Sequoya Children's Book Award. In making these awards, lists of books are first compiled by various individuals concerned with children's literature—such as librarians, teachers, parents, and so on. Students from the fourth through ninth grade then vote on their favorites.

Interestingly, a study using students' judgments found that only four books chosen by students were Newbery Award winners.[26] There were 10 similar books chosen by the six award-granting organizations that used children's judgments. It appears that children from different areas have some unanimity of opinion on what they like. Also, all Newbery-winners may not be ones that interest children. This does not mean that major awards, such as the Newbery, should be abolished, but rather that children's choices should also be considered. The main purpose of these awards is to encourage the writing of good children's literature.

Since the middle 1970s, an annual bibliography of classroom choices of trade books has been compiled under the direction of the International Reading Association–Children's Book Council Joint Committee. Of all the trade books published in the previous year, approximately 500 are selected by a group of educators. The books are then sent to designated classrooms. A team of specialists keeps a record of the children's reactions to the various books. Based on the children's choices, a book is either elected to the bibliography or denied placement on it. The bibliography is usually published in the October issue of *The Reading Teacher*.

Developing Children's Taste in Book Selection

Helping children develop taste in the selection of books is an important goal in the literature program. However, this will not come

[26]Manuel Darkatsh, "Who Should Decide on a Book's Merit?" *Elementary English* 51 (March 1974): 353–354.

about by restricting children's reading or insisting that they only read those books selected for them.

The Nancy Drew, Hardy Boys, and Bobbsey Twins books have been the bane of librarians for decades. Some libraries do not even keep copies, and the mere mention of one of these books may upset some librarians. They arouse such animosity because they are mass produced in accordance with an exact formula. As a result, the vocabulary, plot, and characters are stereotyped—all are almost exactly the same. Although these books have no literary value, many children read and seem to enjoy them. The problem confronting teachers is not whether they should demand that children stop reading these books, but how to get them interested in and reading other books.

Good readers eventually become bored with Nancy Drew, the Bobbsey Twins, and the Hardy Boys series because of their sameness, and leave them after reading just a few. However, some children need further stimuli, such as having teachers introduce other books that they think would interest those students.

A good method of bringing attention to better books is by reading excerpts aloud from them. The teacher should tell the children something about the book—just enough to whet their appetites. The part chosen to be read should help to arouse the children's curiosity and interest. The manner in which the excerpt is read is very important. The teacher must show genuine enthusiasm, both in reading and in telling about the book. If the teacher has done a good job, most of the students will be trying to get the book to read on their own. The teacher should have several copies of the book immediately available.

TREATMENT OF THE ELDERLY IN CHILDREN'S LITERATURE

The treatment of the elderly in children's literature has probably been the most neglected and poorly portrayed of all areas. Interestingly, we are living in an era where a person's life expectancy is the greatest that it has ever been, and as a result the elderly are much more visible and vocal.

Although there is an increased interest in gerontology and increasing benefits for the elderly, old age is a topic that the young and middle-aged would prefer to ignore. This is sometimes not too difficult because with the advent of nursing homes and retirement communities, the elderly are probably more segregated from society today then ever before.

Who can speak for the old? And who speaks to us? . . . No one looks at me—, into my eyes, into the core of me. It is as if I am like all who have lived too long, a being to be tolerated or bypassed or humored. [27]

Stereotypes of the Elderly

Although an analysis of old people in various folktales shows that the elderly actually are portrayed in various ways, when children were asked how elderly people were shown in fairy stories, the children responded; "They are witches." [28] Obviously, these children have been greatly influenced by the portrayal of the old woman as a mean, cross, wicked hag or witch in such famous fairy tales as "Hansel and Gretel," "Sleeping Beauty," and "Snow White and the Seven Dwarfs."

Barnum, in a study of 100 randomly selected books, found that the elderly are discriminated against in contemporary young children's literature. She claims that the elderly "appear less frequently than they should, in view of their proportion in the United States population, and are depicted as disadvantaged in many socioeconomic and behavior characteristics." [29] In analyzing books in which the elderly do appear and in which they play a significant part, Barnum claims that the elderly male and female are shown in stereotyped roles. The elderly are rarely shown engaging in notable or exciting activities; they are rarely shown as interesting or active individuals; they are generally shown as passive or incompetent. [30] This is a rather depressing state of affairs.

[27]"An Old Woman Speaks," in *Aging in America* by Bert Kruger Smith (Boston: Beacon, 1973), p. 2.

[28]Myra Pollack Sadker and David Miller Sadker, *Now Upon a Time: A Contemporary View of Children's Literature* (New York: Harper & Row, 1977), p. 77.

[29]Phyllis Winet Barnum, "The Aged in Young Children's Literature," *Language Arts* 54 (January 1977): 29.

[30]Ibid., p. 32.

On the other side, there are books that portray the elderly in another stereotyped way— that of being omniscient. The elderly are shown to be wise and all-knowing in all matters. This idealized version appears in such books as John Houston's *Akavak: An Eskimo Journey*.

Some contemporary authors are attempting to portray the elderly in more realistic terms. A *Figure of Speech,* by Norman Fox Mazer, is one such book. It is the sensitive portrayal of an independent old man who lives in a separate apartment but in the same house as his children and grandchildren. Jenny, one of his grandchildren, has a warm relationship with her grandfather. Conflict arises when the grandfather begins to become a little senile about the same time that Jenny's brother returns from college—married and needing a place to live.

Literature can help dispel myths concerning the elderly as well as create them. If books present the elderly in a realistic, compassionate, sensitive, and perceptive manner, it is to be hoped that the negative image that many young people have of the elderly will change to a more positive and realistic one. (See the "Children and the Aged" section in the Selected Bibliography for sources that present a bibliography of books with a positive and acceptable image of the elderly.)

TREATMENT OF DEATH IN CHILDREN'S LITERATURE

Death, like old age, is a subject that in the past has been avoided in most children's books. This may be due to the fact that adults feel children are too young to understand death, so it is best that the topic not be broached. However, young children do think about death, but their perception of it usually differs from that of adults. Perhaps if teachers had a better understanding of children's views of death, they could help their students to cope with their feelings and misconceptions.

Young children do not understand the phenomenon of death:

The child of less than five years does not recognize death as an irreversible fact. In death he sees life. Between the ages of five and nine, death is most often personified and thought of as a contingency. And in general, only after the age of nine, is it recognized that death is a process happening to us according to certain laws.[31]

Children beyond the age of nine are becoming more logical, better able to deal with the world of reality, and better able to relate to others. They are becoming more aware of what it is to be alive. At the same time, they are also becoming aware of what it might be not to be alive; they are beginning to grasp the concept of death.

Elisabeth Kübler-Ross in the past decade probably has done more to change our views toward death and dying than anyone else. She has also helped us to learn about the stages that dying persons and their loved ones go through. She feels that children should be raised with an awareness of death, and says that in olden days children were more familiar with death because the aged and infirm lived at home. Today, American families are not as nuclear as in the past or even as in the rest of the world. Many elderly live by themselves and this separation from the grandchildren "deprives the children of an experience of death, which is an important learning experience."[32] She says, further, that "if we help them to face fear and show them that through strength and sharing we can overcome even the fear of dying, then they will be better prepared to face any kind of crisis that might confront them, including the ultimate reality of death."[33] For, she says, "Only when you are not afraid to live will you be unafraid to die. Only when you have lived *your* life fully can you begin to help others do the same, and thus face the moment of *their* death.[34]

If children develop *thanatophobia* (fear of death), bibliotherapy (see following section) may be a viable method of helping these children. Perhaps by experiencing death vicariously

---

[31]Maria Nagy, "The Child's Theories Concerning Death," *Journal of Genetic Psychology* 73 (1948): 7.

[32]Elisabeth Kübler-Ross, "Facing Up to Death," in *Readings in Human Development* (Guilford, Conn.: Dushkin Publishing, 1976–1977), p. 239.

[33]Ibid., p. 241.

[34]Elisabeth Kübler-Ross, *Working It Through* (New York: Macmillan, 1982), p. 137.

through their readings, children may be better equipped for its realities. Few books give as good a treatment of death as *Little Women*, but many boys would not read it. Some good books are being published, however, and these seem to represent a "far healthier and more honest approach than the squeamish skirting of the whole subject that has characterized so much of twentieth-century juvenile literature, for surely this is a vital aspect of life, inseparable from it."[35]

Books on Death

In Lloyd Alexander's *The High King*, death is shown to open doors never thought possible. In Jean George's book *Who Really Killed Cock Robin*, death is presented as a teaching situation. Madeline Polland's book *To Tell My People* presents death as a misunderstanding, whereas Barbara Wersba's book *Run Softly, Go Fast* portrays death as not the worst part of life because it is only after a father's death that the son gains a better understanding of his parent.

Some other favorites teachers might find helpful because of their bibliotherapeutic value are:

Where the Lilies Bloom by Vera and Bill Cleaver, Jr.
Little Women by Lousia May Alcott
The High Pasture by Ruth Harnden
Up a Road Slowly by Irene Hunt
The Big Wave by Pearl S. Buck
The Yearling by Marjorie Kinnan Rawlings

(See the "Children and Death" section in the Selected Bibliography for references that will help in selecting books on the subject of death. See also Table 10.2.)

BIBLIOTHERAPY

If you have ever read a book in which the main character had a problem exactly like yours and if the book helped you to deal better with your problem, you were involved in bibliotherapy.

Bibliotherapy is also regarded as reading guidance given by teachers and librarians to help students with their personal problems through the use of books. Such forms of help are not a new phenomenon, however. As far back as 300 B.C. Greek libraries bore inscriptions such as "The Nourishment of the Soul" and "Medicine for the Mind." Alice Bryan, a noted librarian, in the late 1930s advocated the use of books as a technique of guidance to help readers "to face their life problems more effectively and to gain greater freedom and happiness in their personal adjustment."[36] However, it probably was not until Russell and Shrodes published their articles on the "Contribution of Research in Bibliotherapy to the Language Arts Program" in 1950 that teachers attempted to bring bibliotherapy into the classroom. Russell and Shrodes discussed their belief that books could be used not simply to practice reading skills, but also to influence total development. They define bibliotherapy as "a process of dynamic interaction between the personality of the reader and literature—interaction which may be utilized for personality assessment, adjustment, and growth." They also say that bibliotherapy

is not a strange, esoteric activity but one that lies within the province of every teacher of literature in working with every child in a group. It does not assume that the teacher must be a skilled therapist, nor the child a seriously maladjusted individual needing clinical treatment. Rather, it conveys the idea that all teachers must be aware of the effects of reading upon children and must realize that, through literature, most children can be helped to solve the development problems of adjustment which they face.[37]

(For an understanding of the process, see the "Bibliotherapy" section in the Selected Bibliography.)

---

[35]Evelyn J. Swenson, "The Treatment of Death in Children's Literature," *Elementary English* (March 1972): 401–404.

[36]Alice I. Bryan, "The Psychology of the Reader," *Library Journal* 64 (January 1939): 110.

[37]David Russell and Caroline Shrodes, "Contributions of Research in Bibliotherapy to the Language Arts Program, I," *The School Review* 58 (September 1950): 335.

Uses of Bibliotherapy

Bibliotherapy can be used in both preventive and ameliorative ways. That is, some individuals, through reading specific books, may learn how to handle certain situations before they take place. Other persons may be helped through books to overcome some common developmental problem being experienced.

For whatever purpose bibliotherapy is used, it will only be of value if teachers are knowledgeable of *how* to use it in their classrooms. Teachers should know about children's needs, interests, readiness levels, and developmental stages. A word of caution is, however, necessary. Teachers must recognize that they are not psychologists, and they must be careful that they do not "step on the moral or religious toes of parents" when they introduce bibliotherapy in the classroom. Also, children should never be *forced* to discuss their feelings; children should know, however, that their teachers are available for discussion if they wish to express their feelings.

Bibliotherapy Themes

The kinds of problems that lend themselves to bibliotherapy are varied. For example, being the smallest child in the class or encountering the first day of school can be devastating. Being an only child may cause difficulty for some children. A new baby may bring adjustment problems for others, and going to the hospital may be a frightening event for yet others. Moving to a new neighborhood or the simple dislike of a name can cause problems for a number of children. The death of a loved one, the fear of death, or the divorce of parents cause great anxieties on the part of children, and just growing up can be confusing. These are just a few of the problems suitable for bibliotherapy.

The Teacher and Bibliotherapy

By reading books that deal with themes such as those stated in the previous section, children can he helped to cope better with their emotions and problems. Teachers sensitive to their children's needs can help them by providing the books that deal with their problems. However, since teachers are not clinicians, children who are having serious adjustment problems should be referred for help to the guidance counselor or school psychologist. Also, teachers must be careful not to give children who are anxious about a situation a book that would increase their anxiety. A teacher should also not single out a child in front of the class to give him or her a book that points out that child's defects. Such treatment would probably embarrass and upset the child more.

The school librarian and the special reading teacher may be excellent resource persons to help the teacher to choose books for bibliotherapy purposes. For best results, teachers should work very closely with them. As was stated earlier, teachers should be familiar with the *Elementary School Library Collection,* which is available in most libraries. It has an annotated bibliography of children's books on all themes with both readability and interest levels indicated, as well as resource books for teachers. Another excellent book with which the teacher should be familiar is Sharon Dreyer's *Bookfinder.*

After teachers use *Bookfinder,* the *Elementary School Library Collection,* or the aid of librarians to identify possible books, they should peruse the books themselves to determine whether they meet certain important criteria. Books for bibliotherapy should deal with problems that are significant and relevant to the students. The characters should be "lifelike" and presented in a believable and interesting manner. The characters' relationship to others in the book should be equally believable, and they should have motives for their actions. The author should present a logical and believable plot using vivid descriptive language, humor, adequate dialogue, and emotional tone. The situations presented by the author should be such that minor problems can be separated from main problems. The episodes in the book should lend themselves to being extracted and discussed so that students can formulate alternate solutions. Also, the author should present enough data so that students can discern generalizations that relate to life situations. The book should also be written in such a manner that the readers' imaginations are so stirred that they can "enter the skin of another."

A good teacher, one who is perceptive to the needs of students and who recognizes the importance of individual differences, will be in a better position to determine when a problem lends itself to being presented to the whole class, or when it should be handled on an individual basis. As was stated earlier, when a teacher wishes to give individual children books for bibliotherapy purposes, the children should not be singled out lest they feel ostracized or humiliated. One chance to help the children choose books could occur during a school library period or a class library period. The teacher and/or school librarian could make a few suggestions to a child. The student could then decide on one by reading the first page of a few of the suggested books.

Another way to interest individual students in books for bibliotherapy would be to choose an episode from a book to read aloud to the class. The chosen episode should present the main character in a problem situation. Also, the protagonist should be one with whom the teacher feels a number of students can identify. After the episode is read, a discussion should take place on how the character resolves his or her problems. The author's solution should not be given. The book may then be offered to those individuals who would like to read it. The teacher using this technique should have a few copies of the book available because many of the students will want to read it.

Many times a teacher may find that a number of children in the class share a similar problem. Therefore, the teacher might want to introduce the problem in some way to the class and use a bibliotherapy technique to help the students to cope with their problem. One technique to use is bibliotherapy and role playing.

SCENARIO

The teacher overhears a number of children discussing their younger brothers and sisters in rather disparaging terms. Not only do many of the children seem to feel that their younger siblings get more love and attention, but they also seem to feel that the younger ones "get away" with much more than they can. The teacher decides to use bibliotherapy and role playing to help the students to adjust to and cope better with their problem. After looking through a few books that deal with this theme, the teacher chooses Judy Blume's *Tales of a Fourth-Grade Nothing* to read to the class. This book was chosen because not only does it have most of the criteria discussed earlier, but it also lends itself to being read aloud to the class, and the story will appeal to less mature as well as more mature students.

INTRODUCING THE PROBLEM

The teacher asks the students to draw pictures of their families and of their pets, if they have any, and under each picture to write one sentence that describes the member of the family or the pet. After the children have finished, a discussion concerning the pictures takes place. The teacher asks those children who have younger brothers or sisters to tell the class something about them. Those children who have no brothers or sisters should be called upon to tell about their parents or pets. Some other questions the teacher might ask are:

How did you feel when your mother brought home your new baby brother or sister? If you have no younger brothers or sisters, how do you think you would feel if your mother brought home a younger brother or sister?

BIBLIOTHERAPY AND ROLE PLAYING

The teacher reads aloud Blume's book *Tales of a Fourth-Grade Nothing* to the whole class in a week's time. After the book is finished, the students discuss Peter's relationship to his younger brother Fudge. Students are encouraged to share some of their experiences. After this, the students are told that they are going to do some role playing. Each child who would like to will play the role of Fudge, Peter, the mother, or the father. A scene is set in which Fudge keeps interrupting Peter while Peter is trying to build a model plane. No dialogue is given. The children must spontaneously provide that on their own. After each role-playing scene, the teacher should discuss what took place with the class, and ask for the role-players to give their feelings about the parts. If time permits, the children should reverse roles. It is important that only those children who wish to role-play should. No child should ever be forced to role-play.

BIBLIOTHERAPY AND CREATIVE PROBLEM-SOLVING

Another technique the teacher could have used is bibliotherapy and creative problem-solving. In this method, almost the whole book is read aloud to the class. Before the ending, the students, using clues from the book, try to determine how the main character's problem is resolved. They are encouraged, also, to generate their own solutions. After the ending is read, the students are asked to compare their solutions with the author's. Then they can discuss which they liked better and why.

(See "Role Playing: An Extension of Creative Play" in Chapter 7.)

The following section presents two examples of how a teacher can use bibliotherapy with either role playing or creative problem solving in an upper-primary- or lower-intermediate-grade-level class.

Bibliotherapy can be effective in helping students to better understand themselves and their feelings. When students realize that other persons have similar problems, they are able to cope better with their own. Bibliotherapy also encourages students to try to seek answers in a positive, intellectual, and logical manner.

Books as an Aid in Bibliotherapy

There are a number of excellent books that deal with some of the problems that children may encounter in today's world. Nan Hayden Agle's *Maple Street* is an enlightening story about a young black girl's desire to improve her street and to come to terms with a prejudiced white girl. Mary Calhoun's book *It's Getting Beautiful Now* concerns a boy's emotional problems and drugs. Francine Chase's *A Visit to the Hospital* helps both parents and children in preparing for a stay in the hospital. Gladys Yessayan Cretan's *All Except Sammy* portrays a boy's attempts to win the respect of his musical family.

Perceptive teachers, alert to the needs of their students, should be able to aid them in choosing books to help them cope more effectively with individual problems. As in all matters, the teacher should look for balance in the child's reading habits. A certain degree of escapism is fine, but the child must live in the real world and cannot be in a continuous state of fanciful thinking. (See bibliography for annotated references that will help in selecting literature that portrays life as it is.) Table 10.2 consists of a good sampling of books for bibliotherapy organized by theme.

TABLE 10.2   SOME BOOKS FOR BIBLIOTHERAPY, ORGANIZED BY THEME

Theme	Title	Author	Level
Adoption	*Here's a Penny*	Carolyn Haywood	Upper primary
Aging and Death	*The Granny Project*	Anne Fine	Intermediate
Child who is different	*A Girl Called Al* *Dinky Hocker Shoots Smack*	Constance Greene M. E. Kerr	Upper intermediate Upper intermediate
Childhood Fears	*There's a Nightmare in My Closet*	Mercer Mayer	Preschool
Death	*Run Softly, Go Fast* *The Dead Bird* *My Grandpa Died Today* *Charlotte's Web* *Annie and the Old One* *A Taste of Blackberries* *The Tenth Good Thing About Barney* *That Dog!* *When People Die* *Loss*	Barbara Wersba Margaret Wise Brown Joan Fassler E. B. White Miska Miles Doris Buchanan Smith Judith Viorst Nanette Newman Joanne E. Bernstein and Steven V. Gullo Joanne Bernstein	Young adult Preschool/Kindergarten Primary Upper primary/ intermediate Intermediate Primary Preschool/lower primary Lower primary Primary Upper intermediate
Dealing with a younger sibling	*Tales of a Fourth-Grade Nothing* *Nobody Asked Me if I Wanted a Baby Sister*	Judy Blume Martha Alexander	Upper primary/lower intermediate Preschool
Dislike of Name	*Sabrina*	Martha Alexander	Preschool/early primary
Divorce	*A Month of Sundays* *My Dad Lives in a Downtown Hotel* *It's Not the End of the World*	Rose Blue Peggy Mann Judy Blume	Upper primary/lower intermediate Upper primary/lower intermediate Intermediate
Divorce, loneliness, and the finding of self	*Dear Dr. Henshaw*	Beverly Cleary	Intermediate
Finding of self	*Then Again, Maybe I Won't* *Are You There God? It's Me, Margaret* *Nikki 108* *The Soul Brothers and Sister Lon*	Judy Blume Judy Blume Rose Blue Kristin Hunter	Upper intermediate/ young adult Intermediate Upper intermediate Young adult
First day of school	*Shawn Goes to School*	Petronella Breinberg	Preschool/early primary
Hearing aid	*Keeping It Secret*	Penny Pollack	Intermediate
Illness (in a hospital)	*Elizabeth Gets Well*	Alfons Weber	Primary
Learning-disabled child	*Will the Real Gertrude Hollings Please Stand Up?*	Sheila Greenwald	Intermediate
New baby	*Confessions of an Only Child*	Norma Klein	Upper primary/ intermediate

TABLE 10.2   (continued)

Theme	Title	Author	Level
	Peter's Chair	Ezra Jack Keats	Preschool
	My Mama Needs Me	Mildred Potts Walker	Preschool
Overcoming Fear	*Frizzy the Fearful*	Marjorie W. Sharmat	Preschool
Prejudice	*Maple Street*	Nan Hayden Agle	Upper primary/ intermediate
Transformation of a loner	*Get Lost, Little Brother*	C. S. Adler	Intermediate
Youngest child	*Weezie Goes to School*	Sue Felt Kerr	Primary

POETRY SHOULD NOT BE THE STEPCHILD OF CHILDREN'S LITERATURE

I have a secret from everybody in the
   world-full-of-people
But I cannot always remember how it goes.

In Chapter 9, we talked about the child's delight in words, and the magical quality that they seem to have for the young child. Words trip off the child's tongue glibly. The young child is a natural poet. Tell children a rhyme, and they will laugh and tell you one in turn. The rhyme they give you may be nonsense words, but they don't care as long as the words sound right. While young children seem to have an ear for poetry, in going through the grades something unfortunate occurs: Poetry seems to lose its place in their hearts. The question is, "Does poetry have a place in the school curriculum?" If it does, what can we do to maintain children's early love of poetry?

Poetry's Place in the Curriculum

Poetry does have a place in children's lives and in the curriculum at school. Children's listening experiences should try to cover Mother Goose rhymes, nonsense poems, poems with sensory appeal, and poems that tell a story. Creativity has its origin in children's minds when they begin to respond to the rhythmic beauty of a poem. Enjoyment may be derived from the humor, the fantasy, and the rich store of ideas and emotions expressed in poetry. There is a release from tension; there is sheer joy to be had in listening to literature read with feeling and understanding by the teacher.

Teachers should help guide their students to rich experiences through poetry. In order to do this well, teachers must also enjoy poetry. To spread enthusiasm, teachers must be enthused. The choice of poems should be varied, and the study of poetry should not be made prescriptive; for example, children should not be subjected to memorizing poems for the sake of memorizing. If children enjoy a poem and re-read it many times for sheer delight, they oftentimes will memorize it simply because they want to. To aid in this process, teachers should be concerned with selecting poems that will appeal to children, that will help them to clarify and extend their appreciation of literature and life.

Children should hear poetry for the sheer delight of it, as they would listen to music. Poetry should be read aloud to hear the sound of the words, the lilt of the rhyme, and the swing of the line. Choral speaking, poetry recordings, and combining poetry and music are examples of exercises that would help to enhance children's enjoyment of poetry. As the poet William Yeats once said, "I just heard a poem spoken with so delicate a sense of its rhythm, with so perfect a respect for its meaning, that if I were a wise man and could persuade a few people to learn the art, I would never open a book of verse."

Teachers should be knowledgeable about children's preferences in poetry so that they can wisely select poems for their students. It has been found that children usually prefer the following:

1. Direct discourse to indirect
2. Having the place and time clearly indicated so that they can picture the scene in their minds
3. Humor, but not the satire of adult humor
4. Sincerity
5. Lack of moralizing or preaching

In the presentation of the poem, the following principles, if followed, will help to instill a continuous liking:

1. Teachers should read the poem aloud. Like music, the poem should be heard a few times first.
2. Clear up any baffling words that block the children's comprehension.
3. Wait for children's reaction.
4. Plan the uses of poetry in the classroom.
5. Try to choose the right poem at the right time.

Following are some "don'ts" in teaching poetry:

1. Do not overanalyze.
2. Do not overemphasize word practice.
3. Do not confuse singsong rhymes with poetry.
4. Do not approach children below their level.
5. Do not say, "Oh, everybody should love this poem." What appeals to some will not necessarily appeal to others.
6. Do not emphasize memorization.
7. Do not ask children to recite at length.
8. Do not "force" poetry on children.

Examples of Poetry in the Classroom

Many opportunities present themselves for the introduction of poetry in the classroom. The teacher should take advantage of these mo-ments, remembering that not everyone likes the same kinds of poems. During autumn, when the leaves are starting to turn many different colors, and to fall, the teacher could introduce such poems as James S. Tippett's "Autumn Woods," Carl Sandburg's "Theme in Yellow," Bliss Carman's "A Vagabond Song," Amy Lowell's "The City of Falling Leaves," and Adelaide Crapsey's "November Night."

Rachel Field's "Roads" is excellent for stirring the imagination, and a foggy, drizzly day might be a good time to present Carl Sandburg's "Fog." Young children especially enjoy poems about animals, so such poetry books as *A Dozen Dinosaurs* by Richard Armour and *Good Dog Poems* by William Cole are good ones to present to them. An excellent way to get young children attracted to poetry is through humor. As we have said a number of times, children love silly words and the sound of them; they like rhymes, puns, limericks, and almost all word plays. Many well-known poets such as John Ciardi and Shel Silverstein write delightfully humorous poems for children. Teachers can amuse their children with Silverstein's *Where the Sidewalk Ends* and Ciardi's *The Man Who Sang the Sillies*, as well as Sara Brewton's *Laughable Limericks*.[38]

Many poets are writing for children today, so teachers have an abundance of material from which to choose.

"There is one rule of thumb for the choice of poetry to be used with children: it should be the best available. . . . Poems should employ metaphor and image effectively and delightfully; they should have strong sensory appeal; many should illustrate patterns of repetition and rhyme; all poems chosen for use with children should speak to the child at his level of understanding and experience; but they should also broaden experience and stretch the imagination with new concepts and fresh ways of looking at things.[39]

[38]Joan Mason, "Forum: A Librarian Looks at Poetry for Children," *Language Arts* 59 (March 1982) : 280–283.

[39]Glenna Davis Sloan, *The Child As Critic* (New York: Teachers College Press, 1975), p. 55.

Figures of Speech in Poetry

There is a place for analysis of poems in the language arts program. In poetry, as in prose, if the words are not in the children's listening capacity, or if they do not understand the ideas, or if the figures of speech are meaningless to the listeners or readers, little enjoyment can take place. Although some poems, such as "The Congo" by Vachel Lindsay and "The Raven" by Edgar Allan Poe, can be enjoyed (the former because of its rhythm and the latter because of its eeriness and ability to create a mood) without knowing the complete meaning, this is not so for the majority.

If the purpose of the lesson is to be analysis of poetry, or the better understanding of figures of speech, this aim should be emphasized and not be confused with poetry appreciation. The children should be helped to understand that in order to appreciate poetry fully, they should understand the words and figures of speech used in the poems. The reason many children say, "It just doesn't make sense to me," is because many of the words are just noises to them.

The figures of speech most commonly used in poetry are simile, metaphor, and personification. *Simile* is the comparison of two unlike objects using "like" or "as." *Metaphor* is also the comparison of two unlike objects, but without using "like" or "as." *Personification* is the giving of human characteristics and capabilities to nonhuman things such as inanimate objects, abstract ideas, or animals.

In the poem "There Is No Frigate Like a Book" by Emily Dickinson, when a frigate (a ship) is compared to a book, and coursers (swift horses) are compared to a page of prancing poetry, simile is being used. "Prancing poetry" is also an example of personification. The poet says, "This traverse may the poorest take without oppress of toll." "This traverse" is an example of a metaphor in which a journey is being compared to the reading of a book.

Most children in the primary grades would not be able to understand symbolic figures of speech. However, they will be able to get an understanding of imagery in poetry, if the images that are presented in the poem are nonsymbolic ones. For example, young children would have no difficulty in understanding the poem "What Is Pink?" by Christina Georgina Rossetti.

Upper-elementary-grade students enjoy using *oxymorons*. These are word contradictions, which are used to portray a particular image. For example, "the loud silence was deafening." (See "Creating Word Images: Figures of Speech" in Chapter 11.)

BOOK REPORTING

Before discussing the methods of book reporting, the purposes of book reports must be made clear. For many teachers, the main purpose of the book report is to find out whether the child has actually read the book. A teacher who asks students to make a formal, written book report after every book they have read is

not being realistic, and is actually discouraging children from reading more. The oral book reports discussed in a previous section were used to stimulate other students' interest in books. The students enjoy giving this kind of report because it is based on books of the students' own choosing, and the reports are voluntarily and enthusiastically given. If the purpose of the book report is to discern whether the students have read a particular book, there are many interesting ways that this can be done that are also fun.

Children can present character sketches portraying the main characters in a book, or they can tell about a character to see if the other children in the class, who have also read this book, know who the character being portrayed or sketched is.

Some students might draw caricatures of some of the book characters or a scene from the book they have read, to see if other students can discover the book they had in mind. The alert teacher will note that this type of activity is a hybrid, and allows for the cross-fertilization of language arts with the visual or graphic arts, thus helping to weld the entire elementary-school program into one cohesive whole. This allows for maximum interplay of the various skills and talents of students, which, in turn, will yield the maximum favorable reinforcing response from the students. The teacher should be constantly on the lookout for such activities.

Whatever activity the children choose in relation to their reading, they should not have to do something for every book they have read.

Written book reports as well as oral book reports have a place in the language arts program, because children have to be able to communicate in writing as well as orally. However, written reports should not deter children from reading. Some teachers choose one book on which everyone must write a report, some give the students a choice of books, and some allow students a completely free choice. The latter two methods, where choice is involved, are better than the forced method. Since many students look on the written book report as an onerous task, it becomes unbearable to some if they cannot at least choose the book. The number of written book reports should be kept to a feasible minimum.

Pillar presents a number of novel approaches to stimulate students to write book reports. The approaches are typed on index cards and available for students. Here are some of them.

1. Pretend you are a puppy and have a chance to be adopted by one of the people in your book. Which one would you choose and why?

2. King Kong has just climbed through your bedroom window. He is trying madly to rip apart the book you have just finished reading. You must act very quickly and defend it. Convince him not to destroy it by citing incidents that you enjoyed. Prove to him that this book is worth keeping.

3. Invite one of the characters in your book to dinner. Tell the character why you have selected him or her above the others. Then, leave a note for your mother describing the person and including a few "do's and don'ts" for her to follow so that your guest will feel right at home.

4. You are your book on a shelf in a toy store. What will you say to children to convince them to buy you?

5. Pretend that you are the author of the book you have just finished reading and that it has not yet been published. The editors like your book except for the last chapter. They ask you to write a completely different last chapter. You agree to do so. Remember that it must agree in content and style with the earlier chapters.

6. You are a television commercial writer and have been asked to write a commercial advertising this book to the American public. In not more than two paragraphs, since commercial time is expensive, tell why your book should be read.

7. Since you have the power to transform the major characters in your book into animals and choose to do so, decide upon an animal for each based upon personality traits. Write a letter to each telling why he or she is similar to the animal selected.

8. You are a typewriter that continues to type long after the author has put the final pe-

riod to a story and retired. Is it that you are changing some of the characters and parts of the plot, or is it that you just can't bear to *see* the story end? What do you have to say?[40]

The main objective for written book reports should be similar to oral ones; that is, to stimulate other children into wanting to read the book. This is the best purpose for having students do book reports. (The techniques for writing book reports will be presented in Chapter 12.)

THE SCHOOL LIBRARY AND LIBRARY SKILLS

The school library should be an integrated part of the students' ongoing activities. A number of schools have designed their physical plants so that the library is actually in the center of the building, easily accessible to all classrooms. The library, properly utilized, becomes the students' storehouse of information and a reservoir of endless delight for them.

The atmosphere in the library should be such that children feel welcome, invited, and wanted. The librarian is the individual who is responsible for setting this tone. A friendly, warm person who loves children and books will usually have a library with similar characteristics. Children should feel free to visit the library at all times, not just during their regularly scheduled periods.

An enthusiastic and inventive librarian will, by various means, act as an invitation to children to come to the library. Some librarians engage in weekly storytelling activities for all grade levels. Librarians should encourage teachers and children to make suggestions for storytelling, as well as to share the kinds of books they enjoy and would like. The librarian should also act as a resource person in helping the classroom teacher to develop library skills in students. Once students gain the "library habit," it is hard to break, and it will remain with them throughout life.

Following are some of the library skills that children should achieve in the elementary school.

[40]Arlene M. Pillar, "Individualizing Book Reports," *Elementary English* 52 (April 1975): 467–469.

Primary Grades

In the primary grades children are ready to acquire some library skills that will help them become independent library users. First, the teacher can help primary-grade children to gain an idea of the kinds of books available in the library; for example, fiction and nonfiction books. Definitions of the terms should be given, as well as examples of each type of book. For best results, the examples used should be books with which the children are familiar.

Primary-grade children who have learned to read and can alphabetize can also learn to use the card catalogue. They should learn that there are three kinds of cards for each book: an author card, a title card, and the subject card. The teacher should have samples of these for the children to see and handle. By simulating this activity in the classroom, children will be better prepared for actual library activity. Also, their chances for success in using the catalogue properly to find a desired book will be increased. This utilitarian activity can also be programmed to reinforce knowledge of alphabetizing.

Intermediate and Upper-Elementary Grades

By the fourth grade children can learn about other categories of books in the library, such as biographies and reference books.

Reference Books Children in the elementary grades ask many questions about many topics. Teachers should use some of these questions to help children learn about reference sources. Teachers should help children to understand that it is impossible for one person to know everything today because of the vast amount of knowledge that already exists, compounded each year by its exponential growth. However, a person can learn about any particular area or field if he or she knows what source books to go to for help. For example, the *Readers' Guide to Periodical Literature* will help one to find magazine articles written on almost any subject of interest. There are reference books on language and usage, such as Roget's *Thesaurus of English Words and Phrases*, which would help upper-grade students in finding synonyms and less trite words to use in writing.

The most often-used reference book in elementary school, besides the dictionary, is the encyclopedia. Children should be helped to use the encyclopedia as a tool and an aid, rather than as an end in itself. That is, children should be shown how to extract information from the encyclopedia without copying the article verbatim.

In the upper-elementary grades children should learn that there are many reference source books available in the library that can supply information about a famous writer, baseball player, scientist, celebrity, and so forth. The key factor is knowing that these reference sources exist, and knowing which reference book to go to for the needed information.

Teachers can help their upper-grade children to familiarize themselves with these reference books by giving children assignments in which they have to determine what source books to use in fulfilling the assignment.

THE NEWBERY MEDAL AND THE CALDECOTT MEDAL

The Newbery Medal is given annually to the book published in the United States that has been voted "the most distinguished literature" for children. The Caldecott Medal is given for the book chosen to be the best picturebook of the year. Tables 10.3 and 10.4 give a listing of the Newbery and Caldecott Medal books chosen since 1980:

TABLE 10.3   NEWBERY MEDAL AWARDS

Title	Author	Year
A Gathering of Days: A New England Girl's Journal, 1830–32	Joan W. Blos	1980
Jacob I Have Loved	Katherine Paterson	1981
A Visit to William Blake's Inn: Poems for Innocent and Experienced Travelers	Nancy Willard	1982
Dicey's Song	Cynthia Voigt	1983
Dear Mr. Henshaw	Beverly Cleary	1984

TABLE 10.4   CALDECOTT MEDAL AWARDS

Title	Author and Illustrator	Year
Ox-Cart Man	Donald Hall; Barbara Cooney (illus.)	1980
Fables	Arnold Lobel	1981
Jumanji	Chris Van Allsburg	1982
Shadow	Blaise Cendrars; Marcia Brown (illus.)	1983
The Glorious Flight: Across the Channel with Louis Blériot, July 25, 1909	Alice and Martin Provensen	1984

STUDENT'S NAME:
GRADE:
TEACHER:

DIAGNOSTIC CHECKLIST FOR CREATIVE COMMUNICATION THROUGH CHILDREN'S LITERATURE

PART ONE

	YES	NO
1. The child voluntarily chooses to read.		
2. The child reads: **a.** fairy tales and folktales **b.** adventure stories		

    c. sport stories
    d. biographies
    e. autobiographies
    f. nonfiction stories
    g. mysteries
    h. science fiction
    i. poetry
    j. books depicting various cultures
    k. books to help him or her cope with an adjustment or emotional problem
    l. other

PART TWO

	YES	NO
1. The child usually finishes the book he or she chooses to read.		
2. The child asks for help in choosing a book.		
3. The child chooses books to read that are at his or her independent reading level.		
4. The child readily shares information about the book he or she reads with others or with the whole class.		
5. The child gives oral reports on books he or she has read.		
6. The child presents written reports to the class on books he or she has read.		
7. The child chooses to dramatize or role-play some scenes or characters from books he or she has read.		
8. The child uses ideas that he or she has gained from reading in his or her writings.		
9. The child asks to read to younger children.		
10. The child asks that the teacher read a story to the class.		
11. The child asks to tell a story to a class.		

PART THREE

1. State how many books the child claims he or she reads in a month.
2. State how many books the child claims he or she attempts to read in a month but doesn't finish.

SUMMARY

If teachers have done a good job in other areas of language arts, it should manifest itself in the children's literature program. The teacher who is enthusiastic about books, who provides a good classroom environment, as well as books at all the children's interest and reading ability levels, is setting the stage for a good children's literature program.

The goal in this chapter is for teachers to get children "hooked on books." Various techniques to whet children's interest in books are presented, and the importance of peer and teacher role modeling are discussed. Information is presented on how to initiate a Sustained Silent Reading (SSR) program and how to help children choose books. In choosing books for children, teachers must avoid those books that portray children or adults in a stereotyped role. Teachers should also introduce children to nonfiction books; techniques for doing this are also given.

Some knowledge of readability formulas, which are generally based on sentence length and the number of syllables in a word, should aid teachers in choosing books at their students' reading ability levels. Teachers are cautioned, however, about assuming that a readability formula will correctly predict how a specific individual will interact with a particular book.

This chapter presents a discussion of the use of books to help students cope better with their developmental problems. The treatment of old age and death in children's literature was also discussed.

A discussion on book reporting, poetry, and library skills was also presented. It was suggested that various types of book reporting be used as means to encourage other students to read, rather than as ends in themselves.

Suggestions on how to incorporate poetry into the classroom, as well as kinds of poems that children might like, were discussed. A section on the librarian and library skills was included because the library, which is the reservoir of knowledge, should be available and easily accessible to all children on their own. A "Diagnostic Checklist for Creative Communication through Children's Literature" was also presented.

As a further aid, two examples of children's literature lesson plans follow. Using these as a guide, see if you can construct another plan.

LESSON PLAN I: PRIMARY-GRADE LEVEL

OBJECTIVE

Students will be able to portray a character in a previously read story so that others in the class can tell who the character is.

PRELIMINARY PREPARATION

Witch's hat, broom

INTRODUCTION

"We've read many books and stories together this year. Some of you have also told us about your favorite books and stories. If I were to put on this witch's hat and use this broom as my flying aid, would I remind you of someone we read about? Yes, the witch in *The Wizard of Oz*. Now, let's see if you can guess who I am. I'm not going to use any special materials to help me. I'm getting smaller and smaller; I'm now walking on all fours; I live in a barn, and I have an eight-legged friend. I also have a problem. I see so many hands raised. Who am I? Yes, Wilbur, the pig from *Charlotte's Web*. Now, let's see how many of you can be a character from one of our stories. Although we may speak, we must not name the story or give names of people or places in the story."

DEVELOPMENT

Call on a number of children who have raised their hands. Each child acts out a character, while others try to guess who the character is and the name of the story. After a few children have done this, tell the class, "We will go into groups and play a little game. We will see who can get the other groups to guess the character and story. Remember, we can't name anyone in the story."

Children are grouped and each group is told what their story is. The children choose the characters they wish to portray.

After the groups have decided on who their characters are, and how they will portray them, they are presented to the class. The teacher keeps time.

SUMMARY

The teacher elicits from the students what they have done during the lesson. The teacher asks students to think about some new stories that they would like to have read to the class.

LESSON PLAN II: INTERMEDIATE-GRADE LEVEL

OBJECTIVES

1. Students will take books out of the libarary.
2. Students will be able to describe what a character might look like and to give reasons why the character would behave in a certain way.

PRELIMINARY PREPARATION

Three pictures (differing in body, features, detail) of a possible character. Excerpt from a book (depicting a dilemma).

INTRODUCTION

"Today we're going to be looking at some characters from books and seeing if we can guess the kinds of things they would or wouldn't do. Remember the discussion on *The Indian in the Cupboard?** I told you something about the story, and then I read some excerpts from the book. After that I asked you what you thought Omri would do with his Indian, Little Bear, Bright Stars, the horse, and Boone. Now I'm going to read you an excerpt from another book, and I want you to be thinking about the characters and possible clues to their personalities. Also, I have three pictures here (show pictures and stand them up against chalkboard) and I'd like you to be thinking of which picture best describes the main character, if any."

*Lynne Reid Banks, *The Indian in the Cupboard* (New York: Doubleday, 1981).

DEVELOPMENT

(Read excerpt from book.) "What do you think happened?" *(A few suggestions answered orally.)* "Yes, those could all have occurred. What about those pictures? Did they match your mental images of the characters? Why or why not?" *(Answers.)* "Did any of the things the characters did influence the way you pictured them? Now, I'd like you to write your own ending to the episode, trying to think as the main character would, remembering your mental image of the person and explaining why you think he or she will act in a particular way. If you like, you can also describe what you would do in the situation."

SUMMARY

"We looked at some characters today and tried to discover what they would or would not do in a situation, based on their former actions. Tomorrow we can act out some of our endings, and if some of you would like to read the book to find out how the characters in the book actually acted, you can later report your findings to the class. We can then see how our reasoning and endings compare to the author's. You can keep this in mind while reading any book, and see whether the characters behave in the same way throughout the book."

SUGGESTIONS FOR THOUGHT QUESTIONS AND ACTIVITIES

1. Choose and read a book that you feel primary-grade children would enjoy. Give your criteria for choosing the book. Explain how you would present this book to gain the attention and interest of your students. Do the same for the intermediate grades.

2. Choose and memorize the plot of a story that you feel primary-grade children will find entertaining. Present the story in your own words using videotape. Do a critique of your presentation.

3. You teach an intermediate grade in an inner-city school with a large population of children who speak nonstandard English. What criteria would you use in choosing books for these children?

4. You have been appointed to a special school committee whose function it is to determine criteria for choosing books for your school. You have a limited budget. How would you determine the book-buying criteria? What factors would you take into consideration in determining your criteria?

5. You have been appointed to a committee whose responsibility it is to determine the books that children like to read. How would you go about doing this?

6. You have been invited to speak on bibliotherapy. What books would you choose to discuss in your talk?

7. Critically analyze the Newbery Award Books chosen in the last four years.

8. Using some of the approaches presented in the chapter as a guide, generate three other creative ways to stimulate students to write book reports.

SELECTED BIBLIOGRAPHY

General Books and Articles

Arbuthnot, May. *Arbuthnot Anthology of Children's Literature.* Glenville, Ill.: Scott, Foresman, 1976.

Bennett, John E., and Priscilla Bennett. "What's So Funny? Action Research and Bibliography of Humorous Children's Books—1975–80." *Reading Teacher* 35 (May 1982): 924–927.

Berglund, Roberta L., and Jerry L. Johns. "A Primer on Uninterrupted Sustained Silent Reading." *Reading Teacher* 36 (February 1983): 534–539.

Burke, Eileen. *Early Childhood Literature.* Boston: Allyn & Bacon, in press.

Ciani, Alfred, ed. *Motivating Reluctant Readers.* Newark, Del.: International Reading Association, 1981.

Coody, Betty. *Using Literature with Young Children.* Dubuque: Wm. C. Brown, 1983.

Feirstein, Ben. *Children's Enjoyment through Poetry.* New York: Vantage, 1982.

Gillespie, John T., and Christine B. Gilbert, eds. *Best Books for Children: Preschool through the Middle Grades,* 2d ed. New York: Bowker, 1981.

Glazer, Joan I. *Literature for Early Childhood.* Columbus, Ohio: Merrill, 1981.

Harms, Jeanne McLain, and Lucille L. Lettow. "Poetry for Children Has Never Been Better!" *Reading Teacher* 36 January 1983): 376–381.

Hearne, Betsy. *Choosing Books for Children: A Commonsense Guide.* New York: Delacorte, 1981.

Hopkins, Lee Bennett (Comp.). *The Sky Is Full of Song.* New York: Harper, 1983.

Huck, Charlotte S. *Children's Literature in the Elementary School,* 3d ed. updated. New York: Holt, Rinehart and Winston, 1979.

Keating, Charlotte Matthews. *Building Bridges of Understanding between Cultures.* Tucson, Ariz.: Palo Verde, 1971.

Kimmel, Margaret Mary, and Elizabeth Segel. *For Reading Out Loud! A Guide to Sharing Books with Children.* New York: Delacorte, 1983.

Lukens, Rebecca. *A Critical Handbook of Children's Literature,* (2d ed.) Glenville, Ill.: Scott, Foresman, 1981.

MacDonald, Margaret Read. *The Storyteller's Sourcebook: A Subject, Title, and Motif Index to Folklore Collections for Children.* Detroit, Mich.: Neal-Schuman, 1982.

Tway, Eileen, ed. *Human Ladders for Human Relations,* 6th ed. Urbana, Ill.: National Council of Teachers of English 1981.

White, Mary Lou. *Adventuring with Books: A Booklist for Preschool—Grade 6.* Urbana, Ill.: National Council of Teachers of English, 1981.

Weiss, Jaqueline S. *Prize-Winning Books for Children.* Lexington, Mass.: D. C. Heath, 1983.

Children and Death

Kübler-Ross, Elisabeth. *On Death and Dying.* New York: Macmillan, 1969.

———. *Questions and Answers on Death and Dying.* New York: Macmillan, 1974.

———. *Working It Through.* New York: Macmillan, 1982.

Reed, Elizabeth. *Helping Children with the Mystery of Death.* Nashville, Tenn.: Abingdon Press, 1970.

Children and the Aged

Constant, Helen. "The Image of Grandparents in Children's Literature." *Language Arts* 54 (January 1977): 33–40.

Mavrogenes, Nancy A. "Positive Images of Grandparents in Children's Picture Books." *Reading Teacher* 35 (May 1982): 896–901.

Bibliotherapy

Bernstein, Joanne E. *Books to Help Children Cope with Separation and Loss,* 2d ed. New York: Bowker, 1983.

Cornett, Claudia E., and Charles F. Cornett. *Bibliotherapy: The Right Book at the Right Time.* Bloomington, Ind.: Phi Delta Kappa, 1980.

Dreyer, Sharon S. *Bookfinder.* Circle Pines, Minn.: American Guidance Service, 1981.

Jalongo, Mary Renck. "Bibliotherapy: Literature to Promote Socioemotional Growth." *Reading Teacher* 36 (April 1983): 796–803.

Schrank, Frederick A. "Bibliotherapy as an Elementary School Counseling Tool." *Elementary School Guidance and Counseling* 16 (February 1982): 218–227.

ELEVEN

Written Expression As a Creative Act

INTRODUCTION TO WRITING CHAPTERS

I don't know what I mean until I see what I've said.

E. M. Forster

It is taken for granted that the ability to convey thoughts in written form is necessary for social, utilitarian, and business purposes. It is not generally understood, however, that writing may also be a therapeutic aid for emotional release, as well as a mode of learning and an aesthetic experience. Writing gives us a record of our thoughts so that we can stop to reflect, to analyze, to review, to clarify, to change, and to understand better what we think. Unfortunately, a considerable proportion of young people "do not understand the nature and conventions of written language."[1] This is not surprising since results from the Third National Writing Assessment (1969–1979) show that "neither 13-year-olds nor 17-year-olds receive a great deal of direct instruction in writing or are required to do much writing in school. Very few appear to have access to a writing program that includes prewriting instruction, oral and written feedback on writing assignments, encouragement to write several drafts of papers and opportunities to rework papers after they have been reviewed by teachers."[2] What is most devastating, perhaps, is that the enjoyment of writing seems to decline as students go through the grades.[3]

[1] *Writing Achievement, 1969–1979: Results from the Third National Writing Assessment,* Vol. III: 9-Year-Olds (Denver, Colorado: National Assessment of Educational Progress, December 1980,) p. 48.

[2] Ibid., p. 48.

[3] Ibid., p. 47.

Dr. Ernest L. Boyer, a former United States Education Commissioner, and the principal author of a Carnegie Foundation report on secondary education (released fall of 1983) said that "teaching students to write clearly and effectively should be a central objective of the school." He also suggested that the writing requirement was more critically needed than improved science and mathematics instruction.[4] Many agree with him.

In the 1970s studies of children's language helped investigators in the writing area gain insights into the writing process. The emphasis in writing since then has been on attempting to understand the language strategies that learners use rather than focusing on errors. Educators have felt that as children gain knowledge of the rules of English, they make some natural errors. For example, young children in learning language tend to make errors due to overgeneralizing (see "Stages of Language Development" in Chapter 3). As children develop in their language growth, however, they eventually learn the correct form. (See also "Invented Spelling" in Chapter 13 and "Relationship of Child Growth and Development to Handwriting" in Chapter 14.) The emphasis on process rather than product in writing has influenced how writing is being taught in many schools. It has also dictated a complete recasting of the writing objectives for the Fourth National Assessment of Writing.[5]

An emphasis on process in writing means that learning to write is developmental; that is, such learning takes place over a period of time and a piece of writing usually goes through a number of stages. An emphasis on process does not exclude knowledge of the conventions of writing (mechanics and usage). In addition an emphasis on process does not mean that adult professional writing standards should be imposed on children.

Persons who have difficulty in expressing themselves in writing are handicapped in our society. Authorities on social relations have proposed the thesis that socioeconomic status can be determined by the amount and kind of writing that an individual's job requires. It has been hypothesized that the more writing that people must do on their jobs, the higher their socioeconomic status.

In writing, individuals cannot depend on facial expressions, gestures, or tone of voice to help convey the message. As a result, the words, their organization into sentences, and the punctuation signals used must stand on their own. When writing is judged, a judgment is also being made of the writer. The individual's personality, creativity, schooling, and intelligence are literally "put on the line." Although schools cannot inject creativity into students, they can provide stimulating techniques and an atmosphere where individuals are free to be creative. At the very least, the schools at each grade level should help students to improve their writing to a higher level of acceptability each year.

Although students' writings are generally classified into *practical* and *creative* writing, these are not "natural" divisions. Creative as well as practical writing needs to be functional and requires knowledge of writing skills. The separation of the two is usually done for pedagogical purposes. The more knowledge, background, and imagination students have, the better writers they will be.

[4]Gene I. Maeroff, "Teaching of Writing Gets New Push," *The New York Times* Education Winter Survey, Section 12, January 8, 1984.

[5]*Writing Objectives: 1983–84 Assessment,* National Assessment of Educational Progress, 1982, p. 1.

Practical writing usually means letters, notes, and the necessary mechanics that good writing usually requires. However, even business letters can have some spark that sets them off from others. Wouldn't we all rather receive a creative letter than the more typical cut-and-dried one?

There is no agreement on what constitutes creative writing. When you read something that seems to "get under your skin," that excites, stirs, and makes you "experience," you have probably encountered creative writing.

Regardless of what writing activity children engage in, the teacher must act as a guide, an information center, an encourager, and a stimulator. The teacher must provide an atmosphere conducive to writing and show by his or her behavior that writing is important.

Although, as has already been stated, it is difficult to divide practical and creative writing, it has here been divided into two separate chapters. Chapter 11 will be concerned with the general aspects of writing applicable to both creative and practical writing. It will focus on creative writing in the elementary school. Chapter 12, the second chapter on written expression, will concentrate on practical writing and present a sequential development of writing skills that children should be attaining as they go through the elementary grades.

INTELLIGENCY

I think of the Hippopotamus
As quite an intelligent fellow;
(Not owing to the fact that he's
Very fat; and his teeth are yellow)
I think he's wise
Because of his eyes,
So solemn and big
When opened up wide.
And I also think
(Though I may be wrong)
That he does not boast
That he's more strong
Than any of the other animals
Of the forest
And though a passing tourist
May not envy him,
I do.

Janet M.
Fifth Grade

Creative writers usually have "an itch to write." They allow their imagination to roam freely and give play to it. Their curiosity is never satisfied. They are always searching for the meaning of things and attempting to explain their findings in their own words. Creative writers are explorers; they are always seeking. They are miners, always digging deeper for greater understanding.

Creative writers are aware of the world in which they live. They are sensitive to their environment and are acute observers of it. They are concerned with what is happening around them and have compassion for others. Being perceptive and feeling persons, they are able to "step into the skin of others."

In order to create, they sometimes destroy old ideas. Sometimes they build on past conceptions to generate new ones. They are always open to new ideas and recognize the importance of evaluating their creation as objectively as possible.

Creative writers recognize that creativity takes time. It cannot be commanded or demanded! It is a personal thing.

This chapter will concentrate on some general aspects of writing, including the writing process. It will look at how students' experiences, coupled with the teacher's help, can awaken or stir the creative spark. After reading

this chapter, you should be able to answer these questions:

1. What is the sequence of writing skills in children?
2. What are the differences between revision and editing?
3. What kind of classroom environment is conducive to writing?
4. Can children in the primary grades write creatively?
5. What are some stimulating techniques for creative writing?
6. What are some ingredients necessary for creative writing?
7. What techniques can be used to stimulate children to create poetry?
8. What are some poetic forms that can be used to stimulate children's poetry writing?
9. What is the teacher's role in helping to foster creativity in students?
10. What is the writing process?

SEQUENCE OF WRITING SKILLS IN CHILDREN

When children of about two and one-half first put pencil or crayon to paper, they are entering the initial stage of writing. The desire to convey something of one's own on paper is a necessary first step.

Parents should create a stimulating environment for preschoolers, so that children can scribble and express themselves. After preschoolers have committed themselves on paper, they should be encouraged to tell about what they have drawn or "written." A number of preschoolers try their skills at writing stories, even though they do not have specific hand motor control. (See "Relation of Child Growth and Development to Handwriting" in Chapter 14.) Showing enthusiasm about the child's endeavors will reinforce continuance.

Also, parents should be good role-models for their children. Parents who write will be more prone to have children who write. If parents react negatively to writing letters or "thank-you" notes, this will carry over to their children.

Children usually remain in the scribble stage until they master control of specific muscles. Three-year-olds are often able to make circles, showing that they are gaining control of specific hand muscles. By age five, many can construct other geometric figures, such as squares, which require more precision.

Once the child can make figures such as circles, squares, triangles, and variations of these, his or her written expression takes on a "picture form." Kindergarten children may use these figures to "write a story." Some kindergarten children, who have the necessary hand coordination and mental ability, are able to construct letters or words. Some can print their names in some legible form and write a story about themselves or their families. See p. 205 for an example of such a story.

In the first half of first grade, when children are learning to read and write, teachers should be careful that the children do not spend most of their time in merely imitative writing, that is, the copying of sentences and short stories that the teacher has written. Teachers should encourage children to try to express their own ideas. In this way, children will begin to gain confidence in themselves and feel that what they have to write is important and worth reading by others. When using the language–experience approach, where the written stories are cooperatively developed based on the interest and experiences of the students, teachers should try to capture the children's unique self-expression.

Children love to create, and, as previously stated, many children have been creating their own stories and attempting to convey these in some written form as preschoolers. Teachers need to capitalize on the childrens' creativity. They can do this by giving children the time and opportunity to write and by respecting their ideas. Although the story may be only one or two sentences, it is the child's own creation. Then, by the latter half of first grade, when many students have acquired the specific hand motor control necessary for sustained writing, the children will often write longer stories.

As students go through school, they should be accumulating many firsthand as well as vicarious experiences, and the necessary skills they need for written self-expression.

WRITING ENVIRONMENT

The school plant, the curriculum, school materials, and books are all inert. They only become activated and part of the dynamic learning situation when the teacher and students use them in an effective manner. An attractive classroom, filled with books and children's "published" works, and well organized into a number of learning centers, may be a catalyst for students' writing. If the classroom is a place where exciting things are happening and where children are involved in reading, observing, manipulating, and experimenting, it will be a place where written self-expression goes on.

The quality of the teacher–pupil and pupil–pupil relationships is important in setting the emotional climate of the classroom. If students and teachers are engaged in cooperative endeavors and students feel secure, they will want to write and share their written ideas with others.

Teachers can help establish a secure writing environment by doing some preplanning and by trying to anticipate a number of students' concerns. Children should know where supplies are, where they can go for help, what they can do when they are through, and so on.

TIME FOR WRITING

Students need time to express themselves in written form. Actually writing helps students to be better writers. Five or ten minutes before the lunch hour is not a good time for children to start writing. If teachers spend a great deal of time in preparation and motivating techniques to stimulate the desire to write in children but allow little time for the writing activity itself, the spark, the excitement that has been ignited is hurriedly extinguished. The point to remember is that children should be allowed adequate time to write in class. After getting the proper start in class, many children will work on their own during free time and at home, finishing their compositions because they have become involved with the creative act and want to see the finished product. The option of working on compositions at home should be theirs.

THE WRITING PROCESS

If we were to ask five different persons to explain what they mean by the writing process, it is likely that we would receive five different responses. The *writing process* refers to what we do when we are in the act of writing. That seems simple enough; however, when we attempt to analyze the writing process, we find that it is a complex thinking process analogous to problem solving.

Writing as a thinking act requires that we relate new information to our past experiences or existing information and that we analyze, synthesize, and evaluate this information so that we can present it in a coherent and logical manner. Writing as a thinking act requires

time—time to mull over what we have written, time to dig deeper for greater understanding, time to create new ideas, time to destroy old ideas, time to explore our feelings, and time to evaluate as objectively as possible our creation. As evaluators, we need to be concerned both with the revising and editing process. We need to be concerned with the creative improvement of our present script, as well as with the correcting of technical writing errors such as punctuation errors, capitalization errors, spelling errors, and so on.

When we recognize writing as a problem-solving process, we recognize that writing requires changes, rereading, rethinking, and rewriting. We recognize that writing takes time, thinking, emotional involvement, and commitment to quality. (See "Writing and Reading" in Chapter 8, which illustrates the interrelatedness of the reading and writing process.)

Now, let's look more closely on the writing process, which consists of four stages: prewriting or rehearsing, drafting, revising, and editing.

The *prewriting* or *rehearsing stage* consists of several steps preliminary to the actual writing of the paper. First, we generally begin with a problem or an area that we would like to explore or write about. Next, we have to choose a topic and delimit it. Then, we must determine for whom we are writing this paper because this will determine our style and our format or design for the paper. After we have done this, we need to decide on our central theme, as well as our position on the subject. Note that up until this time, we have not yet begun the actual writing of our paper.

We are now ready to begin the writing of our paper, the *drafting stage*. This part of the writing process is one that requires patience and "sitting power," among a host of other necessary ingredients. It is the stage at which the writer puts down in specific words his or her particular ideas. As we have stated a number of times already, a good writer does not produce a finished, polished version at the first sitting or with the first draft.

Now, in the *revising stage*, the paper is refined through thinking, writing, reading, critiquing, rewriting, rethinking, and so on.

Finally, it requires *editing*, which focuses on the conventions of writing, including word choice and syntax, and the "fine tuning" of final copy for a particular audience.

The writing of various drafts differs from the recopying of a paper. Some writers may be involved in a number of different drafts of their paper; that is, they will go through a number of cycles of prewriting or rehearsing, drafting, and revising before they are satisfied that they have a draft to edit.[1] As one educator has stated, "Composing refers to everything a writer does from the time first words are put on paper until all drafts are completed. Sometimes when a writer must rehearse by writing, there is overlap between the two, composing and rehearsing.[2]

The Writing Process and Instruction

Observing how writers compose, as well as listening to what writers say they do when they compose, have given investigators of writing some insights into the writing process. A number of researchers are now applying what they feel are writing-process techniques to the teaching of writing not only in the upper grades but in the lower grades as well. While teachers should be aware of what researchers are discovering about the writing process, they should be wary when it comes to applying stringent writing-process routines to all children's writing. Even though many students will benefit from participating in some writing-process routines, teachers should not allow any "routine" to become prescriptive. Actually, this would be paradoxical to the essence of the writing process. After all, the writing process applies to what we as individuals do when we are involved in writing. Not all of us proceed in the same way. Therefore, teachers should not expect that all their students should either. For example,

---

[1]See Donald M. Murray, "Writing as a Process: How Writing Finds Its Own Meaning," in *Eight Approaches to Teaching Composition*, Timothy R. Donovan and Ben W. McClelland, eds. (Urbana, Ill.: National Council of Teachers of English), pp. 3–20; Sondra Perl, "Unskilled Writers as Composers," *New York University Quarterly* 10 (1979): 17–25.

[2]Donald H. Graves, *Writing: Teachers & Children at Work* (New Hampshire: Heinemann Educational Books, 1983), p. 223.

some students will spend a great amount of time thinking about what they will write before writing it; whereas others may commit pencil to paper almost immediately. Also, children composers "write to their own length, in their own voices. They *are* writers, but they are sometimes writers of a different kind from adult writers, with their own problems and their own solution."[3] Teachers must be aware of this individuality and of their own expectations that children who imitate the processes of adult writers will necessarily become better writers.

A number of researchers of writing feel strongly that elementary-school children can and should learn the "craft" of writing. Donald Graves, who has done extensive work in writing, states that "many eight- and nine-year-old children can do extensive revisions of a single selection, rewriting well over six to eight drafts to get information the way they want it."[4] This may be, but many children, as well as adults,

[3]Myra Barrs, "The New Orthodoxy about Writing: Confusing Process with Pedagogy," *Language Arts* 60 (October 1983): 832.
[4]Graves, *Writing,* p. 4.

might rebel at having to make so many drafts. Graves would probably agree with the latter statement because he feels strongly both that teachers must know their children well and that the decision to make the revisions should come from the student writer—not imposed by the teacher.

Teachers who use the writing-process routines must respect the individual differences of their student writers. They must be sensitive to the child's efforts and know when to intervene, how to intervene, and how much intervention an individual child needs. If every time a child writes something, the teacher keeps saying, "Is this what you really want to say?" or "I think you can say that better," the child may become inhibited in writing. The child may begin to feel that what he or she has to say is never worthy, a belief that will turn children away from writing. Also, not all writing requires revision. Teachers need to help children recognize when to "let go" as well as when they should continue to revise and "polish."

Now, let's look a little more closely at two student writers to see the writing process in action for them.

SCENARIO

SETTING THE STAGE

Andrew is a fifth-grader in Mrs. Smith's class. He is fortunate to have Mrs. Smith because she is a dynamic, enthusiastic teacher who is as knowledgeable of her subject as of her students. When you walk into Mrs. Smith's classroom, you sense immediately that this is a room where exciting learning is taking place. Conspicuously displayed is a whole shelf of children's bound books that they have "published." Other books are also clearly visible, as well as several learning centers, children's art, and so on. What is most impressive to a visitor, however, is that when you walk into the classroom no one notices you because each child is deeply immersed in what he or she is doing.

The students in Mrs. Smith's class have been reading a number of fiction stories and books, and now they are going to write their own.

PREWRITING OR REHEARSING STAGE

Andrew has been interested in space travel for some time. As a matter of fact, his dream is to become an astronaut. There is almost no book on space travel in the school library that Andrew hasn't read, and the school librarian and Mrs. Smith have just ordered two new books "hot off the press" for him. Andrew had no problem deciding what kind of fiction story he would write. It would be, of course, science fiction. Andrew was excited about his choice, and discussed with Mrs. Smith some of his ideas. He also shared some of his thoughts with his friends. They, in turn, shared some of their ideas with Andrew.

Kathy, however, was in a quandary because she couldn't decide on a topic. She hated to have to choose her own topic and wasn't used to doing it. A transfer student from a school where the teachers always assigned the topic, Kathy had been in Mrs. Smith's class for only a few weeks. She would have to meet with Mrs. Smith for some help.

DRAFTING STAGE

Finally, Andrew decided that he had a good enough idea of the story he wanted to write, so he decided to "give it a try." (This is not Andrew's first attempt at writing in Mrs. Smith's class—it's now the seventh month of the term, and students have been writing since the first day of class.) Andrew worked for a concentrated period of time and seemed oblivious to his surroundings. While he was working, no one interrupted him. Andrew only stopped writing when the lunch bell rang. (Andrew had surmised that it was about that time from the growls in his stomach.) Andrew is the kind of writer who likes to get everything down in his first draft. Kathy, on the other hand, goes through her first draft very, very slowly because she doesn't like to keep revising and making new drafts.

Andrew was so involved with his story that it's all he could talk about at lunch. If he had time during the day, he would try to get back to it. Kathy, however, said that she liked to mull things over. Anyway, there was something bothering her, and she didn't know how to proceed. She discussed her problem with her friend Andrew, who made a suggestion that she said she liked. She wanted to think more about it, however.

By the next day, Andrew had finished his first draft. He had worked on it at home because it had been on his mind. Kathy did not complete her draft until the end of the week.

REVISING STAGE

Andrew reread his first draft to himself rather than to Kathy, who was busy, because he was anxious to see how it "held together." He always liked to go over his material right away. Not Kathy, however, who usually waited for a period of time before returning to her first draft. Anyway, Andrew was used to making more than one draft. He was reading it to see whether he had to make any substantive creative improvements to the story. In other words, he had to decide whether he needed to reorganize any of the material, and whether he needed to add, delete, or change anything. Because Andrew felt "stuck," he decided to meet with Mrs. Smith to discuss his story and to ask for advice. Andrew did this, and, as usual, it paid off. Mrs. Smith listened carefully to what Andrew had to say. She took her cues from him, and then asked some penetrating questions that helped Andrew see more clearly what his problems were. He knew that what he had wasn't exactly what he wanted, but he had not been able to get at the problem.

Andrew now knew what revisions to make; he sat down to write another draft. Actually, Andrew wrote two more drafts before he was finally pleased with his story. He also met two more times with Mrs. Smith to discuss his story.

EDITING STAGE

When Andrew finally felt that he had the story exactly the way he wanted it, he went over his paper to check whether he had made any word-usage, punctuation, capitalization, or spelling errors. (This is the part that Andrew really dislikes.) Mrs. Smith, however, insisted that the final copy should be as free from certain types of errors as possible. A paper or book filled with spelling, punctuation, and other such errors is not one that people enjoy reading, even though the ideas are excellent.

When Mrs. Smith read Andrew's paper, she suggested that he might want to use some other words for variety, and she also picked up some spelling, capitalization, and punctuation errors. In addition, she made some suggestions about sentence structure. After Andrew made these corrections, Mrs. Smith asked him how he felt about his story and whether he felt it was ready for publication. Andrew claimed that he was happy with it and wanted it to be published. (See Appendix A on "Bookbinding for Children's own Published Books," and "Computer-aided Instruction" in Chapter 16.)

If children are involved in publishing their own books or class magazine, they will have a purpose for writing, revising, and editing. The amount of revision that a student will do and the number of different drafts will depend on the student. Therefore, it is imperative that teachers know their students quite well.

Persons revise their material for a number of reasons; it may be that the student feels the writing does not express what he or she intended; it may be that the student gains some new information or insights into the topic; or it may be that the student doesn't like the organization. Whatever the reason, the best revision is that which stems from the writer and not from the direct intervention of the teacher; it "comes because children control their writing."[5]

Graves presents four factors that lead children to make "healthy" changes in their writing:

1. Surround the children with literature.
2. Publish children's writings.
3. Provide children with access to each other.
4. Create direct involvement with the teacher—usually in conference. In the conference, the teacher takes her cue from the student and asks only those questions that "fall within the child's intention for the piece and that he or she feels the child can handle."[6]

Note that the conferences Andrew had with his teacher followed the writing-process sequence, which, of course, makes sense. First, Andrew discussed his ideas with Mrs. Smith; next, he discussed how he would put his story together; then he was concerned with the conventions of writing.

The revision process is a painful one for any writer. Sometimes it's helpful to read aloud the material to determine whether it does express exactly what the writer intends. Other times, it might be advantageous to discuss the writing with another student or the teacher. Other times, it might be best for the student to simply "back off" from the writing, that is, to distance oneself from what was written in order to get a better and more objective perspective on it.

One technique that teachers can use to get students to understand better the revision and editing processes is to cooperatively go over a paper from a previous year and have the students state what they would do to try to im-

[5]Donald Graves, "Teacher Intervention in Children's Writing: A Response to Myra Barrs," *Language Arts* 60 (October 1983): p. 845.

[6]Ibid., p. 845.

prove the paper. The teacher should list the students' suggestions on special large charts, which should be displayed throughout the year. The Revision and Editing Checklists in Chapter 12 (pp. 248–249) are examples of what can be kept on display. Throughout the year teachers should remind their students to review these checklists.

Also, teachers should suggest that their students try to act as uninformed readers rather than the writer when revising and editing their material.

CREATIVE WRITTEN EXPRESSION IN THE PRIMARY GRADES

Children in the primary grades have a multitude of ideas. They love to listen to stories and enjoy creating their own. In kindergarten, children should be encouraged to tell stories about the many different things around them. When teachers listen to their kindergarten and first-grade children, they discover that many of the things they say about the world around them are in poetic form. Young children seem to play with words and to delight in saying and repeating them. Teachers should take advantage of the opportunities that present themselves to record these utterances. Children enjoy listening to and seeing their first creations in print. Their lively imaginations are ready to blossom forth in writing, if they are properly encouraged and stimulated. A number of restraints may act as deterrents, however, learning manuscript and mastering spelling, among others. If every time children write something on paper, the teacher corrects and criticizes it, the children may cease to put their ideas on paper.

On page 211 are some efforts at creative writing by two first-graders at the beginning of the school year. These were displayed, even though they were not perfect. These two children had worked very hard on their stories, and they were looking forward to having them displayed. They had each revised their story once because they felt that they could make it better. Now, they were happy with them. The teacher talked separately with the children about their stories, and he went over some of the conventions of writing with each one. He did not ask them to redo their papers again, however.

By accepting the writing at this point, the teacher is encouraging these children to write again. They should not have to revise or recopy the paper a number of times to achieve perfection. As the term progresses, the teacher will correct the children's papers before displaying them. Also, he will continue to supply them with the punctuation and capitalization skills they need.

Children should be allowed to use any words they wish regardless of whether they can spell them correctly. They should also not be censored or made to choose only a topic the teacher has selected. Primary-grade teachers have a great responsibility, because what they do in school may influence students' attitudes toward writing the rest of their lives.

TEACHER'S ROLE IN CREATIVE WRITING

Teachers can help to foster creativity in students. The attitude and understanding of teachers, as well as their manner of teaching, will influence students' creative development. Teachers who demand one way of doing things will thwart pupils' desires to "look beyond" or to try new paths; teachers who stimulate students to be more divergent, however, will be encouraging their creativity.

When students are helped to realize that if they take the time to search within themselves, they will have worthwhile things to write about, they are being helped to discover they can write.

Stimulating Creative Written Expression

The more creative the teacher, the greater students' chances will be for realizing their creative potential. Teachers cannot inject creativity into their students, but they can provide an atmosphere in which children feel free to explore, to make mistakes, and to take chances.

Motivation is an important facet of creativity and is necessary for all learning. Teachers can create situations, either through using everyday events or through preplanned happenings, to motivate students in wanting to create. Although the best motivation is internal, out-

Matthaew D. W.
I ate an apple
Have an ache
Do You? Have One.
The End.

Julie
I see a mouse? He is scared to look at me

side stimulators can get the individual aroused and involved. Once students are motivated, a mood and desire to write should be created.

Creative writing stimulators can emanate from a variety of media—pictures, literature, tapes, discussion, records, films, dramatic activity, and so on. Motivational devices can be used to heighten awareness on the part of the child and to act as a springboard to stir the students' imaginations.

The teacher must be careful not to expect the same responses from all students. As individuals, children will be motivated by different stimuli, so a diversity of techniques and devices should be used to encourage responses from as many students as possible.

Motivating Techniques A variety of motivating techniques exist to help stimulate creative writing:

1. Hold up a papier-mâché "animal" that has the characteristics of many different animals. Tell the children that this "creature" is very confused. It doesn't know who it is or where it comes from. It needs help from the children. Perhaps they can find a name for it, and tell where it came from, what it does, and how it lives.

2. After reading some books the children can be asked questions that stimulate creative thinking in writing. In fifth or sixth grade the children might read *A Wrinkle in Time*, in which the main characters visit a gray planet devoid of sunlight, inhabited by gray people. The children could then be asked to write on the following problem: How would you as a human being adapt to this gray planet?

3. Hold up a number of pictures and ask students to write creative stories about them. In the primary grades a picture stimulus can be used as an experience story, with the teacher and pupils writing the story together.

4. Ask children to imagine they have an animal that can talk. Ask them to tell of their experiences with this animal.

5. Ask children to imagine they are living in a house of the far-distant future, and tell what this house is like: its furniture, its appliances, its kitchen utensils.

6. Ask children to imagine that they live at the bottom of the sea. Ask them to tell of their adventures. For a fantastic account of such an adventure they can read *Twenty Thousand Leagues Under the Sea* by Jules Verne, and for a scientific account that may seem stranger than fiction they can read Rachel Carson's *The Sea Around Us*.

7. Ask children to imagine that they own a spaceship that can take them to another planet. Ask them to tell of their experiences.

8. Ask children to write an imaginative theme beginning with the sentence, "There is only one hour to wait. . . ."

9. "Who am I?" Students develop biographical mysteries.

10. Ask children to imagine they are machines, and to write a story from the machine's point of view.

11. Have your students write another ending for a book that they have read.

12. Have your students write an adventure for a favorite character in a television situation comedy series.

13. Show your students a metal skeleton key. Tell them that this key has lived through some very strange and frightening adventures. It has seen things that no one has seen. Have the students write one of the adventures and tell what it is that no one has ever seen.

14. Present the students with titles that have nonsense words in them. The students are asked to choose a title and write a story about it. Examples:

The Pringle that Ploobed
A Peropious Gragle
Two Seripitious Flangles
A Visit to Velanious

15. Children can create tall tales to answer these questions:

Why do lions roar?
Why does a camel have a hump on its back?
Why is grass green?
Why do snakes hiss?
Why do mountains have ice caps?

16. Students can make up their own questions for tall tales.

17. Students can write funny stories about topics such as the following:

The light who hated to be turned out.
The kangaroo without a pouch.
The refrigerator that was allergic to food.
The umbrella that was afraid of the rain.
The dog that meowed.
The lion that said, "Peep, peep."
The monkey that was afraid of heights.

18. Have the students write a humorous autobiography.

19. Have the students write a riddle about one of their favorite animals.

20. Have students write a fairy tale about one of these:

A person who lives in a walnut shell.

A magic fan.
The people who live in the sea.

21. Have students make up topics for fairy tales.

22. Have students finish the following "If I . . ." phrase and write a story about one of them:

If I lived on the moon . . .
If I had magic power . . .
If I could be . . .
If I could fly . . .

23. Present the following to your children:

In the book *The Ice-Cream Cone Coot* by Arnold Lobel, there are many strange and rare birds. The author has combined bird parts with everyday objects to make some unusual birds. For example, he's combined a pencil and a parrot to make a Pencilkeet Parrot, he's combined a dollar bill and a dodo to make a Dollarbill Dodo, and he's combined a water glass and a goose to make a Water Glass Goose.

You can use your imagination to combine any animal with any object to make your own special rare animal. Describe your animal and tell something funny about it.

Brainstorming lends itself to providing a warm-up for creative writing, as well as other creative activities. (See Chapter 4 for brainstorming techniques.)

SOME INGREDIENTS FOR CREATIVE WRITING

Experiencing, getting in touch with one's feelings, and having many opportunities to write are necessary ingredients for writing. Ideas are not created in a vacuum. Children need a rich and varied literary environment to which they can add their firsthand knowledge and experiences. Good literature not only gives students models of human thinking but also makes students more sensitive to the elements needed for good writing.

Students need time to write, to incubate and mull over ideas. They need a place where they can write undisturbed by others. Pupils need a classroom environment that is psychologically safe, a place in which they feel free to share ideas with others and to look within themselves.

Description: An Essential Writing Ingredient

Good writers are usually good observers of the world around them. They are perceptive and sensitive to their senses—touch, smell, hearing, taste, and sight. Children need many experiences in these areas. They must recognize the importance of each sense and how each helps them communicate with themselves.

A variety of activities exists to help students become more sensitive, keener observers of their environment, and to help them to develop descriptive ability:

1. Have children close their eyes and put their hands into a number of different bags held near them. Each bag contains a different item—such as a piece of liver, cold spaghetti, or ice-cold grapes. Have the children describe each item. As they do so, the terms they use are put on the board. (Ice-cold grapes elicit very good descriptions.)

2. Each group of students is given a box containing one item. Students must try to figure out what the item is using their sense of hearing.

3. One student comes to the front of the room, while all others close their eyes. The student then describes someone in the class. The children, without opening their eyes, try to guess who the person is.

4. Have the children describe a building that they have to pass on the way to school. After they have described it in writing, the teacher should take the whole class to visit the building to see how accurate the descriptions are.

5. Have the students describe odors that come from the school cafeteria on a particular day.

6. Ask students to describe the sounds of a busy traffic intersection.

7. Have students describe a favorite holiday, telling how it seemed to them when they were about five years old, and comparing how it seems now.

8. Ask students to describe a costume they would like to wear to a ball.

9. Have students describe a character from a favorite television show.

10. The teacher sets up the scenario at the bottom of the page, and the children describe the person they saw.

Exercises in description help children to be more perceptive of the world around them, and aid them to develop characters for their stories.

Creating Word Images: Figures of Speech

People use figures of speech in conversation in order to communicate better, and children are exposed to them from listening to the language around them before they come to school. Depending on their backgrounds, many children will already use word images in their speech.

As with the rest of our speech, the use of word images does not depend on knowledge of their labels. Since children use verbs, nouns, and other parts of speech without knowing their names, so they can use figures of speech. Many students may depend heavily on slang to convey their meaning.

When children begin to read, they encounter figures of speech that help the reader to see vivid word pictures. (See "Figures of Speech in Poetry" in Chapter 10.)

Although students use figures of speech quite well in oral expression, they seem to have more difficulty with them in reading and writing. Perhaps children use such expressions in speech quite naturally and are not aware that they portray word images. Teachers must, therefore, try to get students to recognize that some of the phrases that brighten up speech can also be usefully incorporated in their writing. However, teachers must also recognize that since figures of speech are a form of inference, not all children will be able to work with figurative language. (See "Figures of Speech in Poetry" in Chapter 10.)

Intermediate Grades: Developing Word Imagery The teacher can record a number of expressions commonly used by students, and then ask why and when students use these expressions. The children should be encouraged to generate a number of word images about a specific event. The word images they include in their writing give readers a more lucid picture of the event. One event the teacher might describe for such an activity follows:

A boy and girl are dancing at a school dance. The boy is very clumsy and keeps stepping on the girl's feet. Students, using word pictures, have to express how the boy and girl feel.

SCENARIO

Beforehand, the teacher asks two outsiders each to bring an item into the classroom as he or she is talking to the students. The first person brings in a brown paper bag, the second brings a sheet of paper. The two persons put the items on the desk and leave. Then the teacher looks at the desk, notices the items, and says, "Oh! This isn't mine. It belongs to someone else." The teacher asks the children if they had seen who left the brown paper bag on the desk. The teacher asks them to write a description of the person who brought the item. After the children write their descriptions, some of them are read aloud for comparison. Later the visitor who brought the brown bag is invited into the classroom so that the children can see how accurate their descriptions are.

When students have generated a number of expressive phrases that start with "as" or "like," which compare two unlike things, the teacher states that these figures of speech are called *similes*. After analyzing some of the other phrases given by students which compare two unlike objects or concepts, but which do not start with "as" or "like," the teacher tells students that these phrases are *metaphors*.[7] If students have described inanimate objects with human characteristics, students should be told that these figures of speech are *personification*.

Students can then be encouraged to give further examples of similes, metaphors, and personification. They seem to have the least difficulty with generating and recognizing similes, because they are introduced with "like" or "as." Metaphors seem to be more difficult for students to recognize and make up, because there is no introductory word cue.

---

[7]Often the term "metaphor" is used in a generic (general) sense to cover all forms of figures of speech. Therefore, simile, personification, and so on, might be referred to as metaphors.

Although children in primary grades are both exposed to and frequently use similes such as he is skinny as a toothpick, she is pretty as a picture, she is happy as a lark, he is quiet as a mouse, they do not have to learn the term "simile" for these. However, by fourth grade "simile" can be introduced, and by fifth grade both "metaphor" and "personification" can be learned.

Hyperbole, or "gross exaggeration," can be introduced in the intermediate grades. Again, students use this type of figure of speech in their everyday language, but they must be made aware of its potential in written form. For example, students might say:

> I walked a million miles today.
> I am dead tired.
> He missed by a mile.

Students should be encouraged to discuss how these terms help readers get a clearer understanding of what they are saying. When a writer says that someone "prattled on for an eternity," he or she is not only telling us that the person talked for a very long time, but the writer is also giving us his or her feelings about the event. If

FIGURE 11.1 CHARLIE BROWN HAS DIFFICULTY UNDERSTANDING LUCY'S SIMILE AND METAPHOR.

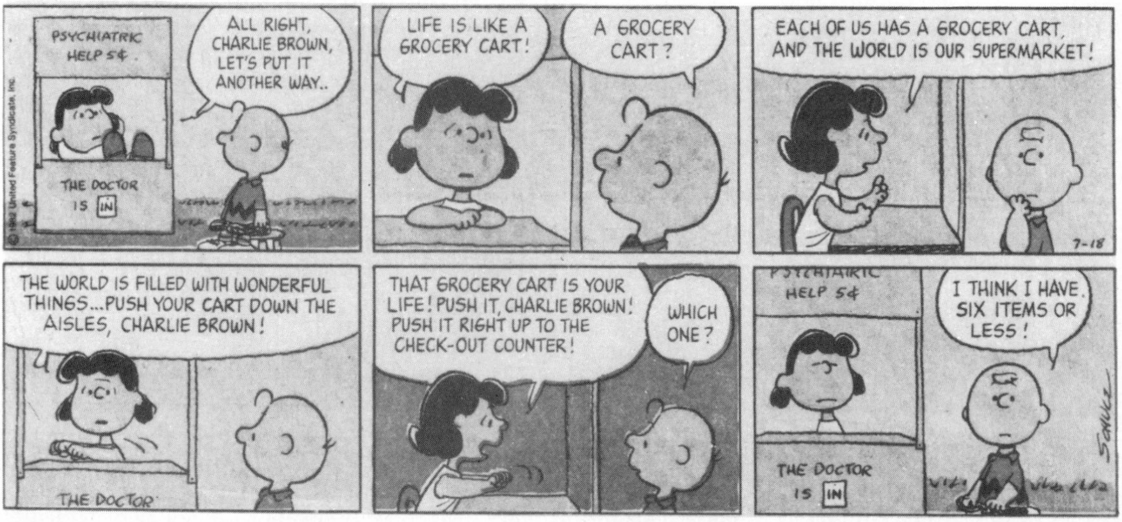

the writer had enjoyed the company of the person talking, the writer would not have said that the person prattled on for an eternity.

Students should be helped to understand the use of hyperbole in advertising. The term "hype" is used very often in our culture, especially about the advertising industry in connection with television and movie advertisements. Exaggerated words such as "blockbuster," "death-defying," "shocker," "stupendous," "stupefying," "sensational," "amazing," and "unbelievable" are often used to describe the production they are promoting. Students should be able to generate many more terms.

Another technique that is frequently used by writers is that of oxymoron. (See "Figures of Speech in Poetry" in Chapter 10.) *Oxymoron* is the combining of contraries (opposites) to portray a particular image or to produce a striking effect. These word contradictions attract our attention and present the author's feelings or ideas indirectly and expressively.

An oxymoron with which students may be familiar is "the poor little rich girl." Usually this word contradiction is accompanied with sarcasm, that is, the person saying it is actually ridiculing the girl while expressing a seemingly sympathetic phrase. In other words, the writer does not feel sorry for the girl. However, it is possible for the phrase "the poor little rich girl" to mean that the girl has a lot of material possessions, but she lacks other things such as love, understanding, or parents.

Some other examples of familiar oxymorons used in sentences follow:

1. Parting is such *sweet sorrow*.
2. A *loud silence* followed the improper remark.
3. This is one of those occasions for *making haste slowly*.
4. She lives in *happy ignorance*.
5. He is suffering from *benign neglect*.
6. They are the *best* of *enemies*.
7. She was *conspicuous* by her *absence*.

The oxymoron "the dawn of night" would probably be one that would be used in connection with Dracula, who would be more interested in the "dawn of night." "Night is day" for Dracula. Students can probably come up with some interesting oxymorons in relation to the adventures of Dracula, one of the living dead.

Avoiding Overworked Phrases

Teachers need to encourage students to avoid using overworked phrases—phrases that have been used over and over again. For many people, it is often easier to use a common phrase than to think of a fresh and original way to say something. For example, in the similes presented earlier, the phrases "pretty as a picture," "happy as a lark," "quiet as a mouse," and "skinny as a toothpick," would be considered overworked phrases.

Children need to be helped to recognize that strong, active, and descriptive words are better than general and static ones. For example, see how the sentence "They removed the obstacle" can be made into a more vivid and graphic sentence by changing the verb "removed" to one of the following verbs: *erased, demolished, obliterated, destroyed, liquidated, wiped out, uprooted, smashed, scattered,* or *displaced.*

Character Development

In developing characters children must be aided in avoiding stereotyping. A researcher who worked with intermediate-grade pupils was trying to help them improve their imaginative writing. The researcher used a short piece, "How to Tell the Good Guys from Bad Guys" by John Steinbeck (*The Reporter,* March 10, 1955). In the piece Steinbeck's son, Catbird, points out to his father that you can always tell the plot of a television Western at the beginning of the program, because the good guy is wearing a white hat and the bad guy wears a black one. The man in the gray hat is either good at the start and then turns bad, or is first bad and then turns good. A reading of this piece opens up an excellent opportunity for class criticism of some of the character portrayals on television.

To develop their critical abilities, children can be asked to watch a number of different television shows to distinguish which characters are one-dimensional or not very realistic, and which characters are multidimensional or more lifelike and realistic. Students can then state what the differences are.

A combination of methods that make a character come to life can be listed as:

1. Describe the characters—how they look and so forth.
2. Show them in action—what they do.
3. Tell what they say—this can lead into attempts at dialogue.
4. Show what other people think about them.
5. Tell what they think about—what goes on in their heads.[8]

Rather than merely requiring pupils to write character sketches, have them present the characters in a happening, so that they are real people in action. Such an event includes all those things that could take place in a given situation or scene.

Developing Suspense

In order to develop suspense, children must learn not to give all their information at once. They must learn to postpone, to give just enough to whet the appetites of their readers. In putting events together children must try to have something in each situation that will heighten the desire of the reader to want to go on with the story. Reporting suspenseful stories will help children learn this technique, as will choosing good suspense stories for analysis to see how the author achieved suspense.

Another technique that the teacher could use is to present students with some examples of themes that entail suspense, and to have them fill in what led up to such a decision. Here are examples of some endings that teachers could use:

I did have friends after all. What a warm feeling it is to belong.

I learned a lesson from all this. You have to trust someone.

The nightmare was over, but we would probably never be the same.

[8]Adapted from Henry Larom, "Sixth Graders Write Good Short Stories," *Elementary English* 37 (January 1960): 20–23.

The animals saved my life. I will be grateful to them always.

It was an exciting adventure and one that I will always remember, but I'm glad it's over.

After what happened, I knew that I would never see them again.

Writing about Events

In order to help children write about situations, events, or scenes, they should be given many experiences. Children might present a short skit, which the rest of the class can then write about, telling exactly what took place and describing the character and the action. The teacher can show a movie or a television clip and the students can write a description of it.

In developing skills in writing there is no set order in which elements must be presented by the teacher. The important thing is that children be aided in mastering writing skills and that they be given *many opportunities to write*.

CREATING POETRY

In Chapter 10 it was stated that children get "turned off" from poetry as they go through the grades. However, if children are properly exposed to poetry and allowed to create it, what delightful creations they can produce!

WHAT AM I?

I am a monster.
No, now I'm a dog!
Now I'm a bluebird,
And now I'm a log!

Now I'm a cat,
Now I'm a rat!

Now a mouse,
In a house!

I'm a lizard
No, I'm a blizzard

Now I've turned into a hat;
And now once again
Into a cat!

Richard

Kenneth Koch in his book, *Wishes, Lies, and Dreams,* demonstrates how he was able to get elementary-school children reading and writing poetry. His formula includes a fundamental belief that all children are able to create poems. They must be encouraged to put their thoughts down, and not fear recriminations because of misspellings, lack of neatness, or improper word usage. There must be a proper classroom environment, as well as knowledge of some techniques for poetry writing.

One technique used to stimulate poetry writing is to ask children to start their own poems with "I wish." According to Koch, "The idea helped them to find that they could do it, by giving them a form that would give their poem unity and that was easy and natural for them to use: beginning each line with 'I wish.' " One of the main problems children have as writers is subject matter, and using a technique like "I wish" encourages children to be "imaginative and free."[9]

Some other successful methods employed were to:

1. Put a comparison or a sound in every line.
2. Write dream poems.
3. Write lie poems; to say something in each line that wasn't true.

Children were helped to write by ". . . removing obstacles, such as the need to rhyme, and by encouraging them in various ways to get tuned in to their own strong feelings, to their spontaneity, their sensitivity, and their carefree inventiveness."[10]

Another technique that helps children in poetry writing is exposure to many poems. "Jump or Jiggle" by Evelyn Beyer can be read as a "loosening up" exercise for the class. This can be followed immediately with Iris Tiedt's poem "What Can You Do?" After each poem is read children should be asked where they think the idea for the poem came from. A poem in a similar vein, "I Speak, I Say, I Talk" by Arnold L. Shapiro, can also be read. At this point children should be asked if they would like to try writing a poem together. To stimulate the class,

PUPPET SHOWS BY STUDENTS DEVELOP WRITING CAPABILITIES.

words in groups of two, similar to those given below, are listed, and the children contribute their ideas orally. Some children may want to write their own pairs, and should be encouraged to do so.

Cows
Dogs

Ants
Worms

Cats
Fish

Boys
Girls

I
Birds[11]

Since teachers do not know which poems will ignite the creative spark in their students, they should expose them to a variety. After listening to Amy Lowell's "Falling Leaves," and a number of other poems about fall, some children wrote poems of their own.

[9]Kenneth Koch, *Wishes, Lies, and Dreams* (New York: Chelsea House, 1970), p. 7.

[10]Ibid., p. 25.

[11]A. Barbara Pilon, "Lighting the Candle to Children's Creative Language Powers," *Elementary English* 50 (April 1973): 568.

As we have stated, teachers must recognize that what stirs one child may not necessarily interest another. Not all students love all the poems presented in class, and teachers should be very careful about "gushing." It's one thing to be genuinely enthused about a poem; it's another to try to force-feed it to students. Children seem to be able to sense sincerity and honesty. Let the children know that you, too, do not "love" all poetry. Since you are sharing poems with the class, ask them to bring in some of their favorites, as well as some of their parents' favorites. This usually sparks an interest in poetry, a necessary first step in the creation of poems.

Poetry of the Senses

The poetry books used by the class should offer sights, sounds, and colors that stimulate children to want to produce their own creations. Mary O'Neill's *Hailstones and Halibut Bones: Adventures in Color* has stimulated many students to create color poems. This prolific writer has also published *What Is That Sound!*, which encourages children to create "sound" poems. Her book *Fingers Are Always Bringing Me News* makes children more aware of utilizing the sense of touch in writing[12] (See "Listening for Appreciation" in Chapter 6 for more on poetry of the senses. See also Chapter 9 for "Vocabulary of the Senses.")

Music and Poetry

The teacher should use a number of different stimuli because it is difficult to determine what will act as a catalyst to creation. Music can stir poetic creation in children because both have their own unique rhythms. Children respond very readily to the sounds as well as the rhythms of music, so music might stimulate children to "hear" poems.

As a result of listening to Tchaikovsky's "Quartet in D Major" some children wrote poems. A sample of a girl's poem reflects the soft sounds, whereas the boy's is preoccupied with the sonorous sounds.

POETRY AND MUSIC

Galloping, galloping, over the hills;
With two Toms, and six Bills.
Boy this is a lot of fun;
I hope we never get done.
Ride and ride all afternoon;
The horses' feet make such a tune.

Bill

POETRY AND MUSIC

Exciting music, soft and low and bouncy; a
    beautiful show.
The violin singing, Oh how lovely.
Never a mistake, skimming along.
Beautiful music, humming a song.

Abbe

Fun with Different Poetic Forms

Children can become excited over the many kinds of literary forms used in writing poetry. Children may even be encouraged to make up their own. To act as guidelines to the great diversity of poetic forms, children should be exposed to the triangle, quadrangle, and diamante poetic forms created by Iris Tiedt;[13] (discussed later in this Chapter). Haiku, cinquain, concrete poetry, and newspaper poetry are other types of poetic forms children can experiment with in their creative endeavors.

Haiku   *Haiku* is one of the oldest forms of Japanese poetry. It consists of three lines composed of seventeen syllables—five in the first and third lines, and seven in the second. Since Japanese and English syllabication are not similar, haiku lends itself more readily to Japanese writing, and the 5–7–5 syllabication pattern is not always adhered to in English.

The most important factor in haiku is the feeling that is supposed to be portrayed in the poem. The themes are usually concerned with beauty and nature. The theme should be clearly stated and the location, time of day, or season is usually incorporated in the poem. Nothing is too insignificant to be noticed by the poet.

The 5–7–5 syllabication cannot be used until children are in the intermediate grades and

[12]Ruth Kearney Carlson, "The Creative Thrust of Poetry Writing," *Elementary English* 49 (December 1972): 1183–1184.

[13]Pilon, "Lighting the Candle," p. 568.

have been exposed to syllables. Therefore, rather than stressing syllables, theme, feeling, and simplicity rendered in three lines can be stressed. Here are some examples *not* based on syllabication:

> The sun—
> brightly afire
> warms all.

> Flowers—
> opening their arms
> to love.

Samples of haiku based on the syllabication pattern include:

THE MORNING MIST

> The morning mist crept
> over my lawn as I slept
> at the crack of dawn.

WINTER

> The sleds flew forward
> like birds flying in the sky.
> We played until dark.

The *tanka* verse is a five-line pattern of Oriental verse arranged in a 5–7–5–7–7 poetic pattern of 31 syllables. Although it has the same qualities as haiku, its form is not as delicate, because of the addition of the two seven-syllable lines.

Lanterne is another syllabic pattern of 1–2–3–4–1, which is arranged in the shape of a lantern. Ruth Carlson discusses both tanka and lanterne verse in her books *Sparkling Words: Two Hundred Practical and Creative Writing Ideas* and *Writing Aids through the Grades*. An interesting variation is that of the *chained lanterne,* which joins several verses in the form of a linked or chained lantern.

Here is one that a fifth-grader wrote:

> Two
> Good pals
> Through the years
> Helping each one
> Chums!

> Two
> Always
> Through the years
> Helping each one
> Pals

> Pals
> A team
> A good match
> Helping each one
> Friends!

Diane S.

Cinquain   *Cinquain* is based on a five-line pattern. People writing in cinquain have varied this five-line pattern; for example, one variation consists of a first line with five words, while each subsequent line has one less word. The result is an upside-down pyramid five lines high, ending in one word.

Another five-line pattern consists of a first line with one word, the second line with two words, the third with three, the fourth with four, while the fifth line reverts to the one-word length of line one. Some persons also give specific purposes for each line, which is helpful in guiding neophyte writers:

> *Line 1:* states the theme
> *Line 2:* describes the theme
> *Line 3:* the theme is in some action
> *Line 4:* gives a feeling of the theme
> *Line 5:* states another word for the theme

Many elementary-level students seem to prefer the second pattern of 1–2–3–4–1, with a specific purpose given for each line. An example is:

> Fog,
> white blanket
> covering the universe
> how still and quiet
> Peace.

Iris Tiedt has invented four new poetry patterns that seem to be successful frames for ideas.[14] The first of these, the diamante (dee ah

---

[14]Iris M. Tiedt, "Exploring Poetry Patterns," *Elementary English* (December 1970): 1083–1084.

mahn' tay), is a seven-line, diamond-shaped poem structured as:

Line 1: subject noun (one word)
Line 2: adjectives (two words)
Line 3: participles (three words)
Line 4: nouns (four words)
Line 5: participles (three words)
Line 6: adjectives (two words)
Line 7: noun, opposite of subject (one word)

A second form by Tiedt is the *septolet,* which consists of seven lines (fourteen words) with this pattern:

Line 1: one word
Line 2: two words
Line 3: three words
Line 4: two words
Line 5: one word
Line 6: two words
Line 7: three words

Tiedt's third form, the *quinzaine,* involves fifteen syllables in three lines (7–5–3) that make a statement followed by a question.

The fourth pattern, called the *quintain,* is a five-line progression of 2, 4, 6, 8, and 10 syllables respectively.

Concrete Poetry *Concrete poetry* seems to be a favorite among children of all ages, who enjoy experimenting with many of the poetic styles utilized by modern poets. Concrete poets are concerned with the arrangement of words on a page and feel that their purpose is to be simultaneously perceived and read. Children can use any object that they desire as their stimulus, and develop a poem using the concrete form of the object as an outline. Stimuli can range from an outline of a cat to a child's hand (see below).

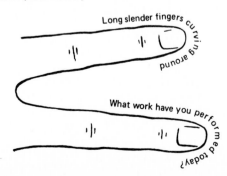

The concrete poem below was written by a child about her kitten.

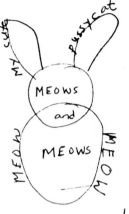

Lisa M. Grade 2

Newspaper Poetry *Newspaper poetry,* a poetic form that can be used to stimulate children's poetry writing, is similar in many ways to concrete poetry. Newspaper poets, like concrete poets, are concerned with the arrangement of words on a page, and feel that these should be simultaneously perceived and read, that is, the visual presentation is part of the poetic experience. However, newspaper poets rely on the appearance of the words and their arrangements for the desired effect, whereas concrete poets are more concerned with a specific object.

Children of all ages enjoy creating newspaper poetry, which involves choosing words from newspapers and magazines that express certain feelings or thoughts. These words can be of various sizes, shapes, and colors. The children arrange them in a pattern that best expresses the thought or feeling they would like to portray.

Constructing newspaper poetry is an enjoyable undertaking. It is a good idea for teachers to construct their own newspaper poems before they attempt this activity in class, because only then will their enthusiasm for this activity be genuine.

On the specified day for the construction of newspaper poems, teachers should make sure that each newspaper poet has an ample supply of newspapers and magazines, paste, a pair of scissors, and *sufficient time*.

To stimulate interest in poetry in which the medium is an important part of the message, the teachers can expose children to some poems by Edward Lear and Alastair Reid. Children will probably delight in Edward Lear's "Nonsense Botany" in which the visual is a very important aspect of the poem. In *Ounce Dice Trice*, Alastair Reid has such poems as "Counting" and "Odds and Ends," in which the visual appearance of the words and their arrangement on the page are part of the poetic experience.

Demons of the Night

These visions, which

haunt

are

sinister,

terrifying

Beyond

fantasy

Teachers can also relate back to their own efforts with newspaper poetry, which should be on display. They should emphasize again that the size, shape, color, and arrangement of the words are part of the poetic feeling, thought, or expression. Teachers could then present a

number of themes that the children could use, but they must be sure to say that these are only ideas or springboards for the children, and that the children can make up their own.

Limericks Most persons especially enjoy listening to limericks. Limericks consist of a five-line pattern. The first, second, and fifth lines of a limerick have three beats and rhyme with one another, whereas the third and fourth lines have two beats and rhyme with each other. Limericks are supposed to be funny, silly, and ridiculous.[15] (See "Listening Appreciation" in Chapter 6.)

> There was a Young Lady of Norway,
> Who casually sat in a doorway;
> When the door squeezed her flat,
> She exclaimed, 'What of that?''
> This courageous Young Lady of Norway.
>
> *Edward Lear*

CAN ELEMENTARY-GRADE STUDENTS DEVELOP STYLE IN WRITING?

Although style in writing is difficult to describe, readers are acutely aware of its absence. The way the writer "turns a phrase," uses words, paints pictures, and incorporates insights are all indications of style.

Students at all grade levels should be acquiring vocabulary and writing techniques that will help them eventually develop their own styles. Some students in elementary school may already have done so; that is, they seem to be able to write with a certain uniqueness despite the lack of many basic skills. Teachers must be ever vigilant for such sudents. They must encourage them to write, and help them to acquire the skills they will need.

In order to acquire style all students must become sensitive to the many nuances of language. They must know when slang is effective, when a slang term can express an idea or thing more effectively than another term. Students must be helped to avoid overworking or "beating to death" particular slang words, such as

[15]See Mary McDonnell Harris, "The Limerick Center," *Language Arts* (September 1976): 663–665, for information on developing a limerick learning center.

"gross," "cool," or "awesome." When these words are no longer fashionable, they actually convey no meaning because of their vagueness. In addition, if writers rely too heavily on slang, they tend to become lazy in word use.

In order to develop style, the student must choose words carefully so that exact meaning is conveyed. Effective use of figurative language is important in style development. Children in the intermediate grades are able to work with simile, metaphor, personification, and oxymorons. (See "Figures of Speech in Poetry" in Chapter 10 and "Creating Word Images: Figures of Speech" in this Chapter.)

While most elementary grades do not as yet have a style of writing, they are in the process of developing such a style of their own. How well they do this depends on a variety of factors, the most important of which is the opportunity to write often.

CHILDREN'S WRITING

By being exposed to the writing of many children, teachers will be in a better position to judge the level and ability of their own pupils. Since children very much enjoy reading other children's creations, and being read to, these may also act as stimuli for children to write on their own. Some schools keep bound volumes of children's works in the school library.

On many occasions, teachers discover they have students with great creative writing potential in their classes. Such students may have gone unrecognized because they are shy or taciturn. "The Flower," is reproduced as an example of creative writing from a young girl who, although very quiet in class, was articulate in print.

THE FLOWER

I looked forward to greeting my sweetheart the day I set out early in the morning to walk to her house. I had done this many a time before so this was not new to me. The houses, the cobblestone way, the tall leafy oaks—everything the same. I walked on with not a care in the world until I saw—the flower. It was, and still is, the most beautiful thing that I have ever seen. The color of it was a soft pure, creamy white that shone like silk. I am not a horticulturist so I cannot tell you its name. It looked somewhat like a rose but much fuller and fluffier. It had many, many petals which gave it a look like a ruffled gown. My words do not do it justice, for it was so beautiful that just one look at it would make its beholders want it like nothing before.

The flower was in a garden of many varied flowers—all of which were very beautiful, but the flower of which I have spoken surpassed all without a doubt. The garden was situated approximately one half mile off the main road, on a dirt path. I had passed the garden before, as I have used it to shorten my journey, but I had not noticed the flower previously. Now that I had seen it though, I decided it would make quite a lovely gift for my beloved. So I hastened to pick it. But it was not to be. Just as I touched the velvet stem, just as I was to pull it from its place, a dog, a monstrous, contemptible, hideous dog jumped up from the ground with such a snarl I had never heard before. I had seen him before but had taken little notice of him. He had seemed a placid enough fellow. But now, this beast that I looked at, surely this was no beast at all, but a demon in disguise. I can remember distinctly a glare in his eyes that froze me in my steps. I thought that now I truly knew what it was to see a dog's lips curl. And oh, that terrible growl I have mentioned before. This was the most remarkable thing about him. His whole body seemed to tremble with it. He started out with a low grumble that grew louder and louder till I thought my eardrums would burst. I thought to myself no lion could outroar this small persistent dog.

After I recovered my sense I wasted no time in escaping from his growls. I was quite lucky in that there was a fence. I shudder to think of my fate had there been no fence.

So, I proceeded to my sweetheart's without the flower. This sequence was to happen many times. Every time I passed the flower and was about to pick it the dog would leap into the air and become a ferocious beast. And each time I passed it, it seemed the flower became more and more beautiful, making it more and more irresistible. You cannot imagine the agony I went through. How I stealthily crept up to the flower, how I held in my hand the graceful stem so many times but each time having to give in to the dog. At night his body haunted my dreams. During the day I heard his unearthly screams persistently. Always on my mind was the flower, the beautiful flower. I feared for my sanity.

I had no idea who was the master of the brute.

Indeed, I often wondered if he possessed one. I had seen not one house along the path. I had always thought the land there unoccupied by humans. Nevertheless, whether occupied or not by humans I knew what I was to do to maintain my sanity. The dog would have to be gotten rid of. From my point of view it was quite a simple task. Not once had I seen any humans about, much less the dog's master. As I have said before the dog was always quiet until I started to pick the flower. The more I thought about it, the easier the deed seemed. I felt better than I had in weeks, but I was anxious to get the deed done with so I could possess the impossible—the flower.

It was a little after noon when I started out to the flower. My legs seemed to acquire a briskness of pace I had never known them to have. When I reached the flower, I stopped for a moment—unsure. In all my time spent thinking of killing the dog I had never given much thought to detail. But then, a wild instinct drove me on. My feet clambered over the fence and before I realized it I was standing on the other side. My heart was pounding furiously as I took a step toward the sleeping dog. I was almost upon him when some instinct of his own must have awakened him for I had proceeded upon him with the utmost of caution. I saw the dog make ready for attack but before he could do so I sprang on him. It was a thrilling battle but I never once doubted as to whom would come out the victor. I was merely a tool for my hate and revenge. They commanded me and I carried out their commands. When I had accomplished my task, I buried the dog in the garden and would have picked the flower then if not for the blood and dirt which covered me like a blanket. I found a stream not too far from the flower and I cleaned myself there. By the time this was accomplished it was quite dark, so I spent the night beside the stream.

Such a lovely night I have yet to see again. It was pitch black, without a star in the sky. I had a great feeling of satisfaction and relief. I was at last free of the hideous beast. My dreams were untormented, my thoughts still on the flower but this time with content for in the morning I would have it for mine.

I arose earlier than usual the next morning and upon doing so rushed to the flower at last. My feelings, I cannot describe, so content, so happy, so joyous was I that morning—until I reached the flower. I thought in frenzy at first that I was in the wrong garden. But no, I remember the bush and trees, everything there the same, untouched, except for the flower. Where could it be? I searched every branch of the bush but not a trace of the flower was to be found. Then, as I hung my head low in despair my eyes caught sight of something under the bush. It was a flower, but surely, surely, not the flower! Its stem was broken and coarse; its petals were crumpled and squashed and had the color of a grotesque brown that seemed to have soaked out all the life that had once lived in the flower. For yes, it was the flower. At the very tip of one of the brown petals was a very minute tinge of white. A white that could not be mistaken. Yet as I touched it, the pureness of the white disappeared and in its place the dullness and drabness of the brown became apparent.

Sharon Anne

STUDENT'S NAME:
      GRADE:
      TEACHER:

DIAGNOSTIC CHECKLIST FOR WRITTEN EXPRESSION AS A CREATIVE ACT

I. DESCRIPTION	YES	No

A. Primary Grades

The child is able to
1. describe a person in the class
2. describe a character from a television show

3. state descriptive words using each of the five senses

4. state descriptive words that appeal to the senses

5. use some word images

B. Intermediate Grades

The child is able to
1. master all items of previous years
2. describe a scene
3. use simile
4. use metaphor
5. use personification
6. use oxymoron
7. use hyperbole

II. CHARACTER DEVELOPMENT	YES	NO

A. Primary Grades

The child is able to
1. describe the appearance of an imaginary character
2. state how other people feel about the imaginary character
3. tell what the imaginary character would say in certain situations

B. Intermediate Grades

The child is able to
1. describe the feelings of an imaginary character
2. show the character in action
3. relate the character to other characters
4. present dialogue between and among characters
5. tell what the imaginary character thinks about

III. POETRY	YES	NO

A. Primary Grades

The child is able to
1. write "wish" poems ("I wish . . .")
2. write "dream poems" ("I dream . . .")
3. write "lie" poems (say something in each line that isn't true)
4. put a comparison or a sound in every line
5. write poems on any topic he or she wants
6. write "sound" poems
7. write concrete poems
8. write newspaper poems

B. Intermediate Grades

The child is able to
1. master all items of previous years
2. write limericks
3. write haiku poems
4. write cinquain poems
5. write tanka and other poetic forms
6. write poems using figures of speech

IV. STORIES	YES	NO

A. Primary Grades

The child is able to
1. write about what he or she would like to be when he or she grows up
2. write an imaginary story
3. finish the statement "If I could fly . . ."
4. finish the statement "If I wore no shoes . . ."

B. Intermediate Grades

The child is able to
1. master all items of previous years
2. write a tall tale
3. choose a topic for an imaginary story
4. choose a title for an imaginary story
5. write a beginning paragraph for a story
6. write a story in proper sequence
7. write a concluding paragraph for a story
8. use dialogue in a story
9. write many and varied imaginative stories
10. produce suspense in his or her stories by not giving all of the information at once

SUMMARY

This chapter has presented some of the ingredients teachers need to develop and implement a good writing program in their classes. For best results in writing, teachers must provide a physical and emotional environment where students do not feel threatened, as well as adequate time and opportunity for writing. Teachers should also know the various writing-process stages, which include prewriting or rehearsing, drafting, revising, and editing, and know how and when to use these in their writing program. In addition, they must know how to guide and help their students.

The teacher must understand that creativity cannot be commanded or taught, but it can be fostered in children by using a variety of motivating techniques. The essentials for putting creative stories together were presented with a major emphasis on description, since the development of children's perceptions of the world is an important factor in writing. In order to interest children in writing poetry, a number of techniques were discussed—such as exposing children to many different poems. Such poetic forms as cinquain, haiku, tanka, lanterne, concrete, and newspaper poetry were presented so that children could experiment with different poetic forms. A "Diagnostic Checklist for Written Expression As a Creative Act" concludes this chapter.

As a further aid, two examples of writing lesson plans follow. Using these as guides, see if you can construct another one.

LESSON PLAN 1:   PRIMARY-GRADE LEVEL

OBJECTIVE

To be able to identify, describe, and project images of an unseen object in terms of its tactile sensory impressions.

PRELIMINARY PREPARATION

"Feel" box. This would be prepared by the teacher before the lesson and would contain a variety of objects that produce sensory impressions. A cardboard box with a "window" cut in it, covered with a curtain, works very well.

INTRODUCTION

Pass around an object (pine cone) for everyone to touch. Elicit descriptions from different points of view from the students. Ask them: What did it feel like? How would you describe it? What do you think it is like to be a pine cone on a tree swinging in the breeze? What do you think it would feel like to have someone pull you off the tree?

Tell the children that they have been spending a lot of time writing. After talking about how writing can be improved, discuss what help is needed in describing things.

Introduce the "feel" box, and explain that there are a variety of objects inside the box and each should produce many sensations. Tell the students that they are going to work with description.

DEVELOPMENT

At this point directions should be made clear. Each student will reach into the box while blindfolded, and the teacher will be sure that they pick up only one object by guiding their hands to an object. Students can hold it, feel it, smell it, and explore all aspects of their objects. After they have held the object for a moment, they are asked to state some words to describe it. The words are put on the board. From these descriptions, children will be asked to name the object.

Some objects that could be used:

a peeled grape	sponge	crumpled tinfoil
cooked spaghetti	toothbrush	chalk
a cotton ball	velvet	flannel
piece of netting	sandpaper	fur
thimble	cornflakes	deflated balloon

After students have had a chance to study their objects, they each contribute a description to be presented to the rest of the class.

After a number of children have used the "feel" box, the children are told they will be divided into groups of four. Each group receives a box with an object inside it. The students describe the object, and from this description other pupils try to guess what the object is.

Each group is given a chance to describe their objects.

SUMMARY

Pull the main points of the lesson together. Help students to recognize the importance of description and how it helps us to "see" an object better. The teacher tells students that tomorrow an object will be chosen and then the class will write about it together, as if the class were the object. Students are asked to think about how they would feel if they were chocolate sundaes or kites flying in the sky. If someone wants to, he or she can borrow the box, collect some new objects, and challenge the rest of the class to guess what they are.

LESSON PLAN II: INTERMEDIATE-GRADE LEVEL

OBJECTIVES

To be able to sell a fictitious product by writing an original slogan and jingle.

To be able to act out (in front of the class) "their own TV commercial" to aid in selling the product.

PRELIMINARY PREPARATION

Large posters containing some of the following famous slogans can be scattered on the walls throughout the room:

You deserve a break today.

Strong enough for a man . . . but made for a woman.

Where's the beef?

You've got a right to chicken done right.

When you care enough to send the very best.

So thick you can eat it with a fork.

Have it your way.

Ring around the collar.

Mounted advertisements from magazines and newspapers.

A tape recording of a well-known TV and radio advertisement.

A box wrapped in plain brown paper with the word TRAZZLE written boldly across the front.

INTRODUCTION

"We have spent some time on critical listening and reading activities, discussing propaganda and bias in relation to advertising. We have discussed the various techniques that advertisers use in promoting their products. Who remembers some?"

Students state the appeal to one's sense of prestige, economy, sex appeal, the use of color, repetition, bold print, and so on.

"We also gave examples of each of these. Who can give one? Yes, the use of a very dignified-looking gentleman surrounded by books and selling pain-killer."

"Listen to this tape recording. A technique is being used that we have not yet discussed." (Tape is played of a jingle with a catchy tune.) "Today we will set up our own advertising companies, decide on a product, determine how to advertise that product using jingles or slogans, and then act the ad out."

DEVELOPMENT

"Before we separate into our advertising company groups, I'd like everyone to look at this poster. What does it contain? Yes, lots of quite well-known selling slogans. Let's see how well we know the products that they are supposed to represent. Very good! You see how the slogan helps you to remember. Now we'll divide into five advertising companies. Each company will be responsible for preparing a slogan or jingle for this product." (Teacher introduces TRAZZLE to students.) "You must decide what TRAZZLE is, and prepare the slogan or jingle that you feel best suits it." *(Students are divided into companies.)*

Teacher walks around room offering assistance. After about a half-hour, or whenever the teacher sees that students are ready, they are asked to present their commercials. The students do not state what TRAZZLE is. The other groups will try to guess the type of product from the slogans or jingles.

SUMMARY

Pull main points of lesson together.

Tell students to think about the kind of television program they would want to use to advertise their products. "Perhaps we will attempt to write such a show ourselves. We'll discuss this next time."

SUGGESTIONS FOR THOUGHT
QUESTIONS AND ACTIVITIES

1. Discuss motivating techniques to stimulate interest in written expression.

2. Construct a creative lesson plan in the area of written expression.

3. How would you stimulate children to write poetry?

4. Discuss a number of topics that could be used to initiate a creative writing lesson.

5. You have been appointed to a committee to judge children's creative writing. What problems do you think you might encounter in this task?

6. You have been invited to give a talk to the annual meeting of teachers in your school system. The suggested topic is how you encourage the creative spark in your students. Write out your talk.

7. Choose 10 poems to stimulate interest in concrete and newspaper poetry writing.

8. Discuss the various stages of the writing process and explain how you would incorporate these routines in your class.

SELECTED BIBLIOGRAPHY

Britton, James et al. *The Development of Writing Abilities,* 11–18. London: Macmillan, 1975.

Dyson, Anne Haas. "Research Currents: Young Children As Composers." *Language Arts* 60 (October 1983) : 884–891.

Florio, S., and C. Clark. "What Is Writing for? Writing in the First Weeks of School in a Second- and Third-Grade Classroom," in *Communicating in the Classroom,* L. C. Wilkinson, ed. New York: Academic Press, 1982.

Graves, Donald H. *Writing: Teachers & Children at Work.* Exeter, N.H.: Heinemann Educational Books, 1983.

Koch, Kenneth. *Rose, Where Did You Get that Red?* New York: Random House, 1973.

Langer, Judith A. "Reading, Thinking, Writing . . . and Teaching." *Language Arts* 59 (April 1982) : 336–341.

Lear, Edward. *Edward Lear's Book of Mazes: Nonsense Rhymes and Limericks.* New York: Sterling, 1980.

Rubin, Dorothy. "Developing Writing Skills," in *The Intermediate-Grade Teacher's Language Arts Handbook.* New York: Holt, Rinehart and Winston, 1980.

———. "Developing Writing Skills," in *The Primary-Grade Teacher's Language Arts Handbook.* New York: Holt, Rinehart, and Winston, 1980.

Squire, James R. "Composing and Comprehending: Two Sides of the Same Basic Process." *Language Arts* 60 (May 1983) : 581–589.

TWELVE

Practical Aspects of Writing

Yes, as Snoopy says, "Good writing is hard work!" Good writing for most of us is usually "99 percent perspiration and one percent inspiration."

Even though creative writers usually have good ideas, imagination, and an itch to write, writing still requires discipline, organizational ability, skill, and time (see "Writing and Reading" in Chapter 8).

Der Techr—
    i no i got som ides but i can't rit em. Hlp.Don

Don is in fifth grade, and he's having difficulties. He has good ideas, but he has difficulty expressing them. He has been in a writing program whose teachers believed that children should choose their own topics and then engage in writing. While they gave Don many opportunities to write, they felt strongly that the major purpose of writing is to express ideas and that teachers should merely stand back and be supportive. They felt that eventually Don would learn the conventions of writing. After all, he spoke quite well and he did enjoy reading.

Unfortunately for Don, his teachers did not realize that many children do not necessarily learn the conventions of writing, even though they are good speakers and readers. Most children usually have to learn the mechanics of writing, and, often, *direct* teaching of these is necessary. The best learning is, of course, based on the student's needs, and the optimum time to learn important editing skills is when the child is engaged in writing and has a need for these skills.

Good ideas, imagination, knowledge of the conventions of writing combined with opportunities to write help children gain writing proficiency. The discussion on creativity in Chapter 4 is important in helping teachers to understand better how to provide an atmosphere that stimulates creativity. Once children sense that creativity is being rewarded, they will attempt to give freer rein to their imaginations. An emphasis on creativity does not diminish, however, a teacher's responsibility for helping students acquire basic writing skills. Creativity and basic skills reinforce one another. A child who has difficulty in spelling, in vocabulary, in writing sentences, in punctuation, and in concept development will probably have difficulty in communicating through writing.

This chapter is concerned with giving teachers the background they need to help students become more adept in writing for various purposes.

After reading this chapter, you should be able to answer these questions:

1. Are creative writing and basic writing skills mutually exclusive? Explain.
2. What writing mechanics does a child usually learn in the primary grades? In the intermediate grades?
3. What are some factors that affect the writing process?
4. Should teachers correct papers while students are in the process of writing?

5. What are the criteria for writing book reports in the primary and intermediate grades?
6. What is the place of the conference in the writing program?
7. How should children's writing be evaluated?

FACTORS AFFECTING THE WRITING PROCESS

Although oral and written language are closely related, there are certain factors basic to the writing process that need to be mastered for good writing. To be successful at written expression, an individual, besides having good ideas, must be able to write somewhat legibly, spell, construct sentences and paragraphs, and have knowledge of word usage. Problems in any one of these areas may interfere with the act of creating through writing. Because of the variables involved, the transition from speech to written expression can be a difficult one. (For example, in Chapter 14 the problems of learning to manipulate a pencil and attempting to move it fast enough to catch a thought are discussed.) Many times the tools that should ease practice of a skill become impediments instead.

Results from the Third National Writing Assessment survey, released in December 1980, suggest that regarding the conventions of writing "the major problems for the majority of students are apparently punctuation, spelling and awkward sentences—three things that present no problems when we speak to one another but come into importance when we write."[1] In discussing the nine-year-old's writing skills, the report stated that "poor writers created many more fragments, awkward sentences, misspelled words and agreement errors than did good writers. Except for fragments, poor writers do not seem to have many more problems with punctuation than good writers. It does appear that while poor writers may have a tendency to end sentences prematurely (fragments), good writers tend not to end them soon enough

---

[1]*Writing Achievement, 1969–79: Results from the Third National Writing Assessment*, Vol. II: 13-Year-Olds (Denver, Co.: Education Commission of the States, December 1980), p. 40.

PEANUTS ®   **By Charles M. Schulz**

© 1958 United Feature Syndicate. Inc.

(run-ons).[2] The writers do emphasize that the report is based on first-draft, timed writing, which would probably underestimate students' writing ability. The report does, however, give us some insights into writing areas in which children need help.

SKILLS NECESSARY FOR EFFECTIVE WRITING

In this chapter, the emphasis is on presenting writing skills that students need, because good writers generally have good writing skills. "Young Americans who do well with basic writing mechanics (such as spelling, punctuation, and sentence structure) also tend to write with the most ingenuity."[3] Even though our approach in this chapter is to look at various skills individually, we do not intend that they be taught as ends in themselves. Rather, they should be taught in relation to what the children are doing in writing and in relation to the whole of their studies.

The needs of individual children often will determine what will be taught. Some of the skills may be taught with the whole class, some in a small group, some in a large group, and some individually. Teachers will have to use judgment on what is best for their children (see "The Writing Conference" later in this chapter).

Some persons feel strongly that skills should never be taught in isolation as exercise drills, but, rather, in relation to students' writing only.

[2]*Writing Achievement, 1969–79: Results from the Third National Writing Assessment,* Vol. III: 9-Year-Olds (Denver, Co.: Education Commission of the States, December 1980), p. 42.

[3]Jane Porter, "Research Report," *Elementary English* 49 (October 1972): 863.

We feel that while skills should be taught relating to writing activities and to their needs, there is nothing wrong with providing extra practice help for those students who are having difficulties with certain skill areas. Often the added practice is just what the student needs to help him or her "overlearn" a particular skill. The student must, however, know the purpose for the practice and see how the specific skill relates to the whole.

Also, teachers should teach directly those skills that they feel their students need; they should not rely merely on incidental learning. The sections that follow should help teachers gain information about the kinds of skills that elementary-grade-level students should be attaining.

Punctuation

Children must learn that punctuation marks give the signals needed for clear meaning in writing. In oral expression, stress, pitch, pauses, and even arm waving help clarify meaning. These punctuation signals replace the various intonation patterns that are used orally:

Punctuation Signals

.	period
,	comma
;	semicolon
:	colon
?	question mark
_____	underlining
!	exclamation mark
—	dash
( )	parentheses
[ ]	brackets
" "	quotation marks

The primary- and intermediate-grade designations in the following outline of punctuation skills are merely approximations. Just when students are ready for the next level will be determined by their individual differences.

In the Primary Grades

1. Period at the end of a sentence
2. Period after abbreviations
3. Question mark at the end of an interrogative sentence
4. Comma in dates
5. Comma after greeting and closing in letters
6. Periods after numbers in a listing
7. Periods after Mr., Mrs., and Ms.
8. Period after an initial
9. Apostrophe in some contractions, such as *can't, she's*
10. Apostrophe in possessive singular, such as *girl's, boy's*

In the Intermediate Grades

1. Mastery of all items of previous years[4]
2. Use of apostrophe in more contractions
3. Use of apostrophe in singular and plural possessives
4. Use of hyphen between syllables in separating a word at the end of the line
5. Use of exclamation mark to express strong emphasis or emotion
6. Use of exclamation mark for a command (optional—a period is often used)
7. Use of a comma to separate items in a series
8. Use of a colon after the salutation in a business letter
9. Use of a comma to set off a quotation
10. Quotation marks before and after a quotation
11. Use of a comma to help make sentences clearer
12. Use of a comma in figures containing four or more digits (optional for four digits)
13. Use of commas with transitional words—such as *however, indeed, that is, for example, in fact,* and so on
14. Use of quotation marks for special words in a sentence
15. Use of quotation marks to set off the title of a

poem, short story, magazine article, chapter, and so on
16. Use of a colon to set off a list of items
17. Use of a colon in writing time, for example, 9:00 P.M.
18. Underlining the title of a book

Capitalization

In the Primary Grades Children in kindergarten and first grade have usually learned that their names start with a "big letter." In learning the letters first-graders are presented with both the capital and lowercase letters. During the primary grades children learn many uses for capital letters. In writing sentences they learn that the first word of a sentence begins with a capital letter and that the greeting is always capitalized in letter writing. From letter writing and working with dates they find that the day and month of the year are also capitalized. In writing experience stories with the teacher, they learn that the title is always capitalized.

Children learn that not only are their own first and last names capitalized but all names are capitalized. Also, titles preceding names are in capital letters, for example, Mr., Mrs., Miss, and Ms. The children discover that the first word of the closing of a letter is capitalized, for example, *Yours truly, Your friend, Sincerely yours,* and so on. States, cities, and streets are capitalized, and whenever children use "I" in a sentence it should always be capitalized. Primary-grade children also notice that the first word of every line in a poem is usually capitalized (except for the poetry of some modern poets).

In the Intermediate Grades Before proceeding into intermediate-level capitalization skills, the children should have mastered all the capitalization skills listed for primary-grade students. They will continue to build their capitalization skills by learning that all names of countries, roads, avenues, streets, towns, and so on are capitalized, as well as any word used as a name, for example, *Mother, Father,* but not *his mother, her father.* Titles of books, poems, stories, movies, and magazines are also capitalized, as well as names of languages, buildings,

[4]This will be determined by the individual differences of students and the school situations in which they study.

institutions, and companies. Intermediate-grade-level students learn to capitalize the first word of a direct quotation, historical periods, names of nationalities, a direction that names a definite area, and, in outlining, the first word of each main topic and subtopic.

Writing Sentences

Learning to write sentences that are clear and make sense is a very important part of the writing program. To write effective stories or paragraphs, children need to be able to write sentences. To do this, children should have practice in oral expression. Starting in the primary grades, children are helped to express themselves so that they can "say what they mean"; this helps them "write what they mean."

Not only do children need many opportunities to express themselves orally, they also must write sentences for clear written expression. Children in the primary grades learn to write simple questions and statement sentences in the active voice. In the intermediate grades they learn to write exclamatory and imperative compound sentences, which may be in the active or passive voices.

Children in both the primary and intermediate grades must learn that a sentence expresses a complete thought and that it is a significant unit of language.

Intermediate-grade-level children learn that a sentence is a word or group of words stating, asking, commanding, supposing, or exclaiming. The sentence contains a subject and a verb that are in agreement in number with one another. It begins with a capital letter and ends with a period (.), a question mark (?), or an exclamation mark (!). For example:

Jennifer is pretty. (statement or declarative sentence)

Who is he? (question or interrogative sentence)

Stop him. (command or imperative sentence)

Help! (expression of great emotion or exclamatory sentence)

Intermediate-grade-level children learn that an *interjection* is a word usually used with an exclamation mark to express emotion, for example, *Oh! Aha!* It is independent of the rest of the sentence. They also learn that some sentences may be as brief as one word, for example,

Stop.
Go.
Help!

When children are taught to write sentences such as the above, they should be helped to recognize that the subject, *you,* is understood and that the punctuation helps give meaning to the sentences.

In the primary grades children write many different kinds of *simple sentences.* They write simple sentences containing the following:

1. Single subject and single verb: *Sharon swims.*
2. Single subject and compound verb: *Sharon runs and swims.*
3. Compound subject and single verb: *Sharon and Seth swim.*
4. Compound subject and compound verb: *Sharon and Seth swim and run.*

In the intermediate grades children are learning to write compound sentences. They learn that a compound sentence contains two or more groups of words that can stand alone as sentences. Each group of words must have its own subject and verb, for example:

My sister is an excellent ball player, and my brother is a good musician.

My sister is a good ball player, but it doesn't interfere with her music.

Each of the compound sentences has two groups of words that can stand alone as a simple sentence because each has a subject and a verb, and each expresses a complete thought.

To combine two sentences into a compound sentence, children learn that they must use a comma with a conjunction such as *and* or *but.*

Primary-grade children, when first learning to write sentences, tend to string many sentences together by adding the conjunction "and." Intermediate-grade children have usually learned to avoid the overuse of conjunctions, but they are more prone to write run-on sentences because of their overuse of the comma. For example, they may take what are properly two sentences and put them together with a comma: *The children all raised their hands, we started to talk.*

In writing sentences pupils learn to avoid certain unacceptable sentence fragments, for example, *Into the store, When she came, And in a second,* and *Although he is.*

In the following list the first sentence is correct, whereas the second example is not.

1. There are a number of birds, such as sparrows, who do not migrate during the winter.
2. There are a number of birds who do not migrate. Such as sparrows.

In order to gain clarity in sentence writing, children must learn that careful placement of words is helpful. For example, how clear are the following sentences?

The girl ran down the street in a green coat.
The baby drank the milk with a smile.

In order to understand the meaning of the sentences better they should be rewritten in the following manner:

The girl in a green coat ran down the street.
The baby, with a smile, drank the milk.

(See "Transformational Grammar's Place in the Classroom" Chapter 15 for a discussion on generating sentences.)

Writing Paragraphs

Even before some children have gained facility in writing sentences, they are attempting to write paragraphs.

A *paragraph* usually consists of a topic sentence followed by a number of related sentences, and usually ends in a concluding statement. The topic sentence is generally the first one in the paragraph. The related sentences tell something about the topic sentence and are arranged in some order to make sense. The beginning of each paragraph is indented.

Paragraphs, like sentences, should have unity and order. If the paragraph is one concerning a sequence of events, then the sentences must be placed in some kind of sequential order. If the paragraph involves an explanation, it must proceed in a logical order such as from cause to effect.

The sentences in the paragraph must also have some kind of coherence so that they flow logically from one to the other. Put another way, sentences must be linked. Some words that help link sentences are *after, then, besides, moreover, however, therefore, as a result,* and *for that reason.* Although linking words are useful connectors, not all sentences in a paragraph need a linking word.[5]

The Topic Sentence The topic sentence is usually the first sentence in a paragraph, and it states the subject of the paragraph. It also usually gives clues to the development of the main idea of the paragraph. From the topic sentence one can anticipate certain events. One can determine that the subsequent sentences will supply supporting details as examples, comparison/contrasts, sequence of events, cause and effect situations, and so on.[6]

It is possible for any sentence in the paragraph to be the topic sentence, and some paragraphs may not even have one. The topic sentence should not be confused with the main idea. The topic sentence usually anticipates both the main idea and the development of the main idea. It may or may not contain the main idea. Even though a topic sentence exists and is stated explicitly (fully and clearly) in the paragraph, the main idea may not be explicitly stated.

The Concluding Sentence A good paragraph does not end with some minor point or detail. It generally ends with some strong point, a conclusive statement, a restatement, or a question relating to what has preceded. In ending a paragraph, try to help students avoid terms such as *In conclusion, In ending, To sum up,* and so on.

Writing a Composition

Children will be at different levels in writing compositions. At all levels, teachers should help them to recognize the relationship between reading and writing, and how one en-

[5]Dorothy Rubin, *Writing and Reading: The Vital Arts* (New York: Macmillan, 1983), pp. 189–190.
[6]Ibid., p. 217.

hances the other. For example, as stated earlier in this chapter and in Chapter 8, students who read widely will have a broad range of ideas from which to draw for their own writing. Also, through reading they will come to recognize what skills are necessary to be a good writer.

A number of children are writing stories and compositions at the primary grades. From listening and from reading stories, they know that a story has a beginning, middle, and end. As a result, many try to incorporate this in their stories; they especially like to write THE END at the end of their stories. Even though children in a good writing program would be involved in writing compositions even at the primary-grade level, it isn't until the intermediate or upper-intermediate grades that teachers would generally teach the formal elements that go into composing. Of course, the choice would depend on the individual differences of the students in the class.

To write a good composition, students must be able to choose a topic that is neither too narrow nor too broad. They must be able to write a topic sentence for an opening paragraph of the composition so that readers will be prepared for what is to follow; they must be able to combine paragraphs so that they are all related to the topic that they have chosen; and they must be able to write a concluding paragraph (see "The Writing Process" in Chapter 11).

The Opening Paragraph Teachers need to help students learn how important and crucial the opening paragraph of a composition is because the opening paragraph helps the reader determine whether he or she wants to continue reading or not. It introduces the reader to the writer and tells something about what the writer wants to say. It also prepares the reader for the rest of the paper. The task is to attract the reader's attention and to get him or her to read on. To do this, the opening paragraph should be brief, to the point, and interesting. The topic sentence, which is usually the first sentence in the opening paragraph, plays an essential role in helping to set the stage for the rest of the paper (see sections on the topic sentence).

Teachers could use samples from literature to illustrate their points. For example, the teacher could bring in a short opening paragraph from a magazine or journal article and state, "Read the following paragraph from 'Would You Obey a Hitler?' by Jeanne Reinert, in *Science Digest:*"

Who looks in the mirror and sees a person ready and willing to inflict pain and suffering on another in his mercy? Even if commanded? All of our senses revolt against the idea.

After the students finish reading the paragraph, the teacher says, "Doesn't it capture your attention? Don't you want to continue reading? Let's analyze what the writer has done:

1. The paragraph is short and to the point.
2. The central idea for the composition is contained in the paragraph so that the reader is prepared for what follows.
3. The writer's technique of using questions gains our attention. (Notice that the questions are rhetorical; i.e., they require or expect no response.)
4. The writer tells us something about his or her feelings."

After analyzing the paragraph, the teacher then says, "Following are a couple of beginning paragraphs taken from the autobiographies of famous persons. The opening tactic used by each writer is anecdotal (referring to a short, entertaining account of some happening that is usually biographical). After reading each one, ask yourself these questions:

1. Did it attract my attention?
2. Did it make me want to read more?
3. Was it short and to the point?
4. Did it give me information about what was to follow?
5. Did it tell me something about the author's feelings?
6. Did it set the stage for the rest of the composition?"

Read the following from *Molly and Me* by Gertrude Edelstein Berg:

I should probably say that I liked school—it sounds better. But the whole truth is, I didn't. I wasn't interested and there was always something I would rather be doing than sitting in a classroom, like, for instance, sitting at home. Besides, I was scared. It wasn't psychological, it was just the way the school looked.

From *Daybreak* by Joan Baez:

Mother tells me that I came back from the first day of kindergarten and told her I was in love. I remember a Japanese boy who looked after me and wouldn't let anybody knock me around. When they gave us beans to eat in the morning I told him they'd make me sick, and he buried them under the table for me.

After the students have analyzed the paragraphs, the teacher should ask them to write the opening paragraph of their autobiography.

The Topic Sentence of the Opening Paragraph The topic sentence in the first paragraph of a composition usually sets the stage for the rest of the paper. It is broader than the topic sentences in subsequent paragraphs because it prepares the reader for what is to follow in the whole composition. The topic sentence of the opening paragraph may give the reader the writer's feelings about the subject or some information as to what the composition is about. Whichever method the writer chooses to use, the topic sentence should catch the reader's attention and make him or her want to read on.

The teacher should expose students to topic sentences from opening paragraphs that attract the reader's attention. The students should be asked to find topic sentences from their readings that they think are good ones. Students should also be asked to generate a number of topic sentences on various themes for the opening paragraph of a composition.

The Concluding Paragraph The concluding paragraph is very special in a composition because it pulls everything in the composition together. It ought to leave the reader with the main thought of the composition and with a feeling of completeness. The writer may use a number of techniques to accomplish this. One method is a simple statement, another is a question, and another is a quotation (see earlier section on writing paragraphs). Teachers should help students notice the similarity between the concluding paragraph of a composi-

tion and the ending of a paragraph. Also, teachers should help their students try to avoid using such artificial terms as *In conclusion, In sum, Finally,* and so on to begin their concluding paragraph. The terms take away from the creativity of the paragraph and do not add anything significant to it.

To help students gain facility in writing concluding paragraphs, teachers can use the same techniques that were given for gaining skill in writing opening paragraphs and topic sentences for opening paragraphs.

BOOK REPORTING

In Chapter 10 it was mentioned that many children look on written book reports as burdensome tasks; which may detract from reading. It was also emphasized that teachers should not require children to do book reports on all books that they read.

Written book reports have a place in the language arts program. In the primary grades the teacher and children can write book reports together when they have all read a book together. The teacher can stimulate this activity by having children tell about some of the things they liked or did not like about the book. The teacher can also ask children if they think other children of their approximate age would like to read the book. If so, the teacher asks how can they let these children know about the book. Should everything about the book be told? Why not?

At the primary level the book report should include the following:

1. The name of the book
2. The author of the book
3. A good beginning sentence that tells something interesting about the book
4. A number of other sentences that further explain why the book should be read, such as something funny in the book
5. The description of a special character
6. A concluding sentence that further encourages children to want to read the book

The report should stimulate interest, but not summarize the whole book so that it need not be read.

In the intermediate grades, even though

most of the children's reports are written to stimulate others to want to read the book, children are also learning that they do not like all the books they have read. They must learn to be more impartial in their reports. Although they did not necessarily like the book, this does not mean that someone else will also dislike it. They also have to share enough information to get the audience interested but not tell the whole story and thereby spoil its enjoyment for others.

At the intermediate level (as at all other levels) students who are asked why they liked a book usually reply, "It was interesting" or "It was good." These comments do not help classmates in deciding whether or not to read a book. Here are some suggestions for helping intermediate-grade students write book reports:

1. State name and author of book.

2. What kind of book is it? For example, is it biography, autobiography, science fiction, war story, mystery, animal story, nature story?

3. Who are the main characters in the story? For example, who is the hero, the villain? What about the characters—are they lifelike or just stereotypes? Which characters did you like or dislike? Why?

4. Is the setting of the story important? Where does it take place? When does the story take place?

5. Very briefly discuss the plot without giving the whole story away. Tell whether it was fast-moving, humorous, whether there was good suspense, and so on.

6. Did the author paint clear pictures? Did he or she describe characters well?

7. What did you like about the book?

8. Are there any particular people for whom you would especially recommend the book?

The teacher can read sample book reports to the class, and students can volunteer which ones they like best and why. It would be worthwhile for teachers in the intermediate grades to write a book report based on a book that all of their students have read, with the participation of the whole class, or with groups of children. (See Chapter 10 for some novel approaches to stimulate children to write book reports.)

Television Reporting

Television, as all educators know, plays an important part in the lives of children. Teachers can use television viewing as an impetus for writing. Children at both the primary and intermediate grades should be encouraged to discuss the programs they watch and review them by writing critically of particular programs.

At the primary-grade level, first-graders can dictate reviews about the shows they have watched either as a group endeavor, using an experience-approach technique, or individually.

At the intermediate level children are able to write their own reports. However, as in book reporting, children should cooperatively develop standards for writing television reviews. (See "Television: Making It Part of the Educative Process" in Chapter 7.)

LETTER WRITING

Most adults, and especially children, love to receive letters. Of all writing exercises, letter writing will be one of the most frequently engaged-in activities for most individuals. Many different kinds of letters have to be written—friendly letters, business letters, invitations, orders, complaints, requests, regrets, apologies, and so forth.

In the primary grades, letter writing can be correlated with a number of other ongoing activities. When first-grade children are learning the days and months, describing the kind of day it is, learning the phonemes and their graphemic representations, the teacher can use letter writing as an ongoing activity each day to review some of the instruction for the handwriting lesson or as part of an experience story, telling about some event or happening in which the children were involved.

Letters should be brief, and they should be written to someone to whom they might actually be sent. In the beginning of the first grade, letters might consist of only one sentence, for example, telling the name of day. Here are some sample letters for first-grade children:

> Dear Mommy and Daddy,
>   Today is Monday.
>   Love,
>   Sharon

> Dear Daddy
>   It is raining today.
>   Love,
>   Carol

Dear Mommy,
    I can make the letter b.
        Love,
        Seth

Many children learn to read and spell the words that are continuously used in letters and their letters usually become progressively longer. Children should be allowed to bring their letters home as well as encouraged to save some so that they are able to see how well they have progressed during the year. It is delightful to hear first-grade children at the end of the year say, "Oh, look at how babyish I was when I wrote that!"

In the primary grades there are many opportunities for writing various kinds of letters. After a trip or after seeing a school play, the teacher and children can write thank-you notes. If a child is out ill, classmates can write friendly letters to him or her. If parents are invited to visit the class to see some class project or play, the class can write invitations.

Children should be encouraged to write many different kinds of letters and to develop the proper attitudes, habits, and skills necessary for letter writing. They should understand that in order to receive letters, they must write them, and that it is discourteous not to answer a letter. They should be helped to develop the necessary skills in letter writing.

In the Primary Grades

1. Answer letters promptly.
2. Proofread all letters.
3. Since a letter is a means of communication, make sure your handwriting can be read easily.
4. Make sure your letter makes sense.
5. Know that there are many different kinds of letters.
6. Use the proper punctuation.
7. Try to make friendly letters interesting.

In the Intermediate Grades

1. Know all the primary-grade skills listed above.
2. Know the forms for different letters.
3. Know that there are five parts to a friendly letter: heading, salutation, body, closing, and signature.
4. Know that a business letter has the same form as a friendly letter, but the inside address is added and, in typed letters, the signature identification is added.
5. Know that headings are conventional.
6. Know that the salutation, closing, and signature in a friendly letter express the relationship between you and the reader.
7. Know that accurate dates and return addresses are important.

Example of a friendly letter:

        172 Rogers Avenue
        Princeton, NJ 08540
        March 10, 1985

Dear Jennifer,

    Your visit is going to be the most exciting event of the year. The whole family is going to come to a picnic in our back yard, and we'll have fried chicken and blueberry pie.
    I can hardly wait for you to come. You'll be sleeping in my room and I can show you my photo album and you can play with my dog Brutus. Come soon.

        Your cousin,
        Tara

Example of a thank-you note:

        January 2, 1985

Dear Andrew,
    I want to tell you how much I enjoyed the picture that you made for me! It is simply lovely. I brought it in to have it framed immediately, and it is now hanging in my study.

    Please give my love to everyone. We are all looking forward to seeing you at the family reunion.

        Love,
        Aunt Florence

Example of an informal invitation:

Room 101
Eaton Elementary School
April 3, 1985

Dear Mr. and Mrs. Jones,

Our class is presenting a play in our room on April 21 from one-thirty to two-thirty. We would be pleased to have you come.

Sincerely yours,
Mrs. Jones's Fifth Grade

Example of a business letter:

1571 Conrad Avenue
Brockley, CA 94501
July 9, 1985

Jones Electrical Company
932 Railing Avenue
Oakland, CA 94604

To Whom It May Concern:

The ABC Corporation in Brockley informs me that you stock the LT-0140 tube for the 1972 model television set manufactured by Grant. The model number is RBC-143V67.

Since the tube is easily replaced, ABC has suggested I order it from you by mail. My check for the cost of the tube plus mailing is enclosed. Please send it to the above address.

Yours truly,
Samuel Potts

OUTLINING

Students in the intermediate grades should be gaining skill in *outlining,* which is closely related to categorizing and classification. Outlining helps students both to organize long written compositions or papers and to study, because it serves as a guide for the logical arrangement of material (see "Notetaking" in this chapter and "Writing as a Mode of Learning" in Chapter 19). However, the skill of outlining should begin to be developed in the primary grades and should continue throughout the grades.

Actually, outlining readiness begins before children come to school. When children learn that certain things go together and certain things do not, they have outlining readiness. Young children tend to overgeneralize. They need to gain skill in making discriminations to be able to classify. Without the ability to classify, they cannot engage in outlining. By the time children come to school, they are usually able to make many discriminations and are beginning to classify (see Chapter 3).

Developing readiness for outlining in the primary grades includes the following skills:

1. Five-year-olds learn to put things together that belong together—blocks of the same size in the same place; clothes for each doll in the right suitcase; parts of a puzzle in the right box; scissors, brushes, and paints in the spaces designated for these materials.

2. First-graders may separate things that magnets can pick up from things they do not pick up by using two boxes—one marked "Yes" and the other marked "No." They can think of two kinds of stories—True and Make-Believe Stories. They can make booklets representing homes, dividing the pictures they have cut from magazines into several categories—living rooms, dining rooms, bedrooms, and so on. They can make two piles of magazines labeled "To Cut" and "To Read."[7]

3. Second-grade pupils continue to put things together that belong together—such as outdoor temperature readings and indoor temperature readings, valentines in individual mail boxes in the play post office, and flannel graph figures made to use in telling a story in the envelope with the title of the story. In addition,

---

[7]Although grade designations are given, teachers must take the individual differences of students into account. Some first-graders may be at a third-grade level; others may be at a first-grade or lower skill-development level.

seven-year-olds begin to understand finer classifications under large headings; for example, in a study of the work of a florist, plants may be classified as "Plants That Grow Indoors" and "Plants That Grow Outdoors." Indoor plants may be further subdivided into "Plants That Grow from Seeds," "Plants That Grow from Cuttings," "Plants That Grow from Bulbs," and so on. After visiting the local bakery second-graders, who are writing and drawing pictures of the story of their trip, can list the details in two columns—"Things We Saw in the Store" and "Things We Saw in the Kitchen."

4. Third-grade boys and girls have many opportunities to classify their ideas and arrange them in organized form. During a study of food in their community one group put up a bulletin board to answer the question "What parts of plants do we eat?" The pictures and captions were formulated by the third-graders in a table:

Leaves	Seeds	Fruits	Roots
cabbage	peas	apples	carrots
lettuce	beans	oranges	radishes
spinach	corn	plums	

The file of "Games We Know" in one third grade was divided into two parts by the pupils—"Indoor Games" and "Outdoor Games." Each of these categories was further subdivided into "Games with Equipment" and "Games without Equipment." After a visit to the supermarket a third-grade class booklet was made by the children with stories and pictures of the trip. The organization of the booklet with its numbered pages was shown in the Table of Contents:

Our Visit to the Food Market

Developing skills in outlining in the middle and upper grades includes several skills. Beginning with grade four, pupils often need to use and make outlines for reporting information found in reading a variety of references; listening to tape recordings, radio, and television; experimenting to find answers to questions; observing; and interviewing people who can help with the question at hand. *As the need for making an outline arises,* pupils may consult their English books to find out about the rules involved. Such suggestions as the following can be put in the pupils' own words and kept on a chart for reference:

Use Roman numerals for the main topics, putting a period after each Roman numeral.

Use capital letters for subtopics, with a period after each capital letter. Indent the subtopics.

Use ordinary (Arabic) numerals for details under subtopics and small letters under the details for less important points. Put a period after each number and letter.

Begin each topic with a capital letter, whether it is a main topic, a subtopic, or a detail. Do not put a period after a main topic, a subtopic, or a detail. Do not put a period after a topic unless it is a sentence.

Keep Roman numbers, capital letters, ordinary numbers, and small letters in straight vertical lines.

Topics are usually phrases, sometimes sentences. Do not mix phrases and sentences in the same outline.

An example of an outline that conveys pertinent information about outlines follows:

I. Main topic
  A. Prime importance
    1. Joins everything under it
    2. Signaled by Roman numeral (I, II, III, and so on)
    3. Begins with capital letter
  B. Example: I. The main topic in outline
II. Subtopics
  A. Grouped under main topics
  B. Related to main topics
    1. Indented under main topic
    2. Signaled by capital letter (A, B, C, D, and so on)
    3. Begin with capital letter
  C. Example: I. The relationship of subtopics to main topics

    A. How related
    B. How written
III. Specific details
    A. Grouped under appropriate subtopics
    B. Represented by Arabic numerals (1, 2, 3, 4, and so on)
    C. Example: I. The dictionary
        A. An important reference tool
        B. Uses of dictionary
           1. Information concerning word
           2. Other useful information

IV. More specific details
    A. Grouped under appropriate Arabic numerals
    B. Represented by lowercase (small) letters (a, b, c, d, and so on)
    C. Example: I. The dictionary
        A. An important reference tool
        B. Uses of dictionary
           1. Information concerning word
               a. Spelling
               b. Definitions
               c. Correct usage
               d. Syllabication, and so on
           2. Other useful information
               a. Biographical entries
               b. Signs and symbols
               c. Forms of address, and so on

V. Types of outlines
    A. Topic outline
        1. Consists of phrases
        2. Useful in preparing either short or long papers
    B. Sentence outline
        1. Consists of complete sentences
        2. Used primarily in planning long papers

Sets and Outlining

An exercise involving sets can be used with both primary- and intermediate-grade students to help them recognize that outlining and classification are closely related. Ask students to think of the set of all the books in the library. This is a very general set:

Next ask students to state the kinds of books one would find in the library. By doing this we are becoming less general:

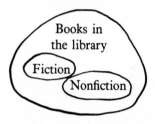

Now ask students to state what kinds of books one would find in the set of fiction books and what kinds of books one would find in the set of nonfiction books:

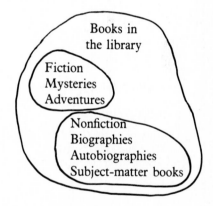

Ask the children to name a particular mystery or adventure book. At this point we are becoming very specific:

Now ask the students to put this information in outline form.

Here are samples of exercises, according to grade levels, that should help children develop the skill of outlining through understanding classification.

PRIMARY GRADES

FAMILY NAMES

Directions: On the line above each group write the appropriate family name or main topic. Although the different groups in this exercise belong to the same general class, the differences between the groups may be indicated by adding a descriptive word to the family name you choose.

EXERCISE

_____

Horse
Cow
Dog

_____

Tiger
Wolf
Bear
Moose
Fox

FOURTH OR FIFTH GRADE

ORGANIZING

Directions: At the head of the exercise is a list of words. Take each word and ask, "Does this word belong in Group I or Group II? When you are sure of your answer, write the word under its main topic."

EXERCISE

Chicago, Arizona, Vermont, California, Los Angeles, Tulsa, Georgia, Baltimore

I. States
   A.
   B.
   C.
   D.

II. Cities
   A.
   B.
   C.
   D.

OUTLINES—TIME ORDER

Directions: Study the exercise list. Select your main topics, and arrange them in time order. Then arrange your subtopics.

EXERCISE

horseback, pioneer forms, modern forms, covered wagon, railway express, pony express, motor truck, airplane

Changes in Transportation

I.
  A.
  B.
  C.

II.
  A.
  B.
  C.

FIFTH OR SIXTH GRADE

LEVELS OF ABSTRACTION

Directions: Here are some items in columns. Each column describes one item. Each word tells you more, or less, information about the item than all the others. Put a "1" in front of the word that tells the least, a "2" in front of the word that tells the next least, and so on until the highest number is placed beside the word telling the most. The word that tells the least is the most general word—such as "animal," whereas the word that tells the most is the most specific—such as "John Doe."

EXERCISE

Example

    3   A—*John Doe*
    1   B—*Animal*
    2   C—*Human*

    ____   A—*Animal*
    ____   B—*Lassie*
    ____   C—*Collie*
    ____   D—*Dog*

    ____   A—*Rock*
    ____   B—*Nonliving*
    ____   C—*Rock formations*
    ____   D—*Mt. Everest*

NOTETAKING

Students are not concerned with notetaking until they begin writing long reports or papers. Then notetaking, like outlining, is taught as a tool. Students in the intermediate grades should learn that notetaking:

1. Is done when writing long reports
2. Is necessary when many different books are to be used
3. Is used to organize material

Students learn to use index cards in notetaking because they are easy to handle and arrange. The cards should contain legible writing and the following information:

1. Name of author, title of book, publisher, date of publication
2. At the top of the card the topic of the report and the subtopic to which the particular note applies
3. The recorded information—a summary, figures, a definition, a quotation, and so on

Intermediate-grade students are learning that notes consist of groups of words that help one remember important material. They learn that notes do not have to be written in sentence form, but book information *is* written in a special form. By the fourth grade the form is as follows: Author's last name is written first, a comma separates the last name from the first name, and the title of the book is capitalized and underlined. A comma and page numbers follow the title. For example:

Wiese, Kurt, You Can Write Chinese, pages 45–50

By sixth grade the bibliography also includes the date of publication. The teacher should initiate a discussion on the importance of knowing this factor.

For practice in notetaking, students read a particular paragraph and take notes on it. Then they discuss the groups of words taken down as reminders of what they read. The teacher collects the paragraphs and asks students if, using their notes, they can give an oral report on what they have just read. The teacher also explains that it is relatively easy for them to give reports on the paragraph because:

1. It is still fresh in their minds.
2. It was not very long.
3. The discussion by many students on the same or similar paragraphs reinforced their recall.

Before students are asked to write a report using notes, the teacher should give them notetaking practice as outlined above with two, three, and more paragraphs on a similar topic from different sources. Students should take notes on these paragraphs and put them together in a short report.

Teachers should also help students recognize that for study purposes, it is a good idea to combine notetaking with outlining; that is, the students should present their notes in some kind of logical order. The outline does not need to be a formal one, but it should make sense and help the student recall a great amount of information. (See "Writing as a Mode of Learning" in Chapter 19.)

THE WRITING CONFERENCE

One of the best ways to help children in writing is to meet with each one and to go over each child's paper together. However, it would not be an efficient use of a teacher's time if he or she met only in a one-to-one situation. There are times when the teacher might want to meet with a few children about some special need that they have, and there are also times when the teacher would want to meet with large groups, as well as with only one child. The amount of time the teacher would meet with each child or with the different groups would depend on the purposes of the conference. At times, it might be just a minute or two to clear up a particular point; at other times, it might be for 15 minutes to half an hour.

When the teacher meets individually with a child, six things should occur:[8]

1. The conference should be *predictable* for the child.
2. The teacher should *focus* on one or two features only.

[8]Donald H. Graves, *Writing: Teachers & Children at Work* (Exeter, N.H.: Heinemann Educational Books, 1983), pp. 271–272.

3. The teacher should *demonstrate solutions*.
4. The *roles should be reversible*; that is, children should also question, comment, and attempt solutions.
5. There should be a *heightened semantic domain* between the teacher and child; that is, the teacher and child are establishing and developing a means of communicating with one another concerning process and subjects. The child gradually becomes more adept at using the language of writing while gaining a keener understanding of what the terms mean.
6. The conference should include *playful structures*; that is, it should include a combination of humor, experimentation, and discovery.

For an effective conference, there must be mutual respect and dialogue between or among the persons involved. During the day, conferences may be initiated by either the teacher or child. There are times when a child needs help, is excited about something, or is "stuck"; the child would then initiate a conference. It could also be that the teacher notices that a number of children or perhaps just one child needs special help; the teacher would then initiate the conference.

When children are writing, teachers should also do some writing, and they should eventually share theirs with their students. Also, teachers should circulate among their students to see what students are doing and to be available for help, for encouragement, or just for receiving information from students about what they are doing.

EVALUATION OF COMPOSITIONS

Evaluation that is ongoing and an integral part of the educative process is most effective when students

1. Are involved in the process
2. Understand the purpose of the evaluation
3. Have a need for it

Evaluation of students' written expression is necessary so that

1. Students can determine whether they are improving in writing.
2. Students can learn how they are performing relative to other students in the class.

3. Teachers can determine how their students compare with other classes.

In the early grades children's compositions should not be evaluated with the intent of giving a grade. However, even in the early grades, teachers and students should be going over papers together, and children should be gaining information about their progress in writing.

The teacher's evaluation of the child's progress is a continuous one. The personality traits that the child shows, the amount of help he needs, his growth in interest, in initiative, in sustained attention to the writing task, in independence, as well as in technical skills of handwriting and spelling are all a part of the evaluation. The teacher's observation of the child's behavior, her anecdotal records, and the writing the child produces form the materials for evaluation. Though the teacher evaluates the child's writing for content and for form, what is happening to the child is more important than what he produces."[9]

By the intermediate grades students' compositions can begin to be evaluated in terms of both content and form, and grades can be given. Merely giving a grade to a paper does not help students; extensive comments about the content and mechanics of the paper are necessary. Encouraging students by praising good ideas, while diagnosing specific writing problems, will do more to help pupils become better writers than awarding a letter or number grade. The teacher, by cooperatively analyzing papers with students, can help them to recognize that, even though their ideas are good, they must be able to express them better in written form or the ideas will not be conveyed to the reader.

Although the emphasis for both practical and creative writing should be on ability to express ideas, basic skills are needed. Children must be helped to realize that basic skills and tools—such as command of vocabulary, knowledge of punctuation, sentence sense, and spelling—are needed for effective communication.

[9]Ruth Strickland, "Evaluating Children's Compositions," in *Children's Writing: Research in Composition and Related Skills* (Champaign, Ill.: National Council of Teachers of English, 1960–1961), p. 66.

The teacher will have to be very careful not to inhibit students who simply put down their ideas, even though they lack many of these tools. Pupils should be encouraged to acquire the tools. If the form of the paper is correct but the quality of the ideas is poor, the teacher should help students clarify their thinking through analysis of their ideas (see "The Writing Conference" earlier in this chapter).

Teachers and students can recognize that the grading of written compositions is not a science, because of its subjectivity. The same paper graded by different individuals can be awarded any grade in the range of "A" to "F" (see Chapter 18 on evaluation). The teacher must be alert for bias or "set" that may creep into the grading of compositions, and should do everything possible to keep an open mind.

An activity that could be used for the fourth grade and above to exemplify this point can also be fun. A short composition, not one belonging to any student in the class, is read. Mimeographed copies of the composition are then given to each student, and they are asked to grade the composition and make comments they think would help the student who wrote it.

This activity serves three purposes. First, students, by sharing their different grades and comments with the class, will verify the subjectivity involved in grading written papers. Second, by analyzing the paper, students should become more critical of their own writing. Third, some criteria for written composition standards can be set up, which might help students in evaluating their own papers (see checklists on revision and editing that follow).

Should a child's composition ever receive a "D" or an "F"? Such a grade means that there is nothing redeemable in the paper—the quality of the writing is poor; the ideas expressed are muddled; the mechanics of writing are non-existent. It means that the child has not made any progress in the composing process. Rather than give the student a failing grade, the teacher should continue to meet individually with such students to discuss their problems. These particular pupils need all the help and encouragement they can get. There should be no pretense that the papers are good. Teachers should, however, help these students know that they can and are expected to do better. After a complete diagnosis of student difficulties, a program to eliminate each one of the problems should be developed. These students need many and varied writing activities. Some may have to start with writing sentences or paragraphs. The important factor is that students' difficulties are analyzed and that something is done to alleviate the problems.

Preventive measures are always more effective than remediation. If *all* teachers provide stimulating techniques, give their students many opportunities to express themselves in written form, and provide basic skill development throughout their teaching careers at school, problems can be prevented.

Revision Checklist

1. Does what you have written express what you wanted to say?
2. Should you add anything?
3. Should you delete some material?
4. Is your material well organized?
5. Is there a better way to organize your material?
6. Is there any new information or ideas that you feel you should incorporate in writing?
7. Are you pleased with what you have written?

The editing checklist that follows is an extensive one. Editing, as already stated, concerns the final polishing of the text. At this point, the writer is concerned with having the most effective word choice and sentence structure to convey his or her message. The writer also wants a text as free from punctuation, capitalization, and spelling errors as possible. The amount of editing material that will be listed on the class checklist would obviously depend on the individual differences of the children in a particular class. In some classes children might have their own individual checklists.

Editing Checklist

1. Have you checked your spelling and looked up any words that you are not sure of in the dictionary?
2. Do you have a period at the end of your sentences that should have periods?
3. Do you have a question mark at the end of your sentences that ask a question?

4. Do you have a capital letter at the beginning of all your sentences?

5. Do you have a capital letter at the beginning of all names and names of things?

6. Have you capitalized "I" whenever you used it?

7. Have you put in commas where you are listing lots of things?

8. Have you put the apostrophe in the proper place in making contractions, such as *can't, don't, isn't, hasn't, I'm*?

9. Have you used the apostrophe in the correct place in writing possessives, such as *Charles's, Joneses', enemies', deer's*?

10. Have you checked for agreement of subject and verb?

11. Have you checked for proper agreement of pronouns with their antecedents?

12. Have you used the active voice whenever possible?

13. Have you avoided the overuse of dashes, brackets, or parentheses?

14. Have you used semicolons in the correct places?

15. Have you checked for run-on sentences?

16. Do you have the proper verb tenses?

17. Do you have the proper verb mood?

18. Are your sentences parallel?

19. Are your sentences complete sentences?

20. Have you indented the first sentence of each of your paragraphs?

21. Have you avoided beginning all your sentences in the same way?

22. Have you used variety in sentence structure?

23. Have you used different types of sentences to portray your ideas?

24. Have you varied sentence lengths?

25. Have you avoided using sentences that are too wordy; that is, can you say the same thing in fewer words or more succinctly?

STUDENT'S NAME:
GRADE:
TEACHER:

DIAGNOSTIC CHECKLIST FOR PRACTICAL ASPECTS OF WRITING

I. PUNCTUATION	YES	NO

A. Primary Grades

The child:

	YES	NO
1. Places a period at the end of a sentence		
2. Places a period after abbreviations		
3. Places a question mark at the end of question sentences		
4. Places a comma to separate day from year (February 11, 1985)		
5. Places a comma to separate city from state (Albany, New York)		
6. Places periods after numbers in a listing (1. candy, 2. cake, and so on)		
7. Places periods after Mr., Mrs., and Ms.		
8. Places a period after an initial		
9. Places an apostrophe in some contractions, such as *can't, he's*		
10. Places an apostrophe in possessive singular, such as *girl's, boy's*		

B. Intermediate Grades

The child is able to:
1. Master all items of previous years
2. Use apostrophes in more contractions, such as *let us/let's, will not/won't*
3. Use apostrophes in singular and plural possessives, such as *Jones's, Joneses', Children's, babies', mice's*
4. Use hyphens between syllables in separating a word at the end of a line
5. Use an exclamation mark to express strong emphasis or emotion
6. Use a period or an exclamation mark for a command
7. Use a comma to separate items in a series
8. Use a colon after the salutation in a business letter
9. Use a comma to set off a quotation
10. Place quotation marks before and after a quotation
11. Use a comma to help make sentences clearer
12. Use a comma in figures containing more than four digits
13. Use commas with transitional words such as *however, indeed, that is, for example, in fact,* and so on
14. Use quotation marks for special words in a sentence
15. Use quotation marks for setting off the title of a poem, short story, magazine article, chapter, and so on
16. Use a colon to set off a list of items
17. Underline the title of a book

II. CAPITALIZATION	YES	NO

A. Primary Grades

The child capitalizes:
1. Persons' names
2. The first word of a sentence
3. The greeting in a letter
4. Days of the week
5. Months of the year
6. Titles of persons such as Mr., Mrs., Miss, and Ms.
7. First word of the closing of a letter
8. Names of states
9. Names of cities
10. Names of streets
11. The pronoun "I"

12. The first word of every line in a poem (except for the poetry of some modern poets)

B. Intermediate Grades

The child capitalizes:
1. All items listed for the primary grades
2. Names of countries
3. Names of towns
4. Names of avenues
5. Names of roads
6. Any word used as a name such as *Father, Mother*
7. Titles of books
8. Titles of poems
9. Titles of stories
10. Titles of movies
11. Titles of magazines
12. Names of languages
13. Names of buildings
14. Names of companies
15. The first word of a direct quotation
16. Names of institutions
17. Historical periods
18. Names of nationalities
19. A direction that names a definite area
20. In outlining, the first word of each main topic, subtopic, and detail

III. SENTENCES	YES	NO

A. Primary Grades

The child is able to:
1. Write simple sentences in the active voice
2. Recognize that sentence fragments are not sentences
3. Recognize that a sentence expresses a complete thought
4. Recognize that a sentence may be as brief as one word such as "Go!" and that "you" is understood in such a sentence
5. Recognize statement sentences
6. Recognize question sentences
7. Recognize command sentences

B. Intermediate Grades

The child is able to:
1. Master all items of previous years
2. Write exclamatory sentences

3. Expand sentences by adding descriptive words
4. Combine sentences
5. Recognize run-on sentences
6. Separate run-on sentences
7. Recognize misplaced modifiers
8. Correct sentences with misplaced modifiers

IV. PARAGRAPHS	YES	NO

A. Upper Primary Grades

The child is able to:
1. Recognize that a paragraph consists of a number of related sentences that develop the main idea
2. Recognize that the related sentences are arranged in some order to make sense
3. State the topic of the paragraph
4. Keep to the topic
5. Know when to begin a new paragraph

B. Intermediate Grades

The child is able to:
1. Master all items of previous years
2. Recognize the topic sentence in a paragraph
3. Write a topic sentence for a paragraph
4. Develop a paragraph using different kinds of details such as examples, comparison/contrast, cause and effect, description, and definition
5. Write a group of paragraphs on a topic
6. Express ideas clearly
7. Express ideas logically
8. Present ideas creatively

V. LETTER WRITING	YES	NO

A. Primary Grades

The child is able to:
1. Write announcements
2. Write friendly letters
3. Write thank-you letters
4. Write get-well letters
5. Write invitations
6. Write the five parts of a friendly letter
7. Address an envelope for a friendly letter including the zip code

B. Intermediate Grades

The child is able to:
1. Master all items of previous years
2. Write business letters using appropriate language
3. Write the six parts of a business letter
4. Order something by mail
5. Write information in a concise manner
6. Write a letter of complaint
7. Write a letter of apology
8. Address a business envelope including the zip code

VI. REPORTING	YES	NO

A. Primary Grades

The child is able to:
1. Choose a topic to report on
2. Choose a title for the topic
3. Keep to the topic
4. Maintain some logical order in reporting
5. Dictate a review about a television show he or she has watched
6. Proofread the report

B. Intermediate Grades

The child is able to:
1. Take notes to write a report
2. Maintain logical order in reporting
3. Find information related to the topic
4. Use the encyclopedia for information
5. Use the card catalogue to find information
6. Write a bibliography
7. Prepare an outline before writing the report

VII. OUTLINING	YES	NO

A. Primary Grades

The child is able to:
1. Make discriminations
2. Begin to classify objects:
   a. Put things together that belong together
   b. Group things under large headings

B. Intermediate Grades

The child is able to:
1. Use outlines for reporting information
2. Use Roman numerals for the main topics

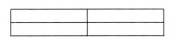

3. Put a period after each Roman numeral
4. Use capital letters for subtopics
5. Indent subtopics
6. Use ordinary Arabic numerals for details under subtopics
7. Use small letters under the details for less important points
8. Put a period after each number and letter
9. Begin each topic with a capital letter
10. Write an outline in phrase form
11. Write an outline in sentence form

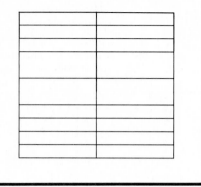

SUMMARY

This chapter has continued to present the ingredients teachers need to develop and to implement a good writing program in their classes. The emphasis in this chapter has been on the development of the conventions of writing. Unless students have knowledge of spelling, punctuation, and word usage, and are able to write in some legible form, they will have difficulty with written expression.

The skills necessary for becoming an effective writer were presented and sequentially developed at both primary- and intermediate-grade levels. Some of the skills included punctuation, capitalization, writing sentences, and paragraphing. Standards for giving book reports, writing various types of letters, outlining, and notetaking for long reports were also discussed.

Evaluation of written expression was reviewed, and teachers were cautioned against giving grades to primary-school pupils for their written work. The writing conference was suggested as one of the best ways to help children in writing, and information on how to have a successful writing conference was given. A "Diagnostic Checklist for Practical Aspects of Writing" was also presented.

As a further aid, two examples of practical writing lesson plans follow. Using these as a guide, see if you can construct another one.

LESSON PLAN I: PRIMARY-GRADE LEVEL*

OBJECTIVE

Students show that they are able to use punctuation marks such as question marks and exclamation points by placing them correctly in sentences.

PRELIMINARY PREPARATION

1. Large cardboard figures of a question mark and an exclamation point
2. Full-page pictures of facial expressions signifying surprise, a questioning or quizzical look, and no discernible expression
3. Transparencies with sentences requiring question marks, periods, and exclamation points
4. Overhead projector

INTRODUCTION

"We've been working with writing sentences, and we've talked about how important it is to know when to end a sentence. We've learned that a period tells us a sentence has ended. Who remembers some other things that we talked about? Good. We said that in speaking we can show surprise by expressions on our faces and also by our voices. I have some pictures that I'd like you to look at. Can someone tell me what kind of expression this person has on her face? Yes, she looks as though she may be asking a question. Can someone make up a question that she may be asking? Good. Let's look at another picture. Yes, he seems surprised. Who can make up a sentence showing surprise? Good. Today we're going to learn about the signals that show surprise and questions in writing. We call these signals punctuation marks."

DEVELOPMENT

"When we are writing question sentences and sentences that express surprise, we can't use our voices or facial expressions to help us get others to understand our meaning. This symbol [*hold up large cardboard symbol*] is called a question mark and this one [*hold up large cardboard symbol*] is called an exclamation point. We use the question mark symbol at the end of question sentences, and we use the exclamation point at the end of sentences that show surprise or some other strong feeling. I'm going to hold up a few more pictures and I'd like someone to tell me which symbol he or she would use. [*Hold up a number of pictures and have children choose symbols.*] Now I'm going to construct a question mark and exclamation point on the chalkboard. After I do so, I'd like you to make three of each of them on your papers. Now we'll see if you can put the correct symbol at the end of the sentences that I'll show you. For example, what symbol would you put at the end of this sentence— *How old are you?* Yes, a question mark. What about this sentence—*Oh, that is pretty!* Yes, an exclamation point. Number your papers from one to five and let's see who can put all the correct signals at the end of each of these sentences." Write on the chalkboard:

1. What is your name
2. I love it
3. This is fun
4. Who is she
5. What color is it

"Let's read each sentence and state what signal it should have. Now I'd like each of you to write one question sentence and one sentence that shows surprise or some other strong feeling."

SUMMARY

Elicit from students when to use a question mark and when to use an exclamation point. Pull together the main points of the lesson.

*This lesson plan was used with an advanced group of third graders. (Exclamation marks are usually not introduced until the fourth grade; however, these children had begun using them in their writing, and they were "overusing" them.)

LESSON PLAN II: INTERMEDIATE-GRADE LEVEL

OBJECTIVE

Students will be able to recognize that notes should fit into only one main topic area.

PRELIMINARY PREPARATION

Overhead projector, transparency of a student's notes, main headings.

INTRODUCTION

"We've discussed the importance of having a good outline when we write a long report or composition. What are some of the reasons we gave? Yes, good. We also talked about the various kinds of outlines. Who remembers some? Good. Today, I'd like you to look at this transparency. It contains notes from a student report called 'Why Accidents Occur.' You don't know this student because she doesn't go to our school. Look for one moment at the notes that this student took and also her main headings. Today we're going to discuss whether this student took good notes and give our reasons for our opinions. From the discussion we should be able to make some suggestions for good notetaking procedures."

DEVELOPMENT

"I'd like everyone to categorize the notes into this student's main headings." Teacher walks around the room while pupils are working and offers assistance. After a while she asks whether anyone is having difficulty classifying the notes. A number of children raise their hands and say that they are. The teacher asks them why. One pupil states that some of the notes fit into more than one main heading, and a number of students agree. Another pupil says that he can't put the notes under the proper heading because he isn't sure about their meaning. The teacher asks some students to read what they have put under main topic I. It turns out that students do not agree. The same is done for main topic II and main topic III. The teacher again asks why this has happened. Students reply that they all interpreted the notes differently, and they could fit under more than one heading.

SUMMARY

The teacher asks students what they have learned that could help them to become better note takers from this activity concerning notetaking and main topics. Students reply that the main topics must be clearly stated and not overlap. The notes must also be precise and exact, so that there is no question as to where they belong.

The teacher then states, "Tomorrow we'll look at this student's notes and main topics again. We'll see if we are able to rewrite them so that they can fit properly under the main headings."

Following are the student's main topics and notes:

Why Home Accidents Occur

I. Failure to see danger
II. Failure to use things correctly
III. Failure to make repairs

Student's Notes

1. Slippery floors
2. Bathroom light switch
3. Cellar stairs dark
4. Ladder broken
5. Medicines on shelf
6. Light cord bare
7. Pots on stove with handles out

8. Throw rugs
9. Using tools carelessly
10. Toys on floor
11. Box on stairs
12. Putting penny in fuse box
13. Curtains over stove

SUGGESTIONS FOR THOUGHT QUESTIONS AND ACTIVITIES

1. A child in a fourth-grade class has good ideas, but also has difficulty in expressing them in a written composition. How would you go about helping this child?

2. A class enjoys writing activities, but most of the students do not revise or edit their papers. What are some things that could be done to stimulate these children to revise and edit their compositions?

3. What are some techniques that can be used to stimulate interest in outlining?

4. You have been chosen to present a talk to teachers in your school on the skills needed for written expression. How would you present this talk so as to gain and maintain audience interest? What skills would you emphasize in your talk?

5. State some creative ways to combine reading and writing.

6. You have been asked to give a talk to your colleagues on the place of the writing conference in the writing program. What will you say?

7. Prepare some fun activities that will help students develop punctuation, capitalization, and sentence-writing skills.

SELECTED BIBLIOGRAPHY

Atwell, Margaret A. "The Evolution of Text: The Interrelationship of Reading and Writing in the Composing Process." Unpublished dissertation, Indiana University, 1980.

Donovan, Timothy R., and Ben W. McClelland, eds. *Eight Approaches to Teaching Composition.* Urbana, Ill.: National Council of Teachers of English, 1980.

Graves, Donald H. *Writing: Teachers & Children at Work.* Exeter, N.H.: Heinemann Educational Books, 1983.

———. *Balance the Basics: Let Them Write.* New York: Ford Foundation Papers on Research about Learning, February 1978.

Gregg, Lee W., and Erwin R. Steinberg, eds. *Cognitive Processes in Writing.* Hillsdale,

N.J.: Lawrence Erlbaum Associates, 1980.

Murray, Donald M. *A Writer Teaches Writing.* Boston: Houghton Mifflin, 1968.

Rubin, Dorothy. *The Teacher's Handbook of Writing/Thinking Exercises.* New York: Holt, Rinehart and Winston, 1980.

_____. *Gaining Sentence Power.* New York: Macmillan, 1981.

_____. *Writing and Reading: The Vital Arts,* 2d ed. New York: Macmillan, 1983.

Sealey, Leonard, Nancy Sealey, and Marcia Millmore. *Children's Writing.* Newark, Del.: International Reading Association, 1979.

Straw, Stanley B. "Assessment and Evaluation in Written Composition: A Commonsense Perspective," in *Research in the Language Arts: Language and Schooling,* Victor Froese and Stanley B. Straw, eds. Baltimore: University Park Press, 1981, pp. 181–202.

THIRTEEN

Gaining Proficiency in Spelling

TEACHER: Spell sago, mucilaginous, ephemeral, cyst, copal.

PUPIL: Why?

TEACHER: Because I say so!

PUPIL: But they are so hard and I never heard them before.

TEACHER: That makes no difference. The harder the words you have at first, the easier spelling will become.

Choosing rare or very difficult spelling words that were almost unpronounceable was part of a lesson illustrated in an early edition of Noah Webster's *Blue Back Speller,* a child's basic primer. Such words as "sago," "copal," and "cyst" were selected for mastery by the elementary-school child. It was not until the latter part of the nineteenth century, when psychologists became involved in determining how children learn to read, that changes in the teaching of spelling also began.

The interaction of reading, language, and spelling was also demonstrated in Webster's *Blue Back Speller.* "Analysis of Sound in the English Language" had to be memorized exactly. It began with this definition:

Language or speech is the utterance of articulate sounds or voices, rendered significant by usage, for the expression and communication of thoughts.

All other explanations were written similarly as if to obscure meaning. Children had to memorize passages without understanding them, since teachers rarely offered explanations. (Perhaps they, too, had difficulty in interpreting the passages.)

The *Speller's* format consisted of a page of the alphabet and a page of syllable combinations. The prose content of the *Speller* consisted of didactic sayings, admonishing children to be good and do their duty. A reading page consisted of several paragraphs, each concerned with an entirely different topic.

A peculiar feature of the book concerned social relations. The "young man, seeking for a partner for life," is advised to "Be not in haste to marry," and the young woman to:

Be cautious in listening to the addresses of men. Is thy suitor addicted to low vices? is he profane? is he a gambler? a tippler? a spendthrift? a haunter of taverns? and, above all, is he a scoffer at religion? Banish such a man from thy presence, his heart is false, and his hand would lead thee to wretchedness and ruin.[1]

[1]Clifton Johnson, *Old Time Schools and School Books* (New York: Dover, 1963), p. 178.

For married people there are suggestions of this sort:

> Art thou a husband? Treat thy wife with tenderness; reprove her faults with gentleness.
>
> Art thou a wife? Respect thy husband; oppose him not unreasonably, but yield thy will to his, and thou shalt be blest with peace and concord; study to make him respectable; hide his faults.[2]

Although Webster combined spelling and reading in one text (along with pre- and post-marital advice), it should be stressed that spelling is not synonymous with reading. (More will be said about this later.) Before Webster's book, which was based on Dilworth's spelling book, spelling in textbooks was not uniform. Even the most highly educated spelled the same word in different ways, as is documented in letters, records, and other manuscripts. Webster brought standardization and order to spelling, almost single-handedly counteracting the chaos that had previously existed.

A woodcut portrait of Webster making him look like a porcupine was used in "Old Blueback." This caused a great deal of controversy concerning the book which helped publicize and advertise it. As a result Webster's *Speller* became very popular.

Before the *Speller* was published, spelling had only been taught incidentally, but Webster's book made it an important subject. Spelling bees were held and prizes were given, which absorbed a great amount of children's time and energy. Spelling bees also became a recreational event, and great competitive exhibitions were held.[3] Although the educational value of these events has been questioned, many vestiges of spelling bees remain to this day.

While spelling is not emphasized as much today as it was in the nineteenth and a great part of the twentieth century, the skill is important for effective communication in writing. Numerous spelling errors detract from the ideas being presented, and the writer who makes many errors is usually looked on as lacking in education.

[2]Ibid., p. 178.
[3]Ibid., pp. 167–184.

Since confusion exists as to the place of spelling in the school program—how it should be taught, and when it should be formally taught—these areas and others will be discussed in order to help teachers to establish an effective and viable spelling program for students.

After reading this chapter, you should be able to answer these questions:

1. How is spelling related to other language arts areas?
2. What is a continuing spelling controversy? Explain.
3. How are words chosen for spelling lists?
4. What criteria should be used for choosing words for classroom study?
5. What are some of the spelling problems that a left-handed child could have?
6. What can the teacher do to stimulate pupils' spelling consciousness?
7. What is invented spelling?
8. What spelling generalizations should be taught?
9. Can you explain the inductive method of teaching spelling?
10. What is the word study plan? Describe the steps involved in this method.
11. What are some possible difficulties in learning to spell? Explain.
12. What is the place of the dictionary in the spelling program?

RELATIONSHIP OF SPELLING TO OTHER LANGUAGE ARTS AREAS

Spelling and reading are related through vocabulary. A child who has difficulty in recognizing a word will have difficulty in trying to reproduce its sequence of letters from memory. Reading and spelling can be seen to be closely related, since many of the abilities required for one are also required for the other. For example, learning to read and to spell requires the ability to discriminate visually among words. Generalizations concerning phonic analysis, structural analysis, and vocabulary development are the same as those in spelling. If vocabulary is poor and articulation not adequately developed, both reading and spelling usually suffer. Spelling and reading are both cognitive processes that require active consumers of information.

Good reading and spelling seem to go together. The more often a word is met in reading, the greater the likelihood that the word will be learned and used in writing. Although there are some good readers who are poor spellers, the opposite is rarely true. Children who have difficulty in learning the relationships between sounds and the symbols that represent them will usually have difficulty in spelling.

Although there are similarities between reading and spelling, the acts of reading and spelling are different. In reading, the child starts with visual symbols and must then think of corresponding sounds, whereas in spelling, one hears the word and has to think of the corresponding symbols. The act of spelling involves encoding (going from sounds to letters), while the act of reading involves decoding (going from letters to sounds). Spelling often requires the motor activity of writing letters to stand for the sounds heard.

Ability to spell enhances a pupil's creative writing, for the pupil does not have to concentrate on the mechanics of words but can be involved in the act of creating.

A CONTINUING SPELLING CONTROVERSY

ENGLISH

I take it you already know
Of tough and bough and cough and dough?
Others may stumble, but not you
On hiccough, thorough, slough and through?
Well done! And now you wish, perhaps
To learn of less familiar traps?

Beware of heard, a dreadful word
That looks like beard and sounds like bird.
And dead; it's said like bed, not bead;
For goodness sake, don't call it deed!
Watch out for meat and great and threat,
(they rhyme with suite and straight and debt).
A moth is not a moth in mother.
Nor both in bother, broth in brother.

And here is not a match for there.
And dear and fear for bear and pear,

And then there's dose and rose and lose—
Just look them up—and goose and chose,
And cork and work and card and ward,
And font and front and word and sword.
And do and go, then thwart and cart.
Come, come, I've hardly made a start.

A dreadful language? Why, man alive,
I'd learned to talk it when I was five,
And yet to write it, the more I tried,
I hadn't learned it at fifty-five.[4]

Author Unkown

A continuing "spelling controversy" is concerned with whether children should be taught spelling based on word lists or generalizations. Linguistic approaches to spelling emphasize the phoneme–grapheme relationships of words and analyzing groups of words by generalized rules. In the analysis, not only must the pupil know that each phoneme has a grapheme representation but the pupil must also learn how to listen for individual phonemes and notice their position and the sequence in which they occur.

Linguistic approaches to spelling instruction are not new. Some schools do not incorporate linguistic principles in the spelling curriculum because administrators believe there is no relationship between the way a word is said and how it is spelled. Because of the innumerable irregularities in spelling words, the subject was taught in the past by rote memorization, without any attempt at phonetic analysis. It was taught with spelling lists based on graduated levels of difficulty and containing words selected for their usefulness in writing. During the past two and a half decades an attempt has been made to emphasize the aural-oral aspect of spelling in relation to vocabulary. It was felt that, by being able to recognize words and *phonograms* or *graphemic bases* (a succession of graphemes that occurs with the same phonetic value in a number of words [at, ack]), children would be able to synthesize a large number of words on their own. As a result, there has

---

[4]Harold G. Shane, *Linguistics in the Classroom* (Washington, D.C.: Association for Supervision and Curriculum Development, 1967), p. 50.

been a greater emphasis on generalizations in spelling. Although there are not many scientific studies in this area, some researchers have attempted to establish sets of rules that would explain spelling.[5]

A study initiated in 1949 at Stanford University found that the phoneme–grapheme representation was regular in 80 percent of the 3,000 words analyzed. This was considered to be too narrow a sample, and it was suggested that if more words were added, the results would verify that the *orthography* (accepted spelling usage) was inconsistent to the point where the study would be considered unreliable.

A second phase was then undertaken, a more extensive study to examine the degree of consistency of the phoneme–grapheme relationships of 17,000 words, closely representative of the American English lexicon of an educated U.S. citizen. Since modern computer technology was used, it was possible to make large-scale analyses that would have been too tedious earlier. It was found that American-English orthography is more consistent with the spoken language than has been thought, especially when several components of the sound system underlying the orthography were examined. These are:

1. **Position in syllables**
2. **Syllabic stress**
3. **Internal restraints; the specific letter that precedes or follows a letter (its environment)**

The investigators did not claim their study made a firm case for the linguistic approach to spelling. It was stated that even though a phoneme is represented by a given grapheme in stressed or unstressed syllables 80 percent of the time, this fact may not help in the spelling of words. The restriction of the phoneme–grapheme correspondences to special positions keeps the results from applying to larger generalizations.

In this next phase of the study of phoneme–grapheme regularity in words, the earlier findings were used to predict the spelling of

17,000 different words. It was found that, by relying on phonological cues alone, researchers could spell over 9,483 words correctly from the list of 17,000. Therefore, even a limited knowledge of the phonological relationships can help provide some ability to spell words, while the additional knowledge relating to *morphology* (the study of the construction of words and parts of words) and *syntax* (the ways in which words are arranged relative to each other in utterances) would be even more helpful to correct spelling.[6, 7, 8]

An ongoing study of "spelling bee" champions confirms that good spellers "draw their information from a full reservoir of knowledge about spoken and written language structure in attempting to spell unfamiliar words."[9] In other words, the good spellers do not merely rely on phoneme–grapheme correspondences; they also use semantic, morphological, syntactic, and phonological information.

Ernest Horn, an authority on spelling, and an opponent of the use of rules and generalizations, claims that there is no justification for assuming that students can deduce the spelling of words from generalizations. For Horn, there is no escape from the need for teaching directly a large number of common words that do not conform to any phonetic or orthographic rule.[10] Horn claimed that:

Like many worthwhile things, there does not seem to be any short cut to learning to spell. Although some phonetic generalizations hold true consistently, e.g., initial consonant sounds like "b," time

---

[5]Ruth H. Weir and Richard Venezky, "Spelling to Sound Correspondences," in *The Psycholinguistic Nature of the Reading Process* (Detroit: Wayne State University Press, 1968).

[6]Richard E. Hodges and E. Hugh Rudorf, "Searching Linguistics for Cues in the Teaching of Spelling," *Elementary English* 42 (May 1965): 527–533.

[7]For the detailed report, *see* Paul R. Hanna et al., *Phoneme–Grapheme Correspondences As Cues to Spelling Improvement* (Washington, D.C.: Office of Education, U.S. Department of Health, Education and Welfare, 1966), U.S. Project No. 1991.

[8]Paul R. Hanna et al., *Spelling: Structure and Strategies* (Boston: Houghton Mifflin, 1971).

[9]Richard E. Hodges, "The Language Base of Spelling," in *Research in the Language Arts: Language and Schooling*, Victor Froese and Stanley B. Straw, eds. (Baltimore: University Park Press, 1981), p. 217.

[10]Ernest Horn, "Some Issues in Learning to Spell," *Education* 79 (December 1958): 229–233.

is better spent in learning to spell needed words rather than learning generalizations. This is true for most spelling rules.[11]

In the late 1960s Horn compared the research on phoneme–grapheme regularity to his own extensive research in spelling. He claimed that the studies (his own and the generalization research) are in substantial agreement on the number of ways in which various phonemes are spelled, as well as on the relative regularity of the spellings of sounds. However, the investigations unfortunately differed in the meaning of the term "regular." In Horn's study *regular* means "the total number of ways in which the sounds are spelled irrespective of the word position or other phonological [refers to speech sounds] or morphological [deals with the construction of words and parts of words] factors."[12] In the linguistic study the term "regular" takes into account the phonological factors of stress and the environmental conditions in words and syllables, including such morphological factors as compounding and affixation and the use of approximately 300 specialized rules.[13]

Although Horn seems to have softened his stance toward the contribution of phonemics to spelling, he still feels that caution is necessary when making conclusions. For example, he says that:

In the evaluation of the claims for high regularity in phoneme–grapheme relations, two limitations should be kept in mind: first, the pronunciations chosen for analysis are those given in Webster's New International Dictionary, second edition. These pronunciations, according to the dictionary, are those found in deliberate and careful speech, elsewhere called formal speech. In many words, these pronunciations vary from those found in informal cultivated speech. Second, the degree of regularity obtained by sophisticated research workers using several hundred rules to guide them, and the use of a computer to perform the tedious analysis, seems far removed from what can be achieved by students with the abilities and tools they have or can be given.[14]

Other researchers claim that although a speller who uses the rules consistently can spell about 80 percent of all phonemes correctly, that speller would only be able to spell about half of the 17,000 most common English words correctly, because these words contain several phonemes.[15]

It is obviously futile to teach a rule in which there are more exceptions than words that conform to a pattern. Therefore, generalizations should only be taught if enough cases conform to the rule. Some studies on phoneme–grapheme relationships have been done with enumerated specific rule generalizations and the percentage of time that words followed the rule. Some investigators have claimed that a rule should not be taught unless it holds true at least 75 percent of the time.[16] However, this should depend on the words. There are some frequently used words that may conform to a rule pattern, whereas a number of less frequently used words may not conform to the same rule generalization. The percentage of these latter words that conform to a rule pattern may not be as high as 50 percent, even though the most often-used words almost always conform to the same pattern. For example, the "silent *e*" rule, which is usually taught in the early primary grades, only has 63 percent applicability.[17] This 63 percent includes many frequently used words that conform to the same rule pattern. Therefore, the rule should be taught as a phonic generalization.

The spelling controversy continues. It seems, however, that it would be best if a bal-

---

[11]Ibid., p. 232.
[12]Ernest Horn, *Teaching Spelling: What Research Says to the Teacher* (Washington, D.C.: National Education Association, 1968), p. 22.
[13]Ibid.

[14]Ibid., p. 23.
[15]Dorothea P. Simon and Herbert A. Simon, "Alternative Uses of Phonemic Information in Spelling." *Review of Educational Research* 43 (Winter 1973): 115–137.
[16]Theodore Clymer, "The Utility of Phonic Generalizations in the Primary Grades," *Reading Teacher* 16 (January 1963): 252–258; and Lillie Smith Davis, "The Applicability of Phonic Generalizations to Selected Spelling Programs," *Elementary English* 49 (May 1972): 706–712.
[17]Davis, "Applicability," p. 709.

anced approach prevailed. Those words that follow phoneme–grapheme patterns should be taught with rule generalizations, whereas those that do not fit any pattern should be taught as separate entities. We must remember also that spelling involves all areas of the language arts, that good spellers use many cues, that spelling permeates all areas of the curriculum, and that spelling is a tool for writing.

WHY CAN'T I SPELL?

This lamant has been voiced by a number of persons. Interestingly, many of these persons are good readers, who are intelligent. Even though there are no simple answers, it may be that these persons have simply not paid attention to the graphic representation of words, and they have not been involved in a developmental spelling program. Even though, as stated earlier, good readers are generally good spellers, it is possible for good readers to be poor spellers. It is possible that some good readers do not attend to the graphic representations of many words because they do not need to read every syllable or even every word to extract meaning from what they are reading. It is also possible that they have been in schools where formal spelling instruction was ignored and where writing opportunities and requirements were few and far between. After all, spelling is a writing tool; the fewer opportunities persons have to write, the fewer opportunities they have to spell.

INVENTED SPELLING

Learning to spell is a complex undertaking that is more than the mere memorizing of words; it is developmental in nature and requires the acquiring and applying of knowledge of spoken and written language.[18] By *developmental*, we mean that learning to spell is ongoing and based on the cognitive development of the child. Correct spelling is learned gradually as the child proceeds through the grades, so that the more information children have about their written and spoken language, the better spellers they are capable of being.

Young children's spelling is based on their limited knowledge of the language system, so when they spell, they may use *invented spelling*. When young children begin asking about the letters adults make to write because they want to write in this way too, they may be on their way to using invented spelling. Not all children will use invented spelling, and the pattern of invented spelling will vary from one child to another. However, from an analysis of children's invented spelling, it appears that they seem to go through certain stages based on the way the individual child hears or pronounces the words. Some researchers in this area claim that children's spelling development parallels the earlier stages of language development. Investigators that hold this language-based hypothesis about how children learn to spell claim that children "internalize information about spoken and written words, organize that information, construct tentative rules based on that information, and apply these rules to the spelling of words.[19]

One researcher in this area has developed a model that shows the four stages children go through before they develop standard spelling.[20] The first is called the *deviant stage* because of the deviant appearance of the child's spelling attempts. This stage usually appears in early kindergarten or first grade, depending on when the child has been exposed to print. Deviant spellings are a random ordering of letters that the child can recall, for example, "btBpA" = *monster*. At this primitive level, the child does not show any evidence of letter–sound correspondence. At the *prephonetic stage*, the child produces one-, two-, or three-letter spellings that show letter–sound correspondence, for example, "MSR" = *monster* and "KLZ" = *closed*. At this stage the child has for the first time linked letter to sound. At the *phonetic stage*, the child's spelling is characterized by an almost perfect match between letters and sounds. The child's spelling includes all sound features as

---

[18]Hodges, "Language Base," p. 218.

[19]James W. Beers, "Developmental Strategies of Spelling Competence in Primary-School Children," in *Developmental and Cognitive Aspects of Learning to Spell,* Edmund H. Henderson and James W. Beers, eds. (Newark, Del.: IRA, 1980), p. 36.

[20]J. Richard Gentry, "Learning to Spell Developmentally," *Reading Teacher* 34 (January 1981): 378–381.

he or she hears and says them. As a result, the child's spelling at this stage does not resemble standard spelling, for example, "MONSTR" = *monster* and "DRAS" = *dress*. The *transitional stage,* which is the final stage in this model, precedes standard spelling. Children arrive at this stage usually in the latter half of Grade One or early in Grade Two. At this stage children are better acquainted with standard spelling, and words look like English, even though they are misspelled. The children are including vowels in every syllable, so phonetic "EGL" for *eagle* at this stage becomes "EGUL."

The *correct stage,* which follows the *transitional stage,* is the stage at which the teacher should initiate a formal spelling program. This program should build on the child's background of experiences. Also, teachers must take the individual differences of their students into account. While some children will be ready for formal instruction in the first grade, others may not be ready until the second (see "Should Spelling Be Taught in the First Grade?" later in this chapter).

DEVELOPING A SPELLING CONSCIOUSNESS

Students need a reason for spelling and a desire to spell correctly. If students do not see the purpose of spelling correctly, and do not develop a spelling consciousness, they usually will not spell correctly. An intermediate-level student whose spelling was so poor that it was difficult to read what he had written was a very creative writer. But it wasn't until the class produced a monthly magazine incorporating their writings and activities that the student made a concerted effort to learn to spell. He wanted other members of the class to be able to read his poems and stories. He had found a purpose for learning to spell.

A spelling consciousness is a desire to spell correctly, the ability to recognize that a word is misspelled, and an awareness that one is unsure about the spelling of the word. Students who make a conscious, concerted effort to look up or ask about any word that they are unsure of are developing a spelling consciousness. Students who have a well-developed spelling consciousness are usually knowledgeable in phonics, have good auditory and visual discrim-

ination, evidence a desire to spell correctly, and use semantic, graphic, syntactic, and phonological cues in determining how to spell an unfamiliar word.

WHAT WORDS SHOULD BE TAUGHT?

The problem of compiling a spelling list is difficult. A first-grade child who comes to school with a speaking vocabulary of approximately 2,500 to 3,500 words may want to know how to spell some of these words. The problem becomes more complex because the child may have from 7,500 to 25,000 words in his or her listening capacity. It is not inconceivable that the child may want to use some of these words in writing.

A 1915 study based on a 1,000-word count of adult literary writing and correspondence found that there were 300 most common words that made up three-fourths of all the writing analyzed. It was also discovered that the first 1,000 most common words made up more than nine-tenths of the material.[21]

During the late nineteenth and early twentieth centuries there was a proliferation of similar studies published in the United States, stating those words that were of the greatest use in written communication. Some vocabulary lists, such as Rinsland's 1945 one, were derived from various types of students' spontaneous writing.[22] It seems that like adults, children employ a few words most often, but that the complete number of words they use is very large.

The question of what factors should be considered in compiling word lists for children has still not been definitively answered. One school of thought is that children should learn to spell those words needed for adult writing. Another is that spelling lists should be composed of words children frequently use.[23] From a psychological point of view, those words should be

[21]Leonard P. Ayres, *A Measuring Scale for Ability in Spelling* (New York: Russell Sage Foundation, 1915).

[22]Henry D. Rinsland, *A Basic Vocabulary for Elementary School Children* (New York: Macmillan, 1945).

[23]Ernest Horn, "Research in Spelling," *Elementary English Review* 21 (January 1944): 6–13; and James A. Fitzgerald, "What Words Should Children Study in Spelling?" *Education* 79 (December 1958): 224–228.

taught that the child needs, has an interest in, and can use. If the child learns words only for a weekly spelling test, and does not use the words again, the chances that the child will retain them are not good. New learning will probably interfere with past learning, and the earlier words may soon be forgotten.

SPELLING IN THE SCHOOL DAY AND CHOICE OF SPELLING WORDS

The allotment of time for formal spelling lessons should not be more than 15 minutes a day, or about 75 minutes a week. With an increase of subject matter in the curriculum at the elementary-school level, the justification for more time is not warranted. However, during the school day there are many opportunities for incidental learning in spelling, and the teacher should take advantage of these. Spelling is related not only to many other language arts areas but to other areas of the curriculum as well. For example, a sixth-grade class in a social studies unit is working with famous people from other continents. The spelling words for the children include:

continent	Asia
globe	India
atlas	Africa
America	Japan
Europe	Israel

During the lesson the teacher asks a question concerning two women leaders whom they have read about and about whom the class has already talked. The teacher says, "I'll give you a hint. One of the women's first names is spelled almost like the country she headed." Many children are able to correctly give Indira Gandhi as the woman, and India as her country.

Another opportunity for choosing spelling words would be at holiday time or in reference to the seasons. Children who want to write about the holiday or season must know how to spell applicable words. The teacher could correlate writing with spelling so that children can use the words and see a purpose for learning to spell them. For example, when children write Halloween stories, they could try to use as many of the spelling words as they can to make good stories.

A teacher can also use children's interests or hobbies as an impetus for choosing spelling words. They may be chosen according to specific generalizations or rules, or grouped around a particular phonogram family.

In addition, teachers can use children's writing to initiate an individualized spelling program. The teacher would have each child keep a record of all the words he or she misspells in written work. Each child would be responsible for his or her own list. The teacher would have children team up and every week or every two weeks, the children would give each other a spelling test based on each child's "spelling demons." The children would be asked to write the words rather than say them aloud because students need to see the graphic representation of the word to determine whether it looks right.

A perceptive teacher should be alert to all of the opportunities that present themselves during the school day for choosing words that students need. The important thing is that a variety of sources should be used, rather than just one specific spelling text or workbook.

SHOULD SPELLING BE TAUGHT IN THE FIRST GRADE?

Some teachers will answer the question of whether spelling should be taught in first grade with a resounding "no." The answer is, however, that it depends on the child. Most first-graders who are reading and writing realize that certain symbols stand for oral sounds. Once they learn to decode the mysterious symbols, they also want to encode them in written form. They want to write stories, and in order to do this they need help in spelling. Teachers can help by spelling words either on the board or on the students' papers. It is difficult to anticipate all the words the first-grader will want or need, especially if the teacher is encouraging creativity. But the sooner teachers help pupils gain needed techniques—such as being critical analyzers of language, gaining skill in phonics, noticing regularities in phonograms or graphemic bases, noticing unusual spelling, and discovering rules—the sooner pupils will become independent spellers.

Teachers of young children need to recognize that children's progress in spelling is based on cognitive development and the amount of print the children have been exposed to. Also, as stated earlier in this chapter, many young children invent spelling to suit their writing needs. "Children's invented spellings evolve from their accumulated experiences with oral language (speech sounds) and the recently acquired familiarity with the alphabet and its use."[24] As a result, a preschooler might spell *truck* as *chruk* because *chruk* is closer to the way the child hears the beginning sound. Interestingly, some investigators of children's acquisition of spelling ability feel that children "are actually more proficient in 'sounding out' words than adults are. Their spellings often appear strange, not because they are random or an indication of poor auditory perception or discrimination, but because adults, as knowledgeable users of the system, have learned to ignore some very real similarities in sounds."[25]

When children begin to write in school, some may still use invented spelling. Teachers should not inhibit children's writing by telling them that they should only use those words that they can spell. Instead, teachers should tell children to try to spell the words as best they can; then after they have finished writing, spelling errors can be corrected. As was stated earlier, the first grade is not too soon to learn how to spell words correctly. Many first-graders are acquiring a spelling consciousness, and they want to know how to spell words correctly.

SPELLING AT THE PRIMARY-GRADE LEVEL

A number of determining factors operate in the grade placement of words: the usefulness of the word, the difficulty of the spelling word, the development of phonic principles, the development of combining forms, the learning of prefixes and suffixes, and the frequency of word use in the child's writing.

Although some words may be considered more difficult than others, often the uniqueness of the word lends itself to making it easier to learn to spell than is true of more common

words. There are many difficult words a primary-grade child uses. But since children use some of these words frequently in their writing, it would be useful for them to know the correct spelling of such words.

An appropriate time for children to learn spelling words that are similar occurs when they are learning certain phonic rules in the primary grades. For example, while children are learning the phonogram *at*, and have already worked with most initial consonants and consonant substitution, they can also learn to spell a number of other words in the *at* family. These words can be put into simple sentences and illustrated with pictures: This is a *cat*.

When children learn open and closed syllables, they can also learn a generalization: Words ending in closed syllables with one consonant preceded by a vowel usually double the consonant before adding endings. For example,

run	running
chat	chatting

TEACHING SPELLING THROUGH INDUCTION AND DEDUCTION

Inductive and deductive teaching strategies lend themselves very well to the teaching of spelling rules. An inductive strategy for teaching spelling generalizations includes the placement of a number of words on the board that portray a regular pattern. Students attempt to discover the generalizations. In order to assure students' discovery of the proper rule, the teacher should continue to put examples on the board that conform to the rule. (See the lesson plan at the end of this chapter for the development of an inductive teaching lesson.)

In the deductive method of teaching a spelling rule the generalization is given first.

[24]Margo Wood, "Invented Spelling," *Language Arts* 59 (October 1982):713.
[25]Jerry Zutell, "Some Psycholinguistic Perspectives on Children's Spelling," *Language Arts* 55 (October 1978): 845.

Then a number of words are examined by students to determine which ones fit the rule.

Inductive and deductive teaching strategies are part of the discovery method. Both require students' discovery of the objective, instead of its explicit statement by the teacher. The discovery technique is conducive to greater learning retention and transfer of learning if it motivates students and encourages them to continue in their endeavors.

Teachers must recognize that not all children can learn through these techniques. The amount of guidance given by the teacher will determine how successful children will be in deriving rule generalizations.

Model for Discovery Lessons[26]

A model proceeding from most difficult to least difficult is presented for developing lessons that help students discover generalizations. In using the model the difficulty of the pattern to be discovered and the abilities of the students must be taken into account. Three other cautions are:

1. Make sure the students can use the examples.
2. Be sure the examples fit the rule. Generalizations

[26]Gary R. McKenzie and Elaine D. Fowler, "A Recipe for Producing Student Discovery of Language Arts Generalizations," *Elementary English* 50 (April 1973): 596.

are rarely *always* true—only usually—and an example that doesn't fit will prevent recognition of the pattern.
3. When children are led through the steps with questions, try to make the questions specific enough so that they will know what to look for.

Teachers first select a principle and then give examples to illustrate the principle, as in the model at the bottom of the page.

Example of a Primary-Grade Exercise to Discover a Generalization Inductively   Children are given a listing of one-syllable words and endings:

run	running
bat	batting
can	canned

The teacher should instruct pupils to look closely at all the one-syllable words, and then look at all the one-syllable words with endings. The teacher should pose two questions: What do all the one-syllable words have in common? What happens to all the one-syllable words when an ending is added? The students should be able to state that all the one-syllable words end in consonants and the consonant is preceded by one vowel. When adding an ending to such words, the consonant is doubled.

After the generalization is learned, children

Most Difficult		Least Difficult
1. Provide students with both positive and negative examples and ask them to describe attributes of the examples.	1. Provide students with positive examples and ask students to describe each one separately.	1. State the rule to students.
2. Ask students to group examples into sets according to patterns. When groups are formed, ask students to state the basis for classification.	2. State that these all illustrate a single rule to be discovered by comparison, or ask, "How are these alike?"	2. Provide an example pointing out attributes in the rule. Repeat with other positive and negative examples.
3. Ask students to compare, within the set illustrating the desired rule, to find the missing pattern.	3. Have students contrast with negative examples. State how all positives are the same, and different from negatives, in the form of a rule.	3. Have students classify new examples and explain choices.
4. State as a rule		
5. Apply as a new test.		
6. Apply to new cases.		

can use deduction on new words to which it would apply.

Add the ending *ed* to the following words:

pin	bat	shop
beg	can	mop

Add the ending *ing* to the following words:

beg	shop	sun
can	get	bet
fan	run	cut
let		

Noun Plural Generalizations

AN ENGLISH TEST

We'll begin with box, the plural is boxes.
But the plural of ox should be oxen, not oxes.
One fowl is a goose, but two are called geese,
Yet the plural of mouse is never meese.
You may find a lone mouse, or a whole nest of mice,
But the plural of house is houses, not hice.
If the plural of man is always men,
Why shouldn't the plural of pan be called pen?
The cow in the plural may be called cows or kine,
But a bow, if repeated, is never called bine;
And the plural of vow is vows, not vine.

If I speak of a foot and you show me two feet,
And I give you a boot, would a pair be called beet?
If one is a tooth and a whole set are teeth,
Why shouldn't the plural of booth be called beeth?
If the singular's this, and the plural these,
Should the plural of kiss ever be written keese?
We speak of a brother, and also of brethren,
But though we say mother, we never say mothren.
Then the masculine pronouns are he, his, and him,
But imagine the feminine, she, shis, and shim!
So the English, I think you all will agree,
Is the funniest language you ever did see.

Anonymous

Here is a list of generalizations for the teaching of noun plurals for grades one through six. These rule generalizations contain many commonly used words that conform to rule patterns. Rules 1 and 3 are usually taught in the primary grades, whereas all others are usually taught in intermediate grades. There is no hard-and-fast rule as to when the rules should be taught.

Noun Plurals That Usually Conform to Rule Patterns

1. An *s* is added to nouns such as tree, airplane, truck, wagon, puzzle, boy, girl, horse, table.

2. An *es* is usually added to nouns that end in *s*, *ss*, *sh*, *ch*, or *x*, making an extra syllable:

bus, buses	bench, benches
glass, glasses	box, boxes
dress, dresses	brush, brushes

3. Nouns that end in *y* with a consonant before the *y*, change the *y* to *i* and add *es:*

baby	babies
story	stories
candy	candies

This rule generalization has many commonly used words that conform to the rule pattern.

4. Nouns that end in *o*, with a consonant before the *o*, usually add *es* to make the word plural:

cargo	cargoes
domino	dominoes
hero	heroes
tomato	tomatoes
potato	potatoes

Some nouns that end in *o* are made plural by adding *s:*

piano	pianos
solo	solos

5. Nouns that end in *f* or *fe* usually are made plural by changing the *f* or *fe* to *ves:*

knife	knives
shelf	shelves

Some nouns that end in *f* are made plural by adding *s:*

chief	chiefs
roof	roofs

Noun Plurals That Do Not Conform to Rule Patterns

1. Some nouns are made plural by changing the letters within the word or adding letters so that the spelling is changed:

foot	feet
man	men

mouse	mice
ox	oxen
tooth	teeth
goose	geese
child	children

2. Some nouns are the same in both the singular and the plural:

bison	bison
deer	deer
grouse	grouse
salmon	salmon
sheep	sheep

More Commonly Taught Spelling Generalizations: Intermediate-Grade Level

1. Words ending in silent *e* usually drop the *e* before the addition of suffixes beginning with a vowel, but usually retain the final *e* before the addition of suffixes beginning with a consonant. A suffix is a letter or a group of letters added to the end of a root word to change its meaning (*ing, ous, ary, able, ion, y,* and so on). Baking—suffix begins with a vowel so *e* is dropped. Blameless—suffix begins with a consonant so the *e* is retained. (See number 3 in the next section for the spelling of words ending in *ce* and *ge* when the suffix *able* is added.)

2. The letter *q* is always followed by *u* in common English words:

queen	quiet	quaint
queer	quick	quite

3. When the sound is long *e,* it is *i* before *e* except after *c,* and when sounded like *ā* as in weight or neighbor, it is *ei*.

		Exceptions
receive	reign	weird
receipt	eight	either
ceiling	believe	neither
conceited	siege	sheik
vein	yield	leisure
neighbor	field	codeine
weight	niece	protein
neigh	brief	

4. In order to retain the hard *c* sound when adding endings beginning with *i, e,* or *y,* add a *k* before the ending:

picknicking	trafficking
mimicker	frolicking
panicky	

Some Spelling Rules for Prefixes and Suffixes

A *prefix* is a letter or a group of letters that is placed in front of a root word and that changes its meaning. A *suffix* is a letter or a group of letters that is placed at the end of a root word and that changes the meaning of the word. Here are some of the most common prefixes and suffixes found in intermediate-grade readers:

Prefixes

in	not, into
un	not
re	back
pre	before
con	with, together
ex	out of, beyond, away from
dis	not
de	off, away from

Suffixes

ness	quality of
less	without, free from
tion	result or product of an act
ful	containing, having qualities of
ish	like
ly	like, in a specified degree or manner
ment	outcome of an action
ous	full of
ure	state of, denoting action
able	capable of

1. The prefix *dis* and the prefix *mis* are spelled with one *s*:

disappear	misunderstand
distrust	mistrust

When the root word begins with *s* there will be two *s*'s, one for the prefix and one for the root word:

dissatisfied	misspell
dissimilar	misstep

2. If a root word begins with *l* or *r,* the negative prefix usually changes to *il* or *ir*:

illegal illogical
irregular illiterate

3. Words or syllables ending in *ce* or *ge* retain *e* before the suffix *able* in order to retain the soft *c* and soft *g* sound, and in all other words ending in a final *e* the *e* is usually dropped:

pleasurable believable
enforceable salable
manageable likable
lovable

STEPS IN LEARNING TO SPELL

These guides are especially useful in helping children learn words that follow no pattern:

1. Look at the word.
2. Pronounce each word correctly.
3. Look carefully at each part of the word as it is pronounced.
4. Say the letters in sequence.
5. Cover the word and try to recall it by first saying it and then spelling it orally and in written form.
6. Check to see if the word is correct.

Spelling Study Plans

The two major study approaches to spelling are the study–test plan and the test–study plan. Investigations of the two plans have invariably found the test–study plan to be superior. Here is a typical test–study plan:

1. A preliminary test is given to determine the child's general spelling-achievement level.
2. A pretest is given at the beginning of each week's instruction, based on a week's list of words.
3. The child's misspelled words become his or her weekly list of words to study.
4. The child follows a series of steps, enumerated in the previous section, in learning to spell the words.
5. The words are presented in context and students usually must put each word into a sentence.
6. At the end of the week, the child is usually given a test to determine spelling mastery of words studied.

The study–test plan is organized in a similar manner except that there is no pretest. Regardless of the child's ability to spell the words, all those in the lesson become the spelling words.

Spelling activities are presented each day during the week, which gives students practice in the spelling, reading, and writing of words. Usually a spelling quiz is given at the end of the week to determine whether spelling proficiency in the words has been accomplished.

Some studies have shown that students do better on weekly review tests when they receive a portion of the words each day and are tested daily on each portion than when they receive all the words at the beginning of the week and do not receive daily quizzes.[27] This procedure is based on sound learning principles because we know that distributed practice is better and tends to bring more sustained learning than massed practice.

Activities and Exercises for the Overlearning of Words Drill and practice in the spelling of words, especially for those that do not follow a pattern, are used so that the child will overlearn correct spelling of the words being studied. Overlearning of the words helps children sustain their learning over an extended period of time, rather than just for a weekly spelling test. Therefore, drill, used for the purpose of helping children gain skills that need to be overlearned, is justified.

However, teachers must be cautioned against having children learn spelling words by writing them 10, 20, or more times. This is a poor practice that develops negative attitudes toward spelling. Many times the students engaged in such an activity will write the word in rote fashion, without thinking. Some inventive student might employ the "mass-production" practice of copying one letter at a time in a straight row down the page in order to finish this onerous task as quickly as possible. This

[27]Herbert Rieth et al., "Influence of Distributed Practice and Daily Testing on Weekly Spelling Tests," *Journal of Educational Research* 68 (October 1974): 73–77.

practice does not help the student to learn to spell.

There are many ways that are fun to achieve overlearning of needed skills. Examples are crossword puzzles, spelling Lotto, anagrams, filling in missing blanks, and others.

The Spelling Test

If the spelling test is used as part of the teaching–learning process, it is being used correctly. The test should be used for diagnostic, review, and reinforcement purposes. Teachers and students can determine through the test specific difficulties the student may be having.

In giving the spelling test the teacher should very carefully articulate each word, present the word in a sentence to avoid confusion with other homonyms, and then repeat the word again. Students should receive knowledge of results immediately after the test, so that they either get reinforcement or can avoid erroneous responses. A good technique, discussed in Chapter 18 "Knowledge of Results," is to have students write their spelling test words twice. One copy is submitted to the teacher; the other is retained for feedback.

Children should not exchange papers after a spelling test. This common practice actually impedes the learning of spelling words and may be detrimental to the individual child. Children need knowledge of their own results—not someone else's. A child who is not doing well does not want to share this with another child. Humiliation does not help children gain positive attitudes toward spelling, school, or themselves.

POSSIBLE DIFFICULTIES IN LEARNING TO SPELL

Difficulties in learning to spell include many factors that may also impede development of word recognition skills. These include:

1. Perceptual problems due to either organic or experiential factors
2. Problems in pronouncing, which might be due to faulty listening
3. Inadequate knowledge in the area of phoneme-grapheme representations

4. Poor visual memory
5. Poor rote memory
6. Not enough exposure to print
7. Not enough time spent in writing
8. An overreliance on letter–sound relationships.

Auditory and visual discrimination are necessary readiness activities for spelling. Unless students are able to hear and see differences between and among letters, they will not be able to spell. Similarly, children who have difficulty pronouncing words may have difficulty spelling them. Studies have shown that children with speech difficulties usually make many spelling errors; spelling errors reflect speech inaccuracies.[28] Substitutions, omissions, distortions, and additions in spelling are usually made by students who make similar speech errors. (See Chapter 7.)

Teachers should also be aware that some primary-grade children's errors may be due not to a lack of knowledge of English phonology but because of their proficiency in sounding out words. This may cause the children to produce some rather "strange" spellings (see "Should Spelling Be Taught in the First Grade?" and "Invented Spelling" earlier in this chapter). Although this may sound paradoxical, it really is not. As was stated earlier in this chapter, recent research in the area of spelling suggests that "the child's growing knowledge of English words is not based on simple letter–sound correspondences but on a combination of phonological and syntactic information as it applies to spoken and written language."[29] In other words, there are many factors that contribute to students' becoming good spellers. One very important factor that has been stressed throughout this chapter and book is that the child be given many opportunities to interact with print.

It appears that primary-grade children's difficulties with beginning spelling may be due to mispronunciations, lack of phonic skills, ina-

[28]James Carrell and Kathleen Pendergast, "An Experimental Study of the Possible Relation between Errors of Speech and Spelling," *Journal of Speech and Hearing Disorders* 19 (September 1954): 327–334; and David R. Stone, "An Analysis of Spelling Errors," *Education* 84 (October 1963): 116–118.

[29]Beers, "Developmental Strategies," p. 40.

bility to make proper phoneme-grapheme relationships, omission of letters, reversing or transposing of letters, insertion or deletion of letters, confusion of words that sound alike but are spelled differently (homonyms or homophones), poor visual discrimination, poor rote memory, poor structural analysis, lack of practice in writing, and perhaps not enough exposure to print.

Spelling and the Left-Handed Child

Oftentimes left-handed students, who have learned to write in cursive with the hook-wrist technique, produce many spelling errors. This occurs because the students tend to cover the first part of the word as they write. They often forget that they have already inserted a letter and repeat it while their hand blocks what they have written. Such students may be prone to delete letters as well if they think they have already inserted the letter.

Since these problems are usually unique to left-handed students using the hook-wrist technique, teachers should be especially vigilant with them. Although teachers should not attempt to change the writing techniques of such students, they should carefully observe their spelling errors. If the errors consist of deletions and insertions of similar letters, the teacher should ask the students to spell the words or-

ally. If they can do so correctly, their spelling errors are probably caused by their method of writing. Such students should be cautioned to be on guard for this kind of error and to get into the habit of lifting their hands from the papers more often. Proofreading papers before they are submitted also helps (see sections on the left-handed child in Chapter 14).

DIAGNOSING CHILDREN'S SPELLING ERRORS

In diagnosing children's spelling errors, the teacher together with the student who is having spelling problems, should analyze spelling errors in all the student's written work and try to determine whether a pattern exists. The teacher should try to discern whether the student's spelling errors are due to an overreliance on phonic generalizations. For example, it is possible that a child well-versed in phonics may apply a rule generalization to an unfamiliar word that sounds the same as one that he or she has met previously. In cases such as this, the teacher should compliment the child on his or her attempt, and then present the child with the correct spelling of the word and explain that the word is an exception to the generalization that the child has learned.

Table 13.1 presents a number of typical spelling errors, causes for the errors, and sug-

TABLE 13.1   TYPICAL ERRORS, CAUSES, AND SUGGESTED CORRECTIVE MEASURES IN SPELLING

Causes	Typical Errors	Corrective Procedures
Incorrect visual image	docter for doctor nitting for knitting familar for familiar	Make pupils conscious of the need to see each letter in the word. Break the words into syllables. Have pupils visualize the words. Look at the word for strong visual image.
Inaccurate pronunciation and inaccurate auditory memory	lighting for lightning pospone for postpone erl for oil chimley for chimney choclet for chocolate	Pronounce each word accurately on initial presentation. Pronounce words in concert with class. Listen for inaccurate pronunciation. Check individual pupils for doubtful enunciation. Repeat several times the part of the word that is difficult to enunciate.

TABLE 13.1   (continued)

Causes	Typical Errors	Corrective Procedures

Insertion and omission of silent letters	lite for light
	lineing for lining
	no for know
	ofen for often
	tabl for table
	gost for ghost
	stedy for steady
	lisen for listen
		Silent letters cause many difficulties in spelling. Since these letters do not appear in an auditory image, special stress must be placed on the visual image.
		    Observe each part of the word and have pupils practice writing the part likely to cause trouble.
		    Provide practice exercises to fix habits of dealing with silent letters.

Confusion of consonant sounds	acke for ache
	parck for park
	gudge for judge
	visinity for vicinity
	sertain for certain
		Practice for correct image of the word.
		    Children need to know that some letters have more than one sound.
		        S may sound like s or z.
		        C may sound like s or k.
		        G may sound like g or j.

Confusion of vowel sounds	holaday for holiday
	turm for term
	oder for odor
	salery for salary
	rejoyce for rejoice
		Have pupils break word into syllables, and look at its parts.
		    Practice for correct visual image of the word.
		    Practice writing the word for the kinesthetic feel of the letters.

Confusion of double vowels	reel for real quear for queer	Double vowels often take the sound of the single letter or another vowel combination.

Inaccurate formation of derivatives	stoped for stopped
	haveing for having
	flys for flies
	sincerly for sincerely
	omited for omitted
		Work for more vivid image of word endings.
		    Emphasize auditory image of endings.
		    Break words into syllables. Have children observe the word in its parts.
		    Call attention to generalizations pertinent to regular ways of adding endings.
		    Stress closer understanding of adding suffixes. Provide practice exercises on word endings.

Reversals or transposition of letters	gose for goes form for from bread for beard	Pronounce the word distinctly. Have pupils listen for sequence of each sound in the word. Practice for correct visual image.

Incorrect meaning—homonyms or homophones	dew for due
	our for hour
	hole for whole
	sum for some
		Illustrate use of the word with commonest meaning.
		    Use pairs of words in sentence to distinguish what each means.
		    Provide practices on homonyms and stress word meanings at all times.

TABLE 13.1 (continued)

Causes	Typical Errors	Corrective Procedures
Phonetic spelling applied to nonphonetic words	bin for been gon for gone sum for some	While spelling embraces phonetics, pupils must be taught to look for numerous exceptions in our unphonetic language. They cannot rely on sound alone. They must realize that their visual memory must be their guide in many new words and word parts.
Confusion of words that are similar in sound	an for and were for where merry for marry effect for affect cents for sense	This error is often due to faulty auditory acuity. Care should be given to enunciation of these words. Pronounce the words in pairs and give the meaning of each.
Lack of acquaintance with phonetic elements	ivlize for result haw for how inbean for imagine	For pupils very deficient in phonetic sense or training, begin work with simple visual–auditory training (attaching beginning consonant sounds to appropriate letter symbol). Use kinesthetic approach also. Provide phonics readiness training.
Poor handwriting	stors for stars temt for tent	Provide practice on letter forms that cause special difficulty. Emphasize accurate formation of each letter Guide pupils in size, shape, slant, and spacing between letters and words.
Nervousness	Inaccuracies due to lack of control for deliberate thinking.	Check child's health. Be sure vision and hearing are not defective. Remove all possible tensions.
Carelessness	Errors due to poor concentration and careless habits of word study.	Stimulate pride in work well done. Praise all improvement.

Source: David H. Patton, "How to Correct Spelling Errors: A Teacher's Diagnostic Spelling Chart," *Education Today,* Spelling Bulletin No. 54 (Columbus, Ohio: Merrill), pp. 364–366.

gested corrective measures. Before looking at the table, remember that a good spelling program is not one that is done in isolation. It should be correlated with the entire curriculum, and children should be given many opportunities to write. Children who are restricted to using words that they know how to spell may write rather unimaginative papers. The teacher must understand this and know what his or her purpose is. And this purpose should be conveyed to the students.

On the other hand, if teachers want to help students correct certain errors that they consistently make, teachers need to bring these to students' attention. Table 13.1 will help teachers do this.

CORRECTING SPELLING ERRORS IN OTHER SUBJECT AREAS

Teachers want to transfer learning from one subject-matter area to another. Using spelling words from mathematics, social studies, and science lessons will help considerably. When a child answers a question correctly, but the answer is marked wrong because of incorrect spelling, the student will probably become resentful and confused because the situation seems unfair. If the teacher wishes to test students' knowledge, misspellings should not count against the subject-knowledge grade. If such errors occur on a spelling test, then misspelled words would count as wrong.

The teacher should correct misspelled words on all written papers, but students will feel more positively toward spelling and will attempt to spell the word correctly in the future if they are not penalized for spelling errors. Seeing the errors and having them corrected immediately on all papers will give students a better chance to stamp out erroneous responses before they have become permanently set in their minds.

DICTIONARY SKILLS

A dictionary is a very important reference book, not only for elementary-school students but for all students. It is helpful in supplying the following information to a student:

1. Spelling
2. Correct usage
3. Derivations and inflected forms
4. Accent and other diacritical markings
5. Antonyms
6. Synonyms
7. Syllabication
8. Definitions
9. Parts of speech
10. Idiomatic phrases

The function of dictionaries is not to regulate but only to describe. This is true for word meanings and pronunciation of words. The lexicographers who compiled the dictionary polled many persons and recorded the ways in which these participants pronounced words. The pronunciation was then recorded by way of diacritical marks under appropriate entries in the dictionary.[30]

Etymology deals with the history of a word. The dictionary is invaluable in supplying the etymology of a word. The semantic approach adds interest to the study of vocabulary because it refers to the way a word has been used in the past; it is the study of word meanings. The dictionary also aids students in choosing the correct meaning of homographs.

Activity to Stimulate Interest in the Dictionary

See how well children can answer these 10 questions using the dictionary. They should use it to find the meanings of words they do not know and then answer each question.

1. In what countries do centaurs live?
2. Where is Mount Everest?
3. Was Prometheus the goddess of fire?
4. Is a songstress a man who writes songs?
5. Is Miss. an abbreviation for Missus?
6. Is haiku a Hawaiian mountain?
7. Did Andrew Jackson fight in the Civil War?
8. Is a statute a work of art?
9. Is a quadruped an extinct animal?
10. Is a centipede a unit of measurement in the metric system?

The questions can also act as stimuli for initiating other activities. For example, looking up "haiku," the children will discover that it is a type of poem, and they may decide to try to write some haiku poems. Some children may want to learn more about Prometheus and other mythological figures, and others may become interested in various mountain ranges.

[30]Leroy Barney, "Dictionary Skills and Punctuation Habits As Aids to Children's Writing," in *Language Arts in the Elementary School: Readings* (Philadelphia: Lippincott, 1972), p. 448.

STUDENT'S NAME:
GRADE:
TEACHER:

DIAGNOSTIC CHECKLIST FOR SPELLING (GENERAL)

I. DICTIONARY	YES	NO

A. Primary Grades

The child is able to:

	YES	NO
1. Supply missing letters of the alphabet		
2. Arrange words none of which begin with the same letter in alphabetical order		
3. List words several of which begin with the same letter		
4. List words according to first and second letters		
5. List words according to third letter		
6. Find the meaning of a word		
7. Find the correct spelling of a word		

B. Grades 3, 4, 5, 6

The child is able to:

	YES	NO
1. Locate words halfway in the dictionary		
2. Open the dictionary by quarters and state the letter with which words begin		
3. Open the dictionary by thirds and state the letter with which words begin		
4. Open the dictionary at certain initial letters		
5. Use key words at the head of each page as a guide to finding words		
6. Use the dictionary to select meanings to fit the context (homographs)		
7. Use the dictionary to build up a vocabulary of synonyms		
8. Use the dictionary to build up a vocabulary of antonyms		
9. Answer questions about the derivation of a word		
10. Use the dictionary to learn to pronounce a word		
11. Use the dictionary to correctly syllabicate a word		
12. Use the dictionary to get the correct usage of a word		
13. Use the dictionary to determine the part(s) of speech of the word		

14. Use the dictionary to gain the meanings of idiomatic phrases

II. SPELLING	YES	NO

A. Primary Grades

1. The child recognizes that letters represent sounds.

2. The child has a need to spell because he or she wishes to write.

3. The child is able to spell a number of words that he or she continually has met.

4. The child can spell a number of words that have similar phonograms (a succession of graphemes that occurs with the same phonetic value in a number of words—often a rhyming unit of a "family" of words). For example, *ake, an, at, ight, ine.*

5. Noun plurals:

  a. The child adds an *s* to nouns such as tree, airplane, girl.

  b. The child adds an *es* to nouns that end in *s, ss, sh, ch,* or *x,* making an extra syllable. Example: bus—buses or busses; glass—glasses; bench—benches; box—boxes; brush—brushes.

  c. The child correctly spells nouns that end in *y* and have a consonant before the *y* by changing the *y* to *i* and adding *es.* Examples: baby—babies; candy—candies.

  d. The child correctly spells nouns that end in *y* with a vowel before the *y* by adding *s* to make the word plural. Examples: boy—boys; day—days.

6. The child can add some endings that begin with a vowel to a closed syllable (one-syllable words) by doubling the consonant before adding the ending. Examples: can—canned; run—running.

B. Intermediate Grades

1. The child has mastery of all items in previous grades.

2. Noun Plurals

  a. The child recognizes that proper nouns follow the regular rules for *s* and *es* plurals. Examples: Bobs; the Joneses.

b. The child recognizes that nouns that end in *o* with a consonant before the *o* usually add *es* or *s* to make the word plural. Examples: domino—dominoes; piano—pianos; auto—autos.

c. The child recognizes that nouns that end in *o* with a vowel before the *o* add *s* to make the word plural. Examples: radio—radios, cameo—cameos.

d. The child recognizes that nouns that end in *f* or *fe* usually are made plural by changing the *f* or *fe* to *ves*. Examples: knife—knives; wife—wives. Some nouns ending in *f* or *fe* form the plural by adding *s*. Examples: chief—chiefs; roof—roofs; safe—safes.

e. The child recognizes that nouns that end in *ff* usually add *s* to the word to form the plural. Examples: staff—staffs; sheriff—sheriffs.

f. The child recognizes that some nouns are the same in both the singular and plural. Examples: deer—deer; salmon—salmon; fish—fish; sheep—sheep.

g. The child recognizes that some nouns do not follow any rule patterns for plurals. Examples: foot—feet; child—children; goose—geese; tooth—teeth.

3. The child recognizes that a multisyllabic word that ends in a closed syllable usually doubles the consonant before an ending beginning with a vowel *if* the accent falls on the final syllable. Example: occur—occurring.

4. The child recognizes that most words ending in final silent *e*, except those ending in *ce* or *ge*, usually drop the *e* before adding *able*.

5. The child recognizes that words ending in final silent *e* usually retain the *e* before adding a suffix beginning with a consonant.

6. The child recognizes that words ending in final silent *e* usually drop the *e* before the addition of suffixes beginning with a vowel.

III. HOMONYMS OR HOMOPHONES	YES	NO

A. The primary-grade child spells correctly such homonyms as to, too, two; so, sew; and red, read.

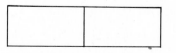

B. The intermediate-grade child spells correctly such homonyms as peace, piece; pore, pour; principal, principle; route, root.

IV. SPELLING CONSCIOUSNESS (PRIMARY AND INTERMEDIATE GRADES)

YES   NO

A. The child generally spells words correctly in most of his or her written work.

B. The child looks up a word that he or she is not sure of.

C. The child asks the teacher about a word he or she is not sure of.

D. The child asks for help in spelling if he or she needs it.

STUDENT'S NAME:
GRADE:
TEACHER:

DIAGNOSTIC CHECKLIST FOR SPELLING (SPECIFIC)

The child makes spelling errors on spelling tests and in written work in the following areas (see Table 13.1 for typical errors, causes, and suggested corrective measures):

SPECIFIC ERRORS   YES   NO

1. Consonants.
  initial
  medial
  final
  blends (clusters)
  digraphs

2. Vowels
    short
    long
    digraphs
    diphthongs
    followed by *r*
3. Prefixes and suffixes
4. Homonyms or homophones
5. Omits letters
6. Inserts letters
7. Doubles letters
8. Noun plurals
9. Monosyllabic words
10. Multisyllabic words

SUMMARY

Spelling should not be taught as an end in itself or for the outmoded belief that the brain is a muscle that needs exercising through memorizing. It should be used as a tool to help children to communicate better through writing.

It has been shown that in order to be an effective speller, certain methods of instruction, attitudes, and understanding must be taken into consideration. Here is a list of some of these:

1. Students have a need to, and want to, spell correctly.

2. Spelling instruction should be systematic, as well as provide for incidental learning.

3. Spelling should be correlated to all subject-matter areas. However, caution should be exercised so that a child who, for example, misspells the word "triangle" in a mathematics test is not penalized in his or her math grade. The word should be correctly spelled for the student, so that the student can correct the error.

4. The test–study technique is superior to the study–test technique. If children are able to spell all the words in a pretest correctly, there is no need for them to spend time studying those words.

5. Spelling words should always be presented in context.

6. Children should be helped to understand that tests are useful for diagnostic and review purposes.

In the first part of this chapter the general aspects of spelling were discussed. It was shown how spelling is related to the other language arts, and how difficulties in one area will affect others. Research and information on the "spelling controversy," involving generalizations and spelling word lists and which method of teaching is more useful, were presented. A dual approach was advocated as the solution yielding the greatest benefits for the most children. It was recommended that generalizations be introduced when enough cases warrant a rule being formed. In discussing spelling consciousness, it was emphasized that unless children have a need and a desire to spell correctly, they may not do so. Also, invented spelling and how children learn to spell were discussed.

The more practical and applied aspects of spelling were presented next. Although the teacher should not spend more than 15 minutes a day on spelling lessons, there are many opportunities for incidental spelling learning. An alert and peceptive teacher would correlate spelling lessons with many of the ongoing activities in the classroom. Methods of teaching spelling through induction and deduction for words lending themselves to generalizations, as well as word study plans, were presented. Spelling difficulties that students might encounter were also outlined. In addition, a section on diagnosing children's errors, with a special look at some problems that left-handed children may have in spelling, was presented.

Two Diagnostic Checklists for General and Specific Spelling were also presented.

As a further aid, two examples of spelling lesson plans follow. Using these as a guide, see if you can construct another one.

LESSON PLAN 1: PRIMARY-GRADE LEVEL

OBJECTIVE

Students will be able to define homophone and give five examples of homophones correctly spelled in a sentence.

PRELIMINARY PREPARATION

A number of humorous sentences composed of homophones are on the board:

I two no the weigh.
No, that is write to.
Hour friend is sew hungry two.
Meat him on the rode
The tail was sew funny.
The heard of cattle is hear.

These sentences would also be on the board, but the underlined word is omitted.

Word	Sentence
meat	1. I like to eat _____ .
meet	2. I have to _____ my friend.
one	1. She has only _____ toy.
won	2. She _____ the game.
hour	1. This _____ seems so long.
our	2. _____ picture is the best.
right	1. John is always _____ .
write	2. I like to _____ letters.
to	1. I am going _____ the zoo.
two	2. I have _____ cookies.
too	3. I want a cookie, _____ .

sew	1. It is fun to _____ clothes.
so	2. I felt _____ sorry for him.

weigh	1. How much does that _____ ?
way	2. Do you know the _____ to town?

INTRODUCTION

"A number of sentences are on the board. Can anyone read them aloud for us? Good! Although you can read them for us, is there something funny about these sentences? Remember, we've worked with words that are spelled alike but have different meanings. Who can tell me what such words are called and give me an example? Yes, homographs, and the example of 'saw' and 'saw' is very good. Today we're going to work with words that are often misspelled because they are mistaken for one another."

DEVELOPMENT

"I am going to give you a number of words in sentences. After you spell the words on your papers, we'll discuss what some of these words have in common."

Give the children the words and sentences shown under "Preliminary Preparation." First state the word, and then the sentence.

Have the children volunteer to pronounce and put in the correct spelling of the word that belongs in the blank. If any errors are made, help to correct them immediately. After all the words have been inserted in the blanks, ask the children what a number of the words have in common. They should come up with the statement that many of the words sound alike, but are spelled differently and have different meanings. Tell the pupils that such words are called homonyms or homophones. Ask them for more examples.

SUMMARY

Pull the main points of the lesson together. Give the students a number of sentences with pairs of homophones and ask them to choose the correct word for the sentence. For example:

1. John is the _____ person _____ help us _____ the letter.
                right/write   to/two   write/right

2. She is the _____ who _____ the game.
            one/won   one/won

3. He has already played _____ games.
            too/two

4. Some girls do not like to _____ .
            sew/so

5. _____ is good for you to eat.
   Meat/Meet

The class might enjoy the following "whimsy." Some children might try to make up their own.

"Well," said Homonym, "it's true
I can't do what you can do,
And furthermore I don't want to . . .

For I had four cents for the fair,
But it didn't make sense to go in where
I'd wear a tie that was not in a knot,
So instead I watched blue smoke that blew
And then flew straightway up the flue.
Now tell me, Homograph, can you
See things from my point of view?
For I, sir, ay yes, I eye a dear deer,
And a hare with a hair that is half of a pair
While I pare a pear beside a new gnu
And shoo a bare bear away from my shoe—
And all this I do at ten to two, too!

Author Unknown

They might also enjoy listening to Eve Merriam's poem "Nym and Graph" about homonyms and homographs, from the book *It Doesn't Always Have to Rhyme.*

LESSON PLAN II: INTERMEDIATE-GRADE LEVEL

OBJECTIVE

Students will be able to derive the hard "c" spelling rule. Students will be able to apply the rule so that they can spell the following words correctly when given orally: mimicking, picnicking, frolicker, trafficker, panicky.

PRELIMINARY PREPARATION

A letter with many spelling errors written on large lined paper:

Dear Miz P,
    I just was askt to apair in a skool pla an i reely wanna. the techa said i ned hlp in spekin if i wan te be init. Plez hlp me.

Ami

INTRODUCTION

"I'd like to show you a letter that someone asked me to read. Perhaps you can help me decipher it. I just can't seem to make it out. What's the problem? Yes, there are so many spelling errors that it's difficult to read. What's the purpose of writing a letter that no one can read?

"In order to help us to become better spellers, we've been working with a number of different spelling rules. Who remembers some of the things we have said, not only about spelling rules but about all rules? Yes, very good! Before we can come up with a rule, there must be enough cases that fit the rule. Who remembers some of the

spelling rules that we have derived? Yes, the 'ie' rule, the soft 'c' and soft 'g' rule before the suffix 'able.' Today, we are going to be involved with a spelling rule that also
concerns some suffixes. Who can tell us what a suffix is?"

DEVELOPMENT

"I am going to give you a list of words to spell. After we all spell them, I'll call on
some volunteers to put the words on the board. After they are on the board, we will
all try to see if we can come up with any rule for these words. Listen carefully while I
give the words. First I will state each word; then I will put it in a sentence; and then
I will restate the word. Here they are:

mimicker	notice
picnicking	ice
frolicking	practice
mimicking	police
panicky	noticing"
trafficking	

Ask for volunteers to put the words on the board. After each word is put down
make sure the spelling is correct. If the "k" has incorrectly been omitted, insert it. Ask
volunteers to pronounce each word. Ask the children to pay particular attention to
the "c" sound at the end of words. For example, "mimicker" and "notice." The two
sounds are different—in "mimicker" the "c" represents a hard sound, whereas in "notice" the "c" represents a soft sound.

Ask the children what would happen to the sound represented by "c" in the
word mimicker if the "k" were left out. For example: mimicer—how would it be pronounced? It would be pronounced with a soft "c." Why? It is followed by an "e." Ask
the children to say what they think the spelling rule is. The teacher should elicit the
following rule: Words that end in "c" add a "k" before "i," "e," and "y" in order to
retain the hard "c" sound.

SUMMARY

Pull together the main points of the lesson and give the students a number of
words to spell to which they can apply the hard "c" rule.

SUGGESTIONS FOR THOUGHT
QUESTIONS AND ACTIVITIES

1. You are involved in a debate on whether to
use spelling generalizations to teach spelling.
Choose one side—either *for* or *against* the use
of spelling generalizations to teach spelling.
Support your argument in a research paper.
2. Think up some spelling activities or games
that are fun.
3. Develop a creative lesson plan in spelling.

4. What do you feel are the best methods that
can be used in presenting spelling words?
Explain.
5. A mother writes a note to her son's teacher
saying that she is most distressed that her son
received a grade of 100 percent on his mathematics paper even though he made many spelling errors when he named the geometric fig-

ures. What do you think about this situation? How would you help parents to understand your position better?

6. How would you correlate the teaching of spelling with the other language arts areas?

7. Observe some preschoolers in the act of writing. Analyze their invented spelling. Observe children at various age levels. Compare the spelling behavior of the children.

SELECTED BIBLIOGRAPHY

Frith, Uta, ed. *Cognitive Processes in Spelling.* New York: Academic Press, 1980.

Furness, Edna. *Spelling for the Millions.* Nashville, Tenn.: Thomas Nelson, 1977.

Gentry, Richard J. "Learning to Spell Developmentally." *Reading Teacher* 34 (January 1981): 378–381.

Henderson, Edmund H., and James W. Beers, eds. *Developmental and Cognitive Aspects of Learning to Spell.* Newark, Del.: International Reading Association, 1980.

Hodges, Richard E. "The Language Base of Spelling," in *Research in the Language Arts: Language and Schooling.* Victor Froese and Stanley B. Straw, eds. Baltimore: University Park Press, 1981, pp. 203–226.

Holbrook, Hilary Taylor. "Invented Spelling." *Language Arts* 60 (September 1983): 800–804.

Manning, Maryann Murphy. *Improving Spelling in the Middle Grades.* Washington, D.C.: National Education Association, 1981.

Rubin, Dorothy. "Developing Spelling Skills," in *The Intermediate Grade Teacher's Language Arts Handbook.* New York: Holt, Rinehart and Winston, 1980.

———. "Developing Spelling Skills," in *The Primary Grade Teacher's Language Arts Handbook.* New York: Holt, Rinehart and Winston, 1980.

Templeton, Shane. "Young Children Invent Words: Developing Concepts of 'Word-ness.'" *Reading Teacher* 33 (January 1980): 454–459.

Wood, Margo. "Invented Spelling." *Language Arts* 59 (October 1982): 707–716.

FOURTEEN

Gaining Skill in Handwriting

"Yesterday we had to write, 'I will be quiet,' a hundred times. I figured out a way to finish fast. First I wrote 'I' all the way down the page, then 'will,' then 'be,' and so on . . ."

"We spend so much time on handwriting. I hate it. Everything must be so exact."

"Even though I get everything right, I still get a poor grade. All because of my handwriting. It's not fair. I'm left-handed and whenever I write, my paper gets all smudged."

"I remember I had just struggled to learn to write one way when before I knew it, they were teaching me another way to write. You would think we had nothing better to do."

"When I grow up, I'll have a secretary do all my writing for me. I'll just speak into a recorder and have it typed."

"I don't see any purpose to it. It's dumb spending so much time on handwriting exercises when there are so many more interesting things to do and learn."

Are the criticisms of these students justified? What is the place of handwriting in today's schools? How much time should be spent teaching handwriting? Should handwriting be taught as an end in itself? What must the teacher know concerning child growth and de-

PEANUTS ®   **By Charles M. Schulz**

velopment when teaching handwriting? What about cursive writing? Is cursive faster than manuscript? Should everyone have to learn to write legibly?

Before answering these questions, let us consider what it would be like if there were no books and if all written material had disappeared. How would scientists do their work if there were no means for record keeping or for putting down findings? For that matter, could anything be preserved through the ages if there were no writing? Obviously, humans without the ability to write would not have been able to advance to the high technological and cultural stage that presently exists.

Before the widespread availability of telephones and personal transportation over good roads, handwritten letters, both personal and business, were the principal means of communication. With the revolution in transportation and electronic communication, plus the widespread availability of low-cost typewriters and word processors, good handwriting has become almost a lost art. The lack of emphasis on handwriting exercises is warranted because of the deluge of knowledge that has taken place. The relative apportionment of time between gaining new knowledge and learning to learn must be weighed against time spent in learning to produce a "fine script." Legible writing is still a necessity, however, for almost all persons in our literate society. Even those who "use recorders almost all of the time" must still get their ideas across on paper at one time or another. Handwriting needs to be taught, but not as an end in itself. It should be a communication tool.

In this chapter the background information necesary for understanding the development of handwriting skill in students will be presented. The sequence of steps for teaching both manuscript and cursive and, finally, the ways of diagnosing specific handwriting problems will be discussed.

After you finish reading this chapter you should be able to answer these questions:

1. How is handwriting related to other language arts areas?
2. What is the relationship of child growth and development to handwriting?
3. Why is manuscript writing used in the early-primary grades?
4. How can the teacher provide a physical and affective environment conducive to producing good handwriting?
5. How does a teacher know whether a child is ready for manuscript handwriing?
6. Should there be a transition to cursive writing? If so, when should this take place?
7. What does research have to say concerning the tools of handwriting?
8. What are the differences between manuscript and cursive writing?
9. How can the teacher help the left-handed child?
10. What are some of the problems that students encounter in cursive writing?

HANDWRITING IN ANTIQUITY

In the days of antiquity, handwriting was a necessity not only for written expression but so that one could learn to read. Children had to copy the "school-boy's book" from the teacher's model. This was their text. For example, a "teacher's copy" contained a series of model passages for children to study. In the early stages of school the teacher would have to copy these passages for the children, but as soon as they could write, they would start copying the lessons themselves. At a later time children would take them down from the teacher's dictation. Since the teaching of reading letters was so essential to the teaching of writing, it was to everyone's advantage that reading and writing be taught together.[1]

In learning to construct letters two methods were employed alternately. One went back to the beginning of the Greek school, and consisted of guiding the children's hands until they got used to the shape of the letter. The other consisted of stamping letters into the waxed surface of a writing tablet and then coaxing students to follow the outlines of the letters with "prickers."[2]

[1]H. I. Marrou, *A History of Education in Antiquity* (New York: New American Library of World Literature, 1956), pp. 215–216.
[2]Ibid., p. 365.

RELATION OF HANDWRITING TO THE LANGUAGE ARTS AND OTHER SUBJECT-MATTER AREAS

Handwriting mixes well with other language arts areas, and with all other subject-matter areas as well. Children who want to communicate their ideas in written form must learn to write and, it is to be hoped, to do so legibly.

Students engaged in listening, discussing, and reading are accumulating many experiences that they might like to share with others through writing. The more activities in which children are engaged, the more opportunities and possibilities will present themselves for writing. Children working with puppets may decide to write their own skits, and the students who read the parts must have legible scripts. Even if the parts of the play are typed, the writing must be legible enough so that the typist can copy it. Announcements of the performances, or invitations that are distributed to other classes, will also have to be written carefully and neatly.

If others cannot read what the student has written because it is illegible or difficult to read, ideas cannot be shared. Students should realize that handwriting is a tool to aid them in conveying their ideas in written form.

Sometimes students "fudge" their handwriting. If a child is unsure of how to spell "receive," both the *i* and *e* in cursive writing can be made to look the same by either omitting the loop in both letters or inserting a loop in both letters. It is then up to the teacher to decide what the letter is. The student may be either deliberately or subconsciously avoiding learning how to write legibly because he or she has problems in spelling. The teacher must relate this student's handwriting problem to spelling difficulties. It is possible that some handwriting problems may be caused by spelling problems.

Influence of Handwriting on Written Expression

Storytelling is basic to the child's development in written expression. Many times, after children speak to the teacher and class about pictures they have brought in, the teacher will write their explanations as captions for the pictures. The children copy these in their own printing.

The transition from oral composition to the complex process of written composition is not so simple, however. Learning how to manipulate a pencil and to form letters in a specific way can be difficult and tension-producing. Learning to move a pencil fast enough to catch a thought is impossible. "Thoughts have to be slowed down to accommodate the pencil."[3] (Although children cannot duplicate their oral fluency in written composition, the accomplishment of writing may be its own compensation.)

The children's composing ability is also slowed during the transition from manuscript to cursive writing. Students must learn a new skill and integrate it into the writing process. Even if children are allowed to "print" after learning cursive writing, they may have lost this original skill through disuse.

If the transition from manuscript to cursive is made too early in a child's life, the child is more involved with learning "how to write" than in actually composing. This raises the question: Which is more important—the sort of handwriting the child uses or the creative process itself? (More will be said about this in a later section.)

RELATION OF CHILD GROWTH AND DEVELOPMENT TO HANDWRITING

Learning to write is not a mechanical, lower-level reflex response, but a thinking process, entailing activity of the cortical nerve areas. Smooth motor coordination of eye and hand, control of arm, hand, and finger muscles are acquired in the process of learning to write and are needed for legible results. Learning to write also requires maturity adequate for accurate perception of the symbol patterns. Writing from memory demands the retention of visual and kinesthetic images of forms not present to the senses, for future recall. . . . From earliest infancy, the eyes guide the hand, and the hand may be considered the instrument which carries out impulses received from the visual organs. The capacity for graphic representa-

[3] Mary J. Tingle, "Teaching Composition in the Elementary School," *Elementary English* 47 (January 1970): 73.

tion, such as writing requires, depends on the motor function of the eye and is coordinated with the eye movements.[4]

Learning to write legibly is a complex skill that requires specific motor muscle control and thinking ability. In order to write legibly, a child must be at a certain maturational level, have had certain background experiences, and be motivated to want to write. The child's perceptual–motor skill development is essential. The term "perceptual–motor skills" refers to the coordination of perceptual processes (the awareness of objects or data through the senses) with motor responses. All observable responses are essentially perceptual–motor in nature, since the motor component is basic to the perceptual component. For example, walking, speaking, and writing are dependent on cognitive direction, on stimuli from the moving muscles themselves, and on stimuli from the external environment.[5]

By the time children come to school they have acquired diverse skills such as speech and walking largely as a result of the maturational process, or internal growth. A number of children may also have engaged in reading and writing. Some preschoolers may have taught themselves to write by inventing their own writing and spelling system (see "Invented Spelling" in Chapter 13). The school's role is to build on this foundation and help children correct any faulty habits that they may have developed. Teachers must be careful, however, that they do not emphasize a child's faulty habits and ignore the child's strengths. The child's early writings were once a satisfactory means of communicating for him or her. Now, in school, it's time to progress to the next phase. Most children understand this and are anxious to learn to write as "grown-ups."

In order to produce a particular letter, children must have a definite mental image of it and of the way in which the strokes are formed.

This serves as a guide for motor development. The image, or perception, which gives meaning to sensations, guides initial practice for motor control and also inhibits the development of faulty habits.[6] If children have an incorrect perception of the letter to be reproduced, obviously they will form the letter incorrectly. The techniques of learning perceptual–motor skills are similar to those used in learning other skills and concepts. For example, concept and motor development involve generalizations and discriminations. In order to write, children's motor responses must develop from a disorganized whole to differentiated part responses. They must then integrate these parts into an organized whole.

Studies have identified a "critical phase" for providing training in the development of motor skills; training before the neural mechanisms have attained a state of readiness (the critical phase) is useless.[7]

In order to have some understanding of the readiness levels for learning handwriting, the teacher should be aware of the sequence of physical development: *cephalocaudal development,* which is development from the head to the tail region (from the top downward), and *proximodistal development,* which is development from the central axis of the body out toward the extremities. Knowledge of proximodistal development is important in understanding left-handed children's problems when they are faced with learning to write from left to right. (This will be further discussed later in this chapter in the section on the left-handed child.) From proximodistal development we know that motor skills that depend on coordination of the larger muscles in the shoulder will appear before specific hand motor skills. From cephalocaudal development we know that children will be able to use their hands before they use their legs.

Teaching handwriting is a most complex task. The child learns to write letters from the

---

[4]Gertrude Hildreth, *Learning the Three R's* (Minneapolis, Minn.: Educational Test Bureau, Educational Publishers, 1947), pp. 583–584.

[5]Morris E. Eson, *Psychological Foundations of Education* (New York: Holt, Rinehart and Winston, 1972), pp. 395–396.

[6]Beatrice A. Furner, "An Analysis of the Effectiveness of a Program of Instruction Emphasizing the Perceptual–Motor Nature of Learning in Handwriting," *Elementary English* 47 (January 1970): 61.

[7]Eson, *Psychological Foundations,* p. 398.

top of the page down and to proceed from left to right. This follows developmental laws and for right-handed people is based on natural development. Human perceptual–motor activity is usually initiated from the one, dominant side of the body, even though humans are bilateral, or two-sided. By the time children enter school they usually show a fairly consistent preference for their right or left hand. There are also preferences in the use of eyes and feet that are usually also established even before attending school. Such preferences concern laterality or sidedness. People are said to have a dominant side if their hand, eye, and foot preferences are similar. When people have a dominant hand on one side and a dominant eye on the other, they are said to have crossed dominance. Individuals who do not have a consistent preference for an eye, hand, or foot are said to have mixed dominance. It has been hypothesized that children who have crossed or mixed dominance may tend to have reversal difficulties in reading and writing, but studies done in this area have not been definitive. Children with crossed dominance can perhaps shift from a left-handed orientation to a right-handed one in writing, but this might cause difficulties for them. (See the next section.)

A teacher can easily test whether a child has crossed or mixed dominance. To determine hand dominance, a teacher can observe which hand the child uses to throw a ball, write, or open a door. The teacher can tell which eye is dominant by observing which eye the child uses to look through a microscope, telescope, or an open cylinder formed by a roll of paper. Foot dominance can be easily determined by observing which foot the child uses to kick a ball or stamp on the floor.

Teachers should be cautioned that crossed or mixed dominance in a child does not mean that the child will have a problem, although the possibility exists. The teacher should give special attention to those children who are having reversal problems by emphasizing left to right orientation for writing.

The Left-Handed Child

A person's preference for one hand and skill in using that hand will determine whether he or she has a dominant hand. Although young children may have mixed hand dominance, as they get older their preference and use of one hand usually increase. The theories concerning why a child becomes left-handed are many, but none are conclusive. Physiologists say the left side of the cerebrum controls the right side and vice-versa. Among those who hold the cerebral dominance theory of laterality, some believe that the child is born either right- or left-handed, and any attempt to change the child from his or her dominant hand will cause emotional problems, such as stuttering and reading disorders. Others claim that handedness is a result of environmental factors, such as training and social conditioning. The heredity–environment debate over handedness has continued for generations without any resolution. Those who believe in the social-development theory of learned handedness believe that since there are many advantages in our culture to being right-handed, it should be trained and not left to chance,[8] especially if the child shows no definite preference. However, today it is generally looked upon as unwise to attempt to change left-handedness in a child.

Children should not be put on the defensive because they are left-handed. They should not be coerced into becoming right-handed, nor should they be continuously nagged about their left-handedness.

Due to the greater naturalness in child-rearing practices since the early twentieth century, there has been a decided increase in left-handedness.

To better understand the left-handed child's problem in writing we must refer to proximodistal development—development from the midpoint of the body to the extremities. Right-handed children move their right hands from left to right naturally. Left-handed children find moving their left hand from left to right against their natural inclination.

Try this simple experiment to illustrate the point: Bring both hands to the center of your

[8]Gertrude Hildreth, "The Development and Training of Hand Dominance: I. Characteristics of Handedness; II. Developmental Tendencies in Handedness; III. Origins of Handedness and Lateral Dominance," *Journal of Genetic Psychology* 75 (1949): 197–275.

body. Now, move both hands out away from your body. The right hand will follow a left to right path corresponding to the English pattern of writing; the left hand follows a right to left path. Ask some left-handed students to write a *t*. Observe carefully how they make the horizontal line. Most of them, unless they have been well conditioned, will draw the line from right to left.

Left-handed children have a greater susceptability to reversal problems—for example, reading the word "was" for "saw"; writing from right to left " ℮ for 9" and ⅂ for 7." (See "Spelling and the Left-Handed Child" in Chapter 13 and "Helping the Left-Handed Child with Writing" in this chapter.)

Gender Differences in Handwriting

Teachers should recognize the maturational differences among all students and between males and females. Girls start school, on the average, more mature than boys, and usually reach puberty about two years before boys. This factor has been used to explain differences in school performance between the sexes. It may well be that girls are readier than boys to learn certain skills such as handwriting that require specific motor coordination. Maturational differences between the sexes may account for the greater number of males who have difficulty with handwriting.

The perceptive teacher does not start all children writing at the same time. Many boys may need extra readiness activities. Pressuring children to attempt a skill for which they are not ready can frustrate them and cause them to develop negative feelings toward the activity. This may also help to explain why so many males dislike handwriting, and usually do not write as well as females.

PERCEPTUAL–MOTOR LEARNING AND HANDWRITING

The way in which letters are formed, accompanied by verbal descriptions, should be emphasized in teaching handwriting. Students should practice the construction of letters based on their observations and the verbalizations, and then should analyze their own errors. Al-

though handwriting skill is based on perceptual–motor learning, many school systems do not use perception in the teaching of handwriting.[9] For example, a 1960 nationwide study of handwriting procedures preferred by teachers reported that copying, exercises and drills, tracing, rhythm exercises, and manual guidance were most favored by teachers, in that order. A commercial system was used as the basis of instruction in 82 percent of all school systems.[10] Although the trend is away from the tracing of letters, it is still being used by a number of commercial handwriting workbooks. As a result, many teachers use methods that emphasize only the motor aspect of handwriting. Children are involved in copying or tracing, without really noticing letter formation as a guide for motor practice.

Should Children Trace?

Although tracing is practiced in school, and is found in most commercial handwriting systems, evidence for its effectiveness is hard to find. Reports showing positive effects are not experientially based.[11] The experimental studies that have been done have all either found no benefit or have reported negative transfer in improving copying or writing performance.[12]

Studies on copying versus tracing as a type of practice in handwriting instruction have shown that copying is superior to tracing at all grade levels.[13, 14] It has been hypothesized that copy-

---

[9]Furner, "An Analysis," pp. 61–69.

[10]Virgil E. Herrick and Nora Okada, "The Present Scene: Practices in the Teaching of Handwriting in the United States—1960," in *New Horizons for Research in Handwriting*, Virgil E. Herrick, ed. (Madison: University of Wisconsin Press, 1963), pp. 17–32.

[11]M. Montessori, *The Discovery of the Child* (Madras, India: Kalak shetra, 1966).

[12]See Marcia Bernbaum et al., "Relationships among Perceptual–Motor Tasks: Tracing and Copying," *Journal of Educational Psychology* 66 (October 1974): 731–732.

[13]Edward Hirsch and Fred C. Niedermeyer, "The Effect of Tracing Prompts and Discrimination Training on Kindergarten Handwriting Performance," *Journal of Educational Research* 67 (October 1973): 81–86.

[14]Eunice N. Askov, "Handwriting: Copying versus Tracing as the Most Effective Type of Practice," *Journal of Educational Research* 69 (November 1975): 96–98.

ing is superior to tracing because the task of copying is more difficult. Children, therefore, must concentrate more, and this makes the letters more memorable. Another reason may be that children must visualize the letter form in order to copy it, whereas in tracing this is not necessary.

Tracing tends to foster bad habits more than anything else. For example, when children see the typical broken line activity found in many workbooks (⊤–┼–) they tend to focus their attention on marking the line, despite the best efforts of the teacher to stress correct starting points for the strokes and the sequence of making the strokes. The broken line receives the children's overwhelming attention and they frequently will carelessly begin the movement of their pencils at any convenient point and will repeat strokes, going back and forth over them in order to "cover" the broken line completely.[15]

If tracing is used in school—and the likelihood is great that it will be because many commercial handwriting systems incorporate it in their programs—teachers should make sure that students are constructing the letters correctly. Some teachers may want to delete this activity entirely.

Importance of Feedback in Learning to Write

Feedback is an important component in learning to write, for it allows the child to detect errors and correct them. The more skilled the individual is, the more quickly and readily the errors are sensed and corrected. Knowledge of results and practice are the two most important ingredients for achieving skill in both cognitive and motor learning. In handwriting, movement is more complex than most people think. Frank Freeman, an authority on handwriting, has pointed out that when we write a single letter or word, the pressure of the fingers on the pencil or pen and the pressure of the pencil or pen-point are continually changing. Feedback is very important in properly sensing when the pressure is incorrect, since changes in pressure

are most complicated and delicate. For example, if the pressures are wrong in force or timing, the movement is incorrect; as a result the letter will be incorrectly formed. The child learns about pressure changes through the feeling of movement.[16] To become proficient at sensing and correcting movement automatically while writing, children must grow internally; they must mature. They also need practice, with knowledge of the results. To attempt to teach children handwriting at ages two or three, when they do not yet have the necessary hand muscle development, would usually be an exercise in futility.

PHYSICAL ENVIRONMENT CONDUCIVE TO HANDWRITING

The physical environment of the classroom is important in the teaching–learning situation, as we have already learned. In teaching handwriting, the furniture must be convenient for the individual child. Lighting is also important. If there is a glare from the sun or from light falling at a certain angle, it will affect the writing position of the child. The teacher should try to arrange the furniture and adjust the blinds so that there is a minimum of glare.

Every child should be able to see a permanent alphabet and a sample of Arabic numbers. The room should have many pictures with words written in manuscript or cursive, corresponding to letters that are being learned in class.

Although it seems obvious that room temperature should be at a comfortable range, so that children are not so hot that their hands perspire when they write or so cold that they have difficulty holding their pencils, this can still be a problem in some schools.

THE AFFECTIVE DOMAIN AND HANDWRITING

Students who feel threatened or are fearful will not be able to write as well as those who feel secure. Although handwriting requires con-

---

[15]Leona M. Foerster, "Teacher—Don't Let Your First Graders Trace!" *Elementary English* 49 (March 1972): 431.

[16]Frank N. Freeman, *Teaching Handwriting: What Research Says to the Teacher*, No. 4 (Washington, D.C.: National Education Association, 1954).

centration (some tension is prevalent in all concentrated activities), the tension should not be such that children can hardly hold their pencils.

The teacher should be warm, understanding, and friendly. Students whose letters are not exact copies of the model should not be embarrassed by having their papers singled out for direct criticism. If teachers observe that a number of errors are recurring, they can either plan a class or group lesson on such errors or work individually with students. Students should feel comfortable in the classroom; they should feel that the teacher will help them with their particular problems, and that they are not expected to produce perfect papers. They should know that everyone's handwriting is not the same.

Students acquire negative attitudes toward handwriting when they are penalized in other subject areas because of it. If a student's answer to a question is correct, but the teacher takes points off the grade for poor penmanship, the child will feel negative about handwriting lessons. The teacher should certainly take note of certain of the student's handwriting difficulties and have a conference with the student. The teacher should point out that illegible handwriting makes it difficult to read his or her paper. The teacher can also tactfully point out that if his or her writing doesn't become more

readable, it might be misinterpreted or other persons might not bother to read the paper.

In this way chances for developing a good attitude in the student toward both the teacher and the lesson will be increased.

Handwriting Exercises As Discipline—No!

Teachers who use handwriting exercises for disciplinary purposes are telling their students that handwriting is a punishment. This type of activity will set students against handwriting activities, deter them from developing a legible handwriting, and adversely influence the handwriting of those who have already mastered a fine script. Using handwriting in this way is poor practice. Some students may even begin to write illegibly as a kind of subconscious revenge on the teacher. Others who stoically bear the punishment learn "how to beat the system"—writing each word down the page as rapidly as possible rather than in sentence form. This can have ruinous results on their handwriting.

CREATIVITY AND HANDWRITING

Since handwriting involves imitating or copying specific forms produced by the teacher or seen in handwriting books, it is a process in conformity, which is the antithesis of creativity. Is it possible to be creative in the area of handwriting? The answer is, Yes, if the teacher works at it; if lessons are stimulating; if handwriting is coordinated with other areas; and if the teacher respects the individuality of students.

In order to stimulate interest in handwriting, a teacher can ask this provocative question: How can illegible handwriting be hazardous to you? Answers might look like this:

1. In following directions—going the wrong way
2. In visiting someone—going to the wrong house
3. In filling a prescription—filling it out incorrectly
4. In following doctor's orders—taking medicine at the wrong time or taking the wrong medicine
5. In writing a note to a friend—misinterpretation of note because of handwriting
6. In taking exams—teacher being unable to read it
7. In taking spelling tests—marking words incorrectly when grading because teacher cannot differentiate between the *i* and *e* or the *o* and *a*, and so on

The handwriting lesson coordinated with other activities can also be creative. Students can become more perceptive to how letters are formed by using their bodies to imitate letters. They can start with simple formations such as the *t* and proceed to more difficult ones. Children who become adept at this game can correlate it with spelling. A number of students can join together to spell words that other students "read" aloud. Or words are suggested to groups of children, which they spell correctly with their bodies.

The children, together with the teacher, can also make up rhymes or jingles with which to practice letter formation in either manuscript or cursive.

Even though models for the proper formation of strokes and letters are given and the students are expected to "duplicate" them, the teacher must recognize individual differences in handwriting. If specimens of many adults' handwriting are made available, it can be seen that no two individuals' ways of writing are the same. These adults may have spent hours copying letters to get them as close as possible to the model, but other factors—such as personality, speed of writing, coordination, and motivation—have affected their handwriting output. This is true even for adults who, during their school days, learned to produce letters as exact replicas.

The teacher should emphasize individual improvement in handwriting rather than similar standards for all. While handwriting scales or standards may be used, attitudes toward handwriting will be improved by respecting the individuality of students and providing realistic goals.

It can be seen that creativity can exist in the handwriting class, but the teacher must provide the proper affective environment, respect individual differences, and provide motivating techniques.

MANUSCRIPT WRITING

Manuscript writing is a simplified form taken from the monks before the invention of printing. It has been called by many different names—print script, unjoined script, script manuscript, Italian cursive, and so on.[17] Today many use the terms "manuscript" and "printing" interchangeably.

Block printing refers to that style of writing where all letters are capitalized: BLOCK PRINTING LOOKS LIKE THIS. In the business world some persons such as salespersons and clerks in stores in the larger cities are required to print. "Printing" to many, however, means manuscript, or to some the use of a typewriter.

Some persons use the term "printing" to differentiate it from writing. This is quite misleading and erroneous. By implying that printing, or manuscript, is not actually handwriting, the impression is given that it must inevitably be replaced by "true" handwriting, or cursive.

Marjorie Wise, an English graduate student, introduced manuscript writing to this country while at Columbia University during the early 1920s. She brought it from England, where manuscript writing was in wide use. The claims for its use by educational authorities in Great Britain and the experiments conducted by authorities at Teachers College, in public as well as private schools, have attributed these values to manuscript writing:

1. It is easy for children to learn because of the simple strokes.

2. Children can obtain satisfactory results early without drill on movement or form.

3. The letter forms are so simple that all of the children can see their difficulties and correct them.

4. The children learn one alphabet for both reading and writing.

5. This type of writing satisfies children's keen desire to write. (One important skill children want to accomplish on entering school is to learn to write.)

6. Unnecessary curves, loops, flourishes, and long joining strokes are omitted; therefore, the results are more legible than in cursive writing. This elimination of extra strokes also speeds up writing.

7. The pen may be lifted when going to the next stroke. This apparently lessens fatigue and the resulting strain on children's immature muscles.

[17]Edith Underwood Conrad, *Trends in Manuscript Writing* (New York: Bureau of Publications, Teachers College, Columbia University, 1936), p. 3.

8. Even children with poor muscular control can produce readable results.

9. The use of simple letter forms lessens the tendency toward children's "eyestrain" in reading and writing. There are fewer movements of the eyes required when reading manuscript writing. In fact, it is as easy to read as typewritten material.

10. Manuscript writing facilitates children's work in beginning reading.

11. Children who have written manuscript for a number of years can equal the speed of those using cursive writing, and in most cases exceed it.[18]

Readiness for Manuscript Writing

The fact that maturation is an important factor in readiness for writing has been stated a number of times. Although maturation is internal growth and cannot be speeded up, there are many readiness activities in which children should be engaged in order to be prepared for formal handwriting. For example, children should participate in working with scissors, in drawing, in making geometric shapes, in working with clay, in using tools, and in other activities that demand the use of eye–hand coordination. Since children's large muscles develop before their hand muscles, children usually may initially use large butcher paper or the chalkboard for drawing and writing. Learning to distinguish left from right is a vital readiness activity for writing. In teaching children to write, the teacher will continuously be stressing the left-to-right progression.

Before formal handwriting instruction begins children should be able to recognize and discriminate between and among letters of the alphabet, should have established a dominant hand, and should have a desire to write. Children should feel that learning to write is very important for them. They must be able to follow directions, have an adequate attention span, be able to make geometric figures (such as circles and squares), be able to make a straight line, and know left from right, that is, that writing starts at the left and proceeds to the right. Another important readiness for handwriting is for children to be exposed to

print. This seems so obvious that, at times, it is not stated.

Most children will want to learn to write because they feel that writing and reading will somehow unlock the door to the adult world. As a matter of fact, as already stated in this chapter, as well as in other chapters, many young children try their hand at writing before they come to school. A number of these preschoolers invent their own writing and spelling system in order to convey their ideas. Also, kindergarten children engage in writing stories, even though they usually have not had formal handwriting or spelling instruction. In addition, many kindergarten children can be seen attempting to write their names and to copy letters from the board or from posters around the room. Most first-graders do not have to be coaxed into learning to write. This desire will soon be dissipated if the handwriting exercise becomes an end in itself, and if children are asked to draw endless pages of strokes, circles, or letters.

When children are first learning to write, all of their efforts will go into attempting to make the letter with the correct strokes. Their reinforcement will be the knowledge that they have correctly completed this task. However, children should always be given a purpose for writing, and activities should be stimulating and interesting. More will be said about this later in the chapter.

Sitting Position

In order to assure that children will be sitting comfortably at their desks, the teacher must make sure that desks and seats are at the correct height for the children. A child should be able to sit erectly with both feet flat on the floor, so that they can sustain his or her weight. The child's forearms should rest on the desk ready for writing. The nonwriting hand should hold the paper in its place and the chair should be close enough to the desk so that the child does not have to bend forward too much. The desk should be cleared of all unnecessary material.

Paper Position

In manuscript the position of the paper is the same for both right- and left-handed chil-

[18]Ibid.

dren. The paper is placed straight in front of the child so that the bottom edge is parallel to the edge of the desk, although many children, especially left-handed ones, find that it may be more comfortable writing with a slight slant.

Position of paper for right- and left-handed children.

Pencil Position

The hand holding the pencil should be relaxed but not so much so that the forearm's muscles do not function properly. The pencil should be held loosely by the thumb and second finger. The side of the second finger touches the pencil, while the index or first finger acts as a guide. The first finger should rest nearer the point of the pencil than the thumb. The thumb and first finger should not be drawn in or tightly pressed against the pencil. The left-handed child usually holds the pencil closer to the point.

Individual differences exist, of course, in the way that both right- and left-handed students may hold their pencils.

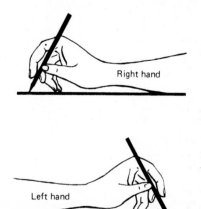

Right hand

Left hand

Handwriting Tools

In the first grade, primary pencils—thicker, rounder, larger, and with softer lead than ordinary pencils—are usually used. Educators generally recommend the use of a pencil with a large diameter because they feel that first-graders lack control of fine muscular coordination. However, this recommendation is based more on subjective observation and evaluation than on scientific data. Very few scientific studies have been done in this area. Interestingly, the ones that have been done have found that the size of the handwriting tool has no effect on the child's writing performance.[19] Since the studies in this area are so few, it is difficult to make any definitive statements concerning pencil size. The best practice would be to have a supply of both primary and regular pencils available. Some children may find pencils with large diameters too awkward to work with and prefer a regular pencil, whereas some children may do better with a primary pencil. Whatever pencil is used, it should be well sharpened and long enough to hold comfortably.

Some studies have been done on whether ballpoint pens, felt pens, or pencils affect the quality and performance of children's writings. According to the studies, it seems that primary-graders perform better with ballpoint or felt pens than with pencils.[20] Furthermore, studies have shown that even first-graders perform better with a ballpoint or felt pen.[21]

From the studies it seems that children in the third grade or lower should be allowed to use either ballpoint or felt pens for writing assignments, especially compositions. They should be allowed to continue the use of pencils for such subjects as arithmetic and spelling, where there is a substantial amount of erasing and where there seems to be no significant differ-

[19]M. E. Wiles, "Effect of Different-Size Tools on the Handwriting of Beginners," *Elementary School Journal* 43 (March 1943): 412–424.
[20]Joseph Krzesni, "Effect of Different Writing Tools and Paper on Performance of the Third Grader," *Elementary English* 48 (November 1971): 821–824.
[21]S. Tawney, "An Analysis of the Ballpoint Pen versus the Pencil as a Beginning Handwriting Instrument," *Elementary English* 44 (January 1967): 59–61.

ence in the child's performance as a result of the writing instrument used.

Paper

Since beginning handwriting involves large, free strokes, children are usually given large sheets of blank newsprint on which to write. The teacher usually makes several parallel folds in the paper creating "spaces" between which letters are formed. As children's hand muscles develop, it is felt that they will become more adept at writing within greater limitations. Therefore as children gain coordination, lined paper is introduced, beginning with spaces about one inch in height. There is generally a dotted or light-colored line running in the middle of the inch to guide the child when making lowercase letters. This type of paper usually alternates light and heavy lines ½ inch apart, and is ruled horizontally on both sides. It is approximately 8½ × 10½ inches. In second grade the paper is approximately 8 × 10½ inches, with alternate light and heavy lines ⅜ inch apart, ruled horizontally on both sides. In grade three students generally use the 8 × 10½-inch paper with alternate light and heavy lines ¼ inch apart, ruled horizontally.

Research on providing special paper for beginning handwriting has been very rare. Two studies, one in 1943[22] and one in 1971,[23] found that the width of the ruled paper had no significant effect on a child's writing performance. A more recent study in 1976 involving kindergarten children also found that the traditional practice of providing special paper for beginning handwriting was not a justified practice.[24] The researchers stated that the width of the writing space (one inch or one-half inch) had no differential effect on the quality of beginning handwriting, and the use of paper with closed ends (vertical lines at the right and left margins to enclose the writing space) did not improve the placement of letters in the writing space.

The D'Nealian Handwriting system incorporates the findings from this recent study into its program. In the D'Nealian program beginning writers start writing on one-half-inch ruled paper with a dotted mid-line, usually referred to as a third-grade writing paper. This paper is used from kindergarten through third grade. At fourth grade in the D'Nealian system the children change to standard notebook paper with about one-third-inch rules, which is a typical size for adult writing.[25] (See "Using Handwriting Workbooks" later in this chapter for more on the D'Nealian Handwriting method.)

Chalkboard

Since children seem to enjoy writing on the chalkboard they should be given the opportunity to do so. While writing at the board children stand at approximately an arm's length from the board, writing at their own eye level. A half-piece of chalk is held between the thumb and first two fingers, and writing proceeds from left to right.

When the teacher uses the chalkboard he or she should make sure that the words to be copied by the children are level with their eyes. The teacher's writing should be clear and legible. In order to achieve firm, bold letters, the teacher also should use a half-piece of chalk and exert sufficient pressure on it. The teacher should make sure that the spacing of letters allows each to be clearly distinguished from any other. He or she should be able to write fast enough so as not to slow down any discussion in progress. It is also important that the teacher write in such a way that he or she does not obstruct the pupils' view of the board. Both right- and left-handed teachers walk from left to right as they are writing on the chalkboard. However, left-handed teachers will have to be especially careful about making their horizontal lines proceeding from left to right, overcoming the natural inclination to go from right to left. The teacher's writing should be of high quality because the children will use it as a model.

[22]Wiles "Effect of Different-Size Tools."

[23]Krzesni, "Effect of Different Writing Tools."

[24]Glennelle Halpin and Gerald Halpin, "Special Paper for Beginning Handwriting: An Unjustified Practice?" *Journal of Educational Research* 69 (March 1976): 267–269.

[25]Donald N. Thurber, *D'Nealian Handwriting* (Glenview, Ill.: Scott, Foresman, 1978), p. 8.

Beginning Instruction in Manuscript Writing

Children need to learn to make the basic strokes and shapes necessary for handwriting. They have already had practice in working with large paper and with making geometric shapes. Now, they will learn to make special shapes using one-inch spaced paper with the half-inch dotted line. The basic shapes needed for lowercase and capital letters consist of:

Children are introduced to the proper construction of the shapes one at a time. Large and lowercase circles can be taught together, as well as large and small vertical lines. The teacher should observe whether students are able to space the shapes properly and keep them within the lines of the paper. Some children may not be able to do this. There will be many other children who are ready to begin handwriting when they enter first grade. This range represents the normal ability span teachers can expect to find in their classes. Teachers must recognize this phenomenon and be prepared to work with a wide range of differences among their students.

In teaching how to write, the teacher will help children make the shapes by giving these instructions:

Straight lines—Start at the top and go down. "We always start at the top and go down."

Circles—Start at the two o'clock position. "Does everyone see the 2 on the clock? Good, we all start at that point and go around this way."

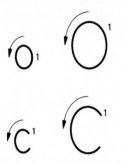

Circles and parts of circles.

The teacher continues in this manner until the children are able to make all the necessary shapes. Children are told, "Each stroke is made separately. Lift your pencil after each stroke."

To give children further practice in making these shapes, and for stimulating interest, the teacher can make some pictures out of circles, lines, and so on. The teacher can then ask children to try to draw other things using the shapes they have learned.

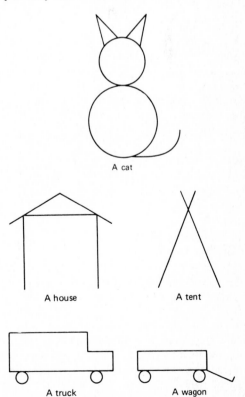

A cat

A house   A tent

A truck   A wagon

TEACHING HANDWRITING IN THE PRIMARY GRADES

Handwriting will be more meaningful if the letters are taught in relation to what is being learned in class. Children should not be taught to write letters in rote fashion, according to the alphabet, but in relation to the spelling or phonics lesson in progress. For example, before teaching the letter *b*, children should have had auditory and visual discrimination exercises for this letter, and they should be able to state words that begin with the letter.

To keep the attention of children, the teacher should pass out paper for writing after children have been shown how to construct the letter. First, the children should be given time to put their first names on the paper. All of the children should have sample nameplates on their desks from which to copy their names. The teacher should then ask children to watch while he or she forms the letter on the board. The teacher might ask some children to volunteer to make the letter with him or her at the board.

The teacher should give explicit instructions on how to draw the letter as he or she constructs it. Children are told to follow exactly what the teacher is doing when he or she writes the letter. After each stroke the teacher stops and looks to see whether any child is having undue difficulty. The lesson proceeds in this manner until the letter is completed.

It is desirable for children who are beginning to write to have a work sample at their desks. This saves pupils from constantly having to shift attention from the board to the desk when copying letters.

Here are some instructional recommendations to help teachers who are working with a perceptual–motor program in handwriting:

1. Develop the appropriate mental set for perceptual learning by involving the children in establishing the problem for each lesson.

2. Guide children to observe the formation of the letter or procedure under study. The child must build a mental image of the letter or feature of writing skill involved (such as spacing or size), as well as how it is formed. This cannot be inferred from a still model presented in a copybook, worksheet, or chart.

3. Provide many guided exposures to the stimulus in order to build perception. For example, guide children to watch the formation of a letter several times, focusing on a different aspect of the formational process each time.

4. Use methods of instruction that require a mental response from each child concerning the formational process, not just motor responses. This facilitates the building of a perception. It can be done through asking children to verbalize the formational process in their own words, having children think about the movement of a letter, or visualize or write a letter as it is described by another child.

5. Use multisensory stimulation. People seem to perceive best through varying modes, and all people appear to respond best to multiple modes. It is important, therefore, to use visual, auditory, and kinesthetic exposure, rather than the simple visual provided by a still model of a letter.

6. Stress self-correction by giving the children a means of comparing their procedure and the desired one. This comparison will serve to build accurate perceptions and can then be used as a basis for practice.

7. In practice, keep the emphasis on comparison and improvement, rather than on writing numerous samples. While a program must provide instruction toward developing speed in handwriting, stamina in writing for longer periods, and fluency, these aspects should be developed separately from direct emphasis on perceptual and motor development of a particular formational procedure.

8. Consistency of letter formation and materials is essential in all writing presented to children and in all performance situations. All teachers from kindergarten through sixth grade should use the style of writing adopted by the school system. A great deal of interference in the building of perceptions occurs when inconsistent models are presented. Further, whenever children see the written form or write, materials should be consistent in line width and style with those used in instruction. Teachers should carefully examine worksheets and workbooks to determine that positive reinforcement is ensured. When children are asked to write on unlined paper, narrow lines, or in too small a

space, negative influences in both perceptual and motor aspects will result.

Whenever possible, the written form should be presented to children on lines to build perceptions of size relationships, spacing, and alignment. Writing on lined chalkboards and using the manuscript or cursive form on lined worksheets and charts facilitate this.

9. Care should be taken to keep expectations in terms of quantity of writing consistent with what children can be expected to achieve. Further examination of the results of this study in terms of speed of writing will be enlightening to many teachers. If the average first-grader can write only 16 to 17 letters per minute, this amounts to only 160 to 170 letters in 10 minutes, or about 30 words. Certainly in terms of motor development, many first-graders could not be expected to write steadily for a longer period than this. Similar comparisons can be made for second- and third-graders.

10. Prior to the development of skills of writing, teachers should consider the positive or detrimental effects to perceptual and motor development of extensive use of unsupervised writing or copywork. Surely many other areas of the curriculum are more crucial than handwriting, and teachers ought not refrain from use of handwriting as a tool when it is important to the child's development in another area. However, many times when copywork is used as a form of independent activity, it is of questionable value to the child and may be detrimental to handwriting. Other activities involving recreational reading, listening, and the like may be more creative and of greater value to the child.

By careful examination of procedures utilized in teaching handwriting and in its use in the classroom, and through application of the procedures suggested above, teachers can improve instruction in handwriting in both the perceptual and motor aspects of learning.[26]

The Handwriting Lesson Related to Other Activities

As has already been stated, children must see a purpose in what they are doing. Rather than having children write lines or pages of a specific letter, stroke, or combination being learned, the teacher should incorporate this action with other activities, such as written expression. In first grade children can write letters to their parents telling them what they have learned. The teacher tells children that although they should try to form all the letters as well as they can, they are expected to pay special attention to the letter they have just learned. (See sample notes and letters in Chapter 12.)

The teacher can easily combine the handwriting lesson with a listening activity. Children can be asked to listen carefully and see how well they can follow directions and how well they can construct the letter *b*. When the teacher has everyone's attention he or she should say, "On the first line make two capital letter *b*s and three small letter *b*s." After the children have finished each line, the teacher can call on individual children who have the correct answers to construct the letters on the chalkboard.

The purpose of good handwriting is legibility. Therefore, the teacher should stress that legibility be carried over to other subject-matter areas—such as spelling, social studies, writing compositions, and so on.

Using Handwriting Workbooks

Many teachers use handwriting workbooks that give explicit instructions on the presentation and formation of each letter. Consistency is important, so the school should use the same series for all its handwriting classes, since the construction of some of the letters differs among different publishers. It can be confusing to learn to construct a letter in one way and in the next grade have to learn to construct it another way. For example, some publishers use whole circles in constructing letters, while others use half-circles or arcs.

Some commercial systems have first-grade children construct capital letters so that they occupy the full space from the top to the baseline. Later on, letters are reduced in size, and capitals occupy slightly less than a full space.

A complete sample of the Zaner-Bloser Alphabet in manuscript form and Zaner-Bloser Numbers follow:

[26]Furner, "An Analysis," pp. 68–69.

FIGURE 14.1   ZANER-BLOSER ALPHABET, from *Handwriting: Basic Skills and Application.* Copyright © 1984, Zaner-Bloser, Inc., Columbus, Ohio.

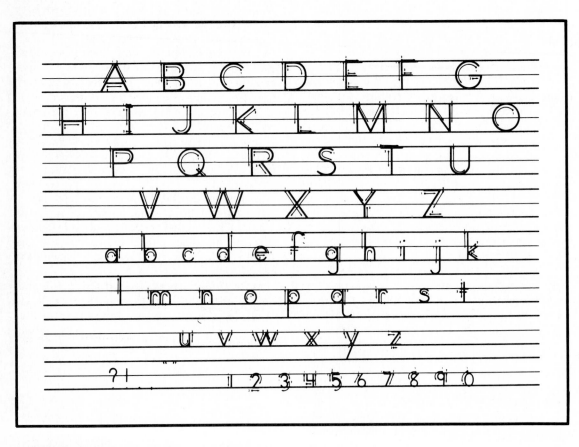

The D'Nealian Handwriting method published by Scott, Foresman deviates from the traditional handwriting systems by making its manuscript letters as similar as possible to their cursive counterparts, which eases the transition to cursive. With the exceptions of *f, r, s, v,* and *z,* manuscript letters become cursive letters with the addition of simple joining strokes.

The D'Nealian method capitalizes on children's desire to imitate adults and their older brothers and sisters. In the D'Nealian method children do not first learn circles, straight lines, and slant lines, and then learn to join these parts into letters. Rather, they start writing immediately. Most of the letter forms are made with a continuous stroke rather than with separate strokes. The beginning writer lifts his or her hand from the paper only after each letter rather than after each stroke. Manuscript letters are slanted, beginning writers use one-half-inch ruled paper with a dotted mid-line (paper generally used in the third grade in most other systems), and spacing is taught from the very beginning.

A sample of the D'Nealian Manuscript Alphabet and D'Nealian Numbers is on p. 303.

TRANSITION TO CURSIVE HANDWRITING

Reasons given against the teaching of manuscript writing in Great Britain in the early 1920s were later cited in support of making the transition to cursive writing in the primary grades in the United States. Such arguments by

FIGURE 14.2   THE D'NEALIAN MANUSCRIPT ALPHABET, from *D'Nealian™ Hand-writing* by Donald N. Thurber. Copyright © 1978 by Scott, Foresman and Co. Reprinted by permission.

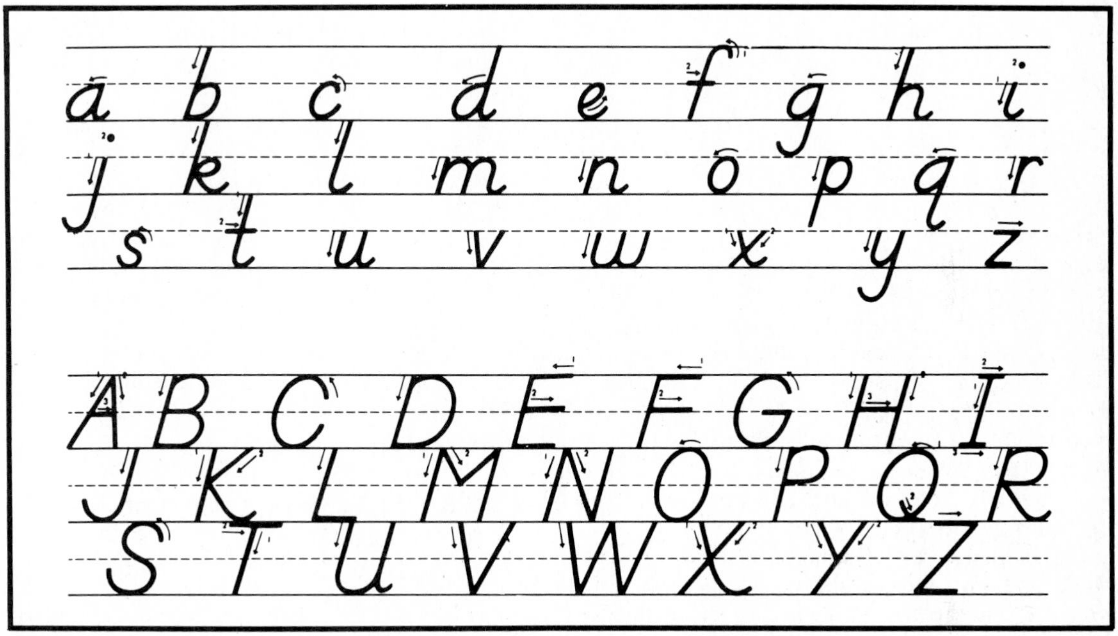

FIGURE 14.3   D'NEALIAN NUMBERS, from *D'Nealian™ Handwriting* by Donald N. Thurber. Copyright © 1978 by Scott, Foresman and Co. Reprinted by permission.

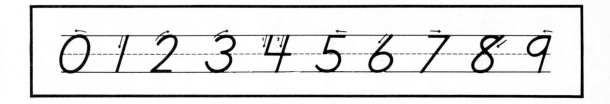

British educators against manuscript writing included:

1. Loss of fluency and speed through the use of the somewhat disconnected letters
2. Inability of children to read the cursive writings of others
3. Resulting uniform stereotyped handwriting and destruction of individuality (Were this the case, grave dangers would ensue in banking and business, making forgery an everyday occurrence.)[27]

Most studies have found no differences in speed beween manuscript and cursive writing. People who learned manuscript can write as

[27]Marjorie Wise, *On the Technique of Manuscript Writing* (New York: Scribner's, 1924), p. x.

rapidly as those who write in cursive.[28] As a matter of fact, it has been stated that people who acquire great speed are usually rhythmical writers, and that manuscript writing is more suitable for rhythm than cursive.[29]

The belief that manuscript writing must be slower may be because an individual's style has become "contaminated" at some time or other with instruction in the cursive style. Children who write in manuscript have not had as much practice as those who are taught the traditional cursive style.[30]

It seems that much of the pressure to change to cursive writing comes from parents and the children themselves. Children observe that their parents and older siblings write in cursive and they want to write that way too. They feel it is too "babyish" to write in manuscript. Parents feel that it is childish to write in manuscript and pressure schools to teach cursive writing. When parents notice children writing in cursive, they feel that somehow the children are "progressing" in learning.

The myths concerning manuscript writing still hold sway, and so cursive writing is taught in most schools sometime during the primary grades. There are a few school systems that allow children to make the transition at the end of first grade or at the beginning of second, claiming that they have the necessary hand development for cursive, but this is poor practice. The children have spent all of the first grade learning to write in manuscript. Most have acquired this skill, and they can now use it as a tool for written expression. If they are made to change at the end of first or at the beginning of second grade, they have had very little time for reinforcement of the skill that they spent all their first school year learning. Looking at it from the viewpoint of the child, the changeover can seem frustrating and useless. Nevertheless, many children do pressure for learning cursive

writing even before they have mastered manuscript.

In view of this discussion, it is probably better to begin the transition to cursive at the end of second or the beginning of third grade. If the school system starts cursive in first grade or the beginning of second, teachers should do the best they can, recognizing that not all children will have the necessary coordination.

Many school systems use commercial handwriting programs, which usually determine at what time the transition to cursive will be made. Even though these programs advocate teaching cursive at specific grades, school systems do not have to follow such suggestions. Workbooks should never be used as ends in themselves or allowed to dictate the kind of program schools should have. Commercial programs should be utilized as aids that are integrated into the whole program.

Differences between Manuscript and Cursive Writing

Manuscript and cursive writing differ,[31] and children should first be made aware of these differences as they make the transition from one to the other. The teacher may write a word on the chalkboard in both cursive and manuscript and try to get the children to see the differences for themselves. After some response, the teacher can write a few more words very carefully in both cursive and manuscript, and note if the children can discern further differences. The teacher can also demonstrate written words on large newsprint paper. With manuscript writing the paper should be put on the board with masking tape in a squared-off position; for cursive the paper should be put in a slanted position.

Cat big jump

[28]Gertrude Hildreth, "Manuscript Writing after Sixty Years," *Elementary English* 37 (January 1960): 3–13.

[29]Wise, *On the Technique*, p. xii.

[30]Gertrude Hildreth, "Simplified Handwriting for Today," *Journal of Educational Research* 56 (February 1963): 330–333.

[31]The differences are for the traditional manuscript and cursive systems. Many of the differences would not apply to the Scott, Foresman D'Nealian method or any other method similar to the D'Nealian method.

Children should state these differences:

Manuscript	Cursive
1. Letters are straight.	**1.** Letters are slanted—parallel to one another.
2. Paper is straight.	**2.** Paper is slanted—to the left for right-handed persons and to the right for left-handed persons.
3. Pencil is lifted from the paper after each stroke.	**3.** Pencil is not lifted from the paper until the whole word is finished.
4. The letters are all separate.	**4.** The letters are all connected.
5. The letter *t* is crossed, and the *i* and *j* are dotted after the completion of the letter.	**5.** The *t* is not crossed, and the *i* and *j* are not dotted until after the completion of the word.
6. Certain letters are more circular.	**6.** Certain letters are more oval—egg-shaped.

Readiness for Cursive

To construct letters in cursive a child must have achieved enough coordination to write in manuscript. He must also have a strong desire to write in cursive, which is often evidenced by the slant a child starts to insert in his or her manuscript writing. Children will also verbalize a desire to "really learn to write."

During the transition stage the teacher should be presenting material in cursive to help children to read cursive writing. They should achieve facility in reading cursive before they attempt to write it. The teacher should also help students acquire the vocabulary and strokes for cursive writing. Again, not all children will be ready for cursive at the same time, so the teacher will have to form groups that will learn cursive at different times.

Paper for Cursive Writing

Grade three uses paper that is $8\frac{1}{2} \times 10\frac{1}{2}$ inches with alternate light and heavy lines $\frac{1}{4}$ inch apart, ruled the long way.

Grade four usually uses $8 \times 10\frac{1}{2}$-inch practice paper. It has $\frac{3}{8}$-inch ruling on one side, ruled the short way, and $\frac{3}{8}$-inch alternate light lines. The ink paper is $8\frac{1}{2} \times 10\frac{1}{2}$ inches with $\frac{3}{8}$-inch ruling on both sides, ruled the short way.

In grades five and six, a similar type of paper is used. Practice paper is usually $8\frac{1}{2} \times 11$ with $\frac{3}{8}$-inch ruling and no margins. The ink paper is $8\frac{1}{2} \times 10\frac{1}{2}$ inches with $\frac{3}{8}$-inch ruling on both sides, ruled the short way.

Position of Paper

In cursive writing right-handed students should slant their papers to the left, and the lower left corner should make an approximately 30- to 40-degree angle with the edge of the desk. The teacher must be especially careful that left-handed children have their papers slanted in the proper position so that they do not develop a hook-wrist position. The paper should be slanted to the right and the lower right-hand corner should make an approximately 30- to 40-degree angle with the desk edge.

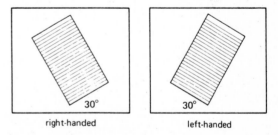

right-handed   left-handed

Paper positions for right-handed *(left)* **and left-handed** *(right)* **children.**

Pencil Position

The pencil position for cursive is similar to that for manuscript.

PRESENTATION OF CURSIVE WRITING IN THE CLASSROOM

Since we know that children should be able to read cursive before they write it, they should have seen many examples of cursive handwriting and the teacher should be presenting lessons mostly in cursive. Differences between the two forms of writing should also have been discovered by the children.

As in manuscript writing, cursive letters are not presented in alphabetical order. There are differences of opinion as to how to introduce cursive, as can be seen by the handwriting programs of various publishing companies. One way is to proceed from the letters that require the easiest and least number of strokes to the letters that require the more complex and greater number of strokes. Another method would be to present those letters most often used by children. Whatever method is used to introduce children to cursive writing, the letters should be put into words at each lesson, so that children can see how they are connected in the word.

The teacher should always stress the importance of legibility and help children see the purpose of the lesson. Although they must first concentrate on learning the proper strokes before cursive writing becomes a communication tool, handwriting should not be made an end in itself. Pages and pages of undercurves, overcurves, upper and lower loops act as a deterrent to developing a "good script." If the children are using the newly learned skills in some activities, such as the following, it will encourage them to try to write their best:

1. Writing a thank-you note to someone
2. Writing to a sick classmate
3. Writing a letter to a friend
4. Writing a letter to parents
5. Making a poster for display
6. Requesting material or information from a firm or organization
7. Writing papers for display on the bulletin board
8. Writing invitations to parents
9. Writing invitations to other classes in school
10. Writing letters to children in other countries, states, communities

FIGURE 14.4   PALMER METHOD HANDWRITING, "Centennial Edition" 1984. Courtesy Palmer Method Handwriting, all rights reserved.

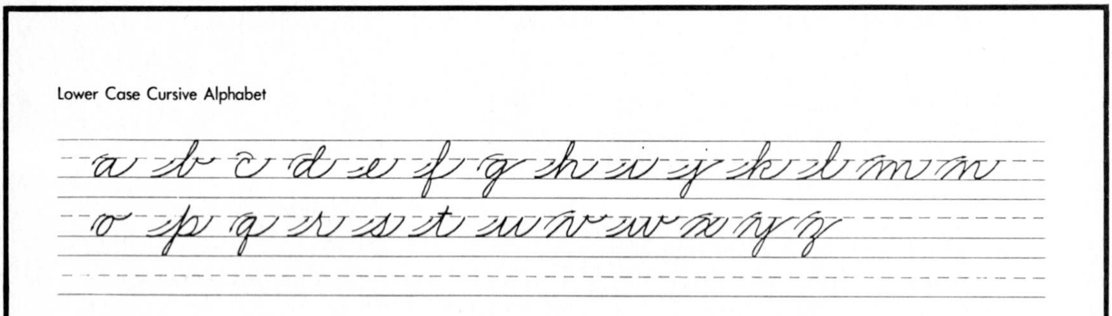

Lower Case Cursive Alphabet

Upper Case Cursive Alphabet

FIGURE 14.5 THE D'NEALIAN CURSIVE ALPHA-
BET, from *D'Nealian™ Handwriting* by Donald N.
Thurber. Copyright © 1978 by Scott, Foresman and
Co. Reprinted by permission.

11. Writing birthday cards
12. Writing cards for holidays
13. Writing reports and creative stories

It should be stressed that cursive writing should be introduced by a method that will "become routine as rapidly and efficiently as possible in order that it may be used functionally by a person to express and record his thoughts and feelings for others to read."[32]

A complete set of cursive letters from two different handwriting systems are shown.

Helping the Left-Handed Child with Writing

Left-handed children need special help not only in the formation of letters and digits but in the positioning of the paper, the placement of their hands, the position of their wrists, the placement of their arms, and the grip of their writing instruments. Although manuscript writing is not much different for left-handed children, the teacher should pay special attention to them to make sure they are following the left–right progression and are holding the writing paper in place with their right hands.

When left-handed children are learning cursive the teacher must be especially careful that left-handed writers avoid the hook-wrist technique by having the paper slanted to the right, opposite to the direction for right-handers. If pupils arrive in an upper grade habituated to the hook-wrist technique, all the teacher can do is make sure that they use a ballpoint pen so that they will not smear their writing. No attempt to change the students' technique should be made at this late stage in their development, as more harm than good may be the result.

Enstrom has done a good deal of research on the writing of the left-handed child, using a camera and sketch pad. From his observations,

[32]Virgil E. Herrick, "Manuscript and Cursive Writing," *Childhood Education* 37 (February 1961): 264–271.

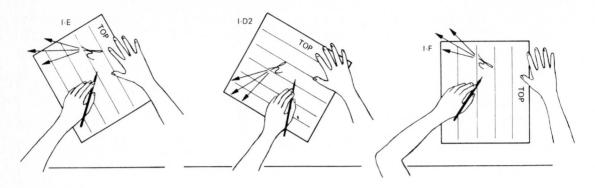

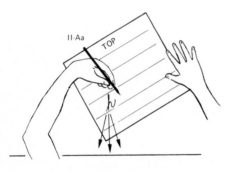

he found that 15 approaches used by left-handed writers could be detected: the position of the paper, arm, pen, and so on. The criteria used to evaluate various techniques employed by the writers were:

1. **The quality of the handwriting product**
2. **The rate of writing**
3. **Ability to produce neat, smear-free papers**
4. **Healthy body posture**

Here are Enstrom's findings and conclusions:

The efficiency testing revealed that in Group I three of the six techniques used are efficient in quality, rate, ability to produce smear-free papers, and considerations of healthful body posture. These techniques are used by 69 percent of the writers in this group. They bear the classification identifications I-E, I-D2, and I-F, and are pictured above, from left to right, in order of desirability:

Only one adjustment in Group II can be recommended, and then only where it seems inadvisable to make radical changes because of habit formation, daily writing pressures, or a pupil's lack of desire to change. Only 20 percent of hooked writers use this more efficient approach, which is 11-Aa above.

While quality and rate are high, the probability of ink-smearing is inherent in this technique. Other variations of the hooked-wrist method either test low or involve possible health hazards, with no advantage in quality or rate—and so cannot be recommended.

The following conclusions can be drawn from the study as a whole:

1. **There are more left-handed writers in the classroom than are usually reported in the literature. This was true in the study area and will probably be found to be universally so as more studies are made. The problem of left-handed handwriting is sufficient in scope to warrant the inclusion of the subject in teacher preparation courses.**
2. **The study clearly revealed the most efficient ways of writing with the left hand. Three of the six**

Group I techniques are superior, all things considered, and are identified, in order of efficiency, as I-E, I-D2, and I-F (see page 308).

3. It can further be concluded that very few, if any, "hookers" can be changed beyond grade four. The best "cure" for the problem is prevention in the first place—a responsibility of primary teachers. Helping the hooker find the most desirable way of writing with a hooked technique is the best answer in advanced grades. The study indicated the best solution for these pupils to be the II-Aa position (see page 308). Instructions for these pupils would be:

  a. Place the paper exactly as a right-handed pupil would place it.
  b. Keep the writing wrist on edge.
  c. Use maximum flexing of the wrist during the writing process.
  d. Ignore all hand-position instructions intended for all other pupils.
  e. Use a ballpoint pen.

  Lest there be misunderstanding, the disadvantages of this position at best should be reviewed: (1) the hand does not move very freely in carrying the work across the page, particularly if the hand perspires; (2) the probability of smearing is inherent in this approach; again, especially if the hand tends to perspire.

4. The study revealed that successful writing with the left hand is strictly a teaching problem, not a pupil problem. Where teachers understand how to help these beginning writers, pupils write successfully, with great speed and ease.[33]

EVALUATION OF HANDWRITING

"To date there still appears to be no generally accepted definition of legibility."[34]

Although teachers and students may use evaluation scales to measure students' hand-

writing, both should recognize that such scales are only guides. That is, students' handwriting should not be expected to conform exactly to the scales. The teacher must allow for individual differences in handwriting, as in all other areas. Individual handwriting improvement, rather than absolute standards, is the criterion that should be used for judging or evaluating progress.

Scientific measuring scales can be useful in helping both teachers and students know what kind of handwriting to expect from students at various grade levels. There are a number of commercial scales used as standards of measurement. In order to determine the level the teacher slides each child's sample along the scale until one is found that comes close.

The Zaner-Bloser publishing company provides a scale for each grade from one through high school. Samples of five degrees of quality are given for each grade: high, good, medium, fair, and poor. To use the scale for grade six—Cursive,[35] the following steps are suggested:

I. WRITING
  A. The teacher writes on a ruled chalkboard a model of the verse.
  B. Students practice writing the verse on lined paper.
  C. Using their best handwriting, students then write the verse again.

II. EVALUATION
  Compare the students' writing to the examples on the scale, and if no more than one element needs improvement, the writing is rated *excellent* (Example 1); if no more than two elements need improvement, the writing is rated *good* (Example 2); if no more than three elements need improvement, the writing is rated *average* (Example 3); if no more than four elements need improvement, the writing is rated *fair* (Example 4); and if five elements need improvement, the writing is rated *poor* (Example 5).

[33]E. A. Enstrom, "Research in Left-handedness as Related to Handwriting," *Public School Digest* 12 (1959–60 School Year).

[34]Victor Froese, "Handwriting: Practice, Pragmatism, and Progress," in *Research in the Language Arts: Language and Schooling*, Victor Froese and Stanley B. Straw, eds. (Baltimore, University Park Press, 1981), p. 228.

[35]*Zaner-Bloser 6 Evaluation Scale—Cursive* (Columbus, Ohio: Zaner-Bloser, 1979).

Here are Examples 1 and 5:

Example 1 — Excellent for Grade Six

The North Wind lives
in a cold, dark cave
in the land of ice-and-snow.
The East Wind lives
in a roofless cell
through which the bright stars glow.

Example 5 — Poor for Grade Six

The North Wind lives
in a cold, dark cave
in the land of ice - and-snow.
The East Wind lives
in a roofless cell through
which the bright stars glow.

SATISFACTORY		NEEDS IMPROVEMENT
☑	LETTER FORMATION	☐
☑	SLANT	☐
☑	SPACING	☐
☐	ALIGNMENT AND PROPORTION	☑
☑	LINE QUALITY	☐

Evaluation of Example 1.

SATISFACTORY		NEEDS IMPROVEMENT
☐	LETTER FORMATION	☑
☐	SLANT	☑
☐	SPACING	☑
☐	ALIGNMENT AND PROPORTION	☑
☐	LINE QUALITY	☑

Evaluation of Example 5.

It is important to mention again that measuring scales can be useful if used properly. Teachers should not employ them as ends in themselves but rather as guides for individual improvement.

Students Set Handwriting Standards

A viable technique for stimulating self-improvement in handwriting is one in which the teacher encourages students to develop their own handwriting standards. Standards that are cooperatively developed can be on display in the classroom. All of the children have their own scales against which they evaluate their handwriting. The students determine which handwriting sample they will use each week to determine if they are making progress. The areas for improvement are discussed with the teacher.

The checklist the class develops may be either general or specific. For example, a general checklist could be stated in this question form:

1. Is my spacing of letters adequate?
2. Is my spacing of words adequate?
3. Are all my letters slanted in almost the same way and direction?
4. Are my letters uniform in size?
5. Did I close all my letters?
6. Do all my looped letters have the proper loop?
7. Are all my letters resting on the baseline?

More specific diagnostic charts and pupil-designed standards can also be used by students to evaluate their handwriting progress. The diagnostic chart can have samples of all strokes necessary for good cursive writing and examples of each. Students can diagnose their handwriting by checking the chart to see whether they are constructing letters correctly by making these strokes properly:

	Example	Letters
1. Undercurve	*↗*	*e i t u*
2. Downcurve	*↙*	*a c d g o*
3. Overcurve	*↘*	*m n v x*
4. Undercurve and retrace	*i*	*s w*
5. Upper loop	*l*	*e l b h k*
6. Lower loop	*f*	*f j p*

Examples of common errors:

1. Failure to close letters	*a d o*	
2. No loops where needed	*l b f*	
3. Letters too close together	*are*	
4. Not enough space between words	*one boy*	
5. Letters are too small or too large	*boy*	

Students should recognize that as they learn new skills in handwriting they are expected to add these to their checklist. Students who have specific difficulties may want to add such problem areas to their checklists, even though they have not been chosen as checklist items for the group as a whole.

TEACHER EVALUATION CHECKLIST

Teachers can use this evaluation chart to determine whether they are teaching handwriting to pupils well:

1. Does each child write legibly and easily?
2. Have I developed good position habits of the body, arms, hand, pencil, and paper in my pupils?
3. Do the children have an appreciation for the value of handwriting as a tool of written expression?
4. Do they take pride in being able to express their thoughts and ideas in good written form?
5. Are the mechanics of handwriting sufficiently proficient among the class so as not to hamper the expression of thoughts and ideas?
6. Do I present my lessons in such a way that the children discover their own errors and willingly proceed to correct them?
7. Are the aims of my handwriting lessons simple, understandable to children, and possible to attain within the scope of one or two lesson periods?
8. Do I encourage proofreading and self-evaluation on the part of the pupils?
9. Has the handwriting of my pupils improved?
10. Has the number of poor writers been reduced?
11. Is my own handwriting always a good model?

Source: Emma Harrison Myers, *The Ways & Hows of Teaching Handwriting* (Columbus, Ohio: Zaner-Bloser, 1963), pp. 142–143.

The teacher may also ask children to save samples of their work so that they, their parents, and the teacher can see the student's handwriting progress.

STUDENT'S NAME:
GRADE:
TEACHER:

DIAGNOSTIC CHECKLIST FOR GAINING SKILL IN HANDWRITING

I. HANDWRITING READINESS (K–1)	YES	NO

A. Concepts and terminology

   1. Location and direction

The child recognizes the following terms:
    a. Above/below
    b. Around
    c. First, second, last
    d. Left/right
    e. Start/stop
    f. Top/middle/bottom

2. Relationships

The child is able to:
    a. Recognize similarities in objects
    b. Recognize differences in objects
    c. Classify objects
    d. Recognize objects that are bigger or smaller
    e. Put things in order

3. Communication

    The child:
    a. Communicates orally
    b. Expresses a desire to write
    c. Attempts to write
    d. Is beginning to read

B. Visual Perception

    The child is able to:
    1. Differentiate between and among letters
    2. Recognize similarities in words and letters

C. Auditory Perception

    The child is able to:
    1. Listen with sustained attention
    2. Follow oral directions

D. Motor coordination

    The child has:
    1. Eye–hand coordination
    2. Large motor control
    3. Specific motor control
    4. A dominant hand
    5. Proper handwriting position

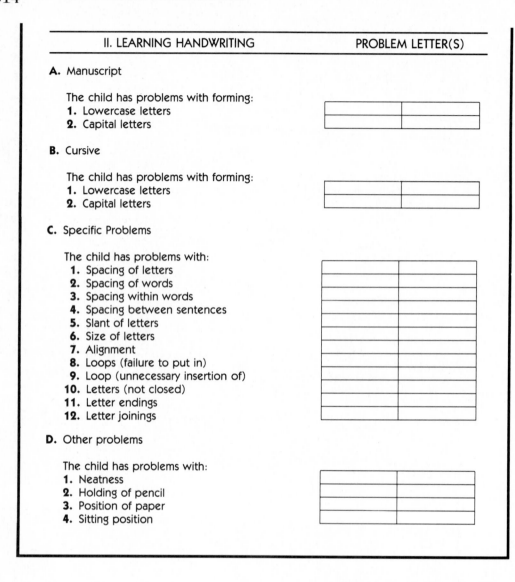

II. LEARNING HANDWRITING   PROBLEM LETTER(S)

A. Manuscript

The child has problems with forming:
1. Lowercase letters
2. Capital letters

B. Cursive

The child has problems with forming:
1. Lowercase letters
2. Capital letters

C. Specific Problems

The child has problems with:
1. Spacing of letters
2. Spacing of words
3. Spacing within words
4. Spacing between sentences
5. Slant of letters
6. Size of letters
7. Alignment
8. Loops (failure to put in)
9. Loop (unnecessary insertion of)
10. Letters (not closed)
11. Letter endings
12. Letter joinings

D. Other problems

The child has problems with:
1. Neatness
2. Holding of pencil
3. Position of paper
4. Sitting position

SUMMARY

The historical, psychological, and general factors concerning handwriting were presented. In order to develop a good handwriting program for all students, it was stated that the teacher must know about the developmental growth patterns of children and, in particular, about proximodistal development. This knowledge of growth from the midpoint to the extremities helps teachers to understand the readiness of students for handwriting, and also gives teachers an insight into some reversal difficulties that the left-handed child may encounter. Providing a good physical and affective environment, one in which children will be comfortable and free from fear, is essential. The teacher must also understand about individual differences in handwriting, and respect individuality. Creativity in handwriting lessons can be achieved by inventive teachers who use stimulating techniques and integrate handwriting with many other ongoing activities.

The manuscript program in handwriting was then given, and the factors necessary for teaching manuscript effectively were presented. The various factors necessary for teaching cursive effectively were discussed in the hope of helping teachers who are unfamiliar with or unaccustomed to teaching handwriting and to give them confidence in their ability to do so.

Specific handwriting problems that cause the most difficulties for students were introduced, and methods for overcoming the problems were discussed. To help in evaluating handwriting, checklists and diagnostic charts were given, so that students can determine whether they are improving. A "Diagnostic Checklist for Gaining Skill in Handwriting" was also presented at the end of the chapter.

The handwriting program presented in this chapter advocates handwriting improvement based on individual differences, not on conformity to absolute standards.

As a further aid, two examples of handwriting lesson plans follow. Using these as a guide, see if you can construct another one.

LESSON PLAN I: EARLY-PRIMARY -GRADE LEVEL

OBJECTIVES

Students will be able to recognize the letter "G g" when orally given as the initial consonant of a word.
Students will be able to state words beginning with the letter "G g."
Students will be able to read some words beginning with the letter "G g."
Students will be able to construct the letter "G g."

PRELIMINARY PREPARATION

A bulletin board is to be filled with pictures beginning with the letter "G g."
A picture of a clown's face with the letter "G" forming the ear.
The following words with blanks in front ___o, ___irl, ___reen, ___ood, ___ame are put on the board.

INTRODUCTION

"We have been constructing alphabet letters and we have talked about how much fun it is to be able to write letters and have our families read what we say. What alphabet letters have we been working with? Who remembers? Yes, an 'F.' Good. Yes, I remember the fish. Can anyone guess what I have for you today? I'll give you a riddle. He makes children laugh. He is at a circus. He does tricks. Who is he?"

"Yes, a clown. Now, yesterday we met the alphabet letter that we are going to work with today. Let's see who remembers what it looks like and what we called it. Everyone look at the clown. The letter we are going to work with is some place on the picture of the clown. When you find it, raise your hand. I'll walk up and down the room so that everyone can see the picture. Has everyone seen it? Good! What is it? Yes, the letter 'G.' Where was it on the clown? Yes, it was the clown's ear. We are going to see how many words we can list that start with 'G g,' and we are also going to learn to write the letter 'G g.' "

DEVELOPMENT

Ask all the children in the class who have a first name that begins with "G" to stand. Ask them to state their names. Ask all children who have a last name that begins with "G" to raise their right hands. Ask children to state their last names. Children who have a "g" in any place in their names are now asked to raise their left hands. Have these children tell where the "g" is in their name by showing their name cards. Next tell the children that you will give them a number of riddles and all the answers have to begin with "G g."

Who can think of a color that starts with "g"?
Who can think of a word that is the opposite of boy?

What word is the opposite of stop?
What do children like to play?
What is the word that is the opposite of bad?

The teacher should then ask children to look around the room and see how many words they can state that start with "G g." After the children have given a number of such words, the teacher tells them that they are going to learn to construct the letter "G g."

"Now let's see how to make the big letter 'G.' Everyone watch. Start at the top, at about two o'clock, go around to the left and stop at about four o'clock. Now make a straight line from the center out. Who would like to try it at the board? Good!"

Give out paper.

Now let's all make it together—'G.' Let's all make a small 'g.' "

Give instructions for the construction of the lowercase "g."

"Who would like to come to the board? Let's all do one together. Good! Who would like to put the lowercase 'g' in the blanks?"

_____ ame   _____ irl   _____ ood   _____ reen   _____ o

"Listen carefully. See how well you can follow directions. On your papers see how well you can make two capital or big letter 'G's, two small 'g's, and one capital 'G' in a row. Do it. What good direction-followers you are, and what good writers you are.* Now let's write a letter telling our parents how well we can write and what we have done."

Dear Mommy and Daddy,
    I can write the letter "G g."
                      Love,
                      Susan

SUMMARY

"What have we done today? We worked out the letter 'g.' We said words that begin with the letter 'g.' Can you figure out what letter we're going to work with tomorrow? I'm going to bring in something that we drink. It comes from a cow. I bet you all know what it is."

*The number of activities would depend on the group of children and their attention span. If children get restless, it is best to stop and pull the lesson together before the letter writing takes place. Also, the emphasis in this lesson is words that begin with a hard "g" sound such as the sound "g" in "gone." If a child has a name that begins with a soft "g" sound as in "George," tell him that yes, his name begins with "g." However, "g" can stand for more than one sound. The "g's" in "George" have a sound different from the "g" in "Gary," even though both names begin with the letter "g."

LESSON PLAN II: EARLY-INTERMEDIATE-GRADE LEVEL

OBJECTIVES

Students will be able to construct these letter combinations with the proper connecting strokes, slant lines, undercurve, downcurve, and spacing: "bl," "st," "cl."

PREPARATION

1. Have on display the proper formation of combinations "bl," "cl," and "st," in the following words: blame, blue, class, clue, clear, steer, stain, stair, star.

2. Have overhead projector available.

3. Put this letter on a transparency:

> 241 Clearview Street
> Clearwater, Florida
> May 10, 1978
>
> Dear Mr. Clancey,
>
> I am answering your advertisement about a job for the summer. I would like an interview. My address is:
> 731 Thompson Street
> Clearwater, Florida.
>
> Sincerely yours,
> John Brown

INTRODUCTION

"We've been writing letters. Who remembers some of the things we said about writing letters? Good, many of you remember the main points we made about the form of the letter. Who remembers another very important statement we made? Good! The letter we write should be easy to read and the word we used was 'legible.' "

Display the transparency of the letter on the overhead projector. Tell the students that they will be concentrating on the construction of some combinations with which they seem to be having difficulty.

DEVELOPMENT

Ask students about the letter on display, and discuss whether the person writing the letter would get the job he wanted. Discuss the students' problems about letter writing, and elicit their comments on specific problems. Choose a few of these problems and practice correcting these.

"A problem we seem to have concerns making the 'bl,' 'cl,' and 'st' combinations. Can you think of a number of words that begin with these combinations so that we can practice them? It would also be fun to make some humorous sentences with the words."

Children may offer such words as:

black	blame	blew	clear	clue	stair	stove	steer
blue	bloom	clothes	claim	clean	stem	store	

These sentences may be offered:
The blue bloom blew in the breeze.
The clean clothes clung to the clothesline.
The steer walked up the stairs to the stove.

Students are asked to observe the teacher while the "bl," "cl," and "st" combinations are constructed in the words blue, bloom, blew, clean, clothes, steer, stair, and stove. Students are then told to construct the sentences, paying special attention to the combinations being practiced. After the children have finished writing the sentences, they are asked to make up their own "funny sentences" using words that begin with the "bl," "cl," and "st" combinations. The teacher tells students that they can share their sentences with the rest of the class by putting some of them on the chalkboard in their best handwriting.

SUMMARY

The main points of the lesson are pulled together. The teacher gets the children to explain what they have done and tells students that tomorrow they will practice some other combinations that seem to be giving a number of children difficulty.

SUGGESTIONS FOR THOUGHT QUESTIONS AND ACTIVITIES

1. A left-handed child in Grade 5 is writing in cursive with the hook-wrist movement. What would you do to help this child?

2. Think up some handwriting activities that will be fun for the class and list them.

3. Develop a creative lesson plan in either cursive or manuscript writing.

4. Should only manuscript writing or only cursive writing be taught? Why? Should there be a transition from manuscript to cursive? If so, how should it be made? Defend your position with research or content from the chapter.

5. You have been appointed to a special handwriting curriculum committee that is charged with the responsibility for choosing the handwriting system to be used in your school. What information would you have to gather in order to be able to make an effective contribution? Would you use a commercial system or would you develop your own? Explain.

SELECTED BIBLIOGRAPHY

Deford, Diane E. "Young Children and Their Writing," *Theory into Practice* 19 (Summer 1980): 157–162.

Foerster, Leona B. "Let's Be Realistic about Handwriting Evaluation." *Elementary English* 51 (May 1974): 741–742.

Froese, Victor. "Handwriting: Practice, Pragmatism, and Progress," in *Research in the Language Arts: Language and Schooling*, Victor Froese and Stanley Straw, eds. Baltimore: University Park Press, 1981.

Horn, Thomas, ed. *Research on Handwriting and Spelling*. Urbana, Ill.: National Council of Teachers of English, 1966.

Howell, Helen, "Write On, You Sinistrals!" *Language Arts* 55 (October 1978): 852–856.

Myers, Emma. *The Whys and Hows of Teaching Handwriting*. Columbus, Ohio: Zaner-Bloser, 1963.

Scribe: A Handbook of Classroom Ideas to Motivate the Teaching of Handwriting. Stevensville, Mich.: Educational Services, 1976.

FIFTEEN

Grammar and Word Usage

We often hear it said that the teaching of grammar is too formal and impractical. Originally grammar was not created to help with teaching nor was it supposed to help children acquire the mechanics of their native tongues. Grammar, then as now, was at the level of linguistics. It was an advanced science that was purely speculative and theoretical.[1]

Although the Western tradition of grammar emanated from the ancient Greeks, the analysis of language dates back as far as 1000 B.C. in India.[2] The science of grammar in Greek antiquity was originally confined to the analysis of poetry. Around the first century B.C., the teaching of grammar expanded to become the methodical study of the elements in language. This subject matter was similar to what we call "grammar."

Although the Greeks were not as successful in analyzing the structure of language as they were in developing Euclid's geometry, Dionysius Thrax did produce an exceptional grammar book, which was in use until the twelfth century. Its use actually extends right up to our own day, since it has influenced all subsequent grammar books. The grammar of Dionysius was an abstract formal analysis of the Greek language, broken down into its simplest elements, and then meticulously defined and classified.[3]

It wasn't until the third century A.D. that some supposedly "practical exercises" in morphology appear on school papyri—there was a writing board with the verb on the back carefully conjugated into all forms (voice, tense, person, and number) of the optative and participle. Although this activity has been determined to be at the level of the primary school, because of the type of exercise used, it was probably part of secondary-school education.[4] Even though the teaching of grammar during the Roman period was intended for the secondary school, somehow it extended downward into the primary school, almost exactly paralleling the situation that exists today.

Despite the knowledge that grammar does not help with speaking or writing (which will be discussed shortly), there is still emphasis on this topic in some schools. Perhaps this is so because of the prestige that has long been at-

---

[1]H. I. Marrou, *A History of Education in Antiquity* (New York: New American Library of Literature, 1964).

[2]Burt Liebert, *Linguistics and the New English Teacher* (New York: Macmillan, 1971).

[3]Marrou, *A History*, pp. 235–237.

[4]Ibid., p. 238.

By Charles M. Schulz

© 1958 United Feature Syndicate. Inc

tached to the term "grammar." In Roman schools the "grammaticus" had more prestige than a mere schoolmaster, even though, measured absolutely, it was not much. Another reason may stem from certain misconceptions. Those persons who believed in faculty psychology (the brain is a muscle that needs to be exercised) felt that grammar was good for mental discipline. If one believed in this theory, then one also believed that exercising the brain would bring about a transfer of learning.

Because grammar was used by the Greeks for the analysis of poetry, it was thought that teaching grammar would help children to interpret literature—which seems logical. It was also believed that knowledge of grammar would help in reading comprehension, in writing, in punctuation, in word usage, and in teaching sentence structure. Although a number of studies in the early twentieth century destroyed this theory,[5, 6] grammar continued to be taught in schools.

In the 1960s it was stated that "teachers have been shown in one experiment after another that the systematic study of traditional grammar has a negligible or, because it usually displaces some instruction and practice in composition, even a harmful effect upon the improvement of writing."[7] Yet traditional grammar is still taught in many classrooms.

Some more recent studies have shown that while traditional grammar still has no positive effect on students' compositions, the teaching of transformational grammar does seem to have some positive results for writing. Teachers are cautioned against inferring from this that the study of grammar will "improve" sentence structure. It was the emphasis on sentence combining practices, associated with grammar study, that produced beneficial results, not grammar study alone.[8]

An often-quoted example, which further lends empirical credence to research proving that traditional grammar does not help children in speaking or writing, is the case of the child who left this message for his teacher after writing for some time on the chalkboard: "Dear Teacher: I have wrote 'I have gone' one hundred times, like you said, and I have went home."

To this day confusion exists about the teaching of grammar—whether it should be taught, when it should be taught, and how it should be taught, and what should be taught. The relationship between grammar and word usage is also not very clear. There is disagreement between linguists and nonlinguists concerning traditional and "linguistic" grammar. Each side is intent on proving the wisdom of its position. Additional complications exist because of the various divisions within the field of linguistics itself—for example, psycholinguistics, descriptive or structural linguistics, and transformationalism.

After reading this chapter you should be able to answer these questions:

[5]Franklin S. Hoyt, "Studies in English Grammar," *Teachers College Record* 7 (November 1906): 1–34.

[6]L. W. Rapeer, "The Problem of Formal Grammar in Elementary Education," *Journal of Educational Psychology* 4 (March 1913): 125–137.

[7]Robert L. Ebel, ed., *Encyclopedia of Educational Research* (New York: Macmillan, 1969), pp. 451–452.

[8]J. C. Mellon, *Transformational Sentence Combining: A Method for Enhancing the Development of Syntactic Fluency in English Composition*, National Council of Teachers of English Research Report No. 10 (Champaign, Ill.: National Council of Teachers of English, 1969).

1. What is meant by the term grammar?
2. What are the differences between grammar and word usage?
3. Should elementary-school children learn the terminology of the new grammar? Explain.
4. Must students know the terminology of traditional or new grammar in order to be able to speak or write better? Explain.
5. Does the teaching of grammar help children in writing? Explain, and give reasons for your answer.
6. What are the major differences between traditional and the new grammar?
7. Should grammar or word usage be taught in school? Explain.
8. What aspects of structural grammar can be used in the elementary-school classroom? Explain.
9. What aspects of transformational grammar can teachers use in their classrooms?
10. What is the place of grammar in the primary grades?

DEFINITION AND ROLE OF GRAMMAR

Robert Pooley, a well-known grammarian, defines *grammar* as:

the study of the way a language is used. English grammar is the study of how English is used. In other words, grammar is the observation of the forms and arrangements of English words as they are employed singly and in combination to convey meaning in discourse.[9]

When a student says, "He ain't no friend of mine" (an example of poor usage), it is as grammatical as "He isn't any friend of mine" (good usage). There is no such thing as good, bad, or poor grammar. Grammar, which is merely descriptive, does not establish any standards and it is not prescriptive.

Nelson Francis, another authority on grammar, seems to have derived his definition from Pooley's. Francis defines grammar as a form of behavior, a field of study or a science, and as a branch of etiquette:

The first thing we mean by "grammar" is "the set of formal patterns in which the words of a language are arranged in order to convey larger meanings." It is not necessary that we be able to discuss these patterns self-consciously in order to be able to use them. In fact, all speakers of any language above the age of five or six know how to use its complex forms of organization with considerable skill; in this sense of the word—call it "Grammar 1"—they are thoroughly familiar with its grammar.

The second meaning of "grammar"—call it "Grammar 2"—is the branch of linguistic science which is concerned with the description, analysis, and formalization of formal language patterns . . . grammar in the first sense was in operation before anyone formulated the first rule that began the history of grammar as a study.

The third sense in which people use the word "grammar" is "linguistic etiquette." This we may call "Grammar 3." The word in this sense is often coupled with a derogatory adjective: we say that the expression "He ain't there" is bad grammar. What we mean is that such an expression is bad linguistic manners in certain circles.[10]

One of the main differences between Pooley's and Francis's definitions of grammar is in the area of "bad grammar." Where Pooley carefully avoids any reference to "bad grammar," Francis, in his linguistic etiquette definition, uses such phrases as "bad grammar" and "bad linguistic manners." Since grammar is not prescriptive, one should avoid using the phrase "bad grammar." Pooley employs the term "usage" to cover the range of choice and discrimination in grammar. In this text "usage" is the term employed when discussing how one *should* speak.

The grammar of most language is discussed in terms of syntax and morphology. *Syntax* is the patterning of words; it is "the way in which words . . . are arranged relative to each other in utterances,"[11] to convey meaning. "The function of syntax is to study the order of

[9]Robert C. Pooley, *Teaching English Grammar* (New York: Appleton-Century-Crofts, 1957), p. 104.

[10]W. Nelson Francis, "Revolution in Grammar" in *Readings in Applied English Linguistics,* 2d ed., Harold Byron Allen, ed. (New York: Appleton-Century-Crofts, 1964), p. 70.

[11]Charles F. Hockett, *A Course in Modern Linguistics* (New York: Macmillan, 1958), p. 77.

words in meaningful discourse and to attempt to explain the relationship between word order and meaning . . . the subject-verb-object pattern of the common English statement is one example."[12] "The cat scratched John" conveys a different meaning from "John scratched the cat," because the order of the words has been changed.

Morphology deals with "the construction of words and parts of words"[13]—for example: ox, oxen; he, they; drive, drove, driven; and girl, girls.

The reason for some of the controversy among educators concerning grammar study may be due to a misunderstanding of terms. Formal grammar study "is *not* instruction in usage, standard dialect, mechanics or writing conventions (such as punctuation, capitalization, etc.), courtesies in speech or writing, spelling, or handwriting."[14]

DEFINING USAGE

Confusion has existed as to the differences between grammar and usage, and the role that usage plays in language. Although individuals who say, "I ain't going no place" and "He don't know nothing" are not considered to have "poor" or "bad" grammar, they are exhibiting poor word usage.

As stated previously, grammar merely "describes" the way an individual speaks; it does not impose standards. Usage, however, "makes choices, expresses preferences, takes sides, creates standards. . . ." Usage is to grammar as etiquette is to behavior. Behavior simply is what people do; etiquette sets a stamp of approval or disapproval on actions or sets up standards to guide actions. Usage involves propriety, idioms, and word choice.

Pooley says:

there is a close relationship between grammar and usage where the propriety of use of certain word forms is governed by the history of its grammatical forms. For example, the past tense of the verb *stick* is *stuck* because of the history of the development of this verb. The irregular form can be explained by reference to historical grammar. . . . When a fifth-grade child says or writes sticked as the past tense of stick, he is following the same process which produced such current past tense forms as "helped" or "wept" from verbs which once had a change of vowels in the past tense. To correct the child at the moment of his use of "sticked" calls for a consideration of propriety—that is, usage—rather than of grammatical history.[15]

See the second half of this chapter for examples, activities, and further clarification of usage.

DEFINING LINGUISTICS

Linguistics is the science of language, and according to linguists, language is speech—the spoken form is more nearly the language than the written form. Linguists are concerned with the empirical study of children's oral language and in developing explanations for their acquisition of language. Their interest in writing is secondary and extends only insofar as writing represents speech. Linguists seek to describe, not prescribe; they tell us how we speak, not how we should speak. They are interested in analyzing sentences uttered by the speakers of the language. The sentence "Go to the store" is a well-formed one; whereas "Store the go to" is not. Linguists are concerned with the rules that speakers follow. Most speakers of a language usually cannot state the rules of their language. It is linguists who find and describe the implied "rules."

Linguistics is not concerned with helping children to acquire language nor in helping them write. It has little to do with the *teaching* of language arts skills, nor can grammar instruction help children acquire speech or writing. By about age three-and-a-half a child has acquired the adult structure of language. He or

---

[12]Pooley, *Teaching English Grammar*, pp. 104–105.

[13]Leonard Bloomfield, *Language* (New York: Holt, Rinehart and Winston, 1966), p. 207.

[14]Stanley B. Straw, "Grammar and Teaching of Writing: Analysis versus Synthesis," in *Research in the Language Arts: Language and Schooling*, Victor Froese and Stanley B. Straw, eds. (Baltimore: University Park Press, 1981), p. 148.

[15]Pooley, *Teaching English Grammar*, pp. 106–107.

she did not need "overt" or "conscious" knowledge of the rules to perform this phenomenal feat.

DEFINING TRADITIONAL GRAMMAR

Traditional grammar has most often been used in schools. It is based on Latin and Greek, leading to the description and analysis of English in terms of these languages. Traditional grammar is prescriptive, in that one must adhere to specific rules:

One such rule forbids the use of the prevalent "It is me." Another commands the speaker or writer never to use who instead of whom. Still another clarifies a point of usage thus: "But means but except when it means except." And never use a conjunction to start a sentence, nor a preposition to end a sentence with. During World War II, Winston Churchill's radio addresses were checked against possible security leaks by an official reader; when this official undertook to rearrange a sentence to conform to this mistaken rule, Churchill asserted himself as follows: "This is the kind of arrant nonsense up with which I will not put."[16]

Instruction in traditional grammar is the classification of the parts of written sentences into nouns, verbs, adjectives, adverbs, prepositions, conjunctions, pronouns, and interjections—which are called parts of speech. It is also concerned with what makes up a sentence, and with the individual's ability to differentiate between phrases and various kinds of clauses.

Here are definitions of the terms most frequently used in traditional grammar:

1. *Nouns:* the names of persons, places, or things
   a. **Proper nouns:** names of particular persons, places, and so on, and usually capitalized
   b. **Common nouns:** all other nouns not capitalized
2. *Verb:* a word that shows action or state of being
   a. **Transitive verb:** requires an object
   b. **Intransitive verb:** does not require an object; for example, the verb "to be"
3. *Adjective:* modifies a noun or pronoun
4. *Adverb:* modifies a verb, adjective, or another adverb
5. *Pronoun:* used in place of a noun

[16]Carl A. Lefevre, *Linguistics, English and the Language Arts* (Boston: Allyn and Bacon, 1970), pp. 21–22.

Diagraming and Parsing in Traditional Grammar

Parsing and diagraming sentences were means of dissecting them into various parts supposedly to help students see the relations among the parts. The sentence: "The happy girl ran swiftly" would be diagramed as:

The sentence: "An old man swiftly ate the apples," which has an object, would be diagramed as:

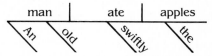

Parsing included further explanation of each word in exact terminology. The verb "ran" in the first example would be explained as: irregular, active voice, indicative mood, past tense, and so on.

Diagraming and parsing are not endorsed as activities in the elementary-school classroom. Nor are they recommended for other students unless they are especially interested in studying and learning about language. Whether or not these exercises are given in the classroom, teachers should be familiar with them, since some language arts programs do include them.

THE NEW GRAMMAR

In order to determine whether differences between old and new grammars are significant, and whether these differences warrant that the new grammar be taught, particularly in elementary schools, a clearer understanding of both grammars must be given. One reason that confusion exists between old and new grammars is because old words, such as "grammar," are being used but new meanings are being stipulated for them. A number of new "grammars" have sprung up in the past few decades, and it is likely that more will be produced. Some of these new grammars are more complete than the old, and are more difficult to use. Noam Chomsky, one of the leaders of the transformational movement, says: "the teaching of new grammar prematurely and abstractly to children incapable of really understanding it would be disastrous, even though the grammar itself might be acceptable to a linguist."[17]

Much of the ferment leading to the present changes in grammar was due to the work of such people as Jespersen and Bloomfield in the early 1900s. Jespersen tried to explain irregularities in the English language. He questioned the "idealness" of Latin or Greek and forced a reevaluation of the source of our standards of usage.[18] Bloomfield also began to describe the language as it was spoken, as it exists, rather than as it should be.[19] Such questioning and attempts at finding answers to perplexing questions relating to traditional grammar paved the way for the new grammars.

The new linguists were not interested in prescribing or in making judgments on what is or is not correct. They were only interested in describing usage. New terms were developed and descriptive grammar was born. Some believe, however, that the new linguists have not been prescriptive only because they are still in the process of determining the rules of the new grammars.

Understanding the Language of the Linguists

Although it is questionable whether children must know the terms that the linguists employ, teachers should have some familiarity with them. This is especially important since a number of English textbooks at the elementary-school level are incorporating some of the new terminology. The task of familiarizing teachers with the new linguistics is not an easy one because of the various systems in existence and the different means of classifying and codifying phonemes. Before elaborating on these points, however, some basic definitions of general terms are necessary for better understanding:

Phonology: A branch of linguistics that deals with the analysis of sound systems of language

Phoneme: Smallest unit of sound in a specific language system; a phoneme is a class of sounds.

Allophones: Variants of the same phoneme; they are phonetically similar to other members of the phoneme class to which they belong. The [p] at the beginning of pin and the [p] at the end of tip are allophones of the phoneme /p/. Brackets are typically used to indicate allophones; slanted lines are used to indicate phonemes.

Suprasegmental phonemes: Pitch, stress, and juncture or pause are significant sound units, or phonemes, because they influence meaning. The term suprasegmental refers to "the vocal effects of pitch, stress, and juncture, which accompany the linear sequence of vowels and consonants in utterances."[20]

Stress: "An accentual system in which the differences are largely in relative loudness or prominence is called a stress system, and the contrasting degrees of prominence are called stresses or stress-levels."[21] Stress can relate to differences in the prominence of various parts of a word or sentence. Some linguists identify three levels of stress, whereas others indicate four. Some linguists also use different symbols to record stress levels.

The accent or stress phoneme with which elementary-school children usually become familiar in their work with the dictionary is the primary stress /'/. They learn that stress is important in helping to convey meaning. For example, the stress or accent in the following words will help determine the meaning of the word:

re cord' (verb): to set down in writing; to make a record

[17]Noam Chomsky and Morris Halle, "Some Controversial Questions in Phonological Theory," *Journal of Linguistics* 1 (1965): 104.

[18]Otto Jespersen, *The Philosophy of Grammar* (New York: Henry Holt, 1924).

[19]Leonard Bloomfield, *Introduction to the Study of Language* (New York: Henry Holt, 1914).

[20]Harold G. Shane, *Linguistics and the Classroom Teacher* (Washington, D.C.: Association for Supervision and Curriculum Development, 1967), p. 110.

[21]Hockett, *Modern Linguistics*, p. 47.

rec'ord (noun): a recording; preservation of something in writing

re fuse' (verb): to reject

ref' use (noun): something worthless[22]

Some dictionaries indicate stress in different ways; teachers should discuss and point out these differences to students in order to avoid confusion.

Pitch: The different frequency levels in utterances. The regulation of the amount of tension on the vocal cords determines the pitch level. The more tense an individual is, the higher the pitch. Although most linguists agree that there are four identifiable degrees of pitch, there is no agreement on the symbols used to record the various pitch levels.

Pitch in combination with stress is necessary in order to convey or receive a message properly. In the following dialogue, while the second and third lines use the identical word, the two sentences do not sound the same, nor do they have similar meanings.

TERRY: What are you doing?

LAURA: Playing.

TERRY: Playing?

LAURA: Yes.

Juncture: The way in which phonemes in a language are joined together in an utterance; the way in which an utterance begins and ends. It is a vocal device for indicating grouping in a linear progression of vowels and consonants, so that divisions into words and constructions—including sentences—can be perceived.[23] Juncture, or pause, is usually divided into four types. Again there is no unanimity among linguists in the use of symbols representing various types of junctures or pauses.

Juncture helps people distinguish between such words as nitrate and night rate. These words sound different because of different transitions between successive vowels and consonant phonemes. The transition between the /t/ and the /r/ of nitrates is muddy. The /t/ of night is clearly finished; then the speaker starts afresh with the /r/ of rates.[24]

Dialect: A variation of a language sufficiently different to be considered a separate entity, but not different enough to be classed as a separate language; these differences occur in vocabulary and pronunciation and, to a limited extent, in grammatical construction.[25]

Graphemes: The written representation of phonemes

Graphemic Base: A succession of graphemes that occurs with the same phonetic value in a number of words (*at, ack, ight, et,* and so on)

Morpheme: The smallest individually meaningful elements in the utterances of a language[26]

Allomorph: A morpheme that is represented by alternate phonemes. For example, the genitive (possessive) English morpheme is represented phonemically by the symbol /z/. But because the pronunciation of this morpheme is conditioned by the preceding consonant, the same morpheme is written differently in different environments. For example, in boy's it is written /z/; in cat's it is /s/, and in fish's it is /iz/.[27]

Affixes: Prefixes added before the roots (bases), and suffixes added to the end of roots (bases)

Morphophonemic system: The ways in which morphemes of a given language are variously represented by phonemic shapes can be regarded as a kind of code.[28]

Syntax: The patterning of words; it is the way in which words are arranged relative to each other in utterances to convey meaning. (In transformational grammar, syntax is divided into two parts: phrase structure rules, which generate deep structures, and transformational rules, which relate deep structures to surface structures. See "Transformational Grammar" later in this chapter.)

---

[22]*Webster's New Twentieth Century Dictionary Unabridged,* 2d ed. (Cleveland, Ohio: World Publishing, 1970), pp. 1508, 1519–1520.

[23]Shane, *Linguistics,* p. 107.

[24]Hockett, *Modern Linguistics,* pp. 54–55.

[25]Pose Lamb, *Linguistics in Proper Perspective* (Columbus. Ohio: Merrill, 1967), p. 138.

[26]Hockett, *Modern Linguistics,* p. 123.

[27]Liebert, *Linguistics,* p. 104.

[28]Hockett, *Modern Linguistics,* p. 135.

The English Phonemic System

The new grammar of English utterances is more complete and complex than the old. The old grammar surprisingly covered only a portion of our English utterances. Linguists have not agreed on the number of phonemes in American-English, nor on the way to represent some of the phonemes, and so a great deal of confusion exists.

People speak differently in different regions of the United States. As a result, linguists record systems of language that are unique to their specific areas. Leonard Bloomfield's system is based on the standard English that prevails in Chicago, and some of the phonemes he records differ from those of other linguists. Some linguists treat suprasegmental features—such as pitch, stress, and juncture—as phonemes; others do not.

Difficulties are further compounded by inconsistencies in the representational symbols used for various phonemes. The same phoneme is written /ʃ/ in I.P.A. (International Phonetic Alphabet), /š/ by Charles Hockett, /ʃh/ in i.t.a. (initial teaching alphabet), /sh/ by Paul Roberts, and /sh/ in some dictionaries.[29]

Some linguists rationalize these differences by saying that consensus is often hard to come by. This may well be, but laypersons should not be expected to make comparisons among experts who differ in something as fundamental as an alphabet. Unlike the case in most other highly technical fields, the lay public in its daily work is intimately concerned with these representational symbols. The average person is in continuous contact with the primary reference work that uses these symbols—the dictionary. If students are taught one system in school, and then find another system in the dictionary or in other sources, their confusion will certainly be justified.

It would appear that linguists have a responsibility to their students, as well as to the public, to agree on a common or standard set of representational symbols from which they may take exception in publications of more limited distribution, such as scholarly journals.

[29]Liebert, *Linguistics*, p. 94.

This is, however, an exceedingly difficult task due to the various dialects that exist in American-English.

English Morphemes

The phonemes of a language have no meaning unless they are combined in certain sequences to form morphemes. Descriptive linguists define morphemes as the smallest element that has meaning. (Some transformationalists, such as Noam Chomsky, disagree with this definition.) Morphemes include word bases, grammatical inflections, and derivational prefixes and suffixes. Morphemes are categorized into free forms and bound forms—"cat" is a free form because it can pattern independently; that is, it can occur in many environments without having any attachments. When /s/, a bound form, is added to "cat" to form "cats," a new morpheme is formed that converys the meaning of more than one cat. Bound morphemes cannot stand independently. They are usually the grammatical inflections and derivational affixes of nouns, verbs, adjectives, and adverbs. This same /s/ bound form can be used to form other meanings—"cat's," meaning possession, and "cats' " showing plural possessive. The single phoneme /s/ in these examples is three different morphemes.

Inflectional affixes are the suffixes that give words the characteristics of tense, number, and gender. The past tense of the verb play is played; the past tense of want is wanted. He, she, it are examples of gender. Number refers to whether something is singular or plural—boat, boats.

Derivational affixes determine in what class a word will be, whether it will be a noun, verb, adjective, or adverb. For example: (base) prince + (affix) ly becomes (adjective) princely.

In order to discern the full meaning of morphemes, they must be seen in context. Although we may know the lexical definitions of the word "saw," unless we hear the word in context we will not be able to determine its meaning. As was already discussed, pitch, stress, and juncture are called phonemes by some linguists because they affect the sound unit and help to give a word its precise meaning. There are ways of expressing words that convey a meaning different from the lexical meaning. The person who says, "Are you kidding!" is definitely not asking a question.

Word Classes

Some of the terms used in traditional grammar are also used in new grammar, but they are presented differently and some new meanings have been stipulated. Nouns, verbs, adjectives, and adverbs are the major parts of speech according to structural linguists, and are categorized as word classes. James Sledd, a structural linguist, defines a noun as:

any word belonging to an inflectional series which is built like "man," "man's," "men," "men's," or "boy," "boy's," "boys," "boys'," on either or both of the contrasts between singular and plural numbers and between common and possessive or genitive cases, and on no other contrasts.[30]

Other structural linguists stipulate numbers to designate nouns, verbs, and so on. Fries assigns 1, 2, 3, and 4 to these terms.[31] Class 1 words fit into the blanks in this pattern: *The _____ carried _____ .* Class 2 words fit into these blanks: *The horse _____ the man;* or into this blank: *The horse _____ brown.* Class 3 words fit into these: *The horse carried the _____ man.* Class 3 words pattern with Class 1 words. Class 4 words are more movable. They fit this blank: *The horse _____ carried the man.* But they may also be moved to other positions; that is, the pattern could be: *The horse easily carried the man;* or *the horse carried the man easily.* Class 4 words pattern with Class 2 words. (Although Fries' complex system, using numbers and other designations to analyze sentences, is not widely followed, many of his concepts are used in other forms.)

[30]James Sledd. *A Short Introduction to English Grammar* (Chicago: Scott, Foresman, 1959), p. 70.
[31]Charles C. Fries, *The Structure of English: An Introduction to the Standard of English Sentences* (New York: Harcourt Brace, 1952).

Function or Structure Words

Function (structure) words, according to structural linguists, include all those words in a sentence that are not classified as major parts of speech. They are used to show the structural or functional relationships of the major parts of speech. They also do not change in form, as form or word classes do. Here is a list of function words that are important for indicating structural meaning; they are used to show the structural relationship of the major parts of speech in a sentence.

Noun markers (noun determiners): Include definite and indefinite articles, possessives, demonstratives, and cardinal numbers. They usually begin a noun group (a noun and its modifiers), serving as a cue that the following word is a noun or functions as a noun. Examples: Articles (a, an, the) are always noun markers: *The* boy ran. Possessives: my, our, your, his, her, their. *My* dress is red. Demonstratives: this, that, these, those. *This* dress is pretty. Cardinal numbers or quantitative terms: one, two, three, and so on; some, many, each, and so on. *One* girl is here.

Verb markers (auxiliaries): Signal that a verb will soon follow. Examples: am, is, has, have, did, will, and so on. He *will* arrive shortly.

Negatives: Indicate that a structural unit is not positive. Examples: not, never, no, and so on. She is *not* here.

Question markers: Usually placed at beginning of sentences to indicate that the sentence is a question. Examples: who, where, what, why, how, whom, and so on. *Who* are you?

Prepositions (phrase markers): Precede noun or noun units combining with them to make phrases that usually act as modifiers. Examples: about, amid, above, across, against, before, into, behind, and so on. They ran *into* the woods.

Qualifers (intensifiers): Precede and modify adjectives and adverbs. Examples: very, rather, quite, considerably, and so on. He is a *very* old man.

Subordinators (clause markers): Usually begin dependent clauses. Examples: subordinating conjunctions (although, before, until, if, when, and so on) and relative pronouns (who, whom, whomever, whichever, and so on). I will not leave *until* you go.

Coordinators (conjunctions): Used to join words having the same or parallel function as in compound subjects. They are also used to produce compound predicates, objects, and compound sentences. Examples: and, but, nor, and so on. The boys *and* girls were happy. We will go with you, *but* we will not enjoy it.

Sentences and Sentence Patterns In order to determine the meaning of sentences, according to structural linguists, it is necessary to know the syntax (the position of words in the sentences) and the morphology (the form of words with affixes and inflectional endings). Sentence pattern or word order would determine whether the word class is a noun, verb, adverb, or adjective. In the sentence "*Vons eat,*" although *Vons* is a nonsense word we know that it is a noun, because it occupies a particular place in a specific sentence frame. Here are five sentence patterns that seem to occur the most frequently in the English language:

1. Pattern: *Noun*   *Verb (intransitive)*
           Birds   fly.

2. Pattern: *Noun*   *Verb (transitive)*   *Noun (direct object)*
           Boys   eat   cake.

3. Pattern: *Noun*   *Verb (transitive)*   *Noun (indirect object)*   *Noun (direct object)*
           John   gave   Jane   the candy.

4. Pattern: *Noun*   *Verb (linking)*   *Noun*
           John   is   a boy.

5. Pattern: *Noun*   *Verb (linking)*   *Adjective*
           Jane   is   pretty.

These common sentence patterns are all declarative, and are given in the active voice.

Special Notes
1. An intransitive verb cannot take an object, and a sentence containing an intransitive verb does not require an object to complete its meaning.
2. A transitive verb can take an object; that is, it can carry over an action from a subject to an object.
3. Verbs such as *be, become, smell, sound, taste, feel, look, seem,* and *appear* are called linking verbs because they often link a subject with a word that in effect renames or describes the subject.

Transformational Grammar

Transformational grammarians build on the work of the structuralists, but they go further into the area of generating sentences. Transformational grammar is concerned more with syntax than the structuralists are. It has formal rules for combining morphemes (the smallest word unit) into simple phrases and for combining phrases into sentences. Noam Chomsky, whose name has become almost synonymous with transformational or generative grammar, in 1957 divided his grammar into three parts:

1. "Phrase structure," the most elemental unit of our language
2. "Transformational structure," which includes "obligatory transformations" and "optional transformations"
3. Morphophonemics[32]

For example, agreement between subject and verb is obligatory, whereas the insertion of adjectives or negatives is optional.

When the obligatory transformations are applied to the phrases in Part 1, and if the appropriate word-form rules of Part 3 are applied, the result would be a grammatical English sentence. If only obligatory transformations are supplied, the sentence will be a kernel sentence. All other English sentences are generated from kernel sentences by optional transformations. For example, the sentence: "The girl eats" is a kernel sentence. It has the attributes of being a simple, active, declarative sen-

---

[32]Noam Chomsky, *Syntactic Structures* (The Hague, Netherlands: Mouton, 1957).

tence with no adjectives, adverbs, negatives, and so on. If we were to change the sentence to the following variations, they would all be transforms of the kernel:

1. **The pretty girl is hungrily eating the red apple.**
2. **Is the happy girl eating that big apple?**
3. **The sad girl is not eating the big red apple.**
4. **The big apple is not being eaten by the pretty girl.**

Kernel sentences consist of noun phrases and verb phrases. They are declarative, active, and affirmative. Transforming consists of sets of rules. Here are some symbols that will be used in diagraming and analysis:

> S: stands for *sentence*
> NP: stands for *noun phrase*
> VP: stands for *verb phrase*
> →: stands for "is made from" or "consists of"
> S→NP + VP

In order to generate a sentence we must choose words from the class of nouns and verbs; for example, "Jane" and "eats." "Girl eating" is the kernel sentence generated, and it would look like this when diagramed:

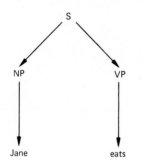

Rigorous rules are presented for combining morphemes into simple phrases. For example: a noun phrase is NP→Determiner (Det.) + Noun. This rule indicates that a noun phrase may be composed of a determiner (article, demonstrative, or possessive) and a noun (common noun, proper noun, collective noun, concrete or abstract, or a pronoun). A verb phrase is

VP→Auxiliary (Aux.) + Verb Expression. Strict rules determine what variety of combinations a verb phrase may contain.

Here is an example of a tree diagram of the sentence "The students will eat the food," using transformational rules:

S→NP + VP

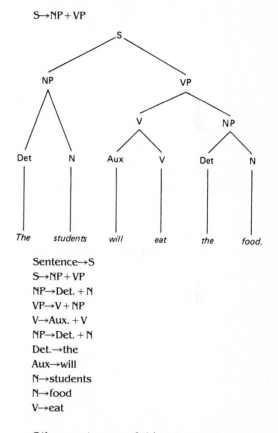

Sentence→S
S→NP + VP
NP→Det. + N
VP→V + NP
V→Aux. + V
NP→Det. + N
Det.→the
Aux→will
N→students
N→food
V→eat

Other sentences of this type can be generated by merely inserting words in each category as required by the rules.

In summary, according to Chomsky the phrase structure rules operate on the vocabulary to produce underlying strings. The transformational rules are the ones that produce the sentence (surface structure). These rules convert one string into another. The underlying phrase marker contains the deep structure from which meaning is derived. The sentences that are produced are the surface structure. In general, apart from the simplest examples, the surface structures of sentences are very different from their deep structures. Chomsky says:

The grammar of English will generate, for each sentence, a deep structure, and will contain rules showing how this deep structure is related to surface structure. The rules expressing the relation of deep and surface structures are called "grammatical transformations." Hence, the term "transformation-generative grammar." In addition to rules defining deep structures, surface structures and the relation between them, the grammar of English contains further rules that relate these "syntactic objects" (namely, paired deep and surface structures) to phonetic representations of meanings on the other. A person who has acquired knowledge of English has internalized these rules and makes use of them when he understands or produces [sentences] . . .[33]

Chomsky also states that the study of grammar is the study of linguistic competence. When one talks of "competence" in grammar, the reference is to the individual's knowledge of grammar, which is considered to be innate (unconscious knowledge). Performance, or the actual observed use of language, involves such factors as memory restriction and extralinguistic beliefs concerning the speaker and the situation.

Special Note

There is still much controversy among linguists concerning transformational grammar and because of this the terms "deep structure" and "surface structure" keep changing.

Comparison of Traditional Grammar with New Grammar

Table 15.1 presents a summary of the differences between traditional and linguistic approaches in grammar.

A linguistic approach is more helpful to teachers and students than traditional grammar because it is based on the English language and it only describes rather than prescribes. However, the emphasis on linguistics in class-

[33]Noam Chomsky, *Language and Mind* (New York: Harcourt Brace Jovanovich, 1972), p. 106.

TABLE 15.1

Traditional	Linguistic
Based on reason, authority, philosophy	Based on careful observation of language data
Concerned with written language, especially great works of literature	Concerned with all phases of language: spoken, written, recorded in any form. Often emphasis on spoken language.
Until recently, considered the language of the vernacular to be inferior. Especially disparaged English because it had few inflections.	Considers the language of all communities of equal value
Attempts to "fix" language into one, unchanging form.	Views language as a constantly changing phenomenon
Has as its purpose the eradication of errors in usage (prescriptive approach)	Investigates language as it actually is used (descriptive approach)
Syntax based on Latin-Greek inflectional system.	Syntax based on English word-order system
Uses form, function, and meaning indiscriminately in defining terminology	Separates form, function, and meaning into different systems; tends to favor form and function over meaning.

Source: Burt Liebert, *Linguistics and the New English Teacher* (New York: Macmillan, 1971), p. 37.

rooms has not extinguished the confusion that exists concerning teaching grammar in school. Although linguistic texts may use different terminology and present their material in different ways, the teacher's emphasis tends toward the prescriptive. Furthermore, the new grammar is highly structured and requires learning parts of speech, so that what started out as merely describing language, with no emphasis on what should or should not be taught (linguistics), has entered the classrooms as a series of prescriptions for teaching via the new grammar.

For example, in a number of linguistic texts, this description would be given for a noun:

A noun is a word like apple, beauty, or desk. That is, it is a word that patterns as apple, beauty, or desk. It is a word that occurs in positions like those in which apple, beauty, and desk occur, such as:

I saw the *apple*. The *apple* tastes good.
I saw the *beauty*. The *desk* is too low.

Traditional grammar would define a noun as:

A noun is a word that names a person, animal, place, thing, or group. Examples of nouns are italicized below.

The *girl* rode the *pony* in the *corral*.

Since researchers have shown that the teaching of grammar does not help in the various language arts areas, how can one, just by changing the terminology and enumerating examples of nouns rather than classes of nouns, justify the teaching of grammar? Linguists have stated that their field is purely descriptive, but it is difficult to reconcile this claim with the many linguistic texts intended for teaching parts of speech. Little evidence exists to support the value of grammar based on linguistics.

Should grammar be taught in the elementary school and, if so, which grammar? Will the new grammars help children in speaking, reading, and writing better than the old grammar? These questions persist into the latter part of the eighties with no definitive answers in sight. Even though studies suggest that formal grammar study does not help students write better, there are those who are loath to abolish grammar instruction. If formal grammar instruction is undertaken, authorities recommend that it not begin until the late elementary grades, that is, about eighth grade.[34] Also, the grammar study should be integrated with writing rather than taught as an end in itself.

THE TEACHER AND WORD USAGE

Young children are self-centered and, according to Piaget, it is not until children must become social that their language becomes more logical and less egocentric. Children coming to school have just emerged from this stage. Language is used in order to communicate, and the more closely the language of children resembles the speech norms of those around them, the more effective will they be in communicating. Similarly, the more opportunity children have to communicate, the more skillful will they become in the use of language.

Since usage is concerned with the way people speak, children can be made to understand that there would be no communication if people involved in listening and speaking did not use common word sounds and meanings.

The emphasis in school should be on using standard English. The range of standard English is broad and includes formal, informal, and colloquial usage. Which type is used depends on the particular situation or circumstance. Formal speech occurs in writing scholarly articles or planned lectures; informal usage is the spoken language of the elementary school. It was Charles Fries, a well-known linguist, who recommended that teachers concentrate on using standard informal usage rather than literary language in teaching children.[35]

When children come to school they speak in a particular way. Children's speech is intimately tied up with their "selves" and their feelings about themselves. Some children come from homes using good speech patterns; others use illiterate speech. Some children speak more immaturely than others. For example, young children tend to overgeneralize and usually regularize irregular verbs. The past tense of "to go" becomes "goed" rather than "went." By the time children come to school, they have often heard the correct past tense of "to go" and it has become a normal part of their speech. If not, the teacher should correct the children, but in such a way that it does not damage their self-concept or deter them from speaking. By accepting what the children have said, by reinforcing their oral statements, and by responding with the correct form of the

[34]Shirley Haley-James, ed. *Perspectives on Writing in Grades 1–8* (Urbana, Ill.: National Council of Teachers of English, 1981).

[35]Charles Carpenter Fries, *American English Grammar* (New York: Appleton-Century-Crofts, 1940), pp. 289–290.

word, the teacher can help the children. If a child says, "I goed to the movies yesterday," the teacher's response might be, "Oh, you *went* to the movies yesterday. Good! Tell me about what you saw." The correct form is emphasized, yet the child's statement is accepted and further conversation is stimulated.

Grammar study is not needed to develop good usage. The teacher does not have to require pupils, orally or in written expression, to learn the principal parts of the verb "to go" in order to speak correctly. Pooley claims that drilling on correct usage of irregular verbs actually results in children's "cheerfully continuing to maltreat these verbs in speech and writing."[36] Since children speak in a specific way, they must be weaned from faulty habits and helped to form others through correction and practice.

Before behavior can be modified so that a habit is changed, students must identify the problem and learn to think about what they are saying. This can be difficult, because when we speak we are concerned with *what* we are attempting to say, rather than the form in which we say it.[37] If the teacher calls attention to the word that needs to be changed, without embarrassing the student, and provides the proper form of usage, the odds in favor of success will increase.

The teacher must be careful to make students feel free to express themselves and not immediately set restrictions for them. Since language is oral, living, and changing, individual differences exist, and there is no arbitrary "good" or "bad." The question is whether the usage is appropriate and based on the situation. If children are constantly reprimanded each time they speak, they soon will speak less.

The teacher should avoid correcting children each time they do not speak in complete sentences. Teachers have been influenced by the definition of a sentence as expressing a complete thought. So when children do not express themselves in a sentence, it is assumed

that they are not expressing a complete thought. Ideas can be well expressed, however, by one or two words or phrases.

Teachers must also be aware that they are models for students, who will often imitate not only a teacher's speech patterns but his or her mannerisms and voice tones as well.

Instruction in Word Usage

Although studies have shown that knowledge of grammar does not help in writing or speaking, a great deal of time is spent on syntax and parts of speech in the classroom. Students are given sentences to dissect—stating which is the noun, verb, adjective, and so on—and grammar is taught as an end in itself. This is not useful. Time is best spent in school on speaking and writing English. The parts of speech may be introduced incidentally when children are working with sentences or sentence patterns.

The main emphasis in the elementary-school grammar program should be on word usage, building and manipulating sentences, and writing. Since studies have shown that word usage helps in writing, the important questions are: What word usage should be taught, and who sets the standards for what should be taught?

Good English is that form of speech which is appropriate to the purpose of the speaker, true to the language as it is, and comfortable to speaker and listener. It is the product of custom, neither cramped by rule nor freed from all restraint; it is never fixed, but changes with the organic life of the language.[38]

This definition of standards is broad, but Pooley's 1960 "particulars," ranging from an elementary level to a more complex one not ordered on any grade-level hierarchy, are excellent and still valid. He claims that some usage

---

[36]Pooley, *Teaching English Grammar*, p. 107.
[37]A. F. Watts, *The Language and Mental Development of Children* (London: George G. Harrap, 1944), p. 65.

[38]Robert C. Pooley, *Grammar and Usage in Textbooks on English*, Bureau of Educational Research Bulletin No. 14 (Madison, Wisc.: University of Wisconsin, 1933), p. 155.

problems are rather easily overcome, whereas others persist into adult life:[39]

1. Elimination of all baby talk and "cute" expressions

2. Correct uses in speech and writing of *I, me, he, him, she, her, they, them* (exception *it's me*)

3. Correct uses of *is, are, was, were* with respect to number and tense

4. Correct past tenses of common irregular verbs, such as *saw, gave, took, brought, ought, stuck*

5. Correct use of past participles of the same verbs and similar verbs after auxiliaries

6. Elimination of the double negative: We don't have *no* apples, and so on

7. Elimination of analogical forms: *ain't, hisn, hern, ourn, theirselves,* and so on

8. Correct use of possessive pronouns: *my, mine, his, hers, theirs, ours*

9. Mastery of the distinction between *its,* possessive pronoun, and *it's, it is*

10. Placement of *have* or its phonetic reduction to *v* between *I* and a past participle

11. Elimination of *them* as a demonstrative pronoun

12. Elimination of *this here* and *that there*

13. Mastery of use of *a* and *an* as articles

14. Correct use of personal pronouns in compound constructions: as subject (Mary and I), as object (Mary and me), as object of preposition (to Mary and me)

15. The use of *we* before an appositional noun when subject; *us* when object

16. Correct number agreement with the phrases *there is, there are, there was, there were*

17. Elimination of *he don't, she don't, it don't*

18. Elimination of *learn* for *teach, leave* for *let*

19. Elimination of pleonastic [redundant] subjects: *my brother he; my mother she; that fellow he*

20. Proper agreement in number with antecedent pronouns *one* and *anyone, everyone, each, no one.* With *everybody* and *none* some tolerance of number seems acceptable now.

21. The use of *who* and *whom* as reference to persons. (But note, *Who did he give it to?* is tolerated in all but very formal situations. In the latter, *To whom did he give it?* is preferable.)

[39]Robert C. Pooley, "Dare Schools Set a Standard in English Usage?" *English Journal* 49 (March 1960): 179–180.

22. Accurate use of *said* in reporting the words of a speaker in the past

23. Correction of *lay down* to *lie down*

24. The distinction between *good* as adjective and *well* as adverb: He spoke *well.*

25. Elimination of *can't hardly, all the farther* (for *as far as*), and *Where is he (she, it) at?*

Pooley claimed that "this list of twenty-five kinds of corrections to make constitutes a very specific standard of current English usage for today and the next few years." He conceded that "some elements in it may require modification within ten years; some possibly earlier." Conspicuous by their absence are these items that were on usage lists years ago and that survive in the less enlightened textbooks:

1. Any distinction between *shall* and *will*
2. Any reference to the split infinitive
3. Elimination of *like* as a conjunction
4. Objection of the phrase "different than"
5. Objection of "He is one of those boys who *is*"
6. Objection of "The reason . . . is because . . ."
7. Objection to *myself* as a polite substitute for *me* as in "I understand you will meet Mrs. Jones and myself at the station."
8. Insistence on the possessive case standing before a gerund

According to Pooley, "These items and many others like them will still remain cautionary matters left to the teacher's discretion. In evaluating the writing of superior students, teachers could call these distinctions to their attention and point out the value of observing them. But this is a very different matter from setting a basic usage standard to be maintained. It is fair to say the items listed in the basic table lie outside the tolerable limits of acceptable, current, informal usage; those omitted from the base table are tolerated at least, and in some instances are in very general use."

Teachers should analyze the speech patterns of children in their classes to determine which speech terms are the most frequently misused. These would then be eliminated by a carefully worked out plan. For example, if children are continually using certain terms incorrectly, a tape recording of their speech could be made. Before it is played back, the teacher can call attention to the term that is being used incorrectly. Since children are habituated to speaking the way they do, they must first identify a bad habit before they can change it. They must also want to change it, and they must get help in doing so.

One motivating technique can be a number of short oral skits in which the teacher incorporates a number of items with which children need help. The skits can be tape-recorded so that the students are reinforced by hearing themselves using correctly stated terms or expressions.

A technique used in the fifth and sixth grades requires a tape recording of a person going for a job interview. The interviewee exhibits incorrect speech usage and colloquialisms. After discussing why this person would have difficulty in getting the job, students can be asked to give some helpful suggestions to him or her for the next interview.

The teacher can also ask children to listen to each other's speech and help plan some word usage lessons based on what they hear.

In order to help children become more sensitive to their language, intermediate-grade students could discuss the importance of speaking well and the role of the linguist. Students can then be told that they are going to be classroom linguists, who describe how someone speaks. The students tape children's speech during many classroom activities, as well as during lunch, free play, and physical education. (All children who are being taped should know about it and give permission for the taping.)

When the tapes are played back, students should be asked whether children use the same kind of English in all activities. They should be encouraged to describe differences that exist in speech in the various activities recorded.

Word Usage Activities: An Emphasis on Diagnosis and Correction

The activities that follow emphasize word usage and the way words are used in sentences rather than diagraming or parsing. Although grade levels are designated, they are not determined by hard and set rules; that is, the abilities and readiness of students will determine whether the concepts should be introduced at a lower- or higher-grade level. Also, the teacher should take into account the individual differences of his or her students; that is, the teacher should only have students work on the word usage problems that they have rather than on those that others have. In addition, teachers should incorporate the word usage lessons into the writing that the children are doing.

Weakness Noted In Pupils' Oral and Written Language	Suggestions for Functional Practice
I. Nouns	
Approximately Grades 3 and 4	
1. Using sentences that are weak and lacking in variety because of careless choice of nouns	Write a sentence on the chalkboard such as "The tiny boat sank." Cover the noun to show how important it is. Find nouns in other sentences. List the nouns in an interesting picture.
	Copy sentences from pupils' work omitting the nouns, such as "_____ grow in south Jersey." Have pupils suggest nouns to fill in the blank (trees, cranberries, vegetables, and so on). Show how the nouns change the meaning of the sentence.
	Suggest nouns that fit a sentence better than other nouns, such as, "A terrified man ran away." "Man" might be changed to "thief," "tramp," and so on. Apply this procedure to pupils' own written work.
	Students may also choose the best noun when several are given: "With a (yell, shriek, cry) of (fear, dismay, terror), the mountain climber fell into the (hole, pit, opening)."
2. Failure to capitalize proper nouns	Change improper nouns to proper nouns to show how meaning can be made more definite: "We consulted a lawyer," or "We consulted Dr. Brown."
	Stress capitalizing of

Weakness Noted In Pupils' Oral and Written Language	Suggestions for Functional Practice	Weakness Noted In Pupils' Oral and Written Language	Suggestions for Functional Practice
	proper nouns. Check own work to make sure all proper nouns have capital letters. Pupils may keep a cumulative list for proofreading and correcting their own mistakes. Such a checklist might include the question, "Are all the proper nouns capitalized?"	**II. Verbs**	
		Grades 3—6	
		1. Failure to recognize the importance of verbs in determining the meaning of the sentence	Show a picture to the class. Write sentences on the chalkboard that describe the picture with blanks for the verbs. Pupils suggest words to fill the blanks and discuss which of these words (verbs) communicate most. Read the sentences with the verbs, then without them, to show how the verb gives life to the sentence.
3. Mistakes in forming plural nouns	As particular mistakes are noticed, the singular and plural forms of the noun should be discussed and rules formulated when possible. For example, to form "stories," change the "y" to "i" and add "es."	Lack of discrimination in choice of verbs	
		Repetition due to meager vocabulary	
	The dictionary can be used to find the spelling of irregular plural forms. Work should be done in spelling class on these difficulties.		Pupils write original sentences about other pictures and decide which words are verbs.
4. Errors in punctuating possessives	Keep a record of errors corrected and discussed to make sure all types of mistakes have been covered: "Jack's boat," "the boys' coats," "the policemen's permission," "James's book".		Pupils can dramatize verbs. Other pupils suggest words that describe the action dramatized. For example, "John tiptoed (or stamped or crept) across the room."
Grades 5 and 6 (Continue with weaknesses listed for Grades 3 and 4)			Appropriate changes of the verb may be suggested to alter the meaning of the sentence. "A man walked down the street," for example, may become "A man shuffled," "A man strolled," "A man hobbled."
5. Omitting commas when nouns are used as nonrestrictive appositives. For example, "Mr. Jones, our neighbor, is away."	Have pupils read sentences orally to show by pauses where commas are needed.		Sentences can be given with a choice of three verbs. Pupils select the verb that fits best. For example, "He (ate, swallowed, devoured) it hungrily." "The crew (planned, plotted, considered) a meeting."
	Use appositives to clarify the meaning of sentences. For example, "Will you invite your best friend to come?" "Will you invite your best friend, Tom Jones, to come?"		Discuss use of effective verbs in sentences pupils have written in letters, newspapers, and so on.
	Use appositives to combine short, choppy sentences into smoother ones. "Mr. Jones had an accident. He is our milkman." "Mr. Jones, our milkman, had an accident."	**Grades 5 and 6 (Continue with weaknesses listed for Grades 3—6)**	
		2. Confusing use of past tense and past par-	Build up a chart showing the principal parts of

Weakness Noted In Pupils' Oral and Written Language	Suggestions for Functional Practice
ticiple. For example, "He seen it." "We have wrote our story." "The vase was broke." "Has the boat sank?" "The birds have went away for the winter."	troublesome irregular verbs. Add to the chart as other verbs give difficulty.

Verb Past | Past
tense | participle
(with no | (with
helper) | helper)

Have pupils read written work (original stories, poems, and so on) as the rest of the class listens for and lists the effective verbs, the past tenses, and past participles used.

3. Failure to make verbs agree with their subjects in number. For example, "You was there, wasn't you?" "Never before has Don and Jim come to the meeting." "He don't care any more." "Each of the men have plenty of money." "I believe everyone of you know the lesson."

Pupils must learn the singular and plural forms of verbs and nouns, and use of a singular verb with a singular subject and a plural verb with a plural subject. The only exception is that "you" takes a plural verb.

Change the noun in a sentence from singular to plural and vice-versa, and have pupils change the verb to fit. Discuss meaning of contractions when they are involved.

4. Mixing tenses in sentences and paragraphs. For example, "The children go to assembly when the bell rang."

Introduce the three tenses by showing an action picture and having pupils tell what happened before, what is going on now in the picture, what is going to happen afterward.

Together check paragraphs pupils have written to find unnecessary changes of tense. Proofreading of their own work helps make pupils conscious of this weakness.

III. Adjectives

Grades 3–5

1. Using weak, ineffective adjectives to describe nouns

Need for vocabulary enrichment

Show pictures of people in different moods. Suggest adjectives to describe each one.

What words would you use to describe your-

self (or some friend of yours) so that a stranger would be able to recognize you when meeting for the first time?

Write a sentence on the blackboard without adjectives. For example, "The dog sprang at the boy." Add adjectives to make the sentence more vivid.

Change adjectives in your own sentences. Substitute "ancient," "antique," "decrepit," "overripe" for "old."

2. Using the wrong article. For example, "A apple."

Find examples in which "a" and "an" are used. Show that "an" always comes before vowel sounds.

3. Failure to make an adjective agree with its noun in number. For example, "Those kind of books are heavy."

Show that "this" and "that" are singular, and "these" and "those" are plural. Have pupils find and correct their own mistakes. Watch for this error in oral expression.

4. Confusing adjectives used for comparison. For examples, "This is the largest ball." (speaking of two balls)

Show that an adjective has two forms when used to compare things. "Henry is smaller than Tom." "He is the smaller of the two boys." "The white kitten is the smallest of the three (more than two) kittens."

Begin to build an adjective chart. Add to it as mistakes are found and corrected. For example, small, young (positive); two things—smaller, younger (comparative); more than two things—smallest, youngest (superlative)

Grades 5 and 6 (Continue with weaknesses listed for Grades 3–5)

5. Using too many adjectives

Compositions lacking in smoothness due to short, choppy sentences

Omit adjectives that are not needed.

Shift adjectives to improve smoothness. For example, "Jeanette is a

Weakness Noted In Pupils' Oral and Written Language	Suggestions for Functional Practice
	worker. She is intelligent and industrious." "Jeanette is an intelligent, industrious worker."

IV. Adverbs

Grades 5 and 6

1. Using weak, ineffective adverbs

Need for vocabulary enrichment

Dramatize adverbs. For example, "Walking across the room (slowly, softly, swiftly, and so on)."

Pupils tell how the actor walked.

Using a sentence, such as "Jennie spoke to Mary," show how adverbs can change the meaning. Insert such adverbs as mischievously, crossly, softly, timidly.

Improve pupils' own sentences by adding and changing adverbs.

2. Using an adjective instead of an adverb. For example, "This pen writes good." "I am real glad to see you." "Walk as slow as you can."

3. Placing adverbs incorrectly. For example, "The poor boy had only one pair of shoes."

4. Using unnecessary adverbs. For example, "These here hens lay very well." "He is not anywhere nearly as tall as I am." "Frank always talks too loudly every time."

Study which words (nouns or verbs) each adverb modifies. Stress the fact that adverbs modify verbs and adjectives and other adverbs.

Placing an adverb correctly involves a knowledge of what verb the adverb modifies.

Discuss these difficulties as they arise, and have pupils cross out unnecessary adverbs.

5. Using double negatives. For example, "He hadn't done no work." "They don't never come on time."

Encourage ways of getting rid of double negatives to express the meaning desired. For example, "He hadn't done any work." "He had done no work." "They don't ever come on time." "They never come on time."

6. Using the wrong degree of adverbs. For example, "John can run fastest" (speaking of two boys). "Which is least im-

Show that adverbs are used in the comparative degree (two), and in the superlative degree (more than two). Find ex-

---

portant, eating or sleeping?"

amples in reading material and written work.

V. Pronouns

Grades 5 and 6

1. Clumsiness of expression and repetition (which can be corrected by using pronouns in place of nouns)

Failure to use "I" last in speaking of several people. For example, "I and Tom and Fred went."

2. Inserting useless pronouns. For example, "Allen he saw the plan."

Using sentences from pupils' work, illustrate the use of pronouns. For example, "Kathy picked up Kathy's pencil from Kathy's desk."

Change to "Kathy picked up her pencil from her desk."

Read sentences without the pronouns to see which ones are needed.

VI. Conjunctions and prepositions

Grades 5 and 6

1. Short, choppy sentences keep the composition from reading smoothly.

Use conjunctions to join two sentences.

Dramatize two actions and have the class tell what happened. For example,

"Barbara wrote on the board." "Tom erased the board." Change to "Barbara wrote on the board and Tom erased it."

Use conjunctions to join the subjects of two sentences. Have two people dramatize the same action. "Tom and Mary erased the board."

Use conjunctions to join two predicates. Have one pupil dramatize two actions. "Tom slipped and fell."

Find conjunctions in reading material or in pupils' own writing. List them:

and	or
but	so
for	yet
etc.	

2. Using incorrect prepositions. Confusing use of "in," "into," and "among."

Write sentences to show the use of prepositions in determining the meaning of a sentence. For example, "The book

Weakness Noted In Pupils' Oral and Written Language	Suggestions for Functional Practice
	is on the table." "The book is under the table." "The book is beside the table." "The book is near the table." Dramatize actions and general sentences like these: "Jim ran around the chair." "Jim ran by the chair." "Sam jumped on the rug." "Sam jumped over the rug." Write sentences with the prepositions omitted; have the class supply the prepositions (into, from, out of, near, up, down, across). For example, "Our cat came _____ the barn." "The boat is going _____ the river." Use "in" when something is already there. For example, "The coat is in the closet." "She came into the room." Use "between" when speaking of two. Use "among" when speaking of more than two. For example, "She divided the pie between Tom and Jim." "She divided the candy among five boys."
3. Using needless prepositions. For example, "Where is the man going to?" "Jim fell off of his bike." "The team will arrive later on." "Where will you be at?"	Read sentences aloud with and without prepositions. Cross out all prepositions that are not needed.

VII. Subjects, predicates, phrases, and clauses

Grades 5 and 6

1. Pupils sometimes use incomplete sentences and need help in completing them. Sentences lack variety.	The only reason pupils must know subjects and predicates is to help them realize when a sentence is complete. Complete unfinished sentences. Break down run-together sentences.

Weakness Noted In Pupils' Oral and Written Language	Suggestions for Functional Practice
	Reverse order of subjects and predicates to vary sentences. Adjective or adverbial phrases may also be used to make the sentence sound better. Substitute phrases for adverbs and adjectives in simple sentences.
2. Misplacing of phrases often confuses the meaning of the sentence. For example, "A girl walked down the street with a blue hat." "We watched the pilot take the plane up with keen interest."	Place the phrase near the word it modifies.
3. Sentences can be enriched by the use of clauses.	Combine short sentences into longer, well-planned ones. For example, "Don had planned a vacation trip. The trip will take three weeks." Change to "Don planned to take a trip that will last three weeks."

Verbs and Nouns as Homographs Some exercises help children be better readers of homographs (words that are spelled alike but have different meanings). (See Chapter 9 for a discussion of homonyms, homophones, or homographs.) Children are given a number of sentences containing homographs used as either nouns or verbs. The emphasis should be on how the word is used in the sentence, since that will determine the meaning of the sentence.

This is a sharp *saw*.
Help me *saw* this tree in half.

You have a long *climb* ahead of you.
Let's *climb* that mountain.

The wounded man left a *trail* of blood.
The police will *trail* him until he is caught.

Adjectives as Modifiers in Writing Written description is very important. Children should be involved in various activities to develop this skill. A useful method of teaching adjectives would be to show them as qualifiers or modifiers, which help a person to describe some object, place, or thing better. By giving examples, children will see how adjectives are used in writing. Children can be asked to describe a picture of a woman. Just stating that the picture is of a woman does not give the class very much information. If it is further stated that she is a tall, fat woman the class is better able to distinguish her from the class of all women.

STRUCTURAL GRAMMAR IN THE CLASSROOM

Activities in structural grammar are concerned with sentence patterns. Earlier in this chapter, five basic sentence patterns were given. The simplest one consists of a noun and verb, such as:

Subject	Predicate
Noun or Pronoun	Verb (Intransitive)
Birds	fly.

If a determiner is added, it would read:

Determiner	Verb
Noun or Pronoun	
The birds	fly.

Children in the third, fourth, or fifth grade can be asked to participate in these activities using the pattern given above:

1. Write sentences similar to the pattern. For example:

People work.
Dogs bark.

2. Choose another word that would fit in the place of "fly" in the sentence "Birds fly" that would make sense.
3. Choose another word that would fit in the place of "birds" in the sentence "Birds fly" that makes sense.

4. Add some words to describe the birds.
5. Add some words to describe "fly." For example, Do the birds fly swiftly or slowly?

The most frequently used sentence pattern is:

Noun	Verb	Noun
	Transitive	
Boys	eat	cake.

Students can be asked to:

1. **Choose another word to replace "boys" in the pattern.**
2. **Choose another word to replace "cake."**
3. **Write two sentences similar to the pattern.**
4. **Add some words to describe "boys."**
5. **Add some words to describe "cake."**

In the sentence pattern:

Noun	Verb	Noun
	Linking	
Mary	is	a girl.

students can be asked to:

1. **Write two sentences similar to the pattern given above.**
2. **Choose another word to replace "Mary" in the pattern.**
3. **Choose another word to replace "girl."**

TRANSFORMATIONAL GRAMMAR'S PLACE IN THE CLASSROOM

Tranformationalists—those linguists who emphasize sentences, the positioning of words in sentences, and the expansion of sentences— seem to offer a fruitful approach to helping students in writing. *Good* teachers, when dealing with supposedly traditional grammar, have always emphasized that the way words are used in a sentence determines the meaning of the sentence.

Teachers in the elementary grades need not use all of the linguists' terminology or rules, but they can help children see how to construct a great many sentences from one sentence in the pattern S→NP+VP. Students can state sentences to fit this pattern, and then transforms (variations) of these sentences can be given. For example, "She is happy" is changed to "Is she happy?" Students need not learn the complicated rules of transformation to make this change.

As children's language expands, due to an increase in short-term memory, the teacher can help them carry this expansion over into their writings. For example, when young children first start writing sentences, they tend to be short and simple:

I can run.
I can play.
I can jump.

As children gain in language competence, they tend to increase sentence length by adding the conjunction "and."

I can run and I can play and I can jump.

Gradually, the teacher helps children to delete the conjunction "and" and the verb "can" and insert commas. Now the sentence reads:

I can run, play, and jump.

The instructor can also teach students to write more descriptively by helping them expand their sentences. "The cat runs" does not tell us very much about which cat is running, where it is running, or how it is running. The addition of certain kinds of words to the sentence will help children with both oral and written communication.

Some activities for both primary- and intermediate-grade students follow.

Primary-Level Activities

1. Given the following words, see how many sentences you can make:

a	funny	happy
the	clown	is
		man

2. Make one sentence out of the following three sentences:

The dog barks.
The cat meows.
The horse neighs.

Intermediate-Level Activities

1. Given the following words, see how many sentences you can make using all the words:

on	who	a
hungry	tired	dog
bag	and	was
car	in	red
brown	slept	the
white	the	and

2. Make one sentence out of the following three sentences:

The sailor is tall and thin.
He walks with a limp.
He became involved in a fight with some men.

As was already stated, knowledge of the terms "adjectives" and "adverbs" or "noun phrases" or "verb phrases" will not make any difference in developing writing skill. Being involved in the act of writing and knowledge of word usage will make a difference. When students are describing something, the teacher can say that "red" is an adjective and, since it tells us something about a noun, it modifies or qualifies the noun. Such comments add to learning and, as in all other areas of the language arts, balance and moderation are key words. Word usage must be taught, but only as a tool to help children to communicate better, not as an end in itself.

TREATMENT OF GRAMMAR IN ELEMENTARY ENGLISH SERIES TEXTBOOKS

From a survey of the treatment of grammar in some of the major language arts series now in use in schools, it appears that grammar holds a prominent position in most of those series. It also appears that many of the series are combining the new grammar terminology with the old or traditional terminology. Almost all of the texts of the 1980s separate grammar from word usage. The emphasis is on sentence patterns, sentence types, and sentence analysis rather than diagraming. Sentences are analyzed in terms of subject-predicate structure, and parts of speech are emphasized. The trend toward the generating of sentences and sentence expansion and combining, which was noticeable in the early 1970s, is continuing, which is good in the author's opinion. The trend away from diagraming is also good; however, the strong emphasis in many texts on sentence structure analysis and the naming of parts of speech is not. The emphasis should be on *sentence writing*. There is nothing wrong with students learning the parts of speech and being able to name them, but continuous drill in this area is not warranted. For example, when children are expanding sentences and using descriptive phrases, the labels for the descriptive words or phrases can be given. However, the naming of the parts of speech should not become an end in itself, nor should the analysis of sentence. Recognition practice helps make students aware of the different types of sentences that they encounter in their everyday reading; it also gives students experience in working with the various sentence types. The key, however, is in giving students the real writing experience needed to generate the various types of sentences.

Teachers and Textbooks

Teachers should not be intimidated by textbooks. They should not be afraid to deviate from the book to try out some of their own ideas. If teachers want to help students be more creative, they will have to behave more creatively themselves. If there is something in the text that violates certain principles or that is not "appropriate" for some students, teachers need not slavishly adhere to the text. On the other hand, if the text presents some ideas that teachers feel are needed and seem promising for their students, teachers should use these as springboards to generate their own ideas. The textbook is only a guide to some of the possibilities that are available to teachers and students. The teacher as the manager, the innovator, and the organizer, based on the needs and interests of the students, is the determiner of what to include rather than the textbook writers.

It appears that an eclectic and pragmatic approach with an emphasis on word usage is the one that is most valuable in the teaching of grammar. Teachers can use vocabulary from traditional grammar, as well as some of the new terminology, and the sentence patterns provided by descriptive grammar can also be used as an aid in gaining insight into language. However, the emphasis should be on speaking and writing, rather than on diagraming or drill on parts of speech. The expansion and generating of sentences from generative transformational grammar, without its accompanying prescriptiveness, are useful in the writing program.

STUDENT'S NAME:
        GRADE:
     TEACHER:

DIAGNOSTIC CHECKLIST IN WORD USAGE FOR STANDARD ENGLISH*

	YES	NO
1. Elimination of baby talk		
2. Correct usage in speech and writing of pronouns such as *I, me, he, him, she, her, they, them* (exception: *it's me*)		

3. Agreement of subject and verb
4. Agreement of pronoun and antecedent: "The men and women went to work. They were late."
5. Correct past tenses of common irregular verbs, such as *saw, gave, took, brought, bought, stuck*
6. Correct use of past participles after auxiliaries: *has gone, had gone, was gone*
7. Elimination of the double negative: "We don't have *no* apples," and so on.
8. Elimination of analogical forms such as *ain't, hisn, hern, ourn, theirselves,* and so on
9. Correct use of possessive pronouns such as *my, mine, his, hers, theirs, ours*
10. Mastery of the distinction between *its,* possessive pronoun, and *it's,* "it is"
11. Placement of *have* (or its phonetic reduction to *v*) between *I* and a past participle
12. Elimination of *them* as a demonstrative pronoun
13. Elimination of *this here* and *that there*
14. Mastery of use of *a* and *an* as articles
15. Correct use of personal pronouns in compound constructions: as subject (Mary and I), as object (Mary and me), as object of preposition (to Mary and me)
16. The use of *we* before an appositional noun when subject; *us* when object
17. Correct number agreement with the phrases *there is, there are, there was, there were*
18. Elimination of *he don't, she don't, it don't*
19. Elimination of *learn* for *teach, leave* for *let*
20. Elimination of pleonastic (redundant) subjects: *my brother he, my mother she, that fellow he*
21. Proper agreement in number with antecedent pronouns *one* and *anyone, everyone, each, no one.* With *everybody* and *none* some tolerance of number seems acceptable now.
22. The use of *who* and *whom* as reference to persons. (But note, "Who did she give it to?" is tolerated in all but very formal situations. In the latter, "To whom did she give it?" is preferable.)
23. Accurate use of *said* in reporting the words of a speaker in the past
24. Correction of *lay down* to *lie down*
25. The distinction between *good* as adjective and *well* as adverb: He spoke *well.*

26. Elimination of *can't hardly, all the farther* (for *as far as*), and "Where is he (she, it) at?"

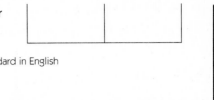

*Adapted from Robert C. Pooley, "Dare Schools Set a Standard in English Usage?" *English Journal* 49 (March 1960): 179–180.

SUMMARY

Some knowledge of the structure of our language is desirable. Structural emphasis can obstruct learning and the love of good language, however, if presented at the wrong time with the wrong approach to the wrong subjects.

There is no evidence that memorization of rules would help the native speaker to improve his acquired capacity to invent and interpret new sentences without recourse to book-learned rules. Such a prescriptive requirement might even undermine the student's creative use of introspection in language study and deprive him of his natural birthright.[40]

Grammar, which is composed of both morphology and syntax, is concerned with the study of the way language is used. Since it is merely descriptive, there is no good, bad, right, or wrong grammar. Word usage is differentiated from grammar in that standards are involved and choices are made in the areas of speaking and writing. Traditional grammar, which is based on Greek and Latin, has been taught in school as a prescriptive system; it is composed of rules from which one cannot deviate. New grammar, which is based on linguists' description of American-English, is replacing traditional grammar in many school systems. However, confusion exists because of the complexity of the new grammar and because of the lack of agreement among linguists on both terminology and methods of classifying the phonemic system.

At the beginning of this chapter a discussion on the source of the new grammars—such as structural and transformational grammar—was given.

Word usage activities, as well as methods of presenting traditional and new grammars in the classroom, were discussed. Activities showing how transformational generative grammar can contribute to children's maturity as writers, if used in a nonprescriptive way, were also suggested.

The treatment of grammar in some elementary-grade English textbooks was discussed. Although a number of authors of such texts disavow the importance of knowledge of grammar in helping students to speak and write better, there is nevertheless an emphasis on parts of speech in some texts. It appears that many books are using an eclectic approach, drawing from traditional, structural, and transformational grammar. A "Diagnostic Checklist on Word Usage for Standard English" was also presented.

As a further aid, two examples of lesson plans follow. Using these as a guide, see if you can construct another one.

[40]Lefevre, *Linguistics, English, and the Language Arts*, p. 323.

LESSON PLAN I: PRIMARY-GRADE LEVEL*

OBJECTIVES

1. Students will be able to recognize when the word "saw" should be used in a sentence.

2. Students will be able to state four sentences using the word "saw."

3. Students will be able to write four sentences correctly using the word "saw."

PRELIMINARY PREPARATION

A picture of a grocery store scene is not visible. A newsprint paper with four pre-pared questions is not visible. A table with a sign saying "Mystery Table" and a large black cloth covering it is in front of the room.

INTRODUCTION

"Yesterday we talked about some of the things we saw on our way to school. Today we will be writing sentences about some of the things we looked at using the word 'saw.' Before we begin, I'd like everyone to look at our mystery table and try to imagine what is under the table cover."

DEVELOPMENT

"There are a number of different things under the cover of the table. I'm going to call on a number of you to come to the table, look under the cover, and then tell us what you saw."

Each child comes to the table and tells what he or she saw. Ask the children why they used the word "saw" rather than "see" when they told about what was under the table cover. Ask them whether it sounds right to say, "A little while ago I see a little doll under the cover," or "A little while ago I saw a little doll under the cover."

Help them to come up with the generalization that the word "saw" is used when something has already taken place, whereas "see" is used when something is presently taking place.

Hang and display the grocery store picture. Ask children to look at the picture closely and see if they can answer these questions:

What did the lady buy?
What kind of machine do we use to find how much our groceries cost?
Where do we go to pay for our groceries?

Cover the picture. Ask the following questions:

What did you see that is good for breakfast?
What did you see that is good to drink?
What vegetables did you see?
What did you see that is not for sale?

Ask children how they would begin each sentence, and why they would begin each sentence with "I saw."

*This lesson plan is only for children who have difficulty with the past tense of *see.*

SUMMARY

Pull main points of lesson together. To determine if they are using the word "saw" correctly, ask children if they can tell about some things they saw on the way to school.

LESSON PLAN II: INTERMEDIATE-GRADE LEVEL

OBJECTIVES

Students will be able to recognize incomplete sentences.
Students will be able to construct sentences that convey complete thoughts.
Students will be able to define "communication."

PREPARATION

On display is an enlarged comic strip labeled "Are They Communicating?" Two scenarios show two cartoon characters saying the following words to one another:

Conversation I	Conversation II
CHARACTER A: "You"	CHARACTER A: "Oh!"
CHARACTER B: "Are?"	CHARACTER B: "You, too?"
CHARACTER A: "I"	CHARACTER A: "Yes!"
CHARACTER B: "They"	CHARACTER B: "Oh!"

INTRODUCTION

"We've been working with improving our sentences so that we can say what we mean better. Who remembers some of the problems we talked about that could take place if someone receives the wrong message? Yes, in an emergency, phoning for help, and so on. Good! We said that if we don't give correct information or complete information we would not get the right kind of help.

"I would like everyone to look at the bulletin board and our two cartoon characters. In which conversation are they having a communication problem? Why? Have any of you ever had any problem in communication? Today, we are going to work with the area of communication and the importance of being able to state and write complete thoughts."

DEVELOPMENT

"Before we can decide if our two characters are communicating, we have to know what 'communicate' means."

During the discussion the teacher should elicit responses from students concerning the meaning of the term "communication." It should be defined as "an exchange of ideas; both the speaker and listener are able to understand and respond to one another."

"Now that we all can define communication, in which conversation in the cartoon are the characters not communicating, and why not?"

A discussion should develop concerning the conversations. Students should recognize that the characters in Conversation I are not communicating because they do not have enough information to be able to respond logically. In Conversation II, even though it is as brief as Conversation I, the characters are communicating because they are conveying a complete thought. Ask students to change Conversation I so that the characters would be able to understand one another using the words they already are saying. A number of different kinds of conversations should be elicited. For example:

CHARACTER A: "You are going, aren't you?"
CHARACTER B: "Are you?"
CHARACTER A: "I probably will, but Chip and Nutty aren't."
CHARACTER B: "They told me that they would be able to go."

After a number of possible conversations have been thought up, put the following phrases and sentences on the board and have the children decide which are complete sentences. Then convert the phrases into complete sentences:

1. The parents named.
2. The baby was.
3. Run!
4. Mary and John.
5. Look!
6. He called.
7. The two girls were.
8. The man ran.
9. She jumped.
10. Running through the woods.

SUMMARY

Pull the main points of the lesson together. Have students give examples of complete and incomplete sentences.

SUGGESTIONS FOR THOUGHT QUESTIONS AND ACTIVITIES

1. You are a teacher in a middle school, grades 4 to 6, who has just been placed on the curriculum committee to help develop the grammar program in your school. What information must you have to be able to make an effective contribution? What kind of program would you advocate? Why?

2. You have just been appointed to a committee whose responsibility is to present to parents the new language program based on transformational grammar. How would you go about doing this in an informative and creative way?

3. Develop a creative lesson plan in the area of word usage concerned with the double negative.

4. How would you help a child who speaks in nonstandard English to acquire standard English sentence structure? Explain.

5. Using knowledge of transformational generative grammar, develop a sentence expansion lesson plan avoiding prescriptiveness.

6. You are to be on a panel that will discuss the merits of the teaching of grammar in your elementary school. What position would you take? Why?

SELECTED BIBLIOGRAPHY

Bach, Emmon. *Syntactic Theory.* Lanham, Md.: University Press of America, 1982.

Bloomfield, Leonard. *Language.* New York: Holt, Rinehart and Winston, 1966.

Carter, Ronald, ed. *Linguistics and the Teacher.* Boston, Mass.: Routledge & Kegan Paul, 1982.

Chomsky, Noam. *Current Issues in Linguistic Theory.* The Hague: Mouton, 1964.

Fromkin, Victoria A., and R. Rodman. *An Introduction to Language,* 2d ed. New York: Holt, Rinehart and Winston, 1978.

Hockett, Charles F. *A Course in Modern Linguistics.* New York: Macmillan, 1969, © 1958.

Kean, John M. "Grammar: A Perspective," in *Research in the Language Arts: Language and Schooling,* Victor Froese and Stanley B. Straw, eds. Baltimore: University Park Press, 1981.

Pooley, Robert C. *The Teaching of English Usage,* 2d ed. Urbana, Ill.: National Council of Teachers of English, 1974.

Rosenberg, Sheldon, ed. *Sentence Production: Development in Research and Theory.* New York: Halsted Press, 1977.

Rubin, Dorothy. "Developing Word Usage Skills," in *The Intermediate Grade Teacher's Language Art Handbook* (New York: Holt, Rinehart and Winston, 1980).

———. "Developing Word Usage Skills," in *The Primary Grade Teacher's Language Arts Handbook* (New York: Holt, Rinehart and Winston, 1980).

Straw, Stanley B. "Grammar and Teaching of Writing: Analysis versus Synthesis," in *Research in the Language Arts: Language and Schooling,* Victor Froese and Stanley B. Straw, eds. Baltimore: University Park Press, 1981.

ENHANCING LANGUAGE ARTS INSTRUCTION

PART THREE

SIXTEEN

Organizing for Instruction

To find one plan of class organization that can be executed effectively by all teachers with all children is as difficult as finding a word to rhyme with orange.

Emmett A. Betts

Teachers' decisions concerning how they will organize their classes for instruction are vital because they will affect the entire teaching—learning program. Teachers certainly should take the individual differences of all the students into account and should try to provide for their individual needs. However, it simply is not practical and is probably not possible to provide a completely individualized program for each student in each specific language arts area. Children need experience in working with small groups, large groups, and with the whole class. Working with various groups helps children gain learnings that they cannot obtain from working individually.

Teachers in organizing for language arts instruction must provide for group instruction as well as individualized instruction. Activities such as choral speaking, creative dramatics, puppetry, plays, discussion groups, and so on all require working with others. In a classroom organized for both individual and group instruction, students learn to work both cooperatively and independently. Being courteous

and respecting the rights of each individual are the basic tenets of any viable program organized for instruction.

GROUPING WITHIN CLASSES

Although a combination of individual and group instruction is advocated, we need to look at each separately to get a better understanding of individualized and group instruction.

Types of Groups

Children are organized into groups to make instruction more manageable. A teacher during any school day usually works with the whole class as a unit, with small groups, with large groups, and with individual students. Some groups are *ad hoc* ones, formed for a specific short-range purpose and dissolved when the purpose has been accomplished, and some groups are ongoing ones.

Student Selection in Groups

Usually the basis for selection in language arts groups such as reading, punctuation, capitalization, word usage, and spelling is the achievement levels of students. During the first few weeks of the term, teachers collect data concerning the achievement levels of each of the students in their classes through observation, informal tests, and formal tests. After evaluating the collected data, tentative groups are organized. The number of groups in a skill area depends on the amount of variability within the class. For some areas, there may be three or four groups; for some, there may only be two groups; for some, the teacher may decide to work with the whole class as a unit; and for some areas, the teacher may have a number of children working individually. The grouping pattern is a flexible one and the groups themselves are recognized as flexible units; children can easily flow from one group to another.

In a number of language arts areas, as well as other subject-matter areas, groups are formed based on interest rather than achievement levels. For some language arts activities such as choral speaking, creative dramatics, role playing, plays, and discussion groups, working in groups allows students of various ability levels to work together. When students have an opportunity to work with others, they usually are able to establish a better basis for mutual understanding and respect.

Student Involvement in Grouping

Student involvement is vital for any program to work effectively. To encourage student involvements, the teacher explains to the students the manner in which the groups are being organized and the purposes for the groups. The students are told that they may ask to move to any group at any time if they feel that they are ready for something another group is learning. Students may also sit in with any other group to either relearn a skill, review a skill, or to learn something that they might have been absent for when it was taught to their group.

At the beginning of the week, the behavioral objectives for each skill area are planned with each group. The behavioral objectives are clearly printed on large newsprint paper. The sheets for all the groups for each area are then clipped together and hung on a small line that has been strung for this purpose. Students are encouraged to go through the objectives at any time to see if there is something that they

would like to learn, relearn, or review. Students then speak to the instructor and make arrangements to come to the group when the specific skill they wish to acquire is being taught. Some students who feel that they are ready for higher-level skills will ask to sit in with another group on a trial basis, or a teacher can invite certain students to sit in with other groups. The main factor is that students have the opportunity to move freely from one group to another. Also, by encouraging students to make decisions about their own learning, teachers are helping students to become more self-reliant and independent learners.

Grade Level   There is no set level to which one can point and say, "*That* is the correct level at which to include student input in grouping decisions." Some intermediate-grade-level children who have never had the opportunity to contribute to planning or decision making will not be ready to work in a program with a strong emphasis on student participation, whereas some primary-grade-level students who have been involved in some planning and decision making will be ready. The teacher will need to involve the inexperienced children gradually in planning and decision making. If teachers encourage some student involvement from the day that children begin school, by the intermediate grades many students should be more independent and involved learners.

Teachers' Responsibility   Involving students in decision making and planning does not mean that the teacher gives up the roles as planner and decision-maker. Teachers are still the individuals responsible for the major decisions in the classroom. If children wish to plan for activities that are neither feasible nor desirable, teachers must help the students to recognize that they cannot do this. Teachers must help the students be responsible and discriminating planners and decision-makers. This is difficult because responsible decision making and planning require value judgments. A number of primary-grade-level students, as well as intermediate-grade-level students, may not be able to make such value decisions. Teachers will obviously have to use their judgment to determine the ability of their students to make certain decisions.

The Stigma Attached to Grouping

The stigma generally attached to grouping is usually discarded when students know that they can move freely from one group to another. By explaining the purposes for the groups and by having the students involved in the planning, students probably will not feel humiliated because they are not at another level. Students do not want to work at their frustration levels; therefore, they usually will not resent working at a lower level, which is at their instructional level. They will also probably not ask to move to a group working at a higher level if they feel that they cannot do the work at that level.

Names usually are chosen for the various ongoing groups rather than numerals, such as one, two, three, and so on. The students usually choose the names for their groups, and this helps give it a sense of identity. When students understand the purposes of grouping and have information about what the various groups are doing, names such as "Bluebirds," "Robins," and "Jays" are not used as cover-ups for fast, medium, and slow. The names never can act as cover-ups—everyone always knows who the fast, medium, or slow "birds" really are.

Teacher Management of Groups

A teacher makes the following remarks to the rest of the class, "Don't bother me now. I'm working with this group. It's their turn now. You've had yours."

Is the teacher who made these remarks a good classroom manager? The answer is probably "No." A good classroom manager is able to deal with more than one situation at a time. A teacher working with a group should be aware of what is going on not only in the group with whom he or she is presently working, but also with the other children in the class. A teacher cannot "dismiss" the rest of the class because he or she is working with a particular group. Even though the children have been provided with challenging work based on their individual needs, the teacher must be alert to what is going on. A teacher who ignores the rest of the class while working with one group will probably have a number of discipline problems. The following scenario presents an example of a good classroom manager. Notice especially how Ms. Mills is able to manage a number of ongoing activities at the same time. Notice how she is always aware of what is going on in her class, and notice how she prevents problems from arising.

SCENARIO

One teacher and six children are seated at a round table engaged in reading. The rest of the class is involved in a variety of activities: A number of children are working individually at their seats or at learning centers; one child is seated in the rocking chair reading; two children are working together; and a group of children are working together in the rear of the room.

The teacher says to her group at the round table, "We've talked about what inference means, and we've given examples of it. Who can tell us what we mean by inference?" A few children raise their hands. Ms. Mills calls on one, and he gives an explanation of inference. "Good," says Ms. Mills. "Now, I'd like you to read the paragraph about Ms. Brown and then tell us what inferences you can make about Ms. Brown. Be prepared to support your inferences with evidence from the paragraph."

Ms. Mills looks at each of the children as they are reading. She then glances around the room. She says, "Judy, may I see you for a moment?" Judy comes to Ms. Mills. The teacher asks Judy in a very quiet tone if she can help her. She says, "Judy, you look confused. What's wrong?" Judy says that she is having trouble figuring out a question. Ms. Mills tells Judy to work on something else for about 10 minutes, and that then she will help her. As Judy goes back to her seat, Ms. Mills again quickly glances around the room. As her eyes catch some of the children's, she smiles at them. Ms. Mills then looks at the children in her group. She sees that they are ready. Ms. Mills asks them what inferences they can make about Ms. Brown. All the children raise their hands. Ms. Mills calls on one of the children. He makes an inference about her. Ms. Mills asks the rest of the group if they agree with the inference. Two students say that they do not agree. Ms. Mills asks all the students to skim the paragraph to find clues that would support their position. Ms. Mills again looks around the room. A child approaches Ms. Mills and asks her a question. Ms. Mills answers the question and then goes back to the group.

After a while Ms. Mills and the group discuss whether they have accomplished what they were supposed to. They then discuss, for a moment, what they will be doing next time. They all go back to their seats. Before Ms. Mills calls another group, she checks off in her plan book the objectives that have been accomplished by the group. She also makes some remarks in her record book about the individual children in the group. Ms. Mills puts down her book and walks around the room to check on what the students are doing. She smiles to a number of the students, says "good" to some others, helps Judy with her problem, and listens in on the group that has been working together on a special project. Ms. Mills asks the group how they are doing and how much more time they will need before they will be ready to report their progress to her and the class. Ms. Mills then goes back to the reading table and calls the next group.

INDIVIDUALIZED INSTRUCTION

The many different types of individualized programs range from informal ones, developed by teachers or teachers and students together, to commercially produced ones. It is beyond the scope of this book to give a description of the organizational patterns or the individualized programs that exist; books have been written on these (see Selected Bibliography). However, a brief description of some of the characteristics of both informal and commercially produced individualized programs would be helpful.

Teacher-Made and Commercially Produced Programs

Teacher-made programs can obviously vary from teacher to teacher. However, most of the programs usually use behavioral objectives, which are taken from curriculum guides, study guides, and instructors' manuals. To accomplish the objectives the teachers usually cull activities and materials from a number of sources. The teacher and student confer periodically, and the teacher keeps a check on the student's progress by keeping adequate records.

A variety of commercially produced or published programs exists, and they have a number of things in common. Most of the programs use behavioral objectives for each curriculum area. Usually each curriculum area is divided into small, discrete learning steps based on graduated levels of difficulty. A variety of activities and materials generally combined in a multimedia approach is used, and usually built into the commercial programs is a system of record keeping, progress tests, and checklists.

Common Characteristics In almost all individualized programs, students work at their own pace. Learning outcomes in individualized programs are based on the needs, interests, and ability levels of the students. Activities are interesting and challenging, and they usually employ a multimedia approach. The activities are based on desired outcomes, students work independently, and there is some system of record keeping.

For Whom Does Individualized Instruction Work?

Students who have short attention spans, who have difficulty following directions, and who have reading problems will obviously have difficulty working independently. Teachers will have to help these students set limited, short-range objectives that can be reached in a brief period of time. For those students with reading problems, the teacher will have to rely very heavily on audio tapes to convey directions. Students who are slow learners (see Chapter 17) will also need special help; special programs will have to be devised for them. Students who have no discernible achievement problems but who have never worked in an individualized program before will also have difficulty unless they are properly oriented to the program. (*Note:* Do not confuse the need to work independently in an individualized program with the need to provide for the individual differences of each student in the class. For example, a child who is a slow learner will usually have difficulty working independently, but the teacher still needs to provide an individual program for this child based on his or her special needs.)

Some Common Sense about Individual Programs

Preparing individual outcomes and a specially tailored program for each student in each specific subject area can be a monumental task. Therefore, what is generally done is to use outcomes and programs already prepared, either informally (teacher-made) or formally (commercially made), and then match these to the needs of individual students. For such an individualized program to work effectively, teachers must have a variety of individualized programs available for their students, and teachers must know the individual needs of each student. (See section on learning centers later in this chapter.)

In the following scenario, an example of how one fifth-grade teacher individualizes instruction in one language arts area is presented.

SCENARIO

In going over Susan's papers Ms. Mills finds that the pupil consistently makes many spelling errors. Ms. Mills decides to have a conference with Susan about this. Ms. Mills begins the conference by praising Susan's ideas and by telling her that she enjoys reading her stories. "However," Ms. Mills says, "you have so many spelling errors that it detracts from the story." Susan says she is aware that she has a spelling problem, but that she has always had a spelling problem. "I guess I just can't spell," says Susan. Ms. Mills tells Susan that since she is a good reader and writer she really should not have a spelling problem. She also tells Susan that since she likes to write, it would be helpful to be a better speller. Susan says that she definitely does want to spell better. "Good!" says Ms. Mills. "The first step to improving in something is knowing that you have a problem." "Let's both look at some of your papers and see if we can come up with a program that will help you. We'll meet tomorrow to discuss this further."

The next day Ms. Mills and Susan have another conference. Ms. Mills asks Susan if she noticed anything special about the words she misspelled. Susan says that she is not sure, but she seems to have problems with word endings. She never knows when to drop a final *e*, change a *y* to an *i*, or double a consonant. Ms. Mills says, "Good, I noticed the same things. Did you know that there are a number of spelling rules that you can learn that will help you? As a matter of fact, in the spelling learning center we have just the program for you. Let's go to the center so that we can look at it together."

Ms. Mills and Susan proceed to the learning center. At the center, Ms. Mills shows Susan a modularized instructional spelling program. The teacher chooses the module that deals entirely with spelling endings. Ms. Mills and Susan go over each step of the module together. The spelling module is composed of the following steps: (1) directions for using the module; (2) pretest; (3) behavioral objectives; (4) learning activities; (5) student self-assessment; (6) postassessment; and (7) recycling.

After going over each step of the module with Susan, Ms. Mills makes sure that Susan is able to operate the audio equipment that is used in the module. Ms. Mills then tells Susan that she can work at her own pace, and that if she needs any help, she should not hesitate to come to her. Susan thanks Ms. Mills and says that she is looking forward to starting as soon as possible. "It looks like fun," she says, "because there are so many different kinds of activities, and I especially enjoy doing word riddles and puzzles."

It is probable that Susan is on her way to becoming a better speller. However, Ms. Mills's job is not over. She must continue to check on Susan's progress and then, together with Susan, determine whether the student is ready to go on to another area or whether she needs further remediation.

Record Keeping

Since Susan is only one of many students in Ms. Mills's class, and since many of the students are working in different areas at different levels, Ms. Mills cannot rely on her memory to recall exactly what each student is doing and at what level each student is working. Ms. Mills, therefore, has established a record-keeping system. She has a folder for each student in the class. In the folder she keeps a record of each student's progress in each area. For example, Ms. Mills, after meeting with Susan, went back to her file drawer to pull Susan's folder. She wanted to record that Susan is attempting to accomplish certain behavioral objectives in the area of spelling. She also wanted to record the specific program Susan is working in and the date that Susan started the program.

Susan's folder contains a number of items; a checklist of activities; a record of standard-

ized achievement test scores, intelligence test scores, criterion-referenced test information, and other diagnostic test information. In the folder there is also a sheet listing the particular behavioral objectives that Susan has attempted to accomplish up to that time. Next to each behavioral objective is the program chosen to

A TEACHER AND STUDENT WORKING TOGETHER.

achieve it, as well as the starting and completion dates.

LEARNING CENTERS IN THE CLASSROOM

The concept of learning centers is not new. Good teachers have always recognized the importance of providing "interest centers" for their students based on their needs and ability levels. However, in the past most of the science, art, library, listening, and fun centers were just "interest attractions"; they usually were marginal to the ongoing teaching–learning program rather than an integral part of it.

As used today, learning centers are an integral part of the instructional program. They are more formalized and recognized as vital to a good individualized program. A set area is usually set aside in the classroom for instruction in a specific curriculum area. Aims for learning centers may be developed beforehand by teachers or cooperatively by teachers and students. Some of the requirements for a good learning center are as follows:

1. Is in an easily accessible area
2. Is attractive
3. Provides for students on different maturational levels
4. Has clearly stated behavioral objectives so that students know what they are supposed to accomplish (outcomes)
5. Provides for group and team activities as well as individual activities
6. Allows for student input
7. Asks probing questions
8. Has some humorous materials
9. Provides activities that call for divergent thinking
10. Uses a multimedia approach
11. Has carefully worked out learning sequences to accomplish objectives
12. Has provisions for evaluation and record keeping

Designing a Learning Center

In the following plan for developing a learning center, notice the similarity to the development of a lesson plan.

1. Motivating technique: necessary to attract attention. This could be realia (real objects), pictures, humorous sayings, and so on. *Example:* Familiar commercials with pictures are listed on learning center bulletin board (propaganda learning center).
2. Behavioral objectives: necessary so that students know what they are supposed to accomplish (outcomes). *Examples:* (propaganda learning center)
   a. Define "propaganda."
   b. Define "bias."
   c. Explain what is meant by a propaganda technique.
   d. List five propaganda techniques.
   e. Describe each of the five propaganda techniques you chose and give an example of each.
   f. Listen to a tape of 10 commercials and identify the propaganda technique used in each.
   g. Listen to a tape of a political speech and state what propaganda techniques the politician uses.
   h. Team up with another student and, using a propaganda technique, role-play a commercial to be presented to the class.
   i. Using one or more propaganda techniques, write a commercial about an imaginary product.
   j. Tape-record the commercial created by you on the imaginary product.
3. Directions to accomplish objectives: necessary so that students know what to do to accomplish objectives. Step-by-step instructions are given for the students to accomplish the objectives. Students are told to:
   a. Read behavioral objectives so that you know what you are supposed to accomplish.
   b. Go to file drawer one, which contains the learning activities to accomplish objective one.
   c. Complete each learning activity and record your progress on each before you go on to the next objective. (This depends on the learning center. In some learning centers, the students must accomplish the objectives in sequence; in others this is not necessary. For the propaganda learning center, some of the learning objectives must be accomplished in order. Obviously, before students can write a commercial using propaganda and bias, they must be able to define "propaganda" and "bias," they must be able to explain propaganda techniques, they must be able to recognize them, and they must be able to give examples.)

CHILDREN WORKING IN A LANGUAGE ARTS LEARNING CENTER.

Summary of Steps in Preparing a Learning Center

1. Select a topic.
2. State objectives.
3. Identify experiences.
4. Collect materials.
5. Prepare activities.
6. Make schedules (which children use center and when).
7. Prepare record forms (each student using center must have one).

Multimedia in Learning Centers

Ms. Mills recognizes that successful individualized programs usually have learning centers that use a diversity of instructional materials to accommodate the individual differences of students. As a result, Ms. Mills has included in each of her learning centers learning sequences that use such instructional materials as textbooks, library books, programmed materials, sets of pictures, realia, commercial and teacher-prepared audio tapes, filmstrips, films, TV, radio, tape recorders, maps, globes, manipulative materials, and games.

The media corner itself is not a learning center, but a conveniently located storage and extra viewing place. Each learning center has its own viewing area. The media corner has two "home-made" carrels, which are helpful for viewing films and filmstrips if the learning center is occupied.

Ms. Mills realizes that she is extremely fortunate to be in a school system that not only recognizes the importance of the use of a variety of media to help students to achieve learning objectives, but which provides the funds necessary to acquire the materials. (She also has a friend who helped her make the carrels for the media center.)

COMPUTER-AIDED INSTRUCTION

Ms. Mills recently read an intriguing short story, which made her stop to think about her feelings toward the influx of microcomputers in education and, in particular, in her very own classroom. Here is the story:

John was still tired and wanted to sleep some more, but a firm voice kept saying, "Time to get up." John stretched and opened his eyes to be greeted by his faithful companion, CIPS.

A MEDIA CORNER IN A LEARNING CENTER.

"Good morning, CIPS, couldn't you let me sleep a little longer?" asks John. "Sorry," says CIPS, "You specifically requested that you be awakened at precisely 7 A.M. It is exactly 7 A.M. Here is your schedule for today. Your outfit for today has been chosen as well as your menus."

"Thank you, CIPS, excellent work!"

John showered, put on the outfit that CIPS had selected and went downstairs to prepare the menu that CIPS had suggested. John always looked good, and he felt that he owed this entirely to CIPS. He didn't know what he would do without CIPS. CIPS saw to it that he was always well-groomed and that his caloric intake was perfect for the amount of activities he engaged in every day.

After breakfast John went to CIPS to get the answer to a very complex problem that he had given to CIPS late the night before to solve. Sure enough, good old dependable CIPS had the solution. John thanked CIPS, put him in his pocket, and went to work.

CIPS is John's personal computer information processing system. CIPS is aware of John's habits, attitudes, desires, physical traits, biological makeup, abilities, and so on. Nothing about John is secret from CIPS. In John's world, anyone who is of any importance has his or her own CIPS. Incredible? Farfetched? Science fiction? Or reality?

Ms. Mills did not dismiss the short story as complete science fiction because at a recent conference she had heard the projections of some specialists in the field of artificial intelligence (the development of computer programs that display "intelligence" by solving problems or engaging in conversation).[1] These scientists talked about the "ultimate computer—the self-sufficient machine,"[2] and predicted that in the 1990s this "machine would learn natural language as people do, gain knowledge and reasoning power through experience, not just spoon-fed instructions, and be able to solve the gamut of problems that humans can solve."[3]

Ms. Mills has a number of mixed feelings

about the recent bombardment of information about microcomputers and their educational value. She knows that computer-aided instruction is not new because when she was in college she learned about a number of programs that have been in existence for quite a long time. She has never been frightened by computer-aided instruction nor does it make her feel unneeded because she realizes that it is mainly a management tool; that is, with the proper program in the computer, she could more effectively manage her class. As a matter of fact, she feels that this would be especially effective for her because she believes in early diagnosis and correction (see Chapter 18).

In terms of application during a language arts lesson, Ms. Mills could have the computer question each student simultaneously through terminals. The students would then answer by menu selection, whereby only one letter or number needs to be keyed to indicate the answer. Ms. Mills could then receive the immediate feedback of the responses of *all* her students. This type of questioning and feedback could be repeated for however much depth or breadth of coverage she wanted. She could not only receive immediate feedback, but she could also see a pattern of the answers. This pattern would help her to immediately discern those areas that proved the most or least difficult for the students. She could also have the computer display for her a pattern of an individual's responses or how well an individual student has done over an extended period of time. She feels the possibilities are innumerable and that she could use the feedback for evaluation and grouping. She would especially love to have the advanced software programs whereby students could type their compositions into the computer, and she would be informed of their individual errors and be given a summary of the entire classes' error profile.

Ms. Mills feels that the microprocessor is one good way to illustrate to students the editing process in action. She has used it with them to write experience stories, and the students enjoyed being able to change words, sentences, and even paragraphs in the story. This does not, however, eliminate the need for the student to have writing skills. The student must

[1]Richard E. Mayer, *Thinking and Problem Solving: An Introduction to Human Cognition and Learning* (Glenview, Ill.: Scott, Foresman, 1977), p. 136.

[2]Ibid., p. 39.

[3]Ibid.

STUDENTS AND TEACHER WORKING WITH A MICROCOMPUTER.

still determine what changes to make, as well as what message he or she wishes to convey. Also, Ms. Mills feels that the availability of word processing software programs that correct spelling, punctuation, and capitalization errors does not make obsolete the need for students to be proficient in these areas.

Ms. Mills can see that another good possibility for computer-aided instruction is to use it in a tutorial manner, that is, in a one-to-one situation with the student. In this manner, the student knows the results in a friendly, nonthreatening way. Computer-aided instruction also diagnoses the student's problem without the teacher knowing it. (Certain programs can be developed so that only the student is aware of his or her language arts problem.) This is done because some students respond better to computer diagnostics than to teacher diagnostics. Such students feel that the computer is more fair and more private and, as a result, relate better to such an impersonal tool. This, of course, is merely one small part of the student's program. Obviously, the teacher will have to know about the student's problems in order to help him or her. (See Chapter 18 for a

discussion of some diagnostic techniques teachers can use, and see also the scenario on pages 357–358.)

There are many factors that cause Ms. Mills to have mixed feelings about the influx of microcomputers in the classroom. First, Ms. Mills realizes that many of the software programs that are emerging are not very good. Yes, students are motivated by using the computer, but, in many instances, the computer is acting merely as an expensive, electronic flashcard. The overlearning of certain concepts is warranted and important, but Ms. Mills feels that there are less expensive and more time-effective ways to achieve certain of her objectives. Also, she does not want her students to spend an inordinate amount of time in front of a computer terminal. She does not feel that the computer program is, or should be, a substitute for

A LANGUAGE ARTS BULLETIN BOARD.

time spent in social interaction, or reading a book or in writing. She feels that the microcomputer can be a good, educational instrument, but she does not want to be carried away in the microcomputer mania that has been sweeping some of the schools across the country. She wants her students to be computer-literate, so she knows that she has to be computer-literate. However, she wants them to learn also that the computer is only as good as the person programming it and that computers cannot think in the way that humans do. She wants to encourage her students to experiment with the computer and to develop their own programs if they want to, but she wants them to recognize that the computer is a tool; it is an aid.

Ms. Mills is fortunate to have her own microcomputer in her classroom. This computer is in her learning center, and she is using it to individualize further her students' instruction. Fortunately for the students in Ms. Mills' class, Ms. Mills does not indiscriminately purchase software or randomly assign students to programs. Ms. Mills always asks the questions "What are my purposes?" and "For whom is this?" Ms. Mills realizes that computer-aided instruction is here, but it is one part of the whole educational program. She realizes that she must integrate it into the language arts program for it to be used effectively. She recognizes its value as an effective motivational tool and uses it accordingly.

BULLETIN BOARDS

Another method of enhancing language arts instruction is the bulletin board. To arouse the interest of students, to use as a motivating technique, and to make the classroom a more pleasant and attractive learning environment, bulletin boards may easily change to reflect projects and activities in the classroom. Students may also participate in the planning and putting together of the bulletin boards.

SUMMARY

How a teacher organizes for instruction will greatly affect the teaching–learning program. In organizing language arts instruction, the teacher ought to provide for both group and individualized instruction. Teachers organize students into groups to make instruction more manageable. However, there are times when the needs of a child will be better served by an individualized program than by group instruction.

Many individualized programs exist. Teachers should be familiar with a number of these so that they can match specific programs to the needs of individual children. Learning centers are an important part of the instructional program and vital to a good individualized program.

In the 1980s many classrooms have microcomputers, and many school systems are providing computer-literacy training for their teachers. Teachers must be discriminating in purchasing computer software programs; they should ask the questions "What are my purposes?" and "For whom is this?"

SUGGESTIONS FOR THOUGHT QUESTIONS AND ACTIVITIES

1. You have been asked to present a talk to your colleagues on "computer literacy" and how you believe microcomputers should be used in the elementary schools. What will you say?

2. Develop a language arts learning center for a grade level of your choice.

3. Explain how you would organize instruction in your class.

SELECTED BIBLIOGRAPHY

Allen, Vernon L. *Children As Teachers: Theory and Research on Tutoring.* New York: Academic Press, 1976.

Brown, James W. *AV Instruction: Technology, Media and Methods,* 5th ed. New York: McGraw-Hill, 1976.

Charles, C. M. *Individualizing Instruction,* 2d ed. St. Louis, Mo.: C. V. Mosby, 1980.

Coplan, Kate, and Constance Rosenthal. *Guide to Better Bulletin Boards.* Dobbs Ferry, N.Y.: Oceana Publishing, 1970.

Flanigan, Michael C., and Robert S. Boone. *Using Media in the Language Arts: A Source Book.* Itasca, Ill.: F. E. Peacock, 1977.

Forte, Imogene, and Joy Mackenzie. *Nooks, Crannies, and Corners: Learning Centers for Creative Classrooms,* rev. ed. Nashville, Tenn.: Incentive Publications, 1978.

Henneman, Dawn. "Hands-On Bulletin Boards." *Instructor and Teacher* (January 1984):34–37.

Mason, George E., Jay S. Blanchard, and Danny B. Daniel. *Computer Applications in Reading,* 2d ed. Newark, Del.: International Reading Association, 1983.

Smith, James A. *Classroom Organization for the Language Arts.* Itasca, Ill.: F. E. Peacock, 1977.

Standiford, Sally N., Kathleen Jaycox and Anne Auten. *Computers in the English Classroom: A Primer for Teachers.* Urbana, Ill.: NCTE, 1983.

SEVENTEEN

Teaching Children with Special Needs

All the children of all the people have a right to an education.

Public Law 94–142

Public Law 94–142 advocates a free appropriate education for all children in the least restrictive environment. This has brought to the fore the importance of the uniqueness of each child. In the regular classroom there is usually a wide range of ability levels, which generally includes the borderline (slow-learning) and the gifted child.[1] As a result of Public Law 94–142, exceptional children may be mainstreamed into the regular classroom. In order to be able to work with such children, all teachers, not just special education teachers, must become more knowledgeable of exceptional children. The more teachers know about the children with whom they work, the better able they will be to provide for their individual differences and needs.

In this chapter, language arts methods are provided that are most applicable for those chil-dren whom teachers currently have in their regular classrooms, such as the borderline child and the gifted child. These methods may, however, also be adapted for mainstreamed children.

Public Law 94–142 requires that exceptional children have individualized programs specially prepared for them. These individualized programs are too varied to be presented in a text with as broad a scope as this one. Teachers who have mainstreamed children in their classrooms are, therefore, encouraged to go to special education texts for more in-depth coverage.

MENTAL AGE SPAN IN THE REGULAR CLASSROOM

While the teacher in a regular classroom usually has students with a mental age span of five years, the span can be greater. Mental age (MA) refers to a child's present level of development; it helps to indicate the child's present readiness. As children progress through the grades the span between the borderline (slow-learning), average, and gifted child gets wider.

While children enter school based on chronological age (CA) rather than mental age, instruction needs to be geared to their mental ages rather than their chronological ages. IQ is calculated as $\frac{MA}{CA} \times 100$, and a child of six, for

[1] Although gifted children are classified as exceptional children, they are generally found in the regular classroom. Borderline (slow-learning) children are not classified as exceptional children in the revised definition of the American Association on Mental Deficiencies.

example, with an IQ of 75[2] has a mental age of 4.5, and a child of six with an IQ of 130 has a mental age of 7.8. (See Table 17.1 on this page.) Obviously, these children need extremely different programs even though both are chronologically the same age.

Even teachers who believe in individual differences and who attempt to develop an individualized instructional program for each child in their class will not be able to build a meaningful program for their students unless they are knowledgeable of the cognitive styles that children at different intellectual levels possess.

THE "AVERAGE" CHILD

The first question that comes to mind whenever anyone labels someone an average

[2]Teachers may have children with IQs as low as 68 in their regular classrooms because borderline children's IQs range from approximately 68 to 85.

child is, Is there really an "average" child? Actually, there probably is not. Every child is an individual and as such is unique. However, for research purposes we tend to look upon the average child as that individual who scores in the IQ range from 90 to 110. Studies are based on averages, and averages are necessary as criteria or points of reference. Only after we have determined the criteria for "average" can we talk about "above or below average."

THE BORDERLINE CHILD OR "SLOW LEARNER"

The borderline child is usually described as a dull, average child who is borderline in his or her intellectual functioning. As already stated, these children's IQ scores range from approximately 68 to 85. As a result, they generally have difficulty doing schoolwork. Borderline children are not, however, equally slow in all their activities or abnormal in all their charac-

TABLE 17.1   COMPARISON OF MENTAL AGES

Grade	CA	75 IQ MA	85 IQ MA	100 IQ MA	115 IQ MA	130 IQ MA
K	5.6	4.2	4.8	5.6	6.4	7.3
1	6.0	4.5	5.1	6.0	6.9	7.8
	6.6	5.0	5.6	6.6	7.6	8.6
2	7.0	5.3	6.0	7.0	8.1	9.1
	7.6	5.7	6.5	7.6	8.7	9.9
3	8.0	6.0	6.8	8.0	9.2	10.4
	8.6	6.5	7.3	8.6	9.9	11.2
4	9.0	6.8	7.7	9.0	10.4	11.7
	9.6	7.2	8.2	9.6	11.0	12.5
5	10.0	7.5	8.5	10.0	11.5	13.0
	10.6	8.0	9.0	10.6	12.2	13.8
6	11.0	8.3	9.4	11.0	12.7	14.3
	11.6	8.7	9.9	11.6	13.3	15.1
7	12.0	9.0	10.2	12.0	13.8	15.6
	12.6	9.5	10.7	12.6	14.5	16.4
8	13.0	9.8	11.1	13.0	15.0	16.9
	13.6	10.2	11.6	13.6	15.6	17.7

Example: An eight-year-old child with an IQ of 115 has a mental age of *9.2.*

$$IQ = \frac{MA}{CA} \times 100$$

$$115 = \frac{x}{8} \times 100$$

$$x = 1.15 \times 8$$
$$x = 9.2$$

teristics. It is difficult at times to differentiate borderline children and children with specific learning disabilities from underachievers produced by disadvantaged environments.[3]

Providing Instruction

Teachers in regular classrooms have many times been frustrated because they have had children who do not seem to be able to learn material that is considered "average" for the specific grade level. Not only is the teacher frustrated, but so is the child. A child with IQ test scores in the 68 to 85 range would have difficulty working at grade level. Because of social promotion (children are promoted according to chronological age rather than achievement) children are moved along each year into a higher grade. As slow learners go through the grades, their problems generally become more pronounced and compounded unless they are given special attention.

The term "slow learner" is probably a misnomer, because the term implies that a child needs more time to get a concept, but eventually will acquire it. Actually, there are some concepts that slow learners cannot acquire no matter how long they work on them because slow learners usually cannot work in the abstract. Obviously, the teacher should not use inductive or deductive teaching techniques in working with slow learners. Slow learners generally can learn material if it is presented at a concrete level. Slow learners usually must be given many opportunities to go over the same concept; slow learners must continue practice in an area beyond the point where they think that they know it, in order to *overlearn* it. The practice should be varied and interesting to stimulate them.

To motivate the slow learners, many games and gamelike activities may be used. Slow learners have a short attention span, so learning tasks should be broken down into small, discrete steps. Generally requiring close super-

vision, they may have difficulty working independently. Distractions must be kept at a minimum, and each task should be very exactly defined and explained. It is necessary to define short-range goals, which slow learners can accomplish, to give them a sense of achievement. Slow learners are usually set in their ways, and once they learn something in one way, they will be very rigid about changing.

The teacher should recognize that individual differences exist within groups as well as between groups. Obviously, there will be individual differences among slow learners.

Language Arts Instruction

In Chapter 3 you learned that children who are advanced in language development have a better chance for success in school than those who are not. Slow development of language is a noticeable characteristic of slow-learning children. The teacher recognizes that these children need many opportunities to express themselves orally and that they learn best at a concrete level. The teacher should, therefore, plan his or her program for slow-learning children to include many *firsthand experiences* where the children can deal with real things. The teacher can take the children on trips to visit farm animals, zoo animals, the firehouse, the police station, factories, railroad stations, farms, and so on. In planning for the trip, the teacher should use the same good practices that are used for all children. The teacher should discuss the trip with the children beforehand and give them the opportunity to help plan for the trip. After the trip the teacher should encourage the children to discuss what they saw. The teacher and children could then cooperatively write an experience story about the visit (see "The Experience Story" in Chapter 8).

In helping slow-learning children acquire new words, the teacher should recognize that these children will learn and retain words that they will use in their everyday conversation more readily than abstract words. It, therefore, helps for the teacher to associate the new words with their pictorial representations, real objects, or actions. Slow learners must repeatedly hear and see these words in association

[3]Samuel A. Kirk, Sister Joanne Marie Kliebhan, and Janet W. Lerner, *Teaching Reading to Slow and Disabled Learners* (Boston: Houghton Mifflin, 1978), p. 3.

with objects, pictures, or actions in order to learn them. As mentioned in the previous section, the children must *overlearn* the word. (Overlearning takes place when you continue practice even after reaching the point where you feel you know something quite well.)

Slow-learning children not only have problems in working with abstract words, they also have difficulty dealing with words in isolation. Cohen's study has shown that the slower students are in academic progress, the more difficult it is for them to deal with words in isolation, unrelated to a totally meaningful experience.[4] Her study has also found that the reading aloud of stories that are at the interest, ability, and attention span level of the children is an excellent means of helping the children to develop vocabulary and sentence sense. After listening to a story, the children should be encouraged to engage in some oral expression activities. All children need many opportunities to express themselves, and slow learners are no exception. A child who feels accepted and is in a nonthreatening environment will feel more free to contribute than one who feels embarrassed.

In providing language arts instruction the teacher should provide opportunities for the slow-learning child to work with other children. Oral expression (speech stimulation) activities such as choral speaking, finger play, and creative dramatics are good for these purposes. The child should be given opportunities to share with the other children; all children seek approval of peers as well as of adults.

THE GIFTED CHILD

Gifted children fall into the category of exceptional children because this group of children deviates greatly from "average" children.

When one talks about the gifted, immediately visions of small children wearing horn-rimmed glasses and carrying encyclopedias come to mind. This is a myth. There are many definitions of the gifted. In recent years the def-

inition of the "gifted" has been broadened to include not only the verbally gifted with an IQ above 132 on the Stanford-Binet Intelligence Scale but also those individuals whose performance in any line of socially useful endeavor is consistently superior.

Marland's national definition in a congressional report alerts educators to the multifaceted aspects of giftedness:

Gifted and talented children are those identified by professionally qualified persons who by virtue of outstanding abilities are capable of high performance. These are children who require differentiated educational programs and services beyond those normally provided by the regular school program in order to realize their contribution to self and society.

Children capable of high performance include those with demonstrated achievement and/or potential ability in any of the following areas:

1. General intellectual ability
2. Specific academic aptitude
3. Creative or productive thinking
4. Leadership ability
5. Visual and performing arts
6. Psychomotor ability[5]

Characteristics

Gifted children, on the average, are socially, emotionally, physically, and intellectually superior to "average" children in the population. Gifted children have, on the average, superior general intelligence, a desire to know, originality, common sense, will power and perseverance, a desire to excel, self-confidence, prudence and forethought, and a good sense of humor, among a host of other admirable traits. Their language development is usually very advanced. They generally have a large stock of vocabulary and delight in learning new words. Many have learned to read before they came to school; they usually have wide-ranging interests that they pursue in extensive depth, they tend to be voracious readers, and they delight in

---

[4]Dorothy H. Cohen, "The Effect of Literature on Vocabulary and Reading Achievement," *Elementary English* 45 (February 1968):209–213, 217.

[5]S. P. Marland, *Education of the Gifted and the Talented* (Washington, D.C.: U.S. Office of Education, 1972), p. 10.

challenge. However, it is possible that without some guidance, a number of gifted students may not read very challenging books.

Instructional Provisions

Gifted children need special attention because of their precocious learning abilities. However, when gifted children are not given special attention, they still usually manage to work on grade level. As a result, gifted children are often ignored. Regrettably, they are actually the most neglected of all exceptional children. Attention is given to those who have "more need." Margaret Mead, the renowned anthropologist, has written about this attitude toward the gifted, which is still applicable today:

Whenever the rise to success cannot be equated with preliminary effort, abstinence and suffering, it tends to be attributed to "luck," which relieves the spectator from according the specially successful person any merit. . . . In American education, we have tended to reduce the gift to a higher I.Q.—thus making it a matter of merely a little more on the continuity scale, to insist on putting more money and effort in bringing the handicapped child "up to par" as an expression of fair play and "giving everyone a break" and to disallow special gifts. By this refusal to recognize special gifts, we have wasted and dissipated, driven into apathy or schizophrenia, uncounted numbers of gifted children. If they learn easily, they are penalized for having nothing to do; if they excel in some outstanding way, they are penalized as being conspicuously better than the peer group, and teachers warn the gifted child, "Yes, you can do that, it's much more interesting than what the others are doing. But, remember, the rest of the class will dislike you for it."[6]

Gifted children, like all other children, need guidance and instruction based on their interests, needs, and ability levels. Although gifted children gain abstract concepts quickly and are intellectually capable of working at high levels of abstraction, unless they receive appropriate instruction to gain needed skills, they may not

be able to realize their potential. Gifted children should not be subjected to unnecessary drill and repetition. They usually enjoy challenge and have long attention spans, so teachers need to provide instruction that will challenge and interest them. One way that teachers can provide for their gifted students so that they can work at their own pace in many areas is through individualized programs (see Chapter 16).

It is interesting to note, however, that the kinds of activities that stimulate gifted students are not significantly different from those that are used in teaching other students. For example, two doctoral dissertations that focused on the literature and composition objectives of the Pittsburgh Scholars Program in English for Grades 10 and 11 present 30 different "Strategies for Teaching Scholars English."[7] The strategies that they present are those that most teachers of English use, and even though these studies concern secondary-level students, the techniques that were used are those that would apply also to upper-elementary-grade-level language arts teachers. The strategies include such techniques as teacher lecture, class discussion, independent project by group or individual, vocabulary enrichment activities, multiparagraph exposition (informational or explanatory writing), comparison and contrast papers, descriptive paragraphs, narrative writing, poetry writing, and research papers.

Although the strategies may not be significantly different from those used by teachers for other students, the manner in which the material is presented should be guided by a knowledge of the characteristics of gifted students. The atmosphere in the classroom should be one in which gifted students are respected as persons capable of independent work and leadership, and the subject matter that is presented should allow for student involvement, choice,

---

[6]Margaret Mead, "The Gifted Child in the American Culture of Today," *Journal of Teacher Education* 5 (September 1954):211–212.

[7]Natalie Apple, "A Study of the Literature Objectives of the Pittsburgh Scholars Program in English, Grades 10 and 11," Doctoral Dissertation, University of Pittsburgh, 1979; Patricia Tierney, "A Study of the Composition Objectives of the Pittsburgh Scholars Program in English, Grades 10 and 11," Doctoral Dissertation, University of Pittsburgh, 1979.

and interaction. Also, the instruction for gifted students should focus on those activities that involve the higher levels of the cognitive domain; that is, gifted children should spend the most time in activities that require analysis, synthesis, and evaluation. They should also be encouraged by their teachers to be intelligent risk-takers, to defend their ideas, delve deeply into problems, seek alternate solutions to problems, follow through on hunches, and dream the impossible dream. In short, gifted students will know that their teachers value their talents if they are provided with challenge commensurate with their abilities.

Language Arts Instruction

In an earlier section, it is stated that gifted children are usually advanced in language learning and that many have learned to read before they come to school. According to Lewis Terman, a noted psychologist who did monumental research on the gifted, nearly half of the gifted children he studied learned to read before starting school; at least 20 percent before the age of five years, 6 percent before four, and 1.6 percent before three years.[8] Most of these children learned to read with little or no formal instruction. Other studies seem to corroborate these findings. However, these findings should not be taken to mean that gifted children can fend for themselves, and that teachers should spend more time with others. It does mean that the teacher must provide alternate programs for gifted children. To not recognize that these children are reading when they first enter school and to make them go through a program geared to "average" children can be devastating.

Also frustrating for a gifted child is to be told, "Put your hand down. You're not supposed to know that yet." Such teacher statements can discourage gifted students from participating in discussions, as well as make them feel ostracized. If the teacher feels that gifted students are dominating the discussion or are answering questions too soon, the teacher should take

stock of his or her program. Perhaps the teacher could have the gifted students be the discussion leaders for certain topics or ask the gifted students to provide special information about the topic that they could share with the rest of the class or group.

Gifted students usually have wide-ranging interests that they like to pursue in extensive depth, and they are generally impatient with detail. Teachers should give their gifted students the time and opportunity to pursue their interests in depth. Also, the teacher should provide a rich and varied program for his or her gifted students because they are usually able to work in a number of activities simultaneously.

While the gifted need opportunities to work with other gifted children, they also need to work with children on all ability levels. Children who work together in activities that tap the special abilities of all the children will usually learn to understand each other better. Speech-stimulating activities such as choral speaking, creative dramatics, and puppetry give gifted children an opportunity to work with children on all ability levels.

Although many gifted students enjoy writing and engage in it frequently for their own pleasure, some may lack basic writing skills. This happens because often it is taken for granted that highly able students have all the basic skills that they need at their fingertips. This is not so. Like other children, they must attain these skills. Also, teachers must challenge their gifted students with stimulating writing activities.

MAINSTREAMING

As discussed earlier, the impetus of mainstreaming was triggered by Public Law 94–142, a federal law that is designed to give handicapped children a "free appropriate public education." It requires state and local governments to provide identification programs, a special education, and related services such as transportation, testing, diagnosis, and treatment for children with speech handicaps, hearing impairments, visual handicaps, physical disabilities, emotional disturbances, learning disabilities, and mental retardation handicaps. Public Law 94–142 also requires that whenever possi-

[8]Lewis Terman and Melita, Oden, *The Gifted Child Grows Up*, Genetic Studies of Genius, Vol. 4 (Stanford, Ca.: Stanford University Press, 1947).

ble, handicapped students must be placed in regular classrooms. *Mainstreaming* is the placement of handicapped children in the least restrictive educational environment that will meet their needs.

Handicapped children who are moved to a regular classroom are supposed to be very carefully screened. Only those who seem able to benefit from being in a least restrictive environment are supposed to be put into one. The amount of time that a handicapped child spends in a regular classroom and the area in which the child participates in the regular classroom depend on the individual child. Some children who are moderately mentally retarded (trainables) may spend time each week in a regular classroom during a special activity such as a story hour.

For mainstreaming to be successful, classroom teachers must be properly prepared for this role, and teachers must enlist the aid and cooperation of every student in their class. Classroom teachers must prepare their students for the mainstreamed child by giving them some background and knowledge about the child. The amount and type of information given will, of course, vary with the grade level. Regular classroom teachers should also have the students involved in some of the planning and implementation of the program for the mainstreamed child.

For example, if teachers are expecting physically handicapped children to be admitted to their class, they can help to prepare their students by reading some books to them that portray a physically handicapped child in a sensitive and perceptive manner. Teachers might read some excerpts from Helen Keller's *The Story of My Life* or Marie Killilea's book *Karen.* After reading the excerpts teachers can engage the students in a discussion of the handicapped child's struggles, fears, hopes, concerns, goals, and dreams. Teachers can then attempt to help the children in their classes recognize that they have feelings, hopes, and fears similar to many handicapped children's. Teachers should also help their students to understand that a child with a physical handicap does not necessarily have a mental handicap. As a matter of fact, many handicapped persons are very intelligent and able to make many contributions to soci-

ety. The teacher can then discuss with the children how they think they can make the new child who is coming to their class feel at home. The teacher might use special films and television programs to initiate interest in the handicapped and to help gain better insights about them. (See section on "Television: Making It Part of the Educative Process" in Chapter 7.)

Besides preparing the children in the regular classroom for the mainstreamed child, an individualized program must be developed for each mainstreamed child in cooperation with the child's parents, the special education teacher, or consultants. The program should be one that provides a favorable learning experience for both the handicapped child and the regular classroom students. That is, the integration of a handicapped child should not take away from the program of the regular classroom children. To assure that this is not done, the NEA in 1975 passed a resolution advocating several measures: modifications in class size, scheduling, and curriculum design to accommodate the shifting demands that mainstreaming creates; appropriate instructional materials, supportive services, and pupil personnel services provided for the teacher and the handicapped student; systematic evaluation and reporting of program developments; and adequate additional funding and resources.

WHO ARE THE EXCEPTIONAL CHILDREN?

The phrase "exceptional children" is applied to those children who deviate so much from "average" or normal children that they require special attention. Exceptional children deviate from the "average" child in "(1) mental characteristics, (2) sensory abilities, (3) neuromuscular or physical characteristics, (4) social or emotional behavior, (5) communication abilities, or (6) multiple handicaps. . . ."[9] More specifically, with slight variation from state to state and author to author, exceptional children have been classified as (1) gifted, (2) educable mentally retarded, (3) trainable mentally retarded, (4) custodial mentally retarded, (5) emotionally

[9]M. Stephen Lilly, *Children with Exceptional Needs: A Survey of Special Education* (New York: Holt, Rinehart and Winston, 1979), p. 17.

disturbed, (6) socially maladjusted, (7) speech-impaired, (8) deaf, (9) hard of hearing, (10) blind, (11) partially seeing, (12) crippled, (13) chronic health cases, (14) multiple handicapped, and (15) learning disabled.

Levels of Mental Retardation

Although there are many definitions of mental retardation, the one that is most generally used is the 1973 revised definition of the American Association on Mental Deficiencies (AAMD):

Mental retardation refers to significantly subaverage general intellectual functioning existing concurrently with deficits in *adaptive behavior,* and manifested during the developmental period.[10] (italics are author's)

"Adaptive behavior" is a crucial phrase in the AAMD definition, and it is one that is often ignored. Many mildly retarded individuals function quite well outside the school environment and their mild retardation is not noticeable. They are able to adapt socially, emotionally, and physically; that is, they have sufficient communication skills, sensory-motor skills, and socialization skills to function in society as independent and self-reliant individuals if they are helped to acquire vocational skills.

The AAMD definition classifies individuals according to the severity of their mental retardation. The scale for determining the levels of mental retardation is based on individual intelligence test scores. (The cutoff for the different levels varies according to the IQ test used.) However, there are also available levels of adaptive behavior that correspond to the intellectual categories of mild, moderate, severe, and profound retardation. (See Table 17.2.)

In the revised AAMD definition, mental retardation refers to an IQ of 67 or below. Children with an IQ above 67 are not considered retarded. A category in the earlier AAMD definition called *borderline* retardation was deleted in the 1973 revision. The IQ range for the borderline

---

10H. Grossman, ed. *Manual on Terminology and Classifications in Mental Retardation,* rev. ed. (Washington, D.C.: American Association on Mental Deficiency, 1973), p. 11.

TABLE 17.2   IQ RANGES FOR THE LEVELS OF MENTAL RETARDATION

	Intelligence Tests	
	Stanford-Binet	Wechsler
Mild retardation	67 to 52	69 to 55
Moderate retardation	51 to 36	54 to 40
Severe retardation	35 to 20	39 to 25
Profound retardation	19 and below	24 and below

level is approximately 68 to 85. This group of children has many times been referred to as *slow learners,* who are between the "average" children and the mentally retarded. Special emphasis has been given to this group of children because most classroom teachers have children in this IQ range in their regular classrooms, but many teachers may not know how to provide for them.

As was stated earlier, there are a number of different definitions of mental retardation that usually have different IQ cutoffs for mental retardation. Whether a child is classified as mentally retarded or not is many times dependent on the definition of mental retardation that is being used. Since different school systems or states may use different definitions of mental retardation, a child may be considered mentally retarded in one school system or state but not in another. School systems also usually use the term *educable* to refer to mildly retarded children, *trainable* to refer to moderately retarded children, and *custodial* to refer to severely and profoundly retarded children.

IDENTIFICATION BIASES OF CHILDREN LABELED "EDUCABLE MENTALLY RETARDED"

It appears that the incidence of educable mental retardation is not equally distributed across all segments of the population. There is a tendency to label more boys as educable mentally retarded than girls. This may be because boys are usually more likely to be mischievous than girls and as a result are more likely to be candidates for referral than girls. There also seems to be a highly disproportionate number of children from lower socioeconomic status homes who are labeled educable mentally retarded. Studies show, too, that minority children are overrepresented in this group.[11]

The teacher is usually the person who first identifies the child as having a problem. Many times, as already stated, the child is referred for special testing because of nonadaptive social behavior. After the referral the child is given a number of standardized tests, of which the IQ test is the most influential in determining whether a child is retarded or not. Since studies have shown that children from minority groups and from lower socioeconomic classes usually do not do as well on IQ tests as children from the rest of the population, it is not surprising to find children from these groups disproportionately represented in the group of children labeled "educable mentally retarded."

It cannot be emphasized enough how careful teachers must be in using such terms as "mentally retarded," "emotionally disturbed," and "learning disabled" to label a child. Once labeled, the child is hardly ever able to shed that label, even though the child has been incorrectly labeled. Often children so labeled continue to function at a particular level because they, themselves, have incorporated the image that others have of them into their own self-concept. (See the section on "Teacher Assumptions" in Chapter 5.)

LEARNING DISABILITIES

The definition of learning disabilities needs special attention because there is so much confusion concerning this term. Researchers have found that the characteristics of children labeled "learning disabled" vary so much that it is impossible to list common characteristics. The way the term is used seems to vary not only from state to state but from school district to school district within a state.[12]

Although there is a great amount of confu-sion and controversy concerning the term "learning disability" and although studies have shown that there is in existence a multitude of definitions and synonyms for this term, there is one definition that is most widely accepted and acted on. The definition that is usually given for learning disabilities is that proposed by the National Advisory Committee on Handicapped Children:

Children with special learning disabilities exhibit a disorder in one or more of the basic psychological processes involved in understanding or in using spoken or written language. These may be manifested in disorders of listening, thinking, talking, reading, writing, spelling, or arithmetic. They include conditions which have been referred to as perceptual handicaps, brain injury, minimal brain dysfunction, dyslexia, developmental aphasia, etc. They do not include learning problems which are due primarily to visual, hearing, or motor handicaps, to mental retardation, emotional disturbance, or to environmental disadvantage.[13]

From this definition, we can see that there does not appear to be any logical explanation for a child's learning disability. Also, the learning disability may go undiagnosed because the child is of average or above-average intelligence, so the teacher thinks that the child is either lazy or lacks discipline.

Teachers should be especially vigilant of those children who are of average or above-average intelligence who are having some kind of learning problems because these children may have a learning disability. Teachers should refer these children for special testing. Teachers must, however, also be leery of labeling youngsters as learning disabled without adequate and substantive documentation. For example, the Black English trial in Ann Arbor showed that the school district had labeled the Green Road children as "learning disabled" and "emotionally impaired" without due consideration to their racial and linguistic backgrounds. Unfortunately, "the staff was handicapped by their inadequate

[11]Lilly, *Children,* pp. 61–62.
[12]Lilly, *Children,* p. 21.

[13]*National Advisory Committee on Handicapped Children: First Annual Report* (Washington, D.C.: U.S. Office of Education, 1968), p. 34.

knowledge of the children's characteristics and the biased nature of the tests that they were using."[14] An example is given whereby the "speech therapists weren't aware that the Wepman test included a number of oppositions that are mergers in the Black English Vernacular: *pin* vs. *pen, sheaf* vs. *sheath, clothe* vs. *clove,* and so forth."[15] (See the following section on "Children Who Speak Nonstandard English.)

CHILDREN WHO SPEAK NONSTANDARD ENGLISH

When children enter school they bring with them the language of their environment, of their family, home, and neighborhood. This first language learning they have acquired is the most deeply rooted, regardless of what other language learning they achieve later in their lives.

As has been stated many times in this text, language is acquired from the utterances of the adults who surround the child. Therefore, the listening process determines the child's speech. As a result, children who hear standard English would learn to speak standard English, whereas culturally different children, who hear another dialect or language, would learn to speak what they hear. Although we must recognize that differences exist in language and help children learn standard English, at the same time we must maintain their dignity and self-respect and be careful not to extend value judgments preferring one language or dialect over another.

As we have said in Chapter 15, linguists cannot completely standardize the phonemic system of the English language because of speech differences in different regions. They describe language based on specific local dialects, and no one of these descriptions is any more correct, or better, than any other. In describing the language of children who speak nonstandard English, it was found that there are a number of phonological, as well as structural, differences between standard and nonstandard English.

[14]William Labov, "Objectivity and Commitment in Linguistic Science: The Case of the Black English Trial in Ann Arbor," *Language in Society* 11 (August 1982):168.
[15]Ibid., 168–169.

It is probably true that facility in standard English is necessary for academic success and for admission into the higher economic community of the culture, but that does not mean that nonstandard English is "bad," nor that the persons who speak it are not worthy. There must be no implication that one language or dialect is inferior to another; learning standard English should be looked on as a useful added skill.

Since it is very important for the teacher to help all children to be able to listen and to discriminate among speech sounds that may seem strange or foreign, it would help teachers to have a better understanding of the difficulties involved if they recognized some language differences. Teachers who know the phonological and syntactic features of nonstandard English will be better able to appreciate the differences between the listening environment of the standard speaker and that of the child who speaks a nonstandard dialect. The teacher with an understanding of dialects will be able to comprehend the child's message and will be more accepting of the child; such a teacher will also be better prepared to plan language arts lessons for this child.

Since there are many dialects of English, and since a student could have grown up with an entirely different language, no attempt will be made to summarize the differences in language here (see the following section). The important thing to be stressed is attitude. Teachers must demonstrate by their attitudes that one language is as good as another, that it is just as useful for people to learn someone else's language as it is for children who speak nonstandard English to learn standard English. Everyone in the classroom can learn from everyone else. Unless the complete classroom environment—physical, emotional, social, and intellectual—reinforces this attitude, very valuable learning opportunities will be lost and actual damage to some students might be done.

The teacher must lead the way. Find out what kinds of language differences exist in the community; check with other professionals who know such communities for information about the varieties of nonstandard English likely to be encountered. Find people who can tutor these languages or dialects, read books and articles on them, listen to recordings, or develop other learning tools. You will find a bibliography of some available materials at the end of this chapter, but that is only a starting point.

Nonstandard English and Its Implications for Instruction

For children to learn standard speech, they must first feel a need to do so. To be successful they must be able to hear differences between sounds. If they hear only nonstandard speech at home, from their peers, and in the school environment, they will not have a need to learn, nor will they hear the differences necessary for learning. Children should be encouraged to express themselves as often as possible early in their school careers, in kindergarten or in preschool organized activities. They should not be criticized. They should not be told, "No, that's wrong. Say it this way." The teacher should repeat the children's sentences in standard English so that they can hear the sentence in a standard structural pattern. When a child says, "Her a good girl," the teacher might say, "Yes, she is a good girl." Unless children learn to hear differences in both the patterns of speech and in the phonemes, they will not be able to reproduce them in standard English. Similarly, unless they learn to hear the sounds and patterns of standard English, they will usually have difficulty in reading and writing.

Schools seem to have had very little effect on teaching patterns of standard English speech to speakers of nonstandard English, as evidenced by the fact that many students leave school knowing only the same speech patterns with which they entered. If a new pattern is to be learned, the process must begin as soon as the children enter school, and there should be direct rather than merely incidental instruction. Such children must have instructors who speak standard English exceptionally well.

Nonstandard English and Listening/ Speaking Instruction

The teaching of standard English to children who speak other languages or dialects is a complex process involving all the language arts areas, but it begins with listening. Since listening and the whole range of aural and oral communications are so important to success in school—and so important to the development of good skills in reading, thinking, and problem solving—it is imperative that attention be given immediately to improving the listening skills of such pupils. These children must be helped with the basic listening skills, and with setting the purpose of the listening they do. The sooner these children get help, the greater their chances for later success will be.

In order to help children who speak nonstandard English to develop sound differentiations, the teacher should emphasize auditory discrimination exercises among initial consonants, final consonants, and phonograms or graphemic bases (successions of graphemes that occur with the same phonetic value in a number of words such as *ight, ake, at, et,* and so on). Examples follow.

Auditory Discrimination Activities "Listen carefully! I am going to say some words that begin like *b*aby and *b*all. Listen and try to pick out all those words that start just like *b*aby and *b*all." Say such lists of three words as:

*b*ook	cake	*b*ox
*b*ang	*B*obby	hat
*b*anana	candy	*b*icycle
*b*aseball	apple	dog

"Now listen carefully; I may be tricky. Does everyone know what tricky means? Yes, it means to fool someone. Well, I may try to fool you. I am going to state a group of words and you will have to pick out all those words that begin like book. Now here's the tricky part. There may be some groups of words that have no words starting like book—cookie, dog, chicken. Are there any words that start like book in that list? No. That's correct. Good! Let's begin."

farm	cow	bear
box	land	school
girl	drum	letter
boy	Tom	bait
cracker	train	drum

"Now, listen carefully as I say some words. Which ones sound alike?"

man   can   tan   book

"Yes, *man, can,* and *tan* sound alike. Good. Now listen again."

look   book   cook   man

"Yes, *look, book, cook* sound alike. Good! Now listen again."

cake   bake   lake   boy

"Listen carefully. I have a riddle for you."

The word I am thinking of rhymes with lake.
It also rhymes with bake.
When mother makes it, I love to eat it.
Who knows what it is?

"Very good! It's *cake.* Listen again."

The word I am thinking of rhymes with man.
It also rhymes with can and tan.
When I am very hot I use it.
Who knows what it is?

"Yes. Very good! It's a *fan.* Listen again."

The word I am thinking of rhymes with mat.
It also rhymes with hat and fat.
It likes to drink milk and says, "Meow."
Who knows what it is?

Other Activities Other activities could involve the taping of standard and nonstandard English sentences between which children are asked to discriminate:

Nonstandard pattern: "She didn't have no money."
Standard pattern: "She didn't have any money."

It is essential that the objective of the lesson is made clear to the children at the start, and that only one pattern is introduced at a time.

In order to give them practice, for overlearning purposes, a good motivating technique is to make this activity into a game. The pupils can be divided into two, three, or four teams. The tape recorder plays four or five sentences in a nonstandard pattern and then four or five similar sentences in standard English. The children on the first team have to differentiate between them and then state all the sentences in the standard pattern. The same procedure is followed for teams two, three, and four. Different sentences are used for each team.

Another technique is to present the students with a standard English pattern, as well as its nonstandard English counterpart. The teacher repeats the standard English pattern, has the children repeat it, and then puts the children in a role-playing situation in which they have to use the standard English pattern.

The teacher can also tape children's conversations. Before playback, the teacher can ask the children to listen for their voices. Next, he or she can have them all say a number of simple sentences in standard English, which would also be taped. The teacher then can play these back so that the children can listen to themselves speaking standard English.

An activity that might be used to develop speaking and listening skills involves directions. In the game, "My turn, your turn," the teacher states some directions. The teacher points at a child and says, "Your turn." The child must then repeat and carry out the instructions.

Another activity includes "mystery" boxes. Numerous commonplace objects are put in the "mystery" box. Children must select an item from the box, state what it is, and compose a sentence in standard English naming the item.

The activities that are chosen should emphasize the aural—oral approach, stimulate interest, and encourage student participation.

The suggestions that have been provided so far for helping children who speak nonstandard English attain standard English are actually adaptations from programs designed to help students who speak another language to acquire English. The emphasis is not on doing away with the student's language but in helping the student add another language, namely, standard English. For the program to be successful, the teacher must know the structure both of standard and nonstandard English—differences in their phonology, morphology, and syntax, as well as the interference points between standard English and nonstandard English.

Pull-out programs, that is, programs where children leave the regular classroom to go for special instruction with a special teacher, are only effective if there is carry-over in the regular classroom. Probably the best way to learn standard English is to be in an environment where it is used all the time. Interaction with persons who speak standard English in a warm, responsive environment coupled with special help within the regular classroom is probably one of the most effective programs for elementary-grade-level children.[16]

A Rich Oral Program A number of studies[17] have found that children who speak nonstandard English make significant gains toward standard English when they are involved in a rich oral program, one that stresses the reading aloud of stories and the active involvement of the children in related oral activities. Teachers, beginning with kindergartners, should plan a program for children who speak nonstandard English that should include the regular and continuous listening to storybooks based on their students' interest and concept development levels. Speech-stimulating activities such as choral speaking, creative dramatics, role playing, individual poetry recitation, discussion, storytelling, and so on should follow the listening to a story so that the children can have an opportunity to express themselves. (See Chapter 7 for more on speech-stimulating activities and "Developing Vocabulary from Literature" in Chapter 9.)

A rich oral program is a necessary first step to prevent reading failure because it helps pre-pare the children for reading. The closer the children's language is to the written symbols encountered in reading, the greater their chance of success. Hearing standard English in the context of something meaningful with which they can identify helps the children gain "facility in listening, attention span, narrative sense, recall of stretches of verbalization, and the recognition of new words as they appear in other contexts.[18]

An excellent technique that combines both listening and speaking uses storybooks that have repetitious phrases and sentences throughout the story. The teacher chooses a familiar story such as the *The Three Little Pigs*, which she or he reads aloud to the children. When the teacher comes to the repetitious parts, she or he pauses, points to the children, and has them say the words aloud. This technique can be done also with poems.

Writing and Children Who Speak Nonstandard English

When children who speak nonstandard English write, teachers must determine (1) if they have a problem in conveying their thoughts in a logical, clear, and creative manner, or (2) if they are having problems in the mechanics of writing. While the latter could interfere with students' written communication, it is not as severe a problem as the one in which the student cannot logically or coherently express himself or herself in writing. It seems logical that students who speak in nonstandard English would probably write in the same dialect, and many do. For example, students who do not include standard inflectional endings on nouns or verbs will usually not include them in their writing, ("Yesterday, the boy work hard, and . . ."). Similarly, those who use a redundant pronoun ("The man, he, . . ."), the double plural of irregular nouns (sheeps, feets) and double negatives ("Jim don't know nobody") will probably do the same in their writing. Teachers need to help these students learn to write in standard English, but they must also respect their stu-

[16]See Carole Urzúa, "A Language-learning Environment for all Children," *Language Arts* 57 (January 1980): 38–44.

[17]Dorothy Strickland, "A Program for Linguistically Different Black Children," Eric # ED 049 355, April 22, 1971; and Bernice E. Cullinan, Angela M. Jaggar, and Dorothy Strickland, "Language Expansion for Black Children in the Primary Grades: A Research Report," *Young Children* 29 (January 1974): 98–112.

[18]Dorothy H. Cohen, *The Effect of Literature*, p. 217.

dents' ideas. If the teacher embarrasses these students and concentrates only on the mechanics of writing, he or she will probably inhibit these students from putting pen to paper.

Sociolinguists have suggested that phonological and grammatical factors may be interfering with nonstandard English speakers' ability to read. Although reading and spelling are related by their use of common word symbols, they are not similar (one requires decoding, the other encoding), as we have seen. However, they both require the ability to discriminate visually and are based on adequate auditory discrimination. It is, therefore, logical to assume that many phonological and grammatical interferences that impede reading also hinder spelling. Studies have shown this to be true.

Some investigators claim that children who speak nonstandard English go through the same sequential stages that standard English spellers do and that nonstandard English children's invented spelling reflects their dialect.[19] This is not surprising. The problem is that children who speak nonstandard English often seem to have many more spelling difficulties than standard English speakers. They are spelling words the way they "hear" and "say" them. Teachers need to be aware of this. And they should not fault children for this: Vowel variations may produce a set of homonyms; for example, pin = pen and beer = bear. Simplification of final consonant clusters can produce another set of homonyms; for example, guest = guess, past = pass, and walked = walk. The weakening of final consonants creates yet another set of homonyms; for example, road = row and seat = sea.

Children who omit the r before vowels, as well as consonants, may produce another set of homonyms; for example, Carol = Cal, Paris = Pas, and guard = god. Those students who omit the l from a word may also be forming another set of homonyms; for example, toll = toe, help = hep, fault = fought, and tool = too. It can be seen that students who hear "toe" for "toll" will certainly have difficulty in spelling or reading "toll."[20]

A student who speaks nonstandard English may spell the plural of "desk" "desses" because desk = des, and a closed-syllable word that ends in s is made plural by doubling the final consonant and adding es.

To minimize confusion teachers need to be familiar with the sound and structure system of persons who speak nonstandard English. The following dialogue between a second-grade student and his teacher aptly exemplifies this point. The child asks his teacher to spell the word "rat." The teacher replies, "r-a-t." The child says, "No, ma'am. I don't mean rat mouse. I mean right now!"[21]

Another problem that children who speak nonstandard English may have concerns the dictionary. Students who look up words under the wrong spellings because of their difficulty in recognizing standard spellings are going to be frustrated. In order to spell words in standard English, these students must be able to hear the phonological differences between standard and nonstandard English, make discriminations between them, be able to pronounce the words in standard English, and also see the words in print so that they can form a visual memory of the words.

[19]Elizabeth S. Stever, "Dialect and Spelling," in *Development and Cognitive Aspects of Learning to Spell*, Edmund H. Henderson and James W. Beers, eds. (Newark, Del.: IRA, 1980), pp. 46–51.

[20]William Labov, *The Study of Nonstandard English* (Champaign, Ill.: National Council of Teachers of English, 1970), pp. 65–67.
[21]Diane N. Bryen, Cheryl Hartman, and Pearl E. Tait, *Variant English* (Columbus, Ohio: Merrill, 1978), p. 207.

SUMMARY

Teachers usually have children with a wide range of ability levels in their classrooms, which generally include borderline (slow-learning) and gifted children. Now, because of mainstreaming, many teachers can expect at some time to have children who are physically handicapped, emotionally troubled, learning disabled, and mildly and moderately mentally retarded. Teachers must, therefore, be prepared for their new role, and an individualized program must be developed for mainstreamed children in cooperation with the children's parents and the special education teacher or the consultant. In this chapter, language arts methods are provided that are most applicable for dealing with borderline and gifted children; however, they may also be adapted for some of the children who may be mainstreamed.

Exceptional children are those children who deviate so much from the average that they re-quire special attention. The category of exceptional children includes the gifted as well as the physically handicapped, the emotionally disturbed, and the learning disabled. Adaptive behavior is an important factor in defining individuals who are mentally retarded. Teachers must be especially cautious in using such terms as "mentally retarded," "emotionally disturbed," and "learning disabled" to label a child. Labels are difficult to shed.

This chapter also presents a special section on children who speak nonstandard English.

SUGGESTIONS FOR THOUGHT QUESTIONS AND ACTIVITIES

1. Prepare a special language arts lesson for a mainstreamed child of your choice. Do the same for a slow learner.

2. You have been put on a special school committee to help develop a language arts program for the gifted students in your elementary school. What suggestions will you make?

3. What types of language arts activities would you prepare to help children who speak nonstandard English?

4. You have been asked to give a talk on mainstreaming. What will you say?

SELECTED BIBLIOGRAPHY

Aiello, Barbara, ed. *Making It Work: Practical Ideas for Integrating Exceptional Children into Regular Classrooms.* Reston, Va.: The Council for Exceptional Children, 1975.

Baskin, Barbara Holland, and Karen H. Harris, eds. *The Special Child in the Library.* Chicago; American Library Association, 1976.

———. *Books for the Gifted.* New York: R. R. Bowker, 1980. Carter, Candy, Chair, and the Committee on Classroom Practices. *Non-Native and Nonstandard Dialect Students.* Urbana, Ill.: NCTE, 1982.

Dexter, Beverly L. *Special Education and the Classroom Teacher: Concepts, Perspectives, and Strategies.* Springfield, Ill.: C. C. Thomas, 1977.

"The Gifted and the Talented." (Special Feature) *Today's Education* 65 (January/February 1976): 26–44.

Hart, Vera. *Mainstreaming Children with Special Needs.* New York: Longman, 1980.

Labov, William. *The Study of Nonstandard English.* Urbana, Ill.: National Council of Teachers of English, 1970.

Labuda, Michael, ed. *Creative Reading for Gifted Learners: A Design for Excellence.* Newark, Del.: International Reading Association, 1974.

Lamm, Stanley S., Martin L. Fisch, and Don McDonagh. *Learning Disabilities Explained.* New York: Doubleday, 1982.

"Mainstreaming." (Special Feature) *Today's Education* 65 (March/April 1976): 18–32.

Paul, James L., Ann P. Turnbull, and William M. Cruickshank. *Mainstreaming: A Practical Guide.* Syracuse, N.Y.: Syracuse University Press, 1977.

Polette, Nancy, and Marjorie Hamlin. *Exploring Books with Gifted Children.* Littleton, Co.: Libraries Unlimited, Inc., 1980.

Spodek, Bernard, Olivia N. Saracho, and Richard C. Lee. *Mainstreaming Young Children.* Belmont, Ca.: Wadsworth, 1983.

Terman, Lewis M., and Melita H. Oden. *The Gifted Child Grows Up.* Genetic Studies of Genius, Vol. 4. Stanford, Ca.: Stanford University Press, 1947.

Tompkins, Gail E., and Lea M. McGee. "Launching Nonstandard Speakers into Standard English." *Language Arts* 60 (April 1983): 463–469.

Turnbull, Ann P., and Jane B. Schulz. *Mainstreaming Handicapped Students: A Guide for Classroom Teachers.* Boston: Allyn and Bacon, 1979.

EIGHTEEN

Diagnosis, the Evaluative Process, and the Language Arts

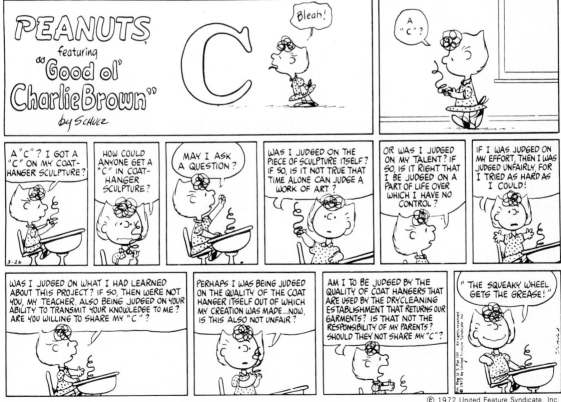

The term "evaluation" seems to bring shudders to most people. Although some individuals may look on evaluation as necessary, it is often considered an intrusion to be avoided for as long as possible. The following remarks were overheard in one school. Do they sound familiar to you?

PERSON A: "Shh, everyone be alert! Keep the kids quiet! We're being evaluated!"

PERSON B: "Oh no! Don't tell me we're being evaluated again. We just finished testing our students."

To some, evaluation, tests, and measurement are synonymous. But they are not.

"Evaluation is the process of delineating, obtaining, and providing useful information for judging decision alternatives."[1] The term "test," which is the narrowest of the three terms, "connotes the presentation of a standard set of questions to be answered. As a result of a person's answers to such a series of questions, we obtain a measure (that is, a numerical value) of a characteristic of that person. 'Measurement' refers to the use of tests, but also observations, rating scales, or any other device that allows us to obtain information in a quantitative form."[2] Evaluation involves making value judgments and is, therefore, larger in scope than measurement, which is limited to quantitative descriptions.

Good evaluation occurs at the beginning, during, and end of the educative process; is based on an adequate collection of data; and is done in terms of desired objectives and standards. Since evaluation is a process carried on by humans, good evaluators avoid emotional bias in their judgments by using a variety of measurement techniques and instruments. It is important to state also that we do not evaluate or measure people; we measure or evaluate *characteristics* or *properties* of people.[3]

---

[1]Daniel L. Stufflebaum et al., *Educational Evaluation and Decision Making.* (Bloomington, Ind.: Phi Delta Kappa, 1971), p. xxv.

[2]William A. Mehrens and Irvin J. Lehmann, *Standardized Tests in Education,* 3d ed. (New York: Holt, Rinehart and Winston, 1980), p. 2.

[3]Ibid., p. 3.

RELATION OF EVALUATION TO THE EDUCATIVE PROCESS

Evaluation is a necessary, ongoing process that should be present throughout the general educational and language arts programs.

Figure 18.1 shows how the evaluative process influences and is influenced by the educational program. It also illustrates the interrelationships between and among the various parts of the educative system.

Although this text is concerned only with the language arts curriculum in the elementary school, it is important for readers to recognize that evaluation of the educational process as a whole will influence the kind of language arts program that will be developed, how it will be taught, and how students and teachers will be assessed. For example, if the Board of Education in a particular school system believes in stringent censorship, it may outlaw certain books. This would affect the objectives of the children's literature program, which would, in turn, affect all the kinds of materials used in the classroom. This would influence the teaching–learning situation. The ramifications are many.

EVALUATIVE CRITERIA FOR THE LANGUAGE ARTS

A good evaluative system should meet these criteria:

1. Determine *what* is to be evaluated in the languate arts program
2. Recognize evaluation as a *means,* not as an end
3. Take into account the *principles* of the language arts program
4. Encompass all *objectives* valued in the language arts program
5. Facilitate *teaching and learning* of language arts
6. Enhance self-evaluation in the language arts
7. Provide appropriate assessments of progress in the language arts
8. Recognize the limitations of assessment techniques

DIAGNOSIS

A good language arts program must have a good diagnostic program because diagnosis

FIGURE 18.1   Evaluation is a continuous and integral part of the educative process.

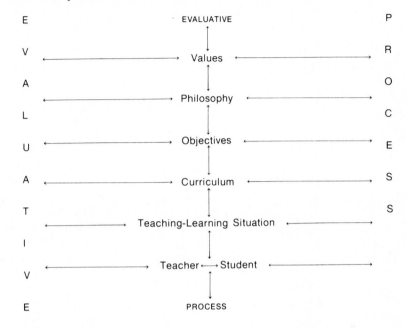

and instruction are interwoven; early diagnosis is essential; and diagnosis is continuous. In a good diagnostic–language arts program, teachers recognize that learning takes place in a nonthreatening atmosphere, that is, a good affective enrivonment. Also, in diagnosis, teachers focus on the individual child because diagnosis is an individual process and a means to correction.

Teachers use both group and individual diagnostic tests and other techniques to learn about students' language arts behavior. A diagnostic test is designed to break down a complex skill into its component parts to help teachers learn about a student's strengths and weaknesses. Criterion-referenced tests are examples of good diagnostic tests because they present a set of behaviorally stated objectives that describe language arts behaviors at rather specific levels. (See "Criterion-Referenced Tests" later in this chapter.)

As previously stated, diagnosis is essential to the language arts program because it underlies prevention; that is, continuous diagnosis

helps teachers nip in the bud an emerging problem. In this text *diagnosis* is defined as the act of *identifying* language arts difficulties and strengths from their signs and then analyzing the cause(s) or nature of the condition, situation, or problem. The first step in diagnosis is identification of signs or symptoms, such as the child's inability to write a sentence correctly, to consistently spell words correctly, to answer questions after listening to a selection, to speak logically, and so on. The second step in diagnosis is determination of the roots of the problem by analyzing the kind of difficulties the child is having. This is done through a careful investigation of the strategies and techniques the child is using in language arts. It may also include looking into individual difference factors (see Chapter 2).

It is important to note that in the first step, we look for both language arts strengths and weaknesses because knowledge of what a child can do is helpful often in giving us insight into a child's language arts problem. In the second step, we generally find that a language arts problem is due to a number of factors rather than to just one. In the identification phase, the teacher examines the student's present status in a particular problem area by describing in detail the student's performance. For example, if a student is having difficulty in writing, the teacher would describe in detail what skills the student possesses, whether the student has word usage problems, spelling problems, vocabulary difficulties, and so on. The teacher would note whether the student writes logically and whether what he or she has to say makes sense. The teacher would determine whether the student is able to write paragraphs so that each has a main idea and whether each of the paragraphs logically develop the central theme of the composition. The teacher could use teacher-made tests or standardized tests to assess further the student's spelling, word usage, sentence sense, and punctuation ability.

In the next step, the determination phase, the teacher tries to find the specific conditions and abilities that underlie the student's performance in a particular area by observing the student during the activity. For example, while writing, does the child display any anxieties? Does the child have writing problems because he or she has not had any experience in writing? That is, perhaps the child has never been asked to write a composition before. The teacher tries to learn from the student about his or her writing experiences in former classes. (See the next section, "Student Involvement.") Next, the teacher tries to determine whether the abilities involved in the specific skill area are causing the difficulty. For example, lack of spelling skills may be due to deficiencies in auditory or visual discrimination (perceptual problems), lack of memory (retention problems), left-handedness (see "Spelling and the Left-Handed Child" in Chapter 13), or nonstandard English speech. Through further diagnostic testing and observation, the teacher tries to determine whether the problem is due to organic or experiential factors. Obviously, if the teacher suspects an organic problem, he or she should make the proper referrals so that the child can see the proper professionals or medical persons. The teacher should also try to determine whether the student's problem in a specific area is due to the student's attitude or motivation.

Student Involvement

The primary purpose for diagnosis is to determine what is causing a student's problem so that a program can be developed to help overcome the difficulty. Student involvement is crucial. Unless the student recognizes that he or she has a problem, understands what that problem is, and is interested in overcoming the problem, correction will be limited.

The teacher can help the student become involved in the following ways:

1. The teacher should help the student recognize his or her strengths as well as weaknesses.
2. The teacher should not overwhelm the student with a listing of all his or her difficulties at once.
3. The teacher should try to elicit from the student what the student thinks his or her language arts problems are, why the student feels that he or she has these problems, and what the student feels are the causes.
4. The teacher and the student together set attainable goals for a specific problem area.
5. Together, the next learning step is determined.

In language arts classes teachers and students usually combine their efforts to develop standards for different activities. Examples of standards by which students can evaluate themselves are presented in the various subject-matter chapters.

Describing Student Errors

So that evaluation is diagnostic, the nature of student errors must be pointed out as clearly as possible. The student should understand exactly what the teacher is saying.

The "Poor handwriting!" on a student's paper will not help a child correct the problem. The teacher should help the student understand that an illegible paper cannot be read and that communication is, therefore, not taking place. Examples of legible handwriting against which children can judge themselves should be available. Teachers should also point out specific problems in constructing letters so that the children can improve in this area. For example, the teacher could say, "In writing the *e* for cursive you are not forming your loop, so that it is difficult to tell the *e* from the *i*." (See the diagnostic checklists at the end of each language arts subject-matter chapter.)

Knowledge of Results

Since feedback is essential in correcting faulty responses, teachers should always go over tests as soon as possible—immediately after the test is the best time. One technique that helps students eliminate errors is to have them write their answers twice. Students fold their papers vertically in half. They then write their answers on one side of the paper and at the end of the test they copy the answers on the other side of the paper, which is then ripped down the creased edge. One sheet is given to the teacher; the other is retained. When the test is reviewed immediately afterward, the student gets immediate knowledge of results.

MEASUREMENT TECHNIQUES FOR DIAGNOSIS AND EVALUATION

Examinations are formidable, even to the best prepared, for the greatest fool may ask more than the wisest man can answer.

C. C. Colton

The positive values of measurement outweigh the negative connotations associated with it. Measurement is useful for diagnostic, review, and predictive purposes. It can be used as a motivating technique for students, as well as a basis for grades and promotion. Through the use of measurement techniques, teachers are also able to reevaluate their own teaching methods.

In order for measurement to be an effective part of the diagnostic and evaluative process, teachers must master varied measurement techniques and be able to administer and interpret them. Such measurements include standardized tests and teacher-made tests. Direct ob-

servation of student behavior is also necessary in order to collect data for valid evaluations.

Criteria for a Good Test

Whatever tests teachers choose, the tests should all meet these criteria:

1. *Objectivity:* The same score must result regardless of who marks the test. Since essay questions do not lend themselves to a high degree of objectivity, the users of such tests should give specific directions for scoring, and should make the essay question as explicit as possible.
2. *Validity:* The appraisal instrument should measure what it claims to measure. There are different kinds of validity, but language arts teachers will be concerned primarily with the content of a test. In order to determine content validity the test should be compared with course content.
3. *Reliability:* The test is reliable if it consistently produces similar results when repeated measurements are taken of the same students under the same conditions.
4. *Suitability:* In selecting or preparing a test, the teacher must determine not only whether it will yield the type of data desired but also whether the test is suitable for the age and type of students and for the locality in which the students reside.

Standardized Tests

Standardized tests are published tests that generally have been constructed by experts in the field and are available from publishers.[4] They are usually developed in a very precise fashion and they should be precisely administered. Standardized tests contain exact instructions on how to administer them, and these instructions are supposed to be followed by all testers.

Confusion may exist concerning the definition of standardized tests because of changes

[4]Oscar K. Buros's *Mental Measurements Yearbooks* are an important source on standardized tests. A teacher can use these reference yearbooks to obtain information about specific tests or to locate tests in specific areas.

in the way the term is currently being used in comparison with how it has been used in the past and is still being used by many, especially in the reading field. Good's *Dictionary of Education,* the *Dictionary of Psychology,* the *Dictionary of Behavioral Sciences,* and the *International Dictionary* all include *norm-referenced* as one of the criteria for a standardized test; however, today the definition does not necessarily include that criterion. Today, a standardized test may or may not be a norm-referenced test. A test is considered to be a standardized test if it is a published test with specific instructions for administration and scoring.[5] Michael Zieky, a senior examiner at Educational Testing Service, defines a standardized test as "any published test in which rules exist such that the test is administered to all examinees under the same conditions.[6] In this text, a test that has been published by experts in the field and has precise instructions for administration and scoring will be considered a standardized test.

Although not all standardized tests have norms, most do. Norms are average scores for a given group of students, which allow comparisons to be made for different students or groups of individuals. The norms are derived from a random sampling of a cross-section of a large population of individuals. The use of a large representative sample of students for research is obviously not possible with a teacher-made test. (See the next section "Teacher-Made Tests.")

Norm-referenced tests are used to help teachers learn where their own students stand in relation to others in the class, school system, city, state, or nation. Although a child may be doing average work in a particular class, the child may be above average when compared to other norms. Similarly, it is possible for a child to be doing above-average work in a third-grade class but to be below average for all third-graders in the nation.

Teachers must be cautious in their analysis of test results. They should not be intimidated by standardized tests and must recognize their limitations. Teachers must determine whether a test is appropriate for their students. If the class has not covered the work in the standardized test, the test obviously would not be valid. Differences in student populations must also be taken into account in interpreting test results.

Another important factor concerns the students themselves. Students who are overly anxious or upset by a test, who are tired or hungry, or who lack motivation will not perform as well as others not burdened in this manner. Such factors will adversely affect test performance. Read Dick Gregory's disturbing words:

The teacher thought I was stupid. Couldn't spell, couldn't read, couldn't do arithmetic. Just stupid. Teachers were never interested in finding out that you couldn't concentrate because you were so hungry, because you hadn't had any breakfast. All you could think about was noontime, would it ever come? Maybe you could sneak into the cloakroom and steal a bite of some kid's lunch out of a coat pocket. A bite of something. Paste. You can't really make a meal of paste, or put it on bread for a sandwich, but sometimes I'd scoop a few spoonfuls out of the big paste jar in the back of the room. Pregnant people get strange tastes. I was pregnant with poverty.[7]

Teacher-Made Tests

Teacher-made tests are prepared by the classroom teacher for a particular class and given under conditions of his or her own choosing.[8] Usually, teacher-made tests are the primary basis for evaluating students' school progress.

Teachers can get quick feedback on student learning behaviors by constructing appropriate informal tests. Since these tests to a large extent help to determine students' grades,

[5]J. Stanley Ahmann and Marvin Glock, *Evaluating Student Progress: Principles of Tests and Measurements,* 6th ed. (Boston: Allyn and Bacon, 1981), p. 285.

[6]Michael Zieky, senior examiner, Educational Testing Service (ETS), Princeton, N.J., 1983.

[7]Dick Gregory, *Nigger: An Autobiography* (New York: E. P. Dutton, 1964), p. 44.

[8]William A. Mehrens and Irvin J. Lehmann, *Measurement and Evaluation in Education and Psychology,* 2d ed. (New York: Holt, Rinehart and Winston, 1975), p. 14.

they must be carefully constructed so that valid results are achieved. For example, if contractions are being taught in class, the test should cover contractions only.

Test Types Tests are usually classified into essay and objective types. The teacher must decide which kind is the most applicable for the area being tested. Although language arts lends itself more to essay tests, both these and objective tests can be used. Objective tests allow for more comprehensive coverage of an area, while essay tests cover subject matter to a greater depth. Objective tests are also more easily graded because there is usually only one correct answer for a given question. Since essay tests are subjective, they are more difficult to grade, Studies have shown that the same essay, graded by different teachers, will receive as many different evaluations as the number of teachers rating the essay.[9] Similarly, an essay graded by a teacher in the morning may receive a different rating if it is graded by the same person in the evening or the next day.

These suggestions may help teachers to determine when to use essay tests:

1. The group to be tested is small, and the test will not be reused.
2. The instructor wishes to do everything possible to encourage and reward the development of student skill in written expression.
3. The instructor is more interested in exploring the students' attitudes than in measuring achievements.
4. The instructor is more confident of his or her proficiency as a critical reader than as an imaginative writer of good objective test items.
5. The time available for test preparation is shorter than the time available for test grading.[10]

In devising essay-test questions the teacher should avoid ambiguity, making the questions as specific as possible, with explicit directions. For example:

> *Poor:*   Explain the poem _____
> *Better:* Compare the poem _____
> to the poem _____
> in terms of the author's ability to portray the idea of "fatalism."

An essay is defined as "a test item which requires a response composed by the examinee, usually in the form of one or more sentences, of a nature that no single response or pattern of responses can be listed as correct, and the accuracy and quality of which can be judged subjectively only by one skilled or informed in the subject."[11] A good example of this type of essay question in an English class is one asking the student to write on "How I Feel about Poetry" or "How I Feel about Poe's Stories." It is impossible to assess correctness of content, and the grader must make a subjective judgment of quality.

Such topics have value when the teacher wants to evaluate students' ability to write logically and to organize the subject matter, as well as when students' ability to use proper word usage and punctuation is to be investigated. If this is the purpose of the essay, students should be told so before the test.

Essay questions are also useful for measuring divergent thinking, since there are no correct answers in a test of this kind. However, the difficulty comes in determining what criteria to use in measuring creativity.

Objective tests include true–false, multiple-choice, fill-in, and matching questions. For example, a fill-in test where students have to put in the correct word could be devised to show understanding of the homonyms "to," "too," and "two." Put the correct word in the following sentences:

> I _____(to, two, too) want to go.
> He went _____(to, two, too) town.
> The children have _____(to, two, too) balls.

[9]B. Claude Mathis, John W. Cotton, Lee Sechrest, *Psychological Foundations of Education* (New York: Academic Press, 1970), pp. 614–620.

[10] R. L. Ebel, *Measuring Educational Achievement* (Englewood Cliffs, N.J.: Prentice-Hall, 1965), pp. 109–110.

[11]*Psychological Foundations*, As cited by J. Stalnaker in Mathis, et al., p. 613.

Criterion-Referenced Tests

Criterion-referenced tests are based on an extensive inventory of learning objectives in a specific curriculum area. The objectives are presented in behavioral terms; that is, they state what behavior the student would exhibit to demonstrate his or her accomplishment of the desired end.

Criterion-referenced tests are designed to diagnose specific behaviors of individual students. They are used to gain more information about the students' various skill levels, and the information is used to either reinforce, supplement, or remediate the skill-development area being tested. The test results help the instructor plan specific learning sequences to help the students master the objective they missed.

Criterion-referenced tests are not norm-based; that is, they do not provide a means for comparing students to a standardization sample or a norm group. Criterion-referenced tests are concerned primarily with mastery of behavioral objectives, which are based on classroom curriculum. On criterion-referenced tests an individual competes only with him- or herself. There is very little difference in appearance between a norm-referenced test and a criterion-referenced test; however, differences do exist, as has already been noted, in the purposes for the tests. Following are examples of a criterion-referenced test question and the related specific pupil behavioral objective. (Note that in criterion-referenced testing *every* test item is related to a corresponding behavioral objective.)

General area: reading comprehension (interpretation)
Specific area: drawing inferences
Behavioral objective: The student will draw inferences about the personality of the main character based on the content of reading material.

The child is asked to read a short story carefully. After the child has finished reading the story, the child is asked to answer questions based on the story. An example of a question based on the given behavioral objective follows:

What can you infer about the personality of Dennis?

The child is then asked to choose the best answer from the given statements.

Criterion-referenced tests can be commercially produced or teacher-made. Many individualized programs use criterion-referenced tests (see Chapter 16). Also, a criterion-referenced test can be administered individually or to a group. (A criterion-referenced test is considered standardized if it is a published test that has been prepared by experts in the field and has precise instructions for administration and scoring.)

OBSERVATION OF STUDENTS' LEARNING BEHAVIORS

The best method for determining whether students have learned something is to observe whether they are actually using what they have learned. For example, it is one thing to be able to pass a paper-and-pencil test on proper punctuation in letter writing, but it is something else to apply these principles when actually writing letters, whether in or out of school. Another example would be the difference between stating the importance of being courteous and giving examples of courteous behavior on a paper-and-pencil test, and behaving in a courteous manner at all times.

Direct observation is helpful to the teacher who wants to become aware of the attitudes, interests, and appreciations of students. For example, teachers can observe whether students are volunteering to participate in discussion and to work in group projects, and whether they voluntarily take books from the library and read them. Teachers can also learn about students' interests by observing what they do in their free time.

So that observations are of value, teachers must be as objective as possible and avoid making generalizations about students' behavior too early in the process of getting to know them. For example, by observing that Jane on one or two occasions is reading mystery stories, the teacher states that Jane likes mysteries. This may be so, but it may also be that she is just "trying them out." Jane may actually like only a few of them and she may read only one or two a year.

Checklists

Checklists usually consist of lists of behaviors that the observer checks as present or absent. Checklists are a means for systematically and quickly recording a student's behavior. They are not tests, although it is possible to present or devise a test to enable the rapid filling out of a checklist of behaviors; in other words, the test is administered to get the result, which is the student's profile. At the end of every subject-matter chapter in this book there is a diagnostic checklist that you can use as an aid in diagnosing students' strengths and weaknesses.

DIFFICULTIES IN GRADING

> FATHER: "Well, Beth, how are your marks?"
> DAUGHTER: "They're under water."
> FATHER: "What do you mean 'under water'?"
> DAUGHTER: "Below C level."

We usually do not joke about our own grades, for they often affect our subsequent learning behavior. Grades may act as positive reinforcement for those students with good grades, but they negatively reinforce those with poor marks. Yet when pupils are overly concerned about grades, the grades may become more important than learning the material.

Grading is a complex topic. Some educators feel that traditional grades should be discarded, and "replaced with something more informative, more diagnostic, and more harmonious with students' own motivations."[12]

The subjectivity inherent in grading brings up the problem of unreliability.

A child returned home from school with his report card for his mother's inspection. "But, dear," she said, "what's the trouble? Why do you have such poor grades this month?" "There's no trouble, Mom," was the quick reply. "You know yourself things are always marked down after the holidays."

Different criteria may be used by different teachers as a basis for grading. For example, one teacher may use a composite of the students' test scores, while another may use the effort exerted by the student in class work. In the second case, a student who receives A's on all language arts papers, but perceived by the teacher as not exerting effort, may not get an 'A' on his or her report card. Some teachers lower the grade if neatness counts in their evaluation. Student absences, lateness, deport-

---

[12]Fred T. Wilhelms, "Evaluation as Feedback," and Clifford F. S. Bebell, "The Evaluation We Have," in *Evaluation as Feedback and Guide,* Fred T. Wilhelms, ed. (Washington, D.C.: Association for Supervision and Curriculum Development, 1967), pp. 6 and 45.

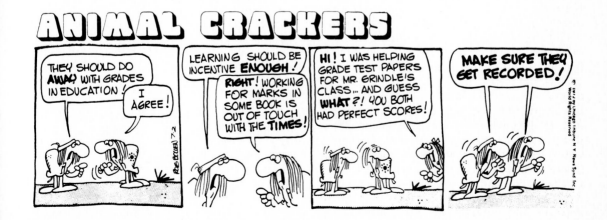

ment, and show of interest can all be factors in determining a grade.

There are teachers who award grades based on pupils' achievement in relation to ability. A child with high ability would be expected to do more than a student with low ability. As a result, low ability children doing less good work might get higher grades than high-ability students doing higher-quality work that was, nevertheless, not up to teacher expectation.

For grades to have any significance and uniformity, school systems must determine the criteria for grading. Students and parents should be informed as to what the criteria are. The grade will be a more accurate evaluation of student performance if a number of valid measurement techniques are used and other information is given.

Other Criteria Affecting Grades

"The teacher said I must learn to write more legibly," she told her father, "but if I do, she'll find out I can't spell."

Should teachers lower grades when a paper is messy or if there are spelling errors if the answers are correct? Should teachers lower grades because of poor handwriting if the ideas are creatively expressed? These questions are important to both students and teachers. Although it is important to recognize the interrelatedness of such factors, and although transference of learning to other areas is desirable, teachers must grade according to the degree that objectives have been achieved. If a teacher cannot decide whether an *i* is an *e* on a spelling test, then the teacher is justified in marking the word incorrect and asking the child to write more legibly. However, in an outlining test, or in the writing of a creative composition, the teacher should not "grade down" a paper with spelling errors or one that is not neat. The incorrect spelling should be corrected by the teacher, although the error will not count in the grade. Neatness is more difficult to handle. However, as children gain respect for their own

work and take more pride in it, it is to be hoped that they will attempt to be neater.

REPORTING PUPIL PROGRESS TO PARENTS

"How is my child doing?" is the question parents most often want the teacher to answer. The method used to report pupil progress will reflect the kind of program prevalent in the school. The report to parents, which consists of specific compartmentalized sections of the curriculum in which a letter or percentage grade is given, probably reflects a curriculum taught in a compartmentalized way. If the report is vague, the curriculum probably is also. If the report is direct, informative, and individualized, an unusual curriculum probably lies behind it. Such a report would consist of a combination of grades and written reports, as well as parent–teacher conferences.

The parent–teacher conference is the most effective way of reporting pupil progress. So that these conferences give the greatest value, teachers should have a progressive sampling of the student's work available. Teachers must be friendly, interested, and allow for an exchange of ideas with parents. It is also important for teachers to recognize that, although they have 25 or 30 students in the class, this particular child is the most important one to the parents because he or she is theirs.

Teachers should help parents understand the grading system and should discuss the children's ranking in relation to the class, national norms, and their own abilities. Most importantly, since this conference is primarily an exchange of ideas, teachers should encourage parents to give some insights into the children that would be helpful in teaching them. Remember, it is doubtful that anyone knows these children better than their parents. If the children need any special help, teachers should point this out to parents and explain precisely what they can do.

Parent–teacher conferences need not take place only during the reporting period. Whenever a need for a conference arises is the right time to call for one. However, teachers should remember that successful parent–teacher conferences require careful planning and effort.

SUMMARY

The evaluative process should be an integral part of the language arts program. It is continuous, beginning at the inception of the language arts program and going on throughout the school year. Effective evaluation is a complex task based on accurate measurement as well as other assessment techniques. It involves more than measurement.

Evaluation is done in terms of desired outcomes. The more explictly such objectives are stated, the more effective the evaluation will be. Behavioral objectives, which are stated in terms of overt student behavior, describe what students will be doing to show achievement of the goals.

Assessment of students' learning behaviors requires an adequate and accurate collection of data and knowledge of diagnosis. Early diagnosis is essential and should be interwoven with instruction. Teachers must know about standardized tests and should be adept at constructing teacher-made tests. One difficulty in grading arises from the different criteria used as a basis for grading. When properly planned, the parent–teacher conference is most effective in reporting pupil progress.

SUGGESTIONS FOR THOUGHT QUESTIONS AND ACTIVITIES

1. You have been chosen to give a talk to your colleagues concerning the importance of diagnosis in the language arts program. What will you say?

2. In evaluating a child's work, what methods would you use to diagnose any problems the child may have? What kinds of procedures would you suggest for alleviating any such problem or problems?

3. As a teacher, how would you evaluate your success in presenting a language arts program to students?

4. You have been selected to serve on a school committee whose responsibility it is to evaluate the language arts program in the school. How will you proceed? (*Hint:* What factors must you take into account? What assessment techniques will you use?)

SELECTED BIBLIOGRAPHY

Ahmann, J. Stanley, and Marvin Glock. *Evaluating Student Progress: Principles of Tests and Measurements,* 6th ed. Boston: Allyn and Bacon, 1981.

Gronlund, Norman E. *Measurement and Evaluation in Teaching.* New York: Macmillan, 1981.

Hillerich, Robert L. "A Diagnostic Approach to Early Identification of Language Skills." *Reading Teacher* 31 (January 1978) : 357–364.

Mehrens, William A., and Irvin J. Lehmann. *Measurement and Evaluation in Education and Psychology,* 2d ed. New York: Holt, Rinehart and Winston, 1975.

———. *Standardized Tests in Education,* 3d ed. New York: Holt, Rinehart and Winston, 1980.

Olmstead, Patricia P., et al. *Parent Education: The Contributions of Ira J. Gordon.* Washington, D.C.: Association for Childhood Education International, 1980.

NINETEEN

Language Arts in Content Areas

Is it possible for a day to go by in a content-area class without any language arts? Without listening, speaking, reading, or writing? Definitely not. Read the following typical teacher statements.

TEACHER: "Class, I want you to write a summary of the science experiment."

TEACHER: "Listen carefully because I'm going to give you information on how to conduct the experiment."

TEACHER: "Each group will be responsible for presenting an oral report on their social studies project."

TEACHER: "Read carefully your assignment. We'll discuss it tomorrow, and we'll probably have a quiz on it on Thursday."

TEACHER: "A special speaker is coming to class on Friday. Listen carefully so that you can ask good questions."

And so it goes . . .

From the teacher's statements, we can see that language arts play an exceptionally important role in the acquisition of content concepts. In other words, competency in the language arts is necessary for competency in content areas, and it is possible that many students have problems in their content-area classes because they have not acquired certain language arts skills. This chapter will discuss and present some techniques that content-area teachers could use in their classes to help students acquire the language arts skills that they need to gain content concepts.

LANGUAGE ARTS SKILLS AS A MEANS TO LEARNING CONTENT

In the elementary grades many teachers teach in a self-contained classroom. The advantages of such a classroom is that teachers have many opportunities to integrate the language arts with the content areas. In a number of school districts, students in the middle- and upper-elementary grades may go to special teachers for various subjects. Even though these teachers may not have as many opportunities as teachers in self-contained classrooms to integrate the language arts with the content area they are teaching, it can and should be done.

The emphasis in any content-area class at any grade level is to attain the concepts of the specific content area; however, the technique includes language arts skills. In other words, the language arts activities are not ends in themselves; they are a means to an end. For example, listening or writing skills are not taught in a content-area class for the sake of having students practice them. They are taught either to help students gain certain content concepts or to show that they have been acquired.

Here are two scenarios that should help you gain a better understanding of the place of language arts in the content areas.

SCENARIO 1: INTERMEDIATE-GRADE SCIENCE LESSON

Ms. Mills, the teacher, tells her fifth-grade students that she had a great deal of difficulty understanding some of their science reports. On a recent test, for example, she had found that many of them had had difficulty expressing themselves in writing and had made a great number of spelling errors. Ms. Mills explains to her students that in her class she is concerned with helping them attain certain science concepts; however, good scientists need to be logical and they need to be able to present reports that are understandable. If they are writing reports that are unclear, it may be that their thinking is unclear. Ms. Milis states further that she will present special guides to the students based on their needs that will help them to attain the necessary skills or strategies to acquire the content concepts.

"But now," she says to her students, "I would like to go over some of your papers with you. First, I would like for us to go over a report that someone a few years ago wrote for me on the same topic. I will put it on the overhead projector. Please read it, and then tell me what you think of it."

After the students have had time to read the report, Ms. Mills asks for their comments. A number of students raise their hands, and Ms. Mills calls on one. The student says that the paper is difficult to read because the writer is not clear. As Ms. Mills looks around the room, she sees many of the other students nodding their heads in agreement. Ms. Mills says, "Good, that's why I chose this paper. Now, I want you to tell me exactly why this report is unclear." After Ms. Mills discusses the unclear report with her students, she asks them to reread their own reports. She asks them to check to see if what they are saying makes sense, and she reminds them of all the pointers they have just discussed. Ms. Mills gives her students time to go over their reports and to revise them accordingly.

The next day, Ms. Mills exposes her students to a well-written report on the same topic. She now asks her students to compare their report to this well-written one. Together, they discuss why the report is a good one.

Ms. Mills is an excellent teacher. She recognizes that the language arts permeates all subject-matter courses and that science is no exception. She recognizes also that science should be taught in a scientific manner and that students in science classes should be encouraged to practice the investigative skills of the scientist. She is providing her student scientists with an environment that is conducive to scientific thought and growth, as well as the skills they need. Good scientists need to be logical; they need to make evaluations; and they need to report their results in an accurate, concise, and complete manner. By using a directed language arts approach to teaching science, Ms. Mills is helping her students to be better writers and better scientists.

SCENARIO 2: INTERMEDIATE-GRADE SOCIAL STUDIES LESSON

Mr. Brown, the teacher, has consistently made a practice of choosing a certain number of words from his students' textbooks and other reading materials to highlight as the "words of the week." When he presents these words to his students, he pronounces each word, puts it in a sentence, and then challenges the students to use their knowledge of context clues and combining forms to figure out the word. If they can't figure out the word, he gives them the definition or asks them to look it up in the dictionary. During the week students can use these words to make up word riddles to challenge their classmates. Also, the words become part of the students' spelling words and students are asked to put the words into sentences that show they understand the meaning. Sometimes Mr. Brown presents the words in sentences to the students and asks them to define the word as used in the sentence.

Recently, Mr. Brown has noticed that a number of his students were having difficulty in such skills as summarizing, categorizing, and outlining. Mr. Brown decided to give the students who lacked these skills direct instruction in them by using relevant content material. He did several things.

Mr. Brown met with the group that was having problems summarizing some of their readings. He told them that he requires students to summarize material that they have read because he has found that this is an excellent way to help them learn and to retain what they have read. Mr. Brown tells his students that he will prove this, but, first, he has to help them learn how to write summaries. He explains the procedures for summarizing information, and reviews with them a technique important to finding the main or central idea of the selection. He gives each student the same selection that they will be reading and tells them that they will practice writing a summary together. After they have written the summary, he explains, he will give them a quiz on the selection. First, however, Mr. Brown goes over some vocabulary words with his students. These are words that Mr. Brown had selected from the passage because he felt that they might be unfamiliar to some of his students.

After going over the words together, Mr. Brown asks his students to read the selection to find its central idea. After they have finished reading the selection, they go over the selection's central idea. Mr. Brown writes this on the board, and then asks the students to try to recall the key details in the selection. He puts these on another board. After the students have finished listing these key details, Mr. Brown asks them to see if there are some details that they feel are not key ones. After a while, a few of the listed details are erased. Mr. Brown then asks the students to put the key details that are left on the board into sentences. Under the central idea, he writes the sentences that are given to him. After the students have finished this activity, Mr. Brown collects the selection that he had given his students to read and gives them a quiz on the material. After the quiz, Mr. Brown goes over the answers with his students. When the students see how well they have done on the quiz, this usually reinforces many to use summarizing as a valuable studying technique.

Mr. Brown, like Ms. Mills, is an excellent teacher. He recognizes that his students who lack certain skills are at a decided disadvantage in attaining content concepts. Therefore, rather than bemoaning the state of affairs, Mr. Brown proceeds to help them acquire the skills they need.

THE DIRECTED LANGUAGE ARTS APPROACH TO TEACHING THE CONTENT AREAS

Even though the major thrust of content-area teachers is *content,* this goal will not be achieved without the language arts. This point has been made a number of times in this chapter already, and it is being emphasized again because it is such a vital one. Also, it appears to be so obvious that persons may not feel that it needs to be voiced. Nothing, however, should be assumed. Most importantly, it should not be assumed that students have the necessary language arts skills to acquire certain content concepts.

Teachers who use a directed language arts approach to teaching content will directly teach any language arts skill that their students need to acquire the content concepts. Nothing would be left to chance or taken for granted. The language arts skills that are directly taught are directly related to content matter at the time. In other words, in a directed language arts approach to teaching content, language arts skills and content are integrated.

A directed language arts approach to teaching content requires students to be active consumers of information, that is, to be actively involved in what they are learning. The direct teaching of any needed language arts skills using pertinent content material ensures this active involvement and helps students to be better learners. The better learners students become, the better strategies they will acquire for processing information, and, consequently, they will become better thinkers.

A User's Guide to a Directed Language Arts Approach to Teaching Content

A directed language arts approach to teaching content is similar to a directed reading approach to teaching content except that other language arts skills besides just reading are directly taught based on students' needs. A directed language arts guide in the content areas can enhance the teaching of any content area because it provides interest, direction, and any strategy students need to acquire the content concepts. It is an aid to better comprehension and communication of information. Following are the general steps for a directed language arts approach to prepare students for the concepts to be taught. (*Note:* This guide should be adapted to suit the uniqueness of the specific content area as well as students. Moreover, not all steps need to be presented for every lesson.)

1. The teacher prepares for the concepts to be taught through five techniques.
   a. *Relating to past experiences of students.* This gives continuity to the lesson. Also, if students can see how what they are to learn relates to what they have already done, this will ease their chances for gaining the new information because they can fit the new information into an existing, meaningful context.
   b. *Using a motivating technique.* This will gain the students' attention. For example, provocative questions, realia, pictures, and so on could interest students in what they will be studying.
   c. *Stating the purposes of the lesson.* This will help give direction to the lesson and help students differentiate between relevant and incidental content. Purposes will also help to furnish organization for the material and provide feedback; that is, at the end of the lesson students will be able to determine whether they have achieved the stated purposes. The purposes also serve as task reinforcers, that is, students who know that they are mastering a set of objectives will achieve more than those whose only reinforcement is a grade at the end of the term.
   d. *Presenting the new terms.* Exposure to new vocabulary will increase the students' ability to acquire the concepts being taught.
   e. *Presenting a special strategy, using relevant content material.* Specific application of strategy to content will provide the special language arts skills that the students will need to acquire the content concepts. For example, if the students will be required to write a summary of the material they have read or if they will be required to write a report on a particular area, the teacher would review with the students the procedures for writing summaries or writing papers. (See Scenarios 1 and 2 earlier in this chapter.)
2. The teacher develops the lesson by using different techniques. For example, the teacher may use

a questioning approach, which requires students to have good listening comprehension to answer questions beyond merely the literal comprehension level. The teacher could present a lecture, which would require the students to be not only good listeners but good note takers. The teacher could also use a discovery approach, which would require students to do deductive and inductive reasoning, as well as to convey information. Whatever approach the teacher uses, it would require the students to be acquainted with and knowledgeable of language arts skills.

3. The teacher prepares the students for their reading assignment. Reading purposes are set; any unfamiliar terms are defined and explained; and highlights of what to look for while reading are given. Also, any special skills that students need to acquire content concepts while reading are directly taught using relevant content material.

4. The teacher summarizes the lesson. The teacher helps students pull together the main points of the lesson by stating the main idea of the lesson and by giving only the important details of the lesson.

Special Note:
Note that the lesson plan format in "A User's Guide to a Directed Language Arts Approach to Teaching Content" is similar to the lesson plan format presented in Chapter 5 and throughout this text. The major differences are found in the preparation step, which includes the presentation of new terms, as well as the direct teaching of any language arts strategy that students will need to acquire the content concepts. (See "Language Arts Teachers, Studying, and Writing as a Mode of Learning" later in this chapter.)

ORAL LANGUAGE IN CONTENT-AREA CLASSES

In many content-area classes, students are not engaged in as much oral language as they should be. This is unfortunate because "thinking aloud" is an excellent way for students to clarify their thinking, as well as to expand their language and thinking skills. Teachers in content-area classes who recognize the importance of oral language will not only give their students many opportunities to engage in discussions, but they will help guide the discussions by providing questions to challenge them to

elaborate their responses and to engage in higher levels of thinking.

Teachers who believe in the importance of oral language will provide a nonthreatening environment where students will feel free to question, to comment, and to say, "I don't understand." One technique that a teacher can use to help students gain proficiency in oral language is to tape a class or group discussion. The teacher then tells the students to listen carefully to each of their statements, questions, and comments to determine whether what they have said makes sense, whether their statements are relevant, and whether the discussion helped them clarify their thinking about the topic. Teachers can also have students discuss which points made the greatest impact and why.

From students' oral language teachers can learn a great deal about their students' thinking. Teachers should be on the lookout for students who can express themselves orally very well, but who do poorly on written tests. These students may have a reading or writing problem rather than a comprehension difficulty. The teacher will then have to try to determine exactly what the problem is. If the content-area teacher feels that this is beyond his or her expertise level, the teacher should refer the student for further diagnosis and help.

Speech-Stimulating Activities

"Whetting Children's Interest in Books" and "Book Reporting" in Chapter 10 present some speech-stimulating techniques that students can use to interest other students in reading books. These same kinds of techniques could be used in content-area classes to help students gain better insights into the content they are studying. Here are some examples that two different teachers have used in their classes.

SIXTH-GRADE SOCIAL STUDIES CLASS

Mr. Davis believes strongly that in order for a country to remain free, students must be good critical thinkers and able to express themselves clearly and logically. Because of this, Mr. Davis engages his students in a number of activities that require them to be good critical thinkers. He prepares his students for these activities by giving them all the strategies he feels they need to gain the most from the activities. Mr. Davis exposes his students to many of the propaganda techniques and helps them to recognize when they are being used. He also helps his students distinguish between facts and opinions. Mr. Davis then simulates a mock debate in class based on the topics they are studying. In the debate a number of students role-play different persons while the rest of the students act as the audience. Responsible for asking questions of the debaters, the audience then votes on the team that they feel has best presented its views.

SIXTH-GRADE SCIENCE CLASS

Ms. Smith's students have been reading biographies about a number of scientists. Some of the students have read about Louis Pasteur's life and contributions to humanity, and have decided to present a puppet show about him. They wrote the script, constructed the puppets, and presented their production to the rest of the class. Another group of students read about Walter Reed and his work to combat yellow fever. This group of students chose highlights from the life of Walter Reed and acted these out for the rest of the class.

After students had had an opportunity to read a number of different biographies about famous scientists, Ms. Smith divided her class into six groups and gave each group the name of a well-known scientist. She told the students that they were to use creative dramatics without speech to get the other groups to figure out the scientist that they were presenting. This activity was an excellent one because it forced the students, first, to determine the key characteristic or contribution of the scientist and, then, to figure out how they could portray this without speech. Even though this would not technically be considered a speech-stimulating activity, it is a good one because it forces students to be more sensitive to their body movements and how they can convey meaning.

LITERATURE IN CONTENT-AREA CLASSES

Good language arts classrooms should be "dead giveaways" because of their emphasis on books and other printed materials. However, this emphasis on books should not be restricted only to language arts classrooms—all content-area classes should have some sections devoted to books and other printed ma-

terial. The classroom, for example, could have one shelf of journals, magazines, newspapers, and so on, and another shelf filled with books. These printed materials should be germane to the particular subject, and students should be encouraged to browse through them. Teachers should also use these as part of their instructional program, as well as for their Sustained Silent Reading program. All teachers could whet their students' appetites for the books on display by labeling them with tantalizing captions. To arouse students' curiosity and stimulate them to go beyond the covers of the book, teachers can also challenge students who have read some of the books to create the captions for the books to motivate other students to want to read them also. The same techniques could be used for articles in magazines and journals.

How to Stock the Shelves

Once content-area teachers have made the decision to have a special corner in their classrooms devoted to books and other printed material, they have to decide on what specific materials to include.[1] One writer suggests the term *starter shelf* for these books and materials because that is most descriptive of the shelf or shelves.[2] The books that are chosen are merely to start the students reading voluntarily. The teacher starts the collection, but the students can contribute to it. The books are changed periodically based on students' interests, needs, and reading ability levels.

The use of the starter shelf will depend on the intent of the teacher, as well as the needs of the students. Some teachers may want to stock the shelves with books relevant to each specific unit that is being studied at the time; others may want to have a core of general books. Some teachers may want to have a sup-

[1]This section draws on Dorothy Rubin, *Teaching Reading and Study Skills in Content Areas* (New York: Holt, Rinehart and Winston, 1983).

[2]Adapted from David M. Bishop, "Motivating Adolescent Readers via Starter Shelves in Content-Area Classes," in *Motivating Reluctant Readers*, Alfred J. Ciani, ed. (Newark, Del.: International Reading Association, 1981): 49.

ply of fiction books related to the topics under discussion; others may want to have only non-fiction books. Some may want to have reading materials on topics of general interest and concern in the particular subject area. Usually, as stated in Chapter 10, teachers use relevant fiction as a stimulus to get students to read informational books.

Teachers must remember that the main purpose of the starter shelves is to get students to read on their own. Teachers should, therefore, not demand that students write a book report for every book that they choose from the starter shelf, nor should teachers require students to read a certain number of books from the starter shelf during the term. The starter shelf should act as a stimulus for students; it should be a place, as already stated, that students go to voluntarily; it should be a place that will "hook students on books."

Nonfiction should be available for primary-grade-level children as well as for children in the intermediate and upper-elementary grade levels. Young children are learning science and social studies concepts that require both hands-on experiences and reading. The books at the lower-primary grades may be picture books that help clarify a concept or that arouse the children's curiosity and stimulate them to ask some questions.

One teacher would list a number of intriguing questions on an easel beside the content-area book shelves. For example, when her fifth-graders were studying about the moon, she had some of the following questions listed: "Can plants grow on the moon?" "Is there water on the moon?" "Does it snow on the moon?" "How long is a day on the moon ?"

This teacher would also have a supply of books available to answer the questions; moreover, she never exerted pressure on the students to answer the questions. However, they almost all made an effort to seek out the answers.

WRITING AS A MODE OF LEARNING

Writing is a means of conveying information. What may not be obvious is that writing is a means of learning. Writing forces us to think about what we have read; it requires us to be logical. "Writing is a way to learn history or science, not just a way to report what has been learned."[3] Writing is a valuable mode of learning,[4] and students in the elementary grades should be gaining this concept of writing. Language arts teachers should help their students recognize that writing is important in all subjects, not just English, and that outlining, note-taking, and summarizing can be helpful study techniques (see Chapter 12). For example, an eighth-grade class produced a newspaper related to their social studies classes. They were learning about the Renaissance, and the newspaper was to be a replica of events that might have taken place at that time. The front page of a paper produced by a highly gifted child is reproduced on page 400. There is humor, knowledge, organizational ability, and hand-work in its production.

LANGUAGE ARTS TEACHERS, STUDYING, AND WRITING AS A MODE OF LEARNING

Many students go through the grades without ever having acquired any study techniques. Usually elementary-school teachers do not spend time in helping children to acquire study skills either because they themselves lack the skill,[5] or feel it is the job of the high school teacher. Many high school teachers do not spend time in this area because they make the assumption that their students have already acquired these skills. As a result, many students may do poorly in school because they have never learned how to study. This is a sad state of affairs. Students should be helped to acquire good study habits as soon as possible before they develop either poor study habits or erroneous concepts concerning studying.

[3]Arthur N. Applegate, *Writing in the Secondary School: English and the Content Areas.* (Urbana, Ill.: National Council of Teachers of English, 1983), p. xii.
[4]Janet Emig, "Writing as a Mode of Learning," *College Composition and Communication* 28 (May 1977): 122–128.
[5]Eunice N. Askov, Karyln Kamm, and Roger Klumb, "Study Skill Mastery Among Elementary Teachers," *Reading Teacher* 30 (February 1977): 485–488.

All teachers should help students recognize that with good study habits, they could spend less time in studying and learn more. It is certainly beyond the scope of this book to go into an in-depth discussion of study habits and study techniques; however, it is important that language arts teachers recognize their responsibility to develop in their students study techniques and writing as a mode of learning.

When teachers are helping students to attain outlining, summarizing, and note-taking skill, they can show their students how these techniques could be effective study tools. A key factor that teachers should convey to their students is that writing can be a learning tool if students stop to think about what they have read before they write. In other words, just copying notes from a book as one is reading will not help students learn the information or retain it over an extended period of time. In order to combine writing with studying, students must read the material, think about what they have read, try to recall the main or central idea of the material, as well as the important supporting details, and then write the information in some understandable manner. Students can write their notes in outline form; they can write a summary of what they have read, or they can make a semantic map illustrating the main points of what they have read. Regardless of what technique students use, the key is to think about the material before writing.

Semantic Mapping (Graphic Organizing) and Studying

Semantic mapping (graphic organizing) is a technique that teachers can introduce to students as a study skill in place of outlining. Semantic mapping requires that students be good critical thinkers to make insightful judgments in selecting material from their reading that will best represent the information and help them recall it. Semantic mapping demands logical thinkers.

Here is one technique students could use. They should first choose the amount of information that they will be studying. This may be a group of paragraphs, a section, a whole chapter, or perhaps just one paragraph. (Usually a semantic map is used for more than one paragraph.) After doing this, the student should read through the whole material that he or she has chosen to study. The student should then try to come up with the central idea of the material, which should be placed in the center of the page. The student should then reread each paragraph. After reading each paragraph, he or she should state its main topic and draw a line from it to the central idea. Important details in each paragraph could be appended to its main topic.

There really is no *correct* way to construct a semantic map. The *correct* way is the one that works for students, and it is important that students recognize this. What works for one student will not necessarily work for another. The test as to whether the semantic map is correct or not comes when the student uses it for study purposes and finds that it does indeed help him or her to recall a significant amount of information. (See Chapter 3 for more on semantic mapping [graphic organizing].)

LANGUAGE ARTS ERRORS IN CONTENT-AREA CLASSES

Should content-area teachers correct students' spelling, word usage, capitalization, or punctuation errors? This question has been asked innumerable times. Another question that has been asked often is whether teachers should lower students' test grades in a content area if they spell the answer incorrectly. These questions are addressed in Chapter 13, "Correcting Spelling Errors in Other Subject Areas" and in Chapter 18, but they will also be discussed here because the emphasis throughout this chapter, as well as throughout this text, is that the language arts should be a concern of all teachers not just the language arts teachers.

In a directed language arts approach to teaching content, the teacher is supposed to help students acquire any skills or strategies that they may need to attain the content concepts. It seems to make sense, then, that students who are having difficulty with the tools they need to express themselves in writing should be helped to acquire these tools.

If teachers note that a number of their stu-

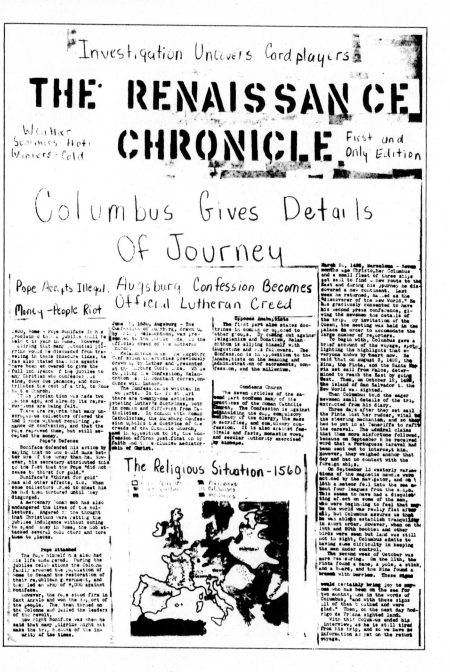

dents are spelling many words incorrectly, they should correct these words on the students' papers and then discuss with these students some steps that they could take to help them to be better spellers. One step would be for the student to discuss their spelling problem with their language arts or English teacher and try to get some help from them. Another would be for the content-area teacher to select a number of words from the students' reading assignments and present these to the students as words that they should learn. If the words that are frequently misspelled are those that are key unit words, the teacher could have these words designated as the "words of the week." The students would then be responsible for knowing the meaning of the words, being able to use the words in a sentence, and for their correct spelling. If students incorrectly use or spell these words, then they would be held accountable

and points could be taken off from their test or composition grade.

It is imperative that teachers make this practice known to students beforehand; that is, students should know beforehand that they will be held responsible for the spelling of the key words on a test or composition. The knowledge that they will be held responsible for correct spelling may in itself act as a stimulus for students to try to be better spellers.

SUMMARY

Competence in the language arts is essential for students to do well in their content-area courses. If teachers suspect that their students lack certain language arts skills that they will need to acquire content concepts, this chapter recommends that they directly teach the needed language arts skills using relevant content. This chapter explains what a directed language arts approach to teaching content entails, and presents a guide with specific steps that content-area teachers can use to help their students

acquire any needed language arts skills. Scenarios were used to illustrate a directed language arts approach to teaching content.

This chapter stresses the importance of oral language in content areas and gives a number of suggestions on how teachers can encourage more oral expression in their content classes. Attention in this chapter is paid also to the question concerning the correction of language arts errors in content courses, as well as how writing can be used as a mode of learning.

SUGGESTIONS FOR THOUGHT
QUESTIONS AND ACTIVITIES

1. Observe a content-area class. Note all the language arts skills that students need to have to do well in the content area.
2. Observe a content-area class. Note any language arts area in which students need help, and prepare a guide for teaching directly a language arts skill using relevant content material. The language arts skills should be one that students need to help them to acquire content concepts.
3. Observe a content-area class. Note the tactics that the teacher uses to encourage oral expression in his or her class.

4. You have been appointed to a special committee in your school. The committee's goal is to make content-area teachers aware of their role in helping students acquire those language arts skills needed to acquire content concepts. What will you recommend that the committee do?
5. You have been asked to give a talk to the content-area teachers in your school district explaining what a directed language arts approach to teaching content areas is. What will you say?

SELECTED BIBLIOGRAPHY

Emig, Janet. "Writing as a Mode of Learning." *College Composition and Communication* 28 (May 1977): 122–128.

Mercier, Lorraine Y. *The Essentials Approach: Rethinking the Curriculum for the '80s.* Washington, D.C.: U.S. Department of Education, Basic Skills Improvement Program, 1981.

Rubin, Dorothy. *Teaching Reading and Study Skills in Content Areas.* New York: Holt, Rinehart and Winston, 1983.

————. *Reading & Learning Power.* New York: Macmillan, 1985.

Seaver, JoAnn Tuttle, and Morton Botel. "A First-Grade Teacher Teaches Reading, Writing, and Oral Communication across the Curriculum." *Reading Teacher* 36 (March 1983): 656–664.

Smardo, Frances A. "Using Children's Literature to Clarify Science Concepts in Early Childhood Programs." *Reading Teacher* 36 (December 1982): 267–273.

Tchudi, Stephen N., and Susan J. Tchudi. *Teaching Writing in the Content Areas: Elementary.* Urbana, Ill.: NCTE, 1983.

EPIOLOGUE

At the beginning, the center, and the end of the educative process is the child, whose proper development is the ideal.

Teachers are the guides, stimulators, energizers, and helpers. They hold keys to unlock the storehouse of knowledge.

Language is the "spiritual food." It is the means by which individuals share thoughts and feelings.

This book has attempted to provide teachers with the language arts skills and knowledge they will need to help students to lead richer, fuller lives. The emphasis has been on the child as an active, curious, imaginative, and creative experiencer of life. Through the language arts, the child's world is expanded. The child grows and reaches new intellectual and emotional heights.

To take a child by the hand and help lead the child into the good life, while safeguarding and fostering his or her uniqueness, is an awesome task. Teachers need all the help they can get. We hope that this book has been one aid.

GLOSSARY

Accommodation. Child develops new categories rather than integrating them into existing ones; part of Piaget's cognitive development process.

Affective environment. Concerned with the feelings and emotional learnings that students acquire.

Affix. Prefix *(which see*)* added before the root word, and suffix *(which see)* added to the end of a root word.

Alliteration. Repetition of usually the initial consonant sound or sounds in two or more neighboring words or syllables.

Allomorph. A morpheme *(which see)* that is represented by alternate phonemes *(which see)*.

Allophone. Variant of the same phoneme *(which see)*.

Ambidextrous. Able to use both hands equally well.

Analogies. Relationships between words or ideas.

Antonyms. Words opposite in meaning.

Articulation. Production of speech sounds.

Assimilation. Continuous process that helps the individual to integrate new incoming stimuli with existing concepts; part of Piaget's cognitive development process.

Association. Pairing of the real object with the sound of the word.

Auding. Highest level of listening that involves listening with comprehension.

Auditory acuity. Physical response of the ear to sound vibrations.

Auditory discrimination. Ability to distinguish between sounds.

Auditory fatigue. Temporary hearing loss due to a continuous or repeated exposure to sounds of certain frequencies.

Aural. Refers to listening.

Base. Same as root *(which see)*.

Behavioral objective. Statement that describes what students will be able to do after they have achieved their goal.

Bibliotherapy. Use of books to help individuals cope better with their emotional and adjustment problems.

Bilingual. Capable of using two languages equally effectively.

Binaural situations. Being in the presence of two or more conversations or sound sources.

Brainstorming. Activity generating many different ideas without inhibition.

Choral speaking. Saying aloud, in unison, of a poem or prose selection by a group.

*Which see refers to the immediately preceding word that is defined elsewhere in the glossary.

Cinquain. Poetic form based on a five-line pattern.

Cognitive development. Growth of thinking processes.

Cognitive domain. Hierarchy of objectives ranging from simplistic thinking skills to the more complex ones.

Combining forms. Roots borrowed from another language that join together or with a prefix, a suffix, or both a prefix and a suffix to form a word; for example, *aqua/naut*. (In a more general sense, also defined as any word part that can join with another word or word part to form a word or a new word.)

Communication. Exchange of ideas.

Composing. Everything a writer does from the time first words are put on paper until all drafts are completed.

Competency-based instruction. Embraces two essential characteristics: learning objectives, defined in behavioral terms; and accountability.

Concepts. A group of stimuli with common characteristics.

Concrete poetry. Poetry whose arrangement of words on a page follow the actual or approximate forms of an object.

Connotative meaning. Emotional senses associated with a word.

Construct. Something that cannot be directly observed or directly measured, such as intelligence, attitudes, and motivation.

Creative dramatics. Informal dramatization by the child using his or her imagination.

Creative process. Wallas's stages of preparation, incubation, illumination, and verification.

Creativity. According to Parnes, knowledge plus imagination plus evaluation; no universally agreed-upon definition.

Criterion-referenced tests. Test items based on an extensive inventory of learning objectives in a specific curriculum area; not norm-based.

Critical listening. High-level listening skill whereby the individual is able to detect bias, propaganda, and so on in oral presentations.

Crossed dominance. Condition in which the dominant hand is on one side and the dominant eye on the other.

Curriculum. Everything in the school environment planned prior to instruction.

Deductive teaching. Method in which students are given a generalization and must determine which examples fit the rule; going from general to specific.

Denotative meaning. Direct, specific meaning of a word.

Derivative. Combination of root word with either prefix *(which see)* or suffix *(which see)* or both; for example, prefix *re* plus root word *play* = *replay*. (*See also* Stem.)

Desist technique. Any technique used to control misbehavior.

Dialect. A variation of language sufficiently different to be considered separate, but not different enough to be classified as a separate language.

Digit span. Amount of words or numbers an individual can retain in his or her short-term memory.

Divergent thinking. Mental ability to solve problems or to "look at things" in many different ways.

Drafting. Part of the writing process; the stage at which the writer puts down in specific words his or her ideas.

Editing. Final stage in writing process; the stage at which the writer focuses on the conventions of writing, including word choice and syntax.

Elaboration in speech acquisition. Means by which baby's word or words are expanded into a complete sentence by parental modeling.

Environmental psychology. Focus on behavior in relation to physical settings.

Equilibrium. According to Piaget, a balance between assimilation *(which see)* and accommodation *(which see)* in cognitive development *(which see)*.

Evaluation. Process of appraisal involving specific values and the use of a variety of instruments in order to form a value judgment.

Exceptional children. Children who deviate so much from the "average" that they require special attention.

Experience story. A basic teaching technique in reading founded on experiences of students.

Function or structure words. All words in a sentence not classified as major parts of speech.

Grammar. The study of the way language is used; composed of syntax *(which see)* and morphology *(which see).*

Grapheme. Written representation of phoneme.

Grapheme—phoneme relation. Letter-sound relation.

Graphemic base. Succession of graphemes that occurs with the same phonetic value in a number of words *(ight, ake, at, et,* and so on); same as phonogram *(which see).*

Haiku. Japanese poetic form consisting of three lines composed of seventeen syllables, 5 in the first and third lines and 7 in the second.

Halo effect. Rater bias that contaminates an individual's perception in the area of evaluation.

Haptics. Nonverbal communication through touch.

Hearing. Lowest level in the hierarchy of listening; the physical perception of sound.

Holophrastic speech. Single-word utterances used by child to express complex ideas.

Homographs. Words that are spelled the same but have different meanings.

Homonyms. Words that sound alike, are spelled differently, and have different meanings.

Homophones. Homonyms *(which see).*

Hyperbole. Gross exaggeration as a figure of speech.

Illumination. Part of the creative process in which the individual achieves an "insight" into the problem.

Imitation in speech acquisition. Process in which child voices the sounds voiced initially by the parent figure.

Incubation. Part of the creative process in which the individual "mulls over the problem."

Inductive teaching. Method in which students discover generalizations by being given numerous examples that portray patterns; going from specific to general.

Inference. Understanding that is not derived from a direct statement but from an indirect suggestion in what is stated.

Intake of language. Listening and reading.

Intelligence. Ability to reason abstractly.

IQ. Intelligence Quotient; mental age divided by chronological age multiplied by 100.

I.P.A. International Phonetic Alphabet.

Juncture. Way in which phonemes *(which see)* in a language are joined together in an utterance; way in which an utterance begins and ends; pause.

Kinesics. Study of the gestures that may or may not accompany speech; message-related body movement.

Language. A learned, shared, and patterned arbitrary system of vocal sound symbols with which people in a given culture can communicate with one another.

Language arts. Major components are listening, speaking, reading, and writing.

Language—experience approach. Non-structured emerging reading program based on students' experiences; incorporates all aspects of the language arts into reading.

Lanterne. Poetic pattern of 1, 2, 3, 4, and 1 syllables in a line, arranged in the shape of a lantern.

Learning center. An integral part of the instructional program that is vital to a good individualized program; An area is usually set aside in the classroom for instruction in a specific curriculum area.

Limerick. A five-line pattern in which the first, second, and fifth lines rhyme with one another, and the third and fourth lines rhyme with each other.

Linguist. Individual engaged in the systematic study of language.

Linguistics. Science of language.

Listening. Middle of hierarchy of listening in which the individual becomes aware of sound sequences, and is able to identify and recognize the sound sequences as words; many times the term "listening" is used in place of auding *(which see).*

Main idea. Central thought of a paragraph; all of the sentences in a paragraph develop the main idea.

Mainstreaming. Placement of handicapped children in the least restrictive environment that will meet these children's needs.

Masking. Factor inhibiting hearing as sounds interfere with the spoken message.

Measurement. Part of the evaluative process; involves quantitative descriptions.

Memory span. Number of discrete elements grasped in a given moment of attention and organized into a unity for purposes of immediate reproduction or immediate use; synonym for digit span *(which see)*.

Metaphor. Comparison of two unlike objects without using "like" or "as."

Morpheme. Smallest individually meaningful element in the utterances of a language.

Morphology. Construction of words and word parts.

Morphophonemic system. Ways in which the morphemes *(which see)* of a given language are variously represented by phonemic *(see phoneme)* shapes; can be regarded as a kind of code.

Motivation. Internal impetus behind behavior and the direction behavior takes; drive.

Newspaper poetry. Arrangement of words on a page that helps express the poet's message.

Objective. An end or outcome; usually used for short-range plans.

Onomatopoeia. Words whose sound suggests the sense.

Oral. Refers to speaking.

Outgo of language. Speaking and writing.

Overworked phrases. Trite phrases.

Oxymoron. Word contradictions that are used to portray a particular image.

Pantomime. Creative dramatics without speech; only facial and body actions are used to convey thoughts or actions.

Personification. Attribution of human characteristics and capabilities to nonhuman things such as inanimate objects, abstract qualities, or animals.

Phoneme. Smallest unit of sound in a specific language system; a class of sounds.

Phonics. Relation between letter symbols of a written language and the sounds they represent.

Phonogram. Graphemic base *(which see)*.

Phonology. Branch of linguistics *(which see)* dealing with the analysis of sound systems of language.

Physical environment. Observable factors in the physical environment that could affect the behavior of an individual.

Pitch. Frequency levels in utterances.

Prefix. An affix *(which see)*; a letter or a sequence of letters added to the beginning of a root word that changes its meaning; for example, *re* plus *play* = *replay*.

Preparation. Part of the creative process relating to the background of experiences.

Prewriting. Part of the writing process; preliminary steps before actual writing is begun.

Principle. Rule or guide.

Projective technique. Method of assessment in which the individual tends to put himself or herself into the test situation.

Proxemics. Study of the effects of space or distance on human interaction; a form of nonverbal communication.

Proximodistal development. Development of the body from the midpoint to the extremities.

Reading. The getting of meaning from and bringing of meaning to the written page.

Rehearsal. Prewriting *(which see)*.

Reinforcement. Any stimulus, such as praise, that usually causes the individual to repeat a response.

Reliability. The extent to which a test instrument consistently produces similar results.

Revising. Part of the writing process; the stage at which the writer is involved with the creative improvement of the text; the writer makes changes, adds, deletes, reorganizes, and so on, in order to say what the writer intends to say.

Role playing. Form of creative dramatics in which dialogue for a specific role is spontaneously developed.

Root. Smallest unit of a word that can exist and retain its basic meaning; a base; for example, *play*.

Simile. Comparison of two unlike objects using "like" or "as."

Semantic clue. Meaning clue.

Sociogram. Map or chart showing the interrelationships of children in a classroom and identifying those who are "stars" or "isolates."

Speech correction. Need for children who must be referred to a clinician for speech help and who are generally not so helped in the regular classroom.

Speech improvement. Applies to the ongoing classroom speech program

Speech stimulation activities. Oral expression activities that help to develop better speech, voice, and body movements.

Standardized tests. Published by experts in the field, instruments that have precise instructions for administration and scoring; usually norm-referenced.

Stem. Any word construction to which an affix *(which see)* can be added. All roots are stems, but all stems are not roots. A stem may consist of a root plus an affix; for example, in *replays, play* is the root, and *replay* is the stem to which the suffix *s* is added.

Stress. Part of the accentual system in which differences in a syllable or words are largely in relative loudness or prominence.

Suffix. Affix *(which see)*; a letter or a sequence of letters added to the end of a root word that changes the grammatical form of the word and its meaning; for example, *prince* plus *ly = princely.*

Suprasegmental phonemes. Significant sound units that influence meaning; include pitch, stress, and juncture.

Syllable. Vowel or a group of letters containing one vowel sound; for example, *blo.*

Synonyms. Words similar in meaning.

Syntax. Patterning of words or the way in which words are arranged relative to each other in utterances.

Tanka verse. Five-line poem arranged in a 5, 7, 5, 7, 7 poetic pattern of thirty-one syllables.

Teaching. Process involving intent, rules, and goals (according to Kingsley Price); no universally agreed-upon definition.

Telegraphic speech. Ability of child to receive and convey a message, even though it is beyond the child's digit span *(which see).*

Topic sentence. Sentence stating the subject of the paragraph.

Traditional grammar. Approach to language based on Latin and Greek, leading to the description and analysis of English in terms of these languages; prescriptive.

Transformational grammar. Approach to language that builds on the structuralists but goes further in the area of generating sentences.

Usage. Way people speak; preferences and choices in language are made according to formal or informal usage.

Validity. The degree to which a test instrument measures what it claims to measure.

Verification. Part of the creative process in which the individual tests the "insight" gained in the illumination *(which see)* phase.

Word classes. Major parts of speech according to linguists; for example, nouns, verbs, adjectives, and adverbs.

Writing process. Activity engaged in by writer; includes prewriting or rehearsing, drafting, revising, and editing.

Appendix A

BOOKBINDING FOR BOOKS
WRITTEN BY CHILDREN

The following section maps out the easy steps to follow in making a handmade book.[1]

Preparation: Decide on the cover size you want and cut two pieces of cardboard to fit. Then select a vinyl-coated fabric wallpaper[2] large enough to cover both pieces of cardboard.

Step 1: Center cardboard covers on wallpaper so that they are about ¼ inch apart and there is a border of about one inch of extra wallpaper around them, then trace with pencil. Paste cardboard covers to wallpaper. (See Illustration 1.)

Step 2: Draw triangle shape at each corner of the wallpaper. Cut off corners of wallpaper. (See Illustration 2.)

Step 3: Fold and paste wallpaper over cardboard. Press firmly until paste sticks. Be neat. Use a sponge. (See Illustration 3.)

Step 4: Finished edges of book cover; all wallpaper edges folded and pasted over cardboard. (See Illustration 4.)

Step 5: Sew or staple 10 pages together. (See Illustrations 5 and 6.)

Step 6: FINISHED BOOK. Paste bottom 2 pages to inside covers of book. Write your full name and room number on inside front page. (See Illustration 7.)

[1]Developed by Ted Lynch, Art Teacher at Community Park School, Princeton, New Jersey.
[2]Cloth may be substituted for wallpaper.

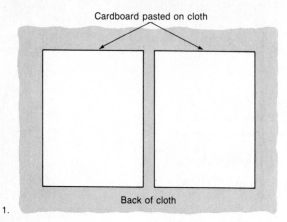

Cardboard pasted on cloth

Back of cloth

1.

Cut off corners of cloth

2.

3. Fold and paste cloth over cardboard on all four sides

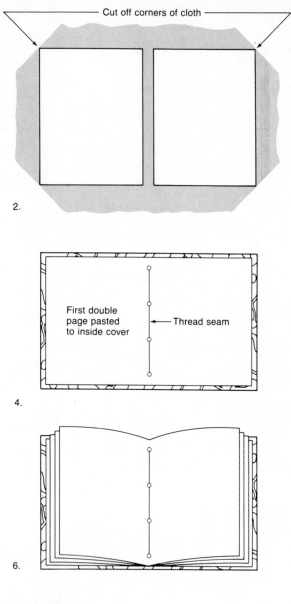

First double page pasted to inside cover ← Thread seam

4.

Thread seam → through other pages

5.

6.

7.

BOOKBINDING

1. Cardboard pasted on wallpaper
2. Triangles cut off each corner of wallpaper
3. Wallpaper partially folded and pasted over cardboard
4. All wallpaper edges folded and pasted over cardboard
5. Pages sewn together
6. Opened book in its finished state
7. Closed book in its finished state

Appendix B

CHECKLIST FOR CHOOSING LANGUAGE ARTS TEXTBOOK SERIES

According to the Educational Products Information Exchange Institute, a nonprofit consumer-supported organization, 95 percent of classroom instruction can be attributed to classroom materials.[1] Even if the percentage is exaggerated, hardly anyone would deny that textbooks play a prominent role in the instructional program. Because of their importance, teachers need to be critical textbook consumers. Although in the past decade children's textbooks seem to be becoming more similar than different, each textbook series is unique in what it tends to stress, the terminology it uses, and usually in the presentation of its material.

The general checklist that follows should help in choosing language arts textbook series.

[1]Donald H. Graves. "Language Arts Textbooks: A Writing Process Evaluation" *Language Arts* (October 1977): 817.

GENERAL CHECKLIST FOR CHOOSING LANGUAGE ARTS SERIES

	Excellent	Good	Fair	Poor
1. *Physical Characteristics*				
a. Print				
1. Clear				
2. Readable				
3. Proper size				
4. Proper spacing between lines				
b. Paper				
1. Good weight				
2. Durable				
3. Nonglossy				

	Excellent	Good	Fair	Poor
c. Binding				
1. Reinforced				
2. Book held firmly in its cover				

2. *Content (General Characteristics)*

	Excellent	Good	Fair	Poor
a. Valid information, i.e., information is related to topic being studied				
b. Covered in proper depth for particular grade level				
c. Based on objectives that have been chosen for specific language arts areas				
d. Emphasis on interrelatedness of listening, speaking, reading, and writing				
e. Emphasis on listening				
f. Emphasis on speech-stimulation activities such as creative dramatics, discussions, puppetry, choral speaking, and so on				
g. Emphasis on creative writing				
h. Emphasis on practical writing skills such as punctuation, capitalization, word usage, and some spelling				

3. *Readability*

	Excellent	Good	Fair	Poor
a. Vocabulary is suitable to particular grade level				
b. Sentence length is suitable to particular grade level				

4. *Features*

	Excellent	Good	Fair	Poor
a. Variety of activities				
b. Creative presentation of material				
c. Objectives presented at beginning of each lesson				
d. Complete index				
e. Glossary—special terms used in text are defined				
f. Bibliographies—include up-to-date materials				
g. Summaries at end of each chapter				

5. *Visual Content or Illustration*

	Excellent	Good	Fair	Poor
a. Charts and graphs are included				
b. Pictures and cartoons included				

	Excellent	Good	Fair	Poor

6. *Treatment of Minorities*

a. Every group of people treated with dignity and respect.				
b. No group stereotyped				
c. Each group accurately portrayed				

7. *Treatment of Gender*

a. Males and females treated as equals				
b. Stereotypes avoided				

8. *Provisions for Individual Differences*

a. Special aids for slow learners				
b. Challenging material for the gifted				

9. *Teacher's Manual*

a. Includes helpful suggestions				
b. Provides extra activities				
c. Provides activities for special children				
d. Provides creative ideas				

Appendix C

FRY READABILITY FORMULA

Expanded Directions for Working Readability Graph

1. Randomly select three (3) sample passages and count out exactly 100 words each, beginning with the beginning of a sentence. Do count proper nouns, initializations, and numerals.

2. Count the number of sentences in the hundred words, estimating length of the fraction of the last sentence to the nearest one-tenth.

3. Count the total number of syllables in the 100-word passage. If you don't have a hand counter available, an easy way is to simply put a mark above every syllable over one in each word, then when you get to the end of the passage, count the number of marks and add 100. Small calculators can also be used as counters by pushing numeral 1, then push the + sign for each word or syllable when counting.

4. Enter graph with *average* sentence length and *average* number of syllables; plot dot where the two lines intersect. Area where dot is plotted will give you the approximate grade level.

5. If a great deal of variability is found in syllable count or sentence count, putting more samples into the average is desirable.

6. A word is defined as a group of symbols with a space on either side; thus, *Joe, IRA, 1945,* and *&* are each one word.

7. A syllable is defined as a phonetic syllable. Generally, there are as many syllables as vowel sounds. For example, *stopped* is one syllable and *wanted* is two syllables. When counting syllables for numerals and initializations, count one syllable for each symbol. For example *1945* is four syllables, *IRA* is three syllables, and *&* is one syllable.

EXAMPLE:

	SYLLABLES	SENTENCES
1st Hundred Words	124	6.6
2nd Hundred Words	141	5.5
3rd Hundred Words	158	6.8
AVERAGE	141	6.3

READABILITY 7th GRADE (see dot plotted on graph)

Average number of syllables per 100 words

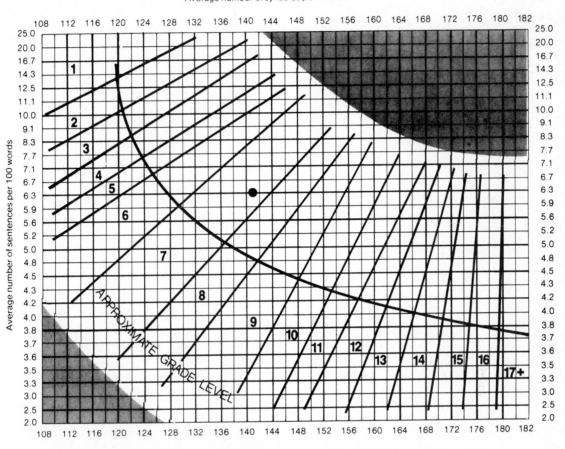

GRAPH FOR ESTIMATING READABILITY—Extended by Edward Fry, Rutgers University Reading Center, New Brunswick, N.J. 08904. Note: This "extended graph" does not outmode or render the earlier (1968) version inoperative or inaccurate; it is an extension. (Reproduction permitted—no copyright)

INDEX

Literary and Photographic Credits

Cover photography by Carol Smith and James Foley.
The author wishes to thank the Monticello Arkansas School System, Ewing Township Public School System, Lawrence Township, and especially Carol Smith for the photography used within the book. Figure 1.2, p. 11, reprinted by permission of Bob Cordray. Cartoon p. 30, copyright Los Angeles Times. Reprinted with permission. Cartoon p. 34, reprinted by permission of Newspaper Enterprise Association. Text 6.2, p. 65, reprinted by permission of the National Education Association. Text pp. 74 & 77, from the English Language Arts Program prepared by the Language Arts Curriculum Committee, Dr. Howard VanderBeek, Chairman, Malcolm Price Laboratory School, University of Northern Iowa, Cedar Falls, Iowa. Text pp. 94 & 95, copyright by the Trustees of Boston University, Boston, Massachusetts. Text pp. 99-101, from *How to Be A Puppeteer* by Eleanor Boylan. Copyright © 1970 by Eleanor Boylan. Reprinted by permission of the publishers, Saturday Review Press/E.P. Dutton & Co., Inc. Text p. 102, "African Dance,"

copyright 1926 by Alfred A. Knopf, Inc., and renewed 1954 by Langston Hughes. Reprinted from *Selected Poems* by Langston Hughes, by permission of the publishers. Text pp. 110-111, copyright © 1971 by Macmillan Publishing Co., Inc. Reprinted by permission of Macmillan. Text pp. 223-224, courtesy of Sharon Anne Rubin. Text p. 268, copyright © 1973 by the National Council of Teachers of English. Reprinted by permission. Text pp. 300-301, from Bernice A. Furner, "An Analysis of the Effectiveness of a Program of Instruction Emphasizing the Perceptual-Motor Nature of Learning in Handwriting," *Elementary English*, January 1970, published by the National Council of Teachers of English, pp. 68-69. Art p. 308, courtesy of E.A. Enstrom, *Public School Digest*, Tri-State Area School Study Council, University of Pittsburgh, Pittsburgh, Pennsylvania. Cartoon p. 389, reprinted by permission of Chicago Tribune, New York News Syndicate, Inc. Copyright 1973. Art p. 400, courtesy of Carol Rubin Smith.